THE LIVERPOOL RIFLES

THE LIVERPOOL RIFLES

A BIOGRAPHY OF THE 1/6TH BATTALION KING'S LIVERPOOL REGIMENT IN THE FIRST WORLD WAR

KEVIN SHANNON

FONTHILL

Dedicated to the memory of all who served in the Liverpool Rifles; in particular, former rifleman, writer, and broadcaster Norman Ellison.

Fonthill Media Language Policy

Fonthill Media publishes in the international English language market. One language edition is published worldwide. As there are minor differences in spelling and presentation, especially with regard to American English and British English, a policy is necessary to define which form of English to use. The Fonthill Policy is to use the form of English native to the author. Kevin Shannon was born and educated in Liverpool; therefore British English has been adopted in this publication.

Fonthill Media Limited
Fonthill Media LLC
www.fonthillmedia.com
office@fonthillmedia.com

First published in the United Kingdom and the United States of America 2019

British Library Cataloguing in Publication Data:
A catalogue record for this book is available from the British Library

ISBN 978-1-78155-701-3

Typeset in 9pt on 13pt DejaVu Serif
Printed and bound in England

Foreword

Raised in Liverpool during the 1950s and '60s, it was impossible to escape war. The numerous bombsites provided an irresistible playground for adventurous children growing up without the distractions of TV and computers. My parents' generation had only just come through the horrors of the Second World War and some items were still rationed; in the background, however, was another group of much older men.

The First World War sealed the fate of my maternal grandfather, invalided out of the Army in late 1917 and condemned to an ever-decreasing quality of life until his premature death. His wife was struck down by a mysterious and fatal tropical disease, contracted during a visit to her brother's ship, recently returned to Liverpool from the Orient. Four years later, my grandfather joined her, orphaning my eight-year-old mother, who was passed round various Lancashire relatives for care until she was adopted by one of her father's stepbrothers in Liverpool.

As a young child, Christmas visits to this side of the family introduced me to a generation too old to have fought in the Second World War, but who had clearly undergone some ordeal of their own. Nearly sixty years later, I can still recall the bronchitic aura that seemed to be their badge. Childhood enquiries were brushed aside by my mother, with brusque replies, such as 'Uncle Bernard was gassed'—making it abundantly clear that further questioning was unwelcome. As an adult, I never did get to talk to these men, as all had passed before I was ten years old. It was only when I began to research this book that I learned that all four 'uncles' served in the KLR, one with the 1/6th.

I have been most fortunate to have had access to the battalion's 'Casualties Book', one of only four surviving examples. This resource is not quite what it sounds, and while it does document killed and wounded, it is actually a record of 'casualties' or 'routine' episodes in the battalion service of every man. If a man does not feature in the resource, then he did not serve overseas with them, though a clerical error resulted in the omission of two, who were transferred shortly after initial deployment overseas—both have been added to the Roll. Initially, this book held information for officers, but post-1916, this was recorded elsewhere and unfortunately has been lost. Fortuitously, 55 Division's A&Q records have provided the names of these later officers.

Upon the formation of the Territorial Force (TF) in 1908, men were given a battalion number of between one and four digits; if a man changed battalions, he was issued a new number and when it became obvious four digits were insufficient, every TF soldier was assigned a new six-digit number on 1 March 1917. It is this later number—if issued—that is used in the narrative and the Roll. As those missing in action were not usually declared dead until a year had passed, many casualties from 1916 have six-digit numbers. Men who were conscripted, or volunteered for the Service Battalions (Pals), received a five-digit number. There are exceptions to this 'norm' in the KLR, but all such with wartime service in the 1/6th held a five-digit number.

Before overseas deployment, the Liverpool Rifles was designated the 6th Battalion. In September 1914, volunteer numbers were sufficient to form a 'Second-line' or 'Reserve' battalion, for the initial purpose of supplying the overseas battalion with trained replacements and also to replace the overseas battalion in its Home Defence role—officially designated the 6th Reserve Battalion. When the 6th deployed abroad, its designation became the 1/6th and the Reserve Battalion became the 2/6th; the 3/6th was formed in Liverpool that May (becoming the 6th Reserve Battalion in April 1916, before being absorbed into the 5th Reserve Battalion in September 1916). Although not strictly accurate, to avoid confusion, I will refer to the subject battalion as the 1/6th, even before their move overseas (pronounced 'First-Sixth'). The multitude of KLR battalions during the First World War was astounding—some forty-nine in total, though not all extant at the same time.

Liverpool's ethnic Welsh population added a complication in that so many shared surnames. Had the KLR so desired, it could have fielded a battalion of Roberts's, nearly two battalions of Jones's, and almost a full battalion of Williams's. If 'Smith' is included, then five battalions could have been populated with just these four surnames. The 1/6th had ninety-five Jones's. Consequently, where confusion is likely, the last three numbers of the individual are placed in brackets after the name. Ranks in the narrative are those held at the time, though those in the Roll are the ranks held on 11 November 1918 and promotions (or demotions) between then and demobilisation have not been applied. If a man holding temporary rank left the battalion, then his temporary rank is the one shown. It is inevitable that there are errors and for that, apologies are issued in advance.

Understanding the actions of the battalion is greatly improved by walking the actual ground, but as most readers are unlikely to be able to do this, I have included coordinates, which can be entered as 'Placemarks' on Google Earth. These are written as degrees, minutes, and seconds, as this format is that most frequently used in a car's Satnav, though, if preferred, it is easily converted to other formats using Google Earth. A combination of this and Google 'Street-View' add a dimension a paper map cannot bring. Where these coordinates are based on map references given at the time, they are as accurate as the original references—though coordinates taken from georeferenced trench maps will be accurate to within 10 yards. If the coordinate is of a trench, then this is either a roughly central position along its length or a part relevant to the narrative. I have also included sketch maps for most of the battalion's sectors. A printout of a 'scanned map' will help the reader follow the action. These maps show the relationship of various positions to each other and, although only approximately to scale, are compiled from information gleaned from a combination of contemporary written and pictorial sources. What maps do not easily show are fields of fire, and having walked the ground, I have used a 'soldier's eye' to comment on these when appropriate. Another change I have made is to the order in which a sequence is described. The British Army lists from right to left, but as most civilians are used to the opposite, I have narrated from left to right.

Sadly, the first draft of this book resulted in no fewer than 300,000 words—far too many for publication—and subsequent editing made it necessary to remove much biographical detail of individuals, most disciplinary cases, and those who departed for reasons of sickness or commissioning. However, every single casualty—fatal or otherwise—is covered in the narrative.

Acknowledgements

This book would not have been possible without the help and patience of my wife, Glynis, whose assistance with research and photography was crucial to its completion. I must also acknowledge archivist Jan Grace from Liverpool Records Office, for her help in accessing the forty as-yet-uncatalogued boxes of Norman Ellison's papers. Many thanks also to Pete Noyce and John Standish for original letters. Finally, many thanks are due to Jay Slater, Joshua Greenland, and all the staff at Fonthill Media, without whom this book would not have been possible.

Contents

Glossary and Abbreviations

4.2 and 5.9	German 105-mm and 120-mm Howitzers. The Imperial designations were used to describe both gun and round
ADMS	Assistant Director Medical Services
AOC	Army Ordnance Corps
APC	Army Pay Corps
A&Q	Administration and Quartermaster
ASC	Army Service Corps
Bde	brigade
Blue-X	gas shells containing diphenylchloroarsine
camouflet	an explosive charge intended to disrupt mining operations
CCS	Casualty Clearing Station
Cheshires	Cheshire Regiment
CRA	Commander Royal Artillery
CRE	Commander Royal Engineers
C/Sgt	Colour Sergeant
CWGC	Commonwealth War Graves Commission
DAH	Disorderly Action of the Heart
DCLI	Duke of Cornwall's Light Infantry
DCM	Distinguished Conduct Medal
DOW	died of wounds
DSO	Distinguished Service Order
FGCM	Field General Court Martial
FOO	Forward Observation Officer
Green-X	gas shells containing phosgene
GRU	Grave Retrieval Unit
GS wagon	general service wagon
HE	high explosive
IBD	Infantry Base Depot

ICT	Inflammation of the Connective Tissue, or Internal Cruciate Tear
IR	Infantry Regiment (German)
KIA	killed in action
KLR	King's Liverpool Regiment
knife-rest wire	a free-standing obstacle consisting of two posts lashed into an 'X'-shape, connected by a longer centre post, all liberally festooned with wire
KORL	King's Own (Royal Lancaster) Regiment
KRRC	King's Royal Rifle Corps
Lifeboat Party	see Second Line
Loyals	Loyal North Lancashire Regiment
L/Sgt	Lance Sergeant—an Acting/Sergeant
MC	Military Cross
MGC	Machine Gun Corps
MiD	Mentioned in Dispatches.
MFP	Military Foot Police
MM	Military Medal
MO	Medical Officer
Monmouths	Monmouthshire regiment
MSM	Meritorious Services Medal
North Staffs	North Staffordshire Regiment
OH	Official History of the Great War. 109 volumes based on official sources.
OP	Observation Post
OR	other rank
OBL	Old British Line
RA	Royal Artillery
RAMC	Royal Army Medical Corps
RDC	Royal Defence Corps
RE	Royal Engineers
RF	Royal Fusiliers
RFA	Royal Field Artillery
RFC	Royal Flying Corps
RGA	Royal Garrison Artillery
Rfn	Rifleman—the equivalent of a Private in a rifle battalion
RSAF Enfield	Royal Small Arms Factory in Enfield
RWF	Royal Welsh Fusiliers (they didn't become 'Welch' till 1920)
RWK	Royal West Kent
Second Line	a proportion of the battalion kept back from the front line as a nucleus to reconstitute the battalion. Also known as the 'B' Team or Lifeboat Party
South Lancs	South Lancashire Regiment

SMLE	Short Magazine Lee-Enfield
SDGW	*Soldiers Died in the Great War* volumes.
SWB	Silver War Badge; also South Wales Borderers depending on context
TMB	Trench Mortar Battery
tool-cart	a two-wheeled utility cart
VC	Victoria Cross
VDH	Valvular Disease of the Heart
Wounded at Duty	A minor wound that is dressed within the unit, the man returning directly to duty
WIA	wounded in action
Yellow-X	shells containing mustard gas
Yorks and Lancs	Yorkshire and Lancashire Regiment

1

August 1914—24 February 1915: Early Days

Before 1908, Home Defence was supplemented by locally organised, part-time Militia and Volunteer units, whose infantry did not serve overseas until the Boer War 1899-1902.[1] The forerunner of the battalion, the 5th Lancashire Volunteer Corps—also known as the Liverpool Rifle Volunteer Brigade—was formed in 1859, from professionals and businessmen of the City; in 1888, they became known as the 2nd Volunteer Battalion, contributing three volunteer companies during the Boer War. The 5th TF Battalion also shared 'Rifles' roots, forming as the 1st Lancashire Rifle Volunteer Corps in 1859, becoming the 1st Volunteer Battalion in 1888—later differentiated from the 'Liverpool Rifles' (the 6th) by the title 'The City of Liverpool Rifles'. Although the 5th lost the official 'rifle' designation prior to the war, the rank 'Rifleman' appears against many of their longer-serving men.

The Haldane reforms of 1907 replaced the Volunteers, Yeomanry, and Militia with the TF and the Special Reserve. The latter, based around the old Militia, was for soldiers who had not served with the Regulars, but had agreed to serve overseas in the event of war. The former were fourteen divisions of locally raised and funded men. There was no obligation for the TF to serve overseas, but men could, if they wished, volunteer to do so. For most Volunteer units, there was little change other than their designation.

In July 1914, the KLR fielded six TF battalions: the 5th, 6th, 7th, 8th (Irish), 9th, and 10th (Scottish). Each was diverse in character and fiercely proud of their traditions and differing dress, sporting no fewer than four different cap badges. The badge of the 6th was the traditional 'Rifles' bugle horn, surmounted by the Lancashire rose. Dress differed also: the 10th decked out in a Forbes tartan kilt, though a khaki kilt-apron was worn in the field. Although the 6th wore the standard khaki, their puttees, buttons, and locally-procured 'webbing' were the black of a rifle regiment; their bayonets were referred to as 'swords'; and the rank of rifleman was held instead of private. Like all rifle battalions, their march pace was 140 per minute, as opposed to the standard 120. Highland regiments, who march to the pipes, have a slower pace of 112 to the minute. With the Liverpool TF encompassing all three paces, this must have made organising a combined march-past an interesting affair. With a large and diverse population to choose from, the TF battalions recruited from different segments of the populace, the 6th retaining their Volunteer practice of only admitting men from professional and white-collar occupations.

The establishment of a TF infantry battalion was set at 1,009 all ranks, twenty-nine of whom were officers, including the 'Regular' adjutant. Recruits were expected to be at least seventeen years old and no older than thirty-five; though sixteen fourteen-year-olds could be enlisted with permission from a parent or guardian, with a discretionary maximum of a further eight—though it was expected that these youngsters would be kept out of harm's way. Recruits had to be at least 5 feet 2 inches tall, though with an average height 8 inches above the minimum, the Rifles towered above most—no doubt attributable to their relatively prosperous background. The 4th KORL, primarily recruited from the mines and shipyards of the Furness district, averaged 5 feet 5 inches; the Lancaster-based 5th KORL were slightly taller at 5 feet 7 inches.

The battalion's selective recruiting policy filtered out most underage recruits and few got away with it. Only three of those later found to be underage were deployed to France with the battalion in February 1915, the rest arriving later, when the selection criteria became less stringent. One of the former, George Broadbent, enlisted in the first rush of patriotic fervour in August 1914. His discharge came about in May 1915, but only after suffering a minor wound that March. After the declaration of war, underage enlistment became endemic, as teenagers desperately tried to get involved. No proof of age was required and recruiting sergeants would take a likely looking lad's word for it if he said he was nineteen. One youngster, who enlisted in the 7th Battalion on 5 August, ended up in court:

> Charged with being an absentee from the 7th King's Liverpool Regiment, William Howard, Boundary Street, Birkdale, was at the Southport court today handed over to a military escort. Detective Lawrence said defendant enlisted in the Territorials on the 5th inst., stating he was 17 years and 4 months old. He did not come up on mobilisation. Witness said his mother told him she would not allow her son to go because he was only 15 years and 8 months old.[2]

In total, forty-four underage soldiers arrived in France, destined for the 1/6th, the majority in March and April 1916. Most were detected before the end of September—many before reaching the battalion. Tragically, the true age of two was not discovered until after their deaths in action. It was not just the young who were guilty, as considerable numbers of older men subtracted years in order to be accepted—some in their late forties. Compulsory registration, under the Military Service Act of January 1916, largely ended fraudulent enlistment.

The Army was fully aware that training could not be as thorough as the Regulars, though the expectation was that, by the time they were needed, they could be brought up to the same standard as their Regular counterparts; men of the National Reserve being used to replace casualties in Regular units.[3]

To begin with, recruits learned basic drill. The lessons of the Boer War were still fresh in the minds of the military and physical fitness and musketry were high on the agenda.

TF infantry spent as much time as possible on the range and all were expected to pass the same stringent annual marksmanship test as the Regulars. In 1914, their rifle was the Charger Loading Lee Enfield (CLLE); the 4-inch-shorter SMLE, issued to Regulars in 1907, had not filtered down to them. The designation as a 'Rifle Battalion' was a source of intense pride and, as might be expected, marksmanship was valued. Prior to the war, the battalion had been represented sixty-seven times in the final stages of the Queen's and King's Prizes at Bisley and achieved '2nd' in the Gold Medal shoot a number of times. At the outbreak of war, the battalion had several members who represented the TF in shooting matches.[4]

Physical training consisted of regular sessions of callisthenic exercises, cross-country runs, football, rugby, and, most of all, frequent route marches. The army of 1914 marched almost everywhere, 10 to 15 miles a routine distance. Falling out of the line of march without permission was judged a heinous crime by officers and senior NCOs alike, who believed it reflected badly upon the unit. Even today, the '10-Mile Bash', part of the Annual Fitness Test for all soldiers, has to be covered in under two hours.

The 980 ORs of a peacetime battalion were not all riflemen, as there were other vital roles to fulfil. Each battalion possessed two Maxim machine guns, requiring one sergeant, one corporal, twelve men, and two drivers. A further twenty-eight drivers were necessary for the horse-drawn transport. Each battalion was allowed eighteen horses for various purposes, two GS wagons, and a machine-gun transport. Specialist sergeants fulfilled the roles of farrier; battalion-cook; pioneer; saddler; shoemaker; armourer; and quartermaster-sergeant. The 6th had the services of S/Sgt William Geekie of the AOC as armourer-sergeant and William Hill of the ASC as farrier. Fourteen Regulars were attached as drivers and medics, though when war was declared, these were supposed to have returned to their parent units, the posts filled internally. However, the Casualties Book lists five ASC drivers and four RAMC medics on the strength when the battalion sailed to France. On a war footing, 'Transport' needed seventy-two animals (fourteen 'riding' horses and fifty-eight draught and pack animals); six GS wagons; eleven limbered wagons; two machine-gun carts; one medical cart; two water carts; and one cart for the Officers' Mess—additional personnel drawn from the manpower available to fighting companies. Transport and Stores comprised around 100 men.

Once mobilised, the two GS wagons allocated under peacetime rules were patently inadequate and additional transport was rapidly requisitioned from civilian owners—often garishly painted and rarely of identical design to its military equivalent. It was no surprise that the rest of the battalion nicknamed Transport, 'The Circus'. RSM James Barnett recounted one amusing consequence:

> The following telegram was received at Batt. Hqrs, Redhill.
>
> 'To all units Southern Army. Send all carts, small arm. Carts, tool. Carts, water. To O.O. Gosport for issue to 6 Division.'
>
> The above was dispatched by our unit and many other units, with the result that the place was congested with all kinds of weird vehicles. To us and to the others, a tool-cart

> was a tool-cart in spite of it having been a bread-van, and a water-cart was a water-cart although its true business was to water the streets of Liverpool.
>
> Of course the vital words omitted were 'military pattern'. Our funny carts were returned to us and in due course handed over to our 2nd Line.[5]

The Annual Camp of the West Lancashire Division was scheduled to begin at Kirby Lonsdale on 2 August 1914. All KLR TF battalions belonged to this division, the 9th and 10th, in the South Lancashire Brigade, the other four making up the Liverpool Brigade. The Advance Party departed Liverpool on Thursday 30 July; the remainder, travelling up on Sunday, met torrential rain at Kirby Lonsdale, receiving a thorough soaking as they marched to camp. Once there, they found most tents, blankets, cooking utensils, and groundsheets already packed for returning to barracks. Newspapers had reported the mobilisation of French, German, and Russian forces in the days prior to camp and rumours of impending war began circulating from the moment they gathered—the lack of equipment only serving to strengthen these. In fact, as the RSM attested, some had already deployed:

> During July 1914, when rumours of war were in the air, in accordance with the precautionary stage period, our Special Service Section, was called out to guard vulnerable points. When the order was sent out, the Section, under Lieut [Thomas] Wilson, 'C' Company, reported for duty in less than two hours; in fact, Lieut. Wilson arrived at Prince's Park Barracks, rigged up in full war kit, in under one hour. The Section proceeded to allotted stations and remained there until after general mobilisation.
>
> These were the first of our men armed and issued with ammunition for the Great War.[6]

Upon their arrival, COs were notified that the troop trains had been detained at Kirkby Lonsdale and further orders were expected returning battalions to their peace stations. Before they got a chance to settle down and dry off, the battalion were ordered home, leaving a rear party under Lt Edward Oliver to pack the remaining kit. The main party marched back to the station, where the RSM observed:

> We saw numerous trains filled with naval ratings, being rushed south. Possibly this was one of the causes of the rumour that Russian troops were passing through England. A chance remark, 'They are rushing troops south', became 'Russian troops etc.'

At Battalion HQ in Prince's Park Barracks, Upper Warwick St, the CO, Lt-Col. H. D. Spencely, retained his Headquarters detail, dismissing the remainder and warning that mobilisation may be imminent. The evening paper for Monday the 3rd reported a dramatic statement made that afternoon by the Foreign Secretary: 'Mobilisation of the Fleet has taken place. Mobilisation of the Army is taking place'.[7] The Mobilisation Notice was received late that night and calling-up notices sent to all ranks, ordering them to report to HQ in the morning. This was also posted at Liverpool town hall on 4 August.[8]

The RSM was alone in the barracks when he received a midnight telephone call from Maj. Fulton, Brigade-Major of the Liverpool Brigade:

> [He] told me to get 100 men at once, issue 100 rounds of ammunition per man and instruct them to report at Exchange Station where a train would be waiting to convey them to Crosby. The matter was extremely urgent as information had been received that some German cruisers were making for the Mersey and it was expected that the Crosby Battery would be attacked. I pointed out that there were no men at the barracks and the battalion was not due to mobilise until the following morning. I was alone in the barracks and furthermore very few of our men lived nearby. However, he stressed the importance of the matter and I promised to do my utmost.
>
> I remembered that the Rear Party left at camp was due back and I kind of kept them up my sleeve.
>
> I had no-one else at the barracks, so I got my wife to standby as telephone-operator-orderly and set out to the home of the nearest man who, as far as I can remember, lived in Madelaine St. [75-yards away] I dug him out and gave him instructions to warn another man who, in turn, was to go to another, and so on, each reporting in turn to me at the barracks.
>
> In the meantime, a phone message came from Divisional Headquarters to the same effect as the one from Brigade and great stress was laid upon its urgency. I reported that action was being taken.
>
> Eventually the Rear Party arrived in the early hours, completely done up. I explained the situation to the officer in charge and he decided that the only thing to do was to take his men to the station. As a matter of fact I am afraid I told him that I had received orders from HQ to send him, but I think, taking everything into consideration, the decision above seems better [a classic RSM ploy]. My next trouble was that the men were famished and had been without food for umpteen hours. My wife fixed up Lieut. Oliver with a snack and I sent out a foraging party to the little shops in the neighbourhood to wake them up and to commandeer food. A varied diet of bread, cakes etc. was obtained. Ammunition was issued to the party and all ranks were mounted on the lorry which had brought up the baggage. With cheers from the thirty or forty people outside the gate, who had assembled how or why is not known, away they went.[9]

The next morning, the battalion assembled and all ranks were given a medical, issued with ammunition, and paid £5 per man—not, as might be expected, in notes, but in gold. Lt John Trench took a couple of men and an empty ammunition box along to the bank in nearby Mulgrave St, withdrawing £3,000 in sovereigns. By 5 p.m., the battalion was in position on the Wirral.

The Liverpool TF, in their Home Defence role, guarded strategically important locations in and around the city; both banks and the mouth of the Mersey; docks; shipyards and marshalling yards; railway stations, bridges, and signals; and power stations, water plants, and munitions factories. It was to these round-the-clock duties that the battalion deployed, with sections assigned to each task. Fortunately, it being the summer holidays, men could be accommodated in schools, with the battalion occupying Blackburne House Girls' School in Hope St (now the Liverpool Institute). The men, many still barely-trained, were given strict orders to shoot anyone who failed to answer their third challenge.

With fear of spies and saboteurs approaching hysteria-level among the civil population, it is hardly surprising that some of the Territorials were edgy; the first tragedy occurring on the Wirral, where the East Lancashire RGA were assigned on guard. On 10 August, twenty-year-old Gunner Louis Morrice was fatally shot at Bidston Hill. Someone thought they had spotted a spy and the guard, under Lt Cook, was turned out to search. Morrice was one of five gunners ordered to beat the thick undergrowth towards the railing that divided the woods from Eleanor Road. Someone gave the order to fire—it was never established whom—and a round from the panicked volley struck Morrice.[10] The next misfortune was on 11 August, when an aged pedlar was shot by a sentry on Red Lion bridge, over the Leeds and Liverpool Canal at Maghull. Sixty-two-year-old William Dawson from Morecambe had failed to respond to the sentry's challenge and died shortly afterwards.[11]

Their duties were taken over by older men from 3/Cheshires on 18 August, and the next day, the battalion marched behind the band through Liverpool to Lord Derby's Knowsley Park estate (the Earl of Derby preferred to be referred to as 'Lord'). The 1,000-strong battalion was accommodated in tents, but lacked the important facility of a water supply. Rfn Norman Ellison recollected that they had to shave in hot tea, or lemonade, and considered it a 'sticky business'.[12] Twenty-one-year-old Rfn Isaac Foulkes gained the accolade of being the first man to be charged for a disciplinary offence, when on 22 August, he was awarded three days' confined to barracks for gambling in camp that morning. A week later, the Rifles moved 2 miles to Earl Sefton's Croxteth Park estate—and although still under canvas, water was available.

Their stay there was short, as camp was packed away on 31 August, men spending the night on the bare ground. Next morning, they boarded a train at Lime Street, bound for Redhill in Surrey. Over the preceding fortnight, much of the Division had deployed on railway guard duties in the south-east, and this too would be the task of the Rifles, guarding 60 miles of the London, Brighton and South Coast Railway. These strategically-vital networks carried most of the men and supplies destined for the Western Front, and with concerns about spies and sabotage, every element of the railway network was guarded. Within hours of their dispersal along the line, an elderly Lewes resident, cycling home in the dark, had a very close call. Unbeknown to the sentry, the old man was deaf and failed to hear the challenge. Fortunately, he dismounted just as the sentry raised his rifle to fire.[13]

Dispersal along a 60-mile span posed challenges: rations had to be portioned out to the various company bases, usually at one of the stations, before distribution to outposts, and few were lucky enough to be billeted in houses, most bedding down in waiting rooms, horseboxes, empty carriages, platelayer's huts, and even in the open. Training was impossible and the maintenance of discipline difficult, especially considering the generosity of residents regarding bottled beer and the attractions of a uniformed young man to local girls. Fortunately, most men kept out of trouble. The first of the disciplinary charges to be levelled there was against one of the more mature and responsible men, father of four, thirty-five-year-old Rfn Francis Owen—though his offence was carelessness rather than obstinacy. He was one of a section from 'G' Company quartered at Balcombe Station, and on their first day there, he accidentally discharged his rifle on the station platform. As the first incident of this type, the punishment given by 2Lt Geoffrey Blackledge reflected this and an admonishment was delivered, the thoroughly-chastised soldier continuing his duties.

At Redhill on 4 September, Rfn Sydney Young was charged with 'insolence to an NCO', by L/Sgt William Heaton. The twenty-four-year-old, who had enlisted on 6 August, was sentenced to eight days' confined to barracks.[14] On 20 September, eighteen-year-old Rfn George Pickles, also discharged his rifle—no doubt scaring the life out of his section-commander, L/Cpl Arthur Le Rougetel, who was standing next to him. He was given seven days' confined to barracks.[15] The word 'accidentally' has been crossed out on his conduct sheet and 'carelessly' substituted. Before too long, the increasing frequency of this potentially-lethal lapse saw 'negligently' become the standard terminology. Just three weeks, later Pickles was in trouble again—this time charged by Sgt Francis Zacharias for 'irregular conduct as a sentry' (German-born Zacharias was naturalised when his parents emigrated to Liverpool). As the punishment levied by Capt. Edward Brocklehurst was a lenient three days' confined to barracks, I suspect his actual crime was either sitting down while on guard, having his rifle slung, or chatting to girls. The last of the disciplinary charges during their time guarding the railway was levied against twenty-year-old Rfn George Robertson, a Territorial since March 1911. C/Sgt William Butler charged him with 'highly irregular conduct—taking apples from an orchard'. The Adjutant, Capt. George Teall, agreed and sentenced the 'scrumper' to five days' confined to barracks.[16]

London-based engineer Mr T. Lockwood-Bunce was surprised to recognise the uniform of the Rifles near Brighton, and having friends in the battalion, he made enquiries as to their whereabouts:

> By the greatest of good fortune, I happened to meet one of the very squad I wanted to see, and was informed that my friends were guarding the railway line a few miles away. Motoring to the spot, I found several of the company at lunch in a platelayer's hut, the remainder being asleep in a tent adjoining. After escaping from a frightfully vigorous handshaking, I was able to ask how matters fared with them, though it was evident from the look of the men, that they were having the time of their lives.
>
> All expressed themselves delighted with their lot. The people in the district seemed to have vied with each other in making a home from home for the men. One lady asked them to send two men to her house every day so they could have the luxury of a hot bath and also asked for their dirty linen and any sewing that was necessary. A station master's wife nearby cooks a hot roast for them each day, and now milk is delivered from a farm morning and evening. Fruit and vegetables have been sent to the camp in abundance, so that beyond the wrench from friends at home and the absence of local news, the Rifles are having a really fine time.[17]

Norman Ellison, whose section included Riflemen Ernest Rowbottom and John Whittle, recorded a similarly-comfortable arrangement with the landlady of the nearby Joliffe Arms, who often cooked their meat for them and local resident, Seymour Hicks, who allowed the men to have hot baths at his home, the 'Old Forge'.[18]

The letter, published in the *Echo*, provoked a caveat from one soldier:

> I have read with interest the letter from Mr T. Lockwood-Bunce, and I may say that my comrades and myself, who form a patrol of the Liverpool Rifles guarding the railway, are highly appreciative of the fact that a Liverpool resident takes so much interest in our battalion. But at the same time, I would like to remove any misunderstanding.
>
> Our work is neither easy nor restful. It is both dangerous and responsible, securing as it does the main lines to the Continent, and it calls mainly for night effort and gives very little time for rest.
>
> Very few of our patrols are so favourably situated and so well looked after as those mentioned by your correspondent. Many of them are working in smoky tunnels and cuttings far away from houses. A false step to them means death, while as for a bath, I should think they have forgotten what one feels like.
>
> We do our work cheerfully and willingly, but I should not like our friends in Liverpool to think that while so many are shedding blood for their country, this fine old regiment is having a glorified picnic.[19]

Just how dangerous was demonstrated on their second day.

Fifty men were based at Haywards Heath station, one of whom was Rfn Cyril Letheren. A clerk with one of the dock companies, he had enlisted in March 1914, two months before his seventeenth birthday. His first day on duty was to prove his last, when he was hit by a train at 3.30 p.m. on 2 September. At the following day's inquest, Capt. John Temple and Sgt James Knight appeared for the battalion. The first witness was platelayer George Downer:

> [Downer was] Working on the down siding when he heard the whistle of a train. There were several sharp whistles. He looked up, and saw the deceased on the four-foot way. He was walking with his back to the engine. Witness shouted and then the deceased was knocked down. He was 20 yards from the engine when witness first saw him. If the deceased had heard the whistle when it was first sounded there might have been time for him to get out of the way, but there was no time for him to do so when he (witness) first saw him.

The inquest continued:

> By the Jury—Deceased never turned his head round once. He was not carrying a rifle?
>
> By Mr Brewer [railway company's solicitor]—Deceased never appeared to hear the train. There is no reason why he should not have walked on the outside of the line.
>
> Henry Dorman, railway porter, said there was no time for the deceased to get out of the way even if he had heard the train.

> Frank Figg, fireman on the engine, said the train left Victoria at 2.04 p.m. It was a stopping train. When he saw deceased he blew the whistle. The driver could not see the man owing to the curve of the line. Deceased was from 15 to 20 yards off when witness first noticed him. Had witness not seen him, no whistle would have been sounded. The train pulled up just clear of the body. The speed was about 30 miles an hour.
>
> Sgt J. A. Knight said deceased was under his orders. He was out on leave, witness having given him permission to go to Haywards Heath. Deceased asked if he might proceed along the line, and witness consented, but warned him to remember his orders and walk on the right side, in the pathway outside the sleepers.
>
> By the Coroner—The deceased was on duty at Balcombe Viaduct, and started from his post there to Haywards Heath.
>
> Mr F. B. Brown, district engineer for the Southern Section of the railway, also gave evidence, and the Coroner said it was difficult to understand why deceased walked in the four-foot way. Evidently he did not realise he was doing a dangerous thing. No blame could be attached to the driver or fireman.[20]

A verdict of 'Accidental Death' was reached.

On Friday 4 September, the platform was lined by an honour-guard, their rifles reversed. As the coffin was loaded onto a Liverpool-bound train, a bugler sounded the 'Last Post' and tears flowed freely from soldiers and civilians alike—who had turned up in large numbers to see the coffin off.

Further down the line at Lewes, the battalion provided an honour guard and bugler on Monday 7 September as a draft of 100 recruits for the Royal Sussex marched behind the local band from the town hall to the station. The platform was thronged with enthusiastic well-wishers and the band, who remained outside the station, played 'Sussex by the Sea' as the train departed.[21] Tragically, it was less than a week before the next fatality, and it was another teenager.

Eighteen-year-old Rfn Harry Liversidge was hit by a train in the morning of 10 September and died soon afterwards. The inquest was held next day at 'the Feathers' in Merstham:

> Harold Stanley Haines, a Rifleman in the 6th (Rifle) Battalion King's Liverpool Regiment, of Blundellsands, Lancashire, identified the deceased and said that when at home he lived with his two maiden aunts. The deceased was stationed at Merstham with part of his battalion.
>
> James Alexander King of Princes Park, Liverpool, a Rifleman in the battalion, said deceased and he were on duty at Merstham, patrolling the line between Merstham Tunnel and Battlebridge. About half-past nine on Thursday morning they were having their breakfast in a hut by the side of the railway line on the south side of Rockshaw Bridge. It was the habit to cry out to passengers in passing trains to throw out newspapers to them. It was their practice to stand by the side of the track, well out of the way of the trains. On this morning the deceased went out of the hut to see if they could get any newspapers, as they heard an up-train approaching. The hut was on the down side. Just

> after the deceased left, witness saw him flung from the track into the ditch. A down-train passed at the same time as the up-train and the former struck him. Witness went to the assistance of the deceased, who was unconscious, but not dead. He died shortly afterwards.
>
> Lieut [Edmund] Buckley of the same battalion was called and the Coroner said they did not want to lose lives in this way if it could be avoided.
>
> The officer said the men had been warned about the danger and instructions had been issued. He added how exceedingly sorry they were to lose the deceased and on behalf of the Commanding Officer and the company officers, he expressed regret at the loss they had sustained.[22]

Ellison's 'billet' was just 6 feet from the rails, in a very steeply-sided cutting at the southern mouth of the Merstham tunnel:

> I lived in a hut made of old railway sleepers at the entrance to Merstham tunnel—a dirty, smoky place that soon made us black as sweeps. This duty was varied with night patrols between the airshafts ventilating the tunnel. They were situated on rough common land, pathless and lonely. I was on patrol one dark night when suddenly behind a clump of furze I saw movement on an indistinct white patch and heard heavy breathing. A face, I thought to myself. I challenged and again. A third challenge was ignored so with my heart in my mouth I lunged at the face with my bayonet.... A cow rose to her feet and made the night hideous with her justifiable protest.[23]

On another occasion, the guard was turned out to chase what turned out to be a straying donkey.

A week later, on 17 September, the battalion lost their third man to the trains. Twenty-three-year-old Rfn Peter Conroy was patrolling the Southerham Bridge, where the railway crossed over the Ouse near Lewes:

> The body was identified by Capt. Ernest Bennet of the 6th Battalion King's Liverpool Regiment. Deceased he said was about 21 years of age [*sic.*] and lived with his parents at 55 Shallot St, Liverpool, and was the sole support of his father and mother. Deceased had been engaged guarding the railway at different spots for about a fortnight, and had been stationed at Southerham since the previous Sunday. The instructions given to the sentries were not to walk in the four-foot way. On this particular duty the sentry was supposed to walk up and down the side pathway of Southerham Bridge between the metals and the rail of the bridge. Conroy was an excellent soldier. Witness added that at the time of the accident there was a very strong wind blowing and with his rifle at the slope, it might have caused him to sway a little as the train passed.

Rfn Thomas Edge testified:

> He saw deceased go on duty about 4 o'clock, and the accident occurred about 4.40 p.m. He had been on the same duty since the previous Sunday. Witness had nothing to do at the time, and hearing a train coming from the direction of Lewes to Eastbourne, he went up the slope to see it pass by. He noticed Conroy walking along to the side of the bridge, coming towards Lewes. His bayonet was fixed and he was carrying his rifle at the slope on his left shoulder. There was a train overtaking deceased from Eastbourne, and noticing that his bayonet was very near the metals, shouted to Conroy: 'For God's sake, look out: there is a train behind you'. The wind was so strong that he did not think he heard him. At all events, he did not appear to take any notice. The train was then close on him and the engine struck his bayonet. Deceased was turned round about three times, and as he fell, must have been struck by some part of the engine. His head was split open and running up to him, witness could see he was dead. He fell clear of the metals onto the path on which he had been walking. The wheels did not go over him. The end of the bayonet was broken off, and it was found on the engine. The train pulled up about 300 or 400 yards down the line.[24]

Cpl Hubert Spargo corroborated Edge's testimony. Capt. Bennet explained that the rifle should have been held on the left shoulder in a straight line, but that after a while, a man's arm became cramped and to ease it, the arm was held out from the body a little, moving the tip of the 17-inch 'sword' nearer to the rails.

The driver of the Lewes-bound train shut off the steam before reaching the bridge, 500 yards from the 10-mph speed limit on the sharp curve leading into Lewes Station and blew the whistle as soon as he saw Conroy, though the driver opined that the soldier had probably not heard him because of the strong wind and the sound of the train coming the opposite way. When questioned about the necessity for anyone to patrol the bridge, Capt. Bennet replied that immediately after the accident, he gave orders that no one was to do this and had instead posted a sentry either side. Men were ordered that if they needed to cross, they were to unfix bayonets and carry their rifle at the trail. The Jury generously donated their fees to Conroy's parents.[25]

There was another fatality that month. The demise of Francis Owen on 26 September was to pit the battalion against the faceless bureaucracy of the Financial Department of the War Office—a struggle that lasted until July 1915. Identification was provided by section-commander, Cpl James Hankey. At the inquest:

> Captain John B. McKaig, commanding 'G' Company, said deceased joined about two months before mobilisation. He acted as cook to the party posted at Balcombe Tunnel. He came to Balcombe about three weeks ago. Witness detailed orders given to the battalion, and also his own personal orders to the men as to walking by the line. Pamphlets were also issued by the railway company, giving instructions to the men. Deceased had always been a careful man. He was apparently returning to his post in the tunnel. He had been off duty and was returning from his billet. He could have gone back by road. It was forbidden to go on the line when not on duty.

> Rifleman [James] Swift said he was on patrol duty about 5.22 p.m. on Saturday. He was about 200 yards south of the tunnel with the patrol. When they saw a down-train coming out of the tunnel, they got up the embankment out of the way of the train. He followed the train with his eye, and saw deceased apparently springing out of the way of the train. Witness was about 150 yards away. The engine caught deceased and hurled him up the embankment, deceased seemed to be jumping out of the way when the train caught him. Witness thought deceased was caught by the square iron plate just behind the buffers of the engine. The patrol ran up the line to deceased. They found he was dead. There was blood on his hand and in his mouth. There was only a slight mark on the chin. The train stopped by the bend by the Red Bridge. Witness did not hear any whistle, or notice any other train. Deceased was in the habit of using the track to get to his post. It was the shortest road to the village. Deceased had had three weeks' experience of the danger of walking on the line.[26]

The War Office determined that Owen had been off duty and declined a pension for his widow and children. The outrage this provoked within the battalion can only be imagined, but supported by the Preston Infantry Records Office, who furnished a copy of the Inquest, and sworn statements from Capt. McKaig and Cpl Hankey—both insisting that Owen had been on duty—the War Office caved in and Mrs Owen got her pension. Tragically, there was still a toll to be paid for the security of the railway network.

On Tuesday 6 October, Rfn Arthur Scarlin was given responsibility for relieving the sentries guarding the railway at Lewisham. That night, after relieving two of the posts, his small squad marching along the 6-foot way stepped around some loose rails lying in the centre of the way. Rfn Thomas Kay described hearing a bang and Scarlin was 'cannoned' into him, pushing Kay into Rfn Ernest Barber, who was marching ahead of them, causing both to stumble. A fast train passed and, looking round, the two men saw Scarlin lying on the 6-foot way, his head grievously injured. Kay insisted he had had not heard the train approach. The thirty-three-year-old died in Lewisham Infirmary the next day.

Sgt Frederick Cavanagh's anger at the London Ambulance Service was palpable:

> It took twenty-five minutes to get Scarlin from St John's station to the infirmary, to which he was wheeled in an open ambulance, with his face exposed and the public gazing at him. He thought it a scandal in the name of civilisation and Christianity. He had enquired of the police and found it was impossible to get either a horse or a motor ambulance. He added that it was disgraceful. 'We,' he said, 'who come from Liverpool expect better things in London, and we are disappointed. In Liverpool we have the proper horsed and motor ambulance services, and we would have had this man to hospital within ten minutes. For a man to be wheeled along the streets as this man was, is revolting to the extreme.'
>
> A police officer stated that the wheeled ambulances were provided with hoods and that it was generally considered advisable to give an injured man as much air as possible.
>
> A medical witness confirmed this view, but in answer to Sgt Cavanagh, said that all the air and room necessary would have been secured in a horse ambulance. The witness added that the case was hopeless from the start.[27]

Accidental Death was the predictable verdict, but the Jury added a rider that trains should whistle on approaching and leaving stations, and that obstructions should be removed where possible. They agreed with Cavanagh's opinion of the Ambulance Service—as did the Coroner. Scarlin's death was the fifth and final railway death for the battalion, though Ellison refers to eight Riflemen losing their lives on the railway.[28] CWGC records indicate only five for the 6th, however, the rank of two railway fatalities suffered by 5/ KLR is shown as 'Rifleman', a vestige from their earlier days.

On 16 October, the local paper announced:

> The War Office have devised a scheme which will relieve Regulars and Territorials from the performing of sentry and other duties on the home railways. They have appealed to the Territorial Force Associations in the country to undertake the new arrangement, which is to call upon National Reserve men in their counties to do this work referred to and the movement is already well-advanced.[29]

The battalion had already left. On the night of 12 October, the RF took over their duties and the battalion moved to Sevenoaks. Their stay there was short, and on 29 October, they continued to Canterbury, joined there by the rest of the Brigade. The other brigades moved to the Sevenoaks in November, forming part of the Outer London defences. The chances of the division deploying to France as a whole were becoming less by the week, increasing numbers being returned to their civilian jobs in strategic munitions industries.

Moves were also afoot to divert men elsewhere. In October, 4th KORL were asked by the War Office if they would like to join the East Lancashire Brigade in Egypt, and tempting though the offer was, they replied that they would rather remain with the West Lancashire Brigade. Despite this response, the War Office ordered them to nominate two companies to go to Egypt. Protests were made, but these companies were withdrawn from their tasks and equipped for warmer climes. However, this order was rescinded at the last minute, their place taken by two companies from a different regiment. A similar move to send the Rifles was made in January, when crates of topis arrived and Brigade asked for the names of men familiar with camels. While Ellison was sure that this heralded a move to Egypt, a more cynical military observer would probably have put his money on a move to the Arctic.[30] As with KORL, nothing more came of this. The first battalion to be parted from the fold was Liverpool Scottish, who went to France on 1 November, joining 3 Division in the Salient. By the end of May 1915, all twelve battalions were serving with other divisions.

Late on 2 November, the battalion were roused from their billets and packed onto a train to Whitstable. The German fleet had been reported in the North Sea and the government was taking no chance of this being the precursor of an invasion. Although some at the time ridiculed this concern, Kitchener's recurring reply was 'I am only prepared to rule out the feasibility of an invasion if I can learn that the Germans regard it as an impossible operation'.[31] Ellison recalled: '... by the light of lanterns, we dug trenches in the smooth, grassy slopes of their seafront—a wet, clayey task that soon had us caked from head to foot'.[32] His company's trenches were at Tankerton.

The battalion was billeted in the town for a few days, returning to the eastern quarter of Canterbury when the Imperial fleet sailed home after shelling Yarmouth. The willingness of locals, woken in the early hours of the morning and asked by Capt. Richard Wainwright and Billeting-Sergeant Charles Skafte to accommodate a couple of tired and muddy soldiers, speaks volumes for their patriotism, as Ellison vouched:

> When it came to our turn—Reggie Smith [William Reginald Smith (763)] was with me—a grey-bearded, upstanding figure of a man, with the South African campaign medals pinned to his dressing gown, an ex-Army surgeon, replied to the billeting-officer's enquiry, 'I shall be proud to have soldiers in my house, Captain, provided they are clean men who will not spit on the wallpaper.' The soldiers he knew were the 'regular' swaddies of Rudyard Kipling; fine tough fighting men, but unvarnished. The war was still too young and the idea of educated fighting soldiers unknown to him.[33]

Billets were not always ideal. Ellison's first in Canterbury was in the house of a woman whose husband was away with the Buffs and she did not want anyone accommodated there. There had been a number of 'incidents', but the final straw was when the rifles belonging to the occupants of the billet were discovered to have had their bolts filled with jam—a deed she rather unconvincingly blamed on her toddlers. Sadly, Ellison recorded neither the comments of the inspecting officer upon discovering the jam, nor its flavour!

A typical day began at 7 a.m., with morning parade and roll call, followed by PT and a short run.[34] Men were granted an hour for breakfast, which ended at 8.30 a.m., the duration necessary due to the difficulties of ration distribution and food preparation. Instead of being fed centrally, uncooked rations were taken by handcart to the various billets and apportioned out to each individual house—a nightmare for the corporal in charge of the detail and his two helpers, faced with problems, such as how to divide one tin of jam between five men in three houses.[35] Breakfast complete, the morning program between 8.45 a.m. and 12.30 p.m. included a route march, drill, and field manoeuvres.

The latter invariably meant practising the two basic formations. In 'artillery formation', men advanced well-spaced apart in single file. Once engaged from the front, they adopted 'extended order' (line abreast), giving more protection from machine-gun fire to their front. Hostile fire from the front when in artillery formation, or from the side when in extended order, was known as 'enfilading fire' and was far deadlier, a single burst potentially dispatching an entire section. Once engaged, they advanced in alternate sections—those not moving providing covering fire. The heavier the enemy fire, the shorter the rushes between cover. When close enough to their objective, men would charge as quickly as possible to overwhelm the adversary by delivering the maximum number of men in the shortest achievable time.

Reconvening at 2.30 p.m., the time until to 4.30 p.m. was occupied by company drill, including a full inspection of uniform, equipment, and weapon. Whenever possible, firing on the range was organised and much time was also devoted to bayonet fighting. After a very welcome brew, men gathered between 5 p.m. and 7 p.m. for lectures on the day's work, or other items of interest. After an evening roll call at 9 p.m., men were dismissed to their billets, with 'lights out' at 10 p.m.

Practice night 'alarms' and deployments also took place—to the great disturbance of billet landladies—and everyone took their share of routine fatigues and guard. Despite inclement weather, training continued apace, the mud-covered men's arrival at their billets causing dismay and alarm to house-proud landladies. Practice deployments took the battalion on day, or night-time, marches to areas that may need to be defended against invasion—companies dispersed along a stretch of coast. News of the German Fleet at sea provoked another move to the coast in December, and an excellent account of one company's stay in the little village of Beltinge—now swallowed up by Herne Bay—was written by journalist and author Mary L. Pendred:

> Our village lies on the coast, two miles off the seaside town of—let us say—Dash. We have no pavements, or even side-walks; no main drainage, no lights save those of the Stores and the Post Office, no amusements outside our homes. We go to bed at ten, or earlier. Few of us have gas laid on in our houses, and have to be content with oil lamps and 'Beatrice' stoves. Our roads are probably the muddiest in England during the wet months of the year, for rain does not sink through the clay soil, which sticks and hardens till it can only be dislodged with a knife. But our air is delicious, and we bask in sunshine when the rest of our isles are wreathed in cloud and fog.
>
> Our houses are scattered, our population sparse, and billets had not been found for all the 200 men of the Liverpool Rifles who arrived here one soaking day last month from our nearest garrison town—(to avoid the censor we will call it Double Dash)—so they had to stand about in the mud and rain for an hour or so, getting wetter and wetter, and making an unconscious appeal to the sympathy of housewives, whose hearts were torn between eager loyalty and the natural dread of strange men in their quiet homes. But the exaction of the King's command (with the offer of 9*d* a night—not to be despised in hard times) was imperative, and by nightfall, a number of men were quartered in bungalows and cottages, as many as could be thus accommodated hospitably, while the rest were sent into unfurnished houses to 'doss down' on naked boards and cook for themselves.
>
> It was quite dark before they were all housed and given their rations for the night. What a night for them! Tired out with marching and standing four or five hours carrying rifles, greatcoats and blankets, extra-weighted by being wet through, they had to make fires in cold grates, from damp coal, before they could feed or rest: and sleep when it came, was taken in damp and steaming coats and blankets!
>
> Neighbours sent in odd tables and chairs, with a camp bedstead or two; but they hardly counted among so many men, for there were twenty or thirty in each empty bungalow. And the loans being haphazard, it was inevitable that some got the lion's share while others had none. Lamps too, were scarce and not of the best, taxing the wit of man to cajole. For what does the city-bred youth know of oil and wick? There must have been language, 'frequent and painful and free' over our old lamps in the empty bungalows that first night!

We saw them as we passed, dim and smoky, mingling their sulky light with the dancing rays of huge fires; saw the rows of sock, trousers, vests, and other garments, stretched on lines across the room to dry; and we wondered what the atmosphere was like inside, the atmosphere our Tommies had to breathe while they slept. And we began to realise, as we had scarcely done before, the minor hardships that soldiers have to bear before their work begins in earnest. Perhaps those hardships, borne in cold blood, without excitement or *éclat*, may be even more trying to a man's spirit than anything they have to endure in actual warfare. Who knows?

They do not complain, bless 'em! 'We have to be hardened, you know, and it's all part of the game,' they say, with a laugh, and we hear them tramp off through the rain or mist to their trenches, five or six miles away, at eight o'clock every morning, singing lustily a ragtime chorus, or their newest song. Now and then, in the writing-room above a garage, that the women of our village have arranged as a soldiers' club, it is true we pick up a spoilt sheet of paper thrown down on the floor, on which is a confession that life is terribly rough, sometimes almost unbearable, but this is in confidence, to mother, sister, wife, or best pal. To the outsider, they make light of every ill.

There were a good many persons in the village who believed we were in danger of an invasion one week, and I think that most of us had a sneaking wish that something really thrilling would happen—something not very bad, but just bad enough to give us a chance of brilliant deeds. I'm sure our Tommies did. They would have liked a German transport to attempt landing a few hundred men in our marshes, and to have had the honour and glory of sniping them off with their long-carried, little-used rifles. But the cry of 'Wolf' which rouse this blood-thirsty expectation has lost its effect now on soldiers and villagers alike. We have fallen back into our normal state of stagnancy, and the boys went back to Double Dash some days ago, many of them declaring that they had enjoyed their stay here immensely, hard work and all.

We did the best we could for them. Every night we had a smoking sing-song in the garage, hung with flags, a huge fire and coffee as refreshment. They sang all their own favourite songs— 'Tipperary', 'Mary-Anne, She's After Me', 'The Spaniard who Blighted my Life', 'Ragtime Cowboy Joe', 'The Ragtime Navvy', 'P.C. 49', 'Little Grey Home in the West', 'Somewhere a Voice is Calling' and 'Land of Hope and Glory' being first favourites. And they sang their own versions. 'It's a Long March into Berlin' and 'D'ye Ken John French'. Nearly all had good voices, and there were several excellent pianists among them, for the Liverpools we saw are mainly recruited from professional and business classes—young men who have left comfortable and even luxurious homes to be hardened into Tommies. And whoever says that the English are not musical should have heard them sing, often in parts and always in perfect time, the choruses of an incredible number of songs. It was a revelation to some of us.

The village now seems asleep or dead now that the boys have gone. They brightened us all up and we loved them. Their behaviour was exemplary, with the rarest exceptions, and they showed themselves immensely appreciative of every hospitality we were able to afford them. Their easy acceptance of all discomfort, their amused pride in their cooking

> and household work, as well as in the trenching, their jolly choruses along the roads, delighted us, and we saw them go with sinking hearts. One little lady was found in tears after the departure of her four nice boys. 'They'll forget me,' she said, 'but I shall never forget them and I shall pray every night for their safety.'
>
> The concert was over, the uproarious ragtime choruses and laughter had all been lost to the *National Anthem*, and we were washing up the coffee cups. A tall boy in khaki jumped up on one of the planks, which laid on orange boxes, formed the seats of our concert hall. 'Anybody know where Blank hangs out? He's dropped his death number.'
>
> He meant the identification disc which every soldier wears in order that his body may be identified, however mutilated, in the field of battle. We looked at each other and ceased smiling. That boy! Was it possible? And the full horror of war surged over us.[36]

As Christmas approached, it had been four months since any had seen home and for most, this was their first time away from families; the expectation of impending seasonal leave was not unreasonable. Sadly, it was not to be—at least not for the Territorials; none of the division's battalions were granted the privilege of a few days at home. Not so the 'Pals', who got their Christmas leave—an injustice that provoked indignant letters in the local press of every battalion in the division. This clearly reached the ears of Lord Derby, who commented upon the matter during a recruiting drive at Bootle on 21 December, explaining:

> He had received lots of letters asking him to do what he could to get the Liverpool Territorials now in Kent sent home for Christmas Leave. He knew how much the men and their relatives would desire this; but to his mind—especially after the Scarborough incident—the territorial on duty guarding the coast in Kent was just as much on active service as the soldiers in France. [The Imperial Navy shelled Scarborough, Whitby and Hartlepool on 16 December.] He had taken on a patriotic duty, and had got to see it through, for the German Emperor would not stop the invasion of this country because the Liverpool Territorials wanted Christmas leave. [37]

With both Rifles battalions away (the 2/6th were in Blackpool with the 2nd West Lancashire Division), the ladies of Liverpool formed a Ladies Work Union to provide the men with 'socks, shirts, underclothing, cholera belts, woollen helmets and mittens'.[38]

After New Year, indications that their time in England was coming to an end became obvious. The battalion was now reorganised from eight into four companies—'A' to 'D'. Beginning with 'D' on 21 January, one company at a time was given five days' pre-embarkation leave, the last to go being 'B', who departed on 9 February. It was fortunate for George Robertson that it was in this order, as he was in trouble again on 21 January. This time, Capt. Bennet had discovered him in a pub, when he should have been working, and he was given three days' confined to barracks—it could easily have cost him his leave.

Men were given another medical and final inoculations. Surprisingly, the jabs were only advisory and at least three must have declined this sensible protection, as they were later invalided home with typhoid. Not all were deemed fit to deploy and some were posted to the 2/6th for reasons of fitness or age. One, who was in the process of being medically discharged, was twenty-five-year-old Rfn Cecil Lewis. On 27 January, he went before a Medical Board at Brighton, his failing eyesight having been detected in late December. The Board considered it was connected to a kidney problem he had suffered five years earlier, which in their opinion was aggravated by the cold and damp conditions at Canterbury. Tragically, before he could be released, he died from kidney failure on 5 February.

On 5 February, new equipment arrived and was issued in a rolling program over the following fortnight. Khaki puttees replaced the black ones and everyone was issued with new boots and webbing; Transport received new wagons, their current hotchpotch manifestly unsuitable for overseas service.

Presumably new rifles (modified CLLE) were also issued, though no surviving record mentions this. From 7 February onwards, one company at a time visited the ranges and it is reasonable to assume that they were zeroing their new rifles with Mk VII ammunition. The battalion did not receive a full issue of Mk VII ammunition until 22 February, but as all Mk VI rounds had been withdrawn three days earlier, it is probable they had some Mk VII left over from the ranges. There were instances of units deploying with unmodified weapons, generating much adverse comment, but as no such mention is made by the 1/6th, it is unlikely they were affected. A report, circulated by 2nd Corps in April 1915, details some of the issues of firing Mk VII ammunition from unmodified weapons:

> With the majority of rifles, it is impossible to fire rapid. A strong hit with the full force of the hand being necessary. In many cases, the extractor does not work when the bolt lever has been raised. I found one case when the full weight of the body was necessary to withdraw the bolt. This is believed to be due to the breach of the long rifle not being fitted to Mark VII S.A.A. The increased charge causing the cartridge to expand more than it did with the Mark VI. The greater resistance of the long barrel would also cause this. The extractor is too weak and also fails to grip the rim of the cartridge. In these cases, the rifles and ammunition were clean and well-oiled. If the rifle gets the least bit dirty, and this is bound to happen on wet or muddy nights, the difficulties are increased. Another fault of the long rifle is that the screw ramp of the backsight is put out of order by the slightest jar. Again, the rifle grenade is not adapted to the long rifle.[39]

The CLLE also required alterations to the rear sight, the Mk VII round having a muzzle velocity around 400 fps faster—thus a flatter trajectory—and to reliably feed the pointed-nose Mk VII, the magazine needed modification. Factories such as RSAF Enfield were working flat out to adapt the CLLE, and in February 1915, this factory alone reworked nearly 28,000 rifles for troops deploying abroad. While with 28 Division on 3 March, the 1/6th was asked to 'list rifles with Mk VII ammunition [concluding] rifles found satisfactory'.[40] This pretty much confirms they received modified rifles before sailing.

On 22 February, the new CO, Maj. Henry Davison, was warned to hold the battalion in readiness for embarkation, the order arriving next day. First Parade at Wincheap in the south-west of Canterbury was at 3.30 a.m. on 24 February, a bitterly cold Wednesday morning, thick flakes of snow cloaking the shivering ranks. Despite the weather, many of the billet landladies turned out to wave their 'boys' farewell. At 6.40 a.m., the first of three trains left for Southampton, the final one departing at 9.50 a.m. It was no insignificant task loading all the stores, animals, and carts aboard ship; only the two-footed walked up the gangplank—everything else was winched aboard, an exercise that was not particularly popular with livestock, which tended to register their disapproval to anyone within range. By 4 p.m., all equipment, thirty-one officers, and 1,094 other ranks were safely aboard SS *City of Edinburgh*, which set sail for Le Havre at 5 p.m.

2

25 February 1915—30 July 1915: A Hard Apprenticeship

Coordinates for this Chapter

Place	Latitude	Longitude
Blauwpoort Farm	50°49′43.30″N	2°54′26.90″E
Brocklehurst-killed	50°49′51.80″N	2°55′49.40″E
canal bridge	50°49′14.40″N	2°53′25.30″E
Canal Post	50°49′1.00″N	2°54′28.30″E
Cavalry barracks, Ypres	50°50′44.10″N	2°53′13.30″E
Chester Farm	50°49′16.10″N	2°54′8.80″E
'D' Coy. 11 July	50°49′22.40″N	2°55′5.50″E
Davidson Dugout	50°49′37.40″N	2°55′26.80″E
dugouts (15 May)	50°50′13.80″N	2°50′59.20″E
Dump	50°49′31.80″N	2°55′27.90″E
farm 'Y'	50°49′46.00″N	2°55′35.50″E
Fosse Wood (Reserve)	50°49′49.10″N	2°55′55.10″E
Gangers' Hut	50°49′42.50″N	2°55′20.10″E
hedge (Sapper rescue)	50°49′47.00″N	2°55′14.00″E
Hill 60	50°49′26.40″N	2°55′43.50″E
Infantry Barracks, Ypres	50°50′53.89″N	2°52′58.50″E
International Tr.—block	50°48′58.10″N	2°55′10.50″E
Jct. 47>47S	50°49′35.60″N	2°56′3.20″E
Knoll Farm	50°49′49.20″N	2°55′41.80″E
Kruisstraat Château	50°50′15.10″N	2°51′22.00″E
Lankhof Farm Château	50°49′22.60″N	2°53′28.80″E
Larch Wood	50°49′36.00″N	2°55′28.40″E
Mount Sorrel	50°49′38.50″N	2°56′34.50″E
Pannenhuisstraat	50°50′30.10″N	2°52′23.20″E

Railway Arch dugout	50°50′0.50″N 2°54′24.10″E	Trench 34	50°49′11.70″N 2°55′6.90″E
Ramparts, Ypres	50°50′44.40″N 2°53′29.70″E	Trench 35	50°49′14.50″N 2°55′16.80″E
Rifle Pits	50°49′46.00″N 2°56′0.20″E	Trench 36	50°49′18.40″N 2°55′25.60″E
road junction 15 March	50°49′34.70″N 2°53′16.30″E	Trench 37	50°49′21.50″N 2°55′34.50″E
Rosenthal Château	50°49′42.00″N 2°53′25.80″E	Trench 38	50°49′26.30″N 2°55′41.10″E
Rozenhill huts	50°48′40.80″N 2°47′2.90″E	Trench 39	50°49′28.20″N 2°55′42.50″E
ruined building (5 May)	50°49′46.10″N 2°55′47.00″E	Trench 40	50°49′30.00″N 2°55′48.80″E
Shrapnel Corner	50°50′15.10″N 2°53′16.60″E	Trench 41	50°49′32.10″N 2°55′45.40″E
sniper-railway cutting	50°49′22.50″N 2°55′44.20″E	Trench 42	50°49′42.30″N 2°55′44.10″E
support post, Zillebeke	50°49′54.50″N 2°55′22.80″E	Trench 47	50°49′34.70″N 2°56′5.50″E
The Bluff	50°48′55.60″N 2°54′53.10″E	Trench 47—barricade	50°49′34.50″N 2°55′56.80″E
The Caterpillar	50°49′19.20″N 2°55′45.30″E	Trench 47 Support	50°49′37.60″N 2°55′54.10″E
The Mound	50°48′33.10″N 2°53′45.60″E	Trench 48	50°49′34.90″N 2°56′14.20″E
Thomas Lewis—killed	50°50′1.50″N 2°55′31.00″E	Trench 50	50°49′37.10″N 2°56′28.60″E
Transport Farm	50°50′8.40″N 2°54′7.10″E	Trench 51 Support	50°49′40.20″N 2°56′23.00″E
Trench 29	50°48′49.40″N 2°55′5.40″E	Triangular Wood	50°48′41.90″N 2°54′27.80″E
Trench 32a	50°49′1.00″N 2°55′13.40″E	Wilson's farm	50°49′56.10″N 2°55′44.50″E
Trench 33	50°49′5.10″N 2°55′5.30″E	Zillebeke *arrêt*	50°49′56.30″N 2°54′53.60″E

The diary entry 'voyage completed without incident' belies the discomfort of the passage.[1] The ship picked up its destroyer escort in the Solent before heading across the Channel, tying-up at Le Havre shortly before 8 a.m. the next day. The crossing had not been particularly rough, but men—prohibited up on deck—were jam-packed below, smoking or lights forbidden, and few managed any sleep. Disembarkation began at 8 a.m., but it was afternoon before everything was offloaded. The morning was cold and frosty, mist sheathing the heights above the town as the men began their march to No. 6 Rest Camp at Harfleur—a facility that was little more than a collection of tattered, leaky tents on a muddy, windswept promontory. Squashed twenty to a tent, mutual proximity kept most tolerably warm. Ellison was less fortunate:

> It was just my luck to be detailed for headquarters-guard on a night of perishing cold: six of us and a prisoner in one tent. Whereas the rest of the battalion packed like sardines some twenty men in a tent, kept reasonably warm, we were half frozen. We all knew the prisoner—one of the best soldiers in the battalion, so we let him out to buy a bottle of whiskey somewhere. I shudder at the thought of what would have happened had we been found out. It helped keep us alive till morning.[2]

When Maj. Davison reported to the camp commander, he was ordered, without explanation, to set aside two platoons to entrain for an unspecified destination at 9 a.m. Why the 91st Reinforcement Battalion required these platoons is unknown, but they rejoined at Bailleul. While at Harfleur, all ranks were issued with goatskin coats, which although they 'stank abominably', due to being improperly cured, were welcomed for their insulating qualities, though soon 'lost' after the snows melted in late-spring.[3]

The battalion paraded at 7 a.m. on 26 February and marched to the goods station in Le Havre, entraining at 1 p.m., though one man was left behind: twenty-four-year-old Rfn Alexander Roberts had briefly been hospitalised with a grumbling appendix at Canterbury; now it flared up again and he was admitted to the Base Hospital in Le Havre. Still unoperated upon, he was evacuated home and medically discharged in June. It was only when he appeared before a Medical Board in January 1918 that his notes were marked 'this case is immediately one for operation.'[4]

The 180-mile journey took an interminable twenty-one hours, a seemingly never-ending transit, with not even the CO informed of their destination. Men were loaded into cattle trucks, forty men and all their kit per wagon, just a pitifully-thin layer of straw on the floor to ease their discomfort. The slatted sides allowed a bitterly cold wind to scythe through (known in Liverpool as a 'lazy wind' because it cannot be bothered to go around, so just goes straight through). Rations consisted of tea leaves—but no means to boil water—hard Army cheese, and the infamous and dentally-injurious biscuit. Rfn Lewis Jones put in a claim for dentures upon demobilisation in January 1919, as on 5 May 1915, he suffered 'loss of teeth, broken by eating biscuits'.[5]

A lengthy stop was scheduled at a station halfway between Rouen and Abbeville, coffee supposedly laid on for everyone. The train halted, officers and men alighted; all were eager for a hot drink, only for the whistle to be blown almost immediately, as the French driver proceeded to pull the train out of the station, chased by the entire battalion—a scene redolent of those stars of 1914 cinema, the Keystone Cops. The CO was the last to board, having raced a considerable distance over signal rods and railway sleepers before managing to jump back on. By some miracle, no one was left behind.

They finally reached Bailleul at 9.30 a.m. on 27 February, and the cold, stiff men marched off to their billets. HQ and three companies were accommodated in the girls' school, the others occupying the lunatic asylum—possibly a portent of events to come? Early the next morning, the two platoons diverted earlier rejoined, complete with an interpreter. *Capitaine* Baron De Rosen was a Polish resident in Switzerland, who travelled to Paris when war was declared, signing up as a trooper of *Cuirassiers*; a larger-than-life character, he became very popular with all ranks.[6] In the distance, a dull rumble of artillery could be heard to the east—the Ypres Salient beckoned.

The battalion joined 15 Bde, 5 Division, the Brigade only just out of the line after ten days in the trenches at Dranoutre (now Dranouter). The Rifles were just one of twenty-six 'unattached' TF battalions arriving that month. Although the TF probably considered themselves trained, it is clear that Chief of General Staff Sir William Robertson thought otherwise. On 4 February 1915, he sent the following memo to all divisions hosting TF battalions:

> The points which experience has shown require special attention are as follows:
>
> Training
>
> (a) More practice required in the use of rifles and machine-guns especially with Mark VII ammunition.
>
> (b) In many cases the men not in hard condition and march discipline generally requiring improvement.
>
> (c) Much practice in entrenching, especially with the entrenching implement required.
>
> (d) The means of keeping up communication not properly understood. Orderlies require more training and the knowledge of telephone equipment slight.
>
> (e) Platoon leading not as good as it should be.
>
> Administration
>
> (a) Lack of proper sense of discipline and the correct chain of responsibility not maintained.
>
> (b) Transport not properly cared for nor well controlled on the march. The billeting of transport not understood. A deficiency of men thoroughly trained in cold shoeing.
>
> (c) Men's boots not well-fitted, many of them too small.
>
> (d) The preparation of indents and the system of supply, generally not understood.
>
> (e) More instruction in billeting required.[7]

Many of these shortcomings were down to a lack of experienced instructors (for all ranks) in England, but on the positive side, these battalions were full of men of extraordinary potential, who were quick to learn and desperately keen to do so. How well this transpired very much depended on the Regulars they received their apprenticeship with. The Rifles were put under the care of 1/Cheshires.

A standard infantry brigade had four battalions, but Robertson—keen not to weaken his brigades—attached the TF as an addition, though five of the brigades had six battalions allocated (four Regular and two TF). The 15th Bde, apart from the battalion and their mentors (1/Cheshires), comprised the 1st Battalions of the Norfolks, Bedfords, and Dorsets. The other TF battalion was the 1/6th Cheshires, who had arrived in December 1914, though a bitter feud had developed between them and 1/Cheshires, and on 1 March, they were removed from the division at the request of the brigade-commander.

The battalion was inspected at Bailleul on 1 March by Brig.-Gen. Count Gleichen, the brigade-commander—though it was his last day in command, as he was replaced by Brig.-Gen Edward Northey the next day. The brigadier, used to Regulars of shorter stature, expressed his amazement at the height of the Riflemen.[8] This was not the only change, as 15 Bde was temporarily attached to 28 Division, and at 10 a.m. on 2 March, the battalion marched into Belgium.

The Brigade was accommodated around Ouderdom. The battalion, who eventually arrived at 2.30 p.m., billeted in 'noisome farmsteads, which at that season were mere oases in a sea of mud', scattered in and around Busseboom.[9] The 17-mile journey had been trying, the roads muddy and deeply-potholed—as the unwary discovered when they found themselves up to their knees in cold, dirty water. The march took longer than expected, as erroneously, they were first sent to Vlamertinghe; then upon arrival, directed back to Busseboom. The highlight of their journey had been in Ouderdom, where the Liverpool Scottish lined the road to greet them, many happy reunions taking place.

Accommodation was basic, most crammed into the lofts of barns, though the abundance of straw for bedding and close proximity of men to one another provided that most precious of resources during a Western Front winter—warmth. Another bonus came from the enterprise of farmers' wives, most of whom sold ration supplements in the form of home-cooked ham, egg, and chips. Conversely, the farms were invariably filthy; a single-storey farm building forming a square around a putrid cess pit, the contents of which exuded an all-pervading stench and hosted legions of flies in the warmer months. The stay at Busseboom was brief for 'A' and 'B' companies, as at 6 p.m. on 4 March, they proceeded to billets in Ypres to begin their induction into trench warfare with 1/Cheshires, one company at a time.

On 4 March, 15 Bde took over the 'B' Sector of the line from 9 Bde, opposite Hollebeke, with 1/Cheshires manning the line. This ran from Trench 32a on the left to the northern bank of the Ypres-Comines Canal on the right. 'A' Sector, on the extreme right of the division, continued from there, towards Triangular Wood; the left of the divisional front at Mount Sorrel.

A major tribulation resulted from the design of these trenches. In areas with a high water table, it was impossible to dig deep before water began to well up—the water table here being less than 2 feet down. In such places, a shallow excavation was made and sandbag walls, known as breastworks, were constructed. These needed to slope at a proper angle to avoid collapse and a minimum thickness of 40 inches was necessary to stop a bullet—consequently the width at the bottom of the wall was much greater. Breastworks were very vulnerable to artillery and a direct hit often destroyed an entire section, crushing defenders under sandbags. Small arms fire constantly eroded the outer sandbags, generating perpetual maintenance, and their new positions lacked drainage and effective top cover. While the small dugouts built into the sandbag walls provided some protection from shrapnel, a hit by HE often collapsed the entire structure, crushing or suffocating the occupants.

Brig.-Gen. Northey inspected the line on 5 March and was concerned with his findings: Northey noted about these former French positions that 'the parapets too high and not bullet-proof, no loopholes for snipers'.[10] Communication trenches were inadequate in design and state of repair, and at the approaches to the Support Line, non-existent.

The two companies approaching Ypres in the gathering dusk, along a road packed with troops and transport, could have had no illusions that they were entering a war zone. The arrow-straight Poperinghe–Ypres road afforded glimpses of shell-rent buildings to the sides, punctuating the bleak flatness of the Flanders countryside; in the distance, the rattle of rifle fire could be heard from the line, delineated by a steady fountain of rising and falling flares. The flash of exploding shells ahead, followed seconds later by the crump of the explosion, served notice that their destination lay well within range of German guns. The poplars lining the roads of Flanders, planted over a century earlier to provide summer shade for travellers, gave the marching columns no protection from the biting wind and heavy rain. Nearer to Ypres, the order 'no smoking' was passed down the line, and as the outskirts of the tortured city were reached, guides met them to escort them to their new billets in the old cavalry barracks.

A 'certain' smell hung about Ypres—one that would become all too familiar when they experienced the front line. In the moat and underground waterways of the city and under ruined and collapsed buildings, the bodies of civilian victims of German shellfire rotted away unburied, the miasma of corruption tingeing everything.

The battalion fared better than the Bedfords. The Regulars were allocated Rosenthal Château (later known as Bedford House), and judging by their report to division, it failed to impress:

> It has been occupied by troops of various nations and was indescribably filthy when we first went there. Suffice it to say that previous occupants had evidently objected to outdoor latrines and had apparently failed to find them indoors. As the château was also subject to shelling, it was no health resort.[11]

Complaints about indiscriminate defecation and the shallow burial of the dead inside trenches were common whenever British troops took over sectors from their European allies. The heavily-damaged Château, comprehensively destroyed by the end of the war, was under direct observation and well within range of hostile artillery, so daytime movement was anathema.

Despite daily shellfire, many civilians remained; sheltering in cellars as shells fell, emerging to continue their business once calm descended again. Although the city was already heavily damaged, the worst was yet to come. Under the streets, the River Yperlee ran in a brick-built culvert, maintaining the level of the moat and draining into the man-made reservoir of Zillebeke Lake. Some weeks earlier, a 'Jack Johnson' (German 15-cm shell) blew a huge hole in the road behind the barracks, revealing a 50-foot-long stretch; the exposed waterway then used for ablutions and watering the horses. There was very little retaliation as the British were woefully short of guns and ammunition, routine expenditure limited to just three rounds per gun, per day.

On 5 March, while 'A' prepared for their first experience in the line, 'B' was hard at work in Ypres. Ellison described the moment the shells began to fall:

> I was on a fatigue party for sandbags this morning and had to go to another part of the town when the Germans opened fire. We could hear the shrapnel playing on the roofs and the children screaming as they bunked to their underground burrows. We saw men looting amongst ruined houses for gas fittings, piping and other odds and ends. I suppose on this game you become something of a philosopher, the odds being enormous against a shell falling on the exact spot you are.[12]

At 6 p.m. on 5 March, 'A' paraded at the barracks and began to make their way towards the 1/Dorsets and the front Line, arriving safely around 11 p.m. Rfn Graham Smith's introduction to the line was exceptionally brief, as within the hour, he was wounded by shrapnel in hip and buttock, and although his wounds were described as 'slight', he was evacuated home, then commissioned into the South Lancs. The rest of the company had a fairly quiet night, and at 5.25 a.m. on 6 March, the CO of the Dorsets reported to brigade that all was quiet—though it did not last.

Trench 32a (International Trench) was shared with the Germans, only a sandbag block separating the protagonists, and was a most unhealthy location. Just after 11 a.m., the Dorsets reported that the enemy had been firing continuously at the loopholes and parapets and by noon, they had lost three killed and seventeen wounded.[13] Two Riflemen were hit in the afternoon; Harry Cooke's wound in the left arm was slight, but he was evacuated home, returning in August. The second, thirty-year-old Liverpool insurance inspector Thomas Jones (988), was more seriously injured, the wound to his left thigh occasioning his medical discharge. 'A' returned to Ypres, arriving at 9 p.m. At 10 p.m., the Dorsets were also relieved, the Bedfords, who sustained three wounded on the way up, taking over the line and the tuition of 'B' Company.

How poor this sector was—and 32a in particular—is well illustrated in a report from the Bedfords:

> At any rate, the front line we took over was more than vague, and the relief was unique in my experience of trench warfare; the trenches, such as they were, seemed to be on no settled plan and were not continuous: as a matter of fact, I believe they were sundry support trenches with perhaps a bit of front trench here and there.

We hold, amongst others, what was termed the 'International Trench'; and the problem was to find out where our nearest friends were to right and left; and where the nearest Germans were not, for they seemed to be in most directions and very close.

The problem was not easy to solve. It was absolutely suicidal to put one's head above the parapet even for a second to look round; and any periscope cautiously raised at once had one or more bullets through it.

On one occasion, a major of my battalion put up a periscope, which was at once perforated, the bullet glancing downwards and slightly wounding him in the head. I took the periscope from him and raised it an inch or two above the surface and immediately got another bullet through it, which sent a tiny splinter into my wrist causing a small vein or artery to spurt blood for a few seconds until stopped by pressure. I handed the periscope on to a captain, [Andrews] who had another try at a different point of the trench, but at once got a bullet through it which was deflected onto his head and caused a fairly serious wound. I think this was the end of this periscope. I give the above and an example of the difficulty experienced in finding out the lie of the land and how the German trenches ran.

The trenches were full of water in places and the Germans kept up an incessant fire on any sandbags which were visible; this in course of time destroyed the sandbags and caused a continual stream of mud and earth to come down at each shot onto the necks or into the eyes of men crowded in the trenches just below the sandbags, and very irritating when continued all day.

We found in due course that the Germans held one end of the International Trench, but that part of the trench had been blocked or fallen in between us and them.

The Germans also held a trench immediately in front of us, and had practically joined up one end of it to the part they held on our right, so as to partially envelop our right at this point.

One trench near here, nearly waist deep in water, had been handed over to us as leading into the German line so we blocked it with wire, and a sentry was posted at our end of it. After a little time however, we explored this trench and found it led away from the Germans; and it proved very useful as a communication trench a day or two later, when the Germans filled in and obliterated some 20 yards of the left of International Trench with heavy *Minenwerfer* shells.[14]

It was here the battalion spent their first sixteen days in the line, the episode with the periscope happening on 8 March, while 'B' was there. The camouflaged loopholes of enemy sniper posts, penetrated the foot of the parapet at an oblique angle, making them incredibly difficult to spot from British trenches directly opposite.

Back in Busseboom, four Riflemen from 'C' were commissioned on 6 March: Harry Mansergh went to 1/9th KLR, dying from wounds in November 1916; thirty-two-year-old Alsager Warburton, Walter Brownell, and Basil Oxenbould were commissioned directly into the battalion.

After dark on 7 March, 'B' filed forward for their introduction to the line, their journey far from straightforward. Their guides repeatedly got lost, and at one point, they became so

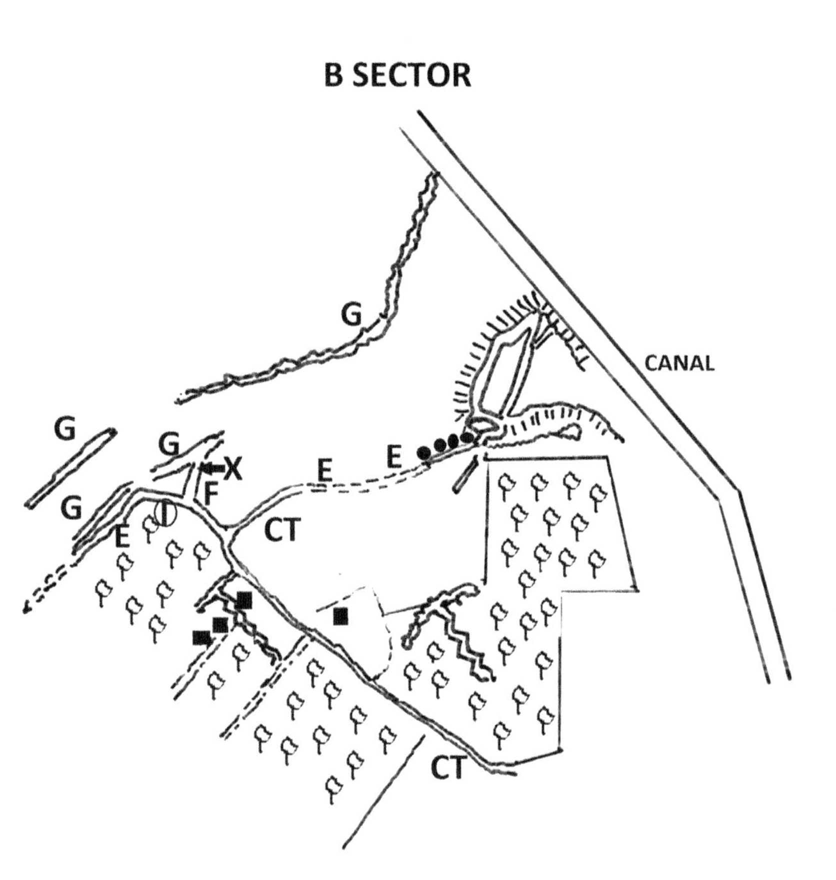

CT- COMMUNICATION TRENCH
G- GERMAN TRENCH
X- BLOCK
■ - DUGOUT
•••• - HEDGE
- TREES
Ⓘ-INTERNATIONAL TRENCH
E- ENFILADED
F- FLOODED

disorientated that the company found themselves between the lines; knee-deep mud on the approach intensified their struggles and it was a full five hours before they reached their destination. 'B' Sector was quiet overnight, though daylight heralded a steady increase in German activity. The Bedfords' HQ was shelled, killing one man, and considerable hostile sniping punctuated the day, killing three and wounding another, though the Rifles escaped unscathed. Sadly, the next morning saw their first fatalities.

Early on the 8th, after the dawn 'stand-to', five Riflemen gathered around a brazier in the front line, frying bacon for breakfast and trying to garner some warmth from the meagre coals. Without warning a shell screamed in and exploded amid them. Twenty-year-old Henry Clarke was killed outright and twenty-nine-year-old Robert Fisher was terribly wounded in the head, dying minutes later. Both were buried behind Trench 32, their graves obliterated in later fighting. Wounded in elbow and scalp, Thomas Furniss was evacuated home, medically downgraded and transferred to the RDC. Norman Ellison and Frank Evans were both knocked unconscious for several minutes by the blast, but remained in the line—their appetite for breakfast severely diminished after being spattered by pieces of their comrades.[15] Wretchedly, the shell, which had fallen short, was fired by a Belgian battery.

Before the end of the day, another six Riflemen were wounded, the most critical being twenty-three-year-old John Pinches, whose wounds to elbow and scalp proved fatal on 20 March. Percy Bird's injury to his left hand was minor and he returned to duty on 18 April. Henry Wilson's wound in his right forearm was more serious, and it was January 1916 before he rejoined. Bank clerk, twenty-seven-year-old Stanley Jones, with the battalion since March 1909, received a sight wound to the neck, returning on 1 April. Later commissioned into the RWF, he was killed in his sleep in 1917 when a shell hit his dugout. With a 'Blighty' wound to his left arm, James Barker did not rejoin. The final casualty, William Goodman, was hit in the left knee, returning ten months later. The cold persisted, and during the afternoon, snow fell, soon turning to slush, making the trenches even more of a quagmire. 'B' was relieved that night by 'C', who had marched to Ypres the previous day.

'C' stayed just twenty-four hours in the line, but still sustained three Riflemen wounded. The Dorsets had relieved the Bedfords at 11 p.m. on 8 March and apportioned 'C' Company's platoons among their own companies. All was quiet until 2 a.m., when forty of the enemy crawled across the narrow stretch of No Man's Land towards 32a. Shortly before the attempted raid, German machine-gun fire began to sweep the parapet, expecting this would keep sentries' heads down. The ploy failed. When the raiders were just 20 yards distant, the defenders opened up with rapid rifle fire and bombs, driving the enemy back. The raiders took cover at the foot of their own parapet, regrouped, and made another half-hearted attempt—with an identical outcome.

'C' Company's three casualties were minor: nineteen-year-old Reginald Periton was able to remain on duty after his wound had been dressed; Herbert Scholefield returned three days later, after a slight hand wound; and Arthur Shaw's shoulder wound led to only five days at the CCS. The Dorsets did not escape unscathed, losing two killed and an officer and ten men wounded before noon the next day. Later that night, 'D' relieved 'C', who returned to Ypres.

'C' Company's woes did not end there, as Rfn Eric Blackburn was admitted to hospital on their return, initially diagnosed as suffering from jaundice. Sadly, it turned out to be cerebral-spinal meningitis, which caused great alarm—all who had been in close contact were placed straight into isolation. 'Spotted fever' caused such dread because it was highly infectious, approximately three out of every four sufferers dying; sadly, this was the case here, the twenty-year-old expiring on 24 March.

For those out of the line, there was no rest. Each day, large working parties carried supplies forward, or toiled on other tasks. On 9 March, 100 men from 'A' worked on road improvements near the canal. This involved clearing away the mud—often a good foot in depth—then laying a solid foundation of wood and faggots, work that continued for a twelve-hour stretch for each fatigue party. The diary records 'casualties, 1 OR wounded'; however, this was an 'injury' rather than a 'wound', Rfn Peter Evans breaking his ankle so severely that he was medically discharged. On 10 March, it was the turn of 'B' to work on the roads, while 'C' provided 100 for a carrying party, two of whom were wounded: L/Cpl Richard Hayward was 'wounded at duty', but eighteen-year-old Rfn Jonathan Donaldson was critically injured, a round going through both thighs. The injury was mortal and he died on 15 March.

'D' Company's first tour of the trenches was casualty-free, though anything but quiet. At 4.45 a.m. on 10 March, the enemy paid particular attention to the parapets of 32a, an activity the Dorsets' grenadiers retaliated to with apparent success. The foe switched tactics, and at 8.05 a.m., the Dorsets urgently requested a pump from brigade, as 32a was filling with water—the enemy having succeeded in diverting their water into it. At 11.15 a.m., the situation remained unchanged, the sounds of German pumping clearly audible. The water level in the right of 32a continued to rise, triggering another plea for a pump and REs to help build drainage—men slaved desperately to prevent the collapse of the badly-weakened parapet. By noon, the Dorsets had suffered ten wounded. Their HQ and reserve company were heavily shelled that afternoon, forcing personnel into the dugouts, but only two were wounded. That evening, 'D' withdrew to Ypres, replaced by 'A'. The Dorsets too were relieved, the Bedfords arriving at 6 p.m. With conditions so bad, twenty-four hours in the line was deemed enough.

The morning after he got back to Ypres, nineteen-year-old Rfn Ernest Eldridge from 'D' sat down and wrote a fairly-sanitised chronicle of his week to his parents in Liverpool:

> When we are on duty for the trenches we are stationed in a barracks not more than four miles from the firing line. We get up about 7.30 a.m. and have breakfast about 8 o'clock, which consists of bacon, tea, bread and jam.
>
> We then go for a wash, either in a lake [Zillebeke] close by the barracks or in a stream which originally ran under the road, but which is now accessible, part of the road having been blown away by a shell. We then clean our rifles, or some such thing. By then it is dinner-time, for which we get stew. (skilly)

After dinner we generally have a rifle inspection, get our equipment together, and as much food as we can pack, as forty-eight hours is rather a long period. Well now, with regard to the trenches.

We leave our quarters at about 6.30 p.m., and for about a mile there is plenty of singing, such as 'Tipperary'. This brings us to a massive bridge over the River—when word is passed down: 'No more singing.' We march on about another two miles to a village which has been a pretty little place, with a church, public hall etc. This place the Germans shell every day, and all that remains of the church is the tower, the clock stopped at three. The churchyard with its memorials of the past, is still intact and the network of rose trees make a very impressive picture.

From this point we are under rifle fire. We now go either to the right or the left, depending on which trenches we are going to occupy. To the left we have a fairly good road for about half a mile, which brings us to the dugouts, which are extensive holes in the ground where the men in reserve go.

If we go to the firing line, we continue the road for about 200 yards, and climb a bank about one and a half feet high and run with heads down about fifty yards. This distance is exposed to the enemy, so one has to be particularly careful.

We then come to what seems to be a ditch with fairly level sides and up to the ankles in mud. We now find that we are in the communication trench, along which we travel for about a quarter of a mile, around corners and up cuts until we see a sentry in front of sandbags some seven feet high, where we hear plenty of cracking. We are now in the front line. [The 'cracking' is caused by bullets breaking the sound barrier.]

During the night, every other man has a fixed bayonet in case of attack, and a continual fire is kept up. At dawn, to which we all look forward, the sky in the distance first becoming hazy, then a faint green, and so on, every man stands-to, that is every man is on duty for an hour, the reason being that every attack is usually made at dusk or at dawn.

During the day little firing is done, and only one man in five is on duty: so we then get a chance of a nap. It is pleasant when the relief arrives, and each of the old party is covered off by his relief. Then the order is passed on 'Relief stand-to.' We then change places.

The next order is for the old party to file out, and we start back on our return journey, arriving back somewhere around midnight.[16]

On 11 March, the enemy began to lob heavy *Minenwerfer* rounds at the junction of 32a and 33—the brigade bound—effectively cutting off the garrison of 32a. What made this bombardment particularly hazardous was the angle the mortar was firing from, allowing it to enfilade both trenches. The Bedfords lost an officer and five men wounded; their neighbours, the 5th RF, had 20 yards of their parapet blown in, killing or burying sixteen men. 'A' Company also suffered: Rfn William Williams (279) and nineteen-year-old Rfn George Battarbee both received 'Blighty' wounds to the arm, and Rfn George Hughes was slightly wounded in the right shoulder. That evening, the company returned to Ypres, replaced by 'B'.

Trench 32a was still under bombardment from the heavy *Minenwerfer* on 12 March, with the Bedfords losing an officer and two NCOs killed and one man wounded. 'B' lost

Rfn Albert Lee, who was wounded in the back and Rfn William Thomas, who was hit in the head and chest. Neither returned. That night, they were relieved by 'D'. The proximity of the protagonists in 32a led to unexpected encounters. One of the battalion's officers slowly raised his head to look over the block just as a German officer did likewise, each glaring in astonishment at the other.[17]

'D' Company's journey forward was far from uneventful and they sustained three casualties on the approach: CSM Thomas McWean was hit in the arm, evacuated home, rejoining in August and Rfn Henry Massey was hit in head and chest and never returned. The most seriously wounded was L/Sgt Charles Batson; the twenty-five-year-old, a former school attendance officer, died the next day.

One officer described his first passage to the Support Line:

> The memory of those early days is still a nightmare. Imagine the company in Indian file, feeling its way in the pitch dark, burdened with ammunition boxes and stores, in addition to pack, goatskin coat and rifle, stumbling into shell-holes, checking at every ditch and hedge and running to catch up between, bogged in mud like treacle, with guides ignorant of the way and an utter uncertainty of what lay before. Now and then, the flash of a bursting shell or the flare of a star-light would show up a ruined farmhouse and the great shell-holes on every side, filled to the brim with slimy water. Presently, bullets began to whistle, and one can hear their flick into the mud. A man is hit; there is a call for stretcher-bearers. Never mind, press on; it is worse than useless to halt. Another is hit, then another. At length, it seems ages (it is, in fact, hours), we see before us, in a low rise among some splintered trees, a few lights, apparently coming from burrows in the earth facing towards us. Weary beyond description, and dripping with sweat, we are told off in small parties to each of these burrows which constitute the shelters of the supports, and are but a few yards behind the front line. The rifle and machine-gun fire is incessant and the bullets make loud cracks as they strike the trees overhead. The firing goes on all night and increases in intensity just before dawn. The burrows, damp and evil-smelling as they are, seem to afford security, which they do not really possess.[18]

In 1970, Ellison wrote that he believed Geoffrey Blackledge was the author, though the former-officer was always evasive when asked, without ever actually denying it.[19] Ellison left record of his own journeys:

> Trench relief was carried out by small parties crossing open ground until you came to the support line. Frequently you were under direct fire so every time Jerry sent up a flare, you stood quite still, or if he opened fire, you threw yourself flat on the ground and waited until the flare burnt itself out. For a minute or so you were semi-blinded by the brilliance of the light. I remember on a particularly dirty night being one of a relief party when up shot a flare and a machine-gun opened out. I went flat in the mud alongside another fellow. When the flare had fizzled out, I said to him 'come on' but he did not

reply. Thinking he had been hit, I got hold of his arm to help him up, when ... the whole lot came off at the shoulder. It was a French *Poilu*, who had lain out there for months.[20]

Once handover was complete, 'B' began the dangerous journey back.

They had not travelled far when Liverpool teacher Rfn Fred Wedlake was shot through the abdomen from behind. The twenty-seven-year-old died at Ypres in the early hours of 13 March and is buried in the pretty Ramparts Cemetery there. Tragically, his brother, Frank, had died of wounds in September 1914, and in a sad letter, his father, George, commented that 'having lost all my sons in this war has nearly killed'.[21]

The Dorsets, who had relieved the Bedfords at 8 p.m. on the 12th, continued to repair 32a overnight, darkness providing little protection. Despite frantic efforts, the trench was still flooding and another plea for pumps was made at 12.15 a.m. on 13 March. By noon, the Dorsets reported three killed and five wounded, and 'D' suffered further loss. Company-Commander Capt. William Montgomery was shot through the head, and although still alive when he was stretchered off, he was declared dead on arrival at 84 Field Ambulance. Rfn James Armstrong's thigh wound was minor, and Rfn Lewis Jones was wounded in the right buttock, rejoining after six weeks. The final casualty before they returned to Ypres late on 13 March was Rfn John Spear; the shrapnel wound to his left thigh was just a flesh wound and he was back on duty three days later—this tour, such a contrast to their first.

'C' left Ypres for the line at 6 p.m. on 13 March, burdened down by sandbags, ammunition, and various trench stores for the Dorsets. In fact, so much needed to be ferried forward that two platoons from 'B' were dragooned into the task. When 'D' reached Ypres, their toil was not over as two platoons were immediately hijacked to carry stores to the Cheshires in 'A' Sector.

Between midnight and noon, the situation remained unchanged, constant sniping, machine-gun fire, and rifle grenades targeting 32a in particular—the Dorsets suffered three killed and five wounded during these twelve hours. 'C', who came out of the line at 6 p.m., had four wounded: Rfn Alexander Balfour was hit in the head, face, leg, and arm and never returned; twenty-one-year-old Rfn Edward Rattray was another to be lost, as he was commissioned after recovering in England from his hand wound; Rfn Charles Topping transferred to the Labour Corps after recovering from the wound to his right foot; and the most critically injured, L/Cpl George Jones, suffered severe shrapnel wounds to his face and both legs. These proved fatal and the twenty-four-year-old died on 20 March.

At 5.15 p.m., a mine explosion was heard to the right, and 'B' Sector was heavily bombarded by German artillery, principally Trench 29, on the right. The mine heralded an attack against 27 Division at St Eloi—the sector adjoining the right bound of the Cheshires. It might be thought that 'C' Company's woes were over once they returned to Ypres, but sadly this was not the case as Rfn M. Ferguson managed to accidentally stab himself in the leg on another man's bayonet and was transferred to the MFP after his recovery in England.

HQ received a telephone call at 3.35 p.m., asking for two platoons to carry ammunition and supplies to the Bedfords in 'B' Sector that evening and another two to provide the same service for the Norfolks in 'A' Sector. At 10 p.m., another 160 men were ordered to Rosenthal Château to take ammunition up to the Cheshires and Dorsets (the latter were positioned to command the canal bridge on the Ypres–St Eloi road in case 27 Division was unable to hold the German attack). Shortly afterwards, another message was received, ordering all the battalion's ammunition carts, machine guns, and reserve ammunition to Brigade HQ immediately. The situation on the right was grave: 27 Division's counterattack had failed and they had lost the Mound—strategically important because of its dominant view over 'A' Sector. The 15th Bde began to line the canal bank with all available machine guns and the two reserve battalions, all facing south in case the flank was turned.

Ellison hated carrying ammunition, describing it thusly:

> A terrible job as the boxes weigh 80 lb and are slung on a pole between two men. You have to go in the pitch dark cross-country, with the result that you spend half your time falling into ditches and water-filled shell-holes and then running like hell until you catch up with the rest of the party. We have all cut our greatcoats down to pea jacket size as we found they used to drag in the mud and weighed us down like ton weights.[22]

An additional complication to any night-time fatigue requiring rifles to be slung was the combination of tall riflemen and the longer-barrelled CLLE. Muzzles frequently got snagged by the overhead telephone wires criss-crossing the trenches—fixed at a height not to inconvenience the much-shorter SMLE-armed Regulars.

The 14th was a bad day for accidents and 'A' bore the brunt: considering the length of the bayonet, uneven ground, and men in such proximity, it is not unexpected that there were a number of 'friendly stab' incidents. However, poor weapon-handling was endemic. Soldiers were taught, and constantly reminded about, procedures, but frequently ignored them: no round was to be in the chamber, unless specifically ordered; safety catches had to be applied whether there was a round in the chamber or not; and the magazine cut-off always had to be across. When cleaning, the magazine must be removed first, followed by the bolt. Reassembly required the soldier to refit the bolt and ease springs before inserting the magazine, all of which—if followed—made negligent discharge virtually impossible.

In his Ypres barrack room, thirty-one-year-old Rfn Thomas Riddick shot himself in his left leg while cleaning his rifle. Unfortunately, he also managed to wound three of his pals with the same round, none of whom returned to the battalion: L/Cpl Charles Caird, sitting to his left, was shot in the thigh; the round passed through him, hitting Rfn Frank Jones (942) in the leg; Rfn Percy Scott, was then struck in the foot, as the bullet deflected downwards. Riddick would normally have faced a FGCM, but sadly, the wound had turned gangrenous by the time he reached hospital in Lincoln on 19 March and his leg was amputated. A needless loss of four good men.

There were casualties among the carrying parties too. 'A' Company's Rfn John Maudsley escaped with a bullet graze to his left arm, though the twenty-four-year-old would not be so lucky the next time. Rfn John Shaw was hit in the left shoulder, returning to 'D' a month later. By 2 a.m. on 15 March, 500 boxes of ammunition were in place at Rosenthal Château, and shortly after, the battalion was ordered to replenish its ammunition carts from 31 Bde's Ammunition Column, half a mile south of Vlamertinghe. By dawn, one company, each man with 200 rounds and a day's rations, was positioned as a reserve force at Brigade HQ, and at 6.30 p.m., two platoons from 'A' were sent to meet guides from the Bedfords at Brigade HQ, to join them in the line. At 7.45 p.m., 100 men with shovels met guides from the Norfolks at the road junction south of the Château and were taken to 'A' Sector to extend the support line towards 27 Division. By now, the situation in front of St Eloi had eased and the battalion's machine guns were withdrawn from the canal bank. At 6.40 a.m. on the 16th, a telegram to 15 and 9 Bde ordered all units to return to their normal stations.[23]

There were just two casualties on 15 March. Twenty-two-year-old Rfn Jonathan Pierce from 'A' was wounded in the chest and evacuated home, returning in September. Rfn George Broadbent of 'C' was less badly injured, the wound to his left knee treated at Saint-Omer. Although he returned to the battalion in mid-May, it was not for long—a dental filling at No. 2 CCS bringing about his downfall. Youngsters may have been skilled at fooling recruiting staff as to their true age, but dentists were savvier and seventeen-year-old Broadbent was sent home.

Although the billets at Busseboom were far from luxurious, compared to the line, it was five-star accommodation—but most of all, men could catch up on sleep. It was also an opportunity to write home, and the day before they returned to the front, L/Cpl Herbert Roberts of 'A' wrote to family in Gwernymynydd, Mold:

> The Germans must have a splendid system, as they spot anybody very easily; if you pass a loophole, they 'get' you passing it. We believe they somehow have their loopholes in the ground and can spot us without being seen themselves. When we fire in the daytime, it's a case of a jack-in-the-box, only twice as quick.
>
> To get something hot in the trenches is a luxury. What I do to boil water is to get an empty jam tin, cut up a candle, cut up small pieces of string, and put a match to it and in a quarter of an hour, you have the mess tin boiled. The journey to the trenches we occupied is much safer from rifle fire than others we have been in, but, of course, nowhere is safe. Going out we passed through a ruined village, and on returning, the place was ten times worse, having been shelled while we were in the trenches.[24]

The battalion left Busseboom when 15 Bde returned to the fray, taking over from 9 Bde either side of the Ypres–Comines railway. Just before midnight on 21 March, the battalion relieved Liverpool Scottish in 'D' Sector, facing Hill 60—the first time they deployed independently. The battalion was responsible for trenches 38–42, all to the east of the railway: trenches 39 and 40 were held by 181 men from 'B' and two machine guns; 'D' put sixty-two men into Trench 38 at the railway cutting, thirty-five into support in Trench 41, and a further fifty into reserve in Trench 42; and HQ occupied Davidson dugout in the railway cutting. 'A' and 'C' remained in reserve at the Infantry Barracks at Ypres.

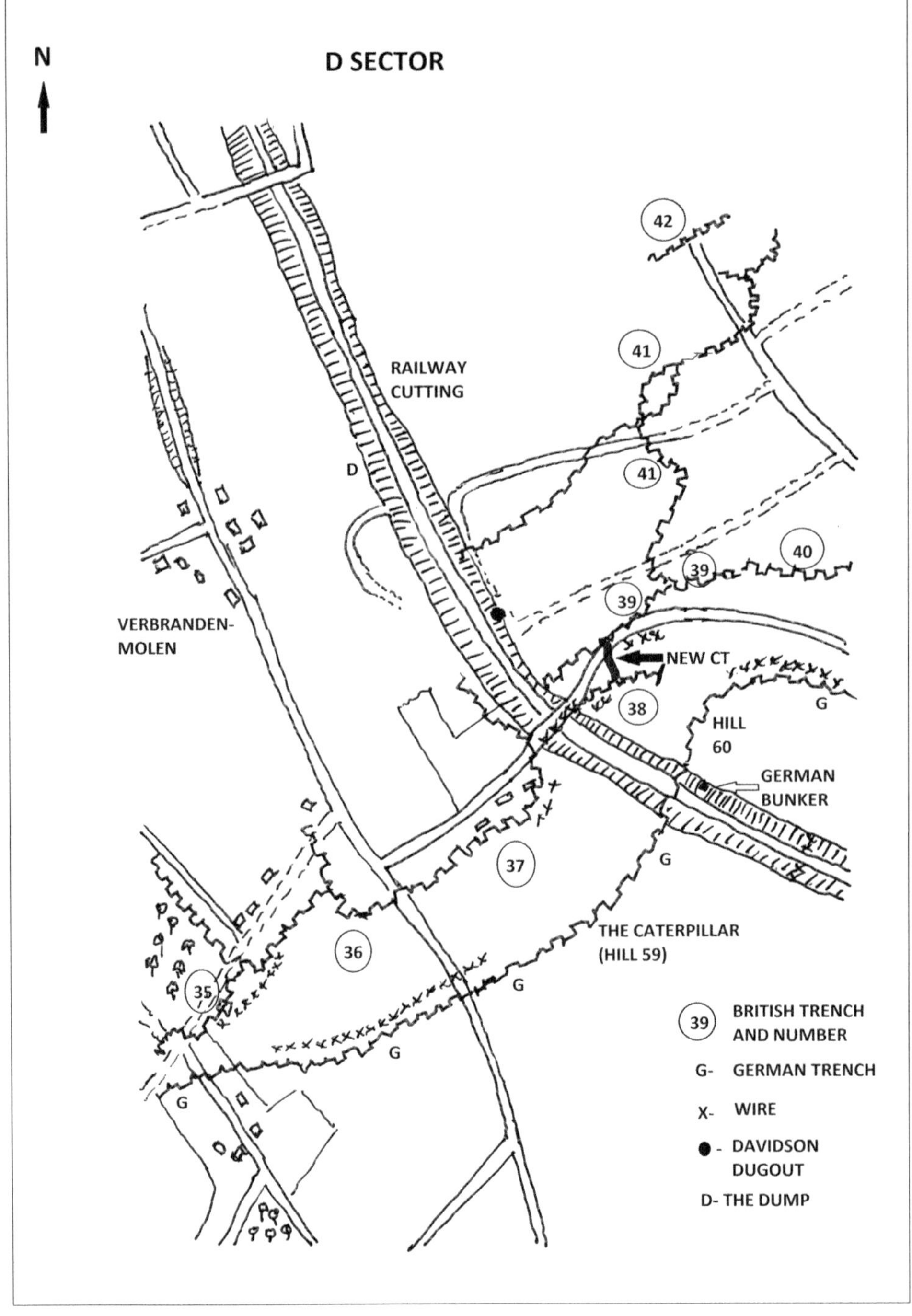
N
D SECTOR
RAILWAY CUTTING
D
42
41
41
40
39
39
38
37
36
35
VERBRANDEN-MOLEN
NEW CT
HILL 60
GERMAN BUNKER
G
THE CATERPILLAR (HILL 59)
39 BRITISH TRENCH AND NUMBER
G- GERMAN TRENCH
X- WIRE
● - DAVIDSON DUGOUT
D- THE DUMP

Hill 60 was a steeply-scarped artificial mound, made by the spoil excavated from the railway cutting, and although only 250 metres long and 5 metres higher than the British front line, it gave the enemy a clear view of the British rear, which was 25 metres lower.

A quiet first night in the trenches was spent improving top cover and traverses. The diary notes one man wounded before noon, an entry unsupported by the Casualties Book—though numbers were admitted to hospital with assorted ailments and injuries. Even after it became light, enemy guns remained inactive, and during the morning, Brig.-Gen Northey toured the battalion's positions. Trench 42 offered little protection for its garrison so, after dark, the fifty men from there were repositioned into dugouts near HQ in the railway cutting.

During the night, men continued working on parapet and parados, but at 4 a.m., heavy firing from the Germans opposite caused the battalion to 'stand-to' in case of attack. In actuality, it was triggered by the sector to the left, who had targeted German lines with a trench mortar bombardment, leading the enemy in turn to believe an attack or raid was under way. 'D' suffered three casualties from this: Rfn Colin Chappell was killed instantly; the twenty-six-year-old from Hoylake had held a peacetime commission with the 5th, but resigned because of a recurring throat illness, re-enlisting in the 6th when war was declared. During 'D' Company's last tour in 'B' Sector, he and another left cover during a bombardment, to rescue a wounded man of the Dorsets who was out in the open.[25] Recently-married twenty-six-year-old Rfn William Williams (871) was mortally wounded (although his death is recorded for 23 March by CWGC, his entry in the Casualties Book has '23' crossed out and '24' entered, so he may actually have died on the 24th). Rfn William Woodyer was shot in the chest and evacuated home and transferred after leaving hospital. 'B' Company's casualties were both serious: Rfn Frank Davies, though wounded in the head, recovered and was commissioned into the Cheshires and killed on 1 July 1916; Rfn Clifford Lymn, hit in the chest, was medically downgraded and posted to the Depot.

The firing soon settled down on 23 March, but at 1 p.m., one of the sentries noticed the Germans working on their trenches on Hill 60 and artillery was notified. After just one round, the enemy ceased their labours and peace descended once more. At 9 p.m., a German gun on Hill 60 shelled the trenches and HQ, and although no casualties are recorded, the next day, Rfn Ernest Fosbrooke from 'D' was admitted to 86 Field Ambulance with shellshock, returning to duty three days later. At 9.30 p.m., 'B' and 'D' were relieved by the others and returned to Ypres.

The fresh companies continued overnight work on the trenches, and frequent outbreaks of small arms fire and occasional shellfire claimed two victims from 'A' before noon on 24 March. Nineteen-year-old Rfn John Phillingham was killed by small arms fire and Sgt Henry Imlach wounded in the arm—the twenty-eight-year-old Argentine-born NCO, one of two Liverpool dentists in the ranks of 'A'. In the afternoon, a shell scored a direct hit on the parapet of Trench 39, flattening a section and occasioning much overnight repair work. The only casualty that afternoon was Rfn Frank Gascoigne, of 'A', who received a minor face wound.

Apart from repairing the break in Trench 39, working parties erected knife-rest wire in front of Trench 38 and restored a communication trench running along the railway cutting between 38 and HQ. One patrol lay up near the German wire, returning a few hours later to report a total lack of enemy activity. Twenty-three-year-old Rfn Robert Nightingale of 'A' was wounded before noon on 25 March. Hit in the back, he was evacuated home and later transferred to the MGC, being accidentally killed with them in February 1918. It is possible that Rfn Arthur Scoins of 'A' was also injured by shellfire on the 25th; the Casualties Book records his admittance to 85 Field Ambulance on 26 March, with bruising of the left shoulder—described as 'wounded, slight'—a common injury when struck, or buried by sandbags sent flying by shellfire. Despite the apparent triviality of his wound, it was June before he returned. There was another 'A' Company casualty from that day, though this was an accidental wounding: twenty-four-year-old L/Cpl Arthur Underwood was accidentally shot in the left foot, evacuated home, and later commissioned into the South Lancs. Around 3 p.m., the enemy began shelling trenches 39–41, the gun 800 yards directly to their front. British artillery replied and the shelling stopped at 7.30 p.m., but not before twenty-four-year-old Rfn Eric Parrington from 'D' received a shrapnel graze to his left thigh, leading to five weeks away from duty.

After dark on 25 March, the companies rotated again. The diary reports that all was quiet during the night, but there was certainly shellfire between the time of relief and midnight, as 'B' sustained three casualties: Rfn W. Davies (104) was hit by shrapnel in the wrist and thigh, transferring to the MFP after leaving hospital; Rfn John Glover was admitted to the Field Ambulance with shellshock, but was returned to duty the following day; and finally, 'B' Company-Commander Capt. George Westby was also hospitalised with shellshock, remaining there a month. It was probably this night that Lt Frederick Bardsley-Powell pledged to 6 Platoon, as they made their way along the railway cutting under heavy shellfire, 'if we ever get out of this, lads, I'll stand you the greatest dinner of your life'.[26] The menu-card for this meal—enjoyed on 20 March 1936—attributes the promise to 20 March 1915, but as the battalion was in Busseboom then, the 25th seems the most likely date. 'C' Company did not escape unscathed, with L/Cpl Samuel Morgan receiving a minor thigh wound; it was a month before the thirty-one-year-old returned.

The morning of 26 March was uneventful and 'D' Sector remained quiet. After dark, work continued on the front line and the communication trench along the embankment. Occasional shellfire caused problems for men out in the open and 'B' lost two Riflemen before midnight. Twenty-seven-year-old William Mountford was killed and John King wounded in the left hip. He was evacuated home, returning in August. 'B' suffered further losses on 27 March, when thirty-four-year-old Sgt James Marshall was killed and four wounded—Rfn Charles Adams in the right elbow; Sgt Richard Annesley in the neck; and Sgt William Watt and Rfn Joseph Williams (098) both received facial wounds. All four returned. In comparison, 'D' escaped lightly, with just Rfn Thomas Colley receiving a very minor wound to his left hand. That evening, 'B' and 'D' returned to Ypres, with 'A' and 'C' replacing them.

After handover, work began; 'A' Company's task was to dig a new communication trench between trenches 38 and 39. In the short time between handover and midnight, Rfn Frank Cooper was wounded in the back and evacuated home, being commissioned into the

Royal Warwicks and killed with them in 1916. 'C' lost Sgt Robert Glendenning, wounded in the left leg. Also on a hospital ship bound for England was Rfn Douglas Horsfall, who sprained his knee working on the communication trench—an injury that occasioned his medical discharge. Fortunately, there were no further casualties that night and 28 March proved remarkably quiet.

Overnight on 28–29 March, the new communication trench was completed and the spell of recent dry weather had also helped considerably in improving the state of the trench floors. Six casualties were suffered by 'A' and 'C' before their relief in the evening of the 29th. Twenty-two-year-old Rfn Arthur Hawitt ('A') and twenty-year-old Rfn John Diggle ('C') were both killed. Rfn Thomas Bannon from 'A' was hit in the left elbow and medically discharged, though the other casualty from his company, twenty-year-old Rfn William Fell, was more fortunate, his minor wound needing just two days treatment. 'C' Company's other two casualties were equally blessed, with Riflemen Christopher Ellison and Eric Harding also returning two days later. At 11.45 a.m., the score was evened slightly when a battalion sniper shot one of his counterparts moving into position in the railway cutting. That night, while waiting for 'B' and 'D' to relieve them, Herbert Roberts sat in his dugout and wrote home:

> It being a bright moonlit night, it is very difficult to keep away from the view of the enemy; although we are well screened by sandbags one cannot be too well screened, snipers have such clever means and ways of getting you, sometimes from behind. It is the constant cry, especially during the day, 'Keep that head down', and it is a rule which even the old hands always remember; but although it is a most important rule to obey and treat with all seriousness, one must have some humour of it. The joke is to add a little to the command by saying, 'There's a man hit in the ankle'.
>
> During the day, the firing is much quieter than the night, as both sides, unless they are looking for trouble, keep completely out of sight, as by the use of the periscope one can easily detect each other's movements when passing loopholes, or when out of the trench.
>
> We are as near to the enemy as to be able to hear them when one raises his voice, although they are well behind their wall of sandbags; the distance between us at this point [the left of Trench 38] is 40 yards. When the bullets continually hit the top of our sandbags, it is time to prepare another to take its place, and when some of us feel like teasing the enemy, which is not always advisable, a *bhoy* next to me, with a noticeable Irish brogue, sent a signal to Fritz by moving a stick from side to side above the trench, which interpreted means 'no hit', or the correct way of putting it is, a 'washout'.
>
> This throws out a challenge to the Fritz boys and they immediately reply by aiming to destroy our bags in earnest, and if they can spoil even one, it is a good piece of work for them, as of course, the bullets then come through and someone passing that spot at the time gets it. The day usually finishes with everyone 'having a go' at each other. Shell fighting is what no-one seems to get accustomed to. It is a fearful business, and one will even notice a regular, who has possibly been all through the campaign, shiver and frown, and remark, 'I can stand bullets all around me, but I can't stand shells'. One does not shiver or tremble with fright always; it is the nerves that get uncontrollable.

> Our forty-eight hours in the trenches are nearly over; and how we look forward with glee for our night's rest in the billet, about three miles away! We are as eager for our floor bed as you are for your spring mattress at home.
>
> I had the experience of going down a mine laid by the Sappers from the trench and burrowed well under the German trench. There are quite a number in the making and when complete—well you can imagine the result. There is only one thought which has to be faced, and that is, will the enemy, who are doing just the same thing, get finished at the mining before we do? While underneath I could hear the talking going on by the Germans, and some singing, so must have been almost touching their feet. We expected to be attacked during the night, but there was nothing doing.[27]

It is extraordinary that the final paragraph of this letter was not expunged by the Censor, as these mines were being prepared for an attack against Hill 60, scheduled for 16 April—eight days after this letter appeared in the papers.

Once 'B' and 'D' took over late on 29 March, their men began repairing parapets and placing knife-rests in the water pooling under the railway bridge. In the early morning, thirty-three-year-old Sgt Joseph Donnan of 'B' was killed, the only casualty up until noon. At 2 p.m., Brigade requested their assistance to rescue a wounded sapper lying on the railway near Zillebeke Arrêt. Although the Arrêt was 1,500 yards distant, the elevation of German positions on Hill 60 brought it into their field of observation. Notwithstanding the obvious peril, eight Riflemen volunteered. Sadly, little reliable information survives—newspaper reports containing clear inaccuracies—though it is possible to make reasonable deductions based on the few known facts, contemporary maps, and the lie of the land.

The rescue began from the dugouts at HQ—the cutting giving rescuers protection over the first 650 yards of their journey. Almost as soon as they broke cover, Hilton Crafter and nineteen-year-old Joseph Lancaster were both shot in the arm. With these two lying wounded in the open, under small arms and artillery fire, there were now three to rescue, and the squad split. Thomas Phillips took Samuel Caffal, Harry Slack, and James Weir in search of the sapper and twenty-three-year-old William Broster, assisted by twenty-one-year-old Eric Dodsworth, tried to reach their two injured comrades. The open ground between them and the casualties was swept by machine-gun fire, so Broster tried a different approach, and although it took him fifteen minutes, he managed to cut his way through a hedge to reach the wounded men via dead ground (the coordinates in the table are for the most likely hedge). Both casualties were recovered without further injury and he and Dodsworth delivered them safely to the Aid Post. Phillips and his team were also successful in finding their casualty, who was evacuated to an Aldershot hospital (possibly Spr J. Winstanley of 38 Field Company, though the only corroborating evidence, a newspaper report, contains several factual errors[28]). Broster and Phillips received the DCM—alas, apart from plaudits in the diary, the others received nothing. Three of these gallant rescuers did not survive the war.

After dark on 30 March, men were tasked to construct more dugouts near HQ in the cutting. During the afternoon and evening of 31 March, the enemy targeted Trench 38 with a *Minenwerfer*, located in an old crater on Hill 60. Fortunately, all sixty rounds fell short and no damage was done. In the hours leading up to their midnight relief by the RWK and Victoria Rifles, another five Riflemen were wounded, though all their injuries were slight: William Sidebotham's and R. Ball's wounds required four days in the Field Ambulance; Charles Jackson was back two days later; George Jones (227), with a scalp wound, was off duty until 18 April; and the final casualty, Humphrey Lewis, suffered a back wound, and it was mid-May before he returned to 'D'. All bar one would feature again in subsequent casualty lists.

The next four days were spent in leaky Nissen huts along the Vlamertinghe–Ouderdom road. While there, a number of men and 2Lt Blackledge, the designated Bombing-Officer, attended a course run by Capt. Johnson VC of the RE, learning how to make jam-tin bombs. These primitive devices were far inferior to the German stick grenade, and throwers, frequently left in doubt as to whether the fuse was lit or not, would toss them at the enemy anyway—habitually receiving them back, with the fuse properly lit. This unfortunate circumstance ended when one of the battalion cunningly substituted an 'instantaneous fuse' (stained black instead of the usual red) and threw it unlit into a German trench, to be rewarded by the sound of an explosion in the enemy trench a few seconds later. After this, no more 'duds' were returned.[29]

The appalling No. 1 Grenade also featured:

> Apart from these home-made jam tins, the only other bomb then available was a fearsome affair of brass on a long stick with ribbons tied to the handle. [The streamers aided the bomb's flight, so it landed detonator-first.] There was even more risk in the throwing of these, for they exploded on percussion and if the thrower managed to avoid hitting the back of the trench as he raised his arm to throw there was still the danger of the ribbons being tangled round his wrist and of the bomb refusing to leave his hand and exploding against the parapet of the trench in front. Altogether in those days, a bomber's life was not a happy one.[30]

Small wonder that the volunteer bombers were thought deranged. Unlike 1917, when each platoon acquired its own bombing-section, they were organised into a single squad of around thirty under an officer and NCO.

At 6 p.m. on 5 April, the battalion left for their new billeting area around Rosenthal Château, as Brigade Support. Their route took them through Ypres, each company spaced ten minutes' apart, leaving the Lille Gate around 9 p.m. HQ, 'B', and 'D' were at the Château, now much cleaner than when the Bedfords first occupied it; 'A' went into dugouts at Chester Farm; and 'C' went into dugouts along the canal bank. At night, 'A' garrisoned Canal Post with fifty men and 'C' provided fifty men and two machine guns for Canal Bridge Post, a commitment also requiring a daytime garrison of ten men to man the Maxims.

The dispositions above are taken from the Battalion diary, though *The Greenjacket*, gives the following for 'B' and 'D':

> After our rest at 'B' Camp, we were moved into Brigade support in Ypres, with 'D' Company in closer support in Blauwpoort Farm, a deserted building situated at that inconvenient distance behind the line which, while attracting occasional shells, is not too far away for frequent bullets. 'B' Company were also in support in dugouts, or scratches in the ground under the embankment of the Comines railway, near Transport Farm, the brigade headquarters.[31]

The accuracy of this is debateable, being written twelve years later and differing much from detailed contemporary information—though these dispositions were taken up on 20 April.

There was occasional hostile artillery, but the only casualty was Reginald Periton from Canal Bridge Post. During the morning of 6 April, he received his second wound in less than a month, a shell splinter hitting him in the back. Losses from sickness were more prevalent that week, with thirteen men evacuated home, never to return.

On the night of 7 April, the battalion was relieved; 15 Bde moved to 'rest' around Reninghelst, with the battalion accommodated in the Rozenhill huts. Another significant change had taken place the night before when 15 Bde returned to 5 Division. For the Rifles, this would be the first time that they actually came under the tactical command of their parent division.

Twenty-year-old Rfn Maurice Moss took the opportunity to finish a 'potted-history' of his last month, for a friend in Liverpool:

> You arrive in the trenches about 9.30 on (say) Tuesday night. From then till 9.30 on Thursday your time is taken up with poking your head up over the top and pot-shooting at old Fritz, and also feeding up as much as possible.
>
> A short time ago, Harrison (my greatest friend) [George Harrison 368] and I were put on a listening post. That is to say, we had to sit half way down the bank, ten yards from a bridge, and if any Germans tried to crawl under the bridge our duty was to pot them. It is a very miserable job as you have to sit still for 12 hours with your feet frozen.
>
> A short time before we were on it, some men of another regiment in our brigade were doing the duty when they saw a sniper crawl through. These snipers are particularly odious, as you would also think if you saw some of their work.
>
> Well they did not shoot right off; they called about a dozen men up very quietly, and then the whole lot peppered him while he was caught in the barbed wire. Best thing for him too.
>
> The other day [6 April] we were in dugouts, about fifty yards from a certain château, and thinking we might find something to improve our dugouts, we paid the château a visit [Lankhof Farm Château]. We had been in there half an hour, when whoo-bang went a shell over the building, and then another. A sergeant came along and told us to run like heaven for the dugout. Well, we got outside and as no more were coming, we started picking up wood once again for our fire, when all of a sudden went another shell in the lake twenty yards behind Harrison and I. Harrison said, 'Run like the devil.' So we ran, not half.
>
> Just as we got well away, a high explosive (it was not a shrapnel) burst ten yards off Periton and a bit caught him in the back. He did not seem much hurt, because

immediately the next one was heard coming, he threw himself flat, then got up and ran to the dugouts. However, he was hit, and it looks like England for him, lucky chap [Periton was commissioned into 7/KLR after leaving hospital].

As you understand, we are not allowed to give away any information, but you may take this from me that we have been in about the hottest part of the front as regards rifle and shell fire up to now. Tomorrow [10 April] we are moving away from this district, having done all we had to, e.g., clearing up some awkward positions left by our Indian regiment.

We are at present on rest in a camp of wooden huts. These huts are in two long rows, so we call the space in between, Wavertree Road. Our number is 31 and there are twenty-seven of us in it. Some fellows try to be funny, as witness the board outside 22. The Sniper's Château they have called it. Our last trench by the way was Lord Street, and the Orderly Room dugout had a notice on: 'No hawkers, no circulars;' also 'Tradesmen's Entrance' on the back of it.

Last Thursday we had a cinematograph show here, three miles from the firing line. Nearly all were 'Bunny' pictures. It went down splendidly. The only rotten part was coming out again onto the Belgian soil. By the way it was in a barn.

Our billets are very comfortable; there are fifty of us together, and a number of cows under the same roof. It is nothing to experience a rat running over your face and if you are lucky enough, you can catch it and throw it on someone else.[32]

On 10 April, 'B' and 'D' were attached to 1/Norfolks, marching to the front line with them at 3 p.m. The rest of the battalion left Rozenhill three hours later, bound for Ypres.

For those with the Norfolks, another new sector awaited, for 5 Division had taken over all of 28 Division's line, a relief facilitated to no mean degree by two of their brigades having been attached to 28 Division. The Norfolks were allocated 'C' Sector—trenches 33–37, sandwiched neatly between their last two deployments. The left bound of 'C' Sector was the railway cutting and, just as in 'D' Sector, most of the line was overlooked by the enemy, particularly on the left. Trench 33 in Ravine Wood and Trench 34 in the ravine itself were unusual in that the cover provided by the thick, fir woods allowed a careful approach to the front line in daylight, and in the supports, men could move about freely, screened from German view. The platoons from the attached companies rotated for two days in the front line, then two days in the support dugouts, a couple of hundred yards behind the front line.

The weather was generally fine, the soggy conditions of the front line somewhat improved, though careless movement was severely punished in the positions overlooked by Hill 60, 800 yards to their left, and Hill 59 (The Caterpillar), directly overlooking trenches 35–37. In the early morning of 11 April, thirty-five-year-old Rfn James Goodyear from 'B' was sniped in the head, dying two days later. Enemy artillery was fairly active after dark until around 2 a.m. During the early hours of 12 April, 'D' Company's Sgt Herbert Dixon was wounded in the chest and evacuated home. Generally, the situation remained quiet and 13 April was casualty-free, despite Trench 34 and its support being heavily shelled at 2.40 p.m.

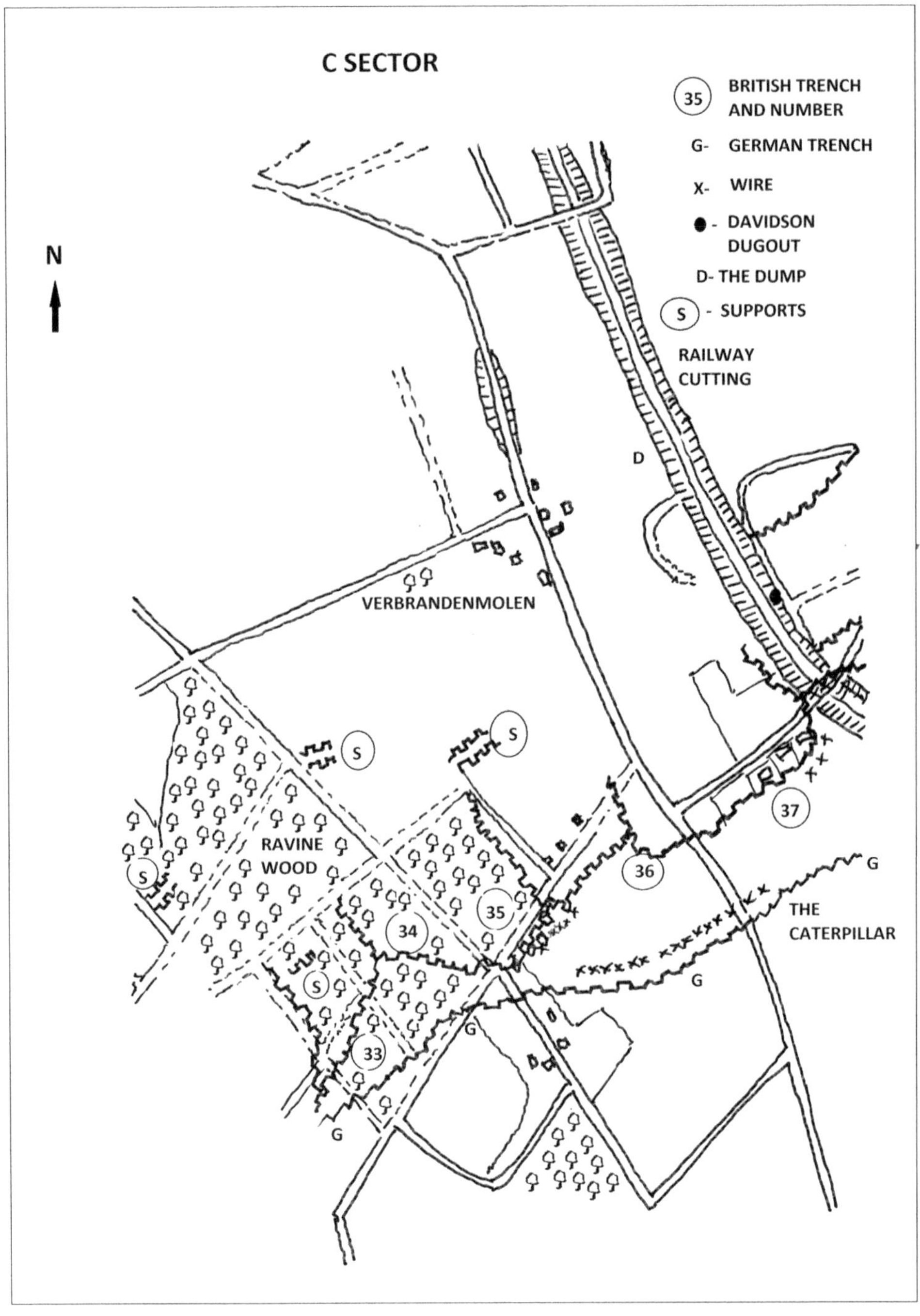
C SECTOR
N
35 BRITISH TRENCH AND NUMBER
G- GERMAN TRENCH
X- WIRE
- DAVIDSON DUGOUT
D- THE DUMP
S - SUPPORTS
RAILWAY CUTTING
D
VERBRANDENMOLEN
S
S
RAVINE WOOD
S
S
35
34
33
36
37
G
THE CATERPILLAR
G
G
G

In Ypres, twenty-five-year-old Sgt Alfred Jones (78) from 'C' was admitted to hospital with enteric fever; sadly, this proved fatal and he died on 25 April. The Ypres contingent laboured behind trenches 39 and 40 in 'D' Sector, constructing new dugouts in the reserve line for the two additional battalions scheduled to assault Hill 60. 'B' lost one man on 14 April, when Rfn William Raws was hit in the leg and evacuated home. 'D' was relieved that evening by 'C', their only casualty before relief being Rfn Sidney Webster, who returned the next day after his minor back wound had been dressed. 'C' Company's first casualty occurred only a few hours after reaching the line: Rfn Wilfred Bowden was hit in the right thigh, returning ten months later.

'C' Sector was probably the quietest stretch of the divisional line on 15 April, yet even so, thirty-four-year-old father of three Rfn Herbert Phillips of 'B' was critically wounded, the gunshot wound to his neck proving fatal on the 19th. On 16 April, 'B' lost another when nineteen-year-old Rfn Stanley Rowland was killed. 'C' Company's Cpl Raymond Russell was wounded in the right thigh and evacuated home, never to return.

In the days leading up to the assault on Hill 60, the battalion was ordered to find more-suitable billets in Ypres, commanders concerned the assault would trigger a German bombardment of the city. Capt. George Teall was billeted with a local doctor and asked their host, a notable authority on the history of Ypres, if he knew of any suitable cellars that could be requisitioned. The antiquarian mentioned a series of long-forgotten railway tunnel-sized subways, deep under the ramparts—former powder magazines from Vauban's seventeenth-century defences. These were located, and though chock-full of accumulated rubbish, space was quickly cleared to accommodate HQ, Signals, the Aid Post, and the Stores.[33]

'A' and 'D' were involved in intensive carrying parties while the others were at the front. On 17 April, they too moved under the Ramparts. The attack against Hill 60 was scheduled to commence that evening, with 1/RWK from 13 Bde making the initial assault. Six charges, totalling over 10,000 lb of explosive, had been laid under German defences in three paired locations. These were detonated in pairs, the first under Hill 60 itself; the second, opposite Trench 38, to the west of the hill, was to be triggered ten seconds later; followed ten seconds after that by the final pair opposite Trench 40.[34] Immediately as the last charge detonated, the British barrage would begin and infantrymen in 'C' and 'E' sectors line their parapets to fire upon German lines. The initial infantry assault began at 7.06 p.m.

To maximise the firepower in 'C' Sector, all men from the reserve dugouts were brought into the front line at noon and the battalion's two Maxims under Lt Hugh Scott-Barrett, sited in trenches 36 and 37. Ellison, with 'B' in the left of the line, described the moment the attack began:

> It was a calm spring evening, quiet with desultory rifle fire here and there. We waited, tense and ready for 7 p.m. Three deep rumbling roars and the seven [*sic.*] mines beneath the Hill were exploded. The crest lifted up bodily to dissolve into dense pillars and spurts of black smoke and dust. 'Keep close into the parapet to escape falling debris,' had been our orders and we crouched low into the base of the sandbag wall. Immediately

> 'band bang bang!!!' ripped out a battery salvo. It was the signal hundreds of gunlayers had been awaiting. A sound that grew louder and louder rose from the hissing rush of escaping steam to a screaming roar which seemed to fill the sky with its concentrated volume. When it reached a pitch beyond which it seemed impossible to rise, it broke in a terrific, rolling C-R-R-RASH which rocked the ground on which we stood. The German lines were quickly hidden in smoke and yellow lyddite fumes, through which sandbags and pieces of debris could be seen spinning into the clearer air above.[35]

Rfn Frederick Bentley of 'B' observed 'columns of earth and flames seemed to leap into the sky'.[36]

Scant small arms fire was returned by the enemy, but he began to shell the front and support lines of 'C' Sector almost immediately. 'B' Company's thirty-two-year-old Rfn William Hipwell was killed and Rfn Arthur Allen wounded in the thigh; Rfn John Hunter was hit in the left hand; and twenty-four-year-old Rfn James Pinnock in the left leg—the only man to return. 'C' suffered losses, too. Rfn Frank Loughran was wounded in the shoulder and twenty-four-year-old Rfn Henry Reeves in the left hand. Their only casualty not to return was Rfn William Lowe, with a shrapnel wound to his left shoulder. His injury was complicated by pneumonia contracted in hospital, and he was evacuated home.

One of 'C', on the right of the line where his view of the mine detonation was blocked by Ravine Wood, wrote:

> At 6.15 p.m., we were at our posts, bayonets fixed in readiness. On the stroke of seven the mines were exploded and although we could not see the effects, we felt them in the tremor of the earth. It was a most uncanny sensation.[37]

The RWK were firmly established on top of Hill 60 by 1.30 a.m. on 18 April. Earlier enemy counterattacks from Hill 59 were severely punished by British artillery and small arms fire from 'C' Sector. Another large counterattack at 3 a.m. was beaten off, but the RWK suffered significant losses and was relieved by 2/KOSB shortly afterwards, though a portion of the hill was retaken by the enemy. 'B' Company's Sgt George Dawson described the initial hours of the attack in a letter to his wife:

> We were about a quarter of a mile from the Hill, but we opened rapid fire. I walked up and down the line for about ten minutes to see if the men were going all right; then as every rifle counted, I took my coat off, got on the parapet and waded in. it took two and a half hours to get the upper hand; by that time, although it was a cold night, we were sweating like bulls. Things then quietened for about an hour.[38]

It was a busy night in the front line:

> We spent most of that night flat on the parapet, firing until the barrels of our rifles became red-hot and blistering to the touch. All night through, a man went up and down the trench

> with a can of oil, which he poured on the open breeches. It boiled and fizzled and made the trench smell like a fish-and-chip shop. There was no barbed wire protecting us, so our job was to keep Jerry in his trenches.[39]

After sustained firing, the rifle bolt become difficult to operate—oil cooled the action and allowed fire to continue.

Some of 'A' and 'D' moved to 'C' Sector supports just before Zero, their task to ferry ammunition forward:

> Our platoon left the place we are billeted in about 6.30, and got up near the firing line pretty quickly. We were put in rotten little dugouts that were expected to fall to the ground. Anyhow ten of us scrambled in and waited till the fatal hour (i.e., 7 p.m.). When that came the ground shook three times violently, and then our old artillery started, and never stopped the whole night, to say nothing of theirs (the Germans).
>
> We were dragged out a bit later to carry ammunition up to the trenches, which was no pleasant job with the shells bursting heaven knows where. A Jack Johnson fell about ten yards from our dugout, and in the wood the row was awful. We took a box each first time and carried and dragged it through the trenches, etc., and then we had a little rest. Sometimes it was too hot to go out. We did the same job three or four times. I think listening to the noise in the dugouts was the worst.[40]

One man in Trench 34 described the majesty of the bombardment:

> The artillery fire lasted all night. Although we experienced some very intense hours, there was, nevertheless, something magnificent about the bombardment. The glorious night, with the new moon shining brilliantly in a cloudless sky; the pine trees with their tops just turning green, in the wood in which we lay; the great and intensely-vivid flashes of light of the bursting shells, the ceaseless roar of the thunder of the guns and the earth vibrating with the force of the explosion, produced a scene one is not likely to forget quickly.[41]

The only casualty among the carrying parties on 17 April was 'A' Company's Rfn Harold Allen. The nineteen-year-old was severely injured in the abdomen by a shell splinter, a wound that proved fatal on the 20th.

During 18 April, under constant artillery fire and volleys of grenades, 2/Duke of Wellington's were gradually pushed off the crest of the hill. At 6 p.m., boosted by 2/KOYLI, they counterattacked, firmly re-establishing themselves on the crest by 7 p.m.

As enemy artillery continued to seek out targets in 'C' Sector on 18 April—the usual HE and shrapnel, interspersed by lachrymatory (tear gas) shells for the very first time—the men in the trenches suffered another eight casualties, three from 'C'. Rfn James Allen was wounded in the abdomen and Rfn Thomas Beveridge, the arm. Critically injured with a head wound was Rfn Thomas Cairns. The twenty-eight-year-old died in England in June—tragically, his only child died six months later.

Once again, 'B' fared worse. Rfn William Thompson, wounded in the right elbow, was the only one of their five casualties to survive: both nineteen-year-old Rfn Reginald Davies and twenty-three-year-old L/Cpl Harry Joynson were killed outright; twenty-three-year-old Rfn Vincent Cama, whose father was part of Liverpool's thriving Italian community, was hit in the head, clinging onto life until the 27th; and twenty-seven-year-old Sgt Charles Skafte, with a shell wound to the abdomen, died at the CCS on the 30th. As if losing an only son was not bad enough, a letter from his grieving father indicates that a silver chain with pendants, a prismatic compass, and his son's wristwatch were stolen while he was in hospital and, 'although their intrinsic value is not great, we should like to have them'.[42] Sadly, this sort of despicable theft was far from uncommon (it was only upon reading Skafte's Service Record that I discovered I'd lived in the same house after leaving the Army—a very strange feeling).

The bombardment against 'C' Sector continued into 19 April, though the only battalion casualty in the front line was Rfn John Pointer, evacuated with shellshock. It was nearly six months before he was deemed fit again. It was not just 'B' and 'C' that suffered over these two days, the Norfolks lost eleven killed and forty-six wounded.[43]

'A' and 'D' spent the night of 18–19 April carrying grenades and sandbags up to 13 Bde HQ, supplies then relayed forward to Hill 60. Men from 'A' also assisted Transport, ferrying 'C' Company's rations up, and were caught by a salvo just past the Lille Gate: forty-two-year-old John Marrison, a divorced father of two and the battalion's Machine-Gun-Sergeant, was killed; Rfn William Bland was wounded in the left knee; Rfn Harry Wallis in both legs; and thirty-two-year-old Rfn Wilfred Desages—the only one of the wounded to return—hit in the left arm (he was later killed, as a captain of the London Regiment, in 1918). Although some rations reached 'C' Sector, drinking water was in very short supply, and despite 'Standing Orders' to the contrary, men resorted to taking water from shell-holes, straining it through handkerchiefs, before boiling it to make tea.[44] (It has to wondered if the numbers subsequently hospitalised with dysentery and enteric fever was not directly related to this practise.)

German fire against Ypres intensified on 19 April, much of it from heavy Howitzers and 17-inch naval guns; damage and casualties among the civilian population was severe. The first shell fell amid a group of children, killing fifteen.[45] Two of 1/5th KORL, who were also in Ypres, described the apocalyptical scene in letters home:

> The destruction of life and property in the town was appalling—men, women, children, soldiers, horses, and practically every living thing blown to bits and houses, hotels and churches blown to fragments. The exits from the town were crowded with horror-stricken refugees. The Germans had no mercy, shell following shell in rapid succession—big thumping naval 17-inch shells, 'Jack Johnsons,' 'coal boxes,' 18-pounders, whiz-bangs and shrapnel.[46]

The second observed: 'We could see in front of us buildings blazing, churches, cattle, men, women and children blown to bits'.[47]

As fire intensified, the surviving civilians fled the city, only to be caught outside by further barrages, targeting all lines of communication. In these shell-blasted streets, men from the battalion under the MO Maj. John Martin performed sterling work under heavy fire, rescuing the wounded and dying—military and civilian—and ferrying them to the Aid Post under the Ramparts. *Capitaine* De Rosen was awarded the French *Croix de Guerre* for his work during these few days.

The bombardment of Ypres was not a reaction to the seizure of Hill 60, but the prelude to a massive German offensive. It was so intense that units in the city were ordered out to prevent further casualties, and although HQ and associated elements remained under the Ramparts, the rifle companies departed at 7.30 p.m. on 20 April, bound for dugouts along a 1,500-yard stretch under the railway embankment, from near Shrapnel Corner, past 15 Bde's HQ at Transport Farm, to just south of Zillebeke Lake (the Brigade diary erroneously reports the battalion there from 16–17 April[48]). For the next thirteen days, every man not with the Norfolks was engaged on constant working and carrying parties, sustaining more casualties than the front line companies, particularly on the evening of 20 April, when one was killed and fourteen wounded. Heavy fire along the roads leading out of Ypres presented the QM Maj. Edward Goulding particular difficulties regarding resupply, but despite this, the brave men of Transport always delivered. Casualties across 5 Division on 20–21 April totalled 165 killed, 769 wounded, and 102 missing—a grave toll.[49]

Those with the Norfolks also had a hot time. During the afternoon of 20 April, the enemy shelled all their positions, though Trench 37 was singled out for special attention, a prelude to another attempt to recapture Hill 60, which began at 4 p.m. Although the Norfolks and Riflemen kept up small arms fire against German positions, intense shellfire, continuing into the evening, caused many casualties: the Norfolks suffered seven killed, thirty-one men and two officers wounded; 'B' Company, who were on the left of the line, had seven wounded and twenty-one-year-old Rfn Gerald Cook killed; 'C', on the right, escaped lightly, only L/Sgt Hubert Spargo being wounded.

The attack succeeded in partially pushing back the Bedfords and the East Surreys. At 4.35 a.m. on 21 April, the sound of heavy small arms fire was heard from the east of Hill 60, as the Queen Victoria Rifles began their counterattack. Initially, this failed to completely push the enemy off the top of the hill, only the right of the feature firmly under British control—though by 7 a.m., the British controlled the crest, leaving only small, isolated pockets of German bombers on the hill. Casualties from the battalion were fewer on 21 April, with only three wounded.

The 22nd was much quieter in 'C' Sector, just two of the battalion wounded in the front line—though the carrying parties of 'A' and 'D' suffered more. Of far greater concern than Hill 60 was the major German attack, which began at 5 p.m., against French positions north of Ypres. This first use of chlorine gas against unprotected French troops resulted in a 5-mile-wide gap in Allied defences, plugged heroically by Canadian and British troops at great cost. The greenish gas cloud was visible from trenches 36 and 37, though at the time, none knew its significance. Very early into this assault, all but one divisional telephone wire was cut, which meant that brigades and battalions received little clear information. It was only in the late evening that warnings about gas were distributed to the front line, though it is obvious from the following document, circulated to all three brigades on 24 April, that the nature of the agent was unknown—the AAQMG Lt-Col Tulloch clearly believing that it was just lachrymatory:

> The effects of the so-called asphyxiating gases used by the enemy are neither fatal nor serious, and beyond temporary inconvenience, no injury is caused to the eye.
>
> Any gas projected towards us must necessarily be speedily diluted by the air and dissipated by the wind, and if the precautions in my wire, No. 903 of 23rd are carried out, very little discomfort should be experienced. All ranks will be informed of this at once.[50]

For the front line troops, the night of 22 April was one of rumour and uncertainty. Nerves were on edge—fear of the unknown gas overwhelming them in the dark; concern that the enemy may be behind them and attack from every side without warning—all played their part in suggesting to sentries that a piece of scrub, or uneven patch of ground, was an enemy soldier creeping up. Frequent bursts of fire rippled up and down every sector as rapid fire was opened upon inanimate objects. Random shrapnel burst over the line, spraying their lethal balls indiscriminately, and every so often, a 'whizz-bang' screamed in and punched a hole in the breastwork. Ellison was delighted when the sun rose on the 23rd:

> No dawn was ever more welcome. Whatever might happen during that day, we could at least see what we were shooting. This was to be my lucky day. Soon after dawn, when we were on the parapet giving them a 'mad minute' of rifle fire, a bullet chipped my ear, grazed my neck and set fire to the woollen helmet I was wearing. The shock knocked me flat to the bottom of the trench but was not a serious wound and I carried on.[51]

The tail-end of a letter written to Ellison's father, by his pal Frank Evans, survives:

> He was lucky. I'm very jealous because it was at my peep-hole that he got it. Please give my regards to Mrs and Miss Ellison, and tell them that the accident [*sic.*] happened at an exciting moment, and the way Norman stood calmly to his firing platform, was admired by us all.[52]

That evening, Ellison, still stone-deaf in one ear, was sent to the Aid Post to get his lesion dressed. However, when the MO learned the wound was twelve hours old and his patient had not had an anti-tetanus, he packed Ellison off to the CCS. The Casualties Book incorrectly records Ellison's arrival at the Field Ambulance on 21 April—the sequence of events in his personal diary and notes from further down the medical evacuation chain all support the 23rd. In total, four of the battalion were wounded in the front line that day, two from each company.

Once away from the front line, casualties were far from safe. While Ellison was waiting at the CCS on the Lille Road, a 42-cm shell demolished an entire farmstead just 400 yards away, and the last ambulance in his convoy was destroyed by a smaller shell.

With the situation to the north far from clear and a distinct possibility the enemy may break through, 5 Division began looking at alternative strategies and sent the following precautionary orders to all three brigades on 23 April:

> In view of the possible withdrawal to the 2nd Line, supplies should not be taken up to present trenches until further orders, and as little 1st Line Transport as possible should proceed east of Ypres.[53]

As part of this plan, over the following three days, companies out of the line were tasked with digging a new defensive switch between the gangers' hut in the railway cutting and Verbrande Molen.

One incredible tale from 23 April involves a teenage Rifleman from 'C', admitted to 14 Field Ambulance with an undiagnosed fever on 14 April. Eighteen-year-old Allan Smith was discharged on 22 April, far from the battalion and still feeling unwell. He set off alone and on foot to find his company. As night fell, weary and hungry, Smith sought shelter, being greeted with scorn by all he asked, who thought him a deserter. Eventually, he was welcomed by a Canadian battalion and, throwing in his lot with them, joined one of their platoons. On 23 April, this battalion counterattacked without artillery support, and although they failed to take their objective, they recaptured some British 4.7 guns and stabilised the line. By the end of this attack, Smith's adopted forty-strong platoon was reduced to four, including himself. He was awarded the Russian Medal of St George (4th Class) for his courage, nominated for it by the Canadians.[54]

In 'C' Sector, although it was now quiet to their left on Hill 60, there were numerous small arms fire and artillery exchanges during 24 April and another two were wounded. Next day, twenty-three-year-old Rfn William Evans (782) of 'B' wrote to his mother:

> For the past sixteen days we have been in the trenches, and there is little chance of relief for some time I am afraid. We have been engaged in some of the hottest fighting of the whole war, and I have seen some stirring scenes. I could never have imagined anything like it. We have had a fair number of casualties. My partner on guard yesterday morning [William Owen] was hit in the chest, rather seriously, but so far I have escaped unhurt, though my coat has been ripped open by shrapnel on the shoulder blade and my rifle has been hit in two places. I feel very thankful to have gone unscathed as long as this, and only hope that I shall be similarly favoured by the grace of Providence in the future. It is Sunday morning and I suppose you are now sitting in church. I wouldn't mind being with you.
>
> There is a lot of hard work before us and the artillery is terrific. However, we have done good work, and have made good advance, which I hope we shall be able to hold. We are a very happy crowd and take things very philosophically, so you need not worry in the least about me, for I won't go before my time.[55]

Twenty-one-year-old Owen succumbed to his wound on 14 May. This was William Evans's last letter.

There were no casualties among the trench garrison on 25 April, the sector having quietened down again. Further north, however, British counterattacks near St Julien failed with very heavy casualties. The only casualty in the trenches on 27 April was twenty-year-old 2Lt Reginald Boult, with 'Blighty' wounds to face and neck.

The front-line companies suffered six casualties on 28 April, four of them from 'C'. Rfn Charles Telford received a bayonet wound to the right arm, when a blast from a shell blew him onto someone's 'sword'. Their only fatality was seventeen-year-old Rfn Archie Waterhouse. When the teenager enlisted in 1913, he had added a year to his age and his deception had escaped notice. 'B' lost two, one of whom, Rfn Joseph Williams (098), must have been feeling more than a little peeved. The unlucky twenty-two-year-old had only rejoined the previous night, after convalescence from his prior wounding. The other was William Evans. Terribly wounded, he died soon after reaching the Aid Post. A direct hit on the parapet of Trench 35 by a 77-mm completely destroyed a section of it, rendering communication with the trenches between there and the railway cutting hazardous to the extreme. In the face of intense rifle fire, 'B' Company's Sgt Clement Tanner stood in the gap and calmly rebuilt the parapet with sandbags handed up to him by members of his platoon, sheltering behind the remaining sandbags.[56]

On 29 April, twenty-two-year-old L/Cpl Harry Leaver was killed and Rfn Frederick Heap so badly wounded in the arm that he was medically discharged. Casualties were light on 30 April, though Rfn Thomas Swallow was extremely unfortunate. The nineteen-year-old was helping to carry a stretcher, bearing a wounded man from the Norfolks, when he was hit in the chest by a random bullet. The round lodged between his heart and a lung and doctors deemed it too risky to remove. He too was medically discharged.

Casualties from the Line, 20-30 April 1915

Name	Number	Status
L/Cpl William Alfred Barnes (B)	240158	WIA: 20/4
Rfn John Blyde (C)	240682	WIA: 28/4
2Lt Reginald Herbert S. Boult (B)		WIA: 27/4
Rfn H. Briggs (C)	2027	WIA: 22/4
Rfn Frederick Cook (C)	1858	WIA: 28/4
Rfn Gerald Noel Cook (B)	2090	DOW: 20/4
Rfn Reginald F. Cox (B)	2815	WIA: 20/4
Rfn Leslie Grierson De Valve (B)	240231	WIA: 20/4
Rfn Robert Duffy (B)	240285	WIA: 20/4
Rfn John D. Edmondson (B)	1764	WIA: 20/4
L/Cpl Arthur Wyn Edwards (B)	1052	WIA: 21/4
Rfn Norman Frederick Ellison (B)	240479	WIA: 23/4
Rfn William Dickson Evans (B)	2782	DOW: 28/4
Rfn Ernest Brideson Harrop (B)	240557	WIA: 20/4
Rfn John Hayhurst (B)	240060	WIA: 22/4
Rfn Frederick Millington Heap (C)	1457	WIA: 29/4
L/Cpl Harry Reginald Leaver (B)	2472	KIA: 29/4
Rfn Clifford Underwood Lloyd (C)	2213	WIA: 21/4
Rfn George C. McElhinney (B)	203972	WIA: 23/4

Rfn William Henry Owen B)	2347	DOW: 14/5
Rfn Ernest Henry Pain (C)	243884	WIA: 23/4
Sgt John Ernest Smith (C)	240074	WIA: 23/4
L/Sgt Hubert John Spargo (C)	1141	WIA: 20/4
Rfn Harold Stirk (B)	1531	WIA: 20/4
Rfn Thomas Swallow (C)	1464	WIA: 30/4
Rfn Charles Tankard (C)	240971	WIA: 21/4
Rfn Charles Donald Telford (C)	1790	WIA: 28/4
Rfn Archie Bryant Waterhouse (C)	1494	KIA: 28/4
Rfn Andrew Horne Watson (C)	240746	WIA: 24/4
Rfn Joseph Theodore Williams (B)	240098	WIA: 28/4

Casualties from Carrying Parties, 20-30 April 1915

Rfn Job H. Bennett (A)	1992	WIA: 30/4
Rfn George H. Brownfield (A)	240396	WIA: 20/4
Rfn John Cooper (D)	240481	WIA: 21/4
Rfn William H. Curwen (A)	241026	WIA: 27/4
Rfn Charles Leslie Dixon (D)	240551	WIA: 25/4
Rfn Thomas Dunning (A)	2133	WIA: 20/4
Rfn Ernest James M. Eldridge (D)	2300	WIA: 20/4
Rfn Thomas G. Findlow (A)	2381	WIA: 20/4
Cpl Frederick D. R. Illingworth (A)	1397	WIA: 20/4
Rfn Frank Edgar Jones (D)	240841	WIA: 24/4
L/Cpl H. Jones (A)	240061	WIA: 20/4
L/Cpl John Leigh Kemp (D)	240182	WIA: 20/4
Rfn Jackson White Kirkbridge (D)	240358	WIA: 20/4
Rfn William A. Mackenzie (A)	240554	WIA: 20/4
Rfn Frank W. Muir (D)	2229	WIA: 22/4
Rfn Richard P. Quilliam (D)	2284	WIA: 20/4
2Lt Thomas Edward Rome (D)		WIA: 20/4
Rfn George Percival Stewart (A)	1723	WIA: 22/4
Rfn Hubert J. Taylor (A)	240501	WIA: 20/4
Cpl Samuel Taylor (D)	240044	WIA: 22/4
L/Cpl William M. Thistlewood (D)	1789	DOW: 20/4
L/Sgt John Harrison Thompson (A)	240110	WIA: 21/4
Rfn William Royle Thompson (A)	811	WIA: 21/4
Rfn Simon Tobias (A)	240456	WIA: 22/4
Rfn Sydney Whiteford (D)	240076	WIA: 20/4
Rfn Herbert Whiteside (A)	1925	WIA: 20/4

'B' and 'C' remained in the line, the others continuing on carrying parties until the evening of 4 May, and although enemy fire against 'C' Sector dwindled considerably, twenty-seven-year-old Rfn Hugh Murdoch from 'B' received a minor wound in the shoulder. At 7.15 p.m., 2Lt Blackledge's 11 Platoon in Trench 37 were horrified to witness thick clouds of chlorine roll across British lines to their left. Brigade reported:

> The enemy let loose gas of white and yellow thick substance by opening nozzles opposite 38, 40, 43, 45 and 46 trenches; this gas was shot in thick volumes, very suddenly onto our trenches taking many men too quickly to admit of their getting their mouth protectors on, the asphyxiation effect being practically instantaneous. The men in Trench 36 were hardly affected, but the gas in front of 36 was driven by the west wind on to Hill 60, where

> nearly the whole of three platoons were affected. Many men who had the pad mouth cover all ready to put on either had not time to adjust it, or were affected through the pad.
>
> It appears that most of the affected men were immediately struck down and unfortunately lay about in the bottom of trenches where the gas soon completely asphyxiated them. Short of always wearing the pads, which is impossible, much practice in hasty adjustment is evidently wanted.[57]

German artillery bombarded British support lines and heavy rifle and machine-gun fire was directed at the Dorsets on Hill 60, whose casualties were heavy—two killed by enemy fire, fifty-four killed by the gas, which incapacitated and hospitalised another 204, and thirty-two missing.[58]

The only Dorsets still on their feet on Hill 60, 2Lt Kestell-Cornish and four men, returned rapid fire, possibly leading the Germans to believe the gas had been ineffective—certainly no enemy infantry attack developed. The OC of the supporting battalion, the Devons, immediately despatched six platoons to aid the Dorsets, the Bedfords moving across as additional support. Blackledge's Platoon also lined the parapet, trying to pick off the German gas-troops handling the nozzles of the gas-dischargers.

Although the gas mostly missed Trench 37, Rfn Clarence Adams from 11 Platoon was evacuated with what was initially diagnosed as appendicitis—only correctly diagnosed as gas poisoning by No. 5 General Hospital six days later. Both 14 and 15 Field Ambulance rushed medical staff forward to assist and forty men from 'A' at the embankment were pressed into service as stretcher-bearers—an experience that haunted many:

> Our last few days have been a nightmare. We have experienced the asphyxiating gases; they are awful. You have not a sporting chance. A week ago we were called out; our men on Hill 60 had been gassed. One regiment suffered heavily. All night long we worked hard carrying them down. In some cases the poor chaps died in our arms; the men all the time being heavily shelled. It was Providence alone that carried us through.[59]

The outlook towards the enemy hardened after their use of gas, an attitude that toughened considerably less than a week later, after the sinking of the RMS *Lusitania*. Many of the crew were Liverpudlians, known to—and in some cases, related to—soldiers in the battalion and quite a few had worked for Cunard before enlistment. The sinking triggered anti-German riots in Liverpool and it was a very bad time for residents with Germanic-sounding surnames, whatever their nationality (around a dozen of the battalion had German-born parents).

There was no effective protection against gas, and the best guidance the government's 'gas-expert'—Professor Haldane—could give was to tie lumps of cotton-wool or gauze around the nose and mouth, or long strips of gents' tweed suiting to be wrapped around the head and tied with tape. Maj. Martin had pre-empted Haldane's advice by devising a chemical solution—probably bicarbonate—which men dipped their handkerchiefs into, before tying it around their face.[60]

At 4 a.m. on 2 May, the battalion were ordered to send 'D' up the railway cutting to Larch Wood to reinforce the Devons. The situation was generally quiet across 5 Division's front, though hostile artillery fire was directed against Ypres, the canal, and directly to the south of Ypres after 5 p.m. The only battalion casualty was L/Sgt Thomas Owen of 'C', who was wounded at duty. 'A' was still heavily engaged on carrying parties on 3 May and again, just a single casualty from the men in the trenches, when 'C' Company's Rfn Frederick Houghton was slightly wounded.

The desperately tired battalion was long overdue relief, and at 4.10 p.m. on 4 May, orders came through that they were to become the Divisional Reserve and, as soon as each company was relieved, proceed independently for Kruisstraat Château, south-west of Ypres, where they were accommodated in the dugouts of 'K' Wood. Seven casualties are recorded for 4 May in the Casualties Book, though the diary notes just four. Ellison's pal, L/Cpl Frank Evans, was wounded in the right thigh. From 'C', Rfn George Batcheldor was wounded in the hand and Rfn Henry Richmond in the thigh, both hit while making their way out of the line. 'D' Company's dugouts along the railway embankment were shelled and Rfn Charles Smith (524) severely wounded in the foot, when a shell burst on top of his dugout, splinters penetrating the roof.[61] The other three 'D' Company casualties may have been in the same dugout: twenty-four-year-old L/Cpl Ernest Parry was wounded in the head, though he was back with his section three weeks later; Rfn Walter Roberts (137) was wounded in the foot; and Rfn Harry Slack in the hand—both returned.

It was 6.30 a.m. on 5 May before everyone reached 'K' Woods, the recent spell of fine weather broken by a heavy downpour, which turned the ground into a slough. Too exhausted to care, or even to eat, the men laid down to sleep. Unfortunately, their rest was brief.

At 8.35 a.m., the Germans began to discharge gas against Hill 60 and trenches 34–47. Unlike on 1 May, this was followed up by an infantry attack, and the Duke of Wellington's, overcome by the gas, were driven off the Hill by 9 a.m. Understandably, with communications down and the devastating effects of concentrated gas, the situation was confused and it was not until 11 a.m. that Division learned that Trench 39 was in enemy hands—and forty minutes later—that 40 and 45 were also believed to have been seized.

Directly as news reached Divisional-Commander Maj.-Gen. Morland, he ordered the Cheshires to counterattack, assisted by the Rifles, who were summoned from Kruisstraat Château and instructed to report to Brigade HQ in the Railway Arch dugout near Transport Farm. The orders reached Lt-Col. Davison at 9.30 a.m., men were woken, and the battalion prepared to move. The companies left independently, 'A', under Capt. Bertram Wedgwood, the first to have reached the Château the previous night, moved out at 10.15 a.m.

Later sources give conflicting details for the events of 5 May: the timings and happenings reported in this narrative are taken from battalion, brigade, and divisional documents, or from letters written by the participants themselves; where there is concern about the accuracy of some details, this is mentioned in the text.

'A' routed along the northern side of the railway embankment leading from Shrapnel Corner to Zillebeke Arrêt and reported at Brigade HQ. Some idea of the gravity of the situation must have been gleaned by the gruesome sights encountered, as they passed a tide of gassed victims drifting back from the line. Wedgwood was directed to report to the OC of the Cheshires in Davidson Dugout. Urged to press on as quickly as possible, they were ordered to leave any wounded behind for the RAMC to collect later.

Leaving Brigade HQ at 12.15 p.m., platoons spaced at five- to ten-minute intervals, the company routed along the northern side of the railway, covered from direct enemy observation by the embankment, and although the enemy was shelling the line with shrapnel, this was fairly localised and did not affect them. As they neared the Arrêt, fire intensified and Wedgwood became concerned about the next stage of their journey, enfiladed by fire from Trench 45 and under direct observation from Hill 60—artillery rounds already bursting directly along their proposed route. He placed his men in cover behind the embankment, while the officers discussed their next move.

Wedgwood chose to divide the company, 1 and 2 Platoon continuing under himself, the others under Capt. William Turner. Wedgwood's force back-tracked along the railway, then headed across the fields to the reverse of the embankment surrounding Zillebeke Lake, giving them cover all the way to Zillebeke village. Turner followed the same route fifteen minutes later. Up until then, their advance had been casualty-free.

The company diverged here, Wedgwood taking the right—the usual route for accessing the front line. This led over a plank bridge and along a hedgerow, but the final 200 yards to the cutting was dangerously exposed, especially to fire from Trench 45. This open ground was crossed in rapid rushes, though two men were killed and thirteen wounded, one of whom was CSM Claude Beechey, shot in the stomach—the round exiting through his back. Although grievously injured, he survived, but was medically discharged. Wedgwood stated:

> For this 200 yards the two platoons were subjected to very heavy machine-gun fire. Considering that this line was only 400 yards from Trench 45 and in view of Trench 40 and Hill 60, from each of which a heavy fire was directed, the casualties do not appear excessive.[62]

Turner transited further left, making use of a shallow valley to hide them from German eyes, and then along a hedge—though they were still left with the quandary of how to cross that final open stretch of ground before reaching the sanctuary of the cutting. Lt Alan Stenhouse volunteered to scout a path but was shot through the upper thigh; it was late that afternoon before he was brought in, close to death from blood loss (the diary records his wounding for 6 May; however, Blackledge describes the date and circumstances as narrated above[63]). Capt. Turner and Rfn Montague Hart, who volunteered to help reconnoitre a safer route, crawled out under heavy small arms fire, but found no alternative, so the final 200 yards was covered at a sprint. These two platoons entered the cutting nearby the Gangers' Hut, suffering a similar casualty toll to the others.

When Wedgwood reported at Davidson Dugout just after noon, he learned that Lt-Col. Scott of the Cheshires had just been mortally wounded while making his dispositions for the attack. Wedgwood was ordered to take 'A' to Trench 42a in support of the Cheshires and KOSB, who were still holding parts of trenches 39 and 40. It was while posting his sections here that Sgt Frederick Cavanagh was shot in the face. Cavanagh and a man from the Cheshires were wounded in what was believed to be dead ground, the shot appearing to have come from just behind the centre of Trench 42a. It was only later that Wedgwood learnt that four Germans—cut off from their own lines—had taken refuge in a tall belt of mustard there. It was probably one of these who had killed Lt-Col. Scott, and when they were unearthed that evening, the brave intruders fought to the death. Shortly after 1 p.m., the enemy broke through between the Cheshires and Bedfords, taking possession of Trench 42. 'A' Company was ordered to 'stand-to' with bayonets fixed.

Capt. Edward Brocklehurst's 'C' Company left Kruistraat next, but when they reached Brigade HQ, they were given the following orders:

> Proceed to Zillebeke village by way of south side of Zillebeke Lake to extend on the far side of the village on either side of the Zillebeke-Klein Zillebeke road and to push on as far as possible.
>
> Information was also given by the Brigade-Major, Capt. M. Barrett, that the enemy were believed to be proceeding down the road towards Zillebeke and that the company might expect to come under fire near the eastern end of the lake.[64]

No. 10 Platoon, under Lt Thomas 'Tim' Wilson, and 12 Platoon, under 2Lt Nigel Ronald, were tasked with spearheading the attack; 2Lt Oxenbould's 9 Platoon and 2Lt Blackledge's 11 Platoon were in support. Capt. McKaig went with the two leading platoons, Capt. Brocklehurst accompanied the others.

Many years later, William Wilson (279) described events:

> Capt McKaig, in a short talk, explained to us that the Germans had broken our line to the extent of capturing a trench and it for us to recapture it. Always a fighter, he told us 'To show them what we had learned in Canterbury.' (This referred to his favourite exercise of one platoon advancing, covered by the firepower of another platoon.)
>
> We started off running alongside Zillebeke Lake but were soon picked up by German field artillery, but only two shots were fired and no-one injured; on reaching the village a pause was taken before moving to the left on the road to Hooge. We were spotted by the enemy and a machine-gun turned on us. Corporal-Bugler (I'm afraid his name escapes me) was killed [father of one, twenty-seven-year-old Cpl Thomas Lewis]. We took shelter on the roadside and moved up [190 yards] towards the front line, happily in the shelter of a farm building. [In Coordinates Table as 'Wilson's farm']
>
> Only No. 11 Platoon was here, and I think Nos. 9, 10 and 12 were to our right. This was a welcome, safe shelter, but not for long; almost immediately an order came from Lt Blackledge for Rfn Wilson and Rfn [Norman] Ross. We went to him and found him talking to Capt. Brocklehurst. He said, 'I want you to go scouting with Capt. Brocklehurst.' Capt. Brocklehurst then said, 'Follow me.' I had never seen him before and these were the only words he ever spoke to us.
>
> We emerged into the field leading up to the front lines and went forward in Indian file. Luckily, there was a sheltered dip for some 30 or 40-yards, but as the dip levelled out,

> we came under sharp bursts of rifle fire. Capt. Brocklehurst quickened his pace and was running towards a patch of somewhat longer grass which would form protection from view, when he fell full-length, face down, without uttering any cry or sound. [175 yards forward of the farmhouse] We followed suit and imagined he had fallen to escape the rifle fire which was ripping the ground around us.
>
> We were evidently hidden from the enemy as this fire soon ceased and I took a look at the Capt. He lay in a quite large pool of blood and was quite dead. Shortly after, a connecting file appeared at the side of the farm [Riflemen Frederick Houghton and Joseph Massey] and Rfn Ross crawled back to them with the bad news. He asked them to find out what we had to do now the Capt. had been killed; they returned to the farm and we saw no more of them.
>
> After an hour or so lying there (luckily it was a beautiful day—weatherwise) we ran back to Zillebeke Lake, slept the night there and picked up our company next morning at the Railway dugouts.[65]

By the time that the two scouts returned to the farm, 11 Platoon had begun their advance further to the left, using a small valley that not only protected them from enemy view, but also hid their progress from the scouts. The other platoons, advancing much closer to the Klein–Zillebeke road, were also out of their line of sight, hence the pair's decision to return to Zillebeke Lake.

Brocklehurst could easily have delegated this dangerous reconnaissance to another officer or an NCO; it was a measure of the man that he chose to risk his own life first. The battalion made a number of unsuccessful attempts to locate Brocklehurst's body. It was discovered by the Yorkshire Regiment sometime later, buried, and the coordinates forwarded to battalion. He has no known grave, any marker was destroyed in later fighting.

Wilson's 'beautiful day' made life less pleasant for those sheltering amid the shell-damaged village in the sweltering heat. After running several miles, the men were hot and thirsty, the atmosphere around them pungent with the stench of rotting animal carcases, swelled to bursting-point in the heat. The buildings acted as a magnet for enemy fire, the constant crack of small arms fire passing overhead, or ricocheting off the brickwork. When McKaig learnt of the death of Brocklehurst, he and 2Lt Ronald went to the eastern edge of Zillebeke, where they found a good view of the terrain the company needed to advance across. Concealed in cover, they examined their route through binoculars.

The ground was quite bare, a few old dugouts and shell holes dotting the area. About 1,000 yards away, the enemy could clearly be seen on the low ridge behind Trench 42a and enemy scouting parties were spotted in two ruined farmhouses either side of the main road, 500 yards away (the later-named Knoll Farm on the left and an unnamed farm to the right of the road, marked with the letter 'Y' on McKaig's sketch map).

Two men remained in the village to guide the supports forward, and Wilson was ordered to advance along the left of the road, Ronald along the right. It was vital neither platoon was observed leaving the village, as they would have suffered grievously from hostile fire if discerned. This was to be the only occasion during the entire war when the battalion was called upon to make an open-order attack across exposed ground without any external fire support.

Fortunately, both platoons managed to exit the village, get into formation—each man 5 yards apart—and begin their advance before the enemy saw them. The platoons soon came under very heavy rifle and machine-gun fire from the ridge behind Trench 42a, and a further pair of machine guns, directly to the front of 10 Platoon. Notwithstanding this, they pushed on in short rushes, one section at a time, the others providing covering fire. One of the first to fall was Lt Wilson. Heartbreakingly, in one section, nineteen-year-old Rfn Arthur Fairbairn and his brother, twenty-five-year-old Archie, were killed within seconds of each other. By the time 10 Platoon reached the hedge-line in front of Knoll Farm, they were reduced from forty to just nine.

Wilson's Platoon suffered much higher losses than 12 Platoon, the two machine guns to their front, scything them down. Ronald's losses, though severe, were minimised because the ground fell away on the right, protecting them from much of the fire from the left. Ronald's men found it impossible to return rapid fire against the enemy on the ridge line because, from their position, the enemy were immediately above and in direct line to British positions in 42a, where they had just seen British soldiers moving into ('A' Company). One particularly troublesome sniper on the ridge was shot by twenty-five-year-old Cpl John Pennington, one of 12 Platoon's top marksmen. Having dealt with this nuisance, he was moving into a better position to deal with the machine gun on the ridge, when the Germans withdrew it themselves.

The lines of advancing riflemen prompted the German scouting parties to evacuate the two farms in 'C' Company's path and retire to their own lines (had they remained, 11 Platoon would have cut them off). On the left flank, Oxenbould and Blackledge initially followed Wilson, then Oxenbould slanted sharply towards the right soon after, aligning his right section to the edge of the Klein Zillebeke road. Twenty-three-year-old Oxenbould was badly wounded shortly after. The volume of fire from the front was such that, around 1 p.m., Capt. McKaig decided it was futile to push on further, especially as the Germans had evacuated the farmhouses. The survivors of 9 and 10 Platoon were ordered to dig in on the left, and 12 Platoon on the right. No. 10 Platoon—now led by Capt. McKaig—selected a line of shell-hole positions on the left of the road, about 100 yards from Knoll Farm, Ronald's platoon level with them to the right of the road. No. 9 Platoon dug in about 100 yards behind Capt. McKaig, the men using their entrenching tools to deepen and connect the shell holes.

The enemy withdrew from the ridge around 3 p.m., possibly because they believed the advance was much stronger than it actually was.[66] Using a shallow valley and a series of hedgerows slanting off to their left, Blackledge's 11 Platoon had advanced 150 yards further than the others, suffering few losses in the process. Their position allowed them to enfilade the Germans on the ridge, who may then have considered themselves in danger of encirclement.

The shallow shell-scrapes provided scant cover. Twenty-five-year-old Cpl Thomas Teague of 10 Platoon was killed as he tried to deliver a message; the act of raising himself up on one elbow being all the opportunity a German marksman needed. Blackledge later remarked:

> It is hard to overestimate what the men of 'C' Company endured during the remaining hours of daylight. Lying flat in the hot sun, they tried to throw up a little cover with their entrenching tools from the storm of bullets that came from the hilltop above, while overhead black shrapnel burst with ear-splitting reports. The groans of the wounded, the smell of explosives and blood, and the huddled bodies of the dead, seared indelible impressions on the minds of all those who survived the experience.[67]

McKaig lauded the courage of those helping the wounded, while the company dug itself in, stating, 'many fine deeds were done in getting the wounded into shell-holes and in getting them out of the fire altogether, as will be found in other appendices'.[68] Sadly, the relevant appendix no longer survives. He made specific mention of Sgt John Milton, Cpl Percy Beausire, and L/Cpl Fergus Ridge, 'whose conduct was most cool', though whether this was for the rescue of wounded or leadership during the attack (or both) is unknown.

The third company to leave Kruistraat was 'B', under Maj. Wainwright. He received orders from Brigade to deploy his platoons in trenches either side of the railway line, near the gangers' hut. No. 5 Platoon led, but as they reached Zillebeke Arrêt, they came under rifle and machine-gun fire and extended to the right. Parties of around five men and an NCO made short rushes along the line until they reached the cover of the cutting. Twenty-two-year-old Rfn Charles Scorgie was the only fatality, though seven were wounded. No. 7 Platoon followed shortly after, and although no one was killed outright, they suffered twelve wounded. One, Rfn Donald McGivering, had a very lucky escape:

> We were on our way up (to the trenches) when I was just hit by a bullet. I say 'just hit' because I was almost missed and my flesh is just bruised. The bullet hit me sideways and glanced off. However, we were on a railway line and could be seen. Two chaps very bravely came and put a bandage on, risking their lives time after time. We got away safely and I am now in hospital. This envelope was torn by the bullet.[69]

It was 3 July before the twenty-one-year-old recovered. One of the pair who bandaged him was a Rfn Williams from Smithdown Road, but unfortunately, this could be one of three in the company.

Company designations in the Casualties Book were not updated prior to this attack and three recorded as 'D' had been moved to 'B'; unfortunately, which three is unfathomable and they appear under 'D' in the table below. The other two platoons remained in support under cover of the embankment at Zillebeke Arrêt, until ordered forward in the evening, neither suffering loss.

The last to report to Brigade HQ was 'D', under Capt. Bennet. Initially, held in reserve in the railway embankment dugouts near Brigade HQ, at 1 p.m., Bennet was ordered to take his company and make contact with 'C'. Bennet followed the same route as 'C', using the cover of Zillebeke Lake embankment, halting at the south-eastern end, then sending Lt Edmund Buckley's platoon on ahead.

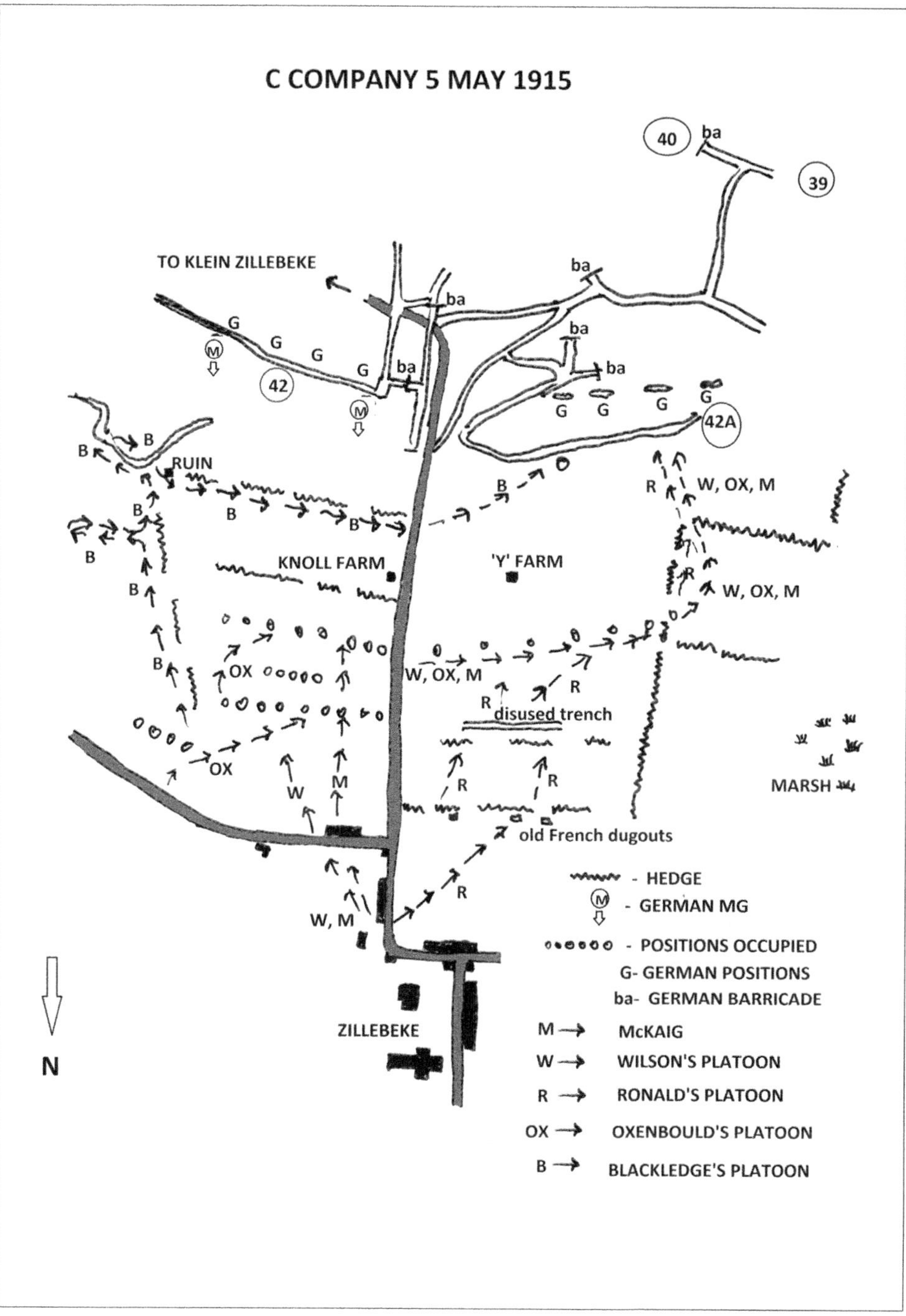
C COMPANY 5 MAY 1915
40
39
ba
TO KLEIN ZILLEBEKE
G
42
42A
RUIN
KNOLL FARM
'Y' FARM
W, OX, M
OX
W
M
R
B
disused trench
MARSH
old French dugouts
W, M
ZILLEBEKE
N
- HEDGE
- GERMAN MG
- POSITIONS OCCUPIED
G- GERMAN POSITIONS
ba- GERMAN BARRICADE
M → McKAIG
W → WILSON'S PLATOON
R → RONALD'S PLATOON
OX → OXENBOULD'S PLATOON
B → BLACKLEDGE'S PLATOON

Buckley approached the outskirts of Zillebeke, where he despatched two small patrols to find 'C', but neither was successful. Buckley then took his men down the right of the Klein Zillebeke road for about 500 yards, where he found some wounded sheltering in an old trench and was directed to Capt. McKaig's shell hole to the left of the road. Another officer described Buckley's arrival:

> About 2.30 p.m., Lt E. C. G. Buckley, of 'D' Company, reached the firing line in order to find out the situation. Bounding from shell-hole to shell-hole, at great risk, he miraculously avoided being hit. Wearing a woollen cap, with his long legs and powerful frame he made the most extraordinary sight, as time and time again, he appeared leaping over the open through the thick of the fire. After a shell-hole conference with Captain McKaig he returned by the same route, to the admiration and wonder of all who witnessed the feat. His escape was marvellous, for the German snipers were deadly with telescopic sights in the strong light.[70]

Second-Lieutenant Alsager Warburton's platoon followed fifteen minutes later, the subaltern particularly keen to help his old company. In a letter home, he described his day:

> I am very sorry to say, 'C' Company and especially my platoon, have taken a nasty knock. Poor old Brockle has been killed and Tim Wilson, and about ten men, all from my old platoon, and quite a lot wounded.
>
> I was sent up to support his company, and got within a 100 yards of his company, but we were all held up by the machine-gun and had to sit tight until the evening. I managed to crawl up to the firing line and found Captain __. [McKaig] We lay in a Jack Johnson hole, full of water, for an hour, trying to work out how to get on, but it was suicidal to move with any troops until after dark, and so I crawled back to my men.[71]

At 5.30 p.m., a runner from Buckley reached Capt. Bennet with details of 'C' Company's dispositions and McKaig's intention to hold position until dark, then move his platoons across the road to connect with 'A'. Bennet forwarded this to Lt-Col. Davison, who, half an hour later, ordered 'D' to advance further down the Klein Zillebeke road and dig in to deny further German advance from that direction.

As the light began to fade around 7 p.m., 2Lt Ronald was ordered to move his platoon through the long, north-south hedgerow to his right, and employ the shallow valley on the reverse to approach Trench 42a, where 'A' was located. Ronald's advance initially caused 'A' some concern—their first intimation being the sight of unknown troops approaching from their left rear. Ronald's platoon came under machine-gun fire from a small group of enemy situated in a patch of scrub just in front of Trench 42a, though escaped without loss.

Leaving a few men behind to tend the wounded, 9 and 10 Platoons began to work their way across the road at 8 p.m.; then, following the same route as Ronald, joined 'A' in 42a. Upon arrival, they found 2Lt Blackledge's platoon had beaten them to it, having found cover from hedge that ran all the way to the road from the ruined building delineating their left flank.

'C' Company's assault was not intended to have been a lone charge: to their immediate right, the Cheshires were supposed to have attacked at the same time, but confusion arising after the death of their CO—the 2IC had only just arrived and was unfamiliar with the ground—affected considerable delay.[72] At 3.30 p.m., Division logged that the Cheshires were moving on trenches 43 and 45 and that the Bedfords had retaken Trench 46. At 4 p.m., KOSB and RWK reached the railway embankment, though by 4.30 p.m., Trench 46 was once more in German hands. The situation was still obscure at 5 p.m., but Maj.-Gen. Morland believed (correctly) that the enemy held all the Zwarteleen Salient, including Hill 60, and trenches 43, 45, and part of 46.[73] As a fighting force, 15 Bde was pretty much spent—a situation exacerbated by 27 Division's artillery—who shelled the Bedfords between 7 and 8 p.m., resulting in 100 casualties. The 13th Bde would continue the counter-attacks at 10 p.m., with 2/KOSB against Hill 60 and 1/RWK to the left.

Ronald was very familiar with the trench layout ahead, and as it was still unclear if the enemy held any portions immediately to the front of the proposed RWK attack, he volunteered to reconnoitre the area to help their CO position his men. One of Ronald's NCOs wrote home about their recce:

> One of our officers was told off—or rather he volunteered to go—to explore a part of some fields in front of us which no-one knew by whom were occupied. Some asserted the Germans were seen a few yards in front. I was asked to go along with the officer, and to bring eight men, so we went away exploring.
>
> We got into a communication trench and crawled on our hands and knees, listening intently for the sounds of any voices, at the same time taking good care to not to make any noise ourselves, in case of being surprised by the Germans, there being so many curves in the trench, and, it being so narrow at this particular part, progress was very slow. The young officer was an example to all, being as cool as a cucumber, and with revolver loaded ready for any emergency. After going some distance, we came across some other communication trenches leading in all directions. Choosing one way, we came to a few Germans who were dead, and by the look of them they had not been killed many hours since. It is supposed that many had been there, but, owing to some being killed, the remainder evidently retreated. We immediately concluded that the fields were in our possession.[74]

This was just one of number of sorties Ronald made that night. He also went out again early next morning, to retrieve the badges of enemy dead for identification purposes.

At 7 p.m., the enemy made another gas attack against trenches 38–40, followed by a half-hearted infantry assault that was easily beaten off by small arms fire. Although the *OH* reports that the gas had 'little effect', it proved fatal for Rfn Allen Haynes of 'B', the twenty-three-year-old succumbing at the Aid Post later that night.[75] He is the only man from the battalion recorded as a gas casualty for 5 May, though Riflemen Harry Fox of 'B' and Charles Nichols of 'D' were both admitted to hospital the next day, suffering from the effects of gas.

After just twenty minutes' bombardment, the attack went ahead at 10 p.m., and despite reaching the top of Hill 60, the KOSB were beaten back by a well-prepared enemy, supported by effective artillery. Just after midnight, 13 Bde accepted the impossibility of holding the Hill, without attacking on a broader front to negate enfilading fire from the Caterpillar and Zwarteleen Salient. British artillery had been utterly inadequate: too few heavy guns, too little ammunition, and barrels so worn that rounds fell on, or even behind, British positions. During 6 May, the Bedfords in trenches 47 and 48, having lost 100 men to friendly fire the previous day, were outraged when British artillery targeted them again.[76] One further, unsuccessful attempt against Hill 60 was made during the night.

CRA Brig.-Gen. J. D. Geddes, humiliatingly aware of the problems facing his heavy guns, wrote to the divisional-commander:

> The situation as regards 4.7″ guns is acute and demands immediate action. On 24 April, ten 4.7″ guns in this division were unfit to fire. They have been gradually replaced and on 5 May we had ten 4.7″ guns in action. They are all 'part-worn' guns and in nearly all cases the rifling towards the muzzle is completely worn away. On 5 May, during the afternoon and evening, the guns were called upon to shoot. The consequence is that 4.7″ shells have been reported dropping behind our lines or bursting on our trenches all over the front held by 5 Division. There was no alternative but to order the 4.7″ guns to cease fire. About 50 per cent of the shell wobble and whistle. I consider it is dangerous and demoralising to fire these guns over the heads of our own troops. The same disaster occurred with both lyddite and shrapnel.[77]

German artillery directed heavy fire against British positions throughout the evening of 5 May, fire that continued overnight, making the rescue of the many wounded lying out in the open perilous. Among those who distinguished themselves, organising rescue parties to bring in the wounded, was Rfn Allan Smith. Helping him was his older brother, Charles, who was commissioned in July.

Just before dusk, 2Lt Ronald, examining the area through binoculars, spotted one of his company lying wounded in a shell hole. Utilising a break in the hostile artillery, he organised a rescue party, retrieving Samuel Lloyd, who was taken to the Aid Post in the railway cutting. Sadly, the twenty-four-year-old, shot through the right thigh, died on 8 July. Just a brief exposure while helping a wounded comrade could be deadly. When Trevor Jones knelt to bandage a wounded pal, he was shot through the chest. The twenty-three-year-old from Egremont died in Boulogne on 12 May. Also from Egremont was twenty-one-year-old Eric Dodsworth; the former Cunard clerk—one of the brave volunteers who had rescued the wounded sapper—was shot through the abdomen when he went to the aid of a wounded pal, dying from his injury the next day.[78] During the night of 5 May, one shell, which burst directly over their dugout, wounded Sgt Milton, L/Cpl Ridge, and six men; fire continued throughout 6 May.

Early in the morning of 6 May, L/Cpl Frank Hargraves, Rfn William Burbage, and Rfn Charles Gladwinfield informed Capt. Wedgwood that they had located five wounded men, who had been lying out in the open all night. One had died, but they moved the others into a shell hole for shelter, where they were collected by a stretcher party. In broad daylight, 2Lt Brownell volunteered to go out into a very exposed position on the far side of the Zillebeke-Klein Zillebeke road, where another casualty lay. Taking water to the critically wounded man, he realised that the only way to move him was by stretcher. The close proximity to the Germans in the end of Trench 45—who constantly deluged the area with bombs—and relentless shellfire falling across the route over the road and around the casualty meant that this would be a suicidal undertaking. Brownell made the heart-breaking decision that the man could not be rescued.

The battalion began to be relieved at 8.30 p.m., the first company being 'C', who marched off to huts at 'E' Camp near Ouderdom. The other companies followed in stages, until, finally, 'D' filed out at 1.20 a.m. on 7 May. All returned via the railway cutting to the embankment near Brigade HQ, with considerable confusion arising as everyone tried to identify their own pack among the piles dumped there on their way forward. Over the following few days, strange assortments of kit were evident and much exchanging went on before everyone had correctly-fitting uniform. Many packs went unclaimed.

Considerable discrepancies exist regarding casualties figures—with a 25 per cent spread and no two sources agreeing. The Casualties Book, which is probably the most reliable, records twenty-nine fatalities and eighty-six wounded (115 overall). Division suffered 3,100 casualties between 1 and 7 May, 1,583 of whom were from 15 Bde.[79, 80]

With Hill 60 in German hands—where it remained until June 1917—the battalion's losses appear pointless. However, their spirited attack plugged a mile-wide gap in British lines—their action leading the Germans to believe British strength was greater than it actually was. The enemy was less than 2 miles from Ypres when 'C' began their advance, and had the foe remained unchecked, the consequences could have been disastrous. These two days gave the battalion confidence in its own abilities and fostered an intense spirit of comradeship between all ranks; no longer feeling like raw troops, they considered they could be relied upon to not only hold trenches, but to attack and advance in the face of heavy opposition.

Very few of the wounded returned, their injuries either precluding further infantry service, or they were commissioned elsewhere. For Rfn George Downie, it was not his thigh wound that brought about his medical discharge, but loss of hearing, preventing the former dental student from hearing challenges from sentries. It is clear from their personal effects that many expected to be commissioned at some time—cataloguing articles, such as privately purchased service revolvers, wristwatches, and prismatic compasses. The effects received by the father of Rfn Stanley Jones (051), who died from a gunshot wound to the abdomen on 7 May, included:

> 1 Identity Disc; 1 Revolver; 1 Collapsible Drinking Cup; 2 Razors; Shaving Brush; Cigarette Case with four Cigarettes; Wristwatch (no fingers or glass); Compass; Stylo Pen; Diary; Booklet; Protractor; 22 Photos; 15 Postcards; 7 Letters; 1 Antipyrin Powder; Safety Pin; 2½ Stamps; 1 piece of Court Plaister; 1 Excess-Fare Railway Ticket.[81]

This may appear to be a comprehensive list, but, suspiciously, no money is recorded.

Disgracefully, it was far from uncommon for valuables—often of immense sentimental value—to be looted. Within a battalion, a man's possessions were sacrosanct, though consumables such as cake and tobacco were shared between his pals—a practice relatives thoroughly approved of. Theft, when it occurred, usually took place further down the chain. In the case of twenty-four-year-old Cpl Sydney Pinnington, the battalion carefully noted all his possessions before sealing these up and passing them through the system for return home. A letter from his father informed Infantry Records that Pinnington's purse was empty when it arrived, though the battalion had earlier written to him, enclosing a full list of effects, noting that the purse containing three 10/- notes and three 5-Franc notes—all of which had disappeared.[82]

The extremely high standards demanded by the battalion, both pre-war and in the final months of 1914, rebounded upon them in that such a high proportion of their sick and wounded were commissioned elsewhere after recovering. Taking into account those killed and those no longer fit, nearly half the 'originals' were lost thus. The only factor keeping the percentage lower than it probably otherwise would have been was that, in 1915, officialdom considered experienced infantrymen far too valuable to withdraw from the Front for the purposes of commissioning—deeming it preferable to commission inexperienced, but educated youths, straight from school. The folly of this policy later became obvious and front-line experience became a prerequisite for a commission—though not before many 'green' subalterns and their unfortunate charges had paid the ultimate penalty.

Casualties from 'A' Company, 5-7 May 1915

Name	No.	Status
Rfn Albert Ernest Alexander	1872	WIA: 5/5
Rfn Eric Ingham Joseph Barrand	240450	WIA: 5/5
CSM Claude Grantley Beechey	36	WIA: 5/5
Rfn Robert W. Butler	2132	WIA: 5/5
Sgt Frederick George Cavanagh	39	WIA: 5/5
Rfn Bernard Stewart S. Courtney	1677	WIA: 5/5
Lt Robert Lyle Dobell		WIA: 5/5
Rfn Harold Gibbs	1417	WIA: 5/5
Rfn William James Herbert	240458	WIA: 5/5
Rfn Arthur Oswald Horner	240559	WIA: 5/5
L/Cpl John Brown Horsfall	1429	WIA: 5/5
Rfn William C. Hunter	1505	WIA: 5/5
L/Cpl Herbert Hyam	240081	WIA: 5/5
Rfn John Francis Jenkins	240288	WIA: 5/5
Rfn Ivor Jones	2062	WIA: 5/5
Rfn Stanley Tynemouth Jones	2051	DOW: 7/5
Rfn Trevor Allport Jones	1351	DOW: 12/5
Rfn Thomas Kay	2135	KIA: 5/5
Rfn Thomas Bell Latham	240902	WIA: 5/5
Rfn Hugh Berwyn Lewis	240405	WIA: 5/5
Rfn Francis Rubenstein Linekar	1914	KIA: 5/5
Rfn Ernest Mason	240281	WIA: 5/5
Rfn John Maudsley	2131	KIA: 5/5
Rfn Walter Millar	240216	WIA: 5/5
Rfn Conrad M. Pakenham-Walsh	1724	WIA: 5/5
Rfn Thomas H. Philipps	240615	WIA: 5/5
Rfn Robert Phipps	240144	WIA: 5/5

Rfn William John Plant	240221	WIA: 5/5
Rfn Percy Postlethwaite	1967	WIA: 5/5
Rfn Herbert Elias Pugh	1299	WIA: 6/5
Rfn George Readle	1898	WIA: 5/5
Rfn William Robertson	1471	WIA: 5/5
Rfn Herbert Sefton	240528	WIA: 5/5
Rfn Richard V. Shepherd	240628	WIA: 5/5
Rfn Alexander Patrick Sheridan	2120	KIA: 5/5
Rfn George Percival Slade	240671	WIA: 5/5
Lt Alan Hugh Stenhouse		WIA: 5/5
Rfn Stanley Wilson Winstanley	240509	WIA: 5/5

Casualties from 'B' Company, 5-7 May 1915

Rfn George Barnes	2286	WIA: 5/5
Rfn James Matthew Braithwaite	2144	WIA: 5/5
Rfn Eric Druce Dodsworth	1722	DOW: 6/5
L/Cpl Frank Dyall*	240258	WIA
Rfn Donald Eastwood	1769	WIA: 5/5
Rfn Harry Fox	1443	WIA: 6/5
Rfn John George Gilbert	1324	DOW: 6/5
Rfn Allen Stanley Haynes	1731	DOW: 5/5
Rfn Robert Jump	1289	WIA: 5/5
Rfn Arthur Towers Lunt*	1696	WIA
Rfn James Walker Lynch	240707	WIA: 5/5
Rfn Donald McGivering	240527	WIA: 5/5
Cpl Harold Dawson Roberts	766	WIA: 5/5
Rfn William Roberts	2150	WIA: 5/5
Rfn Charles Gilbert Scorgie	2082	KIA: 5/5
Rfn John Standish Skyner	1454	WIA: 6/5
Sgt William Watt	3126	WIA: 5/5
Rfn Frederick Edward Wilkins	240357	WIA: 5/5

* = The date of wounding for these two went unrecorded in the Casualties Book, 7 May being the date they were admitted to the hospital in Ypres. The probability is they were casualties from 5 May.

Casualties from 'C' Company, 5-7 May 1915

Capt. Edward Henry Brocklehurst		KIA: 5/5
Rfn Keith Holden Brown	1482	WIA: 5/5
Rfn Gordon Clough	1894	KIA: 5/5
Rfn William Cornes	2399	WIA: 5/5
Rfn Alfred Dixon	240635	WIA: 5/5
Rfn George Gordon Downie	1255	WIA: 5/5
Rfn James Morris Earl	240564	WIA: 5/5
Rfn Arthur West Fairbairn	1329	KIA: 5/5
Rfn William Ritchie Fairbairn	1330	KIA: 5/5
Rfn Albert Fowler	2316	KIA: 5/5
Cpl William Leonard Harrison	1285	WIA: 5/5
Rfn Charles Haswell	240883	WIA: 5/5
Rfn William Hotchkiss	88703	WIA: 5/5
Rfn Edward Highton Hughes	1176	WIA: 5/5
Rfn Trevor Humphreys	1480	WIA: 5/5
Rfn Stanley Robert A. Hutchinson	1336	WIA: 5/5
Rfn Charles Barker Kendall	240174	WIA: 5/5
Rfn George Leslie Key	2287	WIA: 6/5
Rfn Herbert Willoughby Key	240475	WIA: 6/5
Rfn Norman Leslie Kilner	1542	WIA: 5/5

Name	No.	Status
Rfn William Frederick Langham	1564	KIA: 5/5
Rfn George Lawton	1201	KIA: 5/5
L/Cpl Arthur Le Rougetel	1268	WIA: 5/5
Cpl Thomas Lewis	87	KIA: 5/5
Rfn Gerald William Lindsay	1736	WIA: 6/5
Rfn Samuel Turner Lloyd	1614	DOW: 8/7
Rfn Richard Marsh Lyons	240600	WIA: 6/5
Rfn Thomas Simpson McGeorge	240621	WIA: 5/5
Rfn Wilfred Heard Miller	1261	WIA: 5/5
Sgt John Herbert Milton	971	WIA: 6/5
2Lt Basil Henry Oxenbould		WIA: 5/5
Rfn Norman Rutherford Phillips	2306	WIA: 5/5
Cpl Sydney Pinnington	545	KIA: 5/5
Rfn Robert William F. Punt	2409	WIA: 5/5
Rfn Reginald Clive Purvis	1811	KIA: 5/5
Rfn Albert Robert Rashbrook	240770	WIA: 6/5
L/Cpl Fergus Harold Ridge	932	WIA: 6/5
L/Sgt Henry H. E. Royle	1347	WIA: 5/5
Rfn Francis Thomas Ruddle	2541	KIA: 5/5
Rfn Herbert William Scholefield	240919	WIA: 5/5
Rfn Henry Schonewald	1888	KIA: 5/5
Rfn Arthur N. Shaw	2365	WIA: 6/5
Rfn Gilbert Lester Taylor	240337	WIA: 6/5
Cpl Thomas Every Teague	1638	KIA: 5/5
Rfn John Thompson	1922	KIA: 5/5
Rfn John Tilley	240129	WIA: 5/5
Rfn Harold Bennet Whinyates	240354	WIA: 5/5
Lt Thomas Wilson Wilson		KIA: 5/5

Casualties from 'D' Company, 5–7 May 1915

Name	No.	Status
Cpl George Chesshyre Dutton	240085	WIA: 5/5
Rfn Albert E. Fontannaz	2282	WIA: 6/5
Rfn Sydney Baylis Houghton	1832	KIA: 5/5
Rfn Henry Edward Hyde	2813	KIA: 5/5
Rfn Ernest Hugh Jones	240604	WIA: 5/5
Rfn Lewis Vernon Harrison Jones	240243	WIA: 5/5
Sgt Arthur Bertram Moulton	136	KIA: 5/5
Rfn Charles T. Nichols	1497	WIA: 6/5
Rfn Eric Robinson Parrington	2520	WIA: 5/5
Rfn John Parry	1402	WIA: 5/5
Rfn Harry Milton Terry	240620	WIA: 5/5

The battalion remained at 'E' Camp until 15 May, sickness further reducing numbers. The most significant of these was 'C' Company's CSM Joseph Moscrop, hospitalised with 'debility' and returned to England for good. 'Debility', frequently witnessed in records, is best explained as a general weakness of a physical origin—its toll on older soldiers occasioned by endless toil in appalling conditions. One sickness affecting the division in May was influenza and some units were very badly weakened: 5/Cheshires so much so that they were unable to relieve the Devons on 17 May.[83] Over the course of the war, 6 per cent of the Rifles were hospitalised with seasonal influenza, so its impact was not substantial; only 1.8 per cent of the battalion were infected with the deadlier Spanish variety in 1918.

The Greenjacket (1927) reports a draft of men arriving at 'E 'Camp.[84] This is not borne out by contemporary records, with just five officers arriving on 15 May.[85] Amazingly, all the losses suffered by the Regulars of 15 Bde were replaced by 20 May, Brigade reporting that they were actually over-strength.[86] This clearly did not include the Rifles, whose 'strength return' for 12 May catalogued 708 officers and men, significantly less than the 1,125 who sailed in February. In fact, the first OR replacements only appeared on 8 August.

At 11.15 a.m. on 15 May, the battalion was ordered to dugouts east of Kruisstraat Château. Prior to their departure, 150 men from 'A' and 'B' were tasked to work on a support post south of Zillebeke, one of a series of positions in the Zillebeke Switch, protecting Ypres. The remainder of the battalion moved off in stages at 8 p.m., each company ten minutes apart. The working party suffered losses from enemy artillery: from 'A', nineteen-year-old Rfn Albert Jones (162) was killed; twenty-one-year-old Rfn George Hughes (569) and Rfn William Burbage, both wounded in the thigh; and thirty-two-year-old Rfn Harry Robinson wounded in the left hip. Rfn E. Kewish from 'B' was also wounded in the thigh. Only Burbage returned.

On 16 May, fatigue parties began moving small arms ammunition from the Ypres Ramparts to a new dump in the stables at Kruisstraat Château. Men manhandled the heavy boxes up from underground, then carried them through Ypres to a lorry on the road that is now Pannenhuisstraat. The first party of ninety men under Maj. Wainwright left at 3 a.m., and in two journeys, loaded eighty-two boxes onto the first lorry, which departed at 8 a.m. Another party of 100 men under Capt. Bennet left the dugouts at 6 a.m. and loaded a further seventy-eight boxes onto a second lorry, which followed shortly after the first, leaving 400 boxes in the Ramparts to be transferred at a later date. At noon, the battalion were ordered into dugouts on the south-west of Zillebeke Lake, under the command of 8 Bde.

The move was completed by 9.30 p.m., though there was no time to rest, as 400 men were sent to work on the southern section of the Verbrande Molen–Zillebeke line. The battalion's new accommodation was hardly satisfactory, as Ellison recounted:

> They found that perhaps one-tenth could find accommodation there, yet cover from the ever threatening rain and more important, from shell-fire, was of the most urgency. They proceeded to dig themselves in and before nightfall were safely tucked away in a series of shallow holes roofed with groundsheets, sandbags, corrugated iron, or whatever could be scrounged at short notice, each holding two or three men.
>
> For nearly two months they were to remain, unrelieved, in this cramped and comfortless spot, unbathed, never undressed and from Colonel downwards, inexpressibly lousy. The top of the bank was under direct enemy observation from Hill 60, barely a mile distant, and during daylight, our sentries kept a constant watch for aeroplanes. It was amusing to see the entire battalion dive into their burrows like so many startled rabbits, at the first blast of the warning whistle. At night, a patrol saw that no chink of light showed from the carefully shaded candles.

Lice were not the only problem:

> One night I was awakened from the deep sleep of exhaustion by a choking sensation: my face was covered with soil, my mouth crammed with it. For a moment I thought I

> was buried, the fate that every soldier fears, but when I could move, I lit a candle and discovered that a burrowing mole was responsible. It certainly put the wind up me for a little while.[87]

Keeping hidden from aerial observation was testing: men had to eat and it was imperative that company-cooks avoided smoke from the cookers; equally, 700 men occupying a small area inevitably create paths along the ground, detectable on aerial photographs, especially to facilities such as latrines.

Their work was hard and perilous:

> Our duty was to supply large carrying parties for ammunition and mining stores to the front line on Hill 60. This nightly journey—sometimes twice nightly—was a dangerous and detestable job. The open and exposed approach up the railway cutting from Zillebeke Halt was a death trap. Never a journey, but the message 'Stretcher-Bearers' was passed down the ranks. Only those who once formed part of that winding snake of men, overburdened with coils of wire, corrugated iron sheets or balks of timber, stumbling in pitch darkness over sleepers and into shell-holes, with the leading files barely moving, yet those at the rear running in a lather of sweat to keep in touch; with shells arriving punctually every few minutes at recognised danger spots, and overhead the evil swish of machine-gun bullets, can possible appreciate the hardship of the task.[88]

In Ellison's scrapbook, a contemporary photograph of the bridge at the head of this cutting shows extensive bullet-scarring of the brickwork along one side: German machine gunners on the Caterpillar aimed at this particular spot in the knowledge that rounds would glance off along a stretch impervious to direct fire; these tumbling, distorted rounds caused horrendous wounds.

At 8.30 p.m. on 17 May, HQ returned to Ouderdom, but a brief respite for 400 men would have to wait, as they were sent forward to continue the previous night's work. Three Riflemen were wounded before midnight: 'B' Company's Albert Cromer was wounded in the right arm, returning in November. The injuries to the pair from 'A' heralded the end of their time with the battalion. William Fell was commissioned into the MGC when he left his English hospital and nineteen-year-old Thomas Hawitt's abdominal wound—though not fatal—resulted in medical discharge. It must have been a particularly anxious time for his parents, as his older brother, Arthur, had been killed with battalion on 29 March. Tragically, their youngest son, Wilfred, was killed with the Loyals in September 1918, aged just eighteen. The working party returned to 'E' Camp at 3.30 a.m. on 18 May, this brief interlude their last for some time. Sporadic artillery fire slightly wounded Rfn Leonard Alexander above the right eye, though he was back with 'D' a fortnight later.

The battalion returned to the Zillebeke Lake dugouts at 7.15 p.m. on 20 May as brigade reserve. One who did not join them until 2 June was Rfn Eric Brooker, admitted to 15 Field Ambulance on 19 May, suffering from shellshock. The usual carrying parties were demanded and men assisted in wiring the Zillebeke Switch. The only casualty that night was Rfn John Owen from 'B'. Badly wounded in the right foot, he was evacuated home. The entire battalion was involved in carrying parties on 21 May and 'B' lost Rfn Eric Dean, wounded in the right leg. 'A' suffered three casualties in the early morning of 22 May: twenty-one-year-old Rfn Charles Gladwinfield was killed; Rfn William Doyle wounded in the right arm; and twenty-eight-year-old Sgt Henry Imlach wounded for the second time, this time in the left thigh. The battalion was also unlucky enough to lose the services of 2Lt Ronald that day, when he was hospitalised with enteric fever.

Ronald was the second such victim since deployment. 'Divisional Orders' for 3 May had cautioned about this potentially-fatal disease:

> The season of the year during which Enteric is most prevalent is now approaching. It is of extreme importance that sanitation should receive the earnest attention of all ranks, and that men should be constantly warned only to drink water that has been boiled or chemically treated in the water carts, it is however recognised that circumstances prevent the attainment of ideal sanitary conditions, it follows therefore, that Inoculation against Enteric is the principal means whereby the spread of this disease can be checked.
>
> The value of inoculation is probably well understood and recognised throughout the Army. Proofs of this value are abundant. There is a Territorial Battalion (5/Cheshires] in the division which has been some five months [*sic.*] in the country, every individual in the battalion was inoculated before embarkation. This battalion had had no case of Enteric since its arrival on the Continent. Officers Commanding are enjoined to urge the desirability of inoculation on all ranks. Each man of a draft should, on arrival, be specially interrogated and urged to undergo inoculation if he has not already done so.[89]

To be safe, water needs to be boiled for at least one minute—it is doubtful if this ever occurred when men prepared their brews.

The nightly working parties on 22–23 May were casualty free. At 8.30 p.m. on 23 May, 'D' Company and the machine gunners were despatched to join the Norfolks in trenches 35–37, the rest continuing on carrying parties. Although the diary records 'casualties—nil' for 24 May, records show that twenty-year-old Rfn Charles Quayle from 'B' was wounded in the right leg, returning in September. Gas was detected at 3.45 a.m. on 24 May, and everyone donned their rudimentary protection, though the concentration must have been fairly weak, as the gas was released well to the east of Ypres. The battalion also reported heavy shelling around the Menin Road from this direction, and stragglers from units there were seen north of the dugouts at the lake, gathered up and shepherded to Brigade HQ.

The daily pattern of fatigues continued unabated, though casualties increased considerably towards the end of May, particularly on 25–26 May, when several salvoes landed amid parties, killing two—eighteen-year-old Rfn Leonard Blackburn on 25 May and mortally wounding twenty-five-year-old Rfn Harry Barnshaw the same day; just twelve of the twenty-seven wounded returned. By the end of the month, fighting strength had fallen to 645.[90]

Casualties, 25-31 May 1915

Name	No.	Status
Rfn Kenneth Ainslie (C)	1873	WIA: 25/5
Rfn Joseph B. Austin (B)	2077	WIA: 30/5
Rfn Thomas Baker (A)	1424	WIA: 25/5
Rfn Joseph Banning (B)	240958	WIA: 25/5
Rfn Harry Gwillim Barnshaw (B)	1692	DOW: 26/5
Rfn Leonard Blackburn (D)	1511	KIA: 25/5
Rfn Charles Cross (C)	2388	WAD: 25/5
Rfn Ernest Norman Dean (C)	1487	WIA: 27/5
Cpl John Howard Essery (A)	240533	WIA: 25/5
Rfn Malise Ronald Graham (B)	2318	WIA: 25/5
Rfn Thomas Harper (B)	2148	WIA: 30/5
Rfn Matthew Hawksworth (D)	2593	WIA: 25/5
Rfn Charles Jackson (D)	240653	WIA: 25/5
Rfn Edgar Morlais Jones (A)	2010	WIA: 27/5
Rfn Pierce Jones (B)	2056	WIA: 26/5
Rfn William R. Jones (A)	240128	WIA: 30/5
Rfn William Lawson (C)	1237	WIA: 31/5
Rfn William Ledgerwood (A)	240439	WIA: 26/5
L/Cpl Bertram Murray (B)	1683	WIA: 26/5
Rfn Bernard Parry (C)	240095	WIA: 25/5
Rfn Joseph Robert Phillips (C)	240330	WIA: 25/5
Sgt Albert Edward Rankmore (A)	240038	WIA: 25/5
Rfn Mark Revill (C)	2291	WIA: 26/5
Rfn Thomas Francis Reynolds (A)	240172	WIA: 26/5
L/Sgt Thomas Barrett Smith (A)	240063	WIA: 25/5
Rfn Harold William Smythe (B)	240515	WIA: 30/5
Rfn Raymond William Walker (C)	2214	WIA: 26/5
Rfn Samuel Williams (C)	240572	WIA: 26/5
Rfn Frederick Henry Wright (A)	1702	WIA: 25/5

There was little let-up in workload during June, the only variation being that some were employed digging, as opposed to carrying, though casualties decreased during the first fortnight. At 9 p.m. on 3 June, 'A' was attached to the Norfolks, Rfn Reginald Fletcher being wounded at duty the very next day (the company with the Norfolks was rotated every couple of days). At some time before midnight on 5 June, Rfn Martin McGeorge from 'C' suffered a 'Blighty' wound in the right thigh. 'B' lost two wounded on the night of the 7th: Rfn Richard Eastwood hit in the left arm and the infelicitous Rfn Frederick Wilkins, who had only returned from his previous wounding the day before, was hit in the neck. Both were evacuated home.

During the morning of 8 June, the battalion's dugouts were shelled by HE, with one landing right next to Lt-Col. Davison's dugout, nearly blowing it in. Though, no casualties resulted, it was a close thing. The day was oppressively hot, Division recording a temperature of 90 Fahrenheit (32 Celsius) in the shade, and it was no surprise when the afternoon brought a heavy thunderstorm and fifty minutes' torrential rain, which turned their bivouac area into a slough and made the already-difficult nightly trek up to the line even more testing. Just one man was wounded that night, Rfn Alfred Mitchell, who receiving a minor face wound (strictly speaking, the twenty-six-year-old of German extraction was Alfred Mittendorfer. In March 1916, he changed his name by deed poll to Mitchell. After being hospitalised with a broken collar bone in May 1916, the now-sergeant was commissioned into the Dorsets, ending the war as a captain with an MC and MBE).

'A' Company lost Rfn George Bott to a leg wound on 10 June. The twenty-three-year-old was later commissioned into the South Lancs and killed with them in April 1918. There were casualties in other companies too: Rfn William Harrison was critically wounded in the abdomen and stretchered back to Ypres (sadly, the nineteen-year-old from 'D' died later that night), and 2Lt Edward Tyson from 'B' twisted his knee so badly in the slippery conditions that he was evacuated home.

Commanders remained concerned about CLLEs, and the battalion received the following in the early hours of 10 June:

> There have been some reports made recently about the defects of the long rifles, sighted to fire Mk. VII ammunition, and the DOO [Divisional Ordnance Officer] 5th Division has been instructed to carry out an examination of long rifles in charge of your battalion. Will you therefore please arrange for fifty long rifles to be carefully cleaned ready for the examination, which will take place between 4 and 6 p.m. tomorrow, 10th inst. The examination will take the form of the DOO witnessing the firing of 500 rounds of rapid fire from the fifty rifles (ten rounds each)—the rounds being fired into a bank, built up, if necessary.[91]

In the early hours of 12 June, nineteen-year-old Rfn Leslie Dunwell from 'A' was wounded in the hand. Upon his return in December 1917, he was posted to 1/KLR, dying from wounds the following March. The Brigade diary reported that the attachment of one company to the Norfolks ceased on 13 June, though this remained unmentioned in the Battalion's diary.[92] Late on 16 June, Rfn Reginald Fletcher from 'A' got his second wound that month, though this one—to the neck—was more serious and he never returned.

Up until now, there had been a steady trickle of casualties, but late on 17 June, 'A' sustained three wounded: Rfn Arthur Lunt's hip wound was insignificant and he was back nine days later; Rfn Walter O'Donnell's groin wound, however, was much more concerning, and he was evacuated home, his days with the battalion over; and Sgt Robert Purdon's thigh wound also necessitated treatment in England, though he returned in August. Rfn Sidney Webster of 'B' received his second of the war when he was hit by shrapnel in the forehead, returning in November. On 18 June, there was just one casualty, when L/Sgt William Taggart of 'A' was wounded in both hips—keeping him from duty until mid-August. The appalling living conditions and never-ending work was beginning to wear men down, though the British soldier was (and is) remarkably good at maintaining a sense of humour in the most adverse of circumstances. During the day of 20 June, Ellison wrote home from his dugout:

> The dugout I am in at present is cosy as dugouts go, about 5ft by 4ft. It is simply a hole dug in a steep clay bank and boarded over. When three of us get in it is perhaps just a bit squashed but that makes for warmth. Although it is June, the nights are chilly enough. The large parcel ('Wardrobe for Ellison' was shouted out at the mail distribution) greeted me on my return from a particularly disagreeable forty-eight hours in the trenches and so

> was doubly welcome. We had some very heavy thunder rain which soon had everything, including ourselves, covered with liquid clay. Coming back along a communication trench well over our boot-tops in water, the humourist of the company said 'Pass the word along—keep a sharp lookout for submarines'.
>
> The flies in the trenches are a plague, literally millions of them. You can hear them all around you like the drone of a great factory. There are also stinks (more than mere smells) which in comparison, would classify Widnes* as a health resort. 'Nuff said! The other day we went to an old brewery at [Dickebusch] and had most enjoyable hot baths in the beer vats there.[93] [*The stench from the chemical works was still all-enveloping in parts of 1960s Liverpool when the wind blew from there.]

That night saw further casualties: 2Lt Bardsley-Powell was leading his carrying party up the railway cutting when a stray round critically wounded him in the abdomen, and although he survived, his active service was over. Also from 'B', L/Sgt William Heaton was admitted to 15 Field Ambulance with shellshock—severe enough to be sent home. L/Cpl Robert James was wounded in the thigh, the twenty-seven-year-old not returning to 'C' until mid-August. 'D' had two Riflemen wounded on the night of 21 June: twenty-four-year-old Thomas Jones (744), hit in the right thigh, returned to duty in mid-August, and John Broom, who was more fortunate and, once his injury was dressed, continued on duty.

On 22 June near Hooge, 5 Corps continued their operation begun on 16 June, and the division were tasked to divert enemy attention by bombing German positions. The battalion's bombers, under newly-promoted Lt Blackledge, assisted:

> The grenadiers of the 6th Liverpool Regiment were placed at the disposal of the CO 1st Cheshires and in accordance with orders received from him I paraded the battalion grenadiers at 6 p.m. They were split up into small parties to await artillery observation and followed the route NE side of Zillebeke Lake to 51 Support, [in Armagh Wood] where they were met by CO 1st Cheshires who gave me his orders. These were to make no advance but to cause as much inconvenience as possible to the enemy by bombing 46 Support [captured by the enemy on 5 May] from the communication trench from 47 to 46. This was done over the barricade.
>
> Time being short, as many bombs as possible were prepared and I went to the position indicated with twenty men and two lance/corporals.
>
> On arrival at the spot I found that it was impossible to use the heavy types of hand grenade with which I was provided to any great effect, as the German trench (the old 46 Support trench) was from 35–40 yards away. The trench was cleared for about for about 50 yards each side of the point from which the grenades were to be thrown and [I] brought the throwers up in parties of four. About twenty-five hand grenades were thrown and five rifle grenades were also fired. Of the hand grenades, one which reached the enemies' trench failed to explode and was returned by the Germans without effect. Of the remaining hand grenades, I should judge about ten to have been wholly or partially effective, the rest falling short. Of the rifle grenades, three fell in the vicinity of, though

> slightly beyond, the enemy's trench, the other two being difficult to observe owing to the enemy's snipers becoming active. None of the German bombs, of which about ten to fifteen were thrown, failed to reach our bombing point, the only casualty being one very slight wound on the ear caused by a German bomb which fell near the front parapet [unrecorded in the Casualties Book].
>
> The party remained in the trench until 11.30 p.m. when as no further reply came, we left and returned to billets at Zillebeke Lake at 12.15 a.m. the 23rd, without further casualties.[94]

The bombers were delighted to get a chance to retaliate after weeks of merely being a target, though enemy artillery took its toll on carrying parties that night. L/Cpl George Froude from 'A' was wounded in the face, returning in February. The other casualty, from 'B', was twenty-year-old Rfn Robert Jones (533), wounded in the right hand. He too eventually returned, was commissioned into the West Yorks in 1916, and killed shortly afterwards.

It was not just the carrying parties under fire that evening. At 7.30 p.m., Brig.-Gen. Northey was near Verbrande Molen, discussing the digging of a new communication trench with Brigade-Major, Capt. A. L. Ransome when he was wounded in the thigh by a German shell. Temporary charge of 15 Bde was assumed by the CO of 1/Bedfords, Lt-Col. Griffiths, until 28 June, when Lt-Col. M. N. Turner of 1/DCLI was promoted Brigadier. Life on the staff was no sinecure, as Capt. Ransome's predecessor, Capt. W. H. Johnston VC, had been killed in the front line on 7 June.

The 23rd was mostly quiet, though Larch Wood and the Dump were shelled with HE. That afternoon, the battalion was warned that the following night they would relieve the Cheshires and Dorsets in a two-company stretch of the left subsector, opposite Zwarteleen. The night of the 23rd meant carrying parties as usual, but only Rfn Charles Evans of 'B' was slightly wounded.

The move to the front line was completed by 11 p.m. on 24 June, Maj. Wainwright taking command of the front-line companies. Forty men from 'B' took over Trench 47 from the Cheshires and another sixty took over Trench 47 Support from the Dorsets. Thirty-five men from 'C' relieved the Cheshires in Trench 48, another thirty-five going into the Rifle Pits in Fosse Wood (48 Support); they also provided a twenty-man reserve platoon further back in Fosse Wood. HQ occupied Davidson Dugout alongside the Dorsets' HQ. The other two companies remained in brigade reserve at Zillebeke Lake, demand for their porterage services every bit as great. The only casualty that night was nineteen-year-old Rfn Arthur Costello, killed on the way forward with an 'A' Company carrying party.

No doubt one of the more bizarre briefings given to Maj. Wainwright—or any other front-line OC for that matter—concerned the following:

> The French War Office have received reports from various sources that the Germans are employing as projectiles preserved meat tins of French manufacture which appear to have been sent to French prisoners in Germany. The French are anxious to know if there is any truth in these reports, so will you please cause enquiries to be made and report the result by the 27th inst.[95]

The new positions were very exposed, particularly Trench 47, half of which was held by the enemy, just 30–40 yards separating the protagonists. Across a breadth of several hundred yards, the front was held only by isolated posts—hostile infiltration a constant concern at night. These defences were just a single line of sandbagged breastworks, with no parados, and the twists and turns of the line, in part due to the contours, but mainly resulting from German gains on 5 May, meant that there were many spots where enemy snipers could enfilade stretches of the line.

However, geography worked both ways, and battalion patrols probed German defences on a nightly basis, 2Lt Brownell and Cpl Andrew Fitzmaurice gaining a reputation for their daring enterprises. There were no communication trenches accessing the front and the only means of reaching the left of the line was by making a detour of several miles and approaching via Sanctuary Wood, then making a semi-crouched progress along the breastworks of the battalion to their left—much to the annoyance and inconvenience of their neighbours.[96] In reality, the sector was untenable and only held thanks to accurate fire-support provided by Maj. Rudkin and his battery of 18-pounders, which were able to target enemy positions within yards of the battalion, the shells barely clearing the heads of the riflemen.

Their positions were battered by heavy *Minenwerfers* on a daily basis:

> An experience the more terrifying because we had no effective means of reply. Those who were there will remember the huge, unwieldy bombs (called from their shape 'sausages') which the Germans pitched high in the air from their heavy mortars and which burst on the promenade behind Trench 48 with such a rending crash. So regular was this form of bombardment, and so destructive, that there was always a 'sausage-sentry' on duty to watch the sky for the first sign of the *Minenwerfer's* arrival, and he, by his shout would indicate the traverse to avoid. In the scramble for safety that ensued, only too often some poor fellow would misjudge the flight of the bomb or run the wrong way, and such a mistake was usually fatal. It speaks well for the wonderful spirit of the troops that even this form of 'frightfulness' was made the subject of humour as much as it was one for fear.[97]

The night of 24–25 June was quiet, a situation that continued throughout the 25th, though one man was wounded in the early hours of 26 June and another two later that day: Rfn Richard Kent from 'A' received a 'Blighty' wound to the buttocks, but returned in November; from 'B', Rfn Vivian Winstanley was treated in France for his head wound; the third casualty, Rfn Ernest Collins of 'D', wounded in the wrist, was commissioned into the Labour Corps after leaving hospital. At 8.30 p.m. that night, 'A' and 'D' marched up to the line, relieving the others at midnight, they too having a quiet first night in the line.

Though diaries all refer to 27 June as 'quiet', this was obviously a 'comparative' term, as the front-line companies lost three men to *Minenwerfers* that afternoon: twenty-five-year-old Cpl John Dickinson from 'D' was killed; from 'A', twenty-one-year-old Rfn Charles Stockley was seriously wounded in the head, dying on 10 July; and nineteen-year-old Rfn George Duckett, blown through the air by one blast, was left totally dazed and led to

15 Field Ambulance. He was treated for shock, but left with memory-loss and a severe stammer, eventually being medically discharged.[98]

Before being relieved on 28 June, 'D' suffered another casualty, though Rfn William Ford continued on duty after his contusions were dressed. German artillery was considerably more active on the 29th, the rear also coming under heavy fire. One shell penetrated the roof of 15 Bde HQ, though failed to explode—a fortunate detail as the Corps-Commander was visiting at the time. The battalion had six casualties between noon and midnight. 'C' suffered the only front-line casualties: Rfn William Twiss, who was medically discharged due to face and thigh wounds, and Cpl Richard Browne, wounded in the neck and back. The company lost another that day, when twenty-five-year-old Rfn James Spencer was admitted to hospital with dysentery, subsequently diagnosed as also suffering from shellshock and medically discharged a year later. The carrying parties fared worse. Texas-born Rfn William Thomas (049) was evacuated to England with a serious head wound, developed meningitis; he died on 19 July. The other Riflemen, all from 'D', were lost to the battalion after leaving hospital: Ernest Fosbrooke, wounded in the thigh, was commissioned in the East Kents; Alfred Robinson received multiple shrapnel wounds and was transferred to the South Lancs; and Reginald Robinson, wounded in the buttock, was posted to 1/KLR—though he returned to the 1/6th as a Sgt in 1918.

One of the nastier aspects of the war occurred underground: May-July saw intense mining and counter-mining, mostly around trenches 32–38. On 25 June, each brigade supplied fifty men and two officers to begin training under the RE in defensive mining, thus relieving skilled sappers for offensive operations. The battalion's white-collar origins meant they did not supply any of 15 Bde's 'volunteers', though on 30 June, four Riflemen—Leonard Crocker, Robert King, J. W. Smith (108), and Alexander Crabb—were transferred to an RE Signal Company. Crocker died from illness in May 1917.

On 30 June, 'B' in the front line had one casualty, though Rfn John Glover's neck wound was minor. That night, the companies rotated again, with 'A' placing forty men into Trench 47 and a further sixty into 47 Support. 'C', who followed the longer route via Sanctuary Wood, stationed thirty-five men in Trench 48, forty-five in the Rifle Pits, and a thirty-strong platoon in Fosse Wood. Twenty-year-old Rfn Thomas Porter was killed near Mount Sorrel as 'C' wended their way along Trench 50. Buried immediately behind the trench, his grave was lost in later fighting. Rfn Thomas Rowe from 'D' was also wounded before midnight, his arm wound keeping him from duty for nearly a year.

The last night of June saw alterations to divisional sectors, 46 Division moving their right bound south to encompass trenches 49–50. Although this made no real difference to the battalion, who were now on the extreme left of the divisional line, it did mean additional liaison was necessary when accessing the left company's positions. 'A' worked hard on building a parados for 47 Support overnight, and although there was little enemy artillery fire, a number of grenades—all of which fell short—were thrown from the German-held part of Trench 47 and the old Trench 46. The battalion's grenadiers retaliated with two bombs, one of which burst in the enemy trench, after which the foe behaved. At 10 p.m., 2Lt Brownell went out alone from 47 and worked his way quietly towards a German sap,

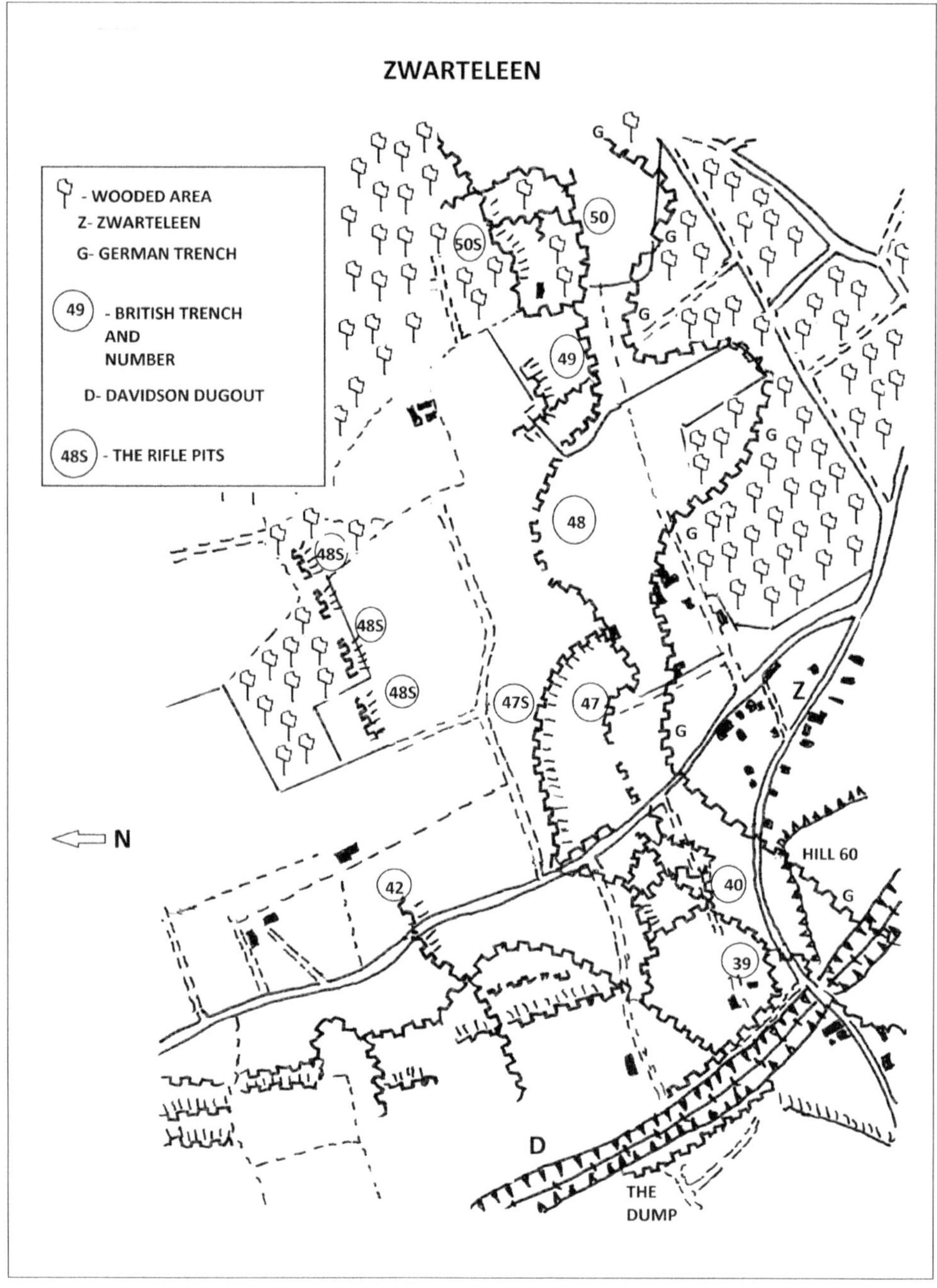

ZWARTELEEN
- WOODED AREA
Z- ZWARTELEEN
G- GERMAN TRENCH
49 - BRITISH TRENCH AND NUMBER
D- DAVIDSON DUGOUT
48S - THE RIFLE PITS
N
50
50S
49
48
48S
48S
48S
47S
47
42
40
39
G
Z
HILL 60
D
THE DUMP

running from the old Trench 46 towards 47. He hunkered down about 15 yards from the sap and watched and listened. Although Brownell heard talking, the enemy did not appear to be carrying out any work. He returned safely shortly before midnight. To the rear, Zillebeke Lake came under fire from gas shells, and despite the gas lingering for hours in the still air, no casualties resulted—in fact, the only casualty on 1 July was Adjutant Capt. George Teall, slightly wounded in the right arm that morning. He continued on duty after it had been dressed.

Most hostile fire on 2 July was directed elsewhere, though Rfn Thomas Colley of 'D' received a head wound, which saw him evacuated home until November. A number were hospitalised with influenza and trench fever in the first few days of July. This first outbreak of trench fever—contemporaneous to the influenza outbreak—resulted in uncertain diagnoses of 'NYD-fever', until it was correctly identified further along the medical chain. Symptoms included headache, dizziness, severe lumbago, stiffness to the fronts of the thighs, and pains in the legs, though chiefly in the shins; symptoms often reappearing in cycles. No cure was found, though it was eventually recognised that lice were responsible for its transmission and the widespread use of chemical disinfestation decreased its incidence. While no accurate figures for the numbers of British troops suffering from trench fever exist—estimates vary—a figure approaching 500,000 would not be far off.[99] Over the war, 6.4 per cent of the battalion spent an average of two weeks in hospital with it.

The companies rotated again late on 2 July, 'B' holding the right and 'C' the left. The weather was hot and sunny on 3 July and some took advantage of this, and a general lack of hostile activity after the morning 'stand-to' and breakfast to sleep in the open behind the parapet during their four-hour rest. Others wrote home:

> I am writing this seated in a trench that has a million flies, the same number of smells, and the reputation of being the nearest to Berlin. A few yards away, it cuts through the ruins of a farm house, in fact, the walls—or what remains of them—are embodied in the parapet [junction of 47 and 47 Support]. Just behind are the rough graves of the farmer and his wife; shot by the Germans as they passed by. Why, I don't know. Today is our 45th consecutive day up here—alternative spells in trenches and dugouts. It is exceedingly hot and the mosquitos are very troublesome. Several fellows have been badly bitten and gone into hospital.
>
> Drinking water is a bit of a problem here. A little way down the trench, a wee burn comes trickling beneath the parapet. It looks clean decent water and is most tempting when your bottle is empty, but it flows from Jerry's lines and we are forbidden to drink it, as maybe it's poisoned.[100]

It was fortunate that the weather was dry as, apart from the lack of shelter, a number of springs, including the one mentioned above, triggered subsidence in long stretches of the parapet of 47 Support. Although the battalion passed a report to brigade about this problem, it does not appear to have been acted upon by the RE.

The lack of activity, which lasted until 4 July, may have been due to new German division moving in opposite them, Intelligence believing that the Bavarians had been replaced on 2 July.[101]

On the night of 4 July, the companies rotated again, 'A' (right) and 'D' (left) manning the line. The 5th began quietly enough, but at 3 p.m., a three-hour bombardment of Trench 38 by *Minenwerfer* and 77-mm began; the Bluff, Trench 42, and Larch Wood were also shelled, though the battalion escaped most of this fire.

The line companies suffered five casualties on 6 July. In the early hours, twenty-year-old Cpl Wilfred Barber from 'D' was critically wounded in the abdomen, dying at Transport Farm the following day. All the others were from 'A': one of Rfn Frank Fraser's fingers was split open by a German grenade and it was eight months before he returned; twenty-year-old Rfn Laurence Cockburn was wounded in the right arm; and Sgt William Stephenson was evacuated home with a head wound. However, the most seriously injured was Rfn John Hayward, also with a head wound, dying on 7 July. That night, the companies rotated. Both Riflemen wounded on 7 July were also from 'A' and 'D', hit on their journey out of the line: George Gibson was slightly wounded in the face, remaining on duty; twenty-eight-year-old Donald Yorke, wounded in the thigh by shrapnel, rejoined 'D' in August.

The 8th began quietly enough for 'B' and 'C', and although there was some hostile fire in the afternoon and evening, the enemy saved their worst for the night. Five casualties were sustained when several salvoes bracketed Trench 50 shortly before midnight, catching the companies withdrawing after their relief by 1/Cheshires. Two were only lightly wounded, the thigh wound of 'B' Company's Rfn John Davies (747) requiring two days at the Field Ambulance and 'C' Company's Rfn Edward Woods remained on duty after his injuries were dressed. Rfn Robert Hopley from 'B' was very badly wounded in the thigh and subsequently medically discharged. Also from 'B', nineteen-year-old Rfn Alfred Lea was killed, as was twenty-one-year-old father of one from 'C' Rfn Jeremiah O'Sullivan—both buried to the rear of Trench 50. The dugouts at Zillebeke Lake also came under sporadic fire and twenty-six-year-old Rfn Robert Jackson from 'A' was wounded in the left thigh.

For most, there was respite from their long spell in the line—apart from 'A', who remained at Zillebeke Lake until 13 July. The others marched to huts in Reninghelst, though 'D' Company's reprieve was transitory, as the very next night, they provided a wiring party for the Norfolks in front of Verbrande Molen (trenches 35–37). 'D' remained in support for the Norfolks, sheltering in dugouts in the north-eastern end of Ravine Wood. Late on 13 July, they accompanied the Norfolks to Reninghelst. On the evening of 17 July, the battalion marched eastwards through heavy rain, 'A' and 'C' into bivouacs in a wood near Dickebusch and 'B' and 'D' into damp dugouts in the woods at Rosenthal Château. The 18th was spent on carrying parties and next day, the battalion marched westwards to the Rozenhill huts. After dark on 21 July, all of 15 Bde marched through Boeschepe into comfortable billets in farms between Abele and Godewaersvelde.

The 27th saw Allan Smith, who had done so well with the Canadians in April, sent to 'Cadet School', rejoining as a subaltern in September. Just before 3 p.m. on 29 July, an advance party, consisting of Maj. Eustace Harrison, *Capitaine* De Rosen, and five NCOs left Godewaersvelde station. The remainder of the battalion departed shortly before 11 a.m. next day, having loaded the seventy-four horses and mules, twenty-three vehicles, and nine bicycles earlier that morning. The 648 officers and men, who now comprised the battalion, indicated a loss of 42 per cent of its strength in just five months. Their departure from the Salient was not so much a 'goodbye' as an '*au revoir*'.

3

31 July 1915—18 November 1915: Vaux

Coordinates for this Chapter

'blue on blue'	49°57′33.40″N 2°48′45.20″E	Point-91	49°58′27.60″N 2°41′35.60″E
Bois Français	49°59′23.40″N 2°43′5.60″E	Post-1	49°56′31.80″N 2°47′26.10″E
Chapeau de Gendarmes	49°58′2.30″N 2°48′28.10″E	Post-2	49°56′30.70″N 2°47′33.20″E
CT NE of Suzanne	49°57′16.50″N 2°46′45.60″E	Post-3	49°56′50.80″N 2°47′40.20″E
Duck Post	49°57′28.70″N 2°47′53.20″E	Post-4	49°57′15.60″N 2°47′21.20″E
Fargny causeway	49°57′49.90″N 2°48′22.50″E	Post-5	49°57′20.80″N 2°47′25.90″E
fourth wood	49°57′42.20″N 2°48′30.80″E	Post-6	49°57′31.30″N 2°47′23.60″E
HQ	49°57′21.30″N 2°47′34.70″E	Post-8	49°57′24.90″N 2°47′42.20″E
La Grenouillère	49°56′50.70″N 2°49′11.50″E	Post-9	49°57′18.90″N 2°47′28.90″E
Lengrenee bridge	49°56′25.50″N 2°47′20.60″E	third wood	49°57′42.30″N 2°48′21.10″E
Moulin de Fargny	49°58′1.30″N 2°48′13.00″E	Trench 76	49°59′20.50″N 2°43′19.10″E
OP—Vaux Woods	49°57′27.10″N 2°47′19.80″E	Trench 83	49°59′24.60″N 2°42′56.50″E
Point-107	49°58′5.50″N 2°41′39.50″E	Usine Saint-Gobain	49°56′33.20″N 2°48′11.60″E

The train reached Corbie at 11.20 p.m. on 30 July and the battalion marched 5 miles north to billets in Lahoussoye (not to be confused with La Houssoye—of which there are three further south). Until now, it had been French-held and 5 Division were the first British troops in what was considered a quiet backwater. The line ran from Bécourt on the left to Lengrenee on the banks of the River Somme on the right. The contrast to the Salient could not have been greater, with verdant, rolling chalk uplands, punctuated by woodlands. Although briefly held by the Germans for a fortnight in September 1914, the countryside was mostly untouched by war. Just 2 miles to the west of Lahoussoye was Pont Noyelles, where the battalion was able to bathe in the river—much appreciated after the foul waters of the Salient.

At 6.30 p.m. on 3 August, the battalion paraded under the acting RSM, Clem Tanner, then marched to billets in Dernancourt, arriving at 10 p.m. RSM William Butler had been admitted to hospital sick that morning and was sent home for treatment on 28 August, travelling on HS *St Andrew*. He would resume his appointment when he returned in January. The 8-mile journey to Dernancourt was the undoing of Lt-Col. Davison: his horse slipped on the pavé, throwing him awkwardly and dislocating his shoulder; he too sailed home on the *St Andrew*. Maj. Harrison assumed temporary command and was officially appointed CO in October.

On 6 August, the battalion, minus 'B', marched to billets at Méaulte. 'B' was far less fortunate, and that evening, they joined 1/Cheshires in Subsector 'C1' (from Trench 83 on the left, to Trench 76 on the right). They were destined as a fatigue party for 174 Tunnelling Company, who were mining at Bois Français. This job was unpleasant enough in the dry, but recent heavy rain made conditions underfoot treacherous, as the French seldom employed duckboards, or any form of drainage in the trenches. Among the labourers was Norman Ellison:

> To crawl on hands and knees along a narrow tunnel twenty feet underground, choked with thick chalk dust and blinded with sweat, dragging a sandbag filled with the excavated debris from the working face to the windlass rope at the foot of the entrance shaft, with air becoming so foul that presently the candles would flicker and die out, was no easy job. Add to this, an undefinable feeling of oppression, of being caged in, intensified by the perceptible earth tremors from the heavy shells and trench mortars bursting on the surface above, and the sure knowledge—could we not hear faintly their pick strokes in the half-hour of 'listening' between our labours?—that the enemy was countermining and it was largely a matter of luck which side 'blew' the other's gallery first, and it will be appreciated why we detested the work.[1]

In addition to the obvious danger and discomfort, the spoil had to be manhandled a long way from the workings before being dumped.

At 8.30 p.m. on 7 August, 2Lt Eric Buckley took two platoons from 'C' to Point-91 to provide cover for a working party from 124 Bty, RFA. Thankfully, the night was quiet and there were no casualties. On 8 August, 112 desperately-needed replacements arrived from England—their first draft since deploying. One newcomer, Rfn Edward Boydell from

Widnes, was only with the battalion a few hours before being carted off to the CCS with an accidental head injury, rejoining a fortnight later. The journey was the nemesis of twenty-one-year-old Rfn David Williams (549). Maj. Martin was not impressed when he examined the former apprentice shipwright, sending him straight to 14 Field Ambulance, then contacting the ADMS:

> In my opinion this man is unfit to march or undertake trench duties. He was sent out from England with a draft for the Battalion, arriving here on 8 August 1915. He had to march only from railhead Méricourt to Méaulte [7 miles] and reported sick with pain in his left foot and inability to march. As his left foot is badly deformed, I am of the opinion that he should not have been passed fit for foreign service and therefore send him before you for your advice please.[2]

The ADMS concurred and Williams, whose foot-deformity pre-dated his enlistment, returned home to munitions work. This was the first example of a medically unfit man being posted to the battalion, but not the last—a year later, the poor standard of many replacements, saw dozens judged unfit at the IBD and returned home.

Substantial working parties were demanded most nights. On 9 August, 100 men went to the Norfolks in the 'C3' subsector, west of Fricourt, assigned to work on the defences. 'B' got respite from their odious duties at Bois Français on 10 August, when they were relieved by 'C', who were in turn relieved by 'A' on 14 August. 'D' went into the line on the 14th to relieve a company of the Bedfords in subsector 'C2' (from the south of Fricourt to trench 84, where it joined 'C3').

Norman Ellison took advantage of some spare time on 15 August to write home from his billet, a hay loft near Méaulte:

> Beer is also a luxury we have not yet discovered since arriving in rural France proper. Nothing to drink but red wine, fearful stuff at best. As I write, there is a very heavy thunderstorm bursting overhead but the sound of Nature's artillery seems very weak compared to ours below.
>
> The other day I was one of a guard at crossroads some little distance outside this place. Our job was to find out the business of everyone who passed. Our guardroom was a deserted inn which the inhabitants had evidently left hurriedly when it was shelled. We explored the place thoroughly and found plenty of crockery, glassware, saucepans etc., so we set about making a good meal. Also I would like to mention that there was a kitchen-garden, fruit trees and a large pigeon loft. Here is our menu for the day:
> Breakfast Bacon and fried pigeons' eggs, jam, bread and butter, tea and coffee.
> Dinner Boiled meat, a stew of two pigeons, carrots, onions, beans and potatoes.
> Tea Stewed prunes, stewed rhubarb and stewed greengages, spring onions and lettuce, bread butter and tea.
> Supper Six boiled pigeons.
>
> I don't think you can beat that for a good day's foraging.[3]

Fortunately, in view of the frequently-thundery weather, the six battalions manning the front line—helped by those in reserve—had made good inroads into draining the trenches and laying duckboards.

At 8 p.m. on 18 August, HQ and 'B' moved into dugouts near Point-107, and 'C' joined the Norfolks in 'C3'. 'B' left Point-107 the following night to relieve 'A' in 'C1'. On 21 August, HQ, 'C', and 'D' went to billets in Méaulte, Transport also moved back from Dernancourt to Morlancourt, leaving the other companies in the dugouts at Point-107 (Albert-Picardie Airport now occupies the sites of Point-91 and Point-107). Two days later, at 8.40 p.m., the Méaulte detachment moved to Morlancourt, the other companies following after their relief later that night.

There had been no casualties since 8 July, and even the front-line battalions found their losses considerably reduced. The weather also played its part and sickness rates were low, with more lost to commissioning than illness and injury combined. They remained at Morlancourt until 1 September, and apart from providing 375 men to the RE on 27 August, for work on the second-line defences, the time was spent training. Protection from gas was now delivered by the PH helmet and all trained on it in a specially-constructed gas chamber. However, accidents marred the time: 'A' Company's Rfn Arthur Edwards (775) and 'D' Company's Cpl John McGill both sustained accidental grenade wounds to the hand; three Riflemen also suffered pickaxe injuries to the hand—James Turford on the 28th, and on 31 August, William McDonnell and Herbert Pugh.

On 24 August, the battalion received orders spelling the end of their time as general labour, as 15 Bde was to take over the 'A' Sector with its four subsectors. On 26–27 August, the CO and two company-commanders spent the night in the trenches of the 'A1' subsector at Vaux, and at 6 p.m. on 1 September, the battalion marched to Suzanne, though without Rfn Thomas Page. Earlier that day, he was kicked in the right leg by a horse, and, while at 13 General Hospital, he was also diagnosed with trench fever and evacuated home. There was one casualty due to enemy action on 1 September, even though the battalion was out of the line: Rfn Sidney Edwards—attached to 174 Tunnelling Company—was wounded in the wrist by shrapnel and medically discharged. The move to Suzanne was completed by 10 p.m., but not everyone remained there, as three machine-gun crews were attached to the Norfolks in subsector 'A2'.

Subsector 'A1' was the quietest in the divisional sector and geographically ideal for an understrength battalion. Situated on a great horseshoe-shaped bend of the Somme, it extended from just to the right of the Moulin de Fargny, along the steep cliffs dominating Vaux, to the bridge at Lengrenee. After a short break, the French sector began at Frise. Marshland and cliffs limited the only place the enemy could attack to along a 4-foot-wide causeway, bridging the river and the marsh between Vaux and German-held Curlu—this being so narrow that a massed attack was inconceivable. The marshland between Vaux and Curlu was over a mile wide, and although the two or three larger channels of the Somme remained fairly consistent, the rest was a maze of constantly-changing channels, pools, and marsh, dotted with wooded islands.

On 2 September, the battalion relieved the Cheshires in 'A1', though Lt Bishop and thirty of his Cheshires remained behind to carry out patrols until the Riflemen learnt the area.

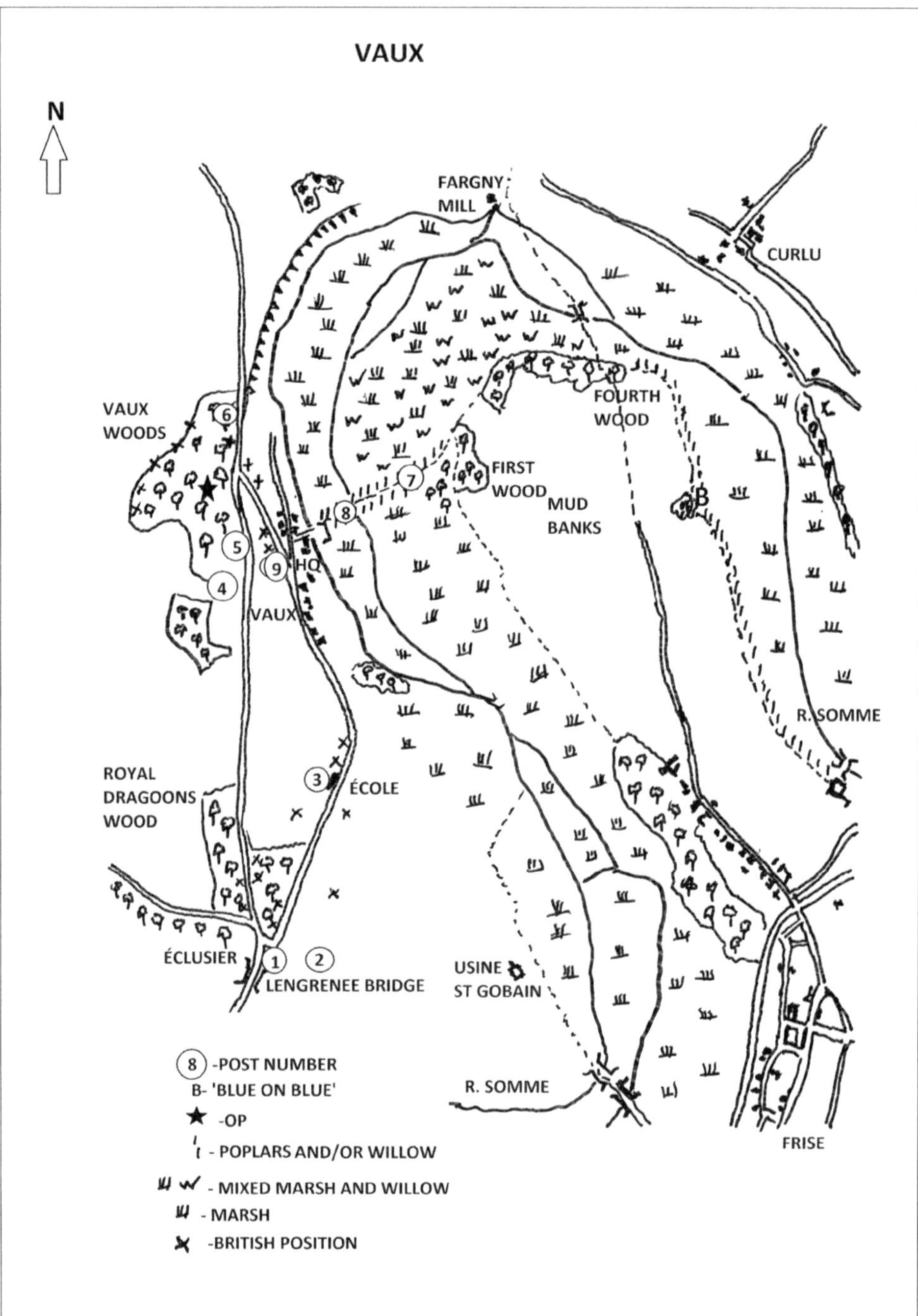
VAUX
N
FARGNY MILL
CURLU
VAUX WOODS
FOURTH WOOD
FIRST WOOD
MUD BANKS
HQ
VAUX
B
R. SOMME
ROYAL DRAGOONS WOOD
ÉCOLE
ÉCLUSIER
LENGRENEE BRIDGE
USINE ST GOBAIN
R. SOMME
FRISE
-POST NUMBER
B- 'BLUE ON BLUE'
-OP
- POPLARS AND/OR WILLOW
- MIXED MARSH AND WILLOW
- MARSH
-BRITISH POSITION

At 3 p.m., two platoons from 'C' under Capt. Turner departed Suzanne for the two key posts on the causeway. Nearest to the enemy was Post-7—better known as Duck Post—a substantial sandbagged strongpoint 700 yards along the causeway and manned by twenty men. Its eastern approaches were cloaked by a combination of osiers and shoulder-high reeds, all of which favoured a stealthy hostile approach. The platoon in Duck Post always posted several layers of sentries, fanning out in semi-circles amid the scrub and reeds to give advanced warning of encroachment; trip wires were positioned to protect these sentries and a 'whistle-code' provided challenge and reply. Sentries needed to be vigilant, identifying anyone approaching, as during the morning of 31 August, the Cheshire's OP on the hill in Vaux woods had spotted a German six-man patrol in No Man's Land, two of whom were wearing khaki.[4] A hollow drum bridge, on the causeway ahead of Duck Post, gave some warning of night incursions along the path as it was impossible to walk on this without making noise. Also on the causeway, 400 yards behind Duck Post, was Post-8, another sandbagged strongpoint—manned by the other platoon from 'C'. Post-8 was the backstop should Duck Post be overrun. The marshland separating Vaux and Curlu contained four areas of woodland, connected by thick scrub, the furthest only 200 yards from the enemy at Curlu. When the rest of 'C' arrived, they were placed in Post-9, on a slight rise to the rear of the village.

The remainder of the battalion departed Suzanne four hours later: 'B', under Capt. Westby, routed along the communication trench north-east of Suzanne to the heights of the Bois de Vaux, standing like a thickly-wooded sentinel above the village. Here they occupied Posts 4–6, along the edge of the woodland to the west of the Maricourt-Carréfour d'Éclusier road. HQ, 'D', and 'A' travelled along the Suzanne-Carréfour d'Éclusier road, dropping off 'D', under Capt. Edmund Buckley, at Éclusier, where they occupied Posts 1–3 in Royal Dragoons Wood and the École de Vaux. It was dark when 'D' arrived:

> A sentry of 'D' Company, who had been employed in peace time in a large Liverpool firm, with a headquarters in Paris, was posted in the dark at the north end of the bridge over the Somme at Vaux-Éclusier [Lengrenee bridge]. At the south end of the bridge was a French sentry, and it was the duty of each to keep in touch with the other. Imagine the amazement of both when the dawn broke, and as daylight distinguished their features, the British sentry recognised in the Frenchman a member of the same firm from the French office![5]

HQ was at Vaux and unusually, forward of the main entrenched positions held by 'B'—a situation made possible by siting HQ on a small island in the marshes, accessible only by a narrow wooden bridge. A very useful OP existed on the heights to the west of Vaux, from where it was possible to observe not just the causeway, but also the main German positions in Curlu. On a clear day, the German sentry standing outside their HQ could be seen. The battalion's single remaining machine-gun was positioned at the OP to cover the causeway.

'B' was housed in dugouts in the wood; 'D' in wicker huts in Royal Dragoons Wood; but 'A' (under Capt. John Trench) and 'C' struck lucky, billeted in the houses of Vaux:

> Vaux was a curious place. The inhabitants had, in their flight, left it as it was, with its boats, nets, ducks and poultry. The Germans rarely shelled it, for there seemed to be a tacit understanding that if the British did not shell Curlu, Vaux was to be left alone. There were no proper trenches for the wide marshes and waterways in front made an attack in force impossible.[6]

Though shellfire was rare, the forthcoming tussle for supremacy in the marshes, currently dominated by an aggressive and experienced enemy, proved bitter.

This relatively unspoilt corner of the war offered opportunities to improve living standards:

> The river abounded in fish and in peaceful days, had supplied eels to the Paris market. All sorts of improvised fishing tackle appeared, whilst those lacking the patience of your true angler, frequently added to their rations by bombing the river [much to the indignation of the keen anglers]. Ducks in a semi-wild state, did not appear on the menu until an ingenious mind baited a spring rat-trap and floated it down amongst them on a board fastened to a line. This was 'easy fishing' as no duck could resist such an easy meal.

One man found an old shotgun in a house and experiments with it, using home-made ammunition, were also tried. It was at Vaux, where Capt. McKaig and RSM Tanner were leaning over the parapet of the bridge, when the following occurred:

> Several of these semi-wild ducks swam underneath the bridge. Captain McKaig remarked, 'Sergeant-Major, I think we ought to get in touch with those ducks.' Tanner replied, 'Well, Sir, the men have already been in touch with them. In fact, sir, I might inform you, that a portion of duck reposes in my belly at this moment.'[7]

Nature also provided its fair share of pests. Mosquitos abounded and the area spawned legions of gigantic rats, frequently observed by moonlight, swarming across the streets. The MO and his fatigue parties worked hard to get the village cleaned up, reducing the rat population, improving drainage, and building improvised showers.

Their first night was quiet, and although the Cheshires pushed patrols into the marshes, no sign of the enemy was found. At 10 a.m., a patrol under Lt Bishop, accompanied by 2Lt Brownell and some of 'C' undergoing their first familiarisation of the area, went out into the marsh towards Frise, returning via Éclusier at 1.15 p.m. After their experiences on the Salient, a day without a single shell being fired seemed remarkably serene. The only casualty was one of the machine gunners attached to the Norfolks: L/Cpl Stephen O'Keefe, wounded in the left arm. Another patrol exited at 7.45 p.m., torrential rain restricting visibility. After an uneventful trip, they returned through the marshes at 10 p.m.

Patrols went out in the morning of 4 September, and again, the enemy failed to manifest himself. That afternoon, recently-commissioned Allan Smith reported back. After dark, the usual sentries were placed forward of Duck Post by Sgt William Winter, little knowing that tragedy was to strike in the early hours. Twenty-seven-year-old L/Cpl Richard Morrish gave evidence at Capt. Teall's Court of Inquiry the following morning:

> On the 5th inst., I was in charge of the two advanced listening posts on the marsh in front of Vaux. The posts should have been relieved at 1 a.m. At about 2.15 a.m., no relief having come, I ordered No. 3083 Rfn R. S. Haworth to proceed to Sgt Winter who was in charge of the Duck Post behind us and to ask the latter to telephone down to see what had happened. I asked Rfn [Richard] Haworth before he started whether he was well acquainted with the system of signals to be used in the passing of other posts. He said he was. I had tested him on them previously and he knew them quite well.
>
> The signals are as follows: the challenger gives one whistle, the challenged replied with two whistles. The challenger shows he has heard by tapping two times on his pouches. The counter-sign is not used after the whistle signals except in the case of patrols returning from the marsh.
>
> I heard the whistle signal and answer as Rfn Haworth passed through the nearest post to mine and did not hear the pouches tapped. He then only had to pass one more post before arriving at the Duck Post.
>
> Shortly after I heard a rifle shot.[8]

Rfn Robert Honderwood, in the centre post on the causeway, confirmed that Haworth gave the correct challenge when he passed through his post. Rfn Robert Colligan continued:

> I was sentry on the listening post just in front of the Duck Post. With me were Rfn [Arthur] Bryning and Rfn [Charles] Kendall. We were lying side by side on the path just behind the barbed wire entanglement.
>
> About 2.04 a.m. by my watch I heard a whistle which I was not quite sure about. After a few seconds there was another whistle. Rfn Bryning replied with two whistles. I heard three taps on the pouches from the man advancing.
>
> The caller than came along the path that winds through the wire entanglement. As he came round the east trench and was only about 6 yards off, I heard the accused Rfn Kendall mumble something and saw his bayonet go up. The next moment he fired and there was a cry from the man advancing and he fell down.
>
> I went back to Duck Post to fetch the Corporal while Rfn Bryning and Kendall remained on the post with the wounded man. I did not know Rfn Haworth by sight.

Bryning also gave evidence:

> Rfn Kendall was on my left and Rfn Colligan on my right. We were all lying close together. About 2 a.m. I thought I heard a whistle and mentioned it to Rfn Colligan. Then after a few moments I heard a very loud whistle. I answered with the usual two whistles, which I made quite loud. I did not hear any taps, but Rfn Colligan said to me, 'There, he taps', or words to that effect.

> I was looking out for the man advancing when I saw Rfn Kendall give a start and raise his rifle. [Had Kendall nodded off?] Almost simultaneously the man came round the bend in the wire and Kendall shouted out 'There he is', or words to that effect. I turned towards Kendall and said, 'don't you dammed fool' and tried to knock his rifle out of his hand. But he fired before I could do so. The man cried out 'what have you done you fool' or words to that effect. I ran up to him and caught hold of him and assisted him.

Kendall cross-examined Bryning:

> 'Why did you not warn me that there was someone coming?' [Bryning replied] 'At the first whistle I was not certain myself, but the second one was so loud that I did not think it necessary to warn you, and as Colligan and I were discussing the first whistle, you could have heard what we said.'

Kendall's defence was brief:

> About 2.05 a.m. I heard a whistle from Rfn Bryning and heard no reply and saw them looking about. Then I saw a shadow come round the wire and it was very dark. So I fired and heard a shout. On going forward I found it to be one of our men.

Twenty-two-year-old Haworth, one of the August draft, died later that day at 15 Field Ambulance. Poignantly, among his effects was one 'bullet-proof shield', though even if he had been wearing the cumbersome item, it probably would not have stopped a .303 round at that range. Kendall was placed under arrest, and at his FGCM on 14 September, he was sentenced to three months' field punishment, to be served at Brigade. Unusually, instead of being transferred after serving his punishment, he returned to 'C' Company.

Morning patrols passed quietly on 5 September, and behind the lines, men weaved withies into screens to hide their woodland positions once the autumn leaves began to fall. On 6 September, men continued to manufacture screens, and now that they were more familiar with the subsector, the battalion's dispositions were altered slightly: 'C' continued to man posts 7–9 with four officers and 105 men, though twenty-five men from 'A' boosted their numbers (the four officers and eighty-one remaining men from that company in reserve in Vaux); 'B', with six officers and 124 men, remained on the wooded hill behind Vaux; and 'D', with six officers and 113 men, stayed around Éclusier. The HQ contingent was thirty-five men—signallers, regimental-police, and pioneers making up the bulk; Lt Blackledge and sixteen bombers were also kept in reserve in Vaux. This was also the last day that L/Sgt Thomas Owen from 'C' wore his third stripe. Capt. Turner had discovered one of the sentries sitting down—in contravention of 'Standing Orders' (no pun intended)—and when he learnt that the NCO had given his permission, Owen was reduced to corporal.

For the first time in the war, the battalion had a dedicated patrol group, comprising 2Lt Maurice Greenhalgh and twenty-six men. Until now, scouts had been selected on a random basis whenever needed, but under the newly-arrived subaltern, they were to be trained as specialists and considering the opposition, not before time:

> The enemy [Bavarian Infantry] had, to some extent gained a mastery over these marshes from the French and the preceding battalions, and they scoured the marsh by day and night, with *Jäger* patrols of 20, or 30 strong, right up to our fortified posts, more than a mile from their base.[9]

To assist in their training, a section of Pathan Scouts from the Indian Army were attached:

> The work they had been engaged upon was a closely guarded secret, but as they were frequently through and well behind the enemy lines, there is little doubt that it was connected with the collection of reports from our Secret Service agents stationed in occupied territory. These Pathans were masters of scout-craft. Dressed in overalls camouflaged with green and yellow paint splashes, with hands and faces likewise disguised and an upstanding fringe of rushes at headgear, they became part of the undergrowth through which they could creep without snapping a twig. Had their orders been to fight, they could have wiped out the enemy patrols with ease, for sometimes, as one of our scouts was creeping along with elaborate caution, his ankle would be seized by a hand, and looking down in alarm, he would see the laughing face of a Pathan, silently enjoying the success of his little joke.[10]

The battalion's scouts set about determining the routes German patrols habitually followed by tying threads across tracks and noting footprints in grass, but would soon discover that they were not the only ones out hunting.

The battalion suffered a casualty at Vaux on 8 September, in most unlucky circumstances: Sgt Arthur Robinson was wounded in the hand by shrapnel from a British anti-aircraft gun shooting at a German plane over Éclusier; fortunately, the injury was not serious and he returned to 'D' in October. In the still dusk air, a German band and voices raised in song could be clearly heard coming from Curlu—an aura of normality and one of the many paradoxes of war. The battalion was relieved by the Cheshires on 9 September and returned to Suzanne.

There, the majority were occupied on working parties: forty men and one officer were designated 'Town Guard'—though 'town' was a grand title for what was a typical French village of one main street, running down a steep hill towards the river, with its adjacent, deserted château. The daily program, requiring hundreds of men for working parties, varied little, though until mid-October, Capt. Teall was in charge as the CO was admitted to hospital with trench fever on 12 September. One hospital admittance that must have caused concern was 'B' Company CQMS, forty-two-year-old Frank Williams, who contracted typhoid. Fortunately, he survived.

Just three days later, Capt. Teall showed he was not going to be a soft touch when he gave Rfn Edward Whitehurst twenty-eight days' field punishment for not complying with an order and insolence to an NCO. Indiscipline, although rare in the line, often increased during so-called 'rest' periods, when men were exhausted by unending working parties.

Immaturity may well have played its part as, in October 1916, Whitehurst was sent home—one of only two pre-war recruits to have lied about his age.

During the evening of 22 September, they returned to the line, their dispositions unchanged. It was quiet overnight, and at 11 a.m. on 23 September, 2Lt Greenhalgh and his scouts penetrated as far as the fourth wood near Curlu, returning at 1.30 p.m. Another patrol ventured to the same area at 3 p.m. and then again at 11 p.m. The identical patrol area was used on 24 September and though times varied slightly, they were clearly setting a pattern. Although the scouts reported no sign of the enemy, eyes had been watching them from the undergrowth.

At 11 a.m. on 25 September, Greenhalgh, Sgt Samuel Morgan, and eight men left Duck Post for another patrol. As they reached the fourth wood, the point came under heavy fire from the centre of the wood. The rest of the patrol extended and went to ground, unable to return fire as the enemy was hidden from their sight by thick undergrowth, and point-man, Rfn Richard Platt, was somewhere to their fore. After about five minutes, thirty of the enemy advanced through the wood, firing as they moved, hitting Greenhalgh, Morgan, and L/Cpl Henry McLaughlin. Although wounded in the left hand, Rfn Guy Davies fought on, urging the others to maintain rapid fire until the enemy retired. Seizing the opportunity, the six fell back to the third wood, taking up a defensive position there.

Alerted by the firefight, Lt Blackledge and his bombers began to advance along the causeway. Satisfied that the other five scouts held a good position, Davies returned to Duck Post, where he met Blackledge's party and guided them forward to where the rest of the scouts were waiting. Refusing medical treatment for his wound, Davies led Blackledge to the ambush site. There, they found Greenhalgh dying, the body of Morgan, and, further forward, that of Platt. Of McLaughlin, there was no sign (he had been captured). When Blackledge investigated the ambush site, he found some discarded shovels and waterproof sheeting, suggesting that the ambushers had been lying out for some time. The bodies of the three dead were carried back, reaching Duck Post at 3 p.m. On their return, Blackledge had to order Davies, who was determined to stay on duty, to get medical attention. It was late January before the brave Rifleman rejoined 'A', the fresh ribbon of a DCM on his tunic.

The 26th was quiet, though an atmosphere of gloom pervaded after their losses, and plans for revenge were afoot. The twenty-two remaining scouts and the bombers were amalgamated into a much larger scouting section of fifty under Lt Blackledge and 2Lt Emmanuel Adam, and in the early hours of 27 September, a sixty-strong ambush party under Lt Blackledge and 2Lt Warburton deployed in the third wood. By 7 p.m., no enemy had showed, so Warburton returned with thirty men, the others remaining in position. At 5 p.m., those in the woods were relieved. Despite the cold and driving rain, the ambush remained out until 3.30 a.m. on 29 September.

At 2 p.m. on 30 September, Lt Blackledge took a thirty-strong patrol to the fourth wood, very nearly suffering the same fate as Greenhalgh's ill-fated party. They were saved by the vigilance of their point-man, Rfn Charles Wilson. Many years later, James Eivers described the action:

> We had just got to the edge of the third wood when Wilson, who was acting 'point', saw a face in the bushes. He gave the alarm and we all fell flat just as Jerry opened fire.

Young Parry was not quick enough and was killed [the fatality was actually twenty-one-year-old Rfn Philip Harris]. We actually could not see anybody, but we had a good idea where the shots were coming from and we replied heavily. One of the Germans got up and commenced to run back, maybe for reinforcements, but we riddled him. You could not miss at fifty-yards range. After the first shot my rifle jammed so I crawled over to Parry [*sic.*] who had been killed, and got his. The sudden burst of fire in such a quiet part of the line, attracted one of our aeroplanes and it came swooping low down to discover the trouble. Afterwards we heard that he had reported great wind-up in Curlu—loading limbers and carts preparatory to quitting [it was probably this movement that attracted the aircraft]. Jerry must have thought we were attacking in force. We continued blazing away for nearly an hour but gradually the German fire became less and finally died away. By this time more of our fellows had come up from Vaux and it was decided to clear the wood. We charged, but they had gone. Rifles, helmets and equipment lay scattered about but they had cleared away their casualties. Great pools and tracks of blood and a field dressing covered with brains, showed they had suffered considerably.

Listening post on the marshes were always a nervy job, but after this scrap it became doubly so. The most advanced sentry was about forty yards ahead of the Duck Post. There you lay hidden in the bushes, absolutely alone, motionless and silent, for two hours on end, with every sense on edge for the least sound. You knew there was nothing between you and the German lines, unless some of our scouts were out, and that probably in the undergrowth about you, their scouts were prowling around. You got an uncanny feeling that unseen eyes were watching and waiting patiently for you to become a good target. The most commonplace happenings—the drip of rain on fallen leaves, the scurryings of rats or waterfowl, became magnified into an invisible enemy attacking your hiding place. Vaux itself was a cushy place, but out on the marshes was a continued strain. No wonder some of the fellows 'saw things' and raised false alarms.[11]

Blackledge withdrew at 5.45 p.m. The successful counter-ambush, just 200 yards from their own lines, must have shaken the enemy as they never sent another patrol out during the six weeks the battalion remained in the line.

The only other casualty was nineteen-year-old Rfn Iorwerth Jones, shot in the right thigh, an injury that occasioned his medical discharge. One of the helmets, property of the 12th Bavarian IR, hung in the Officers' Mess for many years post-war. Wilson was awarded the DCM and Blackledge, the MC—the first of the battalion to be conferred the award.

War correspondent Philip Gibbs visited the battalion shortly after the successful counter-ambush and referred to it in his 1920 book *Now it can be Told*. Unfortunately, he also recorded the battalion as being the Loyals. When he was first guided to the OP by *Capitaine* de Rosen, the soldier on duty there was Norman Ellison, who lent him his binoculars to view enemy positions.[13] He was later taken into Vaux and escorted to Duck Post:

All was quiet when I went along the causeway and out into the wood, where the outposts stood listening for any crack of a twig which might portray a German footstep. I was startled when I suddenly came upon two men, almost invisible against the tree trunks. There they stood motionless, their rifles ready, peering through the brushwood. If I had followed the path on which they stood for just a little way, I should have walked into the German village. But, on the other hand, I should not have walked back again...

Gibbs was critical about the degree to which the French took *laissez-faire*:

It was part of the French system of 'keeping quiet' until the turn of big offensives; a good system, to my mind, if not carried too far. At Frise, next door to Vaux, in a loop of the Somme, it was carried a little too far with relaxed vigilance.

It was a joke of our soldiers to crawl on and through the reeds and enter the French line and exchange souvenirs with the soldiers.

'Souvenir!' said one of them one day. 'Bullet ... you know ... cartouche. Comprenny?'

A French poilu of Territorials, who had been dozing, sat up with a grin and said, '*Mais oui, mon vieux*,' and felt in his pouch for a cartridge and then in his pockets, and then in the magazine of the rifle between his knees.

'*Fini*,' he said. '*Tout fini, mon p'tit camerade*.'

The Germans one day made a pounce on Frise, that little village in the loop of the Somme and 'pinched' every man of the French garrison. There was the devil to pay and I heard it being played to the tune of the French soixante-quinzes, slashing over the trees.[14]

The 'pounce' occurred on 29 January 1916. After a fierce bombardment, the French garrison in the Bois de la Vache was surrounded and forced to surrender.

The battalion laid a strong ambush in the fourth wood on 2 October, though they returned unrewarded on 5 October. On 6 October, Lt Blackledge and 2Lt Adam took a large fighting patrol to reconnoitre right up to the edge of the woodland near Curlu, discovering no evidence of enemy. On 8 October, another patrol went part of the way along the Fargny causeway before returning empty-handed.

At 6 p.m. on 9 October, Lt Blackledge took a sixty-strong patrol, this time to work through the woods towards La Grenouillère—a fresh patrol area. A Court of Enquiry, chaired by Capt Wedgwood, was held at Vaux on 10 October to examine the circumstances leading to a tragic incidence of what is referred to today as a 'blue on blue'. From the testimonies below it is possible to plot exactly where this occurred.[12]

Cpl Herbert Baster was on 'point', with six men, including Riflemen Smith, George Barnes, Alexander Robertson, and John Litchfield:

When we had gone 10 yards along the path to the right of the poplars I sent Rfn Smith to report [to Lt Blackledge] that we had struck the path and were proceeding along it. We then moved along the path for 300 yards and halted. I then sent two men [Robertson and one other] to report on the nature of the ground and with instructions to bring along Rfn Smith who had not returned.

Lt Blackledge continued:

> I sent the messenger back with instructions to Cpl Baster to leave the road and act as left flank guard, working by the river side. I then halted the main body and formed a new point. [L/Cpl Ralph Murrow, Rfn Harry Thomas, and three others]. After a few minutes, I whistled twice as a signal to the left flankers to advance and I thought I heard an answering whistle from them.

Rfn Smith gave evidence next:

> I had a job to find the main party, they were about 30 yards behind I should think. After I had reported, Lt Blackledge told me to get back to Cpl Baster and tell him to halt till the main party came up in touch. On the road back, I could not find Cpl Baster's party, his party had carried on and the main party had stopped. I could not find the path, I did not exactly leave the main party, so when they came up I fell in with them.

When asked if he had reported his failure to contact Cpl Baster, Smith said he had told L/Cpl Thomas Bryson, though this information was not relayed to Blackledge and, more importantly, to Murrow. The track between Baster's point section and the main party was poorly defined where it passed through an open area between the two groups, and in the few minutes that passed before the main party caught up with him, Smith was unable to find the entrance of the path through the woodland leading to Baster.

Shortly after he had sent Robertson to find Smith, Baster recalled:

> I heard two shots and a man fall and call out in English. I could see nothing as it was a very dark night. Thinking we were cut off from the main body, I gave instructions to my remaining three men to take cover. I went to the wounded man, whom I could hear moaning and finding him in a fainting condition, carried him about 20 yards to the left (SW) of the path into thick cover, leaving the wounded man, Rfn Robertson, in [the] charge of Rfn Litchfield. I then made my way up to the main body for assistance. Later on it was discovered that Rfn Barnes was missing, as he had been one of my party, the leading man of my point, I went with a search along the path and found him lying, badly wounded on the right (SW) of the path in cover [he died within minutes].

Murrow explained:

> I was instructed by Lt Blackledge to take charge of a party of four men forming a point. He informed me that Cpl Baster and six men had taken up a position guarding our left flank and from this concluded that there would be none of our own men out in front. I had orders to proceed to the right of the poplars. We had got about [300] yards when I heard a party approaching from the opposite direction. I then said, 'Down boys. There's someone coming.' Before I had finished speaking, the man immediately behind me, Rfn H.

> P. Thomas fired. One of the party approaching then fired and called out in clear English. 'Come on boys, let the buggers have it.' Thinking we had run into a patrol from another regiment, I ordered my men to lie down in extended order. Cpl Baster then came along and told him that we had fired on his party and wounded Rfn Robertson. I only heard two shots fired. On returning to billets I examined Robertson's rifle and found an empty cartridge in the breach.

The Court of Enquiry asked Murrow if orders had been given to shoot on sight:

> Yes, we were told that the [French] regiment on our right had been warned that we were patrolling, and that we should conclude that any troops we met were German and shoot on sight. The usual whistle applied, but in a case of doubt, or hand to hand fighting in the dark, the countersign and sign would be used.

Lt Blackledge countered that no specific orders had been given to shoot on sight, but that men had been told to use their discretion.

Robertson was hit just below the knee in the left leg. After passing through his leg, the round mortally wounded twenty-one-year-old Barnes, lodging near his spine—Robertson's shot hit no one. The Court of Enquiry considered that the reason for the accident was 'A breakdown in communications and loss of touch owing to the operations being carried out in complete darkness and amongst woods. [Brigade judged that] the accident seems to have been a direct result of the officer in command changing his dispositions after the start'.

It must be appreciated that Blackledge and his men had a mere nine days' experience of scouting: their objectives blurred the borders between a reconnaissance and a fighting patrol, and even for a far more experienced unit, to covertly move—and keep in touch with—sixty men through unknown woodland at night was ambitious. War is often a cruel teacher and the lessons learnt, hard.

The remainder of October was spent patrolling and laying ambushes in the fourth wood—all of which were fruitless—the enemy obstinately remaining behind his lines. The weather had turned and frequent mists veiled the marshes at dawn and dusk, with snow falling on a number of days, blanketing everything in white until it began to thaw. Lt-Col. Harrison returned from convalescent leave on 12 October, and on 25 October, 2Lt Eric Buckley was appointed Divisional Transport-Officer. There was also a spate of negligent discharges, with four over a ten-day period, the problem possibly division-wide, as yet another reminder emphasising safety procedures was distributed to all units.

Seventy-nine very welcome replacements arrived on 29 October, and although not enough to replace the losses from earlier in the year, they were more than the numbers eroded by enemy action, sickness, and commissioning. 'C' lost a corporal on 19 October, though the battalion gained a subaltern when Wallace McKaig (Capt. McKaig's younger brother) was commissioned straight from the ranks, bypassing Cadet School. Morale remained excellent and the spirit of the battalion was exemplified by RSM Tanner when he asked the Adjutant for a day's leave. Capt. Teall quite naturally asked him if he intended to spend it in the Transport Lines, or further back at Bray: 'I thought, Sir, that I should like to spend the day in the marsh with the boys [meaning the scouts]'.[15]

On 17 October, Norman Ellison wrote home from his dugout in Vaux wood:

> The rats here swarm everywhere in thousands. Nothing is safe from them. Suspend the food in a sandbag from the roof and as soon as you are asleep they swarm down the string and get at it. At dusk we chase and strafe them with big sticks. I had the record bag the other night—23 inches from nose to tip of tail. Big as a rabbit. When you are bedded down they run over you so you get your face beneath the blanket. Unwholesome brutes. These beds are alarming affairs of wire-netting stretched over a sort of rustic framework. They are comfortable enough when you get to know the hang of them. Although not so warm as straw, they are free from lice, and that is more than a boon and a blessing.
>
> The paths in this wood are all named after the streets of Chester, so you can guess the regiment here before us: Northgate, Eastgate, The Cross and so on. We have done the same with the village below us here. The officers you will find billeted in 'The Angel' [an old estaminet and also 'C' Company's HQ] and they look out upon a very doubtful Exchange Flags. Then there is Dale Street leading to Abercromby Square and a manure heap which would make the original blush. There was a bit of a blaze ['D' Company's HQ] the other day but we rushed out the ancient manual fire-engine still intact in the village and put it out. I think everybody enjoyed the fun. We have been in this dugout now for eight consecutive weeks and it would be rather interesting to see a civilian face—such as they are! Snow has fallen heavily and the whole place is deep in slush.[16]

HQ was 'The Exchange' and 'A' lived in 'Dod's Hotel'.

Just how good a position the OP on the hill was can be garnered from the detailed observations made by 2Lt Ernest Hughes, who carefully noted all German movements behind their lines—almost exclusively in the subsectors to either side of the battalion; though he did note on 4 November that the Germans were demolishing houses in parts of Curlu and civilians were moving about in the village. His sterling work was noticed and he became Intelligence-Officer on 5 November. There were changes in the command structure, too, with Capt. Stanley Gordon getting 'C' Company.

There were only two casualties due to enemy action before the battalion left the line—both 'D'. Late on 6 November, Rfn Philip Davis was wounded in the head by a stray bullet at the Usine Saint-Gobain in 'D' Company's patrol area, and on 7 November, Rfn Joseph Bryans, a machine gunner with the Norfolks, was wounded in the shoulder. There were other losses too: on 2 November, Rfn Thomas Hitchman of 'A' suffered a badly broken leg, bringing about his medical discharge. On 6 November, newcomer Rfn Laurence Wrightson was evacuated, having suffered a nervous breakdown—though not from enemy action—his week with the battalion spent in 'B' Company's dugouts in Vaux Wood. He too was medically discharged. The closest artillery action was two German shells fired into empty ground, just to the south of the Moulin de Fargny, and British artillery fire against a German post between the mill and the Chapeau de Gendarmes. On 11 November, Rfn

John Crouchley of 'C' was hospitalised and evacuated home with shellshock: he had been in the thick of it since their initial deployment; he was one of the attackers on 5 May; and at Vaux, he was one of the intrepid advanced sentries, posted out alone in the marsh. He too was medically discharged. The weather had deteriorated, cold and wet now the norm, and on 13 November, a raging snowstorm.

On 15 November, the first artillery fire to be aimed at the battalion occurred at 12.30 p.m., when a dozen light shells fell in the marsh, forward of Duck Post. At 6 p.m., the Cheshires began to relieve 'D' at Royal Dragoons Wood, and at 11.30 p.m., sentries near the river at Frise were fired upon by fixed rifle battery, so were repositioned nearer the billets. At 8.a.m the following morning, Capt. Buckley marched his eighty men to Bray, where they boarded buses for Bertrancourt—as battalion Advance Party. Later that evening, the machine gunners were relieved, as was 'B' in Vaux Wood, with both groups proceeding to Suzanne. In the morning of 17 November, Lt Geoffrey Hughes marched eighty men from 'B' to Bray and thence by bus to 3rd Army HQ at Beauquesne. The rest of the battalion left for Bertrancourt on 18 November, their time with 5 Division ended. Their employment for the next two months was as 'Army troops' for Lt-Gen. Allenby's Third Army. One man's leisure time was somewhat crimped when on 16 November, L/Cpl William Henry of the Regimental Police found Rfn William Thomas (239) happily ensconced in the latrine with a newspaper—contrary to 'Battalion Orders'—the unfortunate twenty-one-year-old earning three days' confined to barracks.

4

19 November 1915—13 February 1916: Back to the Fold

Army Headquarters needed vast numbers of guards, men on traffic control, typists, clerks, telephone operators, grooms, and general labourers, and the battalion was employed thus across a number of locations. Officers also found themselves posted elsewhere: Lt-Col. Harrison was appointed 'Commandant Army Troops' at Beauquesne, with Capt. Teall taking command. On 21 November, 2Lt Warburton left for good, attached to the staff of 3rd Army, then later to the staff of 164 and 165 Bde, ending the war as a captain with a DSO and MC (Rfn Ernest Ackroyd departed on 2 February to become his batman).

Capt. Trench and 100 men from 'A' were located at the château and small hamlet of Caumesnil—undoubtedly happy to escape the bull surrounding any HQ. Unfortunately for Capt. Bennet's 160 men at Beauquesne, they were in the thick of it. The bulk of the battalion was billeted around the straggling and muddy village of Bertrancourt:

> At Bertrancourt we worked hard, under the Pharaoh-like supervision of General Snow, the Corps-Commander, upon a system of earthworks which had been constructed during the previous summer. Left unrevetted, these were fast melting into mud-pits, under the winter's rain and frost, and were known to the troops as 'Snow's Folly.' They were, in reality, well-sited strongpoints, and it is hoped that out herculean efforts to revet and strengthen them were of some avail later in the war. We learnt the lesson here that an army fights no less with the spade than the rifle.[1]

Those at Caumesnil were employed manufacturing wattle revetment hurdles—a process they had mastered at Vaux, so were able to considerably up the output compared to the previous incumbents, yet still labour for fewer hours in the day, to the mutual satisfaction of all concerned. On Christmas Eve, 2Lt Hughes and fifty men were dispatched to Toutencourt, and on Boxing Day, 2Lt William Davidson and another fifty to Famechon—both under the 10th Labour Battalion. On the same day, 2Lt Buckley and fifty men went to Ampliers and Lt Blackledge took a similar party to Halloy, both coming under orders of the RE. The diminished assemblage at Bertrancourt continued on 'Snow's Folly'.

At Beauquesne, the height of many ensured their demand as guards for Army HQ; equally, the high standard of education and relevant civilian experience meant that many were also appreciated in the myriad of clerical jobs, and by the end of December, eighty-four were thus employed. As Ellison noted, not every job allocation was properly thought through:

> Thus it came about that a joiner and a bank clerk in civilian life, became transformed into cobblers. With hammer and chisel and saw they worked their will cheerfully, if not scientifically, on the men's boots until one day there came along a staff officer's riding boot to be stitched. Neither had the faintest idea how a boot should be sewn but they had a shot at it.... I will not repeat what the S.O. said nor do I think it necessary to explain why our cobblers found themselves on guard duty again.[2]

Ellison and Rfn Cyril 'Skip' Roberts found themselves in an altogether different role, as coalmen to 3rd Army:

> We jumped at it. Not only were we, more or less, our own masters, but we escaped the 'spit and polish' which permeated the whole place. An open dump of some forty tons of coal was in our care. We filled fifty odd bags every morning and delivered them by motor lorry to various châteaux and messes on a 17-mile round. Snow fell on most days, so it became a dirty, slushy job; but it had ample compensations. At most of the larger châteaux there was usually a glass of wine for us: we had free entry to a 'blind tiger'; an estaminet kept open during prohibited hours by the—well, never mind; I will not give them away. A great pot of warm milk, liberally laced with rum, could be found there, simmering on the stove throughout the day, and I know of no better warm beverage when you are half-frozen. You can feel the fire flowing through your veins to the very tip of your fingers and toes. One day I was leaving the château where Field Marshal [*sic.*] Allenby lived, after humping several bags of very wet coal, when I met the great man himself strolling along a path with one of his aides. He looked at me and involuntarily exclaimed, 'Good God, what-?' when his aide whispered something that caused him to burst into laughter. I kept a very straight face and gave him a very stiff and formal salute as he passed.[3]

Those fortunate enough to be on detached duty found the break from normal military routine the perfect panacea for the rigours of life, as Ellison described in a letter to his father:

> This town literally flows with Bass's Pale Ale and Extra Stout. You cannot possibly imagine how we appreciate a pipe and a glass in a snug corner of an estaminet; it is only then that we think of the rough patches we struck 'up there'.
>
> We have now got our mess in working order—fifteen of us—and very snug and comfortable we are. Whittle [L/Cpl John Whittle 447] and I do the cooking and we live like fighting cocks. Every morning we open the ball with porridge, bacon and fried bread, honey or jam and tea. Luncheon mid-day;—steak and onions or mutton, potatoes and another vegetable, milk pudding and jam, cake coffee and cigarettes.

> There just remains time to go out and have a glass of Bass, 'pell-ell' as the natives call it, and voila![4]

No drafts arrived while the battalion was with 3rd Army, but numbers continued to fall due to commissioning, illness, or accident, and between December and April, many of the longest-serving were discharged as their term of service expired (until 'Conscription' began, TF soldiers could only be retained for a year after their term of service had expired). On 7 December, twenty-one-year-old Rfn Richard Clephan was admitted to hospital, suffering from debility. He was treated back in England and subsequently medically discharged, dying after his discharge in April 1917. Twenty-five-year-old Rfn James Hewitt from 'B' was hospitalised after accidental burns in December, rejoining in February. One of the new draft, Rfn Albert Skinner, was returned to England two months to the day after his arrival—his true age having come to light. Few disciplinary charges occurred during their time with 3rd Army, though twenty-one-year-old Rfn William Robertson, who managed to lose his rifle on 30 November, left the OC's office 16*s*/3*d* poorer—nonetheless, he got off quite lightly as rifles cost £3/5*s*.

Whenever possible, men were granted home leave. RSM Tanner's batman acquired a goose and turkey at home in Ireland:

> These he attempted to import live in a sack. The turkey escaped *en route*, but the goose arrived safely after a swim in the railway tank at Abbeville on the way, and a more dishevelled and miserable goose was never seen. The Christmas dinner of the Sergeant-Major was however a great success.[5]

On 20 January, 2Lt Allan Smith transferred to the RFC and soon after becoming an observer, was awarded the MC for safely guiding his aircraft down behind British lines, after his pilot was wounded. He left for England to train as a pilot, tragically dying in a flying accident at Ternhill on 18 March 1917, when the tail of his aircraft broke off when he tried to recover from a steep dive. RSM Butler returned on 21 January and Clem Tanner became CSM 'B' Company. It was not until 25 January that their labours ceased.

Their employment as Army troops came about because the West Lancashire Division was reforming—as 55 (West Lancashire) Division—and its constituent units were being drawn together from around the BEF. The battalion concentrated at Talmas on 25 January and, the next day, travelled by bus to Citerne to join their new brigade. As a TF division, there would be no inequality of treatment for its constituent battalions—something most TF battalions had experienced at some point during their time in the BEF. The 1/6th had been fortunate, in that their mentors saw them as a worthwhile cause whose progress was to mutual benefit. However, at brigade level and above, it is hard not to form the opinion that they were perceived as second-class; while their contribution as additional labour was acknowledged, they were very much at the back of the queue when it came to resources and the tasks allotted. Although there was initial disappointment at the move, their doubts were soon dispelled.[6]

The three brigades comprising 55 Division were 164 (North Lancashire), 165 (Liverpool), and 166 (South Lancashire). The division, under the able command of Maj.-Gen. Hugh Jeudwine, began to congregate on 3 January, the Rifles being the last to arrive. The 164th Bde, under Brig.-Gen. G. Edwards, consisted of 1/4th KORL, Liverpool Irish, 2/5th Lancashire Fusiliers, and 1/4th Loyal North Lancs. The 165th Bde, under Brig.-Gen. F. Duncan, consisted of 1/5th, 1/6th, 1/7th, and 1/9th KLR. The 166th Bde, under Brig.-Gen. F. Green-Wilkinson, included 1/5th KORL, Liverpool Scottish, 1/5th South Lancs, and 1/5th Loyals. Each brigade had its own machine-gun company and trench mortar battery—personnel supplied by their constituent battalions and badged as such, though later that year, all machine gunners were rebadged as MGC. The Divisional Pioneer-Company was 1/4th South Lancs and all divisional troops, with the exception of 2/1 Wessex Field Ambulance, hailed from Lancashire.

Every battalion was seriously undermanned, Liverpool Scottish totalling 454 all ranks. Luckily, drafts for all were on their way from England, though not in the numbers necessary to bring everyone to full strength. The Rifles recorded 757 all ranks upon their arrival at Citerne, including a draft of thirty-eight who had arrived the previous day. Illness and commissioning reduced this to 707 by 8 February (one of the new draft, Rfn Norman Wallace, lasted less than a month, being returned to base as underage on 23 February). The return of Lt Ernest Herschell, who brought nine men with him, did little to address the issue. Among those commissioned was Sgt Zacharias—sadly killed in action with the SWB in November. However, the commissioning of Maurice Moss and Cecil Merriman from 'C' was an investment, as both returned later that year.

Jeudwine had very firm ideas about what he wanted, and a six-page memoranda detailed his initial thoughts. He considered:

> Too great stress cannot be laid on the necessity of developing the moral and soldierly spirit of all ranks. [Training should] develop the confidence of all ranks in themselves, their weapons, their comrades, and their commanders, and to imbue each officer and man with the determination to dominate the enemy, and cause him all the damage and loss possible, whether fighting him in the open or in the trenches.[7]

As a new division, much work was needed before it could operate smoothly as a 'self-reliant fighting force'. Jeudwine indicated that until he gained more experience of their specific needs, his training syllabus was generalised, but once he had more information as to what these were, he would concentrate upon those. His memoranda detailed common elements he desired the division to train towards, giving commanders free rein as to how they achieved the spirit of his instructions. Jeudwine considered those just out of the trenches needed to put extensive effort into smartening their equipment, uniforms, and general demeanour and directed that each day should include time in close-order drill and a march-past of a senior officer.

Fitness was important and each battalion had to carry out at least one route march of a minimum of 6 miles in the first two weeks, and after this, one of no less than 8 miles every fortnight, accompanied by their transport with all equipment properly packed.

Brig.-Gen. Duncan's first inspection did not go well:

> Months of fighting and of detached duty had rubbed the polish off us, and in regard to smartness there was a good deal to be desired. For instance, when the machine-gun limber was inspected the place which should have been devoted to ammunition was found to contain a gumboot and an old sock.
>
> We found General Duncan a fine soldier in every sense. He had commanded a battalion of the Royal Scots, and his standard was high. Of a choleric disposition, he would brook no slackness or lack of soldierly quality. He trained and built his brigade by indefatigable supervision; and in the months to follow he forged an instrument whose subsequent record gave him just cause for pride. We feared him at first, but at length trusted him and valued his approbation; and there were some of us whose affection he secured.[8]

The battalion duly tightened up and once again, an early 'victim' was Rfn Sydney Young. CSM James Knight charged him for having dirty ammunition, earning three days' confined to barracks. The Divisional-Commander was equally hard on his COs, brigade-commanders, and staff-officers, replacing them if he felt they were not up to scratch.

Jeudwine instructed that every officer and man in the division learnt to prepare and throw the No. 1 and Mills grenade and that 'not less than eight men, and preferably one section in each platoon, are to be thoroughly trained grenadiers'. The latter studied more complex tactics and the use of rifle grenades. He established a Divisional Trench Mortar School to train infantrymen in light mortars and Brigade Machine-Gun Schools. Brigade Bombing Schools coached officers and NCOs to act as instructors within their own battalions. The CRE inaugurated an Engineering School to train officers and NCOs in field engineering. Each battalion established its own Sniping Section of at least eight snipers under an officer—this in addition to any 'Company Snipers'. Jeudwine exhorted that snipers and observers must make use of the latest equipment and techniques.

His syllabus emphasised musketry and bayonet training. The former is an obvious skill—it is always a good idea to actually hit what one is shooting at—but the latter was (and still is) controversial. Partly, the criticisms of bayonet drill came from the emphasis placed upon it in basic training, its ascendency due to a lack of instructors, rifles, and knowledge—the bayonet is a cheap and 'easy' thing to teach—and unlike musketry, it could be taught using a wooden rifle. Detractors of the bayonet fail to understand just how effective this weapon is for fostering aggression, something all soldiers need—after all, a soldier's job is to kill; infantrymen do this close up and face to face—not something that comes naturally to most in civilised societies.

Jeudwine initially focused on ten areas of training. Rightly, he was keen that his division kept the initiative, and to do so required fighting patrols, bombing raids, reconnaissance patrols, and the effective use of rifle grenades and sniper scopes. Methods of attacking trenches and, in particular, the indispensable skills of consolidation, protection of flanks, and building blocks in captured trenches demanded repeated practice and refinement.

Infantry needed experience working with friendly artillery and acquiring the skills of advancing under hostile fire. The attack and defence of villages necessitated specialised techniques, as did reconnaissance and scouting. Infantrymen required the proficiency of engineers when it came to the production of wire entanglements, revetments, loop-holes, the construction of trenches, and the repair of blown-in trenches. The use of machine guns for indirect fire and map reading skills for all ranks were instilled. Every one of these aptitudes needed to be so ingrained that men could perform them without thinking—by day or night. In January 1916, the idea that an attack may lead to a breakthrough and end trench warfare was still thought possible, so the division also trained for open warfare.

All ranks received a comprehensive series of lectures by specialists. Included were 'the cooperation of infantry and artillery'; 'marking out of work from a dimension sketch'; the 'extension of working parties'; 'commencement of digging work laid out and wiring'; 'collection of information and its transmission to higher authority'; 'duties and responsibilities of officers, NCOs and men in the trenches'; 'the study of men's comfort, daily inspections of feet and protection against inclement weather'; 'first aid and hygiene'; 'gas and use of smoke helmets'; and, finally, 'morale, discipline and brave deeds'. Jeudwine ardently believed that when a man performed particularly well, news of his deeds was passed around the division as an example to others, and even if the act did not result in an official award, the man should have a certificate to send home to proud families.

Schools for junior officers were established at brigade and division, where officers were given intensive instruction in the skills of platoon-commanders, and also how to operate at higher levels. This education was carried over to men, too—an initiative that paid off, when most battalions at some time or another, ended up with NCOs commanding companies during battle.

One of Jeudwine's great strengths was his readiness to listen to all ranks. He later brought in a policy of all platoon, company, and battalion commanders producing detailed reports of operations—along with their recommendations for improvement. Should a platoon-commander become a casualty, the report would be written by the senior surviving OR, and if the platoon split to carry out separate tasks, the OR in charge of this sub-unit would also complete a report. Many of these original documents have Jeudwine's hand-written notes and comments in the margins. Significant points were then distributed to all units, with recommendations for action.

Problems highlighted rarely reoccurred—indicating that lessons were learned. Frequently, after an action, the General would visit the participants and talk informally to them about it—an aide making notes in the background. The mythology of the First World War would not countenance a general asking ordinary soldiers about how to improve his attack plans, yet the records of 55 Division demonstrate that this is just what happened.

As training intensified, exercises expanded in scope, with brigade schemes encompassing all arms, until the entire division trained as a whole. These not only allowed individual units experience of operating as part of a larger formation, but also gave staff much needed practice. From 4 February, the division marched in stages towards their new sector. At noon on 9 February, they came under the orders of VII Corps and were told that at 10.30

a.m. on 16 February, they would assume command of the Rivière sector, 5 miles south-west of Arras—then held by the 88th French Territorial Division.

One problem facing the ordinary infantryman was the unceasing workload out of the line. Only two of their allocation of three RE Field Companies had been assigned to 55 Division. In a letter to HQ VII Corps on 24 February, Jeudwine repeated a previous request for 1/1st West Lancs Field Company to be reassigned to him:

> This question was raised when the Division formed part of XIV Corps, and Lord Cavan, the then Corps Commander, gave me to understand that action was being taken and that it was only a matter of a week or two before this Field Company would be restored. Matters however do not seem to have advanced and it is possible that the situation is not fully understood.
>
> The only two Field Companies now with this Division have only just come out from home where their training was incomplete, and have no experience of active operations and no training, even at home, in trench warfare. The want of at least one Field Company with experience is most keenly felt.[9]

The problem was amplified because this had been a French sector and there was considerable work to do in the front line and the rear, where most of the accommodation was declared unfit for human habitation by the Divisional Medical Officer; roads and water supplies were also considered inadequate. The 1/4th South Lancs were not trained or equipped as a pioneer battalion, and GHQ even suggested that they return to work as an infantry battalion elsewhere and another pioneer battalion be posted in. The end result of this lack of specialists was that battalions were stretched to their limit, supplying manpower for working parties.

The transition into the sector, with elements of 166 Bde occupying the line, began on 12 February. This area was divided into three sectors, and although sometimes referred to by the names of the area immediately behind them, they were also assigned letters, with 'F' Sector being the left, 'E' Sector the centre, and 'D' Sector the right. Individual sectors were further subdivided into left and right subsectors. Over the preceding week, the battalion had gradually moved nearer, and on 13 February, they gathered at Monchiet. The following morning, the CO and company-commanders reconnoitred the trenches at Wailly. It was time to go back into the line.

5

14 February 1916—30 July 1916: Wailly

Coordinates for this Chapter

Barly	50°15′1.60″N 2°32′47.30″E	Foul Street	50°14′2.60″N 2°43′36.30″E
Bois de Martinets	50°13′59.20″N 2°42′52.80″E	Frog Street	50°14′25.50″N 2°44′14.10″E
Bois des Tailles	49°56′31.66″N 2°40′23.29″E	Halloy	50° 9′24.49″N 2°25′37.81″E
Brétencourt Château	50°14′9.10″N 2°41′51.10″E	Mill Post	50°14′33.80″N 2°43′9.60″E
‘C’ Coy. 23 March	50°14′32.30″N 2°43′38.20″E	Petit Château	50°15′12.30″N 2°44′10.90″E
‘C’ Coy. Wailly	50°14′40.20″N 2°42′56.50″E	raid 28 June	50°14′5.10″N 2°43′56.50″E
calvaire	50°14′35.40″N 2°43′39.30″E	raid—left block	50°14′6.50″N 2°43′58.60″E
Chancery Lane	50°14′20.20″N 2°43′3.70″E	raid—right block	50°14′4.20″N 2°43′55.50″E
enemy cookhouse	50°14′17.40″N 2°44′29.10″E	right bound 8 July	50°13′45.40″N 2°42′43.30″E
enemy OP	50°13′58.80″N 2°44′3.20″E	Sap-A	50°14′8.80″N 2°43′54.20″E
Farm Street	50°14′28.90″N 2°44′18.80″E	Sap-B	50°14′12.60″N 2°44′5.80″E
Flag Street	50°14′5.10″N 2°43′43.20″E	Sap-C	50°14′18.00″N 2°44′10.60″E
Flood Street	50°14′11.80″N 2°43′57.50″E	Sap-D	50°14′22.00″N 2°44′16.20″E

Sap-F	50°14′27.90″N 2°44′29.70″E	Trench 180	50°14′16.10″N 2°44′5.00″E
Sap-G	50°14′29.30″N 2°44′36.60″E	Trench 181	50°14′14.60″N 2°44′2.30″E
Sap-I	50°14′38.80″N 2°44′41.70″E	U/X 105-mm HE	50°15′39.00″N 2°42′1.20″E
Trench 177	50°14′19.50″N 2°44′10.80″E	Wailly Keep	50°14′44.90″N 2°43′29.20″E

The advance party found great contrast between the lives of the poilus and their commanders:

> In the front, the wire defences were poor, the traverses badly-designed, and the trenches morasses of mud; but the support lines and headquarters were soundly built, and the Regimental Commander lived in the château at Brétencourt, within a mile of the German trenches, in undisturbed comfort. The magnificent lunch they served to the officers of the advance party was brought up from the kitchen in a service lift; they slept in luxurious bedrooms with running water laid on; and they could walk in a landscape garden filled with snowdrops and early spring flowers.[1]

Many years later, Richard Wainwright recounted another feature the French CO revealed during their guided tour of the château:

> With great pride the French officer had shown him a bathroom lined with mirrors scrounged from wrecked houses. They were set round the walls at all angles so that his lady friends could display their many charms in a state of total undress.[2]

At 4.30 p.m. on 14 February, the battalion marched to Beaumetz-lès-Loges, meeting guides from the 82nd French Territorial Regiment, who led them to the reserve positions for the right subsector of ‘F’ Sector. The four companies occupied separate locations to the west and south-west of Wailly. They remained in reserve until 18 February, labouring upon communication trenches, dugouts, and the front line. Heavy snow earlier that month had become torrential rain and gusting winds—much to the detriment of the badly-built trenches. Improving these quickly was not only vital for protection from enemy fire, but crucial to prevent sickness:

> The whole trench system was in the most appalling condition. This was a quiet part of the line and so no repairs had ever been done to the trenches; they were knee-deep in liquid mud. The dugouts were foul and filthy; sanitary discipline was conspicuously absent. So during a February of driving snow and sleet, we set about the distasteful task of cleaning out this Augean stable. Only the application of grease [whale oil] outwardly and rum inwardly, saved us from frostbite [trench foot] and worse.[3]

Battalions got through 32 gallons of whale oil per month.

The deep French dugouts—thirty to forty steps underground—were death traps; most were in a state of potential collapse and had no chance of anyone occupying them being able to get out in the event of a German raid. Their place was taken by shallower dugouts, with moderate top-cover.[4]

After dark on 18 February, the battalion relieved the 1/5th in the line. Their dispositions, from left to right, were 'D' under Capt. Bennet; 'C' under Capt. Turner; 'B' under Capt. Gordon; and 'A' under Capt. McKaig. The subsector ran from Frog Street on the left to Flag Street on the right—a frontage of 950 yards. HQ's dugout was near the *calvaire* at the sunken crossroads ½ mile in front of Wailly, which also became the resupply drop-off point. Transport remained at Monchiet.

Fortunately, the line was quiet, though during the afternoon of 19 February, one of the battalion's snipers hit a German sniper who was moving into position—he also shot another German at 6.45 a.m. the next morning. The weekly Intelligence Report observed: '... the enemy are apt to expose themselves a good deal and give good targets for our snipers'.[5]

Quite how *blasé* the enemy was about British snipers is astonishing—displaying unbelievable naïveté. Intelligence Summaries for March substantiate Jeudwine's decision to set up specialist sniping sections, who claimed sixty-four victims. That same month, 55 Division suffered sixteen fatalities from all causes. The Summary for 8 March described one such incident:

> A German shot yesterday dropped a telescope in front of the parapet of sap head R.24c.7.2 [Sap-F]. At 9.25 a.m. a man attempted to pick it up, he was fired at and withdrew. At 9.55 a.m. he made another attempt and was shot by our snipers; as he fell back into the trench the telescope again fell outside the parapet. At 10.05 a bald-headed man made a very cautious attempt to retrieve the article but was shot, the telescope remained outside.

Another example from the Summary of 17 March:

> Our snipers accounted for three Germans. They have considerably more difficulty finding live targets now and have to content themselves with periscopes, twelve of which were broken in the Right Sector in the last twenty-four hours.[6]

To put German casualties from snipers into perspective—with no more than twenty-four British snipers in the line at any one time—enemy losses were the numerical equivalent of an entire British infantry battalion every fifteen months.

The battalion was relieved after dark on 22 February, though the trip back was a struggle: it was bitterly cold and 2 metres of snow had fallen during the day.[7] After relief, HQ moved to Brétencourt Château; 'A' to the Bois de Martinets; 'B' to Brasserie le Fermont; 'C' to Wailly; and 'D' to Mill Post. Further heavy snow fell on 23 February, and with both sides battling the elements, the front remained quiet.

On 25 February, HQ moved to the *calvaire* and 'D' relieved a company of the 1/5th in 'F4', the far left portion of the subsector. It was still bitterly cold and further snowfall filled communication trenches to the brim. The next day, 'B' and 'C' went into the line, relieving two companies of 1/7th KLR—a slight adjustment to the bounds, moving the subsector bound to where Farm Street met the front line. Now on a three-company front, 'B' held the left, 'C' the centre, and 'D' the right. For the first time since manning this sector, enemy artillery was active. On 28 February, a large number of small calibre shells targeted the divisional line, though many were duds—twenty-one of the thirty-seven fired at Three Houses communication trench failing to explode. No casualties were sustained by the battalion, whose greatest concern was a slight rise in the temperature, which began to thaw the snow, making the trenches most unpleasant.

Although hostile artillery ignored 'F' Sector on the 29th, sporadic fire in the afternoon of 1 March slightly wounded Sgt Richard Browne of 'C'. Critically wounded by a sniper that morning, twenty-four-year-old L/Cpl John Jamieson of 'B' died from his head wound the following evening. The 1/5th relieved the battalion at 9 p.m. on 2 March, who occupied reserve billets in Beaumetz until the 8th.

Heavy snowfall on most days made life grim for the large working parties demanded—on 4 March, no fewer than 400 men were required. Lt-Col. Harrison took the opportunity to write MiD recommendations, in recognition for work put in so far. CSM Clem Tanner was one, for the 'good and steady work' of a SNCO, who was 'reliable and full of enterprise' and of great value to the battalion. RQMS William Ward was similarly rewarded. Capt. McKaig was lauded for his 'exceptional qualities in leadership and control of men'; Lt Hugh Barret for his 'consistent good work as Machine-Gun-Officer'; and 2Lt Brownell for his work as Adjutant and as Commandant 3rd Army troops (he was also promoted).[8] Replacements continued to trickle through and another thirty-nine arrived on 4 March.

At 6 p.m. on 8 March, the battalion returned to the line, relieving the 1/5th. Deep snow still blanketed the ground and it continued to be bitterly cold, with clear skies. Hostile artillery fire remained scant, and even on 9 March, when, at 2.30 p.m., British artillery and mortars fired 110 rounds at the German Sap-A and Sap-C (just 50 yards from the battalion's front line), the enemy did not retaliate. The fire was accurate and considerable damage was caused. That night, battalion scouts lay up near Sap-C, but found no indications the enemy was attempting to repair the damage. Here, No Man's Land ran along a valley bottom, British lines in the unenviable position of occupying the forward-facing slope—the main enemy line over the brow. A series of long, German saps ran close to the British front line, with eight facing the battalion, though three were derelict.

Divisional Howitzers and mortars targeted Sap-A again on 10 March, though this time the enemy retaliated with twenty 77-mm against Wailly and the front line, provoking thirty-one rounds of 18-pounder in return. From the outset, Jeudwine instigated a robust policy of retaliation, insisting that any German fire should be returned with interest. During the night of 11–12 March, a reconnaissance patrol investigating Sap-A discovered that the enemy had manned a listening post about 70 yards up from the sap-head—a position previously unmanned—though unlike in many of their advance positions, only human sentries were evident. Intelligence had earlier cautioned, 'from the barking at nights, it seems that many of the enemy's sentries were accompanied by dogs'.[9]

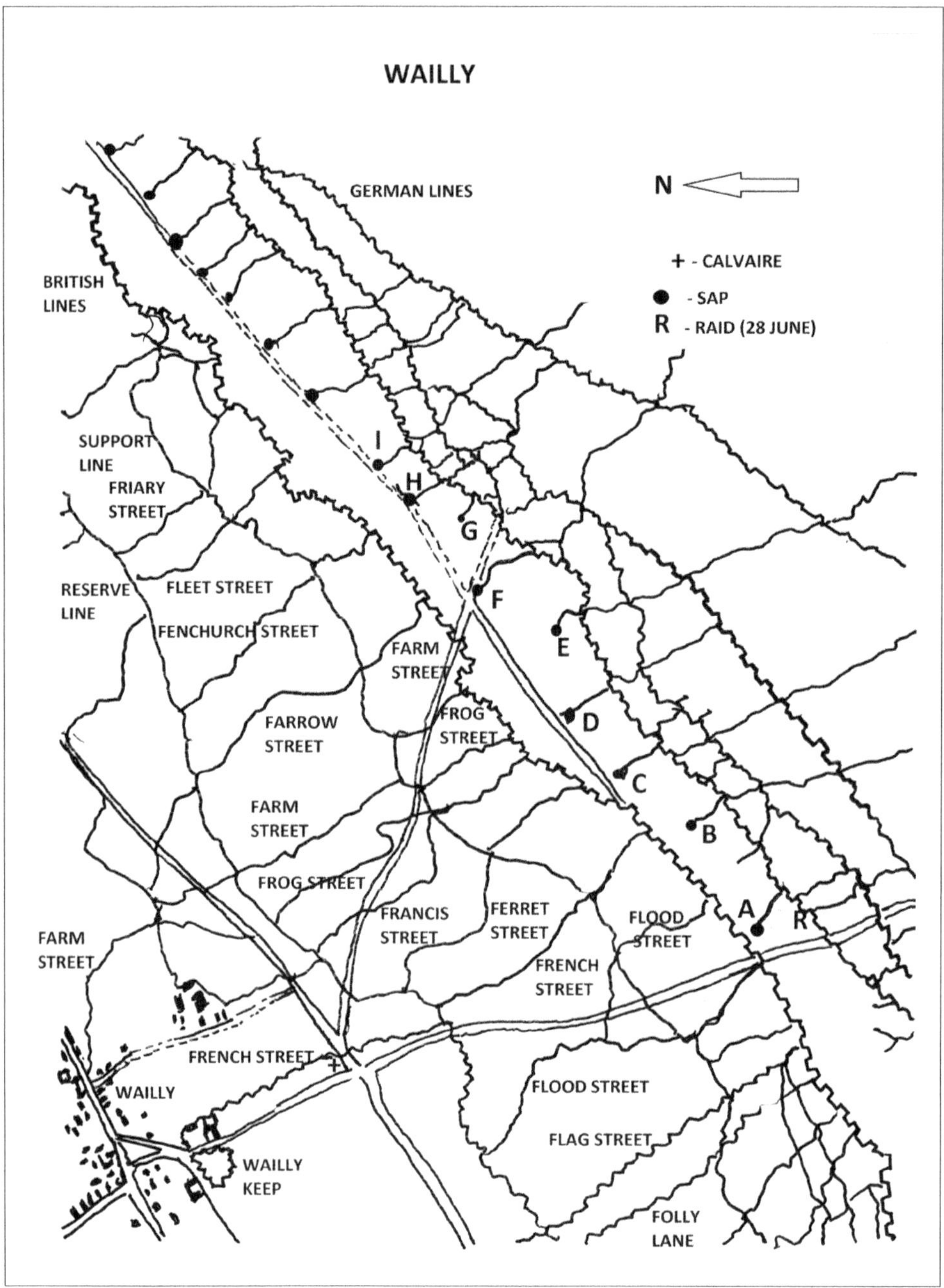
WAILLY
GERMAN LINES
N
+ - CALVAIRE
- SAP
R - RAID (28 JUNE)
BRITISH LINES
SUPPORT LINE
FRIARY STREET
RESERVE LINE
FLEET STREET
FENCHURCH STREET
FARM STREET
FARROW STREET
FROG STREET
FARM STREET
FROG STREET
FRANCIS STREET
FERRET STREET
FLOOD STREET
FRENCH STREET
FARM STREET
FRENCH STREET
WAILLY
WAILLY KEEP
FLOOD STREET
FLAG STREET
FOLLY LANE
A
B
C
D
E
F
G
H
I
R

Artillery from both sides was more dynamic on 13 March, the enemy firing 360 10.5-cm shells and a large quantity of 77-mm into British lines. The left of the battalion's line was hit, killing twenty-four-year-old Rfn Raymond Walker from 'C' and wounding two of 'B'. Rfn Harry Matthews was treated in England for his arm wound; Sgt John Moss was only slightly injured and remained on duty. The next night, the battalion was relieved and returned to Wailly.

While there, Rfn John Caryl was posted to 165 Bde as batman to the chaplain, though not for long, as his time expired a month later. Taking advantage of the offer of choice of battalion and a month's home-leave, for voluntarily re-enlisting, he signed up, and the day after returning, he was posted to 55 Division's band. Batman to a brigade-chaplain sounds cushy—and in a way it was—but he accompanied the chaplain wherever he went, and 55 Division's chaplains cannot be accused of taking a back seat; no fewer than six were killed and four wounded.[10]

The weather had improved considerably and the snow was gone; in fact, 15 March was so hot that some men got sunburnt. One life-saving innovation, issued in early March, was the steel Brodie helmet; though initially unpopular because of its discomfort, it considerably reduced the incidence of head injuries. Wailly was well within range of German guns, as Ellison, now with 'B' Company Stores, described:

> The inhabitants had fled long since; scarce a cottage was undamaged, the church had been reduced to a slender minaret rising above a sea of rubble. During our stay, we strongly fortified the place with hidden machine-gun positions, surprise trenches and barbed wire. Most of the village was well within machine-gun range and was an easy target for artillery, yet, despite an occasional outburst of 'hate', it was a cushy and interesting job infinitely to be preferred to front line duty.
>
> From Wailly, a road led straight though our lines and those of the enemy. Some distance along it, a screen made of straw was suspended across it on two high poles to prevent the enemy looking straight up the village street. McGivering and I had a special duty allocated to us. If the enemy broke through, we had to rush up to this screen, deluge it with a tin of petrol we kept handy for that purpose, and set it alight. On many a night, when artillery exchanges were more lively than usual, Mac and I would crouch in a little dugout by the screen with the precious tin of petrol, wondering if this was going to be our night or not.[11]

Twenty-four-year-old L/Cpl Herbert Young discovered just how vulnerable life in Wailly could be on 16 March when he was unfortunate enough to be hit in the buttock by a spent bullet, though the injury was minor and he was back next day.

The battalion suffered further casualties, when two Riflemen from 'B', on a carrying party to the HQ of 1/5th KLR, were wounded by shellfire on 19 March: William Braithwaite's thigh wound resulted in medical downgrading and transfer; however, the wound in William Barnett's left heel was less significant and he returned three weeks later. On the same day, and also from 'B', nineteen-year-old Rfn Thomas Tushingham appeared in front of Lt-Col.

Liddell of the ASC, OC of the dump where some of the company were working. Charged with 'neglect of duty'—namely being without his rifle—he was awarded three days' field punishment. Tushingham was discharged to munitions work in October, engaged on ship-building at Garston Docks.

On 20 March, the battalion returned to the front line, relieving the 1/5th by 4 p.m. Recent arrival Rfn W. Robinson (814), however, headed in the opposite direction, returned to base as underage. While there, he left camp without authorisation, missing morning parade and his ship home, and was docked four days' pay in consequence. 'C' remained in support, with 'B' on the left, 'D' in the centre, and 'A' on the right. Although the night and next day were reasonably calm, British fire against Sap-B and Sap-D provoked retaliation against 'A' Company, though no casualties ensued.

The 23rd saw a return of the snow, 2 inches blanketing the ground by the following morning. Rfn William Dailey of 'C' was badly scalded on hands and face by boiling water and was transferred to the APC after leaving hospital. The TMB shelled Sap-C on the morning of 23 March and the enemy retaliated against 'D' Company's line and 'C' Company's support position near the *calvaire*. Both suffered three casualties apiece—'C' losing eighteen-year-old Rfn Frank Garland killed and twenty-four-year-old Rfn John Potter wounded in the back. The least injured was Sgt William Winter, whose heel was very badly bruised by a shell fragment. 'D' also had one man killed: nineteen-year-old Rfn Arthur Hudson—the first of the January draft to perish. Rfn John Hallam was critically injured with multiple wounds to chest, abdomen, and right leg, and Rfn John Davies (914) hit in the legs—both survived, but neither returned.

More snow fell on 24 March, much reducing enemy artillery fire—on the whole, a trade-off the men were probably content with. HQ and the *calvaire* received some light shellfire during the early hours of 24 March, though the only casualty was Rfn Thomas Baker, collecting his second wound of the war—though the injury to his buttock was minor and he returned to duty on the 27th. The final casualty before relief on 26 March was Rfn Sidney Webster, wounded at duty on the 25th.

The battalion went into reserve at Beaumetz and Lt-Col. Harrison took the opportunity to grab some well-earned leave in England, temporary command passing to Maj. Wainwright. Capt. Turner also departed for base as an instructor for new drafts.

At 7 p.m. on 1 April, the battalion began their journey back into the line, 'B' remaining in support near the *calvaire*. 'C' manned the left, 'D' the centre, and 'A', the right. Since February, the trenches had been significantly improved: the front line had been deepened and duckboards laid, and work making parapets bullet-proof had progressed well and ten traverses had been constructed. Along the entire subsector, revetting and rebuilding of the fire-step—severely damaged by frost and snow—was well underway. Recesses in the parapet had been fashioned for ready-use grenades and small arms ammunition, and splinter-proof emplacements had been built for four Vickers and six Lewis guns. The construction of splinter-proof shelters for sentries in each traverse was progressing; nine grenade stores and five trench mortar emplacements, with shelters and dugouts for their crews had also been completed.[12]

Relief was not a simple matter of moving one lot in and another out. The day before relief, a reconnaissance was undertaken by officers and senior NCOs. Snipers also moved up twenty-four hours earlier to liaise with snipers from the outgoing battalion. Conversely, outgoing machine gunners remained behind another twenty-four hours before relief by the incoming crews. On their reconnaissance, officers would establish the condition of the wire and parapets and any work in progress. A trench 'log book' was kept and passed on, helping continuity of effort. Arcs of fire and positions of enemy MGs and snipers would be ascertained and any particularly dangerous areas of line highlighted. The position of existing listening posts was passed on and the locations of the small arms ammunition stores, bomb stores, and the general trench stores, and a list of all contained within, had to be obtained. Checking actual stores against the paperwork needed particularly vigilance, as it was not unknown for outgoing units to try to pass deficiencies onto a naive relief.

Methods of communications with the artillery, by phone or visual signals, needed to be shared and procedures to follow in the case of heavy bombardment, attack, or counterattack passed on. The QM needed to identify transport routes and drop-off points for resupply. Of routine, but vital importance was the placement of latrines, water supplies, and available cooking arrangements. All officers needed to know the locations of HQs and be able to brief their company runners accurately enough for them to find them, too. As can be imagined, it was far harder taking over unfamiliar trenches.

After relief, officers and NCOs needed to pass all relevant information to every soldier. Each man carried 120 rounds of ammunition in his pouches, but an additional supply equivalent to 120 rounds per man was kept in the trenches and another 10,000–20,000 rounds at battalion HQ. Reserve ammunition, stored in a dry place in the trench line, was only supposed to be unsealed if there was an attack. Each morning, it was the responsibility of every platoon commander to check to see if the lids on the boxes opened freely and the weatherproofing remained unbroken. Open boxes were used to top up men's ammunition pouches and then returned to stores to be exchanged for new.

Their first night was quiet, but hostile artillery became more active on 2 April, shelling Wailly and nearby communication trenches. 'D', in the centre, had two wounded at duty: Rfn James Thomas was grazed on his right eyebrow by a shrapnel ball—a very close escape; the other was young Rfn Herbert Wilson—exactly how young, the battalion had yet to discover. Cpl Edward Bowman, serving with the TMB, was another casualty—a foot wound ending his infantry days.

On 3 April, the TMB bombarded Sap-D, causing considerable damage, and although the enemy retaliated, their response was feeble. At 8.40 p.m., the men in the front-line 'stood-to' as very heavy small arms fire erupted from German lines in the subsector to their left, the 1/9th KLR replying with rapid rifle and machine-gun fire. This exchange lasted for twelve minutes before calm resumed; the cause of the enemy nerviness was never established. Despite warm weather and clear visibility, German artillery fire remained at a very low level and very little came the battalion's way over the next two days, though the rear was shelled by heavy artillery. One dud 15-cm shell at Rivière was excavated and found to have penetrated 14 feet of earth.

Intelligence believed that the enemy had brought new batteries into the area and the fire was these registering—a view supported when he hit his own lines with the first three 10.5-cm rounds on 6 April, no doubt to the great displeasure of German infantry. The next fifteen rounds landed in and around Blamont. The battalion support line near the *calvaire* was also shelled and 'B' suffered three casualties: Rfn John Gratton was wounded in the head and transferred after leaving hospital; Rfn Richard Woods received minor wounds to his left thumb and right wrist, but remained on duty; and twenty-six-year-old Sgt James Rundle had his leg cut open by a baulk of timber sent flying by a blast, and he only returned in June. 'A' Company's Rfn Walter Parker was also carried to the Field Ambulance that morning after scalding his foot when a dixy of boiling water was knocked over. The final casualty of the day was 2Lt Edward Smith with 165 MGC. He received a shrapnel wound to the head, returning to duty in May.

Although enemy artillery was fairly inactive on 7 April, the small amount of fire directed against 'C' on the left of the line resulted in two casualties. Twenty-eight-year-old Sgt Arthur Edwards was killed and fellow NCO Sgt William Winter became a casualty for the second time in a fortnight, this time multiple shrapnel wounds to leg, thigh, and foot. It was also the last day for CSM Henry Johnson, whose fitness had diminished over the last year. Graded PB, he was transferred to duty with the Command Paymaster in England. At 4 p.m., the battalion was relieved and returned to Wailly.

The weather continued to improve, making life more bearable. Some of the battalion worked on a wiring party in the reserve line during the early hours of 11 March and among these, twenty-one-year-old Rfn Charles Telford was killed and Rfn William Rogers evacuated home with an arm wound. A draft of sixteen arrived later that day, strength rising to a healthier thirty-three officers and 832 men. On the night of 11–12 April, men were once again on working parties and Rfn Cecil Purdon received a minor wound in the knee, returning to duty six days later. Two men were also accidentally injured while digging: Rfn Arthur Pilling suffered a wound to his right leg and Rfn William Eaglesfield a wound to his right hand—both the result of careless pick-axe use by a third party.

At 4 p.m. on 13 April, the battalion returned to the line, this time with 'A' in support near the *calvaire*, 'C' on the left, 'D' the centre, and 'B' the right. The night was exceptionally quiet—the enemy only firing fifty-nine shells across the whole divisional front during the twenty-four-hour period, only nine of which were larger than 77-mm. The sector remained quiet until 16 April, when divisional artillery and mortars began to bombard Sap-C, Sap-D, and Sap-F and another three opposite the left subsector, provoking considerable retaliation. Rfn John Preston from 'C' was wounded in the eye and neck and medically discharged. A number of enemy rounds failed to explode and one, a 10.5-cm HE round that landed a mile behind Wailly, brought some satisfaction to Division. This was from a gun they had previously been unable to locate, but the angle it landed gave them an accurate back-bearing to its whereabouts; scoops in the ground from another two duds pinpointed two further guns.

On the night of 17–18 April, the Liverpool Irish to their right conducted an extremely effective large-scale raid against a sap, and though there was German artillery retaliation, it was mainly directed towards the perpetrators. Wailly was also the target for fifty 10.5-cm rounds, but no casualties were sustained. The 19th was their last day in the line before relief at 10.40 p.m. and a reasonably quiet one, apart from a few shells striking Wailly. Just one casualty ensued, when Rfn William Freeman was wounded at duty, receiving cuts on his nose and right eyebrow from a shell splinter—a narrow escape.

The battalion occupied billets at Beaumetz until 25 April, specialist training and working parties occupying their time. Two Riflemen were lost to the battalion before they returned to the line. One of them, Harold De Valve, the younger brother of Leslie—wounded in April 1915—had only arrived on 15 March, but was found to be underage and sent to base, returning when he attained eighteen and a half years in January. The other, John Robley, went home with eyesight problems, an astigmatism bringing about his medical discharge. Others were discharged, their time expired, but Rfn Lawrence Harding from 'B' became the envy of the battalion when he was posted to the Divisional-Canteen for the remainder of the war.

At 8 p.m. on the 25th, the battalion made their way forward again, 'D' taking their turn in support at the *calvaire*. 'C' manned the left, 'A' the centre, and 'B' the right. The night was quiet, though a number of shells struck Wailly overnight. At 4.45 a.m., a German deserter from the 78th *Landwehr* surrendered to 'A' Company in Trench 180 (it was from him that Division learned the Liverpool Irish raiders had accounted for fifty-seven of the enemy). The weather was once again fine and warm, the recent spell of cool, wet, and windy conditions passed. Despite a general lack of fire, Rfn Arthur Duckett received a 'Blighty' wound to the head from shrapnel.

Hostile artillery remained quiet on 27 April, what fire there was, was directed against battery positions. During the day, the enemy opposite 'A' Company released a number of 'smoke balls'—probably just an unsuccessful ruse to get men to expose themselves to German snipers. Divisional snipers were more productive, killing four of the enemy, including an officer.[13]

On 27 April, a patrol was puzzled by a structure 200 yards behind the head of Sap-F. The object was 4 feet high and 6 feet wide, covered by a tarpaulin, and had a loophole to the front. It stood just outside the wire protecting the sap, but was itself wired and a small trench had been excavated to its front. The patrol used this trench as cover while they inspected it. Later, after the patrol had returned, a light was observed under the sheeting, with sparks flying 20 to 30 feet in the air, seen to its rear. British artillery consequently fired six rounds at it, without apparent effect.

The battalion lost one to shellfire on 28 April, when twenty-eight-year-old Rfn Frederick Birch from 'A' was killed. British snipers were very active in 'F' Sector, and though only one German was killed, ten periscopes were hit. The 29th was also quiet, possibly because the enemy opposite was relieved that night. The only casualty was Rfn Llewelyn Williams of 'B'—with the battalion for only nine days—who was wounded at duty in the evening. On 30 April, a patrol from 'C' reported that the enemy appeared to have been deepening his front line, as a line of fresh white chalk had been thrown up behind Sap-C to Sap-E (confirmation came a couple of days later when the enemy carelessly left their picks and shovels on the parados during daylight). The same patrol also discovered an unmanned sniper's lair behind the bank of the sunken road, to the right of Sap-D.

The battalion was relieved during the afternoon of 1 May and went to Wailly as support. Rfn Arthur Lunt was lightly wounded during the morning, but was back on duty next day. The other casualty—recently arrived Rfn Edward Edwards—was a victim of his own carelessness. The nineteen-year-old from 'B' managed to shoot himself in the left hand while unloading his rifle for cleaning. Fortunately, the wound was not serious and he rejoined on 14 May. There was, however, a penalty to pay for his sloppiness, and his FGCM awarded thirty days' field punishment—the leniency reflecting a belief that his injury was unintentional.

Enemy artillery remained inactive until late on 6 May, when Rfn H. Abbey received a minor shrapnel wound to his right leg. The early hours of 7 May saw further shellfire hitting Wailly, wounding four Riflemen. Two of these, George Nadin—wounded in the right hand—and Edward Peake—hit in the back of the right shoulder—never rejoined. John Roberts (201) remained on duty after the cut to his right hand was dressed and Leonard Windsor—with the battalion for under a month—returned to duty on the 26th.

At 6.45 p.m. on 8 May, the battalion occupied the front line once more, 'C' remaining in support; 'D' on the left; 'A' in the centre; and 'B' to the right. 'D' Company's left (and the right of their neighbours, 1/9th KLR) collected the majority of hostile fire overnight, fifty-one rounds landing in the area—the rest of the divisional line only getting thirty-nine rounds. At 1 a.m. on 9 May, Cpl James McWilliam handed over the duty of 'patrolling NCO' to Cpl William Paton. L/Cpl Vincent Stansfield was on duty in the same traverse:

> I head a Very pistol go off, and not seeing the flare go up, I looked round and saw the flare resting on Cpl Paton's hand, he threw his hand up and the flare fell on the parapet about 1 yard in front. I went to Cpl Paton and bound his hand up.

A 'patrolling NCO' toured the traverses, checking on sentries. Paton explained:

> I had just taken over the patrolling NCO duties from Cpl McWilliam, he handed me a Very pistol, when cocking the pistol before firing, the striker slipped from under my thumb, and the cartridge exploded, entering the palm of my hand. The actions of these pistols is so stiff that both hands have to be used in cocking.[14]

Rfn Donald McMillan corroborated the story at the Court of Enquiry, which found the injury to be a 'pure accident and not the result of carelessness'.

It was four months before Paton returned to duty. As 'trench stores', never leaving the line, Very pistols spent their life exposed to the elements; constant handling wore off much of the cheaply-applied 'coating' and they were frequently rusty and difficult to operate.

'D' Company's patrol during the early hours of 9 May approached Sap-F, and though they could clearly hear an enemy working party there, they could not get near enough to see what was occurring. The TMB targeted Sap-G and Sap-I in the left subsector and

Howitzers bombarded the enemy front line where it crossed the sunken Wailly-Ficheux road—none of which brought any retaliation. Near the *calvaire*, Rfn William Miller, on duty at the road control, was castigated for slovenliness by a senior officer and awarded seven days' field punishment by the CO; Miller more than compensated for this lapse later in the war. 'B' Company's night patrol approached the German lines opposite Flood Street, and though they could hear digging, which continued from 9.30 p.m. until 11 p.m., they were unable to see into the trench.

Enemy artillery was more active on 10 May, and later in the day, 'F' Sector and its rear received most of their attention, though the enemy also directed eighty rounds of 15-cm Howitzer fire onto a dummy position on the Beaumetz Ridge, to the rear of Wailly. The battalion only had two Riflemen injured: James Leamey from Transport was wounded in the buttock and, although he left hospital in August, was attached to an ASC Horse Transport Depot until May 1917; the injuries to Sidney Webster were slight and he returned to duty next day, though must have been fairly disgruntled as it was the third time he had been hit—and it would not be the last either. Early on 11 May, Rfn Charles Ovenden of 'A' was fatally wounded in the head, succumbing at the Field Ambulance later that day. It was also the last day for underage soldier, William Madden, who was sent home.

During the morning of 12 May, one of the snipers noticed a flash of light in the enemy's third line, as sunlight reflected off something partially-hidden by a big block of chalk. Aiming at the chalk block, he split it in two with his first shot to reveal two lenses protruding from a revolving turret. These were hurriedly withdrawn and the turret traversed to leave no aperture facing British lines. The location was noted as a target for the divisional artillery. After midnight, enemy machine guns were active, firing towards Wailly from Sap-F and Sap-C, the latter silenced by the battalion's Lewis guns. One of these machine guns wounded Lt-Col. Harrison, who suffered a minor injury to his hand from a ricocheting bullet. He continued on duty after dressing the injury. Also lightly wounded on 12 May was Rfn Ireson Smith, who returned to duty three days later—though time was running out for the twenty-three-year-old from 'B'. Further to the right of the line, British snipers fired shots at the loopholes in steel plates of what was believed to be a German machine-gun position. The enemy showed their disdain for the marksmanship by using a blue flag on a stick to point out where they had hit the target—whereupon, British Howitzers dropped a salvo directly onto them. Close cooperation between snipers and artillery became increasingly successful in the division.

The night of 12–13 May was quiet, though the enemy continually swept No Man's Land with machine-gun fire. One gun, directly opposite French Street, was silenced by a direct hit from British artillery. When dawn broke, observers noticed fresh chalk thrown up on the mound next to the base of Sap-B and a line of new, black sandbags nearby. Enemy artillery remained subdued and virtually no fire was directed against the battalion. On 14 May, a welcome addition arrived in the form of 2Lt Alfred Broad and seventy-three replacements from England, though they remained behind the lines until the battalion was relieved at 11 p.m. on 15 May.

The battalion went into reserve at Beaumetz, and after resting on 16 May, they practised an emergency deployment to the Corps line at 8.30 p.m. on the 17th, returning at 1 a.m. the following morning. The 18th saw the battalion's machine gunners officially re-badged as MGC, though, in actuality, they had ceased to play any part in battalion life at the beginning of the year. George Palfreyman, who had been put into 'D' when he arrived in April, found himself up in front of the CO, gaining fourteen days' field punishment for not complying with an order; two months later, he was sent home. According to his records, he was nineteen when he enlisted in August 1915; however, he was just fifteen.

Some battalions were not receiving adequate replacements, and on 20 July, eighty men from the 1/6th were 'lent' to the 1/9th until 25 August. Another forty-nine were attached in July—mostly from a draft that came straight from Rouen. Tragically, seven became casualties while attached. Understandably, the men selected were not their most experienced—the majority having recently arrived—and some did not take kindly to the regime: Rfn Arthur Swinnerton refused to obey an order and then reported sick; however, the MO found nothing wrong with him, and the CO of the 1/9th subsequently awarded him seven days' field punishment for the first offence and a further fourteen days' for trying to avoid the consequences by reporting sick.

Casualties While Attached to the 1/9th, 20 May to 25 July 1916

Rfn Joseph Parry Boyd	4253	DOW: 5/7	Rfn Lawrence G. Oldham	4312	WIA: 23/5
Rfn William Fell	241748	WIA: 2/7	Rfn Joseph Stanley Plant	4182	KIA: 13/6
Rfn Joseph Hughes	3771	KIA: 2/7	Rfn Reginald Simister	4049	KIA: 2/7
Rfn Arthur Jones	4245	WIA: 2/7			

On 21 May, the battalion returned to the line, with 'B' in support near the *calvaire*; 'D' on the left; 'A' in the centre; and 'C' on the right. The night and following day were quiet, though something most unusual was witnessed at 2.30 p.m. on 22 May:

> One of our aeroplanes was fired on by machine-guns and was apparently hit as a man was seen to climb out onto the right wing first and then onto the left and worked on some part. The machine eventually disappeared.[15]

On 23 May, Petit Château and Wailly were intermittently shelled by 77-mm for most of the day, wounding four Riflemen. Twenty-year-old Stanley Aspell was critically wounded in both thighs, dying on 27 May and thirty-one-year-old William Marsden, wounded in abdomen and forearm, succumbed on 28 May. The others were evacuated home: Herbert Cockburn, wounded in the groin, and Samuel Smith, wounded in the left arm. At various times throughout the night of 23–24 May, 'A' Company's sentries in Trench 177 reported the sounds of a stationary engine coming from enemy positions opposite—either in the front line or directly behind it. This was heard again between 5 and 7 a.m. on 24 May.

Wailly and Petit Château were again shelled intermittently on 24 May and another three Riflemen wounded. The least seriously injured was W. Longworth, who was wounded at duty; William Williams (279) got his second of the war, though the injury to his left arm was minor and he was back on duty in June; and the most serious case was George Yates, whose thigh wound ended his time with the battalion. There was one other loss—yet another of the April draft discovered underage. Former ticket-collector Frederick Roberts travelled to base to be repatriated and discharged, aged just fifteen.

Another two casualties ensued from shellfire targeting Wailly on 25 May, both from 'D'. Rfn A. Collard's injuries were minor and he returned four days later. Rfn Wilfred Hall's wounds to head and back were critical, the nineteen-year-old dying the following day.

There was scant fire against the battalion on 26 and 27 May, mostly targeting communication trenches and the rear. One of 'D' Company's sentries noted a considerable amount of smoke issuing from a dugout in the enemy second line trenches and it was thought that this may be a cookhouse—its position carefully noted as a future Howitzer target, no doubt to be timed for a mealtime. Both sides were aware of the morale-reducing potential of carefully-scheduled artillery and mealtimes were always a popular option—though not with the recipients. Another stratagem was to target latrine areas half an hour after breakfast. However, division later decided that the dugout had been made to look too obvious, so was probably a decoy.[16]

During the morning of 28 May, 'C' come under heavy fire from Howitzers and though they lost no one, in the support positions, 'B' Company's Rfn Francis Kitson—one of the tallest in the battalion at 6 feet 3½ inches—was wounded at duty. At 5 p.m., the battalion was relieved and returned to support, with 'A' garrisoning Wailly Keep.

Upon their arrival, twenty-year-old Rfn William Gray was given the good news that he was now Battalion-Sadler, a job that would keep him away from the worst. Tragically, he died from illness at the depot in Prees Heath in February 1919, just days after returning for demobilisation. The situation remained quiet until 7.45 p.m. on 30 May, when shellfire wounded three Riflemen from 'C', the most serious being twenty-three-year-old Harry Alcock, whose multiple wounds to arm, leg, and head proved mortal on 3 June. Nathan McManus was only slightly injured and returned to duty the next day, though Arthur Bryning's thigh wound concluded his overseas service. Another from 'C' who landed in hospital was CQMS Harry Wooler, who fractured his hip in an accident. Seven new subalterns arrived on 31 May after inspection by Brig.-Gen. Duncan at Beaumetz, though Lionel Bond, George Harrison, and Norman Phillips were familiar faces, having risen from the ranks.

The first day of June was remarkably quiet until the evening, when a salvo of four shells hit 'B' Company in Wailly. Twenty-three-year-old Rfn Ireson Smith was killed; Rfn Edward Geldard received a minor arm wound; Rfn Thomas Morgan was wounded at duty; and Capt. Westby was evacuated home, once more afflicted by shellshock. That night, a patrol from the 1/5th found an interesting—though futile—effort aimed at encouraging desertion. About 30 yards from one of the sap-heads in 'F' Sector, the enemy had placed a newspaper and a letter on a stick. The letter read:

> Some German soldiers are recognising the land between our and your positions. Our regiment invites you to come to us. We have much, very much food. We have always much to eat, e.g., bread flesch, and other nourishment. Come to fetsch your whisky and cigares. We are gentlemen and will not shoot, when you come. Time is between 7 and 9 in the evening. This has been written by a friend of the Englishmen.[17]

The 1/5th planned a retort for midnight on 3 June.

The enemy sent another four shells into Wailly on 2 June, though failed to hit anyone, the only loss that day being Rfn Frederick Adamson, another underaged soldier from the April draft, who was despatched home.

At midnight on 3 June, the 1/5th attempted a large-scale raid to the right of Sap-A. The raiders successfully formed up behind a bank 70 yards forward of their line, without alerting the enemy, but during the pre-raid bombardment at 12.40 a.m., the TMB dropped two rounds amid them, producing fifty-two casualties and the immediate cancellation of the raid. Enemy retaliation was slight, although they clearly recognised its purpose, as fourteen SOS rockets were fired; it took German artillery eight minutes to respond.

Retaliatory shellfire during the night and next morning struck Petit Château and Wailly Keep, hitting five of 'A': Rfn William Mangan, wounded in the back, and Rfn Charles Thompson, wounded in the right arm, were both evacuated home, only Thompson rejoining; Rfn Frank Abernethy's arm wound left him hospitalised for four months; Rfn Charles Castle received a minor chest wound and sprained ankle, but the twenty-year-old returned to work three days later; and Cpl Thomas Peterson was burned on his side, remaining on duty.

The battalion relieved the 1/5th at 5 p.m., and apart from 'A' going into support near the *calvaire* and 'B' becoming the centre company, the dispositions were as previously. Later that night, during a supply run, Rfn Edward Boydell suffered minor wounds in the left leg and cheek when the enemy shelled the sunken road behind Wailly.

Throughout the next day, the enemy registered the communication trenches leading forward from Wailly, and twenty-two-year-old L/Cpl William Robertson received facial burns from an exploding shell. He was given an eyesight test at the CCS and returned to duty two days later—a remarkably lucky escape. The enemy was clearly carrying out a lot of work on his defences and new wire was visible opposite the battalion's centre and right, new dugouts also being excavated opposite 'D' Company. One enemy patrol was spotted in No Man's Land, near the battalion's right bound, and driven off with rifle and Lewis fire. An enemy machine gun opposite this position also made a nuisance of itself, but was dealt with by divisional artillery during the night.

On 6 June, a draft of eighty-seven arrived. It should have been eighty-eight, but Rfn Charles Iredale was weeded out at the Divisional-School, when the paperwork claiming him back as 'underage' reached HQ. There was very little hostile fire that day, the only departure being Sgt John Kidd MM from 'B', whose commissioning had come through.

The front remained quiet over the following days, though Wailly was shelled between 3 and 4 p.m. on 8 June and three shells landed close to the *calvaire* at 10 p.m. on the 9th. During the night of 8–9 June, a reconnaissance patrol observed an enemy working party labouring on the wire opposite Trench 181 and returned to alert a Lewis team, who dispersed them. Early in the morning of 10 June, an observant sentry noticed sunlight flashing off a binocular lens in a previously-unknown OP, close to the 'decoy cookhouse'. The first casualty of the tour from the front-line companies was on 10 June. Twenty-one-year-old grocer Rfn Hughie Jones is recorded in the Casualties Book as being hit below the left knee by an 'explosive bullet' (this was almost certainly a bullet that had been sent tumbling, by something akin to a glancing strike on barbed wire, rather than an actual 'exploding round'). Although he kept the leg, he was invalided out. A considerable amount of indirect machine-gun fire was directed at Wailly during the night, but without result.

On 11 June, the enemy fired approximately seventy-five shells into 'D' Company's front and support positions, a few of the rounds bursting harmlessly over Wailly. British guns retaliated and calm eventually resumed. At 11.45 p.m. on 12 June, the battalion was relieved and went into divisional reserve at Beaumetz. While there, 55 Division's line was extended to include 'G' Sector. The 164th Bde took over this new length, 165 Bde extending their line to the right.

Training at Beaumetz was not accident-free, and on 22 June, Rfn William Mason was accidentally wounded in the neck, hand, and leg by the premature detonation of a rifle grenade. The battalion also lost Rfn Howard Valentine the next day when he broke a collar bone in a fall. The third injury was to 2Lt Robert Daglish, who sprained his ankle so badly that he was sent home, only returning at Christmas. Yet another underage soldier from the April draft went on his way home, though Rfn John Tunna was far from the last to be unearthed, another twenty-two harbouring the same guilty secret.

Life was about to get considerably more frenetic as orders had been received from VI Corps on 13 June for a series of 'demonstrations' to be undertaken over a period of six days. These were to take the form of bombardments, wire-cutting, and gas attacks, followed by large-scale raids. The six days were termed 'U'–'Z' and all planning was to be complete by 19 June, with 'U' the following day. This strategy aimed to divert German resources away from the offensive planned on the Somme, 8 miles to their south, on 1 July.

On 16 June, fatigue parties from other battalions began to carry 1,898 gas cylinders to the front line—a task that was not completed until 18 June. Jeudwine acknowledged there was no realistic chance of any attack by a single division capturing and holding part of the enemy line. However, in 'E' and 'F' sectors, a length of 2,100 yards of enemy line was vulnerable. With the enemy's main defences on the reverse slope, the fourteen saps on the forward slope were exposed. If these could be seized, the enemy would lose their direct close-range observation and allow the British the tactical advantage previously enjoyed by the foe. Jeudwine was unable to get additional men for his plan, so halved his proposed attack frontage. In the end, no large-scale assault was sanctioned; instead, seven daylight raids across 'E' and 'F' Sectors were substituted, the 1/6th to carry out one of these.

On 22 June, raiders were handpicked and placed into four groups, under Lt William Jones, 2Lts Adam, Thomas Phillips, and Arthur Freestone, with Maj. Wainwright in overall charge—their target, the enemy line to the right of Sap-A. Those not involved continued their ordinary training and undertook carrying parties at night. German artillery had been fairly quiet, but when the TMB began wire-cutting, the enemy stepped up their retaliatory fire. The TMB's positions, Wailly, and the front line received the lion's share and a number of personnel from carrying parties were wounded. On 25 June, L/Cpl George Keates with the TMB was hit in the right hand, spending ten weeks in hospital; Rfn James Murney's wound was minor and he was back on duty with 'D' the following day; and on 26 June, Sgt John Moss was wounded at duty. Despite their labours, men were expected to maintain soldierly standards, and when Rfn Alfred Dixon appeared on morning parade unshaven, he was awarded seven days' field punishment.

The never-ending workload and lack of sleep affected everybody, but one of the most serious offences anyone could commit was falling asleep on guard. One of the March draft, Rfn William Costin, had earlier been caught asleep at his post and faced a FGCM on 26 June. Found guilty, he was sentenced to be shot, the standard punishment for this offence. As usual, his punishment was commuted to six months' imprisonment with hard labour; this was suspended on 17 July and he returned to the battalion—no doubt a wiser man. The last casualty prior to the raid was Rfn George Jones (991), who received a minor shrapnel wound to his left arm on 27 June.

Divisional artillery expended 54,570 rounds on the demonstrations, and on 25 June, British artillery further south began pounding German positions all along the projected line of attack for 1 July, the thunder of guns clearly audible at Beaumetz. At 12.16 p.m. on 28 June, the seven battalions taking part in the raids were put on 'alert', and at 3.40 p.m., 'zero' was confirmed for 5 p.m.

Four parties, each of two NCOs and twenty men, under Lt Oliver, 2Lts Eric Buckley, G. Rothwell, and Walter Penrice, were tasked with discharging a smoke barrage from the front line, using smoke candles and phosphorus grenades. At zero, divisional artillery began its barrage and the gas cylinders were turned on, followed five minutes later by the smoke. The gas was turned off at 5.25 p.m., and ten minutes later, the raiders exited the front line, artillery lifting their fire to enemy supports.

The battalion's raiders were divided into four groups of twenty, each under one of the officers (the Divisional report, forwarded to VII Corps, noted only three officers and seventy men[18]). Accompanying each group was a small detachment of Sappers, equipped with demolition charges—men from each group designated as a protection force for them. Others were tasked to clear dugouts of enemy, and some to establish blocks further along the trench system. Half the force would slant left once enemy lines were penetrated, the others working to the right. In addition, 2Lt Rome and thirty men provided a covering party.

The raiders cleared their own wire without issue, but halfway across No Man's Land, the enemy attempted to set up a machine gun on their parapet. They were seen by the covering party, who immediately laid down accurate fire, killing the crew. The machine gun was captured intact by the covering party, who established themselves on top of the German parapet. The German trenches were 9 feet deep, but the raiders jumped down without problem and each party began its work. The left group bombed their way along until they reached the top of Sap-A, where they encountered stiff resistance and established their block. The enemy made a determined counterattack against this, but were repulsed by the equally-determined raiders and fire from the covering party. The clash was certainly hand-to-hand, as Rfn Sydney Lloyd from 'D' was wounded in the back by a bayonet; 2Lt Phillips was also wounded in this struggle, but continued fighting.

The right group also met strong resistance, but pushed on into a communication trench, and then along for 40 yards before establishing their block. Much credit was given to Rfn Frederick Cowman. The twenty-year-old had only been with the battalion for three months, but when the leading bayonet man was wounded, he stepped in, holding the block alone against all opposition until it was time to withdraw. His courage was rewarded with the DCM and promotion to corporal, and in December, as a sergeant, he returned to England for commissioning, rejoining the battalion in June 1917.

In all, twelve dugouts were bombed, ten of these demolished by the Sappers. Cries and groans were heard coming from the dugouts after the bombs detonated inside, leading the raiders to believe they had inflicted numerous casualties. These dugouts, each having two entrances, were situated under the parapet and were very deep and strongly-built—one even had a brick-lined entrance, though none had any visible means of gas defence (British dugouts were fitted with a gas-curtain at the doorway). At most dugouts, the defenders had been waiting at the entrance, their main means of defence being the ordinary stick grenade—the battalion's report fairly scathing about the effectiveness of this tactic. What is manifest is that enemy wire had been thoroughly destroyed by divisional firepower—a great contrast to the situation that faced the new divisions of Kitchener's Army a few days later.

Fifty minutes after leaving British lines, the raiders returned carrying their booty, which, according to the report, included:

> 1 wounded German [they brought a dead one back also]. 1 machine-gun. 1 bomb-thrower with platform. Many rifles, bayonets, bombs, smoke helmets, a greatcoat, an officer's boots, a pack believed to belong to an NCO, ammunition and a large supply of cigars and cigarettes.[19]

The battalion's losses, while not excessive for a daylight operation, were not insignificant: twenty-three-year-old Lt Jones (an only son) was shot in the head and killed shortly before withdrawal; 2Lt Phillips, wounded in thigh and hand, was evacuated home; and 2Lt Freestone was wounded at duty. Two of the raiders were killed, eighteen wounded, and a further four wounded at duty. One of the 'smoke party' was killed and another four wounded. The bodies of three of the four killed were brought back to British lines, the low ratio of killed to wounded—only one of whom died from his wounds—reflected the speed with which the wounded were retrieved and treated.

Casualties Sustained During the Raid, 28 June 1916

Name	Number	Status
L/Cpl John A. Burtinshaw	2535	WIA: 28/6
L/Sgt Albert Gordon Carr	241678	WIA: 28/6
Rfn James Clayton	214665	WAD: 28/6
Rfn Ernest C. Cleaver	241116	WIA: 28/6
L/Cpl Robert Curwen	2063	WIA: 28/6
Rfn Harold Deane	1656	WIA: 28/6
Rfn Samuel Charles Rhodes Duffy	240232	WIA: 28/6
2Lt Arthur Holland Freestone		WAD: 28/6
Rfn Lawrence Harrison Goadby	240713	WIA: 28/6
Rfn James H. Griffiths	1982	WIA: 28/6
Rfn Percy Harold Harwood	240606	WIA: 28/6
Rfn Walter Peter Hughes	241498	WIA: 28/6
Rfn Hugh Stephen Johnston	241324	WIA: 28/6
Lt William James Jones		KIA: 28/6
Rfn Harry Lavery	241916	WIA: 28/6
Rfn Reginald Ward Lester	241432	WIA: 28/6
Rfn Sydney Lloyd	2208	WIA: 28/6
Rfn George F. Martin	241459	WIA: 28/6
Rfn William McDonnell	3086	KIA: 28/6
L/Cpl Thomas McLean	2040	DOW: 3/7
Rfn Milford G. Parker	4100	WIA: 28/6
L/Cpl Ernest Parry	2348	KIA: 28/6
2Lt Thomas Phillips		WIA: 28/6
Rfn James Hughes Pinnock	240372	WIA: 28/6
Rfn Lewis Rimmer	241056	WIA: 28/6
Rfn William Gordon Rimmer	3956	KIA: 28/6
L/Cpl George Travis Shore	3288	WIA: 28/6
Rfn Arthur Smith	241667	WAD: 28/6
Rfn Francis George Wilson	241915	WIA: 28/6

A number of awards were given for the raid. L/Cpl Robert Curwen, wounded in the shoulder, received the MM, as did L/Cpl William Fairclough—though he escaped unscathed. 2Lt Phillips, awarded the MC, was the last to leave the enemy trench and was wounded a second time on his way back across No Man's Land. He ignored his own injuries to ensure all the other wounded were rescued.[20]

Overall, results were mixed: Liverpool Scottish rightly abandoned their raid when the wind carried the smoke away from their target, making their attack suicidal; the 1/4th Loyals got to within 15 yards of their objective before concentrated fire pinned them down—two of their three officers were killed, the other wounded, and out of fifty-six ORs, they lost nine killed, four missing, and eleven wounded—a high casualty rate. In complete contrast, 1/5th KLR attacked with seventy-one, achieved all their objectives, and suffered only one wounded. The Fusiliers were also successful, though paid heavily; two out of their three officers were missing, the other wounded; nineteen ORs wounded and sixteen missing—the highest casualty rate among the raiders. The 1/7th reached their sap-head, drove the enemy back, but were unable to gain entry—losing seven killed and fourteen wounded in the process. The 1/9th suffered similar casualties, but were successful in taking their target—though one source of considerable annoyance was their inability to get at a number of Germans who retreated into a dugout with a stout door, which defied repeated attempts to break or blow their way in. Of 400 raiders, 136 were missing, killed, or wounded, a casualty rate of 34 per cent.[21]

The planning and post-raid analysis suggest that past lessons had been learnt and that experience from these raids would be used in the future. Apart from successfully cutting all the wire they were asked to, artillery caused significant damage to enemy defences. The gas was less effective, and apart from two the Fusiliers found at the top of Blaireville Wood, there were no German gas casualties. The gas cloud, moving at 3 mph, granted the enemy three minutes to don respirators. The enemy also had plenty of notice of the raids, due to the wire-cutting and the gaps being maintained by repeated bombardment. During the raids, the Germans fired numerous red distress rockets and it was decided that in future, to avoid confusion with British signals, to use 'Japanese daylight signals', which burst with coloured smoke, dropping two white lights. The smoke screen was widely praised for helping cover attack and withdrawal phases—though one group lost direction in it after donning their PH helmets. The division later carried out considerable training in attack and navigation while wearing PH helmets—and its replacement, the box respirator—particularly after this problem was again highlighted in August.

The Sappers were found to be of great value in destroying enemy installations, however, the biggest let-down was communications—failing in every case due to phone wires being cut by enemy fire (a problem that was never satisfactorily solved). The casualty rate was thought considerable, but given the nature of the attacks, with long artillery preparation advertising a coming attack and the failure of the gas to do its intended job, this was not surprising. Jeudwine accepted that in future, surprise was the key element, particularly during daylight. Had the smoke not been so effective, he believed casualties would have been very much higher.[22]

There was no respite, as it was imperative that 55 Division drew as much German attention as possible. Working parties and mock attacks continued daily. No further casualties ensued before the end of the month, though Rfn Walter Shepherd became dangerously ill with typhus and Rfn Samuel Guy with typhoid—neither returned. On 29 June, Maj.-Gen. Jeudwine inspected the raiders, thanking them for their efforts.

On 1 July, twelve officers, each with a pair of NCOs and twenty men, were ordered to lay a smoke barrage for 'Z' Day across the whole 4,000 yards of the brigade sector. Men were stationed in pairs, every 25 yards of the fire trench, and at 7.20 a.m., they discharged a total of 2,482 phosphorus grenades and 3,842 smoke candles at five-minute intervals over two hours.[23] Though orders stipulated every selected man must be thoroughly familiar with these devices, Riflemen James Barnett, John Gill, James Sleightholme, and George Balmer all managed to collect minor burns to hands or face.

Division artillery began to bombard German positions at Zero, though the smoke made observation of the fall of shot difficult. The enemy replied with rifle and machine-gun fire—clearly believing another attack was underway—and their artillery and mortars bombarded the British front line and communication trenches. Although their artillery fire was mainly ineffective, two heavy *Minenwerfers* fired fifty projectiles into the line in front of Wailly, causing heavy material damage, killing three from the smoke parties, and wounding another twelve—two of whom later died. It is probable that it was during this bombardment that Sgt Henry Imlach, whose medical expertise was invaluable, earned his MM, though his citation no longer survives. Division had a general idea of the whereabouts of these mortars and had been trying unsuccessfully to destroy them for some time—their limited arc of traverse suggesting they were hidden in deep shafts.[24] After dark, more working parties filed off with their burdens, hostile artillery fire wounding another three. The uninjured faced an additional 3-mile journey at the end of their labours, as at 11.15 p.m., the battalion moved to Gouy-en-Artois.

Casualties, 1 July 1916

Name	Number	Status
Rfn George Balmer	204776	WAD: 1/7
Rfn James Barnett	241030	WAD: 1/7
L/Sgt Ernest Beeston MM	2295	KIA: 1/7
Rfn Howard Norbury Boase	241610	WIA: 1/7
Rfn Charles Ferguson	240937	WAD: 1/7
Rfn Charles Wilfred Fitzgerald	4099	KIA: 1/7
Rfn John E. Fricker	3781	WIA: 1/7
Rfn John Crofort Gill	240743	WIA: 1/7
Rfn William Henry Greening	242035	WIA: 1/7
Sgt Arthur Griffiths	927	DOW: 9/10
Rfn Arthur Hill	241805	WIA: 1/7
Rfn John Ebenezer Hudson	241433	WIA: 1/7
Rfn John Fred Kneale	241111	WAD: 1/7
Rfn Richard Leonard Maybury	241635	WIA: 1/7
Rfn Hugh Murdoch	2344	KIA: 1/7
Rfn Joseph Purcell	241452	WIA: 1/7
Rfn James Sleightholme	241698	WIA: 1/7
Rfn John James Woods	2222	DOW: 2/7

The battalion remained in reserve until 8 July, never-ending working parties dominating their existence. Twenty-year-old Rfn Eric Brooker, caught smoking while employed on one, gained seven days' field punishment for his sins. At 8.45 a.m. on 9 July, the battalion began their move back to the line, this time much further to the right, in Trenches 162–175. This subsector ran from Foul Street on the left to the right of Blamont Street. The battalion was in place by 4 p.m., 'A' on the left, 'B' in the centre, 'C' on the right, with 'D' in support. HQ moved into a deep dugout in Chancery Lane.

After a recent spell of wet weather, the rain stopped, though it was still cool for the time of year. German artillery was quiet, though shellfire late on 9 July triggered his second evacuation from shellshock for Rfn John Pointer, who was subsequently transferred to the Labour Corps. Three more Riflemen were discovered to be underage and returned to base: John Dawson was only just below the legal age, so was held at 24 IBD until April 1917, whereupon he returned; Herbert Cubbin and Albert Boggiano, were sent home.

Rfn George Millard was posted to 55 Division's Sanitary-Section, which, while not the most pleasant job, was vital in the struggle to keep men healthy. These postings were usually reserved for men whose age or fitness made trench life difficult, though in thirty-two-year-old Millard's case, it was due to eyesight problems, eventually bringing about a move to the Labour Corps.

The spectre of dysentery had long-haunted armies in the field and colossal volumes of excreta and manure conglomerated—its disposal critical. Regulations and practice concerning latrines were well-established and huge amounts of chloride of lime and creosol solution were issued. Latrines were inspected daily and dire punishments meted out to anyone not using the proper facilities. The design of latrines was decreed—eradicating any gap between the hinged seat cover and the bucket below—preventing the ingress of flies. Horse and mule dung was amassed into large, centralised heaps, then burned in designated areas on a daily basis for much of the year. In winter, it was collected into long rows, about 3 yards wide by 2 yards high and buried—a fresh layer of soil covering each addition of manure.[25] Considering the number of animals in a divisional area, this was no mean task and transport-officers were encouraged to induce local farmers to remove as much as possible for fertiliser. Every division appointed a sanitary-officer, who in turn appointed a team of trained men, each responsible for a sub-area. These patrolled daily, reporting on any infractions, often leading to general warnings in 'Divisional Orders', such as 'Cases have recently been brought to notice of excreta being buried by units at their transport lines. This is to cease immediately. All excreta is to be burnt and not allowed to accumulate'.[26]

On 11 July, Liverpool Scottish, to the battalion's right, was relieved by 1/8th Sherwood Foresters of 46 Division, who the following day shifted their line left, one of their companies relieving 'C', who went into billets in Brétencourt. The 1/4th Loyals then relieved 'B' in the centre, who moved into support at the *calvaire*. 'D' was also relieved by the Loyals and, in turn, relieved the 1/5th in the front line from Calvary Street to Liverpool Street—in what had been the right of their line on previous tours. 'A' Company on their right, in the front-line trenches of Clean Street to Liverpool Street, remained where they were. The situation continued quiet, the only casualty being 2Lt Alfred Broad from 'A', evacuated home after being wounded in the right forearm. The following day, two companies of 8/West Riding Regiment, who had just arrived in France, were attached to the battalion for training.

The 13th was another fairly quiet day, with just Cpl Thomas Peterson receiving a minor wound to the right hand and Sgt James Rundle wounded at duty. The calm did not last. When British artillery began a three-hour bombardment of German wire and front line at 5 p.m., the enemy retaliated with 77-mm, 4.2, and 5.9 against front and support lines, and though no casualties resulted, it was an uncomfortable time. At midnight, Lt Blackledge led twelve bombers forward to raid Sap-A; unable to gain an entrance, they bombed it, returning safely at 12.50 a.m.

Further operations simulating a major attack were allotted to 55 and 14 Division, beginning at 3 a.m. on 14 July. Divisional artillery was ordered to cut wire and fire a pre-attack bombardment shortly before Zero. To achieve this, they were allocated 36,000 rounds of ammunition for the guns, 1,000 rounds of 2-inch mortar ammunition, and an 'unlimited' supply of Stokes ammunition. Between 3 and 4 a.m., all Lewis gunners swept the tops of the enemy parapets during their morning 'stand-to'. A smoke screen was also scheduled—the responsibility of the 1/5th King's Own and to their right, 1/5th South Lancs in 166 Bde's 'G' Sector. Initially, all went well, with the enemy lining their parapet and opening rapid fire, but within minutes, the wind veered, blowing the smoke away to the north. German artillery retaliation was moderate and damage was slight.

Little hostile fire occurred on 15 July, until British 18-pounders and the TMB targeted enemy lines and the enemy replied against the battalion's positions with a few 77-mm and light mortar rounds, wounding Rfn George Massey—though his injuries were light.

Rfn Frank Rudd was also wounded in the left arm, but was attached to the TMB at the time and his injuries were accidental. At 11.30 p.m., Lt Blackledge led twenty bombers on another sally, this time to the right of the sunken Wailly–Ficheux road, though the attempt was abandoned when the clouds that had brought the earlier rain disappeared and bright moonlight exposed his group, making further progress futile.

At 8.30 p.m. on 16 July, 'B' made their way forward through the rain to relieve 'A' in Trenches 173–176 and 'C' left Brétencourt to relieve a company of the 1/7th in Trenches 180–183. Half of 'A' joined HQ at the *calvaire*, another platoon at Mill Post, the fourth in Wailly Keep. It must have been clear to all that their time in the sector was drawing to a close, as a reconnoitring party from 5/Dorsets arrived to learn the trenches.

There was a resurgence of activity from enemy *Minenwerfers* and *Granatenwerfers*—replied to with interest—and during the afternoon of 17 July, Sgt James Worthington was accidentally wounded at duty by the premature detonation of a rifle grenade, though he was the only casualty. It was also Sgt Henry Imlach's last day, as he departed for commissioning as a dentist. A brave and effective NCO, he had made substantial financial sacrifice. On 28 December 1915, two months after returning to the front after being wounded—when the battalion was in limbo as 'Army troops'—he wrote to his Company-Commander:

> I beg to apply for my discharge which is due on 31 March 1916. I have been in the battalion since November 1906. I will state the reason for wanting my discharge.
>
> Previous to the war I was in practice as a Dental Surgeon in Liverpool. Being a member of the battalion I was mobilised at the outbreak of war. Since then I've had to pay the rent and taxes on the house in which I carried out my practice. Up to now I've been able to meet the expenses, but now all my savings are gone.
>
> I applied for a dental commission, but have not been successful. I had hoped by that means to meet my expenses.
>
> If I got my discharge, I feel sure I should have more chance of success.[27]

The potential loss of such a good man eventually pushed the right buttons, though it is a pity the process took seven months. Shamefully, many patriotic officers and men faced financial ruin after abandoning successful businesses to help their country in its time of need.

On 18 July, 'C' was relieved and took over Trenches 167–172 from the Loyals; HQ and 'A' moved to Chancery Lane. On 19 July, there was considerably more hostile fire, mainly from 5.9s, though the majority was beyond the battalion's right bound, 100 shells hitting the north-eastern quadrant of Rivière. Some light shells landed around battalion positions and Rfn Albert Smith (122) was wounded in the left arm and evacuated home; he was the last casualty before the battalion departed.

At 1 p.m. on 20 July, after relief by the Dorsets, they relocated to Beaumetz. Leaving there at 9.10 p.m., they marched to Barly, via Gouy and Fosseux, arriving about midnight. Before the battalion next went into the line, another eight underage soldiers would be dispensed with, though two eventually returned. One other loss was Rfn William Jenkins, diagnosed with shellshock on 27 July, returning two months later.

Returned 'Underage', 21 July-4 August (and Month they Joined the Battalion)

Rfn Charles E. Evans	3777	April 16	Rfn Reginald E. Pritchard	3903	March 16
Rfn Charles H. Howard	3397	October 15	Rfn Henry Proudfoot	3766	March 16
Rfn Charles Lawrence	3894	March 16	Rfn Archibald Sides	241714	April 16
Rfn Richard Richardson	241373	March 16	Rfn James Edward Smith	241811	March 16
Mole*			* Mole travelled from Trinidad to enlist.		

At 7.10 a.m. on 21 July, the battalion began their long trek:

> At the end of the first day's march, it was a very tired battalion that cooled its feet in the meadow grass and running streams of Halloy, where some slept under canvas and others in the leaky huts which a platoon of 'C' Company had built in the previous winter. Thence we marched to Gézaincourt, where gloomy apprehensions of our fate began to seize upon those members of our battalion who had by this time received rumours of the inferno for which we were destined. From Gézaincourt we entrained, and after the usual dismal journey overnight, arrived at the railhead at Méricourt and slept in a field by the railway line. From Méricourt [on 30 July] we marched nearer the battle front to a small wood called Bois des Tailles.[28]

6

31 July 1916—29 September 1916: Steel Rain

Coordinates for this Chapter

165 Bde. L bound 8 Aug.	50°0′35.50″N
	2°49′37.30″E
165 Bde HQ (8 Aug)	49°59′8.30″N
	2°46′3.00″E
Angle Wood	49°59′50.40″N
	2°50′2.40″E
‘B’ Coy. Graves	50°3′55.20″N
	2°49′50.40″E
bivouacs (1 Aug)	49°58′33.70″N
	2°44′10.60″E
block in Cochrane Alley	50°0′5.80″N
	2°49′5.90″E
Briqueterie	50°0′6.90″N
	2°47′29.00″E
British/French boundary	50°0′1.20″N
	2°49′20.00″E
Brompton Road	50° 0′56.20″N
	2°49′18.30″E
Bronfay Farm	49°58′4.50″N
	2°44′34.10″E
Cambridge Copse	49°59′6.60″N
	2°46′26.50″E
Carlton Trench	50° 1′30.60″N
	2°47′16.40″E
Casement Trench	49°59′42.10″N
	2°47′21.90″E
Chesney Walk	50° 1′46.60″N
	2°47′50.90″E
Chimpanzee Trench	49°59′54.80″N
	2°48′14.80″E
Citadel, the	49°58′35.40″N
Cochrane Alley	2°42′59.30″E
	50°0′6.10″N
	2°49′4.30″E
Cox	50°3′10.60″N
	2°49′31.10″E
Doubtful Trench	50°0′18.70″N
	2°49′28.00″E
Dublin Redoubt	49°59′41.80″N
	2°47′58.70″E
Dublin Trench	49°59′50.50″N
	2°47′19.40″E
Duncan Alley	50°0′1.00″N
	2°48′24.20″E
Edwards Trench	50°0′3.20″N
	2°49′1.00″E
Factory Corner	50°3′42.50″N
	2°49′30.80″E
Falfemont Farm	50°0′11.70″N
	2°50′20.10″E
Flers Avenue	50°2′32.10″N
	2°49′32.50″E

Flers Trench	50°2′36.40″N 2°49′8.60″E	Oxford Copse	49°59′1.00″N 2°46′27.30″E
Fosse Way	50°2′33.40″N 2°49′40.30″E	Pommier Redoubt	50°0′43.30″N 2°45′16.30″E
Germans' Wood	49°59′38.00″N 2°47′12.80″E	Savoy Trench	50°1′33.20″N 2°47′35.70″E
Gird Support	50°3′34.40″N 2°50′7.60″E	Smoke Trench	50°3′13.70″N 2°49′34.90″E
Gird Trench	50°3′31.00″N 2°50′3.00″E	SP-1	49°59′59.00″N 2°49′20.70″E
Guillemont Station	50°0′57.90″N 2°49′9.00″E	SP-2	50°1′59.70″N 2°47′48.60″E
Hamilton Alley	50°0′31.30″N 2°48′38.20″E	SP-3	50°1′54.30″N 2°47′52.40″E
Jackson Trench	50°0′8.40″N 2°48′54.30″E	Stocker Alley	50°0′14.80″N 2°48′41.30″E
Machine-Gun Wood	49°59′14.80″N 2°46′47.30″E	sunken road	50°3′39.80″N 2°50′14.50″E
Maltz Horn Farm	50°0′6.90″N 2°47′29.00″E	Switch Trench	50°2′22.30″N 2°49′7.10″E
Maltz Horn Trench	50°0′4.50″N 2°48′27.50″E	Tea Trench	50°2′0.20″N 2°47′50.80″E
Montauban Alley	50°0′39.20″N 2°46′56.30″E	Waterlot Farm	50°1′14.50″N 2°48′50.00″E
new trench (for 8 Aug)	50°0′8.70″N 2°49′5.10″E	White Horse Alley	50°0′26.60″N 2°48′40.40″E
NW edge of Guedecourt	50°3′38.60″N 2°50′26.30″E	Wood Lane	50°2′6.50″N 2°47′41.00″E
Orchard Trench	50°1′53.80″N 2°47′47.60″E	Worcester Trench	50°1′57.90″N 2°47′42.70″E
Owens Trench	50°0′27.40″N 2°49′9.30″E	York Trench	50°1′17.00″N 2°47′24.80″E

On 31 July, the battalion moved to the Citadel, and next day, continued east to bivouacs 1,200 yards south-west of Caftet Wood, where they practised battalion attacks that evening. Attack training during mornings and evenings allowed some rest during the baking-hot afternoons, though two working parties were demanded overnight on 2–3 August. The first, fifty-strong, dug a communication trench, later named White Horse Alley, connecting Hamilton Alley to Stocker Alley. The second, 100-strong, carried supplies to the front line—rendezvousing in Death Valley, 400 yards east of the Briqueterie (one of several Death Valleys, this one led to the line near Maltz Horn Farm). Rfn Samuel Carter was wounded in the arm by shrapnel shortly before midnight, and in the early hours of 3 August, Rfn George Massey was hit in the hand; neither returned.

The rolling countryside of wide vistas favoured defence, and adjacent German strongholds provided mutual support and made an attack on any single position demanding. The line to the right of the division was held by the French; 700 yards to their front lay Guillemont, with Ginchy and Delville Wood to the north. The first attack against Guillemont, by 30 Division on 23 July, failed, as did a subsequent attempt a week later. On 8 August, 164 Bde would be on the left of the third attempt to take Guillemont, attacking the village itself, 165 Bde attacking to their right—the brigade bound, an east–west line through the end of the orchard at the southern extremity of the village. The 166th Bde would be held in reserve at the Citadel.

On 55 Division's left, 2 Division would also assault, from Waterlot Farm to Brompton Road, near to Guillemont Station. The enemy, determined to foil the obvious preparations, employed artillery with increasingly fierce intensity behind the lines, particularly during the hours of darkness. The numerous carrying parties, filing through Death Valley on their way forward, performed this miserable task under the threat of ever-impending annihilation.

Training continued throughout 3 August. There were no overnight working parties, though in the evening, six officers and the NCOs practised attacks at Bronfay Farm. The weather cooled on 4 August, to the relief of all. This was the last day in command for Lt-Col. Harrison; utterly worn out and suffering from severe and persistent bronchitis, he was hospitalised on 5 August and sent home. Command passed to Maj. Wainwright, with Capt. McKaig becoming 2IC.

On 5 August, the battalion left for support positions in Dublin and Casement Trench, HQ in Dublin Redoubt, on the western edge of Faviere Wood:

> As the mist of evening rose, the battalion wound its way down the long valley of Carnoy, thick with powdered dust and heavy with the smell of decaying horses. The order of march was: 'A' Company under Captain J. R. Trench; 'B' Company under Captain E. W. K. Bennet; 'C' Company under Captain W. A. Turner and 'D' Company under Captain E. C. G. Buckley. On either side, as we marched, massed batteries of guns flashed and roared deafeningly, and from time to time, shells burst close at hand. Through taking cover, the last platoon of 'D' Company was left behind and lost touch. Captain Buckley went back to find them, only to meet his death from a 5.9 shell bursting close by. Thus ended the career of a greatly-loved officer and as gallant a soldier as the 6th ever possessed.[1]

Twenty-seven-year-old Edmund Buckley, hit in the head by a shell splinter, died at the Aid Post shortly after midnight.

Another killed was twenty-six-year-old Rfn Sydney Young: 'D' also suffered four wounded—neither Rfn Arthur Kirby nor Cpl Thomas Anderson rejoining. 'B' had two wounded, Rfn Lawrence O'Dwyer's hand wound precluding further service with the battalion. The only 'A' Company casualty was Rfn Leonard Clark, though his shellshock was serious enough for evacuation home; 'C' got off the lightest, their only injury being Rfn George Ashley, whose leg was grazed leg by a shell splinter—he was not so fortunate a week later.

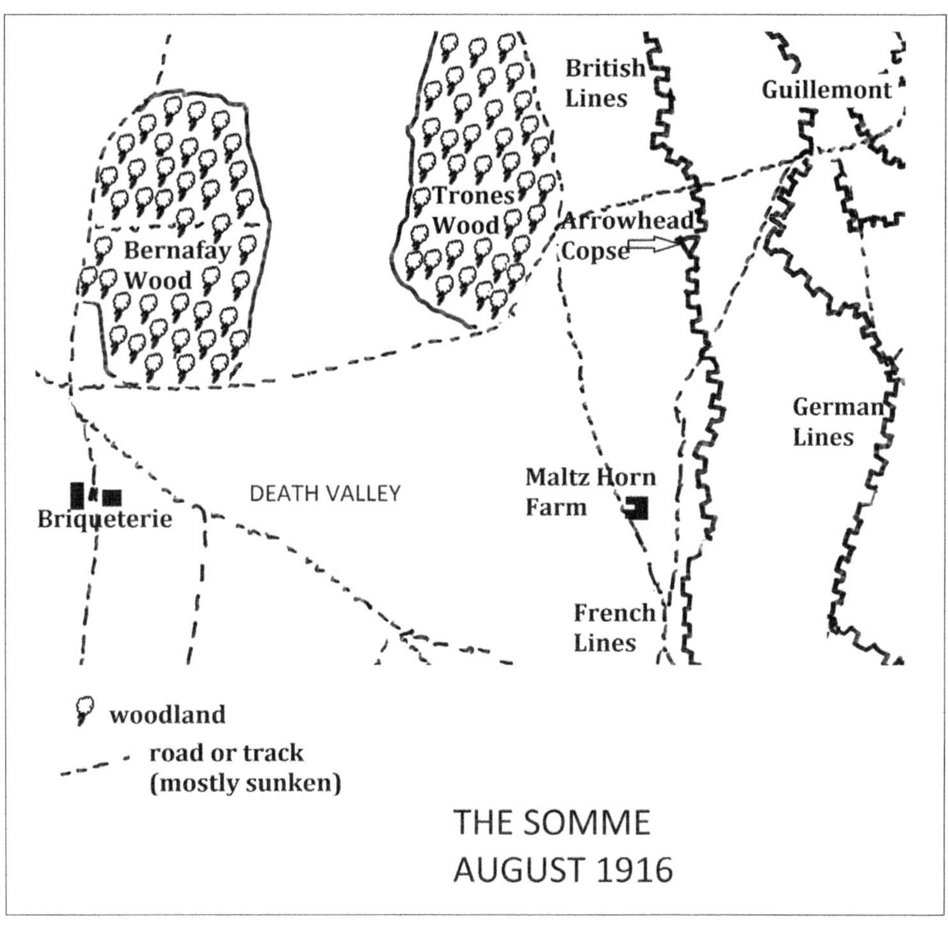

Throughout 6 August, German guns targeted Dublin and Casement Trenches. The only fatality was twenty-eight-year-old Rfn Ernest Barber, who died at the Aid Post later that day. Attached to 165 MGC, he had been manning a Vickers in the battalion's positions. Two Riflemen from 'A' also suffered shellshock: Alfred Brownrigg remained on duty after treatment, though Albert Culverwell was evacuated home. Blackledge's description conjures up a vision of Hell:

> Many of the ranks were occupying nothing more secure than weatherproof shelters of corrugated iron in the old German trenches; and even those who occupied dugouts felt insecure, for the doors faced the direction from which shells came, and the burial of all was possible. And many shells did come, for the German maps had their dugouts placed with precision. Though only on the edge of the battle, the memory of the place sickens. To the right front was the hill of Maltz Horn Farm; on the left and behind us was Montauban with Bernafay Wood in the near foreground, and Trones Wood beyond. In front stretched the yellow desert of Death Valley, a spouting fountain of shells and earth. All around were corpses mummified by the heat or festering foully in the sun.[2]

That night, Capt. Trench took 'A' to dig assembly trenches to the rear of the support line; happily, all returned safely. During the day of 7 August, Dublin and Casement Trenches came under intense bombardment and casualties were substantial. Nine were killed, or died of wounds the same day, and twenty-two-year-old Rfn Fred Foulkes succumbed later. Forty men were wounded and 2Lt Harold Jerrett and Capt. Bennet were evacuated home with shellshock. Second-Lieutenant Harold St George, wounded at duty, was living on borrowed time. The diary records one man missing, Rfn E. Clark, erroneously entered as such; he was wounded in the back and evacuated home. Only one of those killed on 7 August does not have a marked grave: twenty-one-year-old Rfn Brian McBeath is only 'believed to be buried' in Guillemont Road Cemetery, his grave marker lost—though the other six are all in Peronne Road Cemetery. Shamefully, his was another case of valuables stolen during their journey home, as his father angrily corresponded on 15 December:

> Among other things taken from his body before burial were a gold ring, wrist watch, silver cigarette case, field glasses, besides articles of a lesser value than these and it seems strange that none of these are forthcoming or accounted for. It was not their value that concerned me so much, but I and his family would like to have had them as a memento of one who has died for his King and county.[3]

The battalion also lost the services of Rfn Charles Alcock (044), when he was returned to base as underage.

That evening 'A', 'B', and 'C', and one officer and forty men from 'D', snaked through Death Valley to Maltz Horn Trench, as close support for the 1/5th. They were placed under the command of the CO of the 1/5th, Lt-Col. Shute, who was joined in his HQ at the junction of Maltz Horn Trench and Duncan Alley by Capt. McKaig as liaison-officer. For Capt. Turner's 'C' Company, the 'D' Company detail, and Lt Blackledge with his twelve bombers, a perilous task awaited.

At 3.30 a.m. that morning, Brig.-Gen. Duncan and Lt-Col. Shute had met with the French officers, who were to lead a simultaneous French attack against Maurepas on their right. The French, concerned the British advance would veer right, across their line of advance, asked for a jumping-off trench to be dug to the immediate left of Cochrane Alley, near the junction of British and French lines. Stretching off for 300 yards at a 45-degree angle, it compelled the British advance to diverge left. Duncan allocated this task to the 1/6th ('new trench for 8 Aug.' in Coordinates Table).

Lt Thomas Rome and the other forty men from 'D' remained in Dublin Redoubt as runners; a similar party from the 1/7th was positioned south-west of Germans' Wood. Planners included every method of communication possible, though conditions routinely thwarted their efforts: spotting aircraft tried to track progress, with attackers wearing a tin triangle on their backs to help observers distinguish them; flag or light signals were frequently obscured by mist, smoke, and dust—flares and rockets likewise—or the men tasked with sending them had become casualties; telephone wires were cut; and pigeons got lost or were killed. A relay system of runners was by far the most reliable method, though slow and expensive in lives.

A strict route for runners was imposed between the Shute's HQ and Brigade HQ—all having to familiarise themselves with this by day and night. Leaving the 1/5th, they travelled down Chimpanzee Trench to Dublin Redoubt, then along Casement Trench to the Briqueterie-Maricourt Road. From here, they followed the road to the Field Ambulance Collecting Post, thence by a track running 200 yards south-west of Germans' Wood. After passing 100 yards south-west of Machine-Gun Wood, they steered directly between Cambridge and Oxford Copses, before curving back north-west to Brigade HQ.[4] It was not the most direct route, but offered the most cover. Rome's detachment remained on this duty until 13 August, when the battalion was relieved. Unfortunately, it is not possible to differentiate runner casualties from those at the front. Additionally, a wireless station was established in Chimpanzee Trench and seven visual stations distributed across the brigade front.

Due to congestion in the narrow communication trenches, the battalion—laden with supplies for the attack-dumps—arrived later than expected in Maltz Horn Trench. Capt. Turner and his men were immediately sent off to dig. At 12.45 a.m. on 8 August, McKaig became concerned that the rest of his men, ferrying supplies between the dump near Shute's HQ and the forward line, would not have enough time to reach their assembly trench if they were tasked with another journey. Although concurring, Shute decreed they collect another load, take this directly to their assembly trench, and wait until the 1/5th went over the top before occupying the front line. Here, they would wait in support for the 1/5th, already loaded up with the material.[5]

German artillery continued to target front and rear throughout the night, and the digging party, covered by a screen of Blackledge's bombers, excavated furiously while enemy shells exploded all around. One round wounded Capt. Turner, who was fortunate to survive: a large piece of shell casing struck his helmet, which absorbed much of the impact, though it still penetrated to wound him on the head and another cut close to one eye; unconscious, he was stretchered off and evacuated home, receiving a MiD for his work.[6] The digging completed, 'C', now under Lt Oliver, returned to Maltz Horn Trench; the bombers, whose previous orders had dictated a return to Dublin Redoubt, were held at Shute's HQ as a precaution.

The attack began at 4.20 a.m., and at 4.45 a.m., Lt-Col. Shute handed McKaig written orders to take the battalion forward. Shute had heard nothing about the progress of his attacking troops by 5 .25 a.m., though a minute later, a message from one of his companies indicated that they were delayed by enemy bombers and machine guns. Shute ordered McKaig to personally move up to usher forward his two support companies ('A' and 'B') and organise them to hold against enemy counterattack:[7]

> The morning was misty, the air alive, waist high, with hissing machine-gun bullets and the ground rocked with the German shells, which played on our trenches as though on a vast piano. Under such circumstances it can well be imagined that the advance from the support to the front line involved grave casualties and the loss of many valuable lives of both officers and men. Wandering in that haze of death, over broken ground never before seen in daylight, the troops welcomed the magnificent example of courage and

> coolness that was given them by Captain J. B. McKaig. One writer remembers seeing him coming forward through the dawn, quite by himself, with a cane under his arm and a stiff parade walk; and well recollects how the sight of him daring the open brought all the men from cover, and encouraged them to go forward.[8]

'A' and 'B' occupied Edwards Trench and 'C' occupied the old German front line (Jackson Trench).

Shute's concern was justified. In his 4.30 a.m. report, he wrote: 'From one's own judgement of sound, our artillery support did not seem as intense as anticipated—but this may not really have been the case.'[9] The Divisional Artillery, who had been so effective in earlier months, had received no replacement guns and those still in action were worn out, many rounds missing their targets. The barrage maps indicate that most of the heavy artillery was directed against Guillemont itself, and against a line from Guillemont–Falfemont Farm, well forward of 165 Bde's initial objectives.[10]

On the left, 164 Bde fared worse. The 1/4th KORL encountered a strongly-held line of defence in a sunken lane, just 200 yards forward of their jumping-off positions, again not targeted by the initial barrage. They were prevented from reaching this by a double line of barbed wire, erected by the German defenders during the night. While waiting in their jumping-off positions, they had sustained numerous casualties from British guns, aimed at enemy positions 600 yards forward of where the shells actually fell. When they attacked, they were scythed down by artillery, rifle, and machine-gun fire. To their left, Liverpool Irish penetrated Guillemont, but with their right flank open and numerous Germans popping up behind them from deep dugouts with multiple exits, they were surrounded. Virtually the entire force was killed or captured, only two men managing to make their way back (three companies of 1/KLR—attacking to the left of the Liverpool Irish—shared a similar fate).

The 1/5th was the only battalion to make sustainable progress, but paid dearly for their courage. Blackledge's bombers went forward with the rest of the battalion, but on hearing the sound of bombing from Cochrane Alley, hurried there. Cochrane Alley was a half-completed communication trench, connecting the old German line in front of Maltz Horn Farm to the current German line. Once he made contact with the bombers from the 1/5th, Blackledge learned their officer was dead, so he amalgamated both groups under his command. The bombers from the 1/5th were under orders to establish a block in Cochrane Alley and a party of Sappers, led by a corporal, were sent to create this with explosives. The corporal was killed on the way forward, but Sapper Binns took over and led his demolition party into Cochrane Alley, where the Bombing-Sergeant of the 1/5th pointed out where the block was to be blown, 40 yards forward of the trench line captured by the 1/5th. By this stage, Blackledge's bombers were reduced to just five men, but stubbornly clung to this block. The area around Cochrane Alley was a shambles, the torn earth littered with corpses and body parts—some weeks old, others more recent, all blackened by the sun; squadrons of flies feasted on the bloated corpses and the stench was overpowering. In the broad daylight, attempts by runners to report progress proved suicidal, with snipers taking a deadly toll of any trying to cross the many gaps blasted into Cochrane Alley.

While McKaig organised his defences, the survivors of the 1/5th consolidated. A telephone wire was laid to the advanced line, and although Shute was in touch with Capt. Owen, he was having difficulty in accurately determining the exact position of the left of the advance—vital information if the divisional artillery was to provide fire support. Owen was ordered to fix a rifle vertically in the extreme left shell hole, so Shute could take a compass bearing, but the CO was unable to see it. The problem was solved when he arranged for an aircraft to fly over and spot Owen's position at 12.30 p.m. (later known as Owens Trench).

Although Cochrane Alley was perilous for Blackledge's bombers, it was possibly worse for 'A' and 'B' in Edwards Trench; they were subjected to a continuous and accurate bombardment by German Howitzers, who knew the precise range of their former position:

> Those who endured the shelling will never forget the horrible metallic ring which characterised the bursting of 5.9 shells in the hard ground; a sound that would start perhaps a hundred yards down a trench, and advance slowly, traverse by traverse, as the methodical enemy blotted out platoon after platoon—till it was your turn next![11]

Second-Lieutenant Reginald Boult and one man were killed by these shells, another four later dying from wounds; in addition, sixteen were wounded.

'B' Company CSM Clem Tanner was an unequivocal pillar of strength: as a storm of red-hot steel sliced through their positions, he calmly moved up and down the trench, encouraging and reassuring, organising the digging-out of buried men, and supervising the repair of the defences. His great personal example restored the confidence of the shaken men.[12] Among the wounded was Capt. William Davidson, OC of 165 TMB, who had brought his mortars forward, though they had not been used in the attack. The wound in his right elbow was treated back in England. After leaving hospital, he returned to the battalion as a second-lieutenant, having relinquished his temporary rank.

During the day of 8 August, Shute was informed that his left companies would be relieved after dark by two companies of the 1/7th and his right by two companies from the 1/6th. Although the right was reconnoitred by the 1/6th between 8.30 and 9 p.m., the relief never occurred, much to Shute's fury. The Divisional Narrative records just one company of the 1/6th being ordered to relieve the 1/5th during the morning of 9 August, which was carried out as instructed.[13] The failure to relieve is probably connected to the two-page, seventeen-point, hand-written message sent to Shute by Brig.-Gen. Duncan at 5.30 p.m., which contradicts Shute's expectation of a relief by the 1/6th. 'Point-3' of the same message informed Shute that his battalion would be relieved by 'Bert' (1/7th). 'Point-4' dictated that 'Willie [1/6th] to remain about where he is'.[14]

This message also ordered companies from the 1/7th and 1/6th to continue the attack at 4.20 a.m. on 9 August. Shortly after midnight, Capt. Trench was ordered to take 'A' forward and dig a connecting trench from Edwards Trench to Owens Trench. The angle

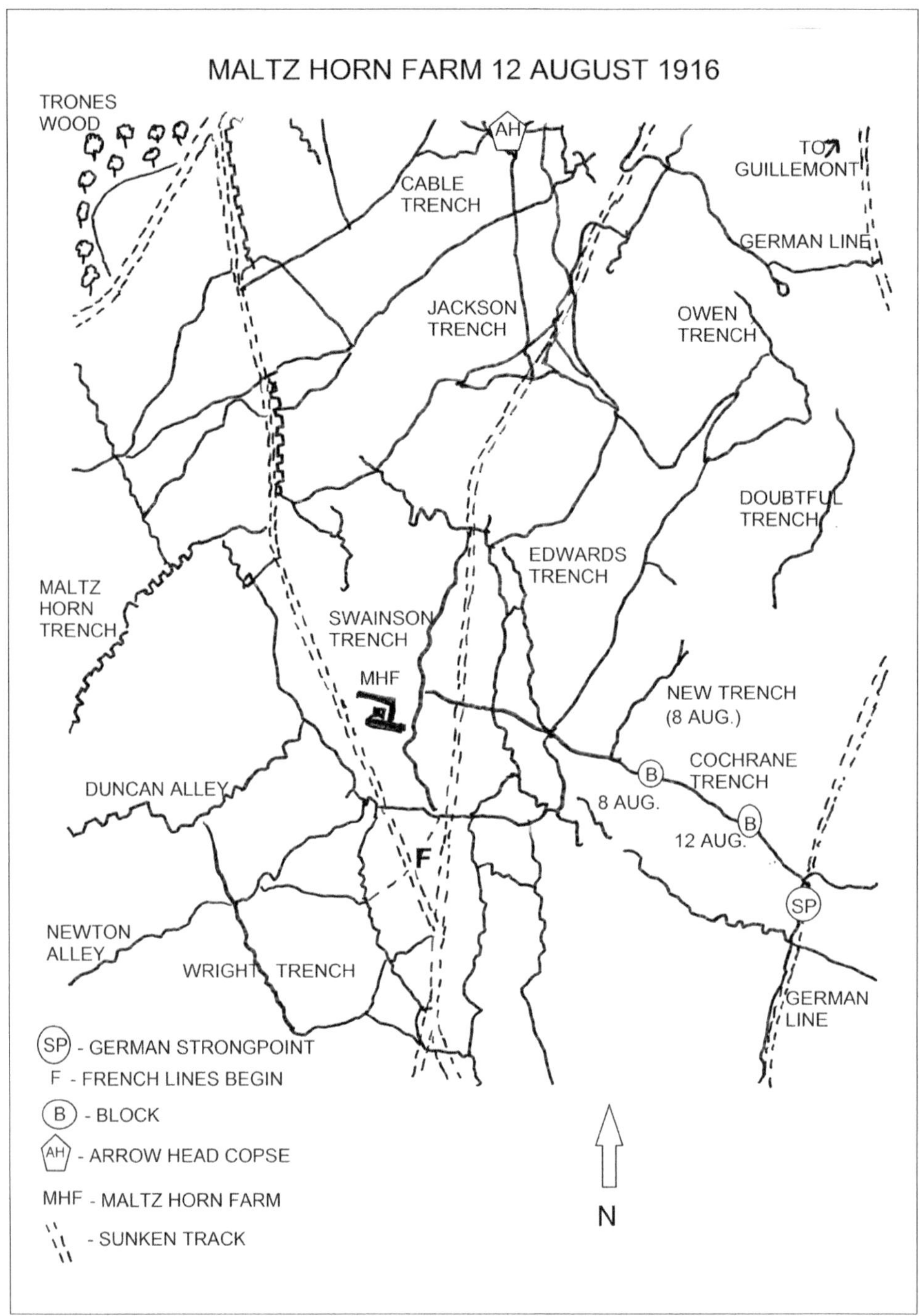
MALTZ HORN FARM 12 AUGUST 1916
TRONES WOOD
AH
TO GUILLEMONT
CABLE TRENCH
GERMAN LINE
JACKSON TRENCH
OWEN TRENCH
DOUBTFUL TRENCH
EDWARDS TRENCH
MALTZ HORN TRENCH
SWAINSON TRENCH
MHF
NEW TRENCH (8 AUG.)
COCHRANE TRENCH
B
8 AUG.
B
12 AUG.
DUNCAN ALLEY
F
SP
NEWTON ALLEY
WRIGHT TRENCH
GERMAN LINE
SP - GERMAN STRONGPOINT
F - FRENCH LINES BEGIN
B - BLOCK
AH - ARROW HEAD COPSE
MHF - MALTZ HORN FARM
- SUNKEN TRACK
N

of this excavation brought them under intense, close-range enfilading fire: Capt. Trench was shot in the left leg; 2Lt Francis Bacon in the abdomen; and Riflemen Charles Castle and Harold Porter were killed. Before the attempt was abandoned, another seventeen were wounded. The attached men from 'D', also part of this detail, did not escape: twenty-two-year-old Rfn Charles Oddy was killed outright; L/Cpl William Bolton—also aged twenty-two—died from his head wound on the 15th; and thirty-year-old married man Rfn Albert Brown (513) succumbed to his hand and leg wounds later that day—a further six were wounded.

Shute's report highlights the confusion prior to this attack:

> The CO's of two battalions [1/7th and 1/9th] and a representative of a third [Capt. McKaig] all arrived at BHQ on the ridge under the impression that these were their Batt. HQ; all seemed in doubt as to their proper location. Explained position as I knew it to them and they 'went out into the night' and moved along to the left [up Maltz Horn Trench] and were lost to sight. During these hours, continuous movements of troops of all kinds up and over the Maltz Horn Ridge, many of whom gave evidence of indecision as to direction and location. Confusion accentuated by the blocking of trenches by working parties, stretcher-bearer parties evacuating wounded, small parties of relieved troops and larger parties of 7th Liverpool going up to relieve or to old front line.
>
> As it got later, about 3 a.m., and still there were troops passing my late Headquarters on the way to the front line, knowing the distance and the difficulties of their traversing that distance, especially under and through an enemy barrage, I called up the Brigade on telephone to ask if the attack at 4.20 a.m. was 'seriously intended' to take place. On being told it was to take place, I formally registered my opinion that the attack had not the slightest possibility of success, unless by an absolute miracle, as many of the troops would barely arrive (if they did arrive) before the exact moment of going over the top, and that such proceeding precluded all idea of any success.[15]

Considering that the enemy routinely eavesdropped on British telephone messages, one has to hope that Shute did not actually announce details about the forthcoming attack over the telephone.

It was not until 6 a.m. that 'C' relieved the 1/5th. As for the attack, the entry in the 1/7th's diary consists of just five words: 'small attack on German trenches'.[16] The Divisional Narrative reported:

> The 7th Liverpool Regiment who probably were somewhat late in starting the attack were prevented from obtaining their objective by heavy machine-gun fire and were obliged to reoccupy their front line of trenches.[17]

No sources recount if the 1/6th also attacked—it is pretty certain they did not.

All day, heavy fire pounded the support trenches, though 'C' in the advanced line got off the lightest: three men suffered shellshock and twenty-four-year-old LCpl Francis Baines was very seriously wounded in the left arm and sustained a compound fracture of the left leg. A resulting infection proved fatal, and he died twelve days later.

'B' lost fifteen wounded and twenty-four-year-old Rfn John Findlow killed. Once again, CSM Tanner displayed utter disregard for his own safety, striding up and down the trench, attending to the wounded, and freeing buried men. Cpl Stephen Bottrill, evacuated to England with shellshock, was unaware that he had been recommended for a MM for his sterling work in the nerve-wracking job as 'listener' while attached to the tunnelling company at Maricourt. The award was gazetted in November, but he never returned. Another who failed to rejoin was Rfn John Colley, who had suffered a minor back wound. While, at 24 IBD, he was discovered underage and sent home.

After dark, 2Lt Adam and the balance of the battalion's bombers made their way forward to reinforce Lt Blackledge in Cochrane Alley.

During the morning of 10 August, 'A' and their attached personnel from 'D' were withdrawn to Dublin Trench; 'C' remained in the advanced trench, and 'B' in support in Edwards Trench—they and the bombers under the command of the 1/7th. 'A' Company's withdrawal did not prevent losses, as two men were wounded and two killed—both only twenty-one-years of age. Cpl John Plumer had only been with the battalion for ten days; the other, L/Cpl Laurence Cockburn, was the brother of Stanley Cockburn, who had been wounded on the 7th.

The forward companies did not escape the fire, though 'C' again fared the best, with just two wounded. Most fell on 'B' Company's positions, killing Rfn Thomas Fisher and twenty-year-old John Davies. Fisher had been on attachment to the 1/9th and had only returned four days earlier. Ten men and 2Lt Rothwell were wounded—the latter remaining on duty after his wound was dressed. The only known casualty from the bombers was 2Lt Adam, with a shrapnel wound to his left knee.

Early on 11 August, HQ advanced to Maltz Horn Trench and Capt. McKaig brought 'A' and 'D' up to the front line, relieving 'C', who went into close support in Edwards Trench; 'B' was withdrawn to Dublin Trench. Additionally, 'A' Company of the 1/9th was put under Maj. Wainwright's control and placed immediately behind Edwards Trench. The bombers were finally relieved by the bombers of the 1/9th and an additional company from that battalion were placed at Maj. Wainwright's disposal in Casement Trench. The reason for the new dispositions was a proposed attack for that afternoon. The 306th French Infantry Bde planned to attack the ravine between Maltz Horn Farm and Angle Wood, and the Rifles were to facilitate this. The battalion's objective was to be a German strongpoint at the end of Cochrane Alley (SP-1 in the Coordinates Table), then entrench 300 yards of the Hardecourt–Guillemont road, towards Guillemont.

Enemy guns continued to seek out targets during the morning, with one shell next to the Aid Post killing the twenty-six-year-old Canadian MO Lt Laurence 'Chick' Evans. At 3.45 p.m., just forty-five minutes before zero, the attack was called off due to a change of French plans. German shelling of the front line was augmented by British guns during the afternoon, as a curt signal from Lt-Col. Marriott to Brigade, timed at 4.20 p.m., indicated:

> Situation report fairly quiet but our front lines have been continuously shelled by our own heavy and light guns. Wind west.[18] [Marriott elaborated in a later, written communication.] Each company in turn has repeatedly reported that out own heavy and light shells were falling on our own lines. It appears to us that an improvement in the system of FOOs would save this unnecessary waste of life and ammunition. It is difficult to prevent demoralisation of troops under such awkward circumstances. The artillery apparently fail to realise that we are constantly trying to move forward.[19]

The situation improved on 13 August—only one of Marriott's companies came under 'friendly' fire that day.[20]

In the evening of 11 August, most of the battalion was withdrawn to Dublin and Casement Trenches, except 'D', who remained in the front line—though, after dark, Lt Ernest Herschell took 100 men to dig communication trenches in the forward area. Apart from the MO, the only fatality on 11 August was twenty-one-year-old Rfn Robert Jones (230), though twenty-two were wounded, four of whom were underage—a detail that, as yet, remained undiscovered.

At 1.15 a.m. on 12 August, word was received that the attack postponed the previous day would go ahead at 5.15 p.m.[21] It was now to be prosecuted by the 1/9th, who had relieved the 1/7th during the night, the latter moving back to Maltz Horn Trench. The 1/5th was to be in support for the 1/9th and the 1/6th was to move into brigade support, between Talus Boise and Cambridge Copse. As the battalion prepared to leave for Talus Boise, the enemy commenced a heavy bombardment on their positions, delaying their departure until 7.30 a.m., though they arrived at their new location without loss from the journey. The bombardment of Dublin Trench resulted in just one casualty: twenty-four-year-old Rfn Edgar Parrington from 'C'. Posted as missing, Parrington's body was never identified. 'D' was not relieved until much later that morning, reaching the reserve area safely around noon.

When the attack began, German artillery immediately targeted the rear, rounds falling on the battalion at Talus Boise, wounding five. The most seriously injured was CSM Tanner, whose wounds to his left side and buttock left him semi-crippled—a huge loss. The same shell wounded Rfn Thomas Pulford in the right side and 'B' Company CQMS Robert Hull in the hand, though his injury was minor and he remained on duty. Sgt Arthur Robinson from 'C' was wounded in the face and left leg, only returning in November 1917. The last casualty was Rfn Francis Wright of 'A', hospitalised with shellshock.

The attack itself, although initially promising, resulted in little gain. Both assaulting companies of the 1/9th attacked in two waves across 400 yards of open ground and were met close to their objective by the enemy. Fierce hand-to-hand fighting ensued and the men from Liverpool, emerging triumphant, began to consolidate. Unfortunately, the French failed to seize Maltz Horn Ravine and the 1/9th found themselves outflanked and suffering increasingly heavy casualties from enfilading fire. Despite reinforcement, it became clear that their shell-hole positions were untenable and they withdrew. An equally determined struggle had seized all of Cochrane Alley: when the bombers eventually reached the road, they found that the trench was completely flattened out for the last few hundred yards and indefensible; consequently, they retired westwards until the trench was deep enough to provide cover, where they built a block. This was the only gain held.

The 1/6th's role in a subsequent attack, at 4.30 a.m. on 13 August, is omitted from brigade and divisional narratives. At 8 p.m. on 12 August, orders reached Talus Boise for two companies to hurry up to Maltz Horn Trench to come under Lt-Col. Marriott's command—the 1/7th occupying the front line while the attack was underway. Shortly afterwards, these orders were amended to just one company, and Lt Oliver brought 'C' forward. At 11 p.m., the 1/7th were relieved by the 1/5th South Lancs, though 'C' remained with the relieving battalion. At 4.30 a.m., 'C', accompanied by 'D' Company of the South Lancs, attacked Doubtful Trench and were met by intense machine-gun fire and a barrage of bombs. Second-Lieutenant Harold St George was seen to fall and Lt Oliver wounded in the head and right shoulder. All attempts to fight their way into the trench failed and both companies retired, with 'C' leaving behind eight dead. Thirty-two-year-old L/Cpl Innes Elden died from his wounds on 15 August and another twenty-four were wounded. The survivors did an astounding job to recover all but two of their wounded, the only exceptions being Sgt Wilfred Lewis and Rfn Thomas Whalley, who were both taken prisoner. The only fatality with a known grave is 2Lt St George, his body buried weeks later by another unit, just 15 yards short of Doubtful Trench.

There are no Operation Orders for this attack, though it is clear from Lt-Col. Marriott's correspondence of 13 August that instructions originated at Brigade:[22]

> The receipt of aeroplane map showing location of Doubtful Trench confirmed various reports of the proximity of the enemy to our front lines and on receipt of orders to consolidate this trench, I emphasised my disbelief to you of airman's statement that this trench was unoccupied. I confirmed this by patrols, and on your order made my dispositions for attacking it. The situation and state of affairs in the trenches and the disorganisation on my right rendered the assembly of troops in their positions for attack very difficult, more so as we were in the middle of a relief, and under the circumstances, the preparation was insufficient. I ought to have stopped the relief and held these troops of 'Walter' [1/5th South Lancs] for the attack. One company of 'Willie' arrived and led the attack. The trench was fully occupied and the attack beaten back. I suggest, as a means of taking this trench, which would be very useful to us, that the troops occupying the front line be withdrawn and the Doubtful Trench dealt with by our own artillery. It is probable that the enemy would vacate the trench and it would be occupied by our own men.

Lt Oliver was awarded the MC for his work as company-commander, and the courage of others was also recognised by awards. CSM Tanner received a long-overdue MM, and RSM William Butler a MiD for his unfailing efforts to get rations and supplies forward through daunting shellfire. The survivors of 'C' rejoined the rest of the battalion at 10 a.m., and at 11 a.m., orders were received to move to Transport Lines, 1,000 yards east of the Citadel.

On 14 August, 'A' and 'B' were sent forward on salvage work, and fifty men from 'D' were employed on the distressing task of burial detail. The balance of the battalion marched west, into billets at Ville-sur-Ancre, joined there at 10 a.m. on 15 August by the others. At 6 p.m., they were inspected by Maj.-Gen. Jeudwine, who expressed his thanks for their work over the preceding fortnight.

When the battalion left their bivouacs on 1 August, their fighting strength was 720 all ranks. The diary records a total of 207 officers and men killed, wounded, or missing between 2 and 13 August, though this fails to paint the full picture, with the Casualties Book detailing 235 for this period. Some of the wounded returned to duty, others never regained their fitness. For some of those with shellshock, their return to duty was rapid; for example, Rfn Matthew Baker of 'C' returned the same day—for others, recovery took years. The battalion escaped lightly compared to some, Liverpool Irish enduring 580 casualties on 8 August alone. Divisional casualties were 3,288 between 2 and 13 August.[23]

Casualties, 2-13 August 1916

Name	Number	Status
Rfn H. Abbey	2407	WIA: 13/8
2Lt Emmanuel Christo M. Adam		WIA: 10/8
Rfn Vivian Maunder Adams	241625	WIA: 13/8
Cpl Thomas John Anderson	240401	WIA: 5/8
Rfn Robert Henry Argue	4154	SS: 9/8
Rfn George K. Ashley*	241412	WIA: 13/8
2Lt Francis Harold Bacon		WIA: 9/8
L/Cpl Francis Slater Baines	1869	DOW: 21/8
Rfn Matthew Baker	241645	SS: 11/8
Rfn Walter Sanders Baker	2392	KIA: 8/8
Rfn Thomas Samuel Ball	241086	WIA: 7/8
Rfn Wilfred Ball	241639	SS: 7/8
Rfn William Ball	241703	WIA: 9/8
Rfn George Balmer	204776	WIA: 8/8
Rfn Ernest Alfred Barber	2037	DOW: 6/8
Rfn Frederick James Barker	241456	KIA: 13/8
Rfn Donald Bates	241660	WIA: 10/8
Capt. Ernest William K. Bennet		SS: 7/8
Rfn George Finch Bibby	240215	WIA: 9/8
Rfn William James Blundell	241815	KIA: 13/8
Rfn John Blyde	240682	WIA: 13/8
L/Cpl William Bolton	2390	DOW: 15/8
Cpl Stephen Noel Bottrill	240524	SS: 9/8
2Lt Reginald Herbert S. Boult		KIA: 8/8
Rfn Wilfred Bernard Bowden	240140	WIA: 8/8
A/Cpl Harold Bretherick	240865	WIA: 13/8
Rfn Francis Xavier Brierton	3557	DOW: 14/8
Sgt Egbert Briggs	1863	KIA: 7/8
Rfn Albert Howard Brown	3513	DOW: 9/8
Rfn Alfred Thomas Brownrigg	240784	SS: 6/8
Rfn James William Brundell	241032	WIA: 8/8
Capt. Edmund Cecil G. Buckley		DOW: 6/8
Rfn John Edwards Burke	240683	SS: 7/8
Sgt Albert Gordon Cadman	240289	SS: 9/8
L/Cpl Thomas Proctor Carr	240125	WIA: 11/8
Rfn Samuel Joseph Carter	241643	WIA: 2/8
Rfn Charles Castle	4424	KIA: 9/8
Rfn James Edward Caunce	4309	SS: 11/8
Rfn George Charles	241001	WIA: 11/8
Rfn Samuel James Cheers	241682	WIA: 7/8
Rfn E. B. Clark	3749	WIA: 7/8
Rfn Leonard Clark	241920	WIA: 5/8
Rfn Peter Clarke	241816	SS: 11/8
Rfn Harold Joseph Claussen	241222	SS: 9/8

Rfn James Clayton	241665	WIA: 9/8
L/Cpl Stanley George Cockburn	1470	WAD: 7/8
L/Cpl Laurence B. Cockburn	1469	KIA: 10/8
Rfn John Colley	3955	WIA: 9/8
L/Cpl Norman J. Cornish	1961	WIA: 11/8
Rfn David Courtie	241616	WIA: 7/8
L/Cpl Richard Innes Cowan	240477	WIA: 9/8
Rfn Thomas Roderick Craig	241024	WIA: 10/8
Rfn John Crebbin	240419	WIA: 7/8
Rfn James O. Cross	4635	WIA: 11/8
Rfn Albert B. Culverwell	3452	SS: 6/8
L/Cpl Robert Curwen	2063	DOW: 8/8
Capt. William Henry H. Davidson		WIA: 8/8
Rfn Arthur Davies	241085	WAD: 7/8
Rfn Harold Davies	241421	WIA: 7/8
Rfn John Glynn Davies	3366	KIA: 10/8
Rfn Joseph Albert Dawson	241320	WIA: 13/8
Rfn Leslie Grierson De Valve	240231	SS: 7/8
Rfn Eric Victor Dean	240984	SS: 7/8
Rfn Alfred Dixon	240635	WIA: 13/8
Rfn Harry Doran	3804	WIA: 7/8
Sgt Hugh Stanhope Elliott	240091	WIA: 7/8
Rfn Charles H. Ellison	241671	SS: 9/8
Rfn Robert Emmett	241793	WIA: 13/8
Rfn Charles Oswald Evans	240463	WAD: 9/8
L/Cpl Francis Gleave Evans	240291	WIA: 7/8
Rfn Frank Arthur Evans	240325	SS: 9/8
Rfn Harry E. V. Evans	241808	WIA: 7/8
Rfn Robert Francis Evans	241970	SS: 10/8
Lt William Laurence Evans (RAMC)		KIA: 11/8
Rfn Paul Farrell	240843	WIA: 13/8
Sgt John Gunning Fazakerley	240101	WIA: 9/8
Cpl Charles Henry Ferguson	240571	KIA: 13/8
Rfn John Walter Findlow	3769	KIA: 9/8
Rfn Thomas Fisher	241908	KIA: 10/8
Rfn George Fletcher	240798	SS: 10/8
Rfn William Frank Ford	240809	WIA: 7/8
Rfn Fred Foulkes	1587	DOW: 18/8
Rfn Edward Geldard	3883	SS: 7/8
Rfn Alexander Gibson	2937	SS: 7/8
Rfn Gerald F. Goodwin	240931	WIA: 9/8
Rfn William Grainger	3446	WIA: 13/8
Rfn John Henry Green	241437	SS: 11/8
Rfn William Griffiths	4494	WIA: 10/8
Rfn James Grogan	241860	SS: 7/8
Rfn Sydney Guilbert***	3666	KIA: 9/8
Rfn Robert H. Hall	3506	WIA: 8/8
Sgt Herbert R. Harraden	1843	WIA: 10/8
Rfn John Hart	4069	WIA: 7/8
Rfn Edward Bromilow Heaton	241742	SS: 7/8
L/Cpl Arthur Newey Henderson	2895	DOW: 9/8
Rfn Paul Henri	241676	SS: 7/8
Rfn Norman George Hill	241362	KIA: 13/8
Rfn Thomas Hill	241423	WIA: 5/8
Rfn Reuben Hoose****	241362	KIA: 13/8
Rfn Alfred Hughes	240953	SS: 9/8
Rfn Frederick Tibbot Hughes	4277	KIA: 7/8
Rfn George Hughes	3984	WIA: 8/8
Rfn Thomas Henry Hughes	241837	WIA: 13/8
Sgt Robert Joseph Hull	240033	WAD: 12/8
Sgt Morris Humphreys	240295	WAD: 7/8
Rfn Harry Hyman	4572	SS: 9/8
L/Cpl Innes Elden Irwin	3468	DOW: 15/8
L/Cpl Charles Jackson	240653	WIA: 11/8
Rfn John Francis Jenkins	240288	SS: 11/8
2Lt Harold Jerrett		SS: 7/8
Rfn Ellis Jevons	4351	KIA: 7/8
Rfn Albert Johnson	242008	SS: 11/8
Rfn Arthur S. Johnson	242014	WIA: 7/8
Rfn Hugh Charles Johnson	241733	WIA: 9/8
A/Cpl Percival Thomas Johnson	240167	WIA: 13/8
Rfn Deiniol Gwynedd Jones	241902	WIA: 13/8
Rfn Ernest Jones	4603	KIA: 7/8
Rfn Griffith Parry Jones	241593	WIA: 11/8
Rfn Robert Lloyd Jones	1230	KIA: 11/8
Rfn Thomas Edward Jones	240744	WIA: 9/8
Rfn James Henry Kent	2337	WIA: 9/8
Rfn Richard Henry Kent	240404	WIA: 9/8

Rfn William Y. Kenyon	240825	WIA: 10/8
Rfn John Hamilton Kerr	241139	WIA: 8/8
Rfn Arthur Kirby	4213	WIA: 5/8
Rfn Henry Kirkland	4051	WIA: 10/8
Rfn Francis Henry Kitson	1745	WIA: 9/8
Sgt Wilfred Lewis	240023	WIA: 13/8
Rfn Richard Lloyd	241792	WIA: 9/8
Rfn Robert W. Longworth	3393	WIA: 11/8
Sgt Norman Percy Maggi	240092	SS: 11/8
Rfn Albert Edward Mason	240916	WIA: 9/8
Rfn George Massey	241601	WIA: 3/8
Rfn Matthew H. Maxfield	2555	WIA: 11/8
Rfn James Maxwell	240747	WAD: 11/8
Rfn Richard Leonard Maybury	241635	WIA: 9/8
Rfn Brian Elstob McBeath	1673	KIA: 7/8
Rfn Donald McGivering	240527	SS: 7/8
Rfn James McMahon	241790	WIA: 8/8
Rfn William Duncan Miller	240989	WIA: 13/8
Rfn John Millington	242045	KIA: 13/8
Rfn Thomas J. Morgan	3757	WIA: 7/8
Rfn William Murray	3831	WIA: 13/8
Rfn Robert Neale	2517	INJ: 7/8
Rfn Charles Oddy	2261	KIA: 9/8
Rfn Lawrence O'Dwyer	241731	WIA: 5/8
Lt Edward Lawrence Oliver		WIA: 13/8
Rfn John Wyndham Onions	3773	KIA: 7/8
Rfn Edgar Parrington	241128	KIA: 12/8
Rfn John Henry Parry	240882	SS: 9/8
Rfn Joseph William Parsons	241711	SS: 9/8
Rfn George Paynter	4028	WIA: 13/8
Rfn Andrew Victor Pearson	3923	DOW: 7/8
Rfn Andrew Peers	242070	WIA: 7/8
Rfn Harry Peers	241933	WIA: 8/8
L/Cpl Percy Sayle Pennington	240114	WIA: 13/8
Rfn John Elliott Pilling	240230	WAD: 11/8
Cpl John Plumer	4457	KIA: 10/8
Rfn George V. Plummer	3845	SS: 10/8
Rfn Henry Poole	4095	WIA: 7/8
Cpl William Porteous	1643	KIA: 7/8
Rfn Harold Morris Porter	4255	KIA: 9/8
Rfn John Charles Potter	240665	KIA: 13/8
Rfn E. Powell	241735	WIA: 8/8
Rfn Thomas Alfred Pulford	241492	WIA: 12/8
Rfn Cecil Howard Purdon	240550	WIA: 9/8
L/Cpl Albert Robert Rashbrook	240770	SS: 10/8
Rfn John Delamere Redmond	240706	WIA: 7/8
Sgt Herbert Wade Roberts	240066	WIA: 7/8
Rfn Frank Henry Roberts	241695	WIA: 9/8
Rfn John Charles Roberts	240201	WAD: 11/8
Rfn William D. Robertson	240530	WIA: 8/8
Sgt Arthur Robinson	240017	WIA: 12/8
Rfn Greig Newton Robinson	241739	WIA: 10/8
Rfn Arthur Rogers	241968	WIA: 9/8
2Lt G. Rothwell		WAD: 10/8
Rfn Herbert Rourke	4414	SS: 7/8
Rfn Alfred Royle	2398	SS: 9/8
Rfn Norman Royle	241415	WIA: 9/8
Rfn John Russell	3792	KIA: 7/8
Rfn Edward W. Sampson	4173	WIA: 7/8
Rfn Arthur George Scoins	240505	WIA: 9/8
Rfn William Scott	241866	SS: 9/8
Rfn William Shields	1876	WIA: 9/8
Rfn Arthur Smith	241667	SS: 7/8
Rfn James Smith	242100	WIA: 5/8
Rfn Rowland Smith	2177	SS: 7/8
2Lt Harold Edgar St George**		KIA: 13/8
Rfn Harry Stacey	241787	SS: 9/8
L/Cpl Vincent Stansfield	240275	WIA: 10/8
Rfn Charles William Steen	241504	SS: 7/8
Rfn George H. Stephens	3944	WIA: 10/8
CSM Clement Tanner	240300	WIA: 12/8
Rfn John Teece	241906	KIA: 13/8
Rfn Harry Parry Thomas	240485	WIA: 9/8
Rfn Thomas William Thomas	241905	WIA: 13/8
Rfn James Martin Thomson	241595	SS: 9/8
L/Cpl Ronald Douglas V. Thorburn	240436	WIA: 9/8
L/Cpl H. Timuthy	240903	WIA: 7/8
Rfn Simon Tobias	240456	WIA: 9/8
Rfn Thomas H. Tobin	241352	WIA: 8/8

L/Cpl Harry Tremayne	240413	SS: 9/8
Capt. John Roy Trench		WIA: 9/8
Rfn Harry Troughton	241319	SS: 8/8
Rfn Cecil Tudor	240195	WIA: 8/8
Rfn Thomas Reginald Tunstall	240839	WIA: 11/8
Capt. William Angus Turner		WIA: 8/8
Rfn Bernard James Tyson	4432	KIA: 8/8
L/Cpl Ernest Tytler	240513	WIA: 13/8
Rfn Ernest Norman Walker	240704	SS: 7/8
Rfn William T. Walton	1963	SS: 7/8
Rfn William Michael John Ward	240845	WIA: 5/8
Cpl Leslie Holland Ward	240622	WIA: 8/8
Rfn Francis Augustus Wareham	240612	WIA: 11/8
Rfn Thomas B. Whalley	241509	WIA: 13/8
Cpl James White	240181	SS: 9/8
Rfn Alexander Williams	240609	WIA: 10/8
Rfn John Lloyd Williams	2841	DOW 9/8
Rfn Alfred Wilson	2363	SS: 11/8
Cpl Frank Musgrove Wilson	240591	WIA: 13/8
Rfn Herbert W. Wilson	3188	WIA: 10/8
Rfn Harold James Winn	240417	WIA: 7/8
Rfn Francis Noel Wright	241969	SS: 12/8
2Lt Georges Wright		WAD: 13/8
Cpl Herbert Young	240539	WIA: 9/8
Rfn Sydney William Young	1686	KIA: 5/8

* = also wounded at duty 5 August ** = also wounded at duty 8 August
*** = attached to 1/9th when killed **** = CWGC record the date of death of Hoose for 12 August, however the Casualties Book notes he went missing during 'C' Company's attack on the 13th.

In view of the casualty toll, a great deal of reorganisation was needed, and 16 August was spent on company training under the new arrangements. At 4 p.m. on the 17th, Transport set off on the long journey by road to Oisemont. Earlier that day, a draft of ten arrived from the Divisional School, and though no doubt welcomed, the battalion was well understrength. The draft should have been eleven, but at the school, Rfn G. Jones (139) was found to be underage and sent home. Before they returned to action in September, the true ages of Frederick Alderson, Frederick Savage, Joseph Cearns, and A. Holden were also exposed, and all four were sent packing.

On 19 August, the battalion left Ville-sur-Ancre for Méricourt, where they entrained for Martainnville, 4 miles north-west of Oisemont. Between then and 30 August, training continued, though a rota system for men longest without leave was established—six officers and 104 men benefitting from seventy-two hours in the seaside town of Le Tréport. As with any time out of the line, illness and injury reduced the roll. On 22 August, Rfn Harry Hyman was badly burned on his chest and right arm and Sgt Albert Edwards broke his ankle, with both returning to England.

At 8.30 a.m. on 30 August, the battalion marched through torrential rain to the station at Pont Remy, thence to Méricourt, arriving at 3 a.m. on the 31st. They bivouacked near Dernancourt, and at 4 p.m., moved into billets around the village, their fighting strength now 803.

At 1.30 p.m. on 4 September, the battalion left for the front line between High Wood and Deville Wood. 'A' took the left of the line in Worcester Trench and 'C', the right in Orchard Trench. 'B', in Carlton Trench (also the location of HQ), provided support on the left; 'D', in Chesney Walk, provided support for the right. Transport moved to the bivouac location of 2 August. Although the companies reached the line by 8 p.m., a very heavy enemy barrage between 8.30 and 9 p.m. delayed completion of the relief and wounded Sgt Norman Maggi in the left hand, Rfn Joseph Parsons in the arm, and Rfn Henry Edwards in the wrist. Rfn William Walton was badly shell-shocked—for the second time in a month—and evacuated home. The rest of the night was quiet, though heavy rain turned the trenches into a morass. These former German positions had been virtually levelled by British guns, and although the occupying troops had begun rebuilding them, there was very little top cover. Some of the trenches continued on into German lines—for example, Worcester Trench, where the combatants were separated by just a few yards of blown-in trench. Lt-Col. Shute, after reconnoitring these on 5 September, commented: 'Trenches are very confusing and complex and the maps issued are not invariably accurate'.[24]

Top priority was to dig seven new 'avenues' leading to the front line from Montauban, bypassing Longueval on their way up. The main route, Montauban Alley—stretching from Montauban to the northern tip of Bernafay Wood—had six 'lanes' branching off to the line, with Turk, French and Milk Lane serving 165 Bde. Division stipulated:

> There must be no less than seven feet of cover in these avenues and a minimum width of three feet at floor level. Trench gratings [duckboards] must be laid throughout. Each avenue is to be provided at intervals of 500 yards with 'runner posts' consisting of small steel shelters let into the side of the avenue.[25]

Although the RE oversaw this work, the labour came from infantrymen.

Rain continued on 5 September and artillery from both sides was active. Seven men were wounded by this fire, only two of whom later returned. Around 9.30 p.m., several gas shells were mixed among the HE and shrapnel, gassing Rfn Edward Evans, who was evacuated home.

On 6 September, orders were issued for the battalion and the 1/7th to carry out a small attack to seize a German strongpoint (SP-2) at the junction of Wood Lane, Worcester Trench, and Tea Trench. Unfortunately, 'Operation Order 39' does not record the time it was issued, though the attackers had little time to prepare.[26]

Lt Blackledge's bombers would assault one strongpoint (SP-1) at 7 p.m., then reorganise and attack Tea Trench from the left while bombers from the 1/7th attacked from the right. At the same time, a 'C' Company party led by 2Lt George Harrison, their numbers boosted by some bombers, would attack another strongpoint (SP-3) at the junction of Wood Lane and Orchard Trench. Any gains were to be consolidated and held.

At 1 p.m., Divisional Howitzers began a four-hour bombardment of Wood Lane and Tea Trench, the 4.9s continuing to fire intermittently until 6.50 p.m. Ten minutes before Zero, the 18-pounders and Stokes barraged Tea Trench and Wood Lane. Precisely at 7 p.m., Blackledge's party advanced, almost immediately coming under heavy fire from the area of the strongpoints, and from snipers and machine guns in isolated shell holes. Fighting continued into the early morning of 7 September, with mixed success: the 1/7th managed to push about 250 yards along Tea Trench and consolidate their gains, but far less was gained by the 1/6th; SP-1 was found not to be a strongpoint at all, with the machine-gun fire originating from a couple of guns north-east of there, though Blackledge made some progress along Tea Trench, which was more a line of shell holes than a proper trench. Second-Lieutenant Harrison's party—also met by very heavy fire—failed to take any ground. One problem the bombers faced was that the final 50 yards of approaches to the German blocks in Wood Lane and Tea Trench were straight, with no traverses to allow them to get within bombing range of the enemy. Wood Lane, heavily damaged north of this junction, was utterly exposed and swept by machine-gun fire, and southwards, the trench was completely blocked by heaps of putrefying German corpses.[27]

Five were killed outright, and twenty-two-year-old Rfn William Thomas (239) died from his wounds on 12 September. His brother, Henry, wrote an angry letter to the War Office on 25 September:

> There are two matters which I beg you to give your best consideration and attention.
>
> Wounded on 6 Sept. my brother died on the 12th inst. at No. 36 Casualty Clearing Station and the only word we received between those dates (and indeed up to the present) was from a Comrade who saw him wounded.
>
> It is difficult to believe that he was not conscious during any part of these six days and yet absolutely no communication of any last utterances—the memory of which would be sacred to the family for all time—have been received from Chaplain, doctor or sister. My mother and father feel very deeply the absence of such communication and I beg therefore to respectfully request that you will cause such enquiries to be made as may remove the suggestion of callousness or slackness which these circumstances seem to us to contain.[28]

With a gunshot wound to the head, it is entirely feasible he never regained consciousness—though it was most unusual for neither the chaplain, nor the nursing sister, to write.

Another twenty-six were wounded, half of whom never rejoined. The failure of Rfn Charles Strange to return was not because of his shellshock—which was minor—but because his anxious parents had informed Infantry Records of his true age and he was sent home from 24 IBD; seven men were also recorded as wounded on 7 September—all probably early morning casualties from this operation rather than from later that day.

Also recorded for 7 September is the wounding of Capt. Alan Perry, the new MO. However, the diary of the 1/5th indicates this happening at 10.15 p.m. on the 6th.[29] During the operation, German artillery began to bombard the rear. Carlton Trench, the HQ of the 1/5th (adjacent to the Aid Post shared by the 1/6th and 1/7th), came under heavy fire. One round scored a direct hit on the entrance of the 1/5th's HQ dugout, blocking the entrance and killing their Adjutant, Lt Saunders—who had just left the dugout to organise an ammunition carrying party for the 1/6th (requested at 9.45 p.m.). The same round wounded Capt. Perry and the MO of the 1/7th, Capt. G. Randall.

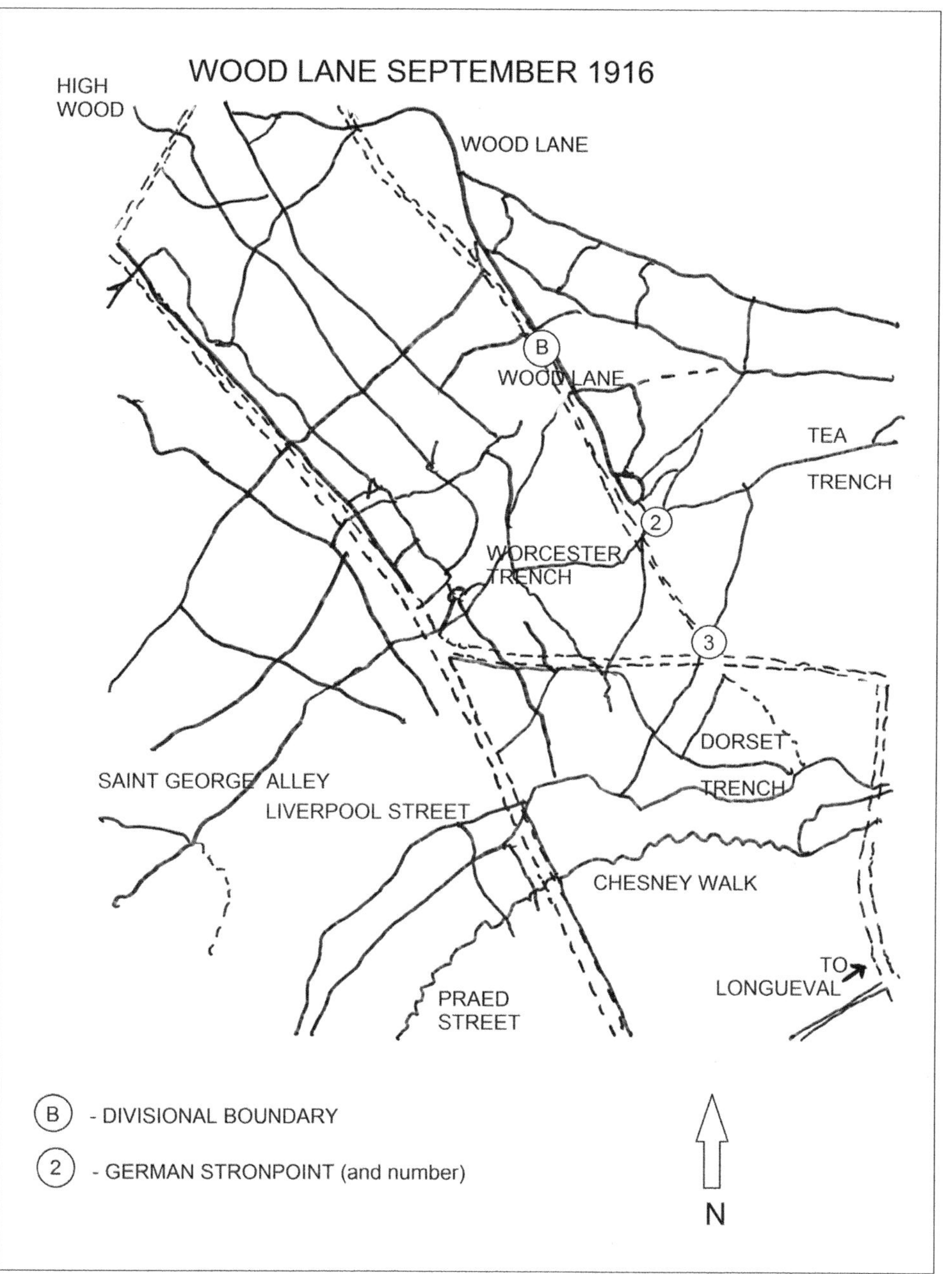
WOOD LANE SEPTEMBER 1916
HIGH WOOD
WOOD LANE
B
WOOD LANE
TEA TRENCH
2
WORCESTER TRENCH
3
DORSET TRENCH
SAINT GEORGE ALLEY
LIVERPOOL STREET
CHESNEY WALK
TO LONGUEVAL
PRAED STREET
B - DIVISIONAL BOUNDARY
2 - GERMAN STRONPOINT (and number)
N

At 5 a.m. on 7 September, the battalion was relieved by the 1/5th and moved into reserve in Montauban Alley. A week later, Shute wrote in his Summary of Operations:

> It seemed to me that quite sufficient [ammunition] had been taken up in the afternoon for any possible developments.' The 6th Liverpool reported that they met with much M. Gun fire and that there seemed to be a fair number of enemy in surrounding points. I took view that the opposition had been magnified, probably mistaking our own MG's fire for that of the enemy.[30]

This was an extraordinary statement to make, especially as he was 1,000 yards to the rear at the time. Shute's written reports frequently tendered negative opinions about the 1/6th—regrettable ill-feeling that may have originated in the mix-up over relief on 8 August, though is more noticeable post 6 September, with Shute probably blaming the 1/6th for Saunders' death. Fortunately, this acrimony eventually faded.

At 7.30 p.m. on 8 September, 'B' returned to the line on a working party to improve the trenches, followed an hour later by 'D'. Two Riflemen were wounded: twenty-year-old John Conway, whose arm wound was minor, and Edward Ryan with shellshock.

On 9 September, the offensive resumed. On the left, 1 Division attacked between the eastern corner of High Wood and the divisional boundary in Wood Lane. The 165th Bde also attacked a 260-yard length of Wood Lane at the left divisional bound. The 164th Bde assaulted Ale Alley and Pint and Lager Trench on the eastern side of Delville Wood, supporting an attack against Ginchy by 16 Division. The bombers of the 1/5th, in cooperation with a company-sized force of the 1/6th under Lt George Hughes of 'D', provided the assault force against Wood Trench.

At 3.29 p.m., the Stokes began firing on the German strongpoint in Wood Lane and the bombers of the 1/5th advanced over the block, constructed in Wood Lane the previous night. The accurate mortar fire caused the German defenders to scatter in all directions, affording British snipers easy targets, though when mortar ammunition ran out at 3.45 p.m., the enemy poured back into their line and drove the 1/5th off.

At 4.45 p.m., the main attack launched and Hughes's men went over the top, with Blackledge's bombers, who had relieved the 1/5th, advancing along Wood Lane from the right to support them (this detail was misreported in Shute's submission to Brigade, which stated that 'our bombers again advanced up Wood Lane to help the 6th'[31]). To the battalion's left, one and a half companies of 2/KRRC also attacked Wood Lane. Blackledge's bombers, supported by a Lewis team from 'D', made good progress along Wood Lane, and though there had been initial opposition, this melted away when the main body attacked.

The attackers came under heavy fire from their right, and only 50 yards into the advance, Hughes was shot in the arm and 2Lt Rothwell in the right thigh and abdomen. Having sustained serious losses, the assaulting force sought cover in shell holes. Rothwell ordered the survivors to make their way in pairs back to Worcester Trench, covered by 'D' Company's other Lewis team, who had come forward to put suppressing fire down on the enemy parapet. By the time all the survivors had returned, that team was down to Rfn David Courtie and Rfn Thomas Argue—who had taken command after their NCO was hit. Courtie took the gun back and then returned to the shell hole, where Argue had remained with Rothwell. Together, they carried the badly-wounded subaltern to safety in Worcester Trench, reaching there at 5.30 p.m. Maj. Wainwright attributed the success of this withdrawal—the enemy unaware that it had taken place—principally to the coolness of this Lewis team.[32]

In Worcester Trench, Hughes refused to be evacuated until he had reorganised for another attack, explaining in detail to the NCOs the orders and objectives he had been given. He also sent word back for more officers to come forward to lead the attack. Shute's report states: '… the 4.45 p.m. attack was a failure so far as the 6th KLR and the bombers were concerned, the KRRs gained their objective and occupied Wood Lane further up'. However, the diary of 2/KRRC makes it clear that they too had been unable to reach Wood Lane due to the intense fire.[33]

Shute sent 2Lt Hose from his battalion to lead the next assault, and at 7.30 p.m., in conjunction with 2/KRRC, the fifty surviving attackers of the 1/6th made another attempt at Wood Lane. With great courage, 2Lt Hose sprinted off far in advance of the rest and was shot dead 30 yards from the enemy trench (Shute, not unreasonably, described his rush as 'impetuous', though paid tribute to his 'splendid spirit' and example[34]). As the force charged, the German garrison, who considerably outnumbered the attackers, left their trench and ran back, pursued by the Riflemen who were now somewhat 'fired-up'. At this point, a German machine-gun team were spotted setting up a gun to the rear and were wiped out by Argue with his Lewis (he was awarded the DCM for this and his earlier deeds). The thoroughly-demoralised enemy laid down their arms and capitulated, though the communication trench they gathered in became so overcrowded that many edged left, 140 surrendering to the KRRC.

Further pursuit was clearly unadvisable, and the attackers set about consolidating. Second-Lieutenants Donald Eastwood and George Harrison came up with the remainder of 'A' and began digging a new trench, as Wood Lane was virtually obliterated—probably why its defenders had been so keen to be elsewhere. Eastwood directed his men to ignore the old German trench and dig an entirely new one in the bank on the enemy's side of the road, which by dawn was 8 feet deep. Twenty of the 1/5th and another twenty-five from the 1/7th came up and assisted with consolidation. At 3 a.m. on 10 September, the enemy began to shell the captured position, but thanks to the depth of their new trench, few casualties were sustained, though to the rear, 2Lt Georges Wright was fatally wounded in the head. Later that day, the battalion was relieved by the 2nd New Zealand Rifle Bde and marched to billets near Bécordel, south-east of Albert.

Casualties had been heavy, with twenty-five fatalities and thirty-nine wounded. Among these, was young Rfn Herbert Wilson, his chest wound thankfully minor, though his age-related deception came to light while in hospital and he was sent home. In the six days since 4 September, the battalion endured 119 casualties, thirty-one of whom were fatalities, sixty-six were wounded, and a further twenty-two suffered shellshock.

Casualties, 4-10 September 1916

Rfn George Norman Abbott	240353	WIA: 7/9
Rfn Henry Ainsworth	241979	WIA: 9/9
Rfn Thomas Henry Grace Aitchison	241180	WIA: 9/9
Rfn Leonard Vionnes Alexander	240625	WIA: 6/9
Rfn Harold Edmund Annison	3589	DOW: 10/9
Rfn Michael U. Atkinson	241526	WIA: 9/9
Rfn Colin James Macbeth Bain	240633	WIA: 7/9
Rfn William J. Ballock	3219	WIA: 6/9
Rfn George Balmer	204776	WIA: 9/9
Rfn Herbert M. Bardwell	1532	WIA: 9/9
Rfn Thomas Bibby	241917	WIA: 6/9
L/Cpl George Bertrand Birkett	240605	WIA: 9/9
Rfn John Blythe	4636	KIA: 6/9
Rfn Samuel Bonner**	242069	WIA: 9/9
Rfn Albert E. Bounds*	241728	WIA: 7/9
Rfn Edward Boydell	240862	WIA: 9/9
Rfn George Henry Bradley	240721	WIA: 9/9
Rfn Max Edwin Bradley	240398	WIA: 9/9
Rfn John Brown	3970	KIA: 9/9
Rfn Alfred Thomas Brownrigg	240784	WIA: 9/9
Cpl Joseph Charles Bryans	240246	WIA: 7/9
Rfn Arthur Burge	240969	WIA: 6/9
Rfn Duncan Campbell	240858	WIA: 10/9
Rfn Albert Gordon Carr	241678	WIA: 6/9
Rfn James Edward Caunce	4309	DOW: 10/9
Rfn Percival Chandler	241468	WIA: 10/9
Cpl Alfred Henry Clarke	2820	KIA: 9/9
Rfn Alfred H. Cliffe	3049	SS: 6/9
Rfn James Cochrane	241809	WIA: 5/9
Rfn John Joseph Conway	242121	WIA: 8/9
Rfn David Courtie	241616	WAD: 10/9
Rfn Herbert E. Crosby	2705	SS: 9/9
Rfn Henry Daniels	241673	WIA: 6/9
Rfn Herbert L. Davis	243883	SS: 10/9
Rfn Bernard Eckford	3892	DOW: 17/9
Rfn Henry Edwards	241776	WIA: 4/9
Rfn Richard John Edwards	241801	WIA: 6/9
Rfn Edward Roberts Evans	240464	WIA: 5/9
Rfn James Percival Evans	241783	SS: 9/9
Rfn Joseph Gladwinfield	241693	WIA: 6/9
Rfn Reginal James Godfrey	241216	WIA: 9/9
Rfn George Guest	241918	SS: 9/9
Rfn Sydney Callow Hampton	4053	WIA: 5/9
Rfn Stanley Hardman	3518	KIA: 9/9
Rfn Ernest Harrison	4168	KIA: 9/9
Rfn Thomas Harwood	241926	SS: 9/9
Rfn Harold Hirst	241620	WIA: 6/9
L/Cpl Gordon Holgate	240514	WIA: 6/9
L/Cpl Herbert Hollinghurst	240580	WIA: 5/9
Rfn John Horan	240650	WIA: 7/9
Rfn Benjamin Rowland Houghton	240995	KIA: 10/9
Lt George Hughes		WIA: 9/9
Cpl Stanley Jones MM	2165	DOW: 20/10
Rfn John H. Joughin	241042	SS: 6/9
L/Cpl Charles Kenneth N. Kemp	240452	KIA: 10/9
L/Cpl Alfred Howarth Kermode	240282	WIA: 9/9
Rfn Harry Lavery	241916	WIA: 9/9
Rfn George Henry Lennie	2563	WIA: 7/9
Rfn Alfred Lodge	241958	WIA: 9/9
Rfn Arthur Millwood Longstaff	4307	DOW: 10/9
Rfn Joseph Lynch	4646	KIA: 10/9
Sgt Norman Percy Maggi	240092	WIA: 4/9
L/Cpl Harry Leonard Mansell	240536	KIA: 10/9
Rfn Charles Marten	3178	KIA: 6/9
Rfn Herbert McAllester	3082	KIA: 9/9
Rfn Joseph McCann	241417	WIA: 6/9
Rfn Donald McGivering	240527	SS: 6/9
Rfn Myer Morris	241825	WIA: 5/9
Rfn William Morton	4417	KIA: 10/9
Rfn William Moss	241404	WIA: 9/9

Rfn Thomas Patrick Murney	240375	WIA: 6/9
Rfn Albert Charles Nadin	240235	WIA: 5/9
Rfn David Nolan	241347	WIA: 10/9
Cpl Stephen O'Keefe	1719	WIA: 5/9
Rfn Joseph William Parsons	241711	WIA: 4/9
Capt. Alan Cecil Perry (RAMC)		WIA: 7/9
Rfn George Walter Pickles	240210	WIA: 9/9
Rfn Mortimer Pim	1658	SS: 10/9
Rfn Joseph Howard Poole	241397	WIA: 9/9
Rfn Harold Reginald Purdon	240548	SS: 6/9
L/Cpl Walter Wilfred Quirk	241339	WIA: 6/9
Rfn John Milligan Riddell	240898	WIA: 6/9
Rfn Thomas E. Roberts	240813	WIA: 9/9
Cpl William Robertson	1471	KIA: 6/9
2Lt G. Rothwell		WIA: 9/9
Rfn Herbert Rourke	4414	WIA: 6/9
Sgt James Robson Rundle	240079	SS: 7/9
Rfn Edward Anderson Russell	240270	SS: 10/9
Rfn Edward Ryan	241519	SS: 8/9
Sgt Alexander Frederick Salmon	240188	WIA: 9/9
Rfn Christian Seiler	4423	KIA: 9/9
Rfn Norman (James) Skeldon	3522	KIA: 6/9
Rfn Harold Skewes	241594	WIA: 9/9
Rfn Douglas Smith	4593	KIA: 6/9
Rfn Archibald Gilbert Speed	4137	KIA: 10/9
Rfn Thomas Harold Spencer	4407	KIA: 9/9
L/Cpl Herbert Charles Stafford	240363	SS: 6/9
Rfn Thomas Steadman	3742	KIA: 9/9
Rfn Charles William Steen	241504	SS: 6/9
Rfn Richard Stopforth	242009	WIA: 9/9
Rfn Charles Strange	4329	SS: 6/9
Rfn Frederick Taylor	241749	SS: 10/9
Rfn Marmaduke Theakstone	240340	KIA: 10/9
Rfn John Thomas	241824	SS: 6/9
Rfn William Harold Thomas	2239	DOW: 12/9
Rfn Thomas Wainwright	3979	KIA: 9/9
Rfn Harold John E. Wallace	242471	WIA: 10/9
Rfn William T. Walton	1963	SS: 4/9
Cpl Leslie Holland Ward	240622	SS: 6/9
Rfn William Andrews Williams	241054	WIA: 6/9
Rfn William Glynn Williams	2045	KIA: 9/9
Rfn William Roberts Williams	2279	DOW: 9/9
L/Cpl Arthur S. Wilson	240356	WAD: 10/9
Rfn Herbert W. Wilson	3188	WIA: 10/9
Rfn John Wilson	3460	WIA: 10/9
Sgt James Rothwell Worthington	240019	SS: 6/9
2Lt Georges Wright		DOW: 19/9

* = shellshock in addition to wounds.

** = attached to 1/9th when wounded.

The battalion remained at Bécordel until 16 September, reorganising and attack-training. On the march to the billets, Rfn John Porter sprained his knee so badly that he was evacuated home and transferred to the ASC. Another who fell out on the march was L/Cpl Robert Colligan, who was consequently deprived of his stripe, serving the remainder of the war as a Rifleman. On 12 September, a draft of 2Lt Harry Gardner and twenty-five men arrived after only six days at the Divisional School—the need for replacements great.

While the division was out of the line, the third phase of the Battle of the Somme began (later known as the Battle of Flers-Courcelette). On 15 September, eight divisions began a north-easterly push on a rough line from Martinpuich to Combles—a renewed offensive notable for two innovations: the first use of the tank and the introduction of the creeping barrage. The Lancastrians would soon add their contribution.

At 2.30 p.m. on 16 September, the battalion departed for bivouacs south-west of Albert, and at 1.30 p.m. the next day, they left for the front at Flers. On a very wet night, they relieved 12/DLI in support at 2 a.m. on 18 September. Enemy artillery had welcomed their return the previous night, mortally wounding twenty-three-year-old Rfn Henry Wilson, who died shortly before midnight. The other casualty overnight was Maj. Wainwright, wounded in the foot by shrapnel. He clung on until the morning, but had to accept the inevitable and was evacuated home, with Capt. McKaig assuming command. Rfn Harry Stacey was also admitted to hospital on the night of the 17th with paralysis of the legs. Having been briefly hospitalised with shellshock on 9 August, his temporary paralysis was possibly triggered by his fresh exposure to the dreadful experience of shellfire. Evacuated home, he transferred to the Labour Corps.

HQ, 'A', 'D', and part of 'C' occupied Fosse Way, and 'B' occupied the nearby Flers Trench. Lt Ronald and the twenty-seven men of his 'C' Company platoon were tasked with building and garrisoning a strongpoint just in front of Flers, at the extreme left of the brigade front, and 2Lt Douglas Colley—who had only arrived on 4 September—and his twenty-five men from 'C' were given a similar task on the extreme right of the brigade front. At 9.30 p.m., the battalion was withdrawn to York Trench, south-west of Longueval. In their brief time in Fosse Way, they suffered thirteen casualties.

Casualties, 18 September 1916

Name	No.	Status
Rfn Joseph Charles Adams	241367	SS
Rfn Thomas J. Ellis	240529	WIA
Rfn Sidney Godfrey	241184	WAD
Rfn John Handley	240720	WIA
Rfn John Arthur Jones	241750	WIA
Rfn Thomas J. McMeakin	2288	WIA
Rfn John Mills	3723	WIA
Rfn Ernest William Owens	241416	WIA
Rfn Walter Meredith Proudlove	1737	KIA
Rfn Robert Edward Railton	4048	KIA
Rfn Walter R. Roberts	241584	WIA
Rfn Thomas Joseph Ruane	241031	WIA
Rfn John R. Ruddock	3989	SS

The Rifles reached York Trench at 1 a.m. on 19 September, remaining there in the cold and wet throughout the day. Intermittent hostile fire resulted in further casualties, including 'B' Company's new CSM Frank Williams. Rfn Percy Harwood was buried by a shell—his body never found. It was not until the early hours of 20 September that they were relieved and retired to bivouac at Pommier Redoubt, near Mametz Wood and out of the line of fire.

Casualties, 19-20 September 1916

Rfn Herbert Adams	241966	WIA: 19/9	Rfn Henry Edgar Dean	241019	SS: 19/9
Rfn Walter Brown	241444	SS: 19/9	Rfn Lewis Charles Evans	242083	WIA: 19/9
Rfn Robert Metcalfe Cooper	241838	SS: 19/9	Rfn Percy Harold Harwood	240606	KIA: 19/9
			Rfn James Readdie	241755	WIA: 19/9
Rfn William Costin	241652	WIA: 20/9	Rfn George Rowlands	240324	SS: 19/9
Rfn Harold Hamer Coupland	242013	SS: 19/9	Rfn Frederick Wilkinson	241615	SS: 19/9
			CSM Frank A. Williams	24	WIA: 19/9
Rfn Frederick C. Daniels	241199	WIA: 19/9	Rfn Llewellyn Williams	241789	WIA: 19/9

The battalion remained in bivouacs until 23 September, rehearsing the forthcoming attack. This would be their first advance behind a creeping barrage, and trials using drummers to simulate the barrage were vital if everything was to go smoothly. The 165th Bde planned a three-battalion attack from Factory Corner on the left to the north-western edge of Guedecourt on the right: the 1/9th on the left, 1/6th in the centre, and 1/7th to the right. This attack was supported by the New Zealand Division to the left and 21 Division on the right. The battalion had two objectives: Gird Trench (including Gird Support) and the sunken road leading from Factory Corner to Guedecourt.

The creeping barrage was provided by shrapnel-firing 18-pounders, though to be really effective, attacking troops needed to be within 50 yards of it—not quite as suicidal as it sounds if the gunners were accurate, as shrapnel was directional, striking the ground forward of the detonation point. However, neither was it totally safe, and an ideally-positioned attacking force was probably going to get casualties from friendly fire—though far fewer than the enemy would have inflicted, if they had not closed up to the barrage. The heavier guns (and spare 18-pounders) would bombard the enemy front line and known strongpoints before lifting to targets further back as the creeping barrage neared the enemy front line. Brig.-Gen. Duncan's plan involved 165 MGC pushing their Vickers forward in the early stages of the attack:

> Even if some are lost, it matters little so long that the machine-guns generally are able to effect their objective of defeating the enemy machine-guns, driving him back, and rendering quick counter-attack very costly.[35]

At 8 p.m. on 23 September, as the battalion marched up to the line, they came under shellfire on the Flers–Longueval Road, wounding five. The only casualty who can be positively assigned to this is twenty-four-year-old Rfn Arthur Johnson; the others were all recorded for 24 September. The chest and back wounds suffered by the farmer from Hale brought about his medical discharge. When they reached the line, the battalion occupied Fosse Way, Flers Avenue, and Switch Trench.

At 7.30 p.m. on the 24th, the battalion journeyed in columns of half companies to their assembly positions in front of Flers. One of 'C' Company's platoons was without a key figure, as Sgt Thomas Davies suffered a serious burn to his left arm during the day and was evacuated home (he was awarded the MM in December—possibly for 13 August). The battalion attacked in two waves: 'B', led by Capt. Herschell, on the left and 'A', under 2Lt Eastwood, on the right; Lt Blackledge's bombers grouped in the centre of the first wave. The second wave—in close support and tasked with consolidating gains—consisted of Lt Rome's 'D' Company on the left and Lt Ronald's 'C' Company to their right. The assembly trenches for the three attacking battalions were named, from left to right, Box, Cox, and Hogshead. Cox Trench had been dug during torrential rain and at great cost by the 1/5th KORL during the night of 21–22 September; only specified to be 4½ feet deep, it provided scant shelter.

During 24 September, the battalion lost another ten wounded and three killed. It is not known if the casualties were from earlier in the day, during the move up, or the occupation of Cox, but as none have known graves, it is unlikely to be the first option. CWGC denotes six killed on 24 September, but entries in the Casualties Book and contemporary letters indicate that the wrong date has been attributed to three: the oldest of those killed on the 24th was twenty-nine-year-old Rfn William Towers, a father of three from the Dingle; twenty-three-year-old Rfn Edgar Gauntlett and twenty-year-old Rfn Charles Hare, who served as 'Charles Ayre', were both single.

There was no pre-attack bombardment, though routine harassing fire was maintained. At Zero (12.35 p.m.), all the division's guns, augmented by 41 Division's artillery, opened up on their targets. As the barrage commenced, the waves advanced across the open to close up to it. Two minutes after Zero, the creeping barrage began to move at a rate of 50 yards per minute. The battalion needed to cross the open for 800 yards behind the barrage and it was not too long before enemy artillery and machine guns responded. At 1.02 p.m., the barrage lifted from Gird Support and the attackers charged. The final objective was seized at 2.11 p.m. and consolidation began.

By 8 p.m., 'A' and 'B' were dug in along the sunken road, 'B' in touch with the 1/9th to their left, who in turn were in touch with the New Zealanders. 'A' could see a platoon of the 1/7th digging in 200 yards to their right, but was not in touch with them. 'C' and 'D' consolidated Gird Trench, with two companies of the 1/7th to their right. About 200 yards forward of Gird Trench, the other three platoons from the company of the 1/7th holding the sunken road were also digging in, but the whereabouts of their fourth company was unknown (it had dropped back to reinforce 7/Leicestershires on their right, who reported the enemy bombing westwards along the road). The Liverpool Irish went forward shortly after 8 p.m. to reinforce the line, one company going to the 1/9th, another to reinforce the 1/7th, the remainder in Smoke Trench. At 10 p.m., a company of the 1/5th reinforced 'C', being deployed to their right on the western edge of Guedecourt; another company reinforced the right of the 1/7th, where the situation was still unclear.

'B' was clearly forward of the sunken road after dark, as a message received by division reported the enemy bombing a British block there around 10.30 p.m. No further details can be found in dairies or reports, but it was probably in Gird Support, near to where 'B'—commanded at the time by Sgt Elijah Roper—buried their dead.

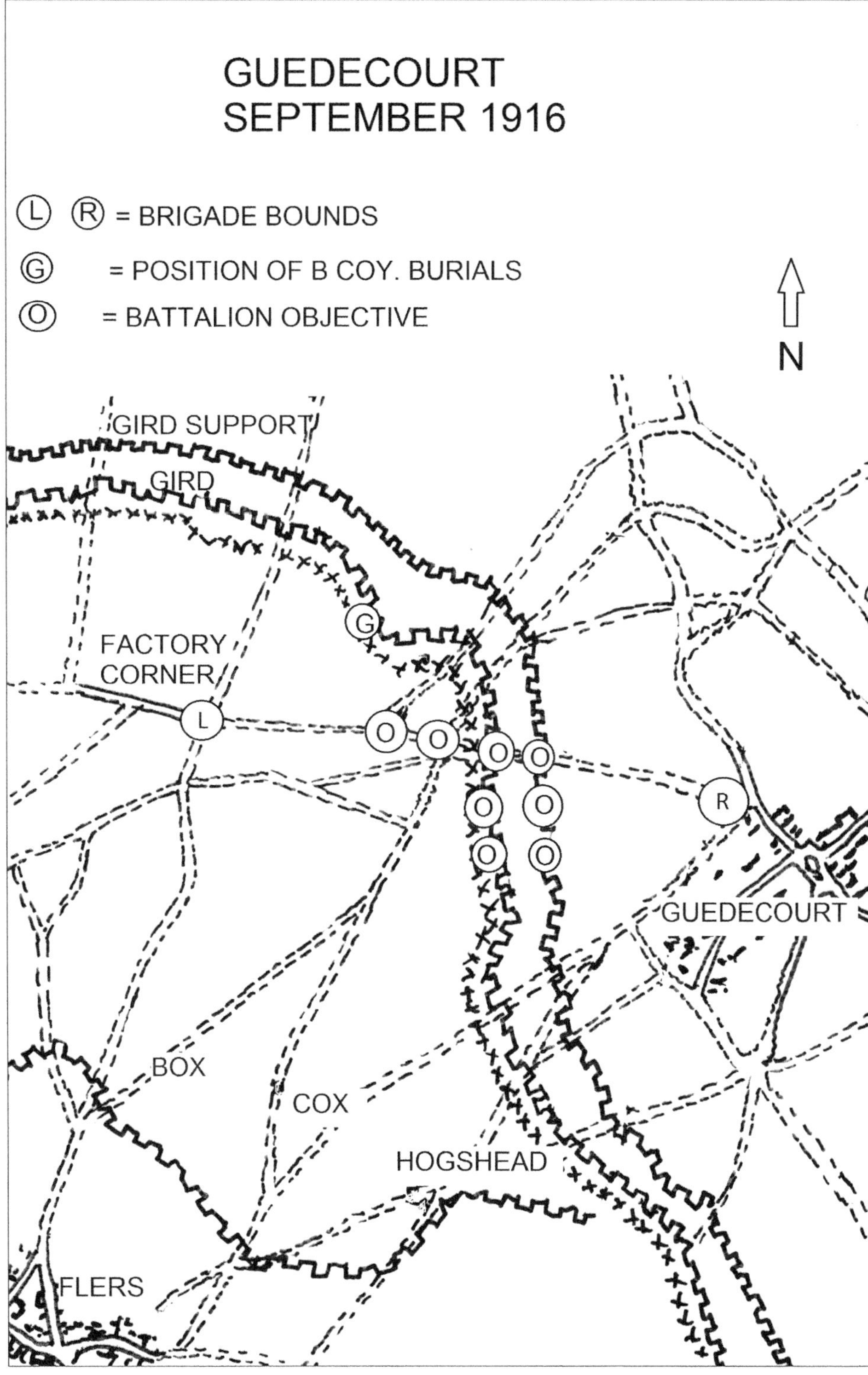
GUEDECOURT
SEPTEMBER 1916
L R = BRIGADE BOUNDS
G = POSITION OF B COY. BURIALS
O = BATTALION OBJECTIVE
N
GIRD SUPPORT
GIRD
G
FACTORY
CORNER
L
O O O O
O O
O O
R
GUEDECOURT
BOX
COX
HOGSHEAD
FLERS

The 1/7th only made contact on their right at 7.45 a.m. on 26 September, after a tank was used to force the surrender of the enemy in Gird Trench—an attack that so upset the foe that, when an RFC observation plane called in artillery fire, then swooped low, adding its machine-gun fire, 370 of the demoralised defenders surrendered to the aircraft.

Casualties among officers were severe, with three company-commanders hit: Capt. Herschell's abdominal wound proved mortal, though Lt Ronald survived his back wound, and Capt. Eastwood remained on duty, his injury minor. Another eight officers were wounded, the most critical being 2Lt Charles Buttery—with the battalion for just five weeks—succumbing to his thigh wound on 1 October. Harry Gardner, wounded in the right hand, had only been with his platoon for a fortnight and Kenneth Bisset and Hugh Withers just a few weeks longer. When officers fell, their NCOs stepped in, many paying severely. Sgt Roper wrote to a sister of his friend, L/Sgt William 'Lawrie' Paton, who was killed during the attack:

> On the dot of 12.30 [*sic.*] every man leapt from his trench with fixed bayonets, and went forward. What a sight, shall I ever forget it? Your Lawrie was on my left. Soon the Germans spotted us and turned their artillery and machine-guns on us. It was a veritable inferno of bursting shells and bullets: men were dropping thick and fast, but on, on, on we pressed. All our Coy. officers were lost but at last we got to our objective. I found myself in charge with only a handful of men. Your brother was one of the handful and I am sure that it must be a little compensation to know that he got through the charge and arrived safe in the captured German position. We soon found that there were some Germans behind us to our right, so we started to drive them out. It was a desperate fight and lasted 50 mins, but we succeeded and captured a colonel, 2 officers and 14 men, all that were left. I am sorry to say that it was in this fight, that your dear brother, my poor old mess mate, was killed. The bullet went through the back of his head just below the right ear and death was instantaneous. If God spares me, I shall be able to tell you the exact spot where he died, also where he is buried. It may interest you to know that the day before the charge, Lawrie, Sergeant [Edmund] Savage (killed in the charge) and myself attended the Holy Communion Service. I must now close as I am so short-handed. Please accept and convey to your dear Mother my heartfelt grief in your great loss.[36]

A nest of snipers in a dugout caused many casualties. Under heavy fire, Roper crawled forward and threw in a bomb, killing two, the remainder surrendering. During consolidation, he took command of 'B' and organised the treatment of the wounded and the burial of the dead—his courage and leadership earning him a DCM. 'B' suffered greatly, with forty-seven (possibly forty-eight) casualties on 25 September, nineteen of whom were fatalities. Following behind 'B' was 'D', who also lost heavily, with fifty-eight casualties, fifteen of whom died.

The volume of fire against the battalion's right was considerably lighter. 'A', the leading company, fared better with thirty casualties, five of whom died. 'C' suffered sixteen casualties, two of whom were killed. The Divisional diary states that 'casualties nearly all occurred while consolidating the position won'.[37] While this may hold true for the other battalions and for 'A' and 'C', it was not the case for 'B' and 'D', most of whose losses occurred during the initial assault against Gird and Gird Support.

Though many great acts of courage were witnessed, regulations often prevented their recognition. Until 1974, the only medal that could be bestowed posthumously was the VC, though a MiD could be given. Twenty-four-year-old Sgt William Broster, DCM, MM, was shot in the stomach during the advance, but despite his great pain, he refused to give in. Throwing off his equipment, he continued to lead his platoon into the attack and was only evacuated when he collapsed at the objective, dying from his wound the next day. Sgt Charles Argent of 'C' and Sgt Albert Rankmore from 'A' were both awarded the MM.

The creeping barrage undoubtedly saved lives and ensured success, though German opposition was patchy—fierce in some places, non-existent in others. The barrage continued on a line 150 yards north of Guedecourt for some time, until it was believed that there was little chance of an enemy counterattack.

The Casualties Book allows clarification between those known at the time to have been killed and those whose deaths were only later confirmed. Of the nineteen confirmed killed at the time, only one has a known grave. The Service Record of 'B' Company soldier twenty-year-old Rfn Frank Williams (4667) includes fascinating correspondence from his father, determined his boy's grave should not be lost.[38]

In 1919, Mr Williams visited his son's battlefield grave. After this was moved to a permanent cemetery in 1920, his son was recorded by CWGC as having 'no known grave'. In 1923, Mr Williams met a representative from the CWGC in Arras, where he was shown the records of the relevant GRU. Seven bodies were exhumed from the map reference where he had visited his son's grave; one attributed to Frank Williams (4661) of the Loyals led Mr Williams to believe there had been a mistake. When it was established there was no such man in the Loyals, the grave was correctly attributed to his son. Today, all seven lie in Bancourt Cemetery, resting together—as they did when they were originally buried—the other six listed 'unknown' (Plot 9, Row A, Grave 20 and Row B, Graves 1–6). As Elijah Roper only buried seven from 'B' on 25–26 September, it is almost certain that the six interred next to Frank Williams are they (Sgt Savage, L/Sgt Paton, and Riflemen Charles Hill, Griffith Jones, Harold Lovett, and Francis Westray).

At 9.30 a.m. on 26 September, the enemy opened a very heavy bombardment of the new front line in the vicinity of Guedecourt, and it was feared it presaged a counterattack from the right, though this did not eventuate. The battalion suffered another dozen casualties, five of whom were fatal. One of the wounded was Lt Brownell, evacuated home with an arm wound, 2Lt Robert Phillips taking over his Adjutant duties. Food, water, ammunition, and medical help were also brought up to the front line. The new MO, Lt Arthur Cardew RAMC, showed great courage and devotion to duty, tending to the wounded under heavy fire, earning a well-deserved MC.

At 9 p.m., the battalion was relieved and withdrew to York Trench. However, one man continued onwards: Rfn Alex Kirkwood of 'B', another of the underaged, was returned to 55 Divisional HQ; old enough not to be discharged, he was posted to 14 POW Company until he was legally old enough to return, in December 1917. The Casualties Book details six casualties for 27 and 28 September, though the diary reports 'none' for these days. Whether the Casualties Book is correct, or the diary is at fault, is debateable, and they have been entered in the table below for the dates recorded in the Casualties Book, which for Rfn Ernest Jones—listed 'missing' on 28 September—corresponds with his CWGC entry. On 28 September, the battalion marched to billets in Buire-sur-L'Ancre, and my own feeling is that all five are probably from the night of 26–27 September.

Between 23 and 28 September, 203 casualties are recorded, fifty-one of whom were fatalities, 143 wounded, and nine with shellshock. Between 1915 and 1918, the percentage suffering shellshock was fairly low: of the 137 diagnosed thus, eighty-nine were from August–September 1916—a staggering percentage for just two months, and probably accounted for by the very poor trenches. Almost exclusively, these were former German positions that had received a battering by British artillery; were shallow, offering little top-cover; with the few dugouts having entrances facing enemy guns. All factors that amplified the impact of very effective enemy fire.

After nineteen months' combat, it was no longer the same battalion. Those who sailed on that cold February day in 1915 felt it, too:

> Something was lost from this time that was never quite recaptured. The feeling that the whole battalion was really a body of pre-War Territorials, taking part in some vast process of annual training, but still almost a club of friends, necessarily became less strong; and as fresh drafts of strangers came and were absorbed into the battalion, the military organisation may have become more efficient, but something of the sheer joy of fellowship, with which we had trained at Canterbury and sailed to France, was lost to be seen no more.[39]

Deploying to the BEF with 1,125, the battalion had lost 251 killed and no less than 1,124 wounded (the latter figure includes some who were wounded more than once). Although some wounded returned, this was more than offset by those lost through injury, sickness, and commissioning; clearly it was not the same battalion. The veterans of the battalion saw the Somme as a watershed because of the sheer number of casualties in two months, many of whom were 'originals'. No less than 50 per cent of all their wounded to date, and 55 per cent of those killed, occurred during these two months.

Casualties, 23-28 September 1916

L/Cpl Charles Frederick Adams	240896	KIA: 25/9	Rfn Robert William Henry Ambrose	3609	KIA: 25/9
A/Cpl Harold Adams	240740	WIA: 25/9	Rfn Robert Henry Argue	4154	KIA: 25/9
Rfn Frederick William Aitcheson	242033	WIA: 25/9	L/Cpl Thomas Campbell Argue	240596	WIA: 24/9
Rfn James Allan	3812	KIA: 26/9	Rfn James Armstrong	240159	WIA: 25/9

Rfn Charles Walter Ayre	4096	KIA: 24/9
Rfn Colin James Macbeth Bain	240633	WIA: 25/9
Rfn Arthur Baker*	241882	WIA: 24/9
Rfn Wilfred Ball	241639	WIA: 25/9
Cpl George Finch Bibby	240215	WIA: 25/9
Rfn Arthur Clifford Bingham	240336	WIA: 25/9
2Lt Kenneth Bisset		WIA: 25/9
Rfn Arthur Diamond Boyd	240266	WIA: 25/9
Sgt William Cropper Broster	2061	DOW: 26/9
Lt Walter Robinson Brownell		WIA: 26/9
2Lt Eric Kelso Buckley		WIA: 25/9
Rfn Neville R. Burrows	242134	WIA: 26/9
Sgt Arthur Bushell**	1675	KIA: 25/9
2Lt Charles Henry Buttery		DOW: 1/10
Rfn Peter Cain	3867	WIA: 25/9
L/Cpl Thomas Proctor Carr	240125	WIA: 25/9
Rfn William E. Cashin	4645	WIA: 25/9
Rfn Thomas George Chambers	242124	KIA: 25/9
Rfn Andrew Clark (M)	241761	WIA: 25/9
Rfn William Killip Cleator	4433	KIA: 25/9
Rfn John Clegg	242067	WIA: 25/9
Rfn Percy Collins	3934	KIA: 25/9
Rfn Richard Conlon	241890	WIA: 25/9
Rfn Robert Cooper	4585	DOW: Jan 17
Rfn Harold Corrin	4555	WIA: 26/9
Rfn David Courtie	241616	WIA: 25/9
Rfn Henry Cowins	240254	WIA: 28/9
Rfn Albert Ernest Cromer	240116	WIA: 25/9
Rfn Herbert E. Crosby	2705	SS: 25/9
Rfn James O. Cross	4635	WIA: 25/9
Rfn Thomas Dalrymple	3581	WIA: 25/9
Cpl John Danily	240555	WIA: 24/9
Rfn Gwilym Ryle Davies	241898	WIA: 26/9
Rfn William Herbert Davies	241992	KIA: 25/9
Rfn Nathan Davis	240537	WIA: 25/9
Rfn Philip Davis	240132	WIA: 25/9
Rfn Robert Edward Draper	241453	WIA: 25/9
Rfn James Durham	242096	WIA: 25/9
Rfn James Morris Earl	240564	WIA: 24/9
2Lt Donald Eastwood		WAD: 25/9
Rfn Wilson Eccleston	241718	WIA: 25/9
Rfn James Elliott	240765	WIA: 25/9
Rfn David Frank Emblen	4223	WIA: 25/9
Rfn David H. Evans	241794	WIA: 25/9
Rfn James Percival Evans	241783	WIA: 25/9
Rfn Stanley Fawcett	240414	WIA: 25/9
Rfn Robert Finnegan	242098	KIA: 25/9
Rfn Frederick Newman Ford	242074	KIA: 25/9
Rfn James Oliver Foster	241623	KIA: 25/9
Rfn Frank Fraser	240618	WIA: 25/9
Rfn Thomas Richard Gaddas	242004	SS: 26/9
2Lt Harry Leonard Gardner		WIA: 25/9
Rfn Edgar Johnstone Gauntlett	4072	KIA: 24/9
Rfn Joseph Gladwinfield	241693	WIA: 25/9
Rfn Richard Griffiths	240163	WIA: 25/9
Sgt William Arthur Hallam	240335	WAD: 25/9
Rfn Douglas Hamar	241740	WIA: 25/9
Rfn Thomas Hankin	241780	WIA: 24/9
2Lt George Harrison		WIA: 25/9
L/Cpl William Arthur Harton	241353	WIA: 24/9
L/Cpl William Frederick S. Hatte	2149	WIA: 25/9
Rfn William F. Henderson	2893	WIA: 25/9
Rfn William C. Hepworth	4455	WIA: 25/9
Capt. Ernest Herschell		DOW: 26/9
Rfn Peter Hesketh	241438	WIA: 25/9
Rfn Charles Douglas Hill	4215	DOW: 25/9
L/Sgt Thomas Reginald Hill	2421	DOW: 26/9
Rfn William John Hill	242021	WIA: 25/9
Rfn Ernest Hitchen	241684	WIA: 25/9
Rfn Albert Christopher Hodgson	241668	WIA: 25/9
Rfn Mark Hodgson	4491	KIA: 25/9
Rfn Reginald James Holmes	4476	WIA: 25/9
Rfn Philip Howorth	240321	WAD: 28/9
L/Cpl Thomas Alfred Hughes	240907	KIA: 25/9

CQMS Robert Joseph Hull	240033	WIA: 25/9
Rfn Joseph E. Ion	241236	WIA: 24/9
Rfn Charles Jackson	4526	WIA: 25/9
Rfn Frank William James	241855	WIA: 25/9
Rfn Arthur Stanley Johnson	241962	WIA: 23/9
Rfn Ernest Beresford Jones	241557	KIA: 28/9
Rfn Frederick Charles Jones	242129	WIA: 25/9
Rfn Geoffrey Jones	241700	WIA: 25/9
Rfn George H. Jones	3991	WIA: 25/9
Rfn Griffith Jones	2192	KIA: 25/9
Rfn J. Jones	3540	WIA: 24/9
Rfn W. Jones	4231	WIA: 25/9
Rfn Wilfred Jones	241720	WIA: 25/9
Rfn William A. Jones	241881	WIA: 25/9
Rfn James George Kay	242107	WIA: 24/9
L/Cpl George Hodgson Keates	241070	SS: 25/9
Rfn Herbert Joseph Keegan	242043	KIA: 25/9
Rfn Henry Kirkland	4051	DOW: 26/9
Rfn Sydney James Kneale	241110	WIA: 28/9
CSM James Arthur Knight	240011	WAD: 25/9
Rfn George Benjamin Langhorne	241803	WAD: 24/9
Rfn Arthur Hermon Lawes	241939	KIA: 25/9
Rfn John James Lee	242118	WIA: 25/9
Rfn William Edward Leech	242082	WIA: 25/9
Rfn George Henry Lennie	2563	KIA: 26/9
Rfn Edward C. Lewis	241622	WIA: 25/9
L/Cpl Herbert Owen Lewis	240133	WIA: 25/9
Cpl Humphrey Lewis	240601	WIA: 25/9
Rfn Herbert Lister	240476	WIA: 24/9
L/Cpl John Robert Litchfield	240534	KIA: 25/9
Rfn Sydney Lloyd	2208	WIA: 25/9
Rfn Harold J. Lovett	4275	KIA: 25/9
Rfn Alexander Lucas	241705	WIA: 25/9
Rfn Edward Lyth	2950	WIA: 25/9
Rfn Thomas Magee (M)	242016	WIA: 25/9
Rfn Harold Egbert Marsden	240790	WIA: 25/9
Cpl Thomas J. Marsden	2865	WIA: 25/9
Rfn Charles Algernon Marston	241964	KIA: 25/9
Cpl James Maxwell	240747	WIA: 25/9
Rfn Richard Leonard Maybury	241635	KIA: 25/9
Rfn Herbert Thomas Mayes	241448	WIA: 25/9
Rfn Francis McDonnell	2709	WIA: 25/9
Sgt Edward McGill	1076	KIA: 25/9
Sgt John Philip McGill	240077	WIA: 25/9
Rfn John Joseph McGrath	2137	DOW: 28/9
Rfn James McKellar	241662	WIA: 25/9
Rfn Nathan McManus	241895	WIA: 25/9
CSM Thomas McWean	240005	WAD: 25/9
L/Cpl Joseph Merrigan	2976	WIA: 24/9
Rfn Malcolm Harding Moses	241993	WIA: 24/9
Rfn Walter Harding Moses	241648	WIA: 24/9
Rfn John Lund Mylrea	240836	WIA: 24/9
Rfn Ernest Neely	240283	WIA: 25/9
Rfn William Henry Niblett	241363	WIA: 24/9
Rfn James Vincent Nicholl	240661	WIA: 26/9
Rfn David John Owens	241666	WIA: 25/9
Rfn Milford G. Parker	4100	WIA: 24/9
Rfn Joseph Henry Parkins	240990	WIA: 24/9
Rfn William Bernard Parkinson	3895	DOW: 1/10
2Lt James Paton		WAD: 25/9
L/Sgt William Lawrie Paton**	1276	KIA: 25/9
2Lt Walter Penrice		WIA: 25/9
Rfn George T. Phillips	241817	WIA: 25/9
Rfn Harold Phillips	241381	WIA: 25/9
Cpl John Elliott Pilling	240230	SS: 25/9
Rfn Mortimer Pim	1658	DOW: 26/9
L/Cpl Percy Postlethwaite	1967	KIA: 25/9
Rfn Ernest G. Pritchard	240859	SS: 25/9
Rfn Samuel Randles	240348	WIA: 25/9
Rfn William John Randles	240145	WIA: 25/9
Sgt Albert Edward Rankmore	240038	WIA: 25/9
Rfn William Redhead	241932	WIA: 27/9
Rfn Leslie John Rees	1807	SS: 25/9
Rfn Charles Reinecke	240146	WIA: 25/9
Rfn Arthur Rider	3529	KIA: 25/9
Cpl Thomas Francis Rigby	240313	WIA: 26/9
Rfn Ernest Roberts	240558	WIA: 25/9
Rfn John George Roberts	241779	KIA: 25/9

Rfn Greig Newton Robinson	241739	WIA: 25/9
Rfn John Robinson	240710	WIA: 24/9
Lt Nigel Bruce Ronald		WIA: 25/9
Rfn George J. Ross	3852	WIA: 25/9
Rfn John R. Ruddock	3989	WIA: 25/9
Rfn George Runacus	241513	WIA: 25/9
Sgt Edmund Douglas Savage**	2270	KIA: 25/9
Rfn Herbert William Scholefield	240919	WIA: 25/9
Rfn Thomas Shallcross	240857	SS: 25/9
Cpl John Alfred Shaw	240179	WIA: 25/9
Rfn Philip Herbert Smart	241167	WIA: 25/9
Rfn Albert Smith	240789	WIA: 25/9
Rfn C. Smith	4360	WIA: 25/9
Rfn Rowland Smith	2177	WIA: 24/9
Rfn William Smith	241778	WIA: 25/9
Rfn Frederick Stockton	241650	WIA: 25/9
L/Cpl John Strutt	3507	KIA: 25/9
Rfn William Henry Sumner	242128	WIA: 25/9
Rfn Herbert Henry Sundwall	241689	WIA: 25/9
L/Cpl Stephen Sutcliffe	240810	WIA: 25/9
Rfn Arthur Watts Swinnerton	3758	KIA: 25/9
Rfn John Thomas	241824	WIA: 26/9
Rfn Samuel Thomas	241896	SS: 25/9
Rfn William Thompson	4380	DOW: 26/9
Rfn Joshua Foden Thomson	241772	WIA: 25/9
Rfn William Towers	4345	KIA: 24/9
Rfn Albert Waddington	241411	WIA: 25/9
Rfn Samuel Walls	4630	WIA: 25/9
Sgt Albert Watson	240143	WIA: 25/9
Rfn Octavius Watson	241653	WIA: 25/9
L/Sgt John Joseph Humphrey Weld	240421	WIA: 25/9
Rfn Thomas Dean Wells	3860	DOW: 27/9
Rfn Francis Allan Westray	3935	KIA: 25/9
Rfn James Whittaker	241018	SS: 25/9
Rfn Arthur Spencer Williams	4503	KIA: 25/9
Rfn Frank Williams	4667	KIA: 25/9
Rfn Robert Charles Williams	241736	KIA: 25/9
Rfn Robert George Williams	241796	WIA: 28/9
Rfn Samuel Williams	240572	WIA: 25/9
Rfn William David Williams	242047	WIA: 25/9
Rfn Eric Wilson	3820	KIA: 25/9
2Lt Hugh Randles Withers		WIA: 25/9
Sgt James Rothwell Worthington	240019	WIA: 25/9

* = attached to the 1/9th. ** = CWGC have the wrong date of death. (M) = attached to 165 MGC.

7

30 September 1916—3 July 1917: Return to the Salient

Coordinates for this Chapter

Location	Coordinates
'B' Camp	50°51′23.30″N 2°47′10.80″E
Bat Trench	50°51′14.80″N 2°55′59.50″E
Beek Trench	50°51′5.10″N 2°55′41.80″E
Bellewaarde Sap	50°51′5.50″N 2°56′20.00″E
Bliss Crater	50°51′13.00″N 2°56′8.80″E
Block-A	50°51′16.50″N 2°56′9.60″E
Block-P	50°51′13.30″N 2°56′16.10″E
Block-Q	50°51′16.30″N 2°56′17.70″E
Block-S	50°51′17.70″N 2°56′15.00″E
C.28.1	50°52′12.90″N 2°55′16.60″E
C.29.2	50°51′54.70″N 2°55′40.60″E
C.29.3	50°51′57.70″N 2°55′38.00″E
C.29.4	50°52′0.60″N 2°55′34.70″E
C.29.5	50°52′3.20″N 2°55′33.40″E
C.29.6	50°52′5.10″N 2°55′30.90″E
C.29.7	50°52′7.20″N 2°55′28.00″E
C.29.8	50°52′9.00″N 2°55′23.60″E
C.29.9	50°52′11.20″N 2°55′19.30″E
Cambrai Trench	50°52′15.50″N 2°55′35.50″E
Cambridge Road	50°51′27.60″N 2°55′42.50″E
Camel Trench	50°52′3.00″N 2°55′52.00″E
Congreve Walk	50°51′56.60″N 2°54′31.80″E
Cotter Crater	50°51′7.40″N 2°56′15.60″E
crater (unnamed)	50°51′13.00″N 2°56′7.70″E
Crater-1a	50°51′2.60″N 2°56′16.80″E
Crater-2	50°51′8.70″N 2°56′12.60″E

Crater-2a	50°51′8.00″N 2°56′13.70″E	Hellfire Corner	50°50′55.30″N 2°55′1.60″E
Crater-3	50°51′14.20″N 2°56′6.70″E	Hopkins Trench	50°52′18.70″N 2°55′14.70″E
Crater-4	50°51′14.90″N 2°56′4.60″E	Hornby Crater	50°51′3.10″N 2°56′18.90″E
Crater-5	50°51′19.90″N 2°56′4.90″E	Horne Works	50°51′1.00″N 2°53′39.70″E
Crater Trench	50°51′12.10″N 2°56′0.20″E	I.5.1	50°51′24.10″N 2°56′0.30″E
Crump Farm HQ	50°51′44.10″N 2°55′42.00″E	I.5.2	50°51′26.90″N 2°55′58.10″E
Culvert, The	50°50′48.10″N 2°56′19.30″E	I.5.3	50°51′29.10″N 2°55′56.40″E
Derby Camp	50°51′27.80″N 2°47′47.30″E	I.5.4	50°51′31.30″N 2°55′54.20″E
disused trench	50°51′18.60″N 2°56′3.70″E	I.5.5	50°51′34.40″N 2°55′51.50″E
École	50°50′53.80″N 2°54′3.20″E	I.5.6	50°51′36.70″N 2°55′49.30″E
‘G’ Camp	50°52′54.70″N 2°45′50.80″E	I.5.7	50°51′38.80″N 2°55′48.40″E
German mine 9 March	50°51′10.00″N 2°56′15.50″E	I.5.8	50°51′41.30″N 2°55′47.10″E
Gordon Crater	50°51′13.60″N 2°56′8.80″E	I.11.1	50°51′10.00″N 2°56′6.90″E
Group-A	50°51′14.00″N 2°56′11.00″E	I.11.2	50°51′12.60″N 2°56′5.20″E
Group-B	50°51′15.10″N 2°56′10.40″E	I.11.3	50°51′16.20″N 2°56′2.70″E
Group-C	50°51′13.70″N 2°56′8.10″E	I.11.4	50°51′18.60″N 2°56′1.30″E
Group-R	50°51′15.40″N 2°56′16.90″E	I.12.2	50°51′3.40″N 2°56′16.10″E
Group-T	50°51′16.10″N 2°56′14.60″E	I.12.3	50°51′5.80″N 2°56′13.70″E
Half Moon Trench	50°51′11.60″N 2°54′44.90″E	I.12.4	50°51′9.20″N 2°56′10.40″E
Haymarket	50°51′33.60″N 2°55′17.50″E	Ice Support	50°51′29.10″N 2°56′21.00″E
Hedge Trench	50°51′1.90″N 2°54′42.90″E	Idea Salient (tip)	50°51′14.30″N 2°56′8.60″E

Idea Switch	50°51′20.40″N 2°56′23.90″E	Prowse Trench	50°51′48.70″N 2°55′4.20″E
Idea Trench	50°51′13.90″N 2°56′10.70″E	Question Trench	50°51′0.40″N 2°56′10.70″E
Identity Trench	50°51′8.60″N 2°56′18.50″E	raid 1 July	50°52′17.70″N 2°55′29.00″E
Idle Trench	50°50′55.50″N 2°56′29.10″E	Railway Farm	50°50′59.70″N 2°55′22.20″E
James Street	50°51′28.80″N 2°55′2.10″E	Railway Wood	50°51′12.70″N 2°55′59.60″E
Jasper Farm	50°52′17.90″N 2°55′53.40″E	Ramparts	50°51′1.80″N 2°53′29.30″E
Jctn Gully Tr./Air Street	50°51′25.20″N 2°55′57.80″E	Rifle Farm Post	50°50′57.10″N 2°55′22.50″E
Jctn Mud Lane and I.12.3	50°51′4.60″N 2°56′13.50″E	River Trench	50°50′52.00″N 2°55′45.60″E
Junction Trench	50°51′6.50″N 2°56′7.00″E	Sap-1	50°51′4.00″N 2°56′14.50″E
Kaiser Bill	50°52′6.80″N 2°55′41.00″E	Sap-1 (head)	50°51′4.50″N 2°56′19.20″E
Lone Farm	50°52′7.50″N 2°55′6.00″E	Sap-2	50°51′8.70″N 2°56′16.20″E
Moat, The	50°51′37.90″N 2°55′58.50″E	Sap-3	50°51′12.70″N 2°56′14.90″E
Mound, The	50°51′46.60″N 2°55′51.80″E	South Lane	50°51′0.10″N 2°55′10.50″E
Mud Lane	50°51′0.20″N 2°55′54.10″E	Strand	50°51′48.00″N 2°55′8.80″E
Mud Lane (end of)	50°51′4.90″N 2°56′14.40″E	Vernon Crater	50°51′7.10″N 2°56′15.60″E
New John Street	50°52′11.00″N 2°55′6.60″E	Vinery, The	50°51′48.10″N 2°54′47.30″E
‘O’ Camp	50°51′59.00″N 2°47′13.70″E	Warwick Farm	50°51′56.20″N 2°55′35.20″E
Park Lane	50°51′31.00″N 2°55′47.00″E	West Lane	50°51′11.30″N 2°56′4.00″E
Piccadilly	50°51′22.50″N 2°55′19.00″E	White Cottage	50°52′14.80″N 2°55′27.30″E
Potijze Château	50°51′44.60″N 2°54′54.40″E	White Sap	50°52′8.90″N 2°55′30.00″E
Potijze left bound	50°51′42.40″N 2°55′46.50″E	‘Y’ Camp	50°51′30.60″N 2°40′53.70″E
Pratt Street	50°52′21.00″N 2°54′47.30″E		

The battalion remained at Buire until 1 October, then marched to Méricourt, boarding a train for Longpré-les-Corps-Saints and thence to billets in Bellancourt. On 2 October, after a short march to Pont Remy, men and equipment were loaded onto a train bound for Esquelbecq. From there, it was 4 miles to billets in Herzeele. On 4 October, the battalion travelled to Poperinghe, then marched to 'G' Camp, between Poperinghe and Woesten—a brief interlude, as next day, they entrained on the light railway at Poperinghe, bound for Ypres.

Two companies went into the Ramparts: one into an old factory, the Horne Works (not to be confused with another Ypres billet, the Hornworks of the old Vauban defences), the other to the École. HQ went into the old Infantry Barracks. Norman Ellison wrote home from the Ramparts on 6 October:

> I have written you previous letters from many queer spots, but the place where this is being written certainly takes the biscuit.
>
> I am way down underground in a wooden-walled alcove off a long tunnel splendidly lit by electric light and as snug and cosy as could be. Up above are the ruins and debris of a once very fine city, now so badly battered and bashed about that it is scarcely recognisable. I have many happy memories of it earlier in the war, but now it is a nightmare![1]

They remained on support until 10 October. Before moving up to the line, RQMS William Ward departed—just one month short of his forty-ninth birthday—his lengthy service ended. CSM Thomas McWean was promoted to replace him.

The divisional front encompassed two sectors—left and right—each subdivided into left and right subsectors. Although strongpoints, communication trenches, and enemy positions were named, fighting trenches received a number based upon their map reference. For example, the left bound of the line was labelled C.28.10. This was because it was in 'Square C', 'Sub-square 28', and was the tenth section from the right within that sub-square. The divisional front encompassed everything south of Pratt Street on the left to the northern side of the Menin Road, at a point known as the Culvert, where, due to marshy conditions, the British line was discontinuous. The right of the continuous British line ended at Crater-1a, the 475 yards of ground between there and the Culvert manned only after dark by a series of small posts known as the Grouse Butts. The main line continued south of the Menin Road, 600 yards further west. The portion nearest the Menin Road was also patrolled by the division to their right, and to avoid misunderstandings, patrols there included a liaison from their neighbours.

It was to Railway Wood the battalion deployed on the evening of 10 October, their left bound at I.11.4 and the right at the Culvert. This subsector was the hottest stretch of the divisional front, opposing sides a mere 20 yards apart in places and constant mining making life precarious.

'B' held the left, with 'A' to their right, and 'C' in support. 'D' was in reserve, with one platoon with HQ in F-13 (South Lane); another in Rifle Farm Post; and a third in F-11 (Beek Trench). The 11th was quiet, though Riflemen J. Wooley of 'C' and Thomas Hill from 'D' both suffered minor facial wounds. That night, a patrol examined the German wire on the south side of the salient in Idea Trench, finding it in very good condition.

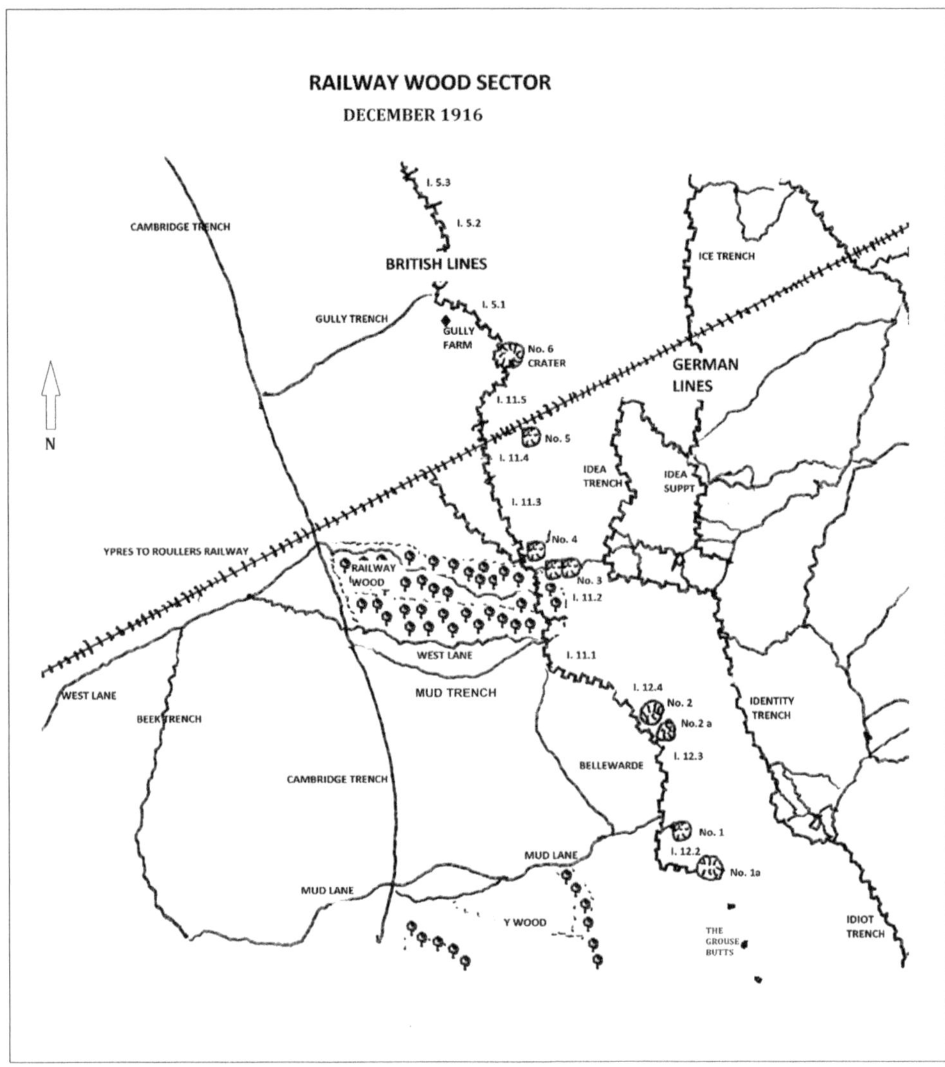

On 12 October, while Maj.-Gen. Jeudwine inspected their trenches, there was intermittent artillery fire, a few rounds falling around F-13, though no casualties resulted. However, between 11.20 a.m. and 1 p.m., forty mortar rounds struck the left of 'B' Company's positions (I.11.3 and I.11.4). Although not physically hurt, two Riflemen were shell-shocked: Donald McMillan and Frank Scarff both returned after six days' rest. When divisional Howitzers retaliated, the mortars ceased. Two night patrols reported that the enemy had been carrying out new work on Idea Trench and also in Idle Trench, opposite the Grouse Butts. On 13 October, 'D' relieved 'B' on the left and 'C' exchanged places with 'A'. There was intermittent enemy fire against F-13 and I.12.3 and I.12.4 on the right, though without result. During the night, an enemy patrol from Identity Trench was spotted approaching Crater-2 and sent scurrying back when two Lewis posts engaged them.

Intermittent fire from 77-mm was directed towards 'C' during the day on 14 October, again without result. However, hostile mortar fire against their right positions killed twenty-two-year-old Rfn Tom Poole and wounded Sgt Harold Crook at duty. At midnight, the battalion was relieved and returned to Ypres, where they boarded a train for Brandhoek, being billeted in huts in 'B' Camp as brigade reserve.

There, twenty officers joined the battalion from the Manchester Regiment and Monmouths; however, fifteen of these parted company within the fortnight. The battalion remained in reserve until 23 October and whenever weather and the demands of working parties allowed, they trained. On 21 October, men learnt to use the new box respirator, a huge improvement over the PH helmet. Corps-Commander of VIII Corps Lt-Gen. Hunter-Weston—nicknamed 'Hunter-Bunter'—inspected them on 18 October. No mention was made in the diary as to the outcome, suggesting it was not a happy time—positive experiences were usually commented upon. The personal diary of Brig.-Gen Stockwell, commander of 164 Bde, leaves little doubt as to the opinion of some senior officers:

> [9 October] COs dining with the Corps-Commander. He is reported mad—dashes about the country inspecting kitchens. Not a Corps-Commander's job. He is a Sapper. [12 October] Tea first then the most astonishing diatribe from Hunter-Weston. He started by saying, almost in words, that none but old generals like himself him knew anything, and that the older ones knew nothing. He preached no trust and spying, and actually spoke the words, 'Remember, I Hunter-Weston, the Corps-Commander, am always watching you, my staff officers are always going round reporting on you.' He then went on about clean frying pans in officers' kitchens etc. The man is mad, egomania. [On 14 October] At the COs class he fell them all in and told them their boots were not clean and some of them filthy—considering half of them had come straight out of trenches and ridden 5 miles I don't wonder—the man is mad.

On 20 October, Hunter-Weston visited just after a torrential downpour caused severe flooding in the trenches; Stockwell noting that the:

> Corps-Commander inspected every latrine seat.—they had just been scrubbed, so he accused officers of peeing on them—then objected to the size of the aperture—too small he said—he then said a slot was to be cut for every officers' private parts and turning to me said, 'This requires your personal supervision'—so I know my job now. He went on this way all round the line. As the trenches built by his beloved 29 Division are falling down everywhere and as this battalion is in trenches for the first time it is rather rough [1/4th Loyals in Railway Wood]. He then started to try and walk me off my legs, by running down the trenches—in the end he dropped his stick and went over it, which slowed him up a bit. Every d...d silly detail, such as the cleanliness of officers' knives—when you are living in a sea of mud were what he fussed about. He is mad and a Sapper.[2]

Drafts from England were not keeping pace with losses, and although dozens destined for the battalion reached 24 IBD, the Casualties Book illustrates that most were diverted elsewhere. During October, only thirty-six arrived, and fighting strength shrank to 664 by the end of the month. Rfn James Rutherford was sent home 'underage' on 16 October, and though there were still another seven, it would be March 1917 before the last was unearthed.

Signals-Sergeant Joseph Smith (036) was severely reprimanded by the CO on 20 October, having transmitted a sensitive message over the telephone during their last stint in the line, risking its interception by German eavesdroppers; though he was too good a soldier to lose his rank over the matter, especially as he had earned the MM while the battalion was on the Somme.

On 24 October, the battalion returned to Ypres, employed on numerous working parties to the front line and the rear. Three days later, the front line beckoned, 'D' taking the left of Railway Wood and 'C' the right. In the early hours of the morning, a 'D' Company patrol entered No Man's Land from the extreme left of the battalion's line, crossed to the enemy wire, and proceeded southward along the outside of it to an unnamed German-held crater, directly east of Crater-3 (in Coordinates Table as 'Group-C'). They found the dense wire in very good condition, with many trip wires and aprons to its front. The patrol lay up 15 yards from the crater, from where loud conversation and laughter could be heard. 'C' sent a patrol to look at the sap head, near the junction of Identity and Idiot Trench, opposite Crater-1 (Sap-1 (head) in Coordinates Table). This was also manned, the sounds of working parties from inside there clearly audible, an alert sentry firing successive flares into No Man's Land.

Hostile artillery was generally quiet on 28 October, just a few scattered 77-mm across the sector. That night, a patrol exited I.11.2 to examine an unnamed crater 50 yards to their front, finding no trace of enemy activity there. On 29 October, enemy artillery became more active and Hellfire Corner, Railway Farm (a.k.a. Rifle Farm), and Railway Wood all came under fire. Rfn Herbert Sundwall from 'D' was wounded in the right thigh by shrapnel, and after leaving hospital, he was posted to 1/KLR (recorded in the diary for the 28th, but other sources place it during the afternoon of 29 October[3]). That night, another patrol revisited the unnamed crater, finding it half-flooded—explaining its disuse.

Conditions were vile, ceaseless heavy rain initiating constant collapse of the breastworks, increasing the already-high workload. Enemy artillery was much quieter on 30 October, their only target being Hellfire Corner, hit by six 10.5-cm shells at 10.15 a.m. One 'D' Company patrol inspected a 70-yard length of disused trench in front of I.11.4–I.11.3, which although only 40 yards away, could not be viewed clearly from the breastworks. The patrol returned, describing it as a series of shell holes, all full to the brim with water. On the night of 31 October, the battalion was relieved and returned to the Infantry Barracks.

Until returning to Railway Wood in the evening of 4 November, everyone grafted hard on working parties and the move to the front line was probably welcomed. This time, 'B' took the left, with 'A' to their right. 'D' manned left support and 'C' the right. 'A' posted one night patrol, tasked with reconnoitring Sap-1. As 'C' had earlier discovered, the sentry here was alert, periodically firing off flares from the sap-head. The patrol found the dense wire still in very good repair, well-supported by 2-foot-high wooden stakes.

On 5 November, heavy rain continued, and apart from a few isolated shells on Railway Wood, hostile artillery was inactive. In the afternoon, a *Minenwerfer* firing from Ice Support targeted Railway Wood, but was soon put out of action by six direct hits from divisional Howitzers. Once it was light, a view of the southern side of the Idea Salient through a trench periscope revealed that, during the night, the enemy had raised the parapet. No patrols ventured out overnight, as 1/5th South Lancs, to their left, were raiding the Mound.

There was very little enemy fire on 6 November, despite 165 TMB firing forty rounds at Identity Trench—directly opposite I.12.4—that morning and another thirty-two rounds at the tip of Idea Salient at 5.45 p.m. (the diary reports one man wounded, though there are no supporting entries in the Casualties Book). At 9 p.m., 'A' sent a patrol to examine the ground between I.12.2 and Crater-2a; apart from hearing a noisy working party near the junction of Identity and Idiot Trench, they returned with nothing to report.

Minenwerfers were very active against Railway Wood on 7 November, and though a number of the trenches were blown in by direct hits, no casualties resulted. The divisional Howitzers retaliated with 250 rounds against suspected *Minenwerfer* positions, their bombardment enhanced by fire from the TMB. A continuation of hostile mortar fire against the left of the battalion's positions on 8 November resulted in five casualties. Twenty-three-year-old Rfn Samuel Owens of 'B' was killed and Rfn Arthur Wakeham shell-shocked; from 'D', Rfn Edward Dutton was mildly shell-shocked, L/Cpl Herbert Stafford wounded in the thigh, and Rfn Archibald Wells wounded in the eye—the latter pair 'Blighty' cases. That night, the battalion was relieved and travelled from Ypres to Brandhoek by train, thenceforth to huts in 'O' Camp.

While there, Sgts William Winter, Joseph Smith, John Pennington, and Thomas Davies; Cpls Ralph Murrow, Samuel Duffy, and William Eaglesfield; L/Cpls Frank Gascoigne and Robert Hartley, and Riflemen David Wilson (338) and Richard Woods were gazetted for MMs. Sgt Ernest Dutton, who was detached to 15 Bde HQ as a clerk, was given a MiD. The MO was presented with the ribbon for his MC; Sgt Roper his DCM ribbon; and Rfn William Williams (024) his MM ribbon. The latter is particularly notable, as twelve days later, he was sent home underage, accompanied by Rfn Charles Botting, whose parents had claimed him back for the same reason. Before the next week was out, another two youngsters also made the trip to the coast: Rfn Robert Longworth and Rfn Edward Ryan.

Time at 'O' Camp was divided between training and working parties. As ever, training had its hazards and Rfn James Murney was accidentally wounded in the right arm by a bomb on 16 November. On 17 November, Lt-Col. McKaig was informed that the battalion was to raid the southern side of Idea Salient, during the afternoon of 28 November, and that Liverpool Scottish would raid Kaiser Bill's Nose in the Wieltje Sector at the same time. Second-Lieutenants Douglas Colley, Maurice Moss, and Frank Pitt were chosen to lead the venture. To the great disappointment of many who volunteered, only eighty-three were chosen and withdrawn for special training. For everyone else, it was business as usual.

On 18 November, the battalion became brigade support in Ypres, 'A' now without Sgt Albert Rankmore, who became CSM of 'D'. The raiders travelled to 'A' Camp near Vlamertinghe, where they built a full-scale mock-up of their target on which to rehearse.

Ypres came under heavy fire at intervals most days, though the enemy held back the worst for darkness, shellfire killing twenty-one-year-old Rfn John Mills on 20 November. He was the only casualty before the battalion returned to Railway Wood on the night of 23 November.

Shortly after relief, the left company sent a patrol to check Crater-5, but found no evidence of enemy mining operations there. Considerable effort was invested into improving the trenches to speed up the movement of men and evacuation of wounded. Although 24 November began quietly, the enemy fired 200 *Minenwerfer* rounds into Railway Wood and the neighbouring sector between 3.30 p.m. and 4.30 p.m. That night, two patrols ventured forth: on the left, they investigated Crater-5 again, which was still unoccupied, then worked their way south to Crater-3, checking the ground; although it was badly cut up and water-logged close to British and German wire, the rest was in remarkably good condition. The right company examined the ground between Crater-1 and Sap-1, finding it badly pitted and very muddy.

The 25th was a day of mist and rain, with very little artillery action. During that night, an enemy sentry launched numerous flares from Sap-2—possibly because he had heard the battalion's working party in Crater-2a, only 50 yards away. This was the planned exit point for the raiders and only 150 yards from where British Howitzers would barrage, so to protect them from friendly fire, shelters were built into the northern face of the crater. Sentries on the left spotted an enemy patrol in No Man's Land, in between Crater-5 and Idea Trench, and they were dispersed with Lewis fire. It was an interesting night for the sentries there, as later that night, two half-starved Russian soldiers surrendered to them. The pair had been captured at Novo Giorgievsk in August 1915 and used as forced labour on the German third-line of defence near Besalare. Escaping from a working party at 11 a.m. that morning, they had hidden in weeds until 7 p.m., before making their bid to reach British lines. Amazingly, after a 6-mile journey through German territory, they reached safety (this episode is erroneously attributed to the night of 26–27 November and also to the 1/5th in the Brigade diary[4]).

Preparations for the raid were progressing well in Vlamertinghe, and a rehearsal was watched by Maj.-Gen. Jeudwine on 26 November. To preserve the element of surprise, there would be no advance bombardment, or destruction of the enemy wire, until an hour before Zero. Though some registration of guns and mortars was necessary, this being carried out over two days, with a day's interval between, beginning on 25 November. It was observed that after the second day, the enemy began registering his own front line with unfused mortar bombs, north of where the raiders intended to enter. As soon as this was perceived, Divisional artillery began to shell the German wire in this location—a very successful ruse, as the German barrage, when it fell during the raid, was well away from the raiders.

Patrols on the night of 26 November checked craters 2, 4, and 5, finding no sign of enemy activity. Between 12.45 p.m. and 4.15 p.m. on 27 November, enemy mortars fired forty-three rounds against front and support lines, severely damaging West Lane where it passed through the wood. British Howitzers and the TMB retaliated, scoring direct

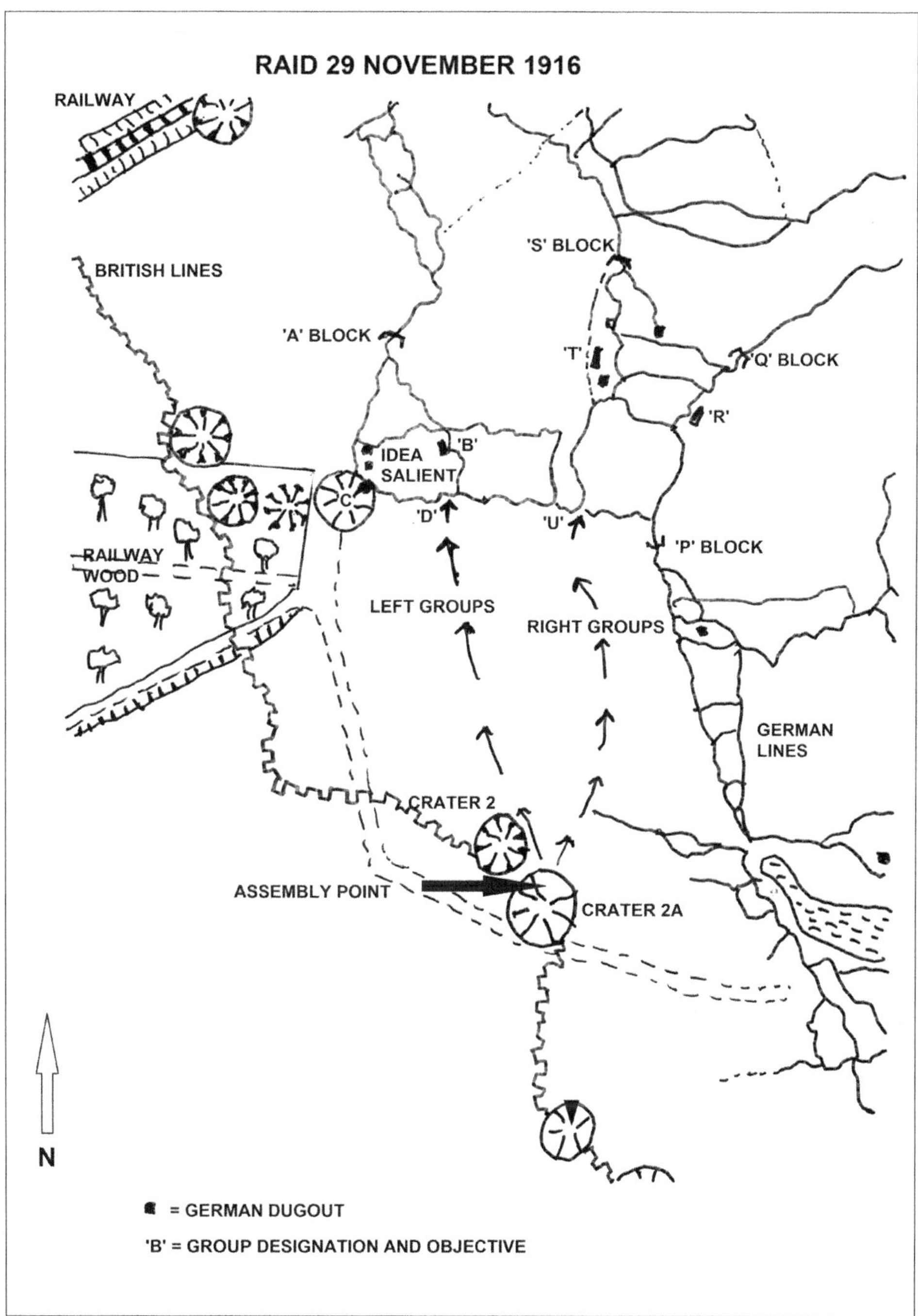
RAID 29 NOVEMBER 1916
RAILWAY
BRITISH LINES
'A' BLOCK
'S' BLOCK
'T'
'Q' BLOCK
'R'
'B'
IDEA
SALIENT
C
'D'
'U'
'P' BLOCK
RAILWAY
WOOD
LEFT GROUPS
RIGHT GROUPS
GERMAN
LINES
CRATER 2
ASSEMBLY POINT
CRATER 2A
N
= GERMAN DUGOUT
'B' = GROUP DESIGNATION AND OBJECTIVE

hits on two *Minenwerfers*. Only listening patrols went out overnight, the one in front of Crater-2a acting as covering party for a working party with a pair of Bangalore torpedoes, who thrust the 13-foot-long devices into the British wire at the intended exit point. Back in Vlamertinghe, the raiding party successfully completed their final rehearsal and moved up to the line.

At dawn on 28 November, thick fog hung over the entire sector, causing visibility down to go down to a few yards. This rendered observation of their fall of shot impossible for the TMB, tasked with breaching the German wire, so the raid was postponed twenty-four hours. Lingering fog so reduced artillery action that only thirteen German shells fell across the entire divisional sector all day. However, at dawn on 29 November, visibility was back to normal.

The raiders were organised into two unequally-sized parties to access two breaches in the enemy wire; four groups ('A'–'D') on the left and six on the right ('P'–'U'). In addition, each party had a 'wire-breaking and entrance group' of an officer and seven men, who would exit first to check the wire had been properly cut by the TMB; if not, they were to complete the breaches with a Bangalore and wire-cutters. A man from each wire-breaking group was given a 100-yard length of white tape to lay to the gap in the enemy wire to guide those following. Both wire-breaking groups would remain at the entrances and form a supporting point, a pair of men, widening each breach in the enemy wire after the raiders had passed through, to speed up egress.

Group-A (an NCO and four men) would access the left entrance, move north 100 yards, and construct 'Block-A' in Idea Trench. Right on their heels, Group-B (an NCO and two men) would clear the trenches around the tip of the salient. Group-C, the 'crater group' (an NCO, four men and two Sappers), would turn left immediately they accessed the German trench, then clear a suspected German position in the crater at the tip of the salient. Group-D (four men) was a stretcher-bearing party, remaining at the entrance with the wire-breakers.

On the right, Group-P (an NCO and seven men) would be the first through the breach. Turning right after entry, they would establish 'Block-P' in Identity Trench to the south of the salient. Group-Q (an officer, NCO and seven men) would establish 'Block-Q', 115 yards up Idea Row. Group-R was a clearing party of an NCO and eight men, accompanied by three Sappers, one of whom was detailed to collect intelligence about the construction of enemy defences. They would clear the length of Idea Row as far as the block, though their main task was to capture a suspected trench mortar. Group-S (an NCO and seven men) would advance the furthest into enemy lines, establishing 'Block-S' in Idea Support—the trench behind them to be cleared by Group-T (identical in composition to Group-R). The final group, 'U', was another four stretcher-bearers.

All identification was removed from the raiders' clothing and they handed over their ID discs. Instead, each man carried an envelope in his left breast pocket, bearing just his name and number. Everyone wore a white band on each arm to distinguish friend from foe.

An hour before Zero, divisional 18-pounders began their bombardment, targeting the rear of the enemy line to begin with before dropping the range to try and draw as many of the enemy as possible into the Salient. Twenty minutes later, the Howitzers joined in, their HE pulverising enemy trenches. Twenty minutes were allowed to give the 2-inch mortars of 165 TMB time to check-register their fire on the enemy wire at the entry points, the rounds having the new Newton fuse (a sensitive contact fuse). One 18-pounder battery was tasked with targeting Identity Trench, just to the right of the raiders, to keep enemy heads firmly down—accuracy essential as this was only 100 yards from the raiders. The Stokes dealt with Sap-2 and a machine-gun position south of it; the heavy mortars targeting German dugouts along the railway line. Six Vickers from 165 MGC provided barrage-fire against enemy lines of approach, expending 17,500 rounds (the 4.2 Howitzers fired 900 rounds; 18-pounders, 4,400-rounds; Stokes, 1,040-rounds; 2-inch mortars, 140-rounds; and 9.45-inch mortars, 6-rounds).

When the Howitzers opened fire, the Bangalores under the British wire were detonated and the raiders in Crater-2a prepared to move out. Only a few splinters from British fire fell inside the crater, causing no casualties. Precisely at 4.50 p.m., the raiders exited, the left party leading. Accompanying them was a Lewis team, who set up halfway between the crater and the entrance points, covering Identity Trench—a second Lewis team remained in Crater-2a in case of any opposition from Sap-2. Speed was of the essence; only thirty minutes was allowed from Zero to withdrawal and there were no means of modifying this. At 5.20 p.m., all guns would cease fire for ninety seconds and three buglers in British lines would play the 'Cookhouse' call to recall the raiders before British artillery began their covering barrage for the withdrawal.

The Bangalores performed impeccably: unfortunately, No Man's Land itself was very heavy-going, considerably delaying progress. The officers of the two entrance groups were each equipped with a torch to guide the others to the breach in the wire and a red lamp to signal back to British lines that all the raiders had entered. Although the first worked well, the red lamp could not be perceived. On the right, the man tasked with laying out the white tape was wounded and his tape blown across, becoming entangled with the left tape, causing most of the right party to access on the left. There was some hostile rifle fire from Identity Trench and Sap-2, and it was probably this that wounded the tape-layer. Second-Lieutenant Colley, in charge of the right entrance group, was killed on his way forward—the right party therefore having no light to guide them to the correct location. The only other source of small arms fire, the crater at the head of the Salient, was distant. Enemy artillery and mortar retaliation was feeble, mostly directed at the stretch of line where the decoy wire-cutting had been carried out. Only a few small-calibre rounds fell near Crater-2a.

With further to go than planned, only a portion of Group-P reached their allocated blocking position, but found they were redundant, Identity Trench having been obliterated by British Howitzers. The other right-hand groups failed to reach their objectives for the same reason—so effective had the Howitzers been that virtually nothing of the trench remained. Group-T, frustrated by their slow progress, took a direct route across open ground, finding two Germans in a shelter; the enemy NCO was killed and the private wounded, dying before he could be brought back.

On the left, Group-A only reached their blocking point at withdrawal time, having been delayed near the left entrance, bombing a deep-mined dugout under the parapet—killing one and capturing four enemy. Group-C found their progress impeded by the devastation, reaching the crater as the time limit approached. Inside the crater was a concrete structure, with five steps leading down. Nearby, a sentry post was found to contain three enemy, one of whom was killed, the others capitulating. A wood-lined concrete dugout, built into the side of the parapet 25 yards east of the left entrance point, yielded six more prisoners. In total, three enemy were killed by the raiders, another four were found dead in the trenches; thirteen prisoners were returned to British lines, two of whom were wounded and a further two killed by German fire on the way back. No machine guns were found, though an empty emplacement was discovered; neither were any trench mortars located.

The Sappers brought their explosives back, the trenches so smashed that no demolition opportunity presented itself. The few surviving sections were very well-built, 7 feet deep, 4 feet wide, and the sandbag parados and parapet revetted with fascines and brushwood. The trenches were floor-boarded and well-drained, with bomb stores built next to the mined-dugout and sentry post.

When the time came for withdrawal, some groups failed to recognise the one-and-a-half-minute pause in British fire—probably because of the volume of enemy fire—though all heard the bugles. Last to leave was 2Lt Moss, commanding the left entrance group. As he returned across No Man's Land, he found a wounded raider and, ignoring the succession of flares and increasingly-heavy small arms fire from Identity Trench, hoisted the casualty onto his back and carried him towards safety. The young subaltern was almost home when he was mortally wounded, collapsing to the ground. Others left cover to assist, but were too late to help the twenty-one-year-old, who died as they reached him. The wounded man was rescued and survived. Unfortunately, his name was not recorded—it could be any one of seven who suffered incapacitating wounds. Had Moss survived, the MC would have been certain, though a MiD was duly awarded.[5] Another recognised was Cpl John Hayhurst, in charge of Group-T, who proved a capable leader.[6] The only surviving officer, 2Lt Pitt, received the MC for his leadership of Group-Q.

The raiders returned to Ypres, but four times during the night, Lt Robert Phillips and Sgt John Handley led small parties into No Man's Land to search for 2Lt Colley, whose fate was unknown. Each time, heavy fire forced them back, thankfully without further loss. Colley was the only one whose body was never recovered. The other dead were buried alongside 2Lt Moss at Vlamertinghe. Twenty-four-year-old Rfn Frank Kitson and Maurice Moss were both 'originals', but twenty-one-year-old Rfn John Casson had only been with the battalion for six weeks. Of the twelve wounded, six of whom were 'originals', only three returned.

Casualties from the Raid, 29 November 1916

Name	No.	Status	Name	No.	Status
Rfn John Casson	5205	KIA	Rfn Charles William Hughes	241029	WIA
Rfn Ernest C. Cleaver	241116	WIA	Rfn Francis Henry Kitson	1745	KIA
2Lt Douglas James Colley		KIA	2Lt Maurice Edgar Moss		KIA
Rfn David William Edwards	241940	WIA	Rfn Thomas Patrick Murney	240375	WIA
Rfn William Edwards	241804	WIA	Sgt Henry Edwin Adey Reeves	240319	WIA
L/Cpl Richard Griffiths	240163	WIA			
Rfn John Rae Milligan Grinton	240647	WIA	L/Cpl John Charles Roberts	240201	WIA
Cpl Walter Bishop Hannah	240443	WIA	Rfn Arthur Smith	241667	WIA
Rfn Reginald James Holmes	4476	KIA	Rfn Harold John E. Wallace	242471	WIA

The rest of 30 November was quiet, apart from *Minenwerfer* fire against Railway Wood—which ceased when divisional artillery shelled their emplacement. In Vlamertinghe, the raiders paraded in front of Maj.-Gen. Jeudwine and Brig. Duncan, who congratulated them, the GOC also reading out a congratulatory message from Hunter-Weston. Expecting the enemy may attempt a retaliatory raid, the battalion was reinforced by a company of the 1/5th during the day, the rest of the 1/5th relieving the battalion that night. Tormented by the thought that their missing subaltern was lying wounded in No Man's Land, Cpl Hayhurst and L/Cpl John Evans made one final, unsuccessful search for twenty-eight-year-old Colley before they left the line.

This tour had been arduous thanks to the weather, a mix of extreme cold and heavy rain and it is no surprise that sickness rates increased markedly, especially for respiratory diseases. During November, forty-five men—approximately 8 per cent of the strength—were hospitalised with illness, twenty-three of whom were evacuated home.[7] With 'A' and 'B' in the Ramparts and 'C' and 'D' in the École, the battalion was shelled daily; however, they were out of the mud and in relative warmth, apart from when on working parties. On 1 December, the raiders attended the funeral for their dead at Vlamertinghe, a solemn occasion.

The battalion remained in Ypres until the night of the 5th, when, boosted by a draft who had arrived the previous day, they were relieved the 1/5th at Railway Wood. The companies in the École were probably thankful to leave, as German Howitzers had pounded their billet for much of the day. 'D' took the left of the front line, with 'A' to their right, 'B' and 'C' in dugouts behind them.

At 9 a.m., and again between 2 p.m. and 5 p.m. on 6 December, 77-mm targeted Railway Wood, but caused little damage. During the afternoon, however, *Minenwerfer* fire, between 3 p.m. and 4 p.m., killed twenty-year-old Rfn William Dilworth of 'C'—the only casualty from enemy action, though Rfn Thomas Turner from 'D' was admitted to the Field Ambulance after accidentally burning both hands. This tour was short, and apart from the hostile fire on 6 December, the enemy was quiet. The battalion was relieved on 8 December and went into reserve at 'O' Camp.

Training was carried out whenever men were not on working parties, such as on 11 December, when 100 men were burying cables. On 16 December, Maj.-Gen. Jeudwine presented medal ribbons for the MM to those gazetted in November and additionally to L/Cpl Percy Johnson, Rfn William Niblett, and L/Cpl Walter Hannah. Second-Lieutenant Pitt was also presented with the ribbon for his MC. In the evening of 18 December, they returned to Ypres.

Next evening, the devastated city was shrouded by a fresh fall of snow, a hard frost numbing the fingers of those on working parties. By 21 December, the snow had gone, replaced by driving rain. In these dreadful conditions, a 'B' Company working party was caught by a salvo of artillery, wounding four. The most serious was Rfn John Carr (651), with the battalion for just nineteen days. Hit in the chest and leg, he was medically discharged. His pal from the same draft, twenty-one-year-old Rfn John Phythian, spent six weeks in hospital with wounds to head and back. Another evacuated home was Rfn Ronald Taylor, his sixteen days at the front resulting in medical discharge after receiving wounds to his left eye, knee, and thigh. The arm wound of twenty-year-old Rfn Thomas Gaddas kept him from duty until March.

In the evening of 22 December, the battalion relieved the 1/5th at Railway Wood. Unfortunately, during relief, the enemy shelled the approach section of the aptly-named Mud Lane, killing three of 'B' and seriously wounding another from 'A'. Two of the dead—nineteen-year-old Rfn William Brown and twenty-one-year-old Rfn Albert Wright—were from John Carr's draft. The third was twenty-three-year-old Rfn David Emblen, who had received a minor wound on 25 September. Rfn Robert Benson was evacuated home with jaw wound, and although he was medically discharged in November 1917, it was for sickness rather than his wound. Once relief was completed, 'B' occupied the left front with 'D' supporting them; 'C' held the right front, with 'A' in support.

Only one patrol was pushed out that night by 'B', checking on a report made the previous night by the 1/5th, who suspected there was a new enemy sap 30 yards to the south-east of Crater-5. On checking, it was found to be a drain running from the enemy line towards the crater, the sounds heard by the 1/5th's patrol, probably a working party clearing this out.

Enemy fire was much reduced on 23 December and the day was notably quiet. After dark, a machine gun in Sap-2 was particularly active, bursts of fire sweeping No Man's Land and Crater-2a. Further south, opposite Crater-1a, a small enemy patrol was spotted, but lost from sight before they could be engaged by the Lewis guns.

For the battalion, Christmas Eve was quiet, most hostile artillery action well to the left, or against the rear at Hellfire Corner. There was a noticeable increase in aerial activity, and German observation aircraft made two attempts to cross British lines, but were driven back by anti-aircraft fire on both occasions. 'C' put out a number of patrols overnight. One, exiting next to Crater-2, noted an enemy working party and machine gun in Sap-2. Another, leaving from the sap at the end of Mud Lane, found it was easily possible to transit between Crater-1a and Sap-1, the ground firm and totally unobstructed by wire. They encountered no enemy patrols, but while they were still out, a number of flares were fired towards Crater-1a and a machine gun in Sap-1 commenced indirect fire towards British positions in the rear, tracer arcing just over their heads.

Christmas Day was far from festive, artillery from both sides in an unseasonal mood, though the only casualty was Rfn William Robertson (530), hit in the left leg and evacuated home. Ypres received the worst of the fire, mainly from 4.2 shrapnel. During the day, Maj.-Gen. Jeudwine visited the entire front line, wishing every man he met a 'Happy Christmas'. Only those behind the lines were able to celebrate Christmas on the day; for the rest, their celebrations were postponed. Sadly, the Christmas mail was delayed by severe storms in the Channel, which also damaged billets and stores in Ypres and Poperinghe. Several patrols were out overnight and one from 'B', near Crater-5, witnessed the enemy digging out the drain again, and also noted considerable movement along Idea Trench, adjacent to the railway line. Much enemy work also appeared to be going on to the south side of Bellewaarde Lake, opposite the Grouse Butts, piles of timber and sandbags visible during daylight.

Daylight on Boxing Day saw a continuance of aerial activity and sentries watched a combat between a Nieuport from 46 Squadron and a Roland. The Nieuport was shot down and crashed just in front of Beek Trench, killing the pilot, Capt. John Nason, and his observer, Lt Claud Felix-Brown.[8] Their bodies were recovered by the battalion and buried at Vlamertinghe. At 3.25 p.m., extensive *Minenwerfer* fire was directed at the ends of West Lane, Beek Trench, Crater Trench, and Railway Wood, though the only casualty was twenty-two-year-old Rfn Harold Ikin, who was wounded at duty. The fire stopped after the TMB retaliated with 150 rounds of 2-inch. After dark, patrols checked the three enemy saps for activity and judged by the considerable amount of talking and shouting that all three were garrisoned in force.

During the afternoon of 27 December, Beek Trench and Mud Lane were shelled, and at intervals throughout the day, 15-cm and 10.5-cm shells sought out targets around I.11.3 and I.11.4. The only casualty was Rfn William Foster, wounded in both hands. That night, the battalion was relieved and returned to billets in Ypres and their delayed Christmas celebration, held on 29 December. Sgt George Owen of 'D' missed this, as on the way out of the line in the early hours of 28 December, he was buried by a shell. Fortunately, his section dug him out—shaken and with a broken collar-bone. It was February before he returned. Although shellfire was directed against the Ramparts on 30 December and also the following day, Owen was the last casualty of the year. The battalion ended 1916 with thirty-three officers and 710 men, slightly down on the numbers from the end of 1915, though the faces on morning parade were now very different.

In the evening of 2 January, the battalion left for Railway Wood. 'D' taking the left front, with 'B' in supporting, and 'A' held the right front, supported by 'C'. Two patrols went forward of Crater-5 and Crater-1a, but returned with nothing to report, the first night in the line passing quietly. Enemy guns ignored Railway Wood, right up until 3 a.m. on 7 January, when the front line was shelled for half an hour—though the battalion suffered no casualties during this tour.

Late on 7 January, the battalion was relieved and marched to 'O' Camp, 165 Bde now divisional reserve. The battalion remained there until 13 January, when they moved to Corps Reserve in 'Y' Camp, a mile west of Poperinghe. That week, two drafts totalling 221 men arrived, though others were lost to sickness and accident. On 14 January, Cpl George Birkett from 'D' was wounded in the face and hand in a bomb accident on the ranges and evacuated home, never to return.

On the same day, a Rifleman from 'B' shot himself in the neck—an injury that fortunately was not serious; a week later, he shot himself again, this time in the right arm. The Court of Inquiry, held on 20 January, reached a verdict that he was of 'unsound mind'. His FGCM for his first self-inflicted injury found him guilty of 'conduct prejudicial of Good Order and Military Discipline [for] carelessly wounding himself in the neck' and sentenced him to forty-two days' field punishment.[9] When he left hospital on 2 April, 24 IBD certified him as fit only for permanent base service. This was not the end of the saga, as three months after joining the Rouen base, he deserted and was on the loose for three weeks before being arrested. The unfortunate man was deemed 'insane' and returned to England for medical discharge. There is no evidence in his records of shellshock, though in November 1916, a year after his arrival, he spent eleven days in hospital complaining of headaches caused by a head injury sustained prior to enlistment.

At 7.30 a.m. on 20 January, the battalion left for Tatinghem, west of Saint-Omer, reaching their billets at 3p.m. While there, they were attached to the 2nd Army School at nearby Wisques. Although some working parties were required, there was time to train—especially important given the influx of replacements and the battalion was in the healthy position of having a strength of 964 when they returned to the line in February. Their location also gave opportunity to get men through specialised courses: sixty went to the Grenade School at Terdeghem; one officer and forty men to the Artillery School at Filques; forty-four to the 2nd Army Sniping School; and fifteen to the Trench Mortar School at Berthen.

At very short notice on 26 January, the battalion returned to 'Y' Camp, where they trained until 17 February. The cold was unrelenting and played its part in elevating sickness levels among those who had been living in hardship for many months. The myalgia suffered by 'D' Company CSM, Harold Willcox had reached the point where he was hospitalised on 17 January, and when he was sent home, L/Sgt Phillip Shaw became Acting CSM. On 29 January, twenty-four-year-old L/Cpl George Jones (227) was admitted to hospital with influenza, dying from pneumonia on 19 February. Rfn George Bradley died in tragic circumstances on 2 February; he had been wounded in the head on 9 September, and after leaving hospital in December, he was posted to Prees Heath as a lance-corporal instructor. He was giving a demonstration of bomb throwing on the 2nd, when the grenade exploded in his hands, killing him and wounding four trainees.

February also saw the departure of Norman Ellison. On 20 January, he attended a course at the Divisional Cookery School, returning on 4 February, keen for his forthcoming home leave:[10]

> We entered 1917 half frozen. I was feeling the winter acutely and realised that my strength was ebbing. My name was on the leave list for late January, [*sic*] so I determined to stick it out. Two of my toes became frostbitten and started to turn black. My leave was only three days away, but my foot was so swollen I could not get the boot off. At last came my leave warrant and a chit to be signed off that I had taken a bath and was free of lice. I certainly could not have a bath in a boot, but found a way of getting that chit signed

> and set off home. It was a nightmare journey. Walking was agony, but I knew that if any Medical Officer spotted me hobbling along, I would be sent to hospital right away. So I marched with the rest of them and at last reached home.[11]

Ellison's affliction was trench foot, which was still referred to as 'frostbite'. Incidences in 55 Division were now rare—so rare that it was considered a case of negligence—prevention measures having proved so effective. Contrary to 'Divisional Orders', some were clearly not having their feet checked on a daily basis, otherwise Ellison's plight would have been detected. Gumboots were 'trench stores' and not individually issued, so it is unlikely men from Stores and Transport received these for their supply journeys and, consequently, endured constantly-wet feet. When he arrived home, Ellison visited his GP in Wallasey and, unsurprisingly, his doctor threw up his hands in horror and insisted he report to the Wallasey military hospital, where he was admitted on 17 February. After convalescence, he was posted to Heaton Park.

Further training accidents occurred. On 7 February, Rfn Samuel Doyle was accidentally wounded in the right ankle—another premature grenade detonation; on the same day, Rfn John Viets accidentally injured his knee. Neither returned. Two of 'B' found themselves in hot water when they appeared in front of the CO. One of the January draft, Rfn Francis Beecroft, was a sentry on the 300-yard range, his duty to prevent passers-by straying into the danger area. For his unbelievably silly lapse in allowing men to wander past the targets while the battalion were firing, he received five days' field punishment; Rfn Henry Edwards received seven days' field punishment for the folly of not having his rifle while on sentry duty. Yet another was found to be underage and departed for home—Rfn James Meredith never rejoined. However, Rfn James Smith (811), who went home underage in July 1916, arrived back with the battalion. When he returned home wounded later in 1917, he wore the ribbon of the MM on his tunic.

On 17 February, the battalion returned to the École, Maj. Gordon taking temporary command when Lt-Col. McKaig went home on leave. The battalion remained there until the evening of 21 February, when they relieved the 1/5th in Railway Wood. 'B' took the left of the front line, with 'D' supporting them; on the right, 'C' were in the front line, supported by 'A'. HQ was in a dugout in Railway Wood.

While the brigade had been out of the line, the enemy blew another mine (Hornby Crater), just 30 yards forward of British-held Crater-1a. As the RE were concerned another mine may be detonated there, the battalion were to man it only during darkness, with a listening party of an NCO and two men—which surely must have been the least-popular duty of all.

Fog over the next few days lessened artillery activity. Patrols on the night of 22 February reported the enemy occupying saps in front of Crater-1a and Crater-2a, but found no hostile patrols in No Man's Land, though working parties could be heard in their front line. The fog made the enemy careless and one of 'B' Company's snipers hit a German in Idea Trench, the victim standing in plain sight. Another sniper took a shot at a sentry opposite Crater-3, though was unable to verify the result. That night, a patrol from 'C' exited Crater-1 to reconnoitre the approaches to Bellewaarde Sap; another from

'B' surveyed enemy wire just south of the railway line, which, although damaged, still presented an obstacle.

Visibility improved slightly on 24 February, bringing an increase in hostile fire, though this remained light until early on 25 February, when a German mine was detonated close to the battalion's line. Maj. Gordon reported:

> At about 5.15 a.m. this morning the enemy blew a mine about 50-yards N. E. of West Lane in No Man's Land.
>
> The FOO at battalion headquarters proceeded at once to the telephone to start a slow rate of fire on our front, but almost immediately the SOS was sent up by right front company. The enemy meantime had opened fire on Railway Wood and West Lane with their artillery and *Minenwerfers*, and also on the right sector. The crater consolidation party immediately moved to the top of West Lane.
>
> I sent the Adjutant up to the front line to gather information, but he could get nothing very definite; for instance, the sentry at I.12.a.05.05 [behind Crater-2] said it had gone up in front of him.
>
> An Officers' Patrol [2Lt George Coleman] had then proceeded out and found the crater which is reported as diameter 20-yards—depth 20-feet already filling with water—it was then reported to me as being 40-50 yards from our front line. I find it is not so much, say 20 or 30 yards.
>
> By this time it was getting very light and on making a personal reconnaissance I decided to cover the new crater with Lewis guns.
>
> As soon as it is dark tonight I shall send out a party to occupy the near lip and to ascertain the distance of the far lip from the Germans.[12]

Despite the subsequent exchange of fire, no casualties were suffered. Although the sending of the SOS signal had been outside the parameters laid down in 'Brigade Orders', Brig. Duncan considered it justified under the circumstances.

After dark, the battalion consolidated the near lip of this new crater, which division named Gordon Crater—to avoid confusion with another recent crater, which was then titled Hornby Crater. Although they were able to wire the near lip and build a small post of sandbags and two steel observation plates, it was not possible to wire the far side as the enemy were engaged in a similar process on their lip. During the night, a covering force for the consolidation party spotted an enemy patrol south-west of the crater, but by the time a fighting patrol reached the area, they had gone.

During the late morning of 26 February, the TMB used their Stokes to flatten the new enemy post on the far lip of Gordon Crater, an activity that was replied to by twenty *Minenwerfer* rounds against the top of West Lane. The enemy post was rebuilt and reoccupied after dark, the foe manning his front line immediately behind it, in sufficient strength to prevent the British seizing the crater. A sniper from 'B' claimed a hit on another German in Idea Trench, though there were no attempts by German snipers to even the score. Later that night, they were relieved and returned to the École—no casualties were sustained during this tour.

The École was lightly shelled during the afternoon of 28 February, wounding Rfn William Spencer in the shoulder, though he returned five weeks later. Although out of the line, the battalion took part in a small operation on the night of 1 March.

Their fighting patrol was one of three from Railway Wood. At 11.30 p.m., the RE blew a mine on the southern edge of Idea Salient; a patrol from the 1/5th was tasked with examining the effects of this and a patrol from the 1/9th tasked with attacking a post near Crater-5. The battalion's sortie of thirteen men and a Sapper, commanded by 2Lt Alfred Balmforth, was to tackle Bellewaarde Sap. Ten minutes after the mine was blown, Corps and Divisional artillery began to bombard enemy positions in its vicinity, the TMB and MGC augmenting the barrage. The guns ceased fire ten minutes later, paused for thirty minutes, then resumed.

Earlier that night, Cpl Edward Jones (929) and the Sapper had entered No Man's Land to place a Bangalore under the wire in front of Bellewaarde Sap. Unfortunately, the moonlight was too bright to approach the strongly garrisoned sap. The intrepid pair tried again later, but were seen by the covering party for a nearby German wiring party. Thwarted, they returned to British lines. Balmforth ordered that they wait until just before the raid, taking advantage of the artillery bombardment to cover their movement. This time, they succeeded.

The three patrols left at 1 a.m., when the guns ceased fire. The battalion were led forward by Cpl Thomas Riley (058), and when they were in position, the Sapper detonated the Bangalore. Unfortunately, as the sap was on a bank, the wire nearest the sap was at an angle to the ground and the explosion failed to sever it all, the patrol subsequently unable to force entry. A bombing contest ensued and some of the enemy, who had been outside their position, were driven back into cover. After all their bombs were expended, the raiders withdrew without casualties, Jones receiving the MM for his earlier courage.

The other patrols fared less well. The 1/9th encountered two strong enemy fighting patrols in No Man's Land, with heavy machine-gun fire forcing their withdrawal and causing one fatality. The 1/5th reached the substantial new crater, which had obliterated nearby enemy positions, but found no sign of enemy—dead or alive—sulphurous fumes still issuing forth from the crater. Raid-commander nineteen-year-old 2Lt William Shield ordered his men back to their lines around the northern side of the crater and took one man with him around the southern side—neither was seen again. Numerous search parties sought the missing pair, all returning empty-handed. Jeudwine seemed uneasy about the role given to recently-arrived Shield, whose 'fitness to command a platoon' had not been formally assessed by Brig. Duncan. The Divisional-Commander personally interviewed the NCOs from the patrol, his handwritten notes recording that he was satisfied they gave 'a clear and connected account of the actions of this party'.[13] However, he ordered an Inquiry into the competence of 2Lt Shield to lead the mission. Although Shield had not been formally assessed, it is clear from his confidential report that he was perfectly capable. Lt-Col. Shute claimed there had been no appropriate alternative, as of the four subalterns available, the other three were unsuitable.

On the evening of 3 March, the battalion returned to Railway Wood, 'D', supported by 'B', on the left, and 'A', supported by 'C', on the right. The night was quiet, as was the following day, though this changed shortly after dark. During the early evening, the sounds of much hammering was heard opposite Crater-1 and Crater-2a, and at 7.10 p.m., the enemy exploded another mine, this time just 80 feet to the east of 2a.

The SOS was phoned through immediately and divisional artillery replied on SOS lines within thirty seconds. The 'Right Crater Consolidation Party' under 2Lt Coleman scrambled from their dugouts in Mud Lane and hurried towards the front line, though were unable to access No Man's Land because some British guns were firing short. As soon as these lifted their fire, the party exited and attempted to negotiate the British wire. Unfortunately, by the time they reached the new crater, the enemy had already occupied it and a bombing contest developed, the Consolidation Party clearly visible in the bright moonlight. Unable to approach nearer, Coleman withdrew, reaching safety without casualties.

Maj. Gordon positioned Lewis guns to impede the enemy as much as possible and contacted the TMB. Unfortunately, only one Stokes was within range, so Gordon decided that their next attempt to oust the Germans would coincide with a pre-planned operation against Crater-5 that the 1/7th had scheduled for 11 p.m. The single Stokes began a pre-attack bombardment of the new crater at 10.50 p.m., though with little effect as it suffered a misfire and the few rounds fired missed by a considerable distance. Nineteen-year-old Rfn James Smith (875) and twenty-year-old Rfn Albert Parry were killed when one dropped short into their trench, at the junction of Mud Lane and I.12.3.

Coleman led his bombers forward under heavy rifle and machine-gun fire, a consolidation party under 2Lt John Fairhurst following in their wake. Some bombers reached the lip of the strongly-held new crater, only to be met by salvoes of grenades. With further progress impossible, Coleman ordered a withdrawal. One of his men was wounded at the lip of the crater and Coleman, the last to leave, carried him back through the hail of fire. Eight were wounded, though all were successfully retrieved. Nineteen-year-old Rfn John Green was missing, his body never found. For his leadership and courage during both attempts on the crater and his daring reconnaissance of the new crater of 25 February, Coleman was awarded the MC. This new crater was later christened Cotter Crater.

Casualties from the Crater Operation, 4 March 1917

Rfn Cecil Lewis Butler	241692	WIA	Rfn Albert Llewellyn Parry	241405	KIA
Rfn John Henry Green	241437	KIA	Rfn David Scroggie	242691	WIA
Rfn Fred Harrison	242664	WIA	Rfn Reginald Edwards	242607	WIA
Rfn Richard J. Jones	242092	WIA	Sergeant		
Rfn James McGough	242748	WIA	Rfn James Smith	242875	KIA
L/Cpl William Elias Owens	240950	WIA	Rfn Charles A. Wilkinson	243637	WIA

Visibility on 5 March was poor all day, snow blanketing the torn ground. A consequent drop in enemy artillery ensued, though 165 TMB and divisional artillery continued to plaster Cotter Crater. Enemy retaliation against West Lane and Junction Trench was quickly silenced by the divisional heavies.

There was little improvement on 6 March, though the Howitzers targeting Cotter Crater scored a number of direct hits. One of the battalion's snipers also claimed a hit on a German who exposed himself there. The same sniper also perceived movement behind a loophole in a steel observation plate and fired an armour-piercing round through it, but was unable to observe the outcome. Enemy light mortars fired a few rounds into Mud Lane and Junction Trench, mortally wounding thirty-eight-year-old Rfn Fred Nuttall, who died the next day. The only other casualty on the 6th was an accidental injury: thirty-seven-year-old Rfn Edward Holt slipped on the snow and fell 15 feet down a mine shaft; traumatised and concussed, the father of one from Manchester was admitted to hospital. Diagnosed as shell-shocked and suffering from trench fever, he was evacuated home and medically discharged. One patrol reported the sounds of considerable work going on inside Cotter Crater; another checked the semi-flooded Gordon Crater, though this was quite unoccupied.

Visibility deteriorated further on 7 March, with strong winds complicating things for the divisional guns targeting Cotter Crater. Just one man was wounded during the day, though Rfn Robert Dixon's wound to his right eye was minor and he was back a week later. That night, most of the battalion was relieved and headed to 'O' Camp. Remaining in the line were two crater consolidation parties, totalling ninety-six men, under 2Lts Harold Oswald and Cyril Vernon. This unlucky group did not reach 'O' Camp until 11 p.m. on 8 March. All of 165 Bde was now in divisional reserve, apart from the infelicitous 165 TMB, who remained at the front, because all of 166 TMB were placed into isolation due to a diphtheria epidemic.

The battalion trained until 17 March. When Lt-Col. McKaig returned from leave on the 16th, he learnt that Brig. Duncan had recommended him for the DSO in the forthcoming 'Birthday Honours' for his leadership of the battalion. Rewarded with a MiD were RQMS Thomas McWean and RSM William Butler, the latter for his untiring energy organising carrying parties to the front line—often under heavy fire—and his rendering of assistance to the wounded.[14] The RSM left at the end of the month, his long and distinguished service finally over. Usually, men who were 'time expired' had their service extended under the Military Service Act, but the RSM was past the age for this. CSM James Knight became the new RSM.

During their time out of the line, Rfn James Cross was sent home, the last of the underaged to be caught and sent packing. One still one remained, but tragically his secret was only revealed after his death. One new subaltern to arrive on 16 March was former Rifleman Ernest Harrop, who took over 2 Platoon. On 17 March, the battalion returned to billets in the École.

Shortly before their return to Railway Wood on 21 March, Rfn Richard Lloyd managed to shoot himself in the right knee. His FGCM sentenced him to the standard forty-two days' field punishment and he was then medically downgraded. Relief went smoothly and 'B' took the left of the front line, with 'D' in support; 'C' went into the right front, supported by 'A'. That night, one battalion patrol investigated Cotter Crater, where the sounds of enemy working parties could be heard. The other, patrolling near Crater-5, found the enemy post to the north-east of there was, as usual, occupied.

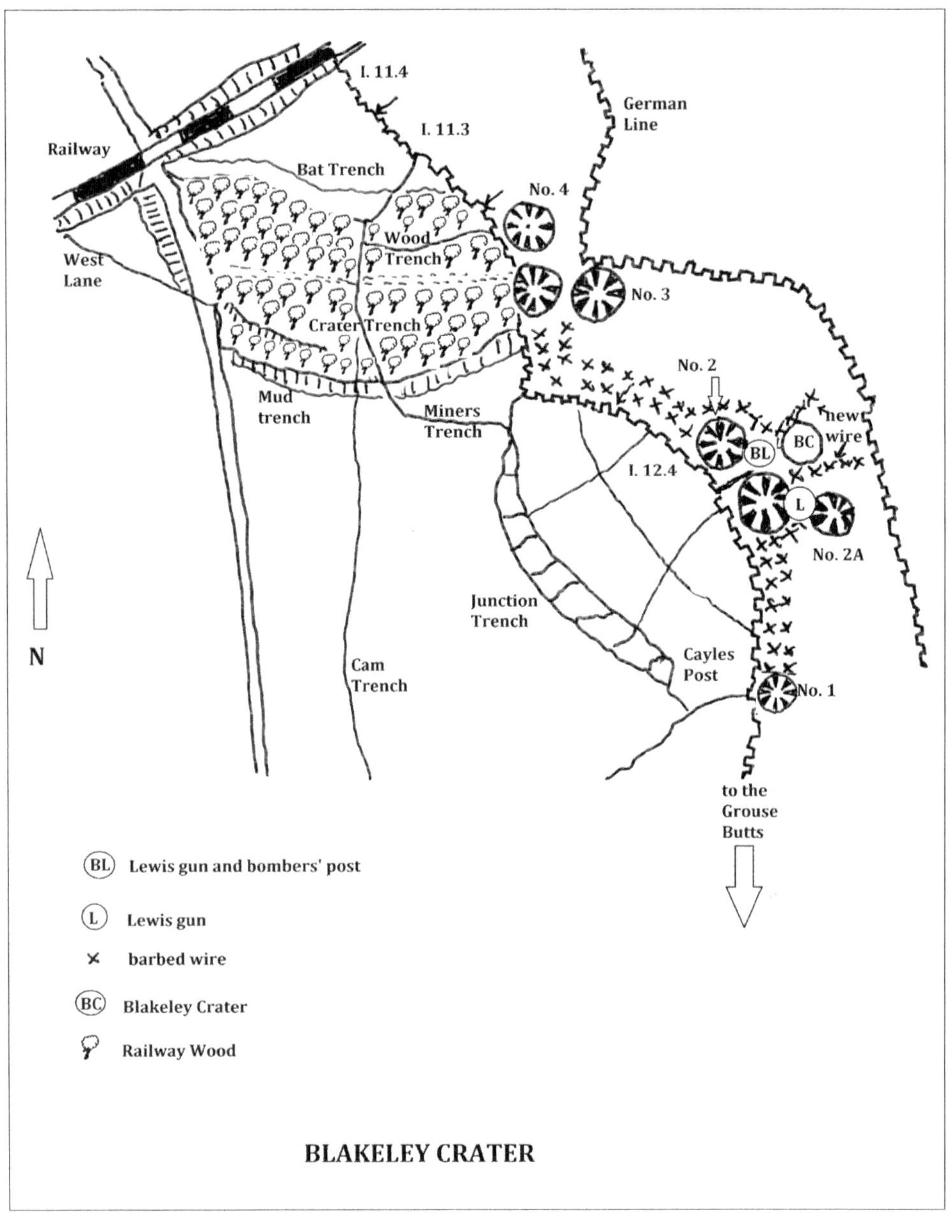

BLAKELEY CRATER

The 22nd was a quiet day, even the sniper who habitually set up in Cotter Crater was for once absent; however, another, positioned on the lip of Crater-5, was making a nuisance of himself. That night, a patrol investigated Blakeley Crater—the result of a German mine on 9 March—30 yards to the east of Crater-2, but found no signs of occupation.

On 23 March, Crater-2, West Lane, and Mud Lane were all shelled between 4.15 p.m. and 6.30 p.m. The TMB continued to target Cotter Crater, Division acutely concerned about the enemy's presence there—its position affording German miners considerable advantage. On 19 March, an enemy camouflet had detonated between Cotter and the British front line, considerably delaying British operations to explode a mine under the lip of the crater. On 24 March, German artillery became more active, targeting West Lane and Beek Trench, wounding Rfn John Sharp in the buttock. Night patrols investigated Crater-5, which was unoccupied, and Sap-1, where a machine gun was positioned, though it only fired about twenty rounds overnight.

German artillery activity diminished on 25 March and there was a success for one of 'C' Company's snipers, who had positioned himself to wait for his German counterpart in Cotter Crater, dealing with him with one shot. The quiet ended at 8.35 p.m., Lt-Col. McKaig reporting that 'the enemy blew a mine opposite the right company sector. The shock felt at Battalion HQ was very heavy, greater than that caused by the blowing of Cotter Crater'.[15] Almost immediately, SOS rockets were fired and a coded telephone message sent to divisional artillery, who responded within a minute of the blast, their rounds dropping a curtain of steel across No Man's Land.

Second-Lieutenant George Tyson, in charge of the crater consolidation party, brought his men forward as soon as the detonation was felt, arriving minutes later. While they hastened to the front, the rest of the battalion went to immediate 'stand-to', as did the TMB. McKaig telephoned the Mining Officer in West Lane, who reached HQ as soon as he had examined the RE's galleries (which were all intact) and then called Brigade to report the mine. Tyson, after consultation with the officer in charge of the right sector as to the source of the blast, led his men into No Man's Land at 8.30 p.m. It was overcast, no visible moon, and extremely dark—so dark that after criss-crossing No Man's Land for an hour, they could not locate the new crater. The 2-inch mortars had been told to standby, but not to fire on Cotter Crater due to it being at extreme range for them, and at 9 p.m., the CO requested the artillery to hold their fire as there seemed no immediate danger. The mortars remained on standby.

The British bombardment was replied to by German artillery, *Minenwerfers*, and *Granatenwerfers* against the front line, Beek Trench, and Junction Trench, continuing on and off into the early hours of 26 March. Twenty-year-old Rfn Herbert Mayes and twenty-four-year-old L/Cpl John Dutton were both killed—Dutton the only casualty from 'D', the others all from 'C'. Second-Lieutenant Vernon was wounded at duty and five men more seriously injured. The gravest of these was thirty-two-year-old Rfn Joseph Cowell, infection to the wound in his right knee proving mortal on 12 April. Twenty-eight-year-old Rfn Walter Bennett was wounded in the ear and it was three months before he returned. Father of four forty-year-old Rfn Henry Crowther was hit in the right elbow and posted away after leaving hospital. Rfn Hedley Booker's hand wounded required treatment in England. The final casualty, also with a 'Blighty' wound, was Rfn James Kane, hit in the legs and fingers.

In addition to the consolidation party, a small patrol left Question Trench to make their way around Crater-1a and Hornby Crater, reporting all quiet at that end of the sector. At 9.30 p.m., 2Lt Balmforth led out another patrol, this time from Crater-2a, to see if the new crater was between there and Cotter Crater—again, the search proved fruitless. At 1.40 a.m., twenty-year-old Cpl Norman Dossor took a small 'C' Company patrol out from

Crater-1, but he too was unsuccessful. Finally, at 3.25 a.m., 2Lt Norman Phillips took another from 'C' to scour the area, finding nothing. It was not until dawn that a very small and quite shallow crater could be discerned, 20 yards to the south-west of Cotter. It did not overlook British lines and there was no evidence that the Germans had occupied it, or done anything to make it defensible.

On 26 March, divisional Howitzers shelled Cotter between 3 p.m. and 6 p.m., the enemy retaliating between 5.30 p.m. and 6.30 p.m., with *Minenwerfers* and *Granatenwerfers* against Junction Trench, Mud Lane, and West Lane. That night, the battalion was relieved and most occupied billets in the École and houses along the Menin Road. Two platoons from 'A' were less fortunate, being tasked to man Hedge Trench and Half Moon Trench (in reality, one long trench cut by West Lane and part of the outer defences between Ypres and Hellfire Corner). On the night of 27 March, they were relieved by two platoons from 'D', who were in turn relieved by two from 'C' on 28 March.

On 28 March, Rfn John Kendal of 'A' was wounded and evacuated home, his arm fractured by shellfire. On the 30th, two platoons from 'B' relieved those in Half Moon and Hedge Trench, and while there, Rfn John Burns received a 'Blighty' wound in the right leg from shellfire.

Concerned that the 1/5th were about to be raided, Lt-Col. McKaig was ordered to send a force to strengthen the right of the 1/5th on 31 March. Second-Lieutenant Donald Eastwood and twenty men occupied positions close to the end of Question Trench and 2Lt Norman Phillips took another twenty into River Trench, near the Menin Road. Around 4.30 a.m., a patrol of the 1/5th encountered a strong enemy patrol near the Culvert and the corporal from the patrol was captured. None of the enemy approached the positions held by the Eastwood or Phillips, and at dawn, they were ordered to rejoin the battalion. One of their party, twenty-one-year-old Rfn Thomas Gaddas, was killed and Rfn John Blundell was wounded in the right hand and evacuated home.

On the night of 1 April, the battalion returned to Railway Wood, 'D' taking the left front, supported by 'B'; 'A' was on the right front, supported by 'C'. HQ occupied a mined dugout in West Lane. 'A' patrolled the northern edge of Blakeley Crater, discerning no sounds of work from within it and found the wire along the lip was very thin. Sap-2 was also approached, the double-sentry post there now extended northwards into Blakeley Crater; the wire on the northern side of this sap was considerably stronger than previously. A machine gun positioned in Identity Trench, close to Sap-2, constantly swept No Man's Land.

A patrol from 'D' entered a sap projecting from Idea Trench, east of Crater-5. The wire around its southern side was weak and no observable work had been carried out there since the 1/7th's raid on 4 March. German sentries could only access it across open ground, the sap blocked between its head and Idea Trench—probably why it fallen into disuse.

Heavy snow on 2 April, hindered hostile artillery, though Crater Trench and West Lane came under fire from a mortar positioned near Idea Switch, giving thirty-eight-year-old Rfn William Carney a minor wound to an elbow. The only other casualty was a self-inflicted injury. Rfn William Holden suffered a slight wound to his left arm, and as the Court of Inquiry judged him blameless, it was probably another premature rifle grenade detonation.

All was quiet on 3 April, the previous day's snow thawing rapidly. Night patrols found little of interest; however, at 4.30 a.m. on 4 April, a muffled explosion was heard from No Man's Land. This turned out to be a small mine, exploded under the eastern lip of Hornby Crater, leaving a shell hole-sized crater. During the day, hostile artillery became more active, but only against sectors to the left of Railway Wood, though persistent trench mortar fire bothered the battalion. This mortally wounded L/Cpl Hugh Clarke of 'A', the twenty-one-year-old dying the next day. In retaliation, fire support was requested from divisional artillery, and within five minutes of its commencement, green rockets were fired from the enemy front line and their mortars immediately desisted. Night patrols investigated Hornby Crater, but the earlier mine had not engendered any enemy activity.

On 5 April, Battalion HQ moved to a dugout in South Lane, with a subsidiary HQ under Maj. Gordon in Railway Wood. The battalion was expecting the discharge of a British mine near the lip of Cotter Crater, but what they got was a German one, detonated near the railway line at 10.56 p.m. An 18-pounder barrage was immediately actioned by the FOO, but when its location behind German lines was determined, the guns ceased fire (almost certainly a planned obstacle to thwart any future British tank attack). At 2.03 a.m. on 6 April, the British mine was blown under Cotter Crater, though failed to break the surface. Realising that one of the charges had failed to ignite, this was successfully fired at 4.50 a.m., damaging the southern lip of the crater. Patrolling was limited by bright moonlight, though one got close enough to Bellewaarde Sap to hear the sounds of a working party there.

On 6 April, the battalion's positions were more or less unmolested by artillery. At 8.30 p.m., a sentry spotted a twelve-man German patrol south of Crater-1a and alerted a Lewis team, who engaged them. Two whistle blasts were blown and the enemy immediately retired. Of interest to all was a discovery made by a patrol in the extreme left subsector of a German booby trap, consisting of two shovels covering a stick grenade. String connected the shovels to the bomb, so that a pull on a shovel would have detonated the grenade.

Although 7 April began quietly, at 5.30 p.m., the enemy carried out a thirty-minute bombardment of the front line and supports. The only casualty was L/Cpl George Langhorne, with a very minor head wound. That night, the battalion was relieved and went to 'O' Camp. It was 23 April before they returned to Ypres.

Time was devoted to training, with numerous working parties interspersed. There were the usual comings and goings—though very few of the former. During the month, fifty-six men were admitted to hospital sick, twenty-nine being evacuated home—a grand total of seven newcomers replacing them. The opportunity was taken to have a serious look at men's fitness, and several dozen—of what the diary rather cynically referred to as the 'old men draft' were medically downgraded by the ADMS on 11 April. This cadre left in early May. One very happy man was Rfn Edward Embley. The forty-year-old father of one from Leigh had been attached to 165 MGC for two months, but on 9 April, he got his dream posting, as a musician with 55 Division's Theatre Company, where he remained for the duration. On 18 April, Rfn George Cornet from 'C', who had arrived three months earlier, was diagnosed with shellshock and returned home.

Time in camp gave senior commanders opportunities to visit and inspect, though Brig.-Gen. Duncan's visit on 9 April was valedictory, as he had come to say farewell. His replacement, Brig.-Gen. L. Boyd-Moss, took over on the 11th. On 10 April, the Corps-Commander visited, though whether or not 'Hunter-Bunter' checked apertures in the officers' latrines for adequate dimensions must be left to the imagination. Finally, on 16 April, Maj.-Gen. Jeudwine inspected, so there must have been considerable cleaning, polishing, and drill practice over this period.

On 16 April, 'D' were on the grenade range when Sgt William Eaglesfield MM suffered that occupational hazard for all instructors, the cack-handed novice:

> A man was in the act of throwing a Mills bomb, when it slipped in his hand, bounced on the top of the 'T' [T-shaped trench of a grenade range] and fell back into a box of bombs, which was lying open on the ground on the near side of the 'T' wall, and lay there with the fuse smoking.
>
> Although he could easily have saved himself by slipping round the wall of the 'T', this NCO rushed forward, picked the smoking bomb out of the box and just managed to get it over the forward wall before it exploded in the air.
>
> His presence of mind and disregard for personal safety undoubtedly saved the lives of one other Sergeant and the thrower, who were in the compartment of the 'T' into which the bomb fell, and probably more who were in the vicinity.[16]

Eaglesfield was awarded the MSM. Commissioned into the Lancashire Fusiliers in March 1918, he tragically succumbed to illness four days after the Armistice.

On 17 April, most moved to 'C' Camp, though 'D' Company went to Proven, labouring for the RE. On 23 April, the battalion moved by train from Brandhoek to Ypres, it was time to return to the Front.

While the battalion was out of the line, 55 Division's sector was expanded left, affecting individual subsector bounds. Though the right of Railway Wood went unaltered, the left was now at the junction of Gully Trench and Air Street, where I.5.1 met I.5.2. This was also the right bound of the Potijze subsector, the left bound of which was now where I.5.8 met I.5.9 near Crump Farm.

It was to Potijze that the battalion was bound, though the short length of their subsector entailed only one company manning the front line, a task given to 'C'. Two platoons occupied the front, the other two were positioned in Cambridge Road, with rapid forward access available along Park Lane. In support, 'B' Company's platoons were spread along James Street, able to access the line on the left via Haymarket, and the right via Piccadilly. 'A', under its new commander Capt. Alfred Balmforth, was with 'D' at the Convent in Ypres.

During the day of 24 April, there was only sporadic hostile fire, until the TMB carried out a 'hurricane bombardment' of enemy trenches near the Ypres–Roulers railway at 10 p.m. In just three minutes, 511 rounds from the Stokes struck German positions, triggering retaliation by *Minenwerfers* against the front line. Divisional artillery then retaliated against the *Minenwerfers*. By 10.35 p.m., all was quiet again. Although the *Minenwerfers* caused slight damage to the line, no casualties ensued.

The 25th was fairly quiet, and although Ypres was targeted intermittently, the front line and communication trenches were only lightly shelled and no trench mortar or rifle grenade activity against battalion positions is reported. However, two men were very seriously wounded that night: twenty-three-year-old Rfn Griffith Jones (593) from 'C' was hit in both legs, dying on 28 April, and Rfn John Blakemore of 'D' suffered wounds to both legs and a hand and died the following day. Entries in the Casualties Book, from the Field Ambulance, denote their admittance on 26 April with 'bomb wounds', suggesting *Granatenwerfers* were possibly the culprits (no raids or aerial bombing occurred).

On 28 April, the battalion sent three strong fighting patrols out to the Moat, halfway between I.5.6 and the enemy Ibex Trench—No Man's Land being 400 yards wide here. The intention was to use one patrol to lure the enemy into an ambush by the other two. The bait was ignored and the patrols returned empty-handed. The enemy had obviously spotted them, as the same time the following night, they barraged around the Moat, hoping to catch a repeat performance.

During the evening of 29 April, the battalion was relieved and returned to the École and Menin Road billets, apart from 'D', who garrisoned dugouts in Hedge and Half Moon trenches. The move to the rear turned out to be perilous, as between 11 p.m. and 2.30 a.m. on 30 April, the enemy hit the École with over 200 5.9 rounds, causing significant damage to the building and wounding six: Transport-Officer 2Lt Wallace McKaig was badly wounded in the leg; also with 'Blighty' wounds were Rfn Francis Fox, hit in the leg; Rfn S. Jones (585), wounded in the left arm; and twenty-one-year-old Cpl George Tinker from Blackpool, whose wounds to back, arms, right leg, and fingers brought about his medical discharge. Less seriously injured was thirty-one-year-old Rfn Charles Neale, an 'original' attached to the Divisional Train (horse-drawn transport); his head wound required five weeks in hospital before he returned to them. The least seriously injured was A/RSM James Knight, who remained on duty. The following day, his appointment as RSM was confirmed and Sgt John Handley became CSM of 'D' Company. Thankfully, 30 April was much quieter.

On 1 May, L/Cpl Jack Fairhurst, in Hedge Trench, was lightly wounded in the left leg. Apart from a false gas alarm at 10 p.m. on 2 May, the rest of their time in reserve was quiet. During the late evening of 5 May, the battalion moved up to the line to relieve the 1/7th in Railway Wood. One casualty on their way forward was Rfn James Nichols, wounded in the arm. He was posted to the 2/9th when he left his English hospital, but he was reposted back in March 1918.

While the battalion had been away from Railway Wood, the underground war had intensified. The obliteration of enemy positions was not the only basis for blowing charges: Camouflets aimed to destroy the galleries of the opposition, preferably when they were occupied by skilled miners; larger charges were detonated to fracture the strata, making enemy tunnelling impossible; and were blown to sculpt the ground surface—either to give a vantage point over enemy positions or deny them the same. All were motives at Railway Wood, 177 Tunnelling Company led by the talented and resourceful Maj. Edward

M. F. Momber DSO, MC, who was responsible for that sector. The major also conducted a series of lectures for infantry officers on how to consolidate captured craters. His death on 20 June 1917 from wounds received on the 18th was a huge loss.

On the night of 5–6 May, a number of patrols deployed. One examined a new crater on the southern side of Bliss Crater, and though the enemy had consolidated the far lip, no activity was observed within the crater itself. On the extreme left, another investigated a disused trench in No Man's Land, finding it much damaged by shellfire, only 2 feet deep, and with no evidence of recent presence. At 4.30 a.m. on the 6th, the enemy blew a small mine on the south-eastern lip of Hornby Crater. No artillery or infantry activity from either side ensued and the proximity to dawn delayed its investigation until nightfall.

The battalion had a quiet day on 6 May, with only isolated shellfire experienced. At 12.20 p.m., a sentry spotted a German wearing a gas mask in Cotter Crater, who disappeared from view before a shot could be taken. Night patrols found Crater-5 unoccupied, though flares were fired from Idea Trench and others from 100 yards south of there. When a patrol investigated the source of the flares in Idea Trench, they discovered the sentry post unoccupied. Further south, another patrol examined the new crater near Hornby Crater, which was about 30 feet in diameter, very shallow, and had no evidence of enemy presence.

On 7 May, Divisional artillery carried out a ten-minute practice barrage against German positions opposite Railway Wood, causing some damage to their trenches—evidently annoying the foe, who retaliated with *Minenwerfer* fire against Bat Trench. This soon ceased when the Stokes targeted the *Minenwerfers*. After the sighting of a German in Cotter Crater the previous day, a sniper positioned with a view over the crater in case of a repeat found his patience rewarded. The new crater next to Hornby Crater was patrolled again that night, finding there was still no activity there. The only other item of interest was a large black dog that wandered over from German-held Idiot Trench, north of Bellewaarde Sap, to investigate the wiring party working in front of Question Trench. The hound evaded capture, but fortunately did not give away the wiring party by barking.

On 8 May, little hostile fire was experienced around Railway Wood. At 9.30 p.m., the RE blew a mine, with the joint objectives of destroying an enemy underground gallery, and of gaining control of another new crater (New Cotter) to the west of Cotter, thus preventing the enemy from mining from there. A consolidation party under 2Lt Vernon left the front line immediately after the blast and secured the near lip (later named Vernon Crater). The enemy was far from complicit and resisted with small arms fire and indiscriminate bombing. There was no infantry counterattack, though snipers made consolidation perilous. By dawn, they had successfully built a T-sap impinging into Vernon Crater; constructed a post at the sap-head overlooking New Cotter; and connected the T-sap to the existing front line. The diary notes two killed and eight wounded for 8 May, though the Casualties Book indicates a greater cost. Three Riflemen from the consolidation party were killed: nineteen-year-old Francis Beecroft, thirty-eight-year-old Harry Lee (both 'B'), and nineteen-year-old Samuel Hankinson of 'D'. Thirteen were wounded, six of whom never returned. Although Rfn John Airey's wound was just a bullet-graze to his left hand, he was also found to be suffering from trench foot; he was sent home because of this and later transferred. The success of this consolidation was due in no small part to Sgt John Horan: aware that the mine was shortly to be blown, he crawled into No Man's Land to cut the barbed wire prior to its detonation, allowing the consolidation party rapid egress; during consolidation—and with total disregard to his own safety—he superintended the digging of the trench leading to the new crater. Although slightly wounded, when a bullet broke his rifle in two, he carried on.[17]

At 4.30 a.m., the enemy detonated a camouflet close to Vernon Crater, causing slight damage to some of the RE's underground galleries. After dawn, a battalion sniper in Vernon Crater shot a German, who had carelessly exposed himself from the knees upwards in New Cotter Crater. The sniper than moved to Crater-2a, observing a new mine entrance in the south side of Cotter Crater. Another German could be clearly seen there, and he too was shot. Shortly after, the sniper claimed his third victim just behind Hornby Crater. Initially, Maj. Momber was delighted with the result, especially when he was told that three enemy miners had been shot from loopholes in the post established to command New Cotter. Both Momber and Capt. Wilkinson RE had earlier offered to build a short gallery connecting that post to the new crater, but had been told their assistance was unnecessary. Hostile artillery action against the front line was minimal on 9 May, though Ypres was shelled heavily throughout the day. At 12.30 p.m., the RE blew a large camouflet near Gordon Crater, though no infantry or artillery action followed.

On 10 May, Capt. James (RE) was asked by Brigade to build the previously-rejected connecting gallery, but by then it was too late. When James visited to reconnoitre the site at noon on 10 May, he was astounded to find that there were in fact no loopholes, and through a periscope, he could see a nearly-completed breastwork, the sandbags stained with the wet, blue clay, only found underground. He watched in amazement, as just 40 yards away, six of the enemy knocked off work and sat down to eat lunch. This breastwork precluded any plans for the gallery. Momber rightly described the situation as "deplorable", as it was quite clear that the enemy was mining inside New Cotter in broad daylight, greatly impinging the chances of success for a British deep mine planned for the end of the month and multiplying the already grievous dangers to his men due to 'absolute neglect in the surface work'.[18] Not only did he worry this activity would foil British mining operations, but as it was a mere 35 yards from British lines, a mine could be detonated under British positions before counter-mining could neutralise it.

During the day, thirty-one-year-old Rfn Edward Jones (740) of 'B' was critically wounded, dying a few hours later at the Field Ambulance. A night patrol found Gordon Crater now occupied, and although there was cracking of the ground above where the camouflet had detonated the previous night, other than that, the surface was little affected. Another patrol at 11.30 p.m. heard considerable activity inside Cotter Crater, and it was decided to conduct a rapid spoiling-operation. No doubt there were some red faces after the fiasco over the gallery—though a daring operation by Sgt Horan and nine men from 'B' went some way towards addressing this.

At 4.32 a.m. on 11 May, under cover of a Stokes and Lewis barrage, Horan led his small party in a dash from the T-sap, through Vernon Crater and into New Cotter. Second-Lieutenant Vernon remained at the T-sap directing the operation. When Horan's men reached the far lip of New Cotter, they began tearing down the sandbag barricade with their bare hands. As this was taking too long—the attackers now under a fusillade of bombs—Rfn George Pover volunteered to return to the line and bring back a couple of Stokes rounds. He succeeded in placing these under the barricade, tamping them with sandbags and detonating them, much to the detriment of the barricade. Sadly, as he withdrew, he was wounded in both wrists. His injuries severe, he was medically discharged in November, a MM awarded for his courage and resource.[19]

As resistance mounted, Vernon joined the party in the crater, and once the Stokes blew, he ordered the raiders back. Almost all this gallant party became casualties: Vernon—who was awarded the MC for this and his successful consolidation on the 8th—was seriously wounded in leg and head, and his leg was later amputated. Also seriously injured was Sgt Horan, wounds to the buttock bringing about his medical discharge. He too was rewarded for his courage during both operations with an MM. Twenty-two-year-old Thomas Leigh and twenty-year-old David Tyson were both missing—their bodies never found.

Hostile fire against Railway Wood was slight during 11 May. West Lane was targeted by shrapnel and the wire in front of Beek trench was shelled, though without damage. That night, a joint operation between the battalion and a group of Sappers from 177 Tunnelling Company was planned. This was to be one of three simultaneous raids across the divisional front; unsurprisingly, the battalion's objective was the mineshafts. Capt. Tyson and 2Lt Harold Robinson were to lead thirty-six men and a demolition party of two officers and twelve Sappers into New Cotter—their objectives to kill or capture any enemy there and destroy the shafts.

The raiders divided into 'A' and 'B' parties. The first, under Capt. Tyson, of two NCOs and sixteen men from 'C' Company, comprised a left and right bombing party, each of an NCO and eight men. Robinson's 'B' Party was similar, his men from 'D' Company. The Covering Party under Capt. Balmforth entailed a Lewis and six snipers in the T-sap; another Lewis in Crater-2a, alongside two snipers; and two sections of grenadiers.

At 10.57 p.m., the TMB began a three-minute hurricane bombardment against both Cotter craters and, as the last round exploded, the raiders left the T-sap for their target, clearly visible in the bright moonlight. Though the mortars ceased fire, the grenadiers and Lewis guns kept up a hail of suppressing fire against the German line. Once inside the crater, the infantrymen held the enemy at bay while the Sappers set charges in both shafts. Six German miners were captured. Inevitably, the shower of bombs began to take their toll, but no withdrawal was made until all the Sappers had cleared. It cannot have been easy to remain in the crater, enemy bombs exploding all around, and when he saw some of 'A' Party wavering, L/Sgt Montague Hart heartened them to hold—courage and leadership rewarded by the MM.[20] Twenty-seven-year-old L/Cpl Alfred Clarke was killed by one bomb, but 'A' Party were unable to retrieve his body. Rfn Robert Dixon was critically wounded in the femur, and although others in 'B' Party managed to carry him back, he died from his wound on the 27th. Another awarded the MM was twenty-three-year-old Cpl William Miller; he commanded one of the small parties in the raid, but after the order to withdraw was given, he noticed L/Cpl Townley (either Ernest or James) struggling to retrieve a wounded man from the crater, and aware that the Sappers' time-fuses were burning down, he returned to the crater and helped recover the casualty.[21]

The arrangements for the evacuation of the wounded worked perfectly. Eight stretcher-bearers waiting at the front line relayed casualties to another eight under the command of Cpl George Langhorne, at the junction of West Lane and Beek Trench. From there, Langhorne's bearers took them to the Aid Post in South Lane, where ten RAMC stretcher teams ferried those treated by the MO to the Field Ambulance. An NCO placed at the entrance to the T-sap, directed walking wounded by way of the front line and along West Lane, avoiding confliction with stretcher-bearers, routing down Mud Lane.

The commander of this highly-successful enterprise, Capt. Tyson, was awarded the MC. It turned out that Cotter was larger than originally believed, but much shallower, and New Cotter much deeper than estimated. At 10 p.m. on 12 May, 177 Tunnelling Company blew another small mine between Crater-2a and Cotter, and although the lip was small, it gave a view into the enemy consolidation on the right-hand side of Cotter. However, the consolidation of this was by the 1/5th, as it occurred during relief. The cost of these two operations was not inconsequential, resulting in the death of seven and the wounding of another twenty-two. Casualty figures recorded in the diary differ from those in their written report to Division, neither of which is supported by details in the Casualties Book, which must be viewed as the definitive.

The raid delayed German plans to thwart Maj. Momber's deep mine, and when this was detonated at 10.35 p.m. on 29 May, it completely obliterated both Cotter craters. The new crater—60 yards wide from west to east and 75 yards from north to south—was easily consolidated and named Momber Crater.

Casualties from the Crater Operations, 8 and 11 May

Rfn John Airey	242044	WIA: 8/5	Rfn Samuel Hankinson	242856	KIA: 8/5
Rfn William Ball	241703	WIA: 8/5	Sgt John Horan*	240650	WIA: 11/5
Rfn Henry John Beale	241658	WIA: 11/5	Rfn Thomas Edward Jones	240744	WIA: 11/5
Rfn Francis Edward Beecroft	242704	KIA: 8/5	Rfn Harry Taylor Lee	242743	KIA: 8/5
Rfn Arthur Bounds	242838	WIA: 8/5	Rfn Thomas Stanley Leigh	241651	KIA: 11/5
Rfn Frederick James Bullock	241931	WIA: 8/5	Cpl Robert Moffat	240040	WAD: 8/5
L/Cpl Alfred James Clarke	240483	KIA: 11/5	Rfn D. Molyneux	242751	WIA: 11/5
Rfn Frederick Stanley	241989	WIA: 8/5	Rfn Arthur Bailey Moor	241458	WIA: 8/5
Clayton			Rfn Harold Phillips	241381	WIA: 8/5
Rfn Robert Colligan	240349	WAD: 11/5	Rfn George Pover	241907	WIA: 11/5
Rfn George Davidson	3887	WIA: 11/5	Rfn James Readdie	241755	WIA: 8/5
Rfn Oliver Edward Deane	242654	WIA: 8/5	Cpl Thomas Arthur Riley	241058	WIA: 8/5
Rfn Robert Henry Dixon**	242847	DOW: 27/5	Rfn Sydney Stent	241996	WIA: 11/5
Rfn John Doyle	241813	WIA: 8/5	Rfn David Albert Tyson	241876	KIA: 11/5
Rfn James Fletcher	242720	WIA: 11/5	2Lt Cyril Harker Vernon		WIA: 11/5

* = Also wounded at duty, 8 May. ** = Wounded, 11 May.

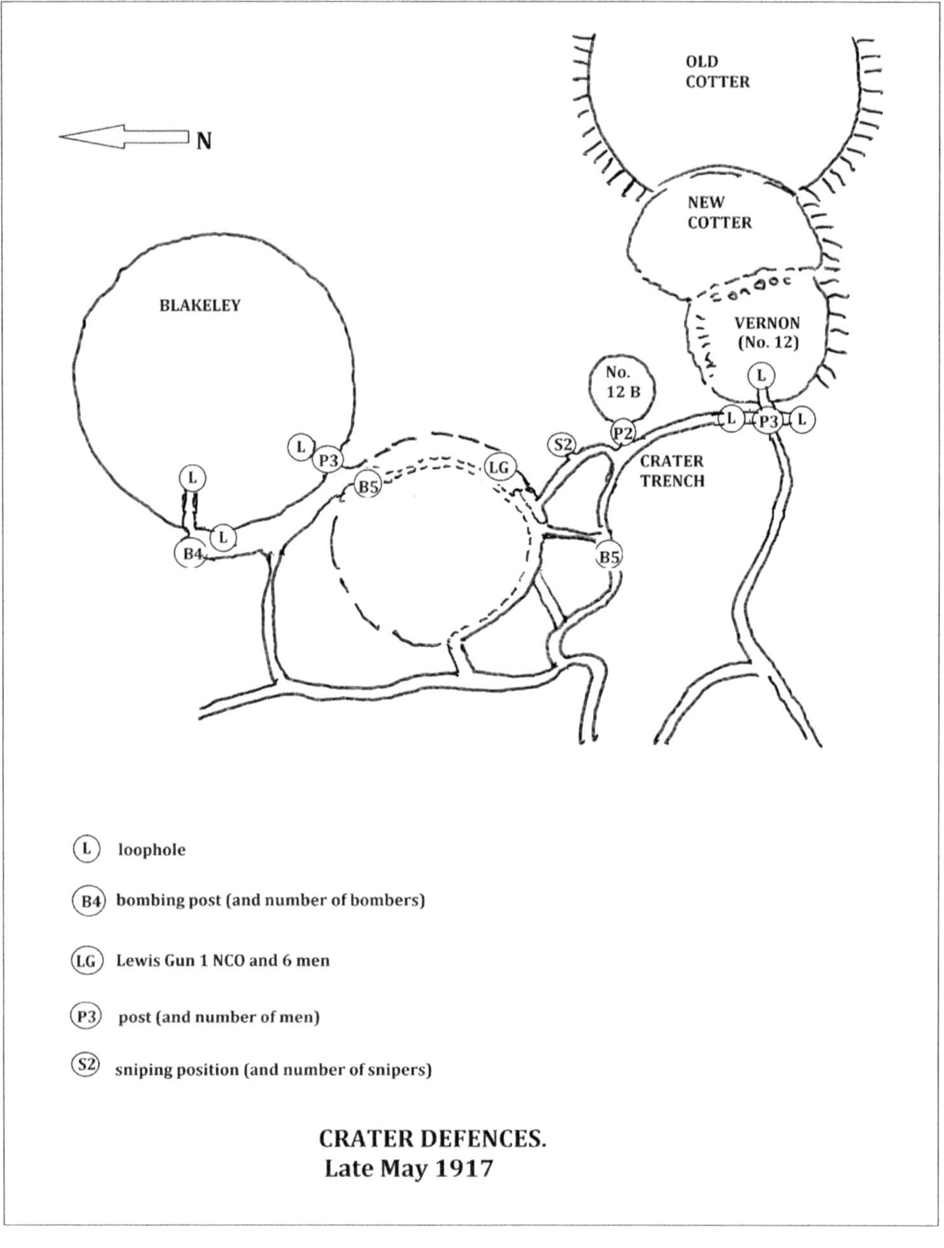

CRATER DEFENCES.
Late May 1917

The battalion moved by train to 'B' Camp, though 'C' was billeted in Proven. The raiders, however, returned to the École that afternoon, where Maj.-Gen. Jeudwine congratulated them on their success. The battalion was overdue a lengthy spell out of the line.

Their first few days were characterised by large working parties; no fewer than 220 men and six officers required for labour on 15 May. However, next day, the battalion paraded and marched to Poperinghe, where they entrained for Millam, 13 miles south-west of Dunkirk.

Training concentrated upon the new platoon organisation. War Office pamphlet *SS143, The Training of Platoons for Offensive Action* was distributed around BEF divisions at the beginning of May, provoking much reorganisation and training. No longer did platoons consist of four rifle sections; bombers became integral to each platoon, as did the Lewis section—usually a junior NCO and six men—doubling later, when each platoon got a second gun. The new bombing section became an equal mix of bombers and riflemen, usually eight men and an NCO; a section of grenadiers, armed with the Hales rifle grenade and Mills No. 23, became part of every platoon; and, finally, a rifle section, whose size varied enormously, though it is unlikely manning ever reached the sixteen laid down within the pamphlet.

This reorganisation gave infantry a flexibility that was unthinkable in 1914 and the tactics developed would feel familiar to a modern infantryman. Battalions advanced behind a creeping barrage in 'wave' formation, usually with two companies forward, two behind. Each company was subdivided into two waves, the first comprising half the force, with 70 yards between each wave (later modified to 100 yards) and 12 yards between each section line. Platoons advanced in artillery formation until they came under fire from their front, when they quickly adopted extended order; when enemy fire became effective, men advanced in a series of rushes. Once the objective was within range of the grenadiers, they and the Lewis section engaged the target to their front, diverting attention from the bombers and riflemen carrying out a flanking attack; alternatively, the rifle section was also used for fire suppression, the bombers alone attacking from the flanks. Further changes would be occasioned in June 1918 by *O.B. 1919*, the 4th Edition of the War Office *Battle Organisation* pamphlet, reducing the platoon to three sections, with the logical amalgamation of grenadiers and bombers.

A tragic accident marred 22 May. After training ended, men washed off the sweat and grime of their day's exertions by swimming in the nearby Canal de Haute Colme; twenty-one-year-old Rfn Walter Hughes got into difficulty and drowned. Two further accidents also resulted in casualties, though fortunately, none were fatal. Capt. Bennet, assisted by 2Lt William Goffey and recently-arrived 2Lt Geoffrey Chavasse, oversaw the Inquiry. The first incident, a premature detonation of a rifle grenade, wounded Capt. Blackledge in the chest, thirty-year-old Rfn John Clough in the face and right arm, and Rfn Thomas Whitter in the left arm. Manxman L/Cpl Sydney Kneale gave witness:

> On 7 June 1917 at No.2 Training Ground, Merkeghem, I was instructing in Rifle Grenade Firing under the supervision of Capt. Blackledge, who was sitting about five yards to the left of the men firing. Rfn Clough was acting as firer and Rfn Whitter acting as loader of the grenade. Before firing, Cpl [Thomas] Ball tested the grenades and detonated them [i.e. inserted the detonator], handing them over to me saying all precautions had been taken. I handed Rfn Whitter the grenade, which was a Hales 20. Rfn Whitter put it in the barrel of the rifle and tested it to see that it worked loosely in the bore, which it did. He then took the grenade out of the rifle, and Rfn Clough loaded with blank and applied the safety catch. Rfn Whitter then put in the grenade and again tried it to see that it worked loosely. He then took out the safety pin and got down flat on the ground as ordered.

> I reported to Capt. Blackledge 'ready to fire'. Capt. Blackledge blew his whistle and I gave orders to 'release safety catch', 'first pressure', 'fire'. I was lying down when giving orders to fire and the next thing I knew was a violent explosion giving me the feeling of being pushed into the ground. I jumped up and found Rfn Whitter wounded in the head [*sic.*]. I then saw Capt. Blackledge was wounded and went over to him. I overheard Capt. Blackledge say to Lt Eastwood, who had come up, 'that everything had been in order', or words to that effect. Both men had previously fired Hales grenades. This was the second grenade to be fired through that rifle on the 7th. I examined the rifle immediately and found it in good working order.[22]

Robert Hartley was nearby:

> I am Bn. Sniping-Sergeant and all the snipers being with their companies, I was watching my company practicing with bombs. I was sitting in a pit about 3-yards from the man firing the rifle grenades. I heard orders given for firing and was watching for the flight of the grenade. I saw the grenade burst about 2-feet from the rifle.[23]

That same day, 'A' were throwing live Mills bombs, supervised by 2Lt Cecil Merriman. That evening, after practice had ended, L/Cpl Albert Hornby checked the boxes of grenades in the limber prior to submitting his evening return. 'D' Company CSM Albert Rankmore was in his billet when he heard an explosion just outside and ran out to find Hornby wounded in the leg, L/Cpl Isaac Foulkes wounded in a leg and arm, and Cpl Richard Lee and Rfn James Mernock both wounded in the head. Rfn John Conway, who was 5 yards from the limber, talking to Lee and L/Cpl Henry Farnham, recalled:

> I saw L/Cpl Hornby sitting on the pole of the limber with a Mills box open beside him. I then heard him call out 'this bomb is fizzing' and saw him throw it away. We ducked and after the explosion I saw that Cpl Lee, L/Cpl Hornby, L/Cpl Foulkes and Rfn Mernock had been wounded.[24]

Merriman described earlier activities:

> Four complete boxes of bombs were withdrawn from the limber. The boxes were detonated one at a time, there never being more than one box detonated at any one time. We used two complete boxes, from the third box, nine bombs were used. The three remaining bombs of the third box were defective, in that the detonator could not be inserted, one of which was used for practice throwing and collected with bombs used for that purpose. The remaining two were put each in the box and the three detonators were placed in their tin box. The fourth box was returned to the limber intact.[25]

Cpl Thomas Riley was ordered to check all the boxes after the accident, finding none of the remaining bombs were fused. However, instead of three 'defective' bombs, only two were in the box—though there was a tin containing three detonators. Riley determined that it was these detonators that were wrongly-sized and destroyed them to prevent future accidents.

Before being taken to the MO, Hornby told the CSM that he had found the grenade on its own in a box, and it had started fizzing immediately as he had picked it up. As he looked down in horror at the bomb, he realised it had no pin and hurled it away. Unfortunately, it exploded before it had travelled very far.[26] Though someone was clearly at fault, the Inquiry was unable to ascertain whom.

At 6 a.m. on 11 June, the battalion paraded and marched to Esquelbecq, their 'rest' over. Reaching 'B' Camp at 2 p.m., they prepared for going up to the line that night. While they were at Millam, there had been a significant event on the Salient. On 7 June, Plumer's Second Army seized the Messines Ridge in a brilliantly planned and executed attack. Senior officers in the division had been briefed about this in early April and warned that, if successful, they would be continuing the offensive to the north. On 26 May, detailed plans of their future objectives were presented to brigade-commanders.[27] The planned offensive also heralded an administrative move to XIX Corps, Fifth Army, on 12 June; VIII Corps (and Hunter-Weston) being moved from the Salient for the duration of the offensive. For the battalion, this heralded a change from their usual trenches, as from the night of 15–16 June, the right divisional boundary ended at the Ypres-Roulers railway, north of Railway Wood—a welcome adjustment.

At midnight, the battalion marched to Brandhoek, then onwards by train to the level crossing at Vlamertinghe, there they continued on foot to relieve the Liverpool Irish in the trenches at Potijze, a relief only completed at 5.15 a.m. on 12 June. The subsector ran (inclusively) from C.28.1 on the left to C.29.2 on the right. 'D' held the front line, with 'B' in reserve in Congreve Walk and 'A' in reserve in Prowse Trench. 'C' were in support in dugouts in the Potijze Road—quite literally, as the dugouts at Wieltje and Potijze were deep-mined below the actual road surface, the pavé affording additional protection. HQ was situated in a dugout in the grounds of Potijze Château. Rfn Frederick Lloyd was wounded in the neck prior to midnight and evacuated home. Although enemy artillery was active during the night, no further losses resulted.

During the afternoon and night of 13 June, enemy artillery shelled the battalion's front line, though it was heaviest around Warwick Farm. During the day, thirty medium *Minenwerfer* rounds fell across the area between Lone Farm and Warwick Farm, one critically wounding Rfn Fred Battersby from Oldham, who died shortly afterwards at the Aid Post. Far less seriously injured was Rfn Frederick Duffin, whose arm wound required nine days off duty.

On 14 June, hostile artillery targeted the battalion's rear, seriously wounding two Riflemen in Congreve Walk; Joseph McGivern suffered 'Blighty' wounds to scapula and thigh, though twenty-five-year-old Hubert Russel succumbed to his back and thigh wounds the following day. That evening, 'A' took over the right half of the front line, the company bound being C.29.6; the relieved half of 'D' went to Warwick Farm. Night patrols found little to report, apart from a gap of several hundred yards in the wire in front of Cambrai Trench, a 10-yard-wide gap in the wire at the apex of Kaiser Bill's Nose, and a small gap in front of Camel Trench. Both patrols reported that enemy sentries seemed particularly nervous, repeatedly bombing their own wire throughout the night.

The 15th saw increased hostile artillery, particularly at 7.30 p.m., in retaliation for British fire against the German line. A patrol on the left entered White Sap, the head of which was only 60 yards from C.29.7. This semi-derelict position had long grass growing inside its head, though the base was occupied, a sentry there firing off flares, and throwing bombs into his wire.

On 16 June, a few mortar rounds hit Lone Farm and Warwick Farm, but the majority of hostile fire—directed across the front line—was from artillery and very heavy at times. The only fatality was eighteen-year-old Rfn Joseph Camm of 'A', his true age only discovered after his death (he had arrived in November 1915). Six were wounded, though Rfn Robert Pearce was a cyclist-orderly on detachment to 164 Bde HQ, multiple shrapnel wounds ending his overseas service. The other five returned. Rfn Jonathan Nickson of 'D' was wounded in the face; from 'A', Riflemen Harold Escolme and William Lloyd both suffered minor finger wounds; Rfn William Marsden, a wound to his left thigh; and L/Sgt Francis Gloyne had back wounds. The battalion also lost the services of 'A' Company CQMS William Henry, who was posted to Divisional HQ.

Once again, enemy artillery was active on 17 June, particularly in the rear: HQ was shelled; the right of the front line struck by HE and gas; and Prowse Trench was also hit. Second-Lieutenant Edward Griffin suffered minor wounds and two Riflemen from his 10 Platoon were also wounded, neither seriously—Joseph Yoxall's arm wound was patched up at the Aid Post and he was back on duty the next day; George Goffey, also with an arm wound, returned in early July. No patrols went out that night, though the enemy once again, nervously bombing his own wire, discharging random rifle shots into No Man's Land.

There was heavy rain and thunder on 18 June and although hostile artillery fire was much reduced, three Riflemen were wounded. Of these, only W. Stott, wounded in the right hand, returned, the others—George Phillips, hit in a finger, and Gilbert Price, wounded in neck and arm, were evacuated home.

Further artillery fire around the Vinery and *Granatenwerfer* fire against New John Street on 19 June, produced another casualty. Rfn William Niblett MM from 'C' was hit in the left arm. At 5.30 a.m. on 20 June, a sentry in C.28.1 spotted a German carrying a bag clamber quickly over the parados of Cambrai Trench, on the extreme left of their line, from where, a few minutes later, seven *Granatenwerfers* were fired. Considerably less hostile fire struck battalion positions this day, though the opposite was true for the other subsectors and Ypres. On 21 June, German artillery switched their fire back to the battalion. Rfn Albert Harrison of 'B' was wounded in the right thigh and evacuated home; from 'D', eighteen-year-old Rfn Robert Hall was hit in the right ankle; and twenty-one-year-old Rfn John Marsden was hit in the left cheek—both rejoining several weeks later.

During the early hours of 22 June, the battalion's front, supports, and HQ came under a very heavy bombardment, activity that continued throughout the morning until divisional artillery retaliated with 1,304 rounds at noon. Riflemen Albert Pritchard, twenty-year-old Frank Scarff, and thirty-year-old William Smith (878) were all killed, and nineteen-year-old John Williams (661) died from his wounds at the Aid Post. Edwin Stevenson was badly shell-shocked.

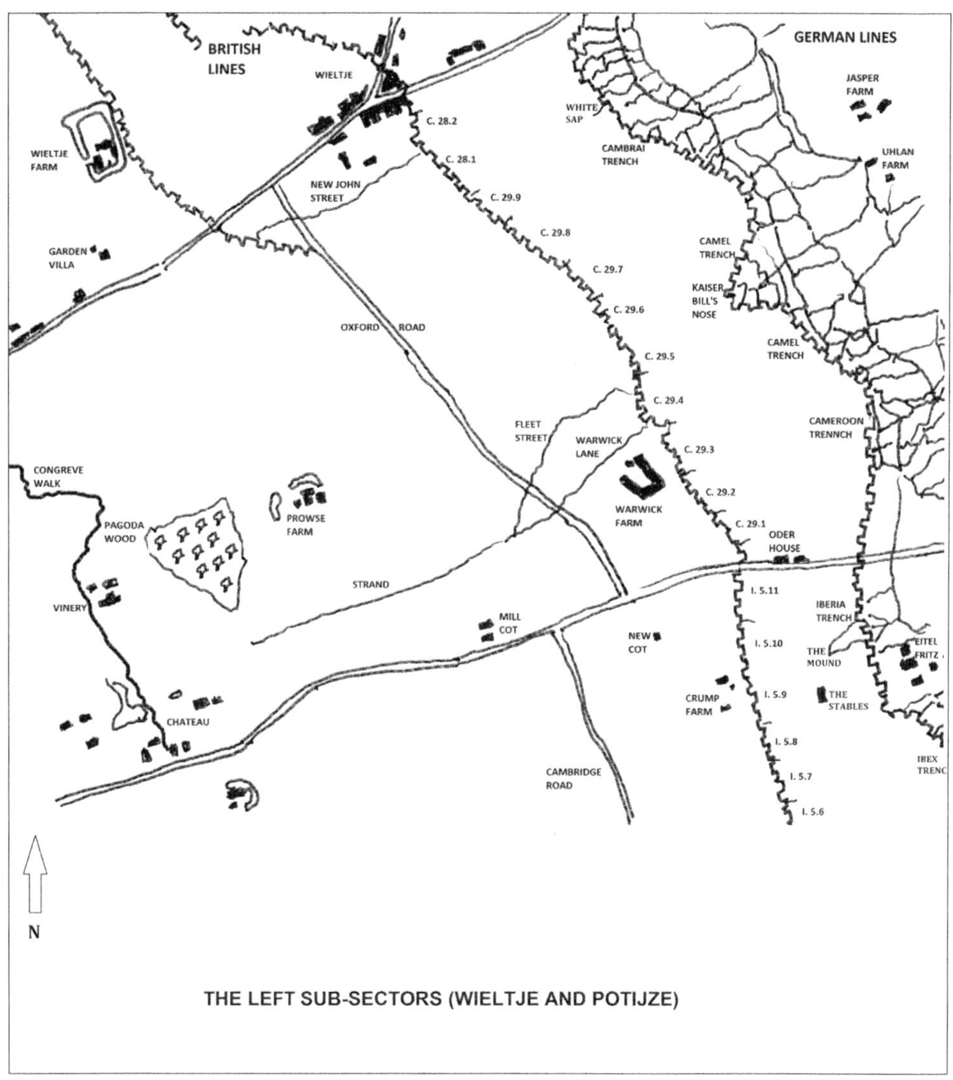

THE LEFT SUB-SECTORS (WIELTJE AND POTIJZE)

German fire sought out positions throughout the day on 23 June, initiating further casualties. The rear and HQ had also been subjected to gas for much of the night, resulting in one man being gassed (unrecorded in the Casualties Book). Shellfire during the day killed twenty-one-year-old Rfn John Conway outright and twenty-three-year-old Rfn Thomas Bibby died at the Aid Post. In addition, nine were wounded. The battalion only fielded a small reconnaissance patrol that night, who observed an enemy working party busy improving Camel Trench, opposite C.29.4.

If the casualties from enemy fire were not bad enough, Rfn Alexander Simon from 10 Platoon managed to accidentally shoot himself in the right foot—in what was probably the only possible way to have a negligent discharge while still following laid-down procedures. Cpl James Lube gave evidence at Simon's Court Martial:

> On 23 June, I was taking over my post near Strand about 10 p.m., Rfn Simon being one of my party. I told them to lead along the trench and went myself to the post to arrange relief. I then returned to my party and just when I reached the Rifleman, who had his back to me, I heard his rifle go off and he turned and hopped along the trench past me. I did not see him doing anything with his rifle and the first I heard was the report. I followed him to the dugout near the post, where he was stopped and found he was shot through the foot. I did not hear him say anything about the cause of the accident.
>
> I have known him 6 months, during which time he has been in my platoon. He is not a young man and is very nervous, but a steady, reliable man. I am satisfied that he would not deliberately injure himself.

Simon also testified:

> On arriving in front line I was ordered to load my rifle by the NCO in charge [L/Cpl Percy Whalley]. When loading I pointed rifle upwards and was told by the NCO that I should be hurting someone and to point it down [Whalley had found himself looking straight down the muzzle]. The cartridge got jammed and in trying to push the bolt home the rifle went off and shot me in the foot.[28]

The FGCM agreed that the thirty-nine-year-old father of four had not intended to shoot himself and when Simon returned from four weeks in hospital, he served the lenient foÅurteen days' field punishment awarded for his carelessness.

Casualties, 23 June 1917

Rfn Thomas Bibby (A)	241917	DOW	Sgt Frederick Douglas Lees (C)	240380	WIA
Rfn Frederick H. Bricknell (A)	242782	WIA	Rfn Thomas Percival Lever (D)	242007	WIA
Rfn John Joseph Conway (A)	242121	KIA	L/Cpl William Alex. Mackenzie (A)	240554	WIA
L/Cpl Henry Charles Farnham (A)	240917	WIA	Rfn Alexander Simon (C)	243639	S/I
L/Cpl Edward Griffiths (D)	240388	WIA	Rfn David Thomas Williams (D)	240748	WAD
L/Cpl John Hegarty (A)	242695	WIA	Rfn Owen James Williams (A)	242885	WIA

On 24 June, large numbers of German aircraft were manifest and six balloons were flown opposite the battalion, the enemy seeking evidence of the offensive being renewed. Their artillery again sought out targets in front line and supports, wounding three of 'B'. The injuries to Rfn William Waterhouse were minor and he remained on duty, but Rfn Arthur Todman suffered multiple shrapnel wounds and was medically discharged; Sgt Edward Qualtrough, wounded in the left hand, returned a week later. 'D' also lost their CSM to shrapnel that night. Albert Rankmore was seriously wounded in the right shoulder—a 'Blighty' wound that resulted in Home Posting after leaving hospital—Sgt John Shaw becoming acting CSM. At 4.30 p.m., a sentry in C.29.7, observing the enemy line through

his periscope, noticed movement around Jasper Farm. At 700 yards distance, he could not clearly make out what they were up to, but they seemed to be marking something out on the ground. About an hour later, another party was observed fixing a number of thin poles into the ground, Division believing they were probably for telephone wire.

Only two patrols were out from 55 Division that night. One, a fighting patrol of two officers and nineteen men, used artillery cover to rush a reported enemy working party, labouring on a disused trench in No Man's Land, to the left of the battalion's subsector. Upon reaching the location, they found it was just some loosely-wired shell-holes and no signs of recent activity. This patrol was despatched because of an important piece of work begun that night, wiring Hopkins Trench, 75 yards forward of the British line and stretching across the Wieltje–Gravenstafel Road. This was to be an advanced jumping-off trench for the attack planned for 31 July, though it was later described by the company-commander, whose position it became, as little better than a 'ditch'.[29] To avoid presenting the enemy with an advanced position, Hopkins Trench needed wiring and 2Lt McLaren was allocated the task. Accomplished over six nights, the labourers were from various 165 Bde battalions, including large parties from the Rifles. McLaren's MC citation noted:

> The work was urgent and was continually interfered with by heavy enemy bombing, but notwithstanding, this officer by personal example and disregard of self, impressed his men with the importance of the job and satisfactorily completed same. In addition to the above, this officer has been charge of the Brigade Wiring Party since February last and has been responsible for all the wiring done on the front of the brigade. He has cheerfully and resolutely continued his work under all conditions, and it is in a great measure due to him that the wiring of the front was successfully and carefully strengthened and renewed.[30]

Enemy fire intensified on 25 June, over 500 10.5 cm and 15 cm hitting Warwick Farm and communication trenches near Lone Farm; the front line was also heavily shelled. Considering the volume of fire, it is fortunate that only two casualties resulted, neither serious. Rfn Charles Whittaker was wounded in the fingers and L/Cpl Leslie Davies suffered a face wound. 'D' Company Storeman Rfn Frederick Woodmansey was also admitted to the Field Ambulance with a lacerated injury to his hand, which took some time to heal. When he attended 24 IBD in October, he was classed PB and transferred to the AOC. Although the battalion deployed one night patrol, heavy rain and darkness reduced visibility to the point where nothing could be discerned.

Enemy artillery remained active on 26 June; however, their rate of fire diminished. Only Rfn George Marland from 'B' was wounded, though his head wound was a 'Blighty' one. That night, a patrol investigated White Cottage, a ruined house in No Man's Land, but were bombed from somewhere to the rear of it. As the cottage was 60 yards from German lines, the patrol believed there must have been an enemy post in the vicinity, but further searching revealed nothing.

The forward area was lightly shelled during the morning of 27 June, inflicting ten casualties on 'C' and 'D'. Thirty-nine-year-old Rfn Isaac Hilton was killed, as was nineteen-year-old 2Lt Samuel Rideal—a young subaltern from Manchester who had only arrived ten days earlier; and Lt Geoffrey Burton's wounds were minor and he returned within days. Of the other wounded, only three returned. Hostile fire on 28 June was lighter than usual, the battalion again suffering disproportionally, with five casualties from 'C'. Rfn Ernest Foxcroft was killed, none of the wounded returning. That night, a 'D' Company patrol led by CSM Shaw investigated a sap protruding from Cambrai Trench, directly opposite C.28.1. They found the enemy wire running from there, southwards to White Sap, very strong, making close investigation of the sap and the line south of there impossible. Luckily, an enemy sentry in a position just north of White Sap launched numerous flares, enabling the patrol to make an accurate description of the wire, and revealing a considerable number of trip wires in No Man's Land.

Casualties from Shellfire, 27-28 June 1917

Lt Geoffrey Bunnell Burton (C)		WIA: 27/6	Sgt Albert Edward MacMaster (D)	240065	WIA: 27/6
Rfn Robert Metcalfe Cooper (D)	241838	WIA: 27/6	Rfn Charles Madden (C)	242862	WIA: 28/6
			Rfn William Henry Moody (C)	241844	WIA: 28/6
Rfn Ernest Foxcroft (C)	241605	KIA: 28/6	Sgt Francis Murphy (D)	240582	WIA: 27/6
Rfn Samuel E. Gittins (C)	241923	WIA: 28/6	L/Cpl Walter O'Connor (C)	242050	WIA: 27/6
Rfn Sidney Godfrey (C)	241184	WIA: 28/6	Rfn Arthur Oliver (C)	242792	WIA: 27/6
Rfn Isaac Lucas Hilton (C)	242828	KIA: 27/6	2Lt Samuel Rideal		KIA: 27/6
Rfn Arthur S. Johnson (D)	242014	WIA: 27/6	Rfn Robert James Unwin (C)	242903	WIA: 27/6

There was little enemy artillery fire on 29 June, though Prowse Trench and communication trenches were targeted, and HQ was heavily shelled for half an hour at 8 a.m. Thirty-two-year-old Rfn George Howarth (Haworth in some records) was badly wounded in the left knee, the father of two from Oldham medically discharged. Also eventually medically discharged for his foot wound was Rfn William Milroy. Rfn Rufus Dunn sustained minor wounds to face and thigh, and though he was soon back on duty, fate was not to be so easily cheated.

On 30 June, the battalion went unmolested, though one fatality not recorded in their returns was that of Rfn Frank Phillips. He had been shipped home in August 1916 for hearing loss and medically discharged. On 30 June, he died from cancer at the tragically-young age of twenty-one.

There was a raid planned for just after midnight. Second-Lieutenant Cowman, CSM John Shaw, and thirty-six men intended to enter Cambrai Trench and Cambrai Support to secure identification.

At 1 a.m. on 1 July, the raiders slipped out of the front line to await the barrage, due fifteen minutes later. As they negotiated British wire, they were met by a shower of bombs, Cowman the first to be wounded. CSM Shaw took command and the combined fire of the raiders and Lewis guns in the front line drove the ambushers off. Shaw led the raiders to their assembly point near White Cottage and was mid-way through reorganising them when they were attacked again, the CSM being slightly wounded. At this same moment, the British barrage opened up and Shaw led the raiders up close to it as the enemy retired. When the barrage lifted, the raiders advanced, but, approaching the small gap in the wire made by the artillery, were met by further salvoes of bombs, mounting casualties forcing their withdrawal.[31] While Shaw successfully evacuated all the wounded, Rfn James Sleightholme began a 'one-man-war':

> I then went forward and heard someone calling. I went to it and found a German stuck on their wire. I tried to pull him off without success so I shot him through the breast. I then searched his pockets (1 trousers and two coat-tail) which were empty. He had no breast pockets. His tunic seemed blue and he had white braid on his epaulettes. I could not get them off.
>
> I then went a little to the left and found a gap in the wire which was about 6-feet wide—the rest of the German wire was in very good condition. I then lay on the parapet and heard running in the trench. I saw two parties of about five each—one going to the left with a machine-gun, the other to the right.
>
> I bombed the left party first and then went towards the party on the right and threw a bomb amongst them which I think must have had good effect. I then made my way into No Man's Land where I returned to our lines with some of our men whom I met.[32]

CSM Shaw was awarded a Bar to his MM and James Sleightholme the MM. Although none of the raiders were killed, sixteen suffered wounds.

There was considerably more shellfire during the day of 1 July and Ypres was targeted by German heavies. Fire against the battalion caused six casualties to 'C': Rfn Michael Conway from Manchester was killed and five wounded. During the day, divisional guns cut another gap in the wire, hoping to dupe the enemy into believing another raid was planned. At 11 p.m., they and the Stokes began a ten-minute shrapnel barrage on No Man's Land, hoping to catch any enemy laying out in ambush. When the guns ceased, No Man's Land was swept by Vickers and Lewis fire and when these ceased fire at 11.30 p.m., two patrols led by 2Lt Norman Phillips and Sgt Eaglesfield left to get identifications from any German casualties. Both patrols returned empty-handed around 1.30 a.m.

Casualties, 1 July 1917

Rfn Reginald Abraham*	242605	WIA
Rfn Wilfred Bernard Bowden	240140	WIA
Rfn Christopher Brennan*	242523	WIA
Rfn James Henry Brown	242836	WIA
Rfn Michael Conway	242652	KIA
2Lt Frederick Gregory Cowman*		WIA
Rfn Archibald Crooke*	242614	WIA
Rfn Donald S. Croxton*	240805	WIA
Rfn Herbert L. Davis	243883	WIA
Cpl James Joseph Eivers*	240341	WIA

Rfn Hugh Evans*	242849	WIA	Rfn William Moston*	242752	WIA
Rfn Michael Furey*	242893	WIA	Rfn Harold Robson*	240800	WIA
L/Cpl John Fred Kneale*	241111	WIA	A/CSM John Alfred Shaw*	240179	WIA
Rfn George Lincoln	242860	WIA	L/Cpl George Nicholson Thomas*	242097	WIA
Rfn Herbert L. Macnicoll*	241392	WIA			
Rfn James Martin	242863	Gassed	Rfn Henry James Vick*	241696	WIA
Rfn Peter Morris	242865	WIA	Cpl Herbert John Webster*	240343	WIA

*= raider.

There were Germans in No Man's Land, but ambush was not their aim. Soon after the patrols returned, raiders rushed the battalion's front line and a short, but violent fight ensued. Although three of the enemy succeeded in entering the front line, they were soon ejected, one of whom was wounded. About an hour later, another raider surrendered himself and, as it got light, a third could be seen lying in No Man's Land. The decision was taken to bring him after dark. Four 'C' Company casualties are recorded for 2 July, though whether from shellfire, or the German raid, is indeterminable. L/Cpl James Cochrane was wounded in the right arm; Rfn William Evans (660) in the shoulder and Southport gardener, Rfn Hugh Gregson in the chest. Only Rfn Charles Edwards, with a minor wound to the right leg, rejoined. This was their last day in the line, as 1/4th KORL relieved them at 1.15 a.m. on 3 July. There was, however, one final casualty, as Rfn Robert Williams (796) was wounded in the left arm by shrapnel shortly before departure. His injury was not serious and he returned to duty on 8 August.

After relief, the battalion went to Derby Camp, west of Vlamertinghe. At 4.30 p.m. that day, they were on the move again, entraining at Brandhoek for Lumbres, south-west of Saint-Omer. Arriving at 8 p.m., they marched to billets in Quercamps. When they returned to the Salient, the entire division would be on the offensive.

8

4 July 1917—3 August 1917: The Battle of Pilckem Ridge

Coordinates for this Chapter

Apple Farm	50°52′35.70″N 2°56′32.40″E	Lone Street	50°52′11.80″N 2°55′18.60″E
Bank Farm	50°52′45.30″N 2°56′37.40″E	Magazine	50°50′50.50″N 2°52′45.40″E
Battalion HQ (advanced)	50°52′18.00″N 2°55′49.50″E	Oxford Trench	50°52′4.90″N 2°55′10.20″E
Cambrai Drive	50°52′25.30″N 2°56′3.40″E	Pagoda Street (end of)	50°52′8.90″N 2°55′24.70″E
Cambrai Reserve	50°52′15.20″N 2°55′51.00″E	Plum Farm	50°52′27.70″N 2°56′20.90″E
Camel Reserve	50°52′13.80″N 2°55′53.40″E	Pommern Castle	50°52′40.40″N 2°57′0.60″E
Camel Support	50°52′11.10″N 2°55′48.10″E	Rat Farm	50°52′39.70″N 2°56′4.80″E
Durham Redoubt	50°50′52.10″N 2°51′5.30″E	Red Rose Camp	50°51′24.70″N 2°48′18.80″E
George Peach (burial)	50°52′47.00″N 2°56′38.00″E	Schuler Farm	50°53′19.80″N 2°57′13.50″E
Jasper Farm	50°52′17.90″N 2°55′53.40″E	Somme	50°52′56.80″N 2°57′3.40″E
Kansas Cross	50°53′8.80″N 2°57′45.40″E	Uhlan Farm	50°52′14.90″N 2°55′56.00″E

On 8 July, the battalion moved to Grand Difques, training on the new platoon organisation and ‘wave’ formations. Rehearsals were made against spitlock trenches of their objective, the creeping barrage simulated by drummers advancing at the predetermined pace (spitlock trenches are marked out with tape, or just have the turf cut away).

Some personnel had remained near the front. Twenty-year-old Cpl Norman Dossor, attached to 2/1 West Lancs RE, was killed on 12 July; on 17 July, L/Cpl Hugh Williams, on detached divisional duty, was wounded in the right shoulder by shrapnel and evacuated home; another casualty was thirty-one-year-old Rfn Charles Neale—his second wound while with the Divisional Train. Upon recovery, he was posted to 13/KLR and killed with them on 31 August 1918. While at Grand Difques, 111 replacements arrived, bringing the fighting strength to 977 officers and men. For many of this latest draft, and for the eighty-eight who had arrived in the last week of June, there was little time to fully assimilate them into their new platoons. Although some were experienced soldiers from other battalions—posted in after recovering from wounds—the majority were novices, and by 3 August, a quarter had become casualties.

At 7.30 a.m. on 21 July, the battalion marched to Saint-Omer and boarded a train for Poperinghe. By the early hours of 22 July, they were ensconced in Red Rose Camp, west of Vlamertinghe. In the days leading up to the attack, massive amounts of food, water, ammunition, and other supplies were stockpiled in advance dumps, the majority of the porterage provided by infantrymen. The battalion spent the 22nd in camp, resting after their journey—though L/Cpl James Jones's day was less relaxing, as he was up in front of Lt-Col. McKaig after over-contributing to the profits of one of Grand Difques' estaminets on their last night there. He marched out a Rifleman, but got his stripe back three weeks later.

On 23 July, every man was involved in working parties near Potijze. Rfn Joseph Fry, attached to Brigade HQ, was caught out by a mustard gas shell, resuming his duty there on 5 August. The following day, every man ferried supplies forward through intense artillery fire. Three Riflemen from the working parties became victims of this—all from the July draft. Twenty-two-year-old Austin Boyle from Ormskirk was killed, George Kane was wounded in the face and arm, and William Annett was wounded in the face and fingers. Fortunately, the working parties on the 25th escaped without loss, despite continuing shellfire.

At 2 p.m. on 26 July, the battalion moved: HQ to 'B' Camp; 'A' and 'D' to positions in Durham Redoubt; and 'B' and 'C' went to Ypres, the former in the Ramparts, 'C' in the Prison and Magazine.

On 27 July, most of the sector was shelled and four Riflemen wounded: James Plant, another recent arrival, was diagnosed with shellshock, returning on 11 August; Thomas Morris (887) of 'A' received a minor head wound, but was back on duty next day; it was November before 'B' Company's William Harris rejoined after his arm wound; and the leg wound of 'D' Company's Charles Parslow resulted in medical downgrading and transfer. Thankfully, 28 July was casualty-free, though for 'C', who had escaped unscathed on the 27th, the respite was fleeting.

The 29th began as another warm and fine day, the RFC finally having gained superiority over the actual front, beat off all German attempts to send aircraft over in daylight. Enemy artillery was less than active, though the front line was shelled intermittently during the morning. Ironically, after weeks of warm and dry weather—so dry that bullets ricocheted off the soil—torrential rain fell around 10 a.m., flooding shell holes in No Man's Land and making movement difficult behind the lines.

Above: Pre-war camp. Though all are wearing black puttees, not all have the 'Rifle Battalion' black buttons. (*Author's collection*)

Below: Seven of the 'Originals'. Probably taken on Lord Derby's Knowsley Park estate, in the last two weeks of August 1914. (*Author's collection*)

Above: Informal group at a pre-war camp. (*Author's collection*)

Below: The 2/6th in late September 1914, marching back to Upper Warwick Street through Sefton Park, after Church Parade at St Paul's in Belvedere Road. Many of these men were later posted to the 1/6th as replacements. (*Author's collection*)

Above: 'H' Company, probably late August 1914. (*Author's collection*)

Below: A group from the 1/6th who were posted to the 2/6th after recovering from wounds or sickness in British hospitals. (*Author's collection*)

Above: 165 TMB in France, twenty-one of whom are wearing the 'Rifles' cap badge. (*Author's collection*)

Below: A group of eight lance-corporals from the battalion. Possibly from mid-1918. (*Author's collection*)

Above: Hill 60 today. The heavily damaged bunker was built long after the battalion had departed the area. (*Author*)

Right: Three brothers in 55 Division. One of the two green rectangle patches, denoting the 1/6th, can be seen on the upper right sleeve of the Rifleman on the left. The seated brother is in the 2/5th Lancashire Fusiliers, the third in an unknown KLR battalion. (*Author's collection*)

Above: Belgian postcard showing the 'Jack Johnson' crater that exposed the River Yperlee in Ypres. The battalion got water from here for washing and watering their horses in 1915. (*Author's collection*)

Below: Belgian postcard showing a sprinkling of snow on heavily-damaged Ypres in 1915. (*Author's collection*)

Above: French postcard of Vaux, the steep hill leading to the road and the beginning of Vaux Woods on the left. The damage from artillery was caused after the battalion had departed. (*Author's collection*)

Below: French postcard showing the ruins of the Moulin de Fargny. (*Author's collection*)

Above: French postcard overlooking the German defences of Curlu-Hem, illustrating the steep terrain dominating the river. (*Author's collection*)

Below: French postcard of the shattered remnants of Longueval in late 1916. (*Author's collection*)

Above: French postcard of La Bassée, reached by the battalion on 3 October 1918. (*Author's collection*)

Right: British postcard of a 'Tommy' of the East Lancs, on sentry duty. This photograph was taken in one of the Givenchy Saps in late January 1918. (*Author's collection*)

Above: Looking across No Man's Land towards Barnton Road from Old Man's Corner. (*Author*)

Below: Looking back from the front line at Givenchy. The tree-covered Spoil Bank is on the left of the picture. (*Author*)

Above: Windy Corner today. (*Author*)

Below: Part of a 1918 panorama of Givenchy, showing the pile of rubble that used to be the church. (*Jeudwine Papers, Liverpool Record Office*)

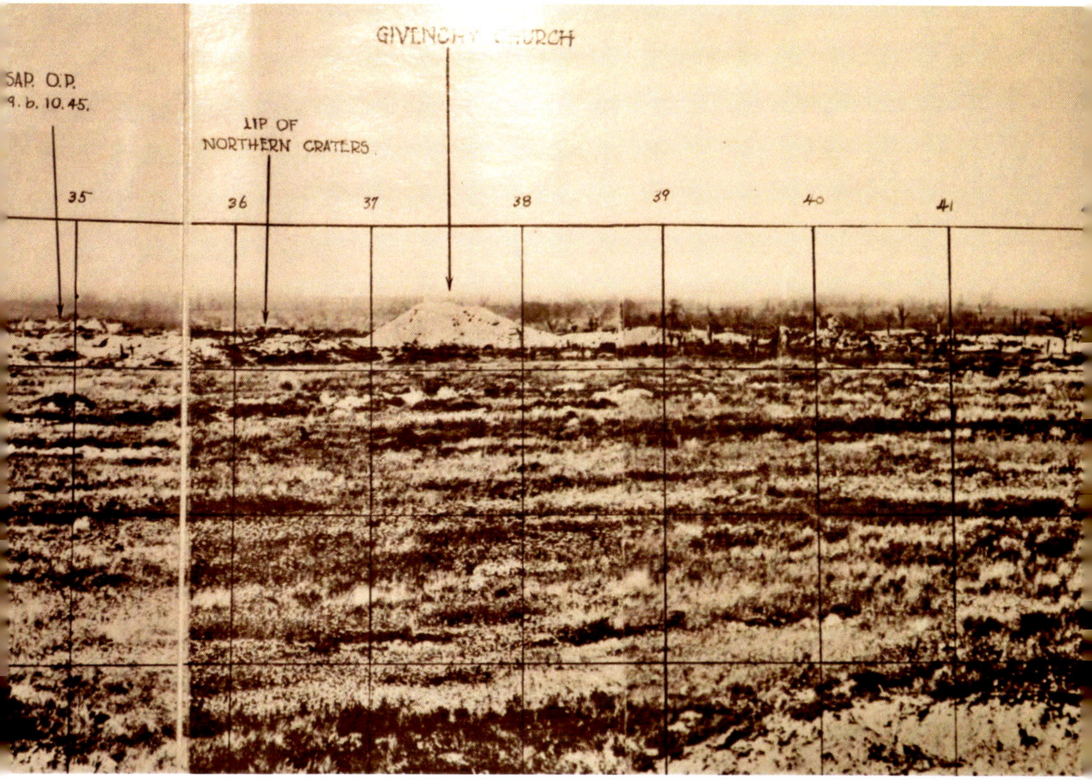

Above: Oblique aerial photograph of Quinque Rue, Barnton Road, and Tee, the OB Line and Cheshire Road. (*Jeudwine Papers, Liverpool Record Office*)

Left: Twenty-two-year-old L/Cpl Eric Brooker, one of the 'Originals'. Evacuated home on 5 May 1917 with ICT of the foot, he was later transferred to the Pay Corps. (*Author's collection*)

Opposite: On the left, Rfn Frank Breese of 31 Claribel St, Toxteth. He joined the battalion on 3 December 1916 and was invalided home after been wounded in the foot on 31 July 1917. (*Author's collection*)

Above: Looking south towards Hill 35. The battalion attacked from right to left, roughly parallel to the road. (*Author*)

Left: Norman Ellison on a home leave. Soldiers on leave from the BEF took their rifles with them, though it was forbidden to take ammunition home.
(*Ellison Papers, Liverpool Record Office*)

Abeele, August 1915.
Standing, left to right: Frank Evans (390), John 'Jim' Fazakerley, and Norman Ellison.
Seated: Cyril 'Skip' Roberts.
All four survived the war.
(*Ellison Papers, Liverpool Record Office*)

Meeting of the 'Old Insufferables' November 1934. Norman Ellison (left) and Skip Roberts (right). (*Ellison Papers, Liverpool Record Office*)\

Above: The 'Old Insufferables' in 1934. Norman Ellison, Philip Smart, Thomas Wiggins, Richard Kent, Skip Roberts, and George Lowes—all from the 1/6th; Herbert Copland (Tank Corps), Robert Lowes (Liverpool Scottish), and George Preston (Cheshire Regiment). George Lowes was the only one still with the battalion at the Armistice. (*Ellison Papers, Liverpool Record Office*)

Below: The menu card for the celebration dinner at the Stork Hotel on 20 March 1936, for the survivors of 6 Platoon. (*Ellison Papers, Liverpool Record Office*)

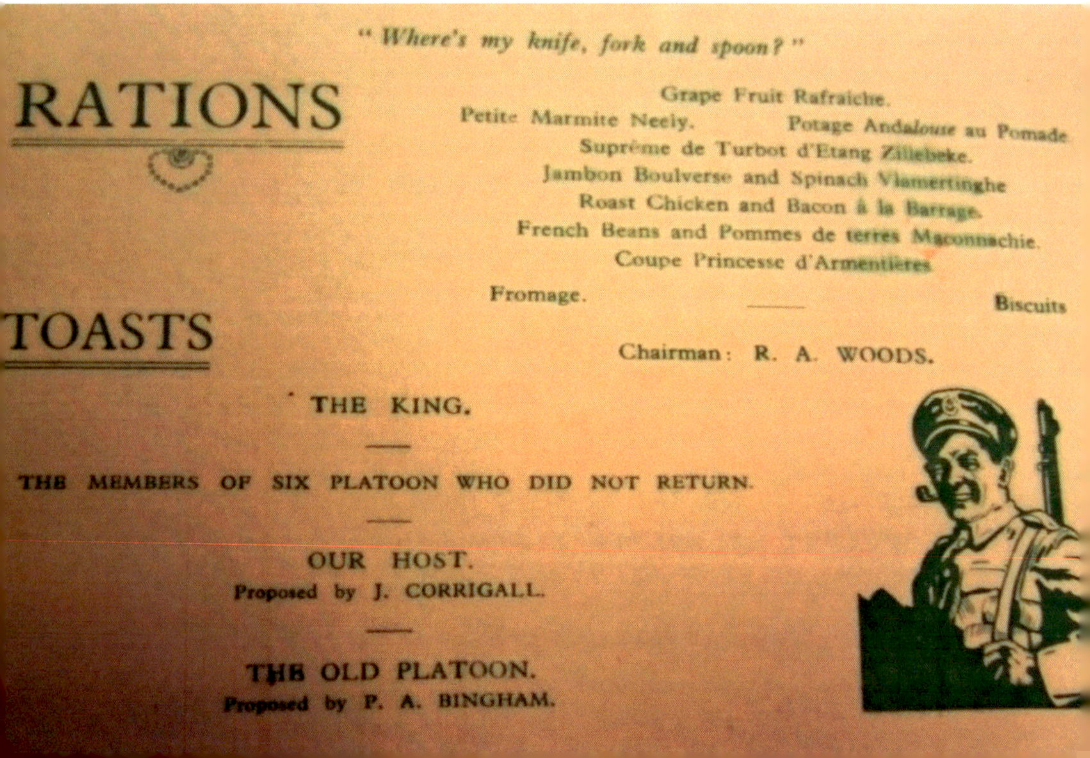

"Where's my knife, fork and spoon?"

RATIONS

Grape Fruit Rafraiche.
Petite Marmite Neely. Potage Andalouse au Pomade
Suprême de Turbot d'Etang Zillebeke.
Jambon Boulverse and Spinach Vlamertinghe
Roast Chicken and Bacon à la Barrage.
French Beans and Pommes de terres Maconnachie.
Coupe Princesse d'Armentières

Fromage. —— Biscuits

TOASTS

Chairman: R. A. WOODS.

THE KING.

THE MEMBERS OF SIX PLATOON WHO DID NOT RETURN.

OUR HOST.
Proposed by J. CORRIGALL.

THE OLD PLATOON.
Proposed by P. A. BINGHAM.

At 8 p.m., the companies set off for the line. HQ established itself in the Cart Dugouts in Oxford Trench; 'B', 'C', and part of 'A' took up positions in Congreve Walk; and 'D' set up in Bottle Trench. The balance of 'A' held the front line from the end of Lone Street to the end of Pagoda Street, approximately 300 yards of trench, which were to be the battalion's assembly positions for the attack. In addition, 'B' and 'C' supplied 150 men for working parties. There was a great deal of shelling and the battalion suffered fifteen casualties. It is likely that five of the six, whose company was not recorded in the Casualties Book, were also from 'C'. Nine were killed outright, or later died from wounds caused by shrapnel or HE, apart from nineteen-year-old Rfn Thomas Brennan, who died from the effects of mustard gas on 20 October.

Casualties, 29 July

Rfn Vivian Maunder Adams (C)	241625	DOW: 1/8
Rfn Wilfrid Barton	260009	WIA
Rfn Thomas Brennan	260007	DOW
Rfn Charles Browne	260003	KIA
Rfn Rufus Dunn (C)	242846	KIA
Rfn George Goffey (C)	241636	WIA
Rfn William Hardy	200187	WIA
Rfn William Henry Hewitt (C)	241756	KIA
Rfn Ephraim John Humphries	50005	KIA
Rfn William Jennings	49950	WIA
Rfn Thomas Jones (C)	242506	KIA
Cpl James Edward Lube (C)	240416	DOW: 30/7
Cpl William Duncan Miller (C)	240989	WIA
Rfn Thomas Smith (C)	242902	WIA
Rfn Joseph Yoxall (C)	242785	KIA

At 9 p.m. on 30 July, the battalion took up its assembly positions. With the 'Lifeboat Party' safely behind the lines, Lt-Col. McKaig fielded twenty officers and 505 men for the attack. Prior to moving forward, 'D' sustained three wounded: Sgt George Owen was wounded in the left arm and back; Rfn Alfred Rodgers suffered a face wound; and recent arrival Rfn John Parker was hit in both arms and a thigh and medically discharged.

The night was dark and damp, the eerie wailing of gas shells, fired by the thousand into German rear and battery areas, adding to the tension. There was very little reply from enemy artillery, but constant outbreaks of flares and rockets along the entire length of his line was testament to German nervousness. At intervals, the night was punctuated by sudden flurries of small explosions as German sentries hurled grenades into their own wire—triggering similar outbreaks in neighbouring sectors.

The attack, scheduled for 3.50 a.m., involved four corps from Fifth Army, Second Army, and the First French Army. The objectives were titled the 'Blue', 'Black', and 'Green' Lines—each being attacked in that order. To the battalion's front, the Blue Line, almost 1,000 yards forward of the British front line, was level with the coordinates for Cambrai Drive in the Coordinates Table. The Black Line—a further 1,200 yards forward—was about 300 yards in advance of Bank Farm; the Green, just past Kansas Cross—a total advance of 3,600 yards if all went well. Once the Blue Line was captured, the second series of waves would move through and attack and consolidate the Black Line, the final series of waves leapfrogging them to seize and consolidate the Green Line.

The 165th Bde would initiate the attack on the right of the divisional front, with 166 Bde to their left. In 165 Bde's first waves, the battalion was on the left, the 1/5th to their right. To the battalion's immediate left was 1/5th KORL of 166 Bde. Both brigades were tasked with seizing all enemy positions up to and including the Blue Line, then consolidating. An hour and a quarter after 'Zero', the remaining battalions from these two brigades would advance to assault and consolidate the Black Line. At Zero plus six hours and twenty minutes, 164 Bde would attack the Green Line.

Although it may appear that the initial waves had the hardest job, tasked with overrunning the first three lines of enemy trenches, the German policy of 'defence in depth' made the assignments of subsequent waves more challenging. Conditions in the Salient and the increasing effectiveness of British artillery had forced the enemy to accept that placing large numbers of defenders in a solid Front Line would result in mass casualties, especially if the attack began with a series of large mines. Consequently, the front was lightly held by strongpoints, supported by a loose line of occupied shell holes in the *Stutzpunkt* Line—each garrisoned by a few troops armed with machine guns. The siting of these mutually-supporting strongpoints allowed enfilading fire against attackers advancing across the open ground. Some 1,600–2,200 yards behind, the enemy constructed another three lines of trenches, designated the Artillery Protective System. This comprised concrete bunkers for approximately 15 per cent of the defenders in the forward trenches, another 35 per cent being accommodated in bunkers in the second line, the remainder in the third line. All approaches to the System were well wired, with wide avenues for counterattack troops set within it.

German defensive tactics, apart from the obvious use of artillery, was to disorganise any attack with machine-gun fire from the shell hole positions, then either as the attacking force reached their objective—or just before—counterattack with troops from dugouts within the Artillery Protective System. If necessary, this would be followed by heavier counterattacks by specially-trained '*Eingreif*' units. The widely-dispersed enemy garrison emphasised the need for British tactics to incorporate mopping-up parties to clear all dugouts and shell holes within a laid-down area, preventing their garrisons popping up after the assaulting troops had moved forward and engaging them from behind.

On the left, 'A' formed the first two waves, 2 and 1 Platoon leading, with 4 and 3 Platoon in the second wave, the latter designated 'moppers-up'. On their right was 'D', with 14 and 13 Platoon, followed by 15 and 16, the latter also 'moppers-up' (the Lewis sections from the mopping-up platoons advanced with the companies in the third and fourth waves). Behind 'A' on the left, 5 and 6 Platoon from 'B' composed the third wave, 8 and 7 Platoon in the fourth. To their right, 'C' placed 9 and 10 Platoon in the third wave and 11 and 12 in the fourth. The first wave would advance through the German front line to attack the supports; the 'moppers-up' clearing the front line, while the rest continued. The third and fourth waves were to take the German reserve line, then consolidate at the Blue Line. While they waited for the attack to begin, these waves sheltered in the ditch immediately behind the parados of the British front line, moving into the front line when the leading waves vacated it.

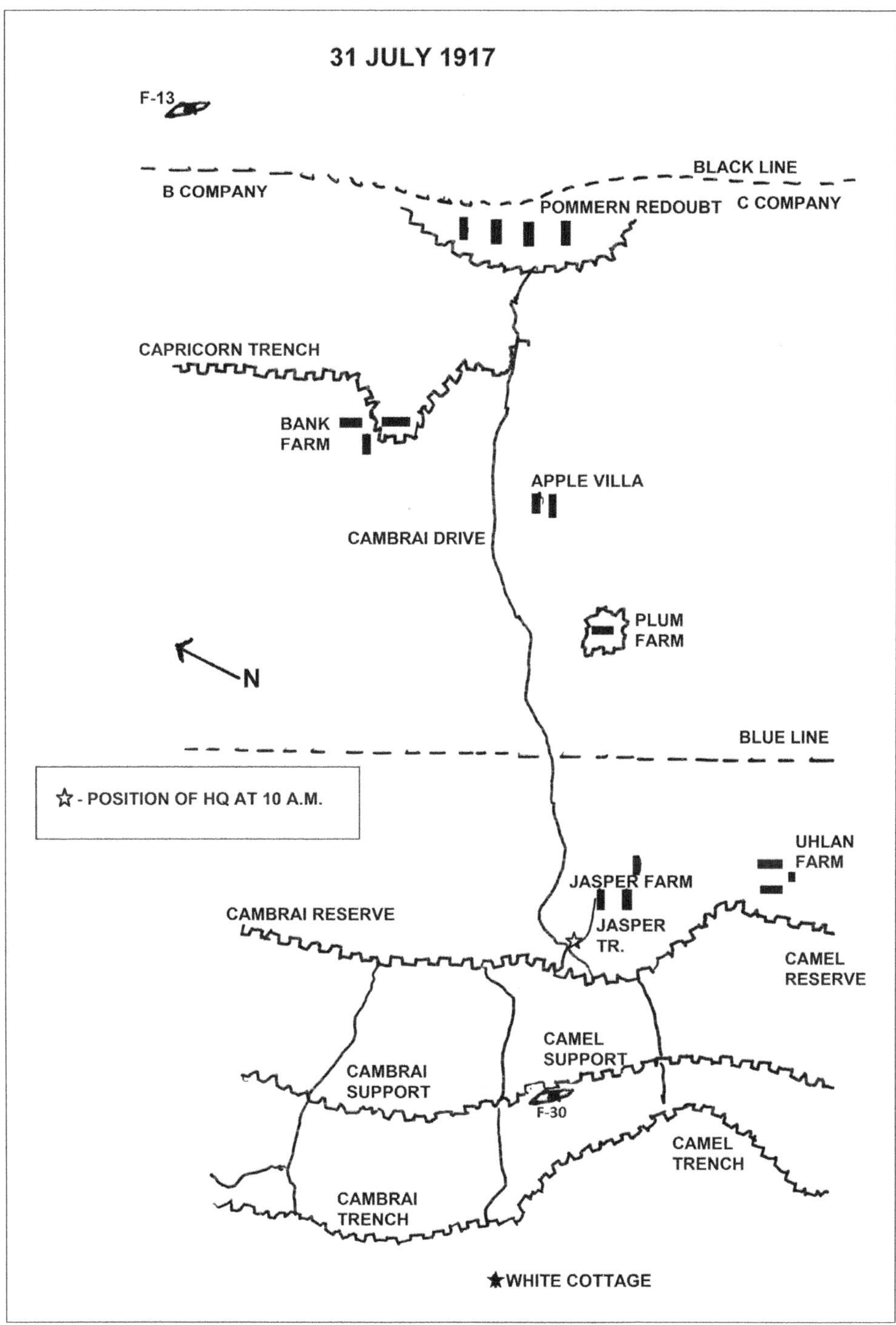
31 JULY 1917
F-13
BLACK LINE
B COMPANY
POMMERN REDOUBT
C COMPANY
CAPRICORN TRENCH
BANK
FARM
APPLE VILLA
CAMBRAI DRIVE
PLUM
FARM
N
BLUE LINE
☆ - POSITION OF HQ AT 10 A.M.
UHLAN
FARM
JASPER FARM
CAMBRAI RESERVE
JASPER
TR.
CAMEL
RESERVE
CAMEL
SUPPORT
CAMBRAI
SUPPORT
F-30
CAMEL
TRENCH
CAMBRAI
TRENCH
★WHITE COTTAGE

Individual platoons cut gaps in the British wire during the night, though for L/Cpl Walter Whitelaw of 13 Platoon, it was a tense time:

> I took up position with my Bombing Section on the right flank of the battalion on the night of 30th July, having the 5th Bn. KLR on my right, with whom I had established connections. Preparatory to the attack I took two men Rfn [Jack] Fairhurst and Sutcliffe out in front of the trench to make a gap in the wire [either Joseph or William Sutcliffe—both recent arrivals]. Whilst doing this I saw three figures some distance away, so withdrew party and made enquiries as to any of our patrols being out and gained the information that 1/5th KLR had sent a patrol out. We then proceeded to finish gap in wire and just on completion, a German machine gun was turned directly on us, but we succeeded in regaining trench unhurt.[1]

Despite orders about maintaining silence, there was some unwelcomed noise, as L/Sgt James Turford of 5 Platoon observed:

> My company moved up from reserve into our battle posts, our position being between Lone Street and Pagoda Street. We remained here until Zero, perfect silence being maintained by all ranks. A few minutes before Zero a number of whistle blasts could be plainly heard from our rear, these I took to be signals for direction to the tanks which were already moving up.[2]

Company-Commander 2Lt James McLaren also commented upon this:

> Previous to Zero Hour (3.50 a.m.) the enemy seemed very uneasy heavily bombing his own wire, this might very easily have been accounted for by the blowing of whistles and shouting while the tanks were placed in position.[3]

Men tried to sleep, though for most, this must have been impossible and the issue of a hot cup of tea at 2.45 a.m. was most welcome.

When the creeping barrage began, the leading companies advanced towards the gaps in the wire, the constriction forcing them into artillery formation. Almost immediately, their carefully-rehearsed movements went awry. Second-Lieutenant Robert Daglish commanded one of 'D' Company's leading platoons:

> At Zero Hour when the barrage opened I took my platoon out through gaps previously cut in the wire. These gaps caused a good deal of confusion as the men had to go out in file and then into line. While we were crossing No Man's Land the enemy was bombing his wire.
>
> When I got to the German wire I found myself separated from my platoon who I had been calling out to follow, but owing to the noise, they could not hear and had got too far to the right. (this I found out afterwards) I was in front of the first line with my runner, so I carried on and must have passed over my objective (Camel Support) partly owing to the darkness, but chiefly it being obliterated by artillery fire.

> I then carried on to junction Camel Reserve and Jasper Trench, where I collected a few men and went on and bombed a support in Jasper Trench. I then went to find the rest of the company and found 'A' Coy. on my left and went back to the dugout and found 5 prisoners who I searched and sent down under a wounded man.
>
> While there, my CSM turned up and told me that there was only 1 other officer left in the Coy. so I took charge and after finding out where the rest of the company were, sent in reports of estimated casualties and dispositions. My dispositions then were one platoon in original German front line, remainder in Camel Reserve and Coy. HQ in a concrete dugout in Jasper Trench which I had bombed previously but no-one was inside. The situation up to now was fairly quiet but about Zero plus about 1 hour and 30 minutes, enemy put a heavy barrage on original front line which moved back to Camel Reserve.[4]

His Company-Commander, 2Lt James Grove, was killed on the way to the support line and 2Lt James Paton badly wounded.

Sgt Albert Macmaster of 14 Platoon also found it difficult to keep his bearings:

> At Zero the barrage opened and we immediately started off, each section getting through the gaps previously cut in our wire and then extending out into battle formation. It being dark at the time it was rather difficult to keep direction. I eventually found myself close to Uhlan Farm along with one of our corporals. Realising we had gone beyond our objective we turned back and as it was now breaking day, I was able to collect most of my platoon together and took up a position in Camel Reserve with 'C' Coy on my left and the 5th King's on my right. After searching all of the dugouts and trenches to make sure none of the enemy were hiding, we stood by until about 10 o'clock when I received orders to take up a position with my platoon in the Blue Line, where we were joined later on by the rest of company.[5]

When L/Cpl Whitelaw reached his objective, he realised he was alone:

> On reaching Camel Support, the remainder of my section missing so attached myself to the 5th and mopped up CT, dugouts round about. On my return I found two of my section who had done good work in mopping up. After this, together with portions of various platoons under Mr Chavasse proceeding to dig in directly in front of [not inserted—probably Jasper Farm]. Here we were repeatedly shelled, having one man killed.[6]

Jack Fairhurst, one of Whitelaw's missing grenadiers, reported:

> After Zero had very little trouble until we reached Camel Support where we started to dig in as per programme, after mopping up ground in front. Here we were subject to moderate shell fire which appeared to be mostly aimed at a tank [F-30 'Flaming Fire'] which had become disabled. An enemy machine gun was rather active and was the cause of a few of our casualties around here.[7]

On the battalion's extreme left, 2 Platoon found direction-keeping equally challenging, veering left across the front of 'A' Company 1/5th KORL until they were steered back on course.[8] KORL had assembled forward of the British wire in No Man's Land, allowing them to begin their advance in extended order—making it much easier for platoons to keep in touch.

L/Cpl Thomas Riley (058) described 1 Platoon's progress:

> As we neared the enemy trench we were met with a scattered volley of bombs, which did little or no damage. We passed over the front trench, which as far as we could see was empty, and then pushed on to our objective, i.e., the support line. As soon as the barrage lifted we pushed into the ruins of the enemy support, but here also none of the garrison could be seen. A small party of them were visible making their way back to their reserve, on which L/Cpl [Henry] Daniels and myself opened rifle fire, but the result could not be observed owing to the uncertain light.
>
> As soon as 'B' Coy passed through us, our bombers cleared the trench tramway and CT to Cambrai Reserve and on their return the platoon was reorganised and continued digging in. The Lewis gun team then moved to the Blue Line to reinforce 'B' Coy according to programme. Platoon HQ was established in a concrete dugout, which was afterwards made Coy HQ. We remained in the position where we had dug in until about 1 o'clock when the Coy moved up to the Blue Line, our Lewis gun team here reformed the platoon. During the morning, a considerable number of shells were flying about, being attracted apparently by some in the vicinity of our positions. The enemy trenches were almost unrecognisable owing to the battering by our artillery and it was difficult to make out exactly where we were.[9]

Company-Commander Capt. Alfred Balmforth fell at the German front line, with 2Lt Ernest Harrop taking command upon reaching the support line. No. 2 Platoon also lost their commander before the support line, though their anonymous post-battle report does not stipulate exactly where:

> The bombers found all dugouts, with one exception, destroyed by our bombardment on their way to the reserve line where they joined up with the rest of the platoon. The grenadiers were not called upon to fire and reached the support line with only one man missing, believed wounded. The riflemen on reaching the German wire were ordered to open out with rapid fire as a number of Boches were throwing bombs into their wire, this they did and the bombing ceased, their men then carried on to the support line and joined up with the rest of the platoon. The Lewis gun team was disorganised owing to the leader and four men being casualties, the gun was put out of action owing to the bursting of a shell in the support line. Those men who had reached the support line were taken charge of by 2Lts Harrop and [William] Smith and were instructed to dig themselves in.[10]

Cpl Herbert Hyam of 14 Platoon got too far ahead:

The barrage opened with a terrific roar. Yelling to my men to get over, I got over myself and led the way through the gap in the wire, which I had previously cut. On getting in front of our wire we spread out in order to get in touch with the people on our flanks, then advanced. I kept on steadily with my attention on our barrage, not noticing that I was getting ahead of the wave. When I found myself on the German parapet, a little to my left I heard a number of bombs going off. On looking round I found I was about 30 yards ahead of the first wave, and that our chaps were bombing his front line. Fearing that I should be taken for a Boche, I made my way very cautiously back in the wave and assisted in beating back a party who were putting up some resistance.

After the barrage had lifted from his support line, we proceeded to mop up dugouts and shell holes, which contained small parties of enemy, who also put up a slight resistance. On passing over Camel Support, I encountered two Boche, being forced to put them out of action, as I was unable to stop to tackle them, and take them prisoner. I then thought it time to try to find some of my section.

Whilst looking round I met Mr Daglish, who was also trying to collect his platoon. Together we attacked a dugout, but with no result. I left my officer to search for some of the men. On reaching Camel Reserve I met Cpl [John] Coates, who was apparently looking for his men. We proceeded together and came across a dugout, which we suspected had a number of Boche in. On ordering them to surrender, nothing happened, but we heard movements inside. On their refusing when being ordered a second time, we lobbed a couple of bombs inside. When the smoke had cleared we entered and found four dead and one very badly wounded. We bandaged him up, but while we were clearing the other bodies out, he died.

On proceeding a little further, we came across CSM Handley, who directed us to Mr Daglish. After a short spell, we were sent to find out something about our platoons' casualties. Just after searching about a little, I found the remains of my platoon digging in alongside of 'C' Company, from where they were compiled to take cover in Camel Reserve, owing to the heavy shelling at that spot. I returned to Coy. HQ with my report.[11]

Coates recounted his advance prior to meeting Hyam:

On reaching the enemy's first line, we found a little resistance, but opened fire from the hip, which was very effective. Here we waited until the barrage had lifted off the support line and then made a rush for same. Unfortunately, we found a little resistance between the front and support line, snipers in shell holes. I killed two of these myself and then carried on. Unfortunately, I went past my objective (Camel Support) and found myself with three others of 14 Platoon in front of Jasper Farm. The three men I sent out under L/Cpl [Henry] Eccles mopping up, while I went to try and find the rest of my company.[12]

Eccles led 14 Platoon's grenadiers:

I and my section consisting of five men, proceeded through a gap in our own barbed wire, which I had cut previously around midnight. One of my section was hit before leaving

> our own trenches. We were able to push our way over No Man's Land fairly easily owing to the light proceeding from our own bursting shells and the enemy's flares. At first the enemy bombed heavily their own front line, particularly the left flank, but on our approach they rapidly retreated to their support lines. In No Man's Land I did not notice any hostile machine gun fire, but the enemy did a considerable amount of sniping. The enemy's wire caused us no trouble. On attaining our objective in Cambrai Reserve, I got together three men and carried on mopping-up. Traversing the trench railway, we bombed dugout and what looked like the remains of a *Minenwerfer* position. While in the trench railway we worked along towards Jasper Farm, several of our own company were sniped hereabouts. After all opposition had been overcome we started digging in about 20 yards in front of the old German support line, the ground being soft we rapidly dug a deep trench.[13]

L/Cpl William Matthews, who led 13 Platoon's grenadiers, received the DCM for dealing singlehandedly with four snipers:

> On leaving trench with section, two of which I kept in view up to 50 yards in front of enemy front line. On nearing trench found four Boche in shell hole. On hesitating to surrender I shot them. In front of this hole saw wounded officer whom I failed to identify. On reaching trench saw nothing but effectiveness of our shells. On leaving for support line found I was out of touch with section and noticed large gaps on left of company. When nearing support line was held up by bombs on enemy wire. On entering trench found small parties busy mopping up. On barrage lifting from reserve line moved up for purpose of mopping up, here I saw untouched concrete dugouts and machine gun also trench materials. I again got in touch with platoon here and moved up to Jasper Farm, here meeting Platoon-Sergeant who gave orders to dig in. After digging for several hours received instructions to move up to the Blue Line.[14]

CSM John Handley was another who found himself too far forward:

> The night of suspense ended rather abruptly as one had only 25 mins warning before Zero when the company had to get into exact position, rations had to be served out etc.
>
> According to my synchronising time, the barrage was a few seconds late and then started first on each flank, some distance away, our own sector being enveloped as it were.
>
> All the troops were eagerly waiting for the signal and climbed out of the trench, scrambled thro' our own poorly-cut wire and went forward with excellent spirit. The cutting of narrow lanes thro' our own wire was a mistake in as much as the avenues of passage were too small and the battle formation was almost completely broken up as far as the first two waves were concerned. The next two waves, 'C' Company, must have found our wire no obstacle after we of 'D' Company had rolled it down with our persons and so over in No Man's Land, they caught us up and got mixed with our own rear sections. Getting thro' the wire rather quickly myself, I found I was in front of the

company, rather than between the first and second waves. However, observing that my part of the line was behind those on right and left, I led forward shouting, "Come on 'D' Company, get up to the barrage." What appeared to me to be a wave followed until we reached 50 yards from the German line, where I got down on one knee, just as in the practice manoeuvre and looked at my watch and waited for 4 minutes. At 4 a.m., at the time the barrage lifted perceptively and right to time, and with a shout I dashed forward. I tripped over some German wire, fell and immediately, as if I had pulled some signal cord, bombs began to burst all round me and looking up, I saw the thin parapet a few yards away, flare lights being shot up vertically from the trench and Huns shoulder to shoulder and head and shoulders over the parapet throwing bombs. Straight to my front, one Bosche fired point blank at me but missed. I looked round to find what support I had, but found myself alone and saw clearly-dim forms, apparently in the middle of No Man's Land. I dropped back out of bombing range and shouted the men to come forward. Then fired a few shots myself and threw two Mills bombs, one of which I am certain exploded inside the German trench and observed the flash. On help arriving I went forward, bomb barrage had then ceased, and jumped into the trench.

What proved to be the next difficult task then commenced. I went up and down the trench trying to locate Jasper CT. Eventually I went up Cambrai Drive and failing to trace Cambrai Support, eventually reached the reserve trench. Here I picked up seven Bosche and returned with them to Cambrai Support, en route to which two of them were sniped by their own men, probably they intended shots for myself. The Bosche had wind right up and squealed like pigs. I handed them over to a wounded K.O.R.L man.

From this point I made my way back to Jasper CT, at the junction of which I looked for some remnants of Company HQ. Of CHQ there were none, so I proceeded to sound the situation myself. Soon finding Sgt Burden I asked for his report and returned when I found a little higher up Jasper CT, Mr Daglish with five prisoners. Sgts [Herbert] Webster and [Edward] Qualtrough soon afterwards turned up and finding they had not searched Cambrai and Camel Support sent a Sgt with a party each way from the CT. I then heard a rumour of Mr Chavasse and Sgt Macmaster being near Jasper Farm so despatched a runner for their reports. On the arrival of other reports, I made that out for the company which Mr Daglish signed and sent it down by a wounded man.[15]

'A' Company's second wave, faced few problems during their advance, as L/Sgt Herbert Lewis reported:

No. 4 Platoon joined in the general attack at 3.50 in the morning of the 31st Ult. We met with very little opposition, took 3 prisoners and commenced to dig in on the German support line. After clearing up Cambrai Walk from the German Support line to the German reserve line. While digging ourselves in our Lewis gun team was put out of action by a shell, two being killed.[16]

Sgt George Webb's platoon captured a number of prisoners:

> No. 3 Platoon comprised the Moppers-Up of the left half of the battalion going over the front line at 3.50 a.m. on the 31st July. We entered the enemy front line which was very battered about and in some places unrecognisable. From out extreme right hand man we cleared the trench and dugouts (2 which were intact) and sent back about 15 prisoners. The party detailed who came up White Sap encountered no prisoners. We remained in the trench as ordered until about 1 p.m. when we joined the remainder of the company in the German support line in order to take up a position in the Blue Line.[17]

In 'D' Company's second wave, was 9 Section, 15 Platoon (Cpl John Dawson and Riflemen James Elston, James Murney, Frank Gammons, John Mather, and Thomas Emery). Dawson described their advance:

> When the barrage opened out on the 31st ult. my section advanced across No Man's Land in the second wave. As we approached Camel Trench a sniper was spotted partly holding up the first wave. The sniper quickly retired on being bombed and the line was formed up again—carrying on. On arrival at Camel Trench, we worked along to the left looking out for Jasper CT. We carried on along Jasper CT, bombing dugouts and collecting prisoners which were sent to the rear. We came across one dugout which gave us some trouble, being practically full of Germans. We told them to come out which they refused to do, so we promptly threw a few bombs into the dugout. Those that were not wounded at once surrendered.
>
> We carried on again down Jasper CT past Camel Support until we came to the Loop. Here I posted a sentry to report to 'C' Company bombers who were closing the Loop. On arrival at Camel Reserve I looked for Mr [Norman] Phillips to report. About five minutes after our arrival I spotted some German bombs being thrown at our men from a couple of concrete dugouts half left from the junction of Jasper CT and Camel Reserve. We moved to tackle this stronghold with the aid of another party. The other party managed to get the rear while we rushed the stronghold from Camel Reserve. When we were near the enemy they threw up their hands and surrendered. There were one or two wounded Germans inside the dugouts, also two German Red Cross men. Shortly afterwards my men were split up to help the company to dig. Four of the section were digging one trench just in front of Camel Reserve. Whilst on this job, Emery (one of the section) was killed by a shell. The remainder of the section, including myself, were sent to a strongpoint just in front of Jasper Farm. After a few hours in this position we were sent to reinforce the Blue Line.[18]

No. 15 Platoon's Lewis section, comprised Cpl Ernest Carline, L/Cpl Eric Foster and Riflemen Ellis Garner, Robert Cooper, Frederick Duffin, and newcomers, William Ormrod and Joseph Gerrard. Carline reported:

> The team got safely over our parapet and moved behind the barrage until we reached what we considered to be Cambrai Supports, but which turned out to be Cambrai Reserve. The team then mustered five, L/Cpl Foster being killed and Rfn Gerrard missing. [he'd

lost touch] I then reported to Mr Chavasse after placing Lewis gun in position in front of trench in shell hole. I then proceeded with Mr Chavasse to bomb dugouts, of which a few were holding out and sniping out men in the back as they passed over, also they were firing artillery flare signals (red) to the rear of their lines. The most resistance was met at Jasper Farm dugouts (afterwards occupied by BHQ). Under cover of rifle grenades, we (a 5th KLR Sergeant, myself and Rfn Garner) approached the dugouts. Give and take bombing followed until one of our bombs must have exploded in a case of their bombs (judging by the reports). A party of 'C' Company under Mr Phillips had by this time come up on the other side, the enemy then turned and surrendered to them, there being about 12 unwounded and 5 wounded Germans, there was also some dead lying about, but I think our artillery was responsible for that. Under orders from Mr Chavasse, I collected all 'D' Company I could find and dug in in front of trench.[19]

After L/Cpl Evan Griffiths was mortally wounded, Rfn Henry Cowins took over 15 Platoon's grenadiers:

On the opening of the barrage on the 31st the word was given to 'get over'. Rfn [Harold] Robson leading, myself following with Cpl Griffiths and other two men bringing up the rear. When we reached the Boche front line the whole of the section became mixed up with other parties. Soon after this, Cpl Griffiths was wounded, two men were missing probably wounded. This left three men including myself. These were Rfn Robson, [Edward] Boon and myself. Robson became mixed up with some of 'C' Company and helped to dig in with them afterwards, joining this platoon later in the day. Boon on reaching Camel Reserve took three prisoners and proceeded with them to the rear.

I carried on with a man from another company along Camel Reserve. We came across one dugout and seeing a German crouching in the door, I jabbed him in the rear with my bayonet, at which he screamed, jumped out of the doorway and flung up his hands. Telling the other man to cover him, I yelled into the dugout for any others to come out. They came out, six in all, and I searched them for weapons whilst the other man stood a little way off covering them. Finding nothing, except what seemed to be a German calling-up paper, which I still have. I then decided to take them back. On the way back to the German front line I found one of our men lying wounded in the arm. I dressed and asked him if he could walk, but he said he was too weak, so I made one of the Germans, who had his oil-sheet, spread it on the ground and laid him on it, making four of them carry him. A little further on we came across Rfn [William] Jones, the SM's batman, with a wound in the leg. I made one of the other Germans carry him on his back. Progress was very slow with the improvised stretcher and just when we got to our old front line, the enemy opened a barrage on it and Congreve Walk, making it absolutely impossible to move one way or the other. After the barrage had died down we proceeded and after 5 hours of heavy going reach the Dressing Station where we left the wounded men. We then carried on with the prisoners to a point on the road where they were handed over to the MPs. We then returned and the other man went to find his company and I to find mine. I couldn't find mine, but found 'A' Company and from them next day I found the company. When I got back I found that Robson and Boon were both with the company, who were on duty in the Blue Line.[20]

No. 16 Platoon's acting Platoon-Commander, Sgt Joseph Burden, reported:

At Zero the moppers-up went over the parapet. It was quite dark, but the Hun evidently expected some sort of attack, as he sent up a shower of Very Lights and dropped light shells in our wire. Our wire delayed the first wave over, so the Coy. arrived at the Hun front line very messed up. I am certain L/Cpl [Herbert] Macnicoll and Cpl [Edward] Heatley were the first in the trench coming up against 10 Huns. These Huns were very shaken, one turned to run and got a Mills in the back, the other Huns threw 3 bombs, one of which wounded both Cpls. On arrival of more comrades the Huns ran, the Cpls capturing three. Sgt [Ernest] Thomas arrived by a Hun MG, the gunner of which ran away. A 5th KLR officer and Cpl claimed and took the gun as they said Thomas was in the 5th sector. Rfn [Allan] Bruce shot two Huns. I arrived at the trench alone, saw a Hun lying in the trench, he moved on being kicked, but clung to his rifle, he was mad with fear, but I persuaded him to let it go. I then took another one prisoner, also in terror, saying his prayers in the trench. I found one of my men wounded, so made these two made these two Huns carry him back. It was now almost light so I collected my platoon and sent them off in pairs patrolling the ground between the Hun first and second line. In all, my platoon captured 10 Germans, five of them wounded. L/Cpl [Frederick] Aitcheson failed to arrive at the trench and is missing. I went over with him in the centre of the platoon. Just on the Hun trench he delayed owing to own barrage and I'm afraid got caught in it. I called to the men to follow and I know most did at once. I sent my reports into my OC at intervals. I collected my whole platoon and put them into concrete dugouts. The men were in fine spirit and very willing. Word came to move up to Jasper Farm and then up to the Blue Line, where we dug in.[21]

Heatley and Macnicoll were awarded the MM. Macnicoll, who led 16 Platoon's bombers, submitted his own report:

My section was on the right of the platoon which was acting as moppers-up for the rest of the company. On the way over No Man's Land all my section, except one man, got lost. This man followed on until the German wire, after that I could not find him. At this point I found Cpl Heatley. Cpl Heatley and myself dropped into the German front line. When we got in there were none of our men to be seen. Cpl Heatley and I advanced along a trench and had not gone five yards when we came to a concrete machine gun emplacement with two Germans in, also machine gun in. I got the first German out and made him stand by while I got the other out. While bending down to get the other out, the first Hun bolted. The second did the same and got 15 yards away and I threw a bomb which caught him in the back, but did not explode immediately, but dropped to the ground and then burst.

It must have wounded him very badly for he was found by the 5th King's when they went down the CT. I followed the Germans and met eight more making their way towards the CT. When they saw Cpl Heatley and I they threw a bomb which went over our heads, they also threw a second one which also went wide. They threw a third which wounded Cpl Heatley and I slightly. Then Cpl Heatley called out to some of the 5th King's to follow up, they had arrived in the meantime. We then rushed the Boche and got three of them. Then we met Rfn J. [John] Fox out of my section and handed the prisoners and told him to report to Sgt Burden that we had got in touch with the 5th King's. We went along the trench and found two wounded. We got one along, the other was very badly wounded. We met Sgt Burden and he told us off in twos to patrol between the German lines for machine guns and Huns, but we found nothing. Sgt Burden then got the platoon and called the roll to see who was wounded and missing. He then put us into concrete dugouts till we had got orders to the Blue Line.[22]

'B' was led by 2Lt McLaren:

At Zero Hour our artillery opened a magnificent barrage and our men climbed over the top, but were rather handicapped getting through our wire, but once clear pushed on well until they were held up by a machine gun about Jasper CT. This was put out of action by an NCO on the right of the company.[23]

The troublesome machine gun was dealt with by 7 Platoon's Sgt Walter Hannah:

On reaching German front line we came under machine gun fire. We however carried on until we came to Cambrai Reserve where we were held up by heavy machine gun and rifle fire. I at this time was on the right flank of my company. From my position here I saw an opportunity of getting to the rear of the machine gun that was holding my comrades up. I seized the opportunity and working to the rear tackled the gun. (As I was working in towards the machine gun I saw Lt McLaren forming the company up to charge the same) With the help of two men I managed to quieten this gun: we had to kill the gunners to do so. I then tackled a dugout near to the MG emplacement and from it got 1 officer and 25 O/ranks, including 2 enemy medical men wounded. I sent these prisoners back under escort of two slightly wounded men.[24]

Hannah received the DCM.

No. 5 Platoon progressed well until Cambrai Support, as L/Sgt James Turford reported:

My platoon formed part of the third wave, our objective Camel Reserve. It was quite dark when we went over and I first thought that the darkness might cause some disorganisation, but am pleased to say that such was not the case and I am now of the opinion that our casualties—which were very, very slight up to reaching objective—might have been greatly added to had we made the first stage of attack in a clearer light.

In my opinion, the barrage was almost perfect, for we met with no opposition until we reached what I took to be the remains of Cambrai Support Trench, where we came under machine gun fire from Jasper Farm, the gun or guns here immediately dealt with and I proceeded with my platoon—my officer Mr [Harold] Robinson being killed—to our objective. There, under the direction of Mr McLaren (OC Coy.) we consolidated our position. It was quite daylight when we reached our objective. The enemy barrage or searching fire did not commence until probably half an hour after Zero. From time of reaching objective, we were in touch with 'C' Company on right and the left brigade also in easy communication with our Battalion HQ at Jasper Farm.[25]

Cpl George Bibby added:

We crossed over the enemy front line without any opposition and we were near our objective which was Camel Reserve when we came under machine gun fire and it was here our Platoon-Commander was killed and our Platoon-Sergeant took command. Our objective was very much broken up by artillery and was not recognisable.[26]

Turford led 5 Platoon until relief.

Cpl Thomas Wright reported that only the Platoon-Commander and one Rifleman from 6 Platoon were wounded before they reached their objective. Platoon-Sergeant Charles Jackson observed: '... our barrage was perfect and one had a very difficult job to find what was once trenches'.[27] L/Cpl Arthur Nickson, in charge of 6 Platoon's grenadiers, reported losing two of their five personnel in the initial advance:

A few minutes after leaving our position in our line, I missed two of my section, [John] Holden and [John] Charnock and failed to locate either during the remaining time before occupying Camel reserve. Before occupying Camel Reserve, myself and Cpl Wright tried to destroy an enemy sniping party (probably two Boches) but just as we tried to near the dugout used by the Boches, someone—probably one of 'C' Company, threw a bomb into the dugout and this took effect, killing both of the Boches. This being the only signs of resistance, our way was made to our objective Camel Reserve and we consolidated along with the remainder of 'B' Company.[28]

Charnock was diagnosed with shellshock and Holden (023) wounded in the left leg.

As 'C' Company-Commander Capt. George Tyson admitted, their waves became mingled:

As there was a company in front of 'C' Company, some difficulty was caused in getting out and through the wire in order to be up to the enemy front line before losing the barrage. I consider it necessary to practice getting out over a trench and then forming up into a line. A great many sections and platoons went over No Man's Land in file.

The German lines were reached, but from my own experience I found difficulty getting some men forward, probably owing to the fact that they were not too sure of the barrage and not having enough experience. I considered Zero Hour was a little early owing to it being dark and men seemed to lose touch, although on the other hand, I think that more casualties might have been caused had it been very much lighter.[29]

Platoon-Sergeant Albert Rashbrook of 9 Platoon commented:

[Upon leaving the trench] Things were not at all satisfactory at this point, the gaps in own wire not being too plainly marked and the 2nd Wave got mixed up with the first owing to the latter not finding the gaps. With the result that instead of lines advancing, we started in little groups of 15-20 men. The whole success of the operation seemed to rest with the fact of the men knowing where they had to go, as between our front line and the German front line things were absolutely a mix up, but after passing the first line the men began to sort themselves out.[30]

The commander of 10 Platoon, twenty-four-year-old 2Lt Edward Griffin, went missing at some point during the advance, his fate never determined; their report written by twenty-two-year-old L/Cpl Thomas Shallcross observed:

No obstacles were encountered up to our reaching the enemy's second line. The chief difficulty being the light. If Zero Hour had been a ¼ hour later, we should have benefitted. The wire in front of his third line was very thick in places and although only knee-high, caused some confusion.

The enemy's entrenchments were practically demolished, only the concrete slab dugouts being intact. I saw no mined dugouts. The first Germans I saw were at Jasper Farm where they put up a half-hearted resistance. They threw bombs and had shot some of our men who had passed their concrete dugouts without noticing them. The dugouts were labelled 'Stoestrupp' (Counter-attacking troops) Dugouts to our front half left (Apple Farm) were blown up by a mine [*sic.*]. Luckily the enemy had no direct observation of our foremost position when we were in support. He shelled his own CT's to a nicety, also Pommern Redoubt and Plum Farm.

At intervals he put a very heavy barrage about 350 yards to our rear between Pommern Redoubt and Plum Farm. Resistance—we encountered no enemy barrage going over until we reached our objective at Jasper Farm. Infantry resistance was practically nil.[31]

Shallcross was not the only one to believe that mines were involved. The CO of 1/5th KORL also wrote about mines heralding the start of the attack—testament to the efficacy of the divisional heavy artillery.

No. 16 Platoon's Lewis section attacked with 'C'. L/Cpl Harold Price described their advance:

On leaving the trench, I led my section through the gap in the wire, but when half way across No Man's Land the 5th Battalion KLR appeared to be heading over to the left and

> so I was cut off from five of my section. I carried on with my remaining gunner and when entering the enemy trench, I heard a Bosch yelling and on looking down, I saw a revolver pointing at me from a small doorway in a German dugout. I forced him to lower the weapon with my sword and ordered him to surrender. This he refused to do, so I shot him and left a man to guard the dugout. We two then carried on to the support line where I picked up two more gunners and saw Mr Daglish. Finding that 'D' Coy. had carried on to the reserve line, I took my men forward to there and met L/Cpl [Eric] Foster who had also been cut off from rest of his team. A party of 'C' Coy were then bombing and rifle grenading some of the Boche who were holding out in the reserve line. These men were doing considerable damage by sniping and MG fire. My party entered Jasper CT and a few moments later, the Boche party surrendered. In the meantime, L/Cpl Foster went to pick up his spare parts bag and was killed. I then picked up No. 1 of L/Cpl [Edward] Dutton's team (Rfn [Arthur] Pasco) and attached him to my crew. We then carried on to our objective along Jasper CT and met Mr Chavasse and part of 13 & 14 Platoons, among them being the remainder of my Lewis gunners. After obtaining some spades, we dug a strongpoint in a shell hole about 30 yards from the trench. Rfn [Walter] Newton (No. 1) showed great coolness and courage getting the gun to its objective and into position through the MG and sniping fire with his No. 2.[32]

L/Cpl Thomas Hill from 16 Platoon's other Lewis section described the events that resulted in his award of the MM:

> My section was attached to 'C' Coy for the stunt. We arrived at our objective which was the Blue Line. We got our gun into action immediately on arrival. While digging in a shot was fired and man wounded next to me and another shot a second later killed another comrade. I told my men to lie down and located two wounded Huns sniping our chaps, so I ran out killed one, then the other because he looked crafty, both their rifles were loaded. One of my men was wounded by a shell and the gun also being put out of action. I carried on a rifle section until I took over another gun which had the team put out. I did a bit of first aid in the front line.[33]

L/Cpl John Burke was in charge of 7 Platoon's grenadiers:

> In accordance with instructions I worked to my left, the German front line was nothing but a mass of shell holes. I carried until the Reserve Line where I dropped in with the King's Own. I advanced again working over to my right, then the word came along that we were held right by a farm. I fired some rifle grenades into the farm and we carried on to Camel Reserve where we captured some 25–30 prisoners including an officer, many Germans wounded or killed. We captured a trench mortar gun and a large store of mortar bombs and a store of body shields which we tried to build a parapet with. A few bullets were flying about, but I should think they were fired from a good distance judging by the way the bullets fell.[34]

Second-Lieutenant Albert Jones's 8 Platoon encountered few problems:

> When the first system of enemy trenches were reached, one saw at a glance the deadly power of our own artillery—the ground was levelled out—and it was difficult to find our position. So far we met with little or no resistance until an enemy machine gun came into action at approximately Jasper CT, when a flank movement was ordered by the Company-Commander and it was so disposed of, and we were able to push on to our objective. No. 8 Platoon under my command worked its way up Cambrai Drive and the flanks thereof—establishing a strongpoint at C24. C. 0.0. [100 yards in from the right bound of the Blue Line] and a block on the drive 30–40 yards further on. Immediately in front of the position was a thick belt of German wire 15–20 feet in depth which proved a great obstacle to troops passing through to the Black Line. Our casualties as yet had been very slight and one might add that the men arrived at their objective quite fresh.
>
> [After the 1/9th] had passed well over, we experienced a great deal of sniping and increased enemy machine gun fire—the latter coming from Bank Farm—I afterwards learnt—and was disposed of by the tanks. An explosion occurred in Plum Farm, also Rat Farm, as yet the enemy barrage was weak.[35]

For 11 and 12 Platoon in the fourth wave, maintaining formation proved challenging, as 2Lt James Killey (11 Platoon) confessed:

> It would have been useful if the platoon had practiced getting out by sections in file and then forming line and if the section commanders had been more practiced at quickly getting their sections into formation. The German lines were reached and passed without much difficulty and after seeing that the platoon was in touch with the right bodies on both flanks, a position was taken up midway between Jasper Farm and Plum Farm as arranged. Suitable shell holes and positions for the sections were chosen and the men were started digging in and improving their cover, casualties attended to, flares lit, report sent in.[36]

In his written submission, one of Killey's men—Rfn Herbert Donaldson—suggested that other factors aggravated the poor formation-keeping:

> My first impression on going over the trench was that the first man over carried on straight on instead of extending to the right or left, waiting for the remainder of their respective sections. This together with the large amount of wire underfoot, caused the men to advance in file rather than in line. Owing to the bad light and terrific noise, it was impossible for section commanders to remedy the straggling.
>
> On my direct front, a small party of Germans were throwing bombs, I should say about a dozen in all. Also a *Granatenwerfer* machine was fairly active.
>
> On reaching the front line I noticed the terrible condition of the trench, the only untouched shelter being a small two-compartment concrete dugout. Proceeding, I observed one or two broken tanks between the first and support lines. The men appeared

> to be rather reluctant to keep up to our barrage and advanced haltingly in bounds instead of steadily at regular intervals. As I reached my objective I saw the smoke of a train behind the ridge quarter right from Jasper Farm. All enemy shells on the first day seemed to be of the same calibre, about 5.9 and it was not until the following day that he started using light stuff. His concrete dugouts in his support line and his reserve line seemed to be untouched.[37]

Cpl John Roberts (201) of 12 Platoon also commented about the muddle:

> The only thing that seemed to trouble our men on jumping out of our trenches was the darkness and when the second wave went over a good number of the first wave were found still trying between them. A number of men lost their direction and joined anybody's party instead to find the gaps in our wire. The men seemed to walk about in groups of 12 or so and a big gap of trying to find their own section. On reaching the German support line quite a lot of men laid down and seemed quite hazy of what to do. Not much of the German wire was left uncut and the trench had suffered from our barrage. Two dugouts of concrete were the only things left standing in the front line of trenches. These were full of prisoners and 2 or 3 inches of water in them. No more dugouts were seen, only surface ones. Quite a good number of steel body covers were lying in bundles of 12 in Cambrai Reserve.[38]

The battalion completed its consolidation of the German reserve line, and platoons from 'B' and 'C' established strongpoints at the Blue Line, casualties relatively few so far.

At 4.55 a.m., the 1/9th passed through 'B' fifteen minutes ahead of schedule, allowing them ample time to reorganise at the Blue Line before their advance to the Black Line. Ten minutes later, they left the Blue Line for their objectives of the *Stutzpunkt* Line and Pommern Redoubt. At 8 a.m., 164 Bde also passed through 'B' Company's positions on their way to the Green Line. Two hours later, Battalion HQ moved to an advanced position at the junction of Cambrai Reserve, Camel Reserve, and Jasper Trench, close to Jasper Farm.

Consolidation continued, as 2Lt Killey reported:

> Digging was continued, good depth being obtained, the men had a meal and a few of them were told off to sleep. There was some shelling, but it was mostly going further back and a few casualties from stray MG bullets. This continued until about 11 a.m., when the platoon was called upon with the company to reinforce the 9th KLR in the Black Line.[39]

The attack against the Green Line was going awry, mainly due to losses from enfilading fire from both flanks, neighbouring divisions having made less progress. Another factor from around midday, was the weather. The rain returned and by evening became a deluge, turning the churned earth into a swamp; the torrent continuing—autumnal rains having arrived an unpredicted two months early.

In late morning, 'A' and 'D' were ordered to the Blue Line (narratives supply contradictory times, varying between 11 a.m. through to 1 p.m., though the diary states that all four companies received their orders at the same time). 'B' and 'C' were sent to reinforce the 1/9th at the Black Line—the diary erroneously states 'A' and 'C'—all four companies advancing through increasingly-heavy shellfire.

Upon reaching the Blue Line, 'A' reorganised into two platoons of approximately twenty-five men apiece, and began to consolidate the left of the line. Their positions were shelled very heavily at intervals and one Lewis team was hit, both gun and team—two of whom were killed—put out of action.

Second-Lieutenant Daglish took 'D' forward:

> We found the Blue Line in good condition and continued to dig in to a good depth, the necessity of which was shown a few hours later when the enemy put a heavy barrage on the Blue Line, but as we were pretty deeply dug in, we had few casualties. A clump of German wire and pickets (barbed and concertina) came in very useful and I had 20 coils put out in front of my section of the Blue Line where there were still remnants of German wire, but not enough to make a serious obstacle.[40]

Cpl Dawson of 15 Platoon, concerned about congestion, took matters into his own hands:

> As the trench was overcrowded, I ordered my men and other men I had collected to dig a new trench joining up with the main trench. We were heavily shelled, but by unsparing efforts and ceaseless energy on the part of the men, we managed to get very good cover. We stayed in the trench all night, a guard of 6 men were posted under me to keep a sharp lookout whilst the remainder of the men tried to get a bit of a rest. During the night, rain fell heavily, flooding the trench.[41]

Second-Lieutenant McLaren's 'B' Company occupied the left of the Black Line:

> I received word to take the company forward and reinforce the 9th Kings at Bank Farm. We started forward in artillery formation, but on account of the enemy wire this formation soon broke up, but the company arrived without casualties and took up a position on the left flank of the 9th, a party being told off to consolidate shell holes in front for Lewis gun positions.[42]

To their right was Capt. Tyson's 'C' Company:

> The company went up in artillery formation under heavy shell fire, which I consider the safest way to move and owing to our keeping fairly large intervals no casualties were caused. We arrived and reported to OC 9th King's and took up position in a newly dug trench in advance of the Frezenberg Line. Strongpoints were dug and occupied and as good cover as possible was obtained.
>
> I then found that the line, that was being held by another company of the 6th, ['B'] was not in touch with the left flank, for a matter of 90 yards, we therefore spread the

> men out and got in touch with the South Lancs. Two German dugouts were available and arrangements were made to relieve men from each post for two hours for rest and warmth, the men being given an issue of rum twice a day. This I found had good results owing to the excessive wet.
>
> The enemy was seen from time to time at the top of the ridge (The Somme) 500 yards away and a counter-attack was expected. We had great difficulties in keeping the Lewis guns and rifles clean, but managed to get them to fire. We had however, two machine guns in good condition.[43]

Apart from the far left at Schuler Farm, 164 Bde held most of the Green Line by 2.15 p.m., but their situation was critical. Around 3 p.m., the enemy counterattacked near Schuler Farm. The Brigade held as long as possible, scavenging ammunition from the bodies of the dead and from knocked-out tanks, but once this was expended, they had no option but to carry out a fighting withdrawal with the last of their rounds, consolidating a line of shell holes about 200 yards forward of the Black Line.

British artillery and machine guns smashed this counterattack, inflicting severe losses on the enemy and for the rest of the day provided an umbrella for those at the front. The appalling conditions became more of an impediment to the enemy than for the defenders, German weapons becoming choked with mud as they struggled forward. Casualties in 164 Bde were very heavy and both flanks were open. Consequently, at 4.15 p.m., they were ordered to fall back to the Black Line, from where they were eventually withdrawn—the last elements being relieved at 11 a.m. on 1 August, the other brigades holding the line.[44]

As the counterattack began, Sgt Jackson's 6 Platoon engaged the enemy:

> We were then ordered to stand-to once again, as we could observe the enemy massing his troops on the ridge about 6–700 yards away and he was shelling our position very heavy. We saw the enemy scouts making towards our position, so our officer gave the word to open fire and as we had five machine guns and two Lewis guns with us, they didn't get very close to our lines before we drove him back again over the ridge and we must have caused a great many casualties as no-one could have lived under such heavy fire and we had plenty of ammunition, which I must say had been sent to us very quickly from the rear.[45]

'B' Company's two Lewis guns inflicted serious losses upon the enemy. Cpl Thomas Corlett commanded one:

> On the evening of the 31st my gun caused some casualties to Germans who were probably massing for a counter-attack about 300 yards in front. I moved to the left flank of 'B' Company on the 1st and remained in that position until we were relieved.[46]

The other Lewis was commanded by twenty-year-old Rfn Frederick Joughin. When the enemy began to advance, he took his gun to a better position 30 yards forward and brought deadly-accurate fire to bear on them. Despite the heavy shellfire seeking out his exposed position, he remained without rest or relief in appalling conditions until the battalion was relieved. For his courage and determination, he was awarded the DCM (not related to Joseph Joughin, who was awarded the MM). Known to have been wounded in the head during this counterattack was Cpl Harold Winn from 'B', who was medically discharged in November.

Resupply for the Black Line was difficult—carrying parties struggling with their loads through the mud. Parties from the Blue Line ferried it forward. Cpl Coates was on one such gruelling detail:

> This finds us about teatime and the company digging in in the Blue Line. At this point, six men under my control were sent to 'B' Company with ammunition, the position of whom I was not certain. After a lot of enquiring I found they were in the front line (Black Line). I first of all, under sniper and MG fire, rushed up to find out exactly where they wanted the ammunition, leaving my men under cover. After I had found the spot, I rushed my men up one at a time and succeeded in getting away without any casualties.
>
> Then I returned to the Blue Line with my men and started to dig in. we had not been digging long when we had a shell put in the middle of us, killing one and wounding four.[47]

Sgt Turford was desperate for flares:

> Supplies of ammunition, bombs, loaded Lewis gun pans, and rifle grenades were good, but Very lights were not forthcoming until later. I journeyed twice to (Beek?) Farm (Brigade Dump) for these lights but they did not arrive until after darkness. Had anything untoward happened, the supplies which we carried might not have been sufficient.[48]

Divisional artillery was outstanding, they and the MGC providing first-class fire support. At times, shells fell short onto some of the advanced positions in the Black Line, but it was impossible to signal the guns to extend their range due to communication difficulties. Although telephone wires were laid, these were cut so frequently that the only means of communication was by runner, a method that became progressively slower—prompting 2Lt Killey's plea that 'some flare or rocket signals to the artillery to lengthen range would appear to be very necessary'.[49]

Perhaps the men's greatest trial was the weather, as witnessed by CSM Handley:

> This trench was shelled intermittently during the evening from the front when one man was killed and three wounded. During the night the trench was completely enfiladed by a light gun, probably a 13-pdr. It caused us much sense of insecurity, but caused no damage.
>
> It commenced to rain [even harder] about midnight and for officers and men a new paragraph and a new enemy, for it proved the most trying thing and all that was worth writing about from this time to relief on the evening of the 2nd inst. By 6 a.m. on the 1st, the trench was ankle-deep in water, legs and thighs were soaking, groundsheets were clogged with much mud. It was also cold. We could not sit down in the water, so

> crouched down in the trench and tried to snooze. Later in the morning it was decided to outpost the Blue Line [a Lewis, NCO and six men] and withdraw the garrison to the cover of [Jasper] Farm after a wire entanglement had been put out. By this time the men were waterlogged and the idea of merely shifting position was repellent and the order to work struck them like a thunderbolt. However, they gradually warmed up to the work and good work was done under L/Cpl Macnicoll, Cpl Hyam and L/Cpl [Frank] Richards, the first named NCO putting out apron of barbed concertina about 40 yards long in about 10 minutes or a quarter of an hour. The main garrison then returning to cover after I, with guides, had searched the ground in rear for cover, which we found a very fatiguing thing.
>
> At 5.30 p.m., the Bosche counter-attacked and we had to man the Blue Line in force, which we did for about three hours. At this stage the men were pretty exhausted and all more or less suffering from rheumatism or ague. A Lewis gunner had to be helped to the Dressing Station through rheumatism. At 8.30 p.m. the garrison was withdrawn to an outpost left, and from this time until relief, the uneventful monotony of two hours up to their knees in mud and water and four hours in Jasper Farm trying to make a rifle appear out of a mud-stick, was the lot of the Other Ranks of 'D' Company. Owing to the difficulty in cleaning rifles and to casualties, the first outpost was not relieved till about midnight. They had been in the trench from 5.30 to 12 p.m. and they staggered into the farm like drunken men. One man did collapse and several were on the point. NCOs and men were exhausted, shivering and numbed in body and mind and one had to repeat an order several times to make them understand and then they would stare blankly, or after hesitation obey the order slowly. Such was their state and that of each successive old relief as it came in after two hours up to the knees in water, under shell fire and after a perilous and exhausting scramble in the mud to and from the Blue Line. Surely no dismal trench ever had a more fitting name. It was under these conditions that each and all of us learned the value of rum. Tee-totalers were not to be found and better prayers said over those tots of rum than saintly maidens ever muttered after a sip from the communion cup. The liquor was not ill-used. We did not drink to drown—we drank to float.
>
> The new relief went forward each time without a murmur, altho' I could tell from the looks on their faces, that many would have walked to their deaths with a more pleasant mien. As CSM, my job was never more unpleasant and never before did my duty go more against the grain. My lot was a king's to theirs and even mine was almost unbearable. Throughout it all however, their spirits did not waver, tho' often the flesh was weak. They all knew it was for the great advance and all bore it willingly. At times the attempted joke almost moved one to tears, when one thought of such gallant spirit strangled by such dismal conditions.[50]

The supply of rum was maintained due to the bravery of Transport, who faced appallingly-heavy shellfire conveying it forward. In the early hours of 2 August, Lt Geoffrey Burton was critically wounded by a 5.9 on his way back from delivering the spirit, dying on 3 August.

The quagmire much reduced the effectiveness of enemy HE, though L/Cpl John Kneale's 8 Platoon, on the left of the Black Line, suffered casualties from an unlucky round:

After dark I again received orders to move my platoon (all senior NCOs having become casualties) further to the left of the light railway where we again dug in. A shell landed in our trench killing several men. I immediately went along the top of the trench to a Lewis gun position and gave orders to the gunner to keep a field of fire to the right.[51]

The 350-yard journey from Jasper Farm to the Blue Line proved perilous, as witnessed by Jack Fairhurst:

At 10 a.m., 1 August, the platoon was taken out to rest, except for this section which was kept behind as a post. During the six hours they were there, the men kept in cheerful spirits which was very commendable under the circumstances. This line had become a very hot position as it was subject to an enemy straff [*sic.*] at intervals of twenty minutes. The section was relieved at 8 p.m. for a three hours' rest and after leaving Jasper Farm almost ran into a shell which wounded four of the section. The remainder carried on in the Blue Line until relieved next morning and were in a rather exhausted condition.[52]

L/Cpl Whitelaw's section also suffered losses returning from respite:

About 8.30 p.m. my post was withdrawn to rest and clean rifles which was done in Jasper Farm. After returning to Blue Line after resting we slightly lost our direction in the dark and three men were slightly wounded and went to Dressing Station—one being returned to duty [James Brookes].[53]

Sgt Burden was keen that his men's fortitude was recognised:

Cpl Heatley still carried on until again wounded in the knee and unable to walk so I sent him down. L/Cpl Macnicoll carried on until the battalion was relieved, doing good work—he was my only NCO and so a lot was asked of him. The wiring was praised by the CSM. We were both buried once but not hurt. The rain spoilt the operations, the men being in great form. Our total casualties for the whole platoon were 1 killed, 7 wounded and 2 missing. L/Cpl Macnicoll has been wounded on 6 occasions, having taken part in every fight and raid the battalion has been on [the Casualties Book only details one previous wounding]. L/Cpl Hill, Lewis Gun attached 'C' Company did very good work, one time going out 30 yards to a shell hole killing two snipers, Rfn H. B. [Herbert] Wren a company-runner of my platoon, did most of the running for the company and never failed to carry out his orders with the utmost dispatch.[54]

Those at the Black Line also suffered greatly in the conditions, 2Lt Killey reporting:

One German dugout was available and arrangements were made to relieve two men at a time from each post for two hours' rest and warmth. The enemy was seen from time to time at the top of the ridge some 300 yards away and a counter-attack was expected

> at any time. This position was held until about noon on 2nd August, when platoon was relieved, the men being completely exhausted through lack of rest and the incessant rain and cold. The rifles were in very bad condition and there was no opportunity of keeping them dry, one of the Lewis guns was out of action and one had been destroyed by a shell. The line was however held with 2 Vickers guns and good resistance could still have been made in a counter-attack.[55]

It was only on 1 August that German artillery succeeded in accurately ranging on the new positions, though only nine of the battalion's casualties are recorded for that date. However, 2Lt Jones wrote:

> On the 1st inst. we had many casualties (26 killed/wounded) the enemy artillery having succeeded in finding our trench in a number of places. The trench was practically a quagmire and we were continually shelled by the German heavies, which caused a number of casualties amongst us.[56]

Clearly, there are dating inaccuracies concerning casualties; one was probably twenty-four-year-old Rfn George Peach from 'C'—his entry in the Casualties Book includes information from the Burial-Officer of XIX Corps, dated 6 August, reporting his burial on the Black Line, 60 yards from Bank Farm.

Two whose wounding was recorded for 1 August were Rfn Charles Donnelly from 'C' and Rfn Fred Haigh—both were gassed and neither returned. Also from 'C', L/Cpl John Puddicombe was evacuated home with an eye wound, dying from pneumonia at the depot in Oswestry in April 1918. Though only suffering from contusions (and no doubt shock) after being buried by a shell on 1 August, Rfn R. Stewart was posted to the 1/9th after leaving hospital later that month.

An abandoned tank, about 100 yards forward and to the left of 'B' Company, was occupied by German snipers on 1 August. Even so, Sgt Hannah volunteered to rescue a wounded soldier lying in a shell hole 200 yards forward of their position. Mr McLaren granted permission to make the attempt, NCO and casualty regaining the relative safety of the Black Line. Just after dawn on 2 August, the snipers attempted to re-enter the tank (F-13 'Falcon'). Cpl Corlett's Lewis team allowed the six enemy to almost reach cover before opening fire, killing four and sending the other two into flight.

At 12.40 p.m. on 2 August, preceded by a heavy bombardment, the enemy counterattacked again. The formidable firepower of the entire divisional artillery, supported by every available Vickers, utterly annihilated both attempts.

Salvation came on 2 August. The companies in the Blue Line were relieved after dark—deliverance for 'B' and 'C', having arrived earlier at 1.30 p.m., in the shape of Capt. Eastwood, Capt. Rome, and a composite force from Transport and the Lifeboat Party. However, these two companies were only allowed to withdraw to the original front line, which, at the time, must have felt like a luxury hotel to the exhausted men. CSM Handley described the journey back to Congreve Walk after 'D' was relieved by 107 Bde later that night:

> After what appeared to us a lifetime, we were relieved and the remnants struggled back past the derelict tanks, literally dragging one limb after the other to Congreve Walk, from which place after a spell we quitted for Vlamertinghe. It was pitiable to see men struggling across our captured ground and some had to rest at intervals before they could continue.[57]

Rfn Frederick Duffin was hapless enough to be badly wounded by shrapnel on his right elbow as he made his way back.

Henry Cowins, Robert Robinson (037), and three of their comrades who were unable to walk remained long after the others reached the rear:

> Nothing further happened until the battalion was relieved and then two men had to stay behind with three men suffering from trench feet. Bearers were expected to arrive the same night. By 6 o'clock the following night they had not arrived. I then set out, leaving Robinson behind, to find these bearers. I found an MO, who had them brought down the same night. I arrived at the battalion the next day [3 August], Robinson arriving a couple of hours after.[58]

The battalion waited in Congreve Walk until the afternoon of 3 August, then marched to Vlamertinghe, where buses transported them to Watou. Tragically, on their way out, nineteen-year-old Rfn Thomas Wyldes was killed by shellfire.

All ranks displayed exceptional resilience, in circumstances that would have reduced most grown men to tears. Multiple reports describe the cheerfulness of all—up to their knees in cold, wet muddy water, with shellfire falling all around and snipers making life precarious. Unbelievable perhaps, but there comes a point—several stages beyond utter misery—when hysterical humour takes over and the ordinary British soldier shines. For recent arrivals, unhardened to the terrible effects of artillery, the horror must have been immeasurably worse.

The diary reports thirty-one fatalities, forty-two missing, and 149 wounded. With hindsight, it is possible to slightly reduce this to 216—sixty-two fatalities and 154 wounded. Forty of these were 'originals', leaving just 259 remaining out of the 1,125 who had crossed the Channel in February 1915. Of the 197 casualties listed for 31 July—though many were indisputably from later—only four died from wounds, a statistic that says more about the inability to find and evacuate wounded than it does about life-saving medical treatment.

Fatalities, 31 July 1917-3 August 1917

Rfn Arthur Adams	49980	KIA: 31/7	Capt. Alfred Balmforth		KIA: 31/7
Rfn William Aspinall	242475	KIA: 31/7	L/Cpl Joseph Banning	240958	KIA: 31/7
Rfn Matthew Baker	241645	KIA: 31/7	Rfn James Barnett	241030	KIA: 31/7
L/Cpl Thomas Samuel Ball	241086	KIA: 31/7	L/Cpl John Gordon Bean	241503	KIA: 31/7

Rfn William Ronald Bentley	242684	KIA: 31/7
Rfn Thomas Bicknell	242706	KIA: 31/7
Rfn Arthur Joseph Boag	242273	KIA: 31/7
Rfn George Lewis Booth	49927	KIA: 31/7
Rfn Charles Arnold Briggs	49991	KIA: 31/7
Rfn George Alfred Brock	49984	KIA: 31/7
Rfn Alfred Britton Burrows	260005	KIA: 31/7
Lt Geoffrey Bunnell Burton*		DOW: 3/8
Rfn Thomas Crane	241575	KIA: 2/8
Rfn David F. Dales	48582	DOW: 7/8
Rfn William Henry Davies	242618	KIA: 31/7
L/Cpl Leslie Grierson DeValve	240231	KIA: 31/7
Rfn James Thomas Downs	49933	DOW: 12/8
Rfn Henry Edwards	241776	KIA: 31/7
Rfn Thomas Emery	202281	KIA: 31/7
Rfn Harold Escolme	242593	KIA: 2/8
Rfn Fred Fosbrook	49937	KIA: 31/7
L/Cpl Eric Crockett Foster	242136	KIA: 31/7
Rfn Charles Henry Green	50003	KIA: 31/7
2Lt Edward Stanley Griffin		KIA: 31/7
L/Cpl Evan Griffiths	240909	DOW: 13/8
Capt. James Percival Grove		KIA: 31/7
Rfn Franklin Wilcox Haworth	241479	KIA: 2/8
Rfn Thomas Henry Hughes	241837	KIA: 31/7
Cpl William Walter Kenneth Hume	240034	KIA: 2/8
Rfn Robert Archibald Jackson	240442	KIA: 1/8
Rfn William Jackson	241925	KIA: 31/7
Rfn Harry Jennings	59538	KIA: 31/7
Rfn Alfred Edward Jones	59367	KIA: 31/7
Rfn Frank Edgar Jones	240841	KIA: 31/7
Rfn William Herbert Jones	241619	KIA: 31/7
Rfn John Hamilton Kerr	241139	KIA: 31/7
Rfn Thomas James Matthews	242625	KIA: 31/7
Cpl Robert Arnold Millard	240410	KIA: 31/7
Rfn David Pagan	41839	KIA: 31/7
Rfn Henry Patton	242132	KIA: 31/7
Rfn George Frederick Peach	241847	KIA: 31/7
L/Cpl Joseph Ralph	242113	KIA: 31/7
2Lt Harold Percival Robinson		KIA: 31/7
Rfn Charles Simpson	49973	KIA: 31/7
Rfn Arthur Smedley	242766	KIA: 31/7
Rfn Lawrence Stafford	242677	KIA: 31/7
Rfn George Henry Stockdale	201874	KIA: 31/7
Rfn John Spillman Swaine	242592	DOW: 10/8
Rfn Henry Albert Swinney	57846	KIA: 31/7
Rfn Charles Whittaker	242770	KIA: 31/7
Rfn Charles Wilcock	242786	KIA: 31/7
Rfn John Henry Wood	41557	KIA: 31/7
Rfn Daniel Bertie Woodward	42718	KIA: 31/7
L/Cpl Harold Woosey	241953	KIA: 31/7
Rfn George Albert Wragge	49979	KIA: 31/7
Rfn William Wesley Wright	240925	KIA: 2/8
Rfn Thomas Wyldes	49377	KIA: 3/8
Rfn Joseph Young	43490	KIA: 31/7

* = fatally wounded on 2 August (other DOW recorded wounded on 31 July).

Wounded, 31 July 1917–3 August 1917

L/Cpl Frederick William Aitcheson	242033	WIA: 31/7
Rfn Leslie Aked	241611	WIA: 31/7
Rfn Richard Alty	330593	WIA: 31/7
Rfn Russell Scott Anderson	240608	WIA: 31/7
Rfn John William Angus	47198	WIA: 31/7
Rfn John A. Armitage	49981	WIA: 31/7
Rfn Thomas Ashton	260002	WIA: 31/7
Rfn Rowland Atkin	49918	WIA: 31/7
L/Cpl Arthur Baker	241882	WIA: 31/7
Rfn William Ball	241703	WIA: 31/7
Rfn Stephen Myles Barker	242837	WIA: 31/7
Rfn Fred Baugh	241840	WIA: 31/7
Rfn Horace O. Beard	49929	WIA: 31/7

L/Cpl Robert Bell	240444	WAD: 31/7
L/Cpl Arthur Gordon Blood	240451	WIA: 31/7
Rfn J. Blood	49986	WIA: 31/7
Rfn Harold Blount	240447	WIA: 31/7
Rfn Whiteley Booth	49930	WIA: 2/8
Rfn Frank Utten Breese	240846	WIA: 31/7
Rfn Richard Bretherton	242705	WIA: 31/7
Rfn James William George Brookes	49922	WAD: 31/7
Rfn Teddie Brown	49924	WIA: 31/7
Rfn Walter Brown	241444	WIA: 31/7
Rfn John Burns	200659	WIA: 31/7
Rfn George E. Callon	242332	SS: 31/7
Rfn William W. Carte	242841	WIA: 31/7
Rfn George Carter	241644	WIA: 31/7
Rfn John Charnock	260013	SS: 2/8
Rfn Harold Collier	260012	WIA: 31/7
Rfn Robert Colligan	240349	WIA: 31/7
Rfn Frank Cope	240465	WIA: 31/7
Rfn Thomas Cowell	242710	WIA: 31/7
Rfn John William Cox	49994	WIA: 31/7
Rfn John Crawford	59227	WIA: 31/7
Rfn Fred Cryer	49932	WIA: 31/7
L/Cpl Arthur Davies	241085	WIA: 31/7
Rfn Ernest Davies	49995	WIA: 31/7
Rfn William Davies	241967	WIA: 31/7
Rfn John Dawson	241435	WIA: 31/7
Rfn Joseph Dilworth	242594	WIA: 31/7
Rfn Albert Edward Dixon	49996	WIA: 31/7
Rfn Charles Donnelly	242655	WIA: 1/8
Rfn Alfred Doran	242491	WIA: 31/7
Rfn John Samuel Doyle	240861	WIA: 31/7
Rfn Frederick George Duffin	241941	WIA: 31/7
Rfn John Duffy	242657	WIA: 31/7
Rfn John Dunn	242716	WIA: 31/7
L/Cpl Edward Dutton	242106	WIA: 31/7
Rfn Henry S. Edgar	59343	WIA: 31/7
L/Cpl Edward Stanley Edwards	241114	WIA: 31/7
Rfn Clifford Ellis	49997	WIA: 31/7
Rfn William Henry Espley	49934	WIA: 31/7
Rfn Cecil Evans	19641	WIA: 31/7
Rfn Charles Evans	242658	WIA: 31/7
Cpl Andrew Myles Fitzmaurice	240303	WIA: 31/7
Rfn Bernard Flanagan	201985	WIA: 31/7
L/Cpl Isaac Foulkes	242646	WIA: 31/7
Rfn Alfred Fyles	32561	WIA: 31/7
Lt William Goffey		WIA: 31/7
Rfn Herbert Greenwood	242723	WIA: 31/7
Rfn William E. Griffiths	241841	WIA: 31/7
Rfn Fred William Haigh	50012	WIA: 1/8
Rfn Harry Hanson	242726	WIA: 31/7
Rfn Robert Hargreaves	242736	WIA: 31/7
Rfn William Hargreaves	260026	WIA: 31/7
Rfn Samuel Harp	49940	WIA: 31/7
Sgt Montague Hart	240315	WIA: 31/7
Sgt Robert Harold Hartley	240583	WIA: 31/7
Cpl Edward Heatley	240308	WIA: 31/7
Rfn John Holden	260023	WIA: 31/7
Rfn Ernest Holland	50010	WIA: 31/7
Rfn William Harold Hughes	242727	WIA: 31/7
Rfn Joseph Jackson	240977	WIA: 31/7
Rfn William Jackson	260027	WIA: 31/7
Rfn Thomas Jennings	49949	WIA: 31/7
Rfn James Johnston	241858	WIA: 31/7
A/Cpl Edgar Jones	241420	WIA: 31/7
Rfn Henry Watkin Jones	242465	WIA: 31/7
Rfn John Arthur Jones	241750	WIA: 31/7
Rfn William Henry Jones	56707	WIA: 31/7
Rfn Robert Kelly	242629	WIA: 31/7
Rfn Charles Barker Kendall	240174	WIA: 31/7
Rfn William Keneley	330675	WIA: 31/7
Cpl Alfred Howarth Kermode	240282	WIA: 31/7
Rfn Imrie Alexander King	240491	WIA: 31/7
Rfn William J. Kirby	330559	WIA: 31/7
Rfn William Arthur Latham	200176	WIA: 31/7
Rfn Herbert Lister	240476	WIA: 31/7
Rfn J. T. Longmore	49952	WIA: 31/7
Rfn Thomas Magee	242016	WIA: 31/7
Sgt Norman Percy Maggi	240092	WIA: 31/7
Sgt James Marginson	260001	WIA: 31/7

Rfn Ernest A. Mason	241414	WIA: 31/7
Rfn Thomas J. McDermott	202740	WIA: 31/7
Rfn Eugene McGowan	27287	WIA: 31/7
2Lt Cecil H. Merriman		WIA: 31/7
Rfn Ernest Mitchell	49955	WIA: 2/8
Cpl Robert Moffat	240040	WIA: 31/7
Rfn William Morriarty	200761	WIA: 31/7
Rfn William George Morris	260029	WIA: 31/7
Rfn James Neary	201521	WIA: 31/7
Rfn Charles Nixon	49961	WIA: 31/7
Rfn George Norman	241025	WIA: 31/7
Rfn John Norminton	241899	WIA: 31/7
Rfn Walter Nowell	242755	WIA: 31/7
Rfn Alfred Gerald O'Leary	242075	WIA: 31/7
Rfn Charles Padley	241753	WIA: 31/7
Rfn Wallis T. Pascoe	49958	WIA: 1/8
2Lt James Paton		WIA: 31/7
Rfn Thomas H. Pearce	240257	WIA: 31/7
Rfn Robert John Pickering	242473	WIA: 31/7
Rfn Joseph Henry Plews	241882	WIA: 31/7
Rfn Charles Poole	49963	WIA: 31/7
Rfn Patrick Price	52703	WIA: 31/7
L/Sgt Ernest G. Pritchard	240859	WIA: 31/7
L/Cpl John French Puddicombe	241612	WIA: 1/8
Rfn Thomas William Purcell	242760	WIA: 31/7
Rfn John Quinn	242057	WIA: 31/7
Lt Richard R. Rathbone		WIA: 31/7
Rfn William Redhead	241932	WIA: 31/7
Rfn Charles Reinecke	240146	WAD: 31/7
Rfn Walter Henry Riddell	200198	WIA: 31/7
Cpl Thomas Arthur Riley	241058	WIA: 31/7
Rfn Lewis Rimmer	241056	WIA: 2/8
Rfn Arthur Rogers	241968	WIA: 31/7
Rfn Arthur J. Rooley	49967	WIA: 1/8
Sgt Ernest Sayer	241536	WIA: 31/7
Rfn Gilbert L. S. Scott	241722	WIA: 31/7
Rfn William Scott	241866	WIA: 31/7
L/Cpl Frank Ernest Sharples	242005	WIA: 31/7
Rfn Thomas Shaw	48990	WIA: 31/7
Rfn Edward Shipsides	242900	WIA: 31/7
Rfn Samuel Thomas Henry Smith	240594	WIA: 1/8
Rfn Albert Smith	240789	WIA: 31/7
L/Cpl William Spencer	242689	WIA: 31/7
Rfn Charles William Steen	241504	WIA: 31/7
Rfn R. G. Stewart	201032	WIA: 1/8
Rfn W. Stott	242810	WIA: 31/7
Rfn Alfred Strange	242678	WIA: 31/7
Rfn Frederick Taylor	241749	WIA: 31/7
Rfn John Thwaite	49977	WIA: 31/7
Rfn Simon Tobias	240456	WIA: 31/7
Rfn Fred H. Tolson	49978	WIA: 31/7
Rfn Ralph Tyson	242122	WIA: 31/7
Rfn James Upton	241240	WIA: 31/7
Rfn Arthur Walker	242331	WIA: 31/7
Rfn John Warburton	242773	WIA: 31/7
L/Cpl Francis Augustus Wareham	240612	WIA: 31/7
Rfn Fred B. Weall	260042	WIA: 31/7
Rfn George Hughes Whamond	242884	SS: 31/7
Rfn Samuel White	242882	SS: 1/8
Rfn Abraham Wilson	242772	WIA: 31/7
Cpl Harold James Winn	240417	WIA: 31/7
Rfn Stanley Woodward	242881	WIA: 31/7

9

4 August 1917—27 September 1917: The Battle of the Menin Road Ridge

Coordinates for this Chapter

battery position	50°52′48.60″N 2°57′16.90″E	Martha House	50°53′1.70″N 2°57′47.50″E
Capitol, the	50°52′54.60″N 2°57′40.90″E	Mersey Camp	50°51′38.50″N 2°47′45.60″E
Gallipoli	50°52′53.60″N 2°57′25.80″E	Pilgrim	50°52′49.50″N 2°57′28.10″E
Gallipoli Copse	50°52′54.60″N 2°57′52.00″E	Schuler Farm	50°53′19.80″N 2°57′13.50″E
Hill 35	50°52′48.70″N 2°57′22.70″E	Schuler Galleries	50°53′14.60″N 2°57′9.90″E
Hill 37	50°52′49.90″N 2°57′56.80″E	Snag, the	50°52′52.80″N 2°58′3.60″E
Iberian	50°52′39.80″N 2°57′21.20″E	Somme	50°52′56.80″N 2°57′3.40″E
Irma	50°52′38.50″N 2°57′28.00″E	Sulva	50°52′50.90″N 2°57′28.80″E
Kansas House	50°53′9.20″N 2°57′34.10″E	Transport Lines	50°51′6.30″N 2°48′15.70″E
Kaynorth	50°52′33.10″N 2°57′33.70″E	unnamed strongpoint	50°52′47.50″N 2°57′30.60″E
Keir Farm	50°53′1.00″N 2°57′36.30″E	Waterend House	50°52′32.90″N 2°57′54.30″E
Lens	50°52′47.50″N 2°57′17.40″E		

On 6 August, the battalion marched to Abele, where they entrained for Audruicq, arriving at 3 p.m. From there, it was just 2 miles to billets in Zutkerque. It would be 16 September before they returned to Vlamertinghe, the time in the rear dedicated to training, concentrating on using the new platoon organisation to overcome isolated strongpoints in the *Stutzpunkt* Line.

Conditions during the last attack had affected the health of many, particularly regarding trench foot, which had been unavoidable in the conditions and a number of sufferers were admitted to hospital. Others, such as Rfn Abraham Wilson contracted trench nephritis and returned home. Though he was fortunate to only have a mild case, he was posted to the 1/5th on his return and captured in April 1918. One of the June draft, Rfn George Green, was awarded the MM for 31 July, but his health had suffered and he was admitted to hospital on 12 September and graded PB. One to leave temporarily was former mill worker Rfn Frederick Musk. The father of one from Rawtenstall was, at forty-two years of age and 4 feet 11 inches in height, not best-suited to infantry life. He was posted to Divisional Traffic Control in late August—though was probably not best pleased to be posted back again a month later.

While the division trained, others made two attempts to advance from the Black Line, but little was achieved. The 55th Division was to make the next effort on 20 September. The first objective, known as the Dotted Red Line, ran from halfway between Schuler Galleries and Schuler Farm on the left, through Gallipoli to Kaynorth, where the divisional bound with the South African Bde lay. The second objective, the Yellow Line, ran from the western edge of Schuler Farm, through Keir Farm and the Capitol, to the divisional bound at Waterend House. The final objective was the Green Line of 31 July. Once again, 165 Bde would be on the left of a two-brigade initial advance.

When the battalion returned to the line, their strength was 791, 200 fewer than was available for 31 July. Although 125 men and nine officers joined at Zutkerque, they had only arrived two days before leaving the area and there had been little opportunity to assimilate them—fifty-four would fall in the forthcoming attack. One newcomer, Rfn Septimus Kersey, was only born in February 1900, but his true age remained a secret, even after being wounded in both legs a fortnight after arriving. On 15 September, the battalion entrained at Audruicq, bound for Vlamertinghe. Arriving at 5.30 p.m., they marched to a mixed camp of huts, tents, and bivouacs, 500 yards south-west of Vlamertinghe, all of 165 Bde accommodated in the immediate area.

At 1.15 a.m. on the 16th, the camp was shelled by high-velocity guns, but no damage or casualties resulted. Later that morning, fifteen low-flying enemy aircraft dropped a number of bombs—again without result—though clearly the Germans were extremely uneasy about the build-up of forces. That same morning, all officers and NCOs visited Divisional HQ in Mersey Camp, to view the large-scale model of the area to be attacked on 20 September.

On 17 September, the overcrowding at the camp was eased when the 1/7th and 1/9th moved to the old British line, those previously under canvas occupying the vacated huts. That evening, the troops in camp were being entertained by the Brigade Band when six high-velocity rounds struck the camp, and although no material damage was caused, one of the audience, Rfn Thomas Chesworth, had his thigh shattered by shell splinters. Tragically, the nineteen-year-old from 'C' died soon afterwards.

On 18 September, Rfn Thomas Tonkinson was accidentally injured, suffering a lacerated forehead. Normally, an injury of this nature was not a 'Blighty' one, but shortly before any major offensive, wards were cleared of minor cases in preparation for an influx of casualties, Tonkinson becoming a lucky beneficiary. After dark, the battalion led by Maj. Gordon, with Capt. Blackledge as 2IC and Adjutant Capt. Robert Phillips, boarded the light railway at Vlamertinghe for St Jean. From there, they filed forward to their pre-assembly positions. Along the journey, between St Jean and Congreve Walk, twenty-six-year-old Rfn Francis Wright was killed by shellfire.

'A', under 2Lt McLaren, and 'C', under 2Lt Norman Phillips, occupied Congreve Walk, HQ in Oxford Trench dugouts; 'D' led by Capt. Rome and 'B' under Capt. Eastwood went into the OBL between Pagoda Street and Strand. Twenty-one officers and 510 other ranks comprised the attacking force, the balance under Lt-Col. McKaig, remaining in Transport Lines, a mile west of Vlamertinghe. This time, 165 Bde's attack would be initiated by the 1/9th (on the left) and the 1/7th (on the right), both charged with capturing the Dotted Red and Yellow Lines. The 1/6th, on the left of the brigade front, would leapfrog through the 1/9th to seize the Green Line—the 1/5th doing likewise to their right. 'B' (on the left) and 'D' (on the right) were in the fifth and sixth waves; behind them, 'A' (on the left) and 'C' (on the right) comprised the seventh and eighth waves.

There was no long interval to allow the leading battalions to seize their objectives, before the following waves advanced against the Green Line. Instead, both battalions would advance slowly behind the first four waves, leaving their battle positions at Zero; if necessary, lingering on Hill 35 after the leading waves had captured it, to await the creeping barrage to cover their assault. This arrangement, agreed between the 1/5th and Maj. Gordon, was to mitigate casualties from the inevitable German counter-bombardment, and was, on the face of it, sensible, though it had unintended ramifications and probably accounts for why later reports carry so few battalion-specific details of the events.

Facing 165 Bde was a low ridge, its twin summits of Hill 35 and Hill 37 separated by a low saddle; on its slopes, a multitude of strongpoints, whose arcs of fire interlocked with those on the flatter ground. Most strongpoints consisted of a cluster of concrete pillboxes, augmented by interconnected, camouflaged shell hole positions, containing snipers and machine guns. Aerial reconnaissance had failed to detect the shell hole positions, but the craters to their front were filled with tangles of wire, preventing their use as cover and these were visible on the photographs.

The initial waves would have to contend with fire from Gallipoli, Lens, Iberian, and Kaynorth. The defences of Lens, on the forward slope of Hill 35, were enhanced by three concrete pillboxes and a machine-gun position, 300 yards to its front; 40 yards to the left of Lens was a concrete battery position, a cause of considerable confusion. The name 'Lens' on the maps could be taken to apply to both positions. and even though a comprehensive ten-page breakdown of enemy defences—distributed on 12 September—warned about this

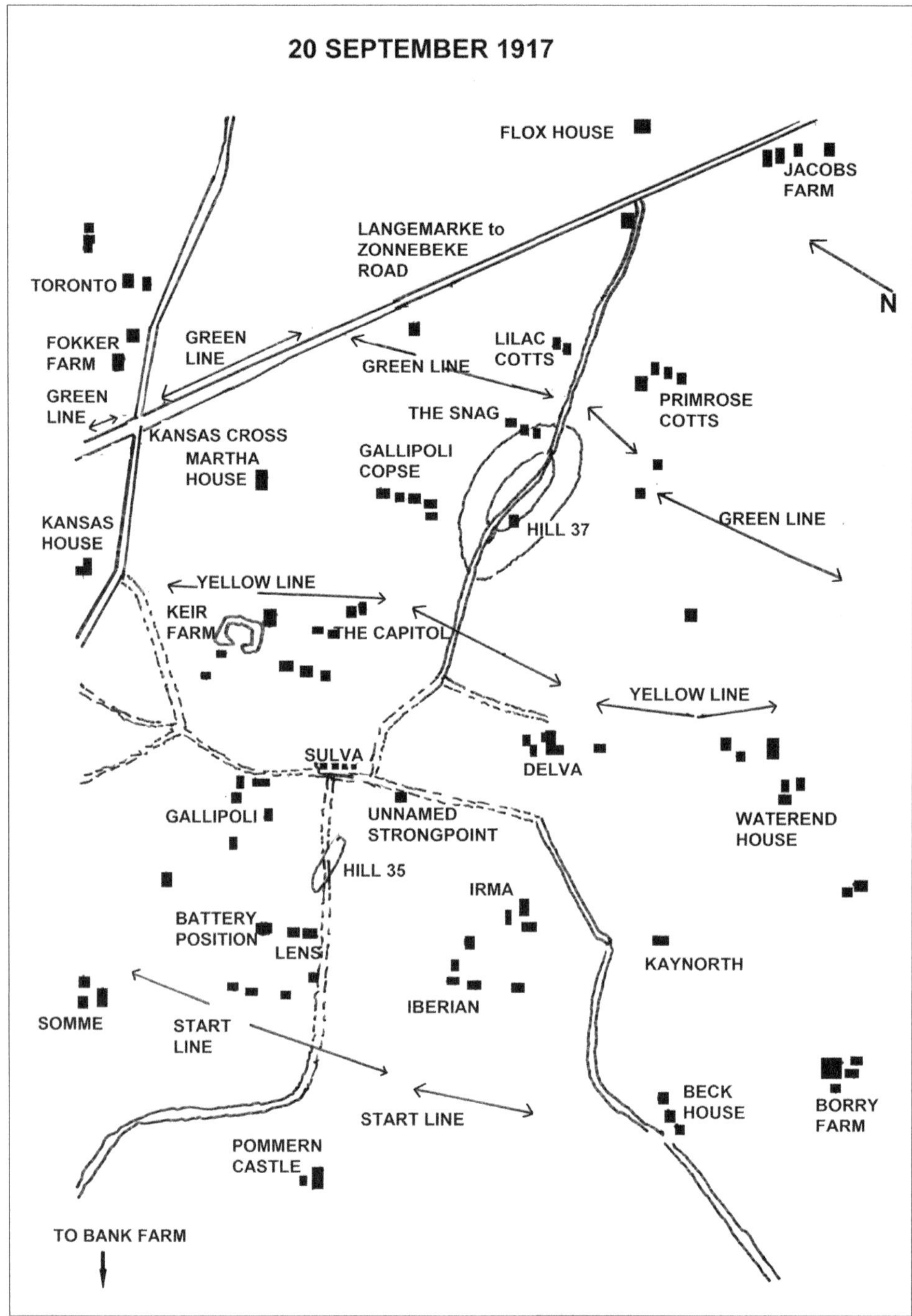
20 SEPTEMBER 1917
FLOX HOUSE
JACOBS FARM
LANGEMARKE to ZONNEBEKE ROAD
N
TORONTO
FOKKER FARM
GREEN LINE
GREEN LINE
GREEN LINE
LILAC COTTS
PRIMROSE COTTS
GREEN LINE
THE SNAG
KANSAS CROSS
MARTHA HOUSE
GALLIPOLI COPSE
KANSAS HOUSE
HILL 37
GREEN LINE
YELLOW LINE
KEIR FARM
THE CAPITOL
YELLOW LINE
SULVA
DELVA
GALLIPOLI
UNNAMED STRONGPOINT
WATEREND HOUSE
HILL 35
IRMA
BATTERY POSITION
LENS
KAYNORTH
SOMME
START LINE
IBERIAN
START LINE
BECK HOUSE
BORRY FARM
POMMERN CASTLE
TO BANK FARM

confusion, it is evident from after-battle reports that some had paid little heed.[1] Although Iberian did not have additional defences to its fore, the three concrete pillboxes of Irma, 150 yards behind, provided considerable supporting fire. In addition, six knocked out British tanks littered the slopes around Hill 35, Division correctly believing these had been fortified as strongpoints.

At dusk on 19 September, 2Lt George Coleman and guides from each platoon went to their proposed battle positions, and after a careful reconnaissance, Coleman taped along a line from Pommern Castle to a point a few hundred yards west of Somme. He indicated the start position for each platoon, allowing the guides to place notice boards showing the flanks of their platoons.[2]

As night fell, a gentle drizzle descended, turning to steady rain by 11 p.m. Generals Gough and Plumer—concerned by the change after weeks of sun—conferred as to whether or not to call off the attack. After further consultation with meteorologist, Lt-Col. E. Gold, and divisional commanders as to the suitability of the ground, they were advised it was 'go-able' and that apart from the risk of thunderstorms, the weather was likely to be fair in the intermediate future.[3] This rain presented great difficulties for platoons, trying to find their positions in the poor visibility. Capt. Rome ruefully commented:

> From that time [midnight] to nearly Zero, I spent my time collecting small parties of men who were wandering round looking for their units. I had my company HQ in a shell hole, which I made my runners deepen. An hour before Zero the Germans started sending over a lot of light HE which was very disturbing and caused a few casualties. I was very glad that the shell hole had been deepened.[4]

The first company left the OBL for their battle positions at 11 p.m., but it was 4 a.m. before the last reported themselves in position. As 'D' left the OBL, L/Cpl Jack Fairhurst was mortally wounded in the abdomen, dying less than an hour later.

At around 5.20 a.m., twenty minutes before Zero, enemy artillery began to shell the battle positions, and unlike Rome's experience, Cpl Donald Bates of 7 Platoon stated that the 'whizz-bang barrage did little damage to the men in my vicinity'.[5] However, for L/Cpl William Reidy of 'A', the shellfire must have left its scars:

> An hour before Zero I was buried in a trench by a shell, which burst nearby. I lay helpless for some hours until I was released by a corporal of the King's Own. I was covered from head to foot with mush and had lost my box respirator.[6]

The darkness and broken nature of the ground had an immediate effect on formation-keeping. On the left, 2Lt James Pilgrim of 6 Platoon observed:

> Owing to the light being bad, I kept up as near as possible to the 9th King's. at 5.50 a.m. I noticed that the 9th Kings were losing direction and seemed to be working too much to the right and a big gap was caused so I moved my platoon up into the gap and at 6 a.m.

was taking part in the fighting and eventually arrived just north of Lens and assisted in clearing the dugouts at that point.[7]

L/Cpl Thomas Kenny of 'B' found himself separated:

I, a corporal and two men, discovered very shortly that we were lost, being on the extreme left of the battalion. We pushed on however, with shells etc. bursting all around us. Soon we lost the corporal [Arthur Regan, wounded in the back] and three of us carried on until we reached a shallow trench where we found some of 'C' Company, also some of the 9th King's.[8]

Another from 'B' was L/Cpl Joseph Levey:

I thought we were heavy laden as my men were very tired before they had gone very far and when we got near Hill 35, we found out that our bombs were no use to us. It was no use throwing bombs at a concrete dugout, but I may say they came in very handy later on. I thought the Lewis guns were not much use as the Lewis gunners were getting sniped. I thought if they could have gone over behind the battalion they could have done very useful work. I thought all the men were too bunched up all the time and that caused a lot of casualties as it made a good target.[9]

The situation facing 'D', to the right of 'B', was little better, as Capt. Rome admitted:

At Zero I moved forward intending to see that my mopping-up platoon got well started and then to cut across to my two platoons that were detailed to attack and take Hill 37. I had not gone more than 100 yards, when I saw fighting had started in front of me and very close. I could not see our barrage owing to the darkness, and I am afraid a number of men ran into it and became casualties. As the fighting had become very furious, a number of men were getting knocked out. I pushed on to my moppers-up platoon, on reaching their position I found a great deal of confusion, both attacking and supporting Bns had become mixed.[10]

The cause of the hold-up—and subsequent intermingling—was a determined resistance by the enemy garrisoning Lens.

Sgt Edward Heatley and Cpl Frank Richards, on the right of 'D' Company's line, bypassed the delay:

On the opening of the barrage we advanced on the left of 'C' Company of the 5th KLR. When we found our own battalion was held up at Lens and did not affect us, we thought it best to carry on in the hope of joining the Bn immediately it came up. We eventually arrived at our objective, the right slope of Hill 37.[11]

No. 4 Platoon began in the wrong position, then advanced diagonally across the battlefield. L/Cpl John Hulme explained:

> In my opinion I fancy 4 Platoon was somewhat out of their allotted position, for instead of being in rear, we seemed to be somewhat on the right front of the remaining three platoons of 'A' Company. When the attack started we were told to get up and go forward. I got my section up, consisting of three men and went forward, keeping touch with Mr [Arthur] Conibear my Platoon-Officer. It was quite dark at the time in regards of seeing much of what was happening, it soon cleared up and coming sight of the enemy's position, we found ourselves about 60-80 yards on the left of Gallipoli, with another strongpoint to the left about 200 yards, but very few men in the intervening space. I only had two of my men left. It was almost impossible to keep a number of men together going forward on account of the ground being so closely pitted with large shell holes. Direction was also easy to lose unless one's eye was glued on some recognised object in the direction to be taken.[12]

L/Cpl John Burke of 7 Platoon's grenadiers arrived in front of Lens to find:

> A large number of the 9th King's in shell holes about 100 yards from the Lens concrete dugouts, which were putting up strong resistance (machine guns and snipers). After about a quarter of an hour, Cpl [Donald] Bates called my attention to Germans coming out from the dugout on the right so we went straight for them at the same time. Mr McLaren came forward with his company, pushing up all the men from the shell holes as they went. Germans were rushing from the back, but one or two Mills bombs were thrown, so I shot two Germans from 30–40 yards' range. Going round to the back we sorted out as many prisoners as we could, then I felt for a Mills grenade, but found I only had Hales. I shouted for a bomb, but nobody had any, so I took out the pin of a Hales grenade, eased back the collar and removed the two studs, and with as much care as I could, threw it into the dugout.[13]

Rfn William Lee and 14 Platoon's Lewis section became separated during the attack on Lens:

> 'The LG Section went over at Zero on the 20th. No. 1 was wounded whilst taking the first strongpoint and while Cpl [L/Cpl Walter] Newton and myself were assisting him, the Corporal was killed by a sniper. That only left [Peter] O'Rourke and myself, as the rest of the section had got separated. So we carried on attaching ourselves to various corporals until the objective was taken and finding ourselves with the 1/5th L. N. Lancs, who were on the left and with whom we had to stay until relieved. When we had finished advancing there were three of us together from the 1/6th KLR, [Rfn Edward] Welsh the Sanitary-Man having joined us close by the objective. The officer in charge of the Lancs was a Mr Davies and one NCO, a Sgt Collier took our names in case anything was said about getting detached from our Bn.'[14]

Sgt Alfred Rashbrook, leading 9 Platoon, was wounded in elbow, so Cpl Alfred Dixon took over. Dixon wanted to outflank Lens and conferred with one of 'C' Company's recently-arrived subalterns:

> We were held up at Lens Redoubt, where I found 2Lt [Wilfred] Huish. He consulted with me and agreed that our only chance of getting forward was on the flank. I took a number of men with me and advanced on the right flank, where an officer of the REs refused to let me go forward with my men because he said, 'he wanted all available men to dig in and form a last line of resistance.' I was engaged on this work until 1 p.m., when I started to go forward again and try to find the battalion.[15]

Huish had his own problems:

> The enemy's shelling was the cause of a certain disorganisation in the waves, so that on reaching the foot of Hill 35, where the advance was temporarily held up by the crossfire of machine guns, the men of the 1/9th, 1/7th and 1/6th KLR were mixed up and there were also some men of the King's Own and I found myself with only half a dozen of the 1/6th KLR.
>
> The advance being temporarily checked, I left my men in a shell hole while I went to neighbouring shell holes in search of men of the 1/6th. My search proved unsuccessful and on returning to join the men I had left waiting I was unable to find them. I therefore endeavoured to get a few men of other regiments, whom I found in adjacent shell holes, to follow me round the flank of Hill 35, which appeared the only way to advance, as we should then be only subjected to machine gun and snipers from one side instead of the crossfire which caused so many casualties on the top of Hill 35. These men however, seemed to think that they should only follow their own officers and I was obliged to go round the flank by myself in hope of gathering some men there and pushing on, I managed to gather together about half a dozen and one Lewis gun and arrived near Gallipoli Farm just after it had been taken [captured by the 1/9th at 8 a.m.].[16]

Sgt Herbert Hyam of 'D' also decided the only forward was by a flanking movement:

> At Zero, we all went forward until we came upon the 9th KLR, who were held up at Lens. We could not avoid intermingling with them and I found a number of each battalion around me. Finding we could not advance at the spot I was in, I worked my way across to the right flank to see if it was possible to move forward at that point and outflank the position.
>
> Coming upon a big shell hole with a number of the 9th KLR in, I endeavoured to urge them on, Cpl Carline assisting me. We managed to get a party together and moved off to the right, intending to work round to the flank of the strongpoint and by doing so, to get out of the enemy's arc of fire. After proceeding about 15 yards, I saw Cpl Carline fall, with a bullet through either his head or chest. On looking round, I saw practically the whole party put out. I immediately took cover. Shortly after this, the position was rushed and taken.[17]

Hyam's report was misfiled under 'C' when the *Jeudwine Papers* were originally catalogued. With Carline was L/Cpl Henry Lane:

> I lost touch with my section immediately we left our position and went forward with Cpl Carline until we were held up at Lens. Cpl Carline went round to the right and I worked round to the left, from shell hole to shell hole, sniping as I went. When the garrison of Lens surrendered I met Mr Garnsworthy and L/Cpl [Walter] Whitelaw.[18]

Lens was taken around 7.40 a.m. by 2Lt Randall Garnsworthy, an action that earned him the DSO: 'I saw the 9th make a rush at Lens, but could not take it, so I advanced with the men and took it, capturing two machine guns and about 40 prisoners'.[19]

The fighting was still ongoing when Capt. Rome reached Lens:

> [I saw] two officers take the situation in hand. At this point, Maj. Gordon came up and established HQ in a local shell hole. The Adjutant got wounded and while out getting information was wounded again and sent to the Dressing Station. Maj. Gordon ordered me to carry on in his place. He ordered Capt. Eastwood [later killed on Hill 35] and Mr McLaren to push on with what men they could collect and try and keep up with the barrage. Then Maj. Gordon decided we could do no good where we were, so we started to move forward in short rushes, from shell hole to shell hole. We had three other men with us, my CSM and two runners. In our first dash forward, my CSM was badly wounded and the two runners were killed, the sniping being very accurate [CSM John Shaw died]. We worked our way onto Hill 35 where another fierce fight was going on to take a very strong German position consisting of six concrete dugouts supported by enfilade fire from two [knocked out] tanks. By the personal bravery of Capt. Eastwood, Mr [Norman] Phillips, Mr McLaren and Mr Garnsworthy, the position was taken, the Germans coming out waving a Red Cross flag. But they were all shot as the men were mad at losing so many of their friends. Here Maj. Gordon established his HQ and still it was no use pushing on, as the general situation was uncertain. We first of all had to find out where we were. I thought it was Lens, which proved to be right, being confirmed by two battery-commanders who came up later. It's officers state that there is a mistake on the map and the battery position on our side of Hill 35 is shown as Lens is quite wrong. [Here, Jeudwine added a large '!' in blue pencil.] However, to avoid confusion we called the place Hill 35 Strongpoint ['battery position' in Coordinates Table].[20]

When Maj. Gordon and the Adjutant moved forward, Capt. Blackledge stayed at Bank Farm Dugout with instructions to collect all possible information and forward it to the Brigade, remaining there until he received word to join the Advanced HQ at Gallipoli—bringing the Signal-Officer, RSM, and HQ detail forward with him. What news did filter back could not have filled him with confidence:

> The first information I received after Zero was from 2Lt Coleman, who returned wounded, and stated that the whole battalion had been used up in the attack on Hill 35 before the tanks were taken. I saw from this that more troops would be needed to press on to Hill 37, so passed the information to the OC 5/North Lancs [Reserve Battalion]. He warned two of his companies to advance and be ready to reinforce the line. Very little other information was received of any kind from the front and I was unable to give any news to the Brigade for several hours.[21]

Some of the battalion bypassed to the left of Lens, joining elements of the 1/9th to attack Gallipoli and its nearby defences. One such was L/Cpl Herbert Macnicoll, leading 16 Platoon's grenadiers:

> My section and I left our position at Zero. On the way over, two of the section got wounded by German shell fire. We were then held up by a concrete pillbox on Gallipoli. By that time, the 6th and 9th battalions were all mixed up. The Germans were sniping and firing machine guns all the time.
>
> While trying to get on the flanks I lost one of my section. The remaining man and I were going forward and we found a Lewis gun of the 9th King's, which we took forward with us. The concrete boxes were rushed and about twelve Germans and two machine guns were taken out of one. When we saw our men getting the prisoners, we advanced again, on to Hill 37. I then met L/Cpl [James] Bryans and he told me that a German machine gun was in a small trench on the right. I then fired the Lewis gun on it to try and keep him low, but he still kept on firing. Then I asked Cpl Bryans if he had any rifle grenades and he said, 'yes'. I then fired two. Fritz did not open out again, so we advanced. I do not know if the grenades hit their mark or not. We got forward again 50 yards and another machine gun fired on us from left. We dropped into a shell hole and called out to some of our men for reinforcements, but they did not come forward. All that were there, was a full Cpl of the 6th, L/Cpl Bryans and myself with three men of the 6th with a Lewis gun. We only had two pans for the Lewis gun and one rifle grenade. While looking out to see if I could see any of our fellows, I caught sight of ten Germans who were coming out of a pillbox. I put the Lewis gun on them and four dropped, the rest made for the dugout. I used half a pan on them, so we only had one and a half pans left, so said we would have to get back for reinforcements. Nobody seemed to know if there were any officers left, so I went back [to Gallipoli] and could not see any of our officers, so I reported to an officer of the 9th King's and he said reinforcements had been sent for. I then tried to get back, but could not. Found Cpl [George] Salt and done post with him until relieved.[22]

L/Cpl Henry Lane and Salt were sent 300 yards further forward, to the Capitol:

> Here we found two German machine guns, one of which we mounted on the dugout steps. As this seemed to be one of the most forward of our positions, we held it with six

men who by now had come up. We held this position until we were relieved and handed the guns over to the relieving party.[23]

With Lens and the enemy-held tanks overcome, the battalion needed to push on to its own objectives, though the way forward was still far from clear. Capt. Rome began to consolidate around Lens, despatching groups of men forward:

We found we had got a very good position indeed and could command both flanks of Hill 35 and we could also see Hill 37 and the ground between the two hills. Many small parties by this time were coming into our position, which were at once pushed forward on both flanks of the hill to work forward to join our men in front. We could see that we had men in Gallipoli, but there only appeared to be very few there. Maj. Gordon sent a message back to the Bn in close support to at once send two companies forward as the situation had become obscure owing to the mixed state of the troops. After a short delay they came forward in good order and did just what was wanted. What men we had at our disposal we dug in and got the machine gun positions so as to cover both flanks.

Maj. Gordon went out to inspect our right flank and was sniped in both legs. I managed to get him away on a stretcher. He told me to take over and carry on in his plan. A party of RE came up to dig a strongpoint at Gallipoli. I saw the officer in command and explained the situation and told him to dig a strongpoint where he was, which he did. He started the men working and was killed. I found myself the only officer left with about fifty men from two different brigades. The sniping had become very bad indeed. I found that some men have no idea about following the paths of least resistance on the ground. They will stand on the highest piece of land in the neighbourhood. However, by posting men at certain known danger points to shout at these men, we managed to reduce the casualties.[24]

Maj. Gordon was carried to the rear by a stretcher party, led by 'A' Company's Cpl Henry Daniels:

After leaving the Black Line at Zero, I made in the direction given me with my bombing section until we were held up in front of Gallipoli Farm. I then found out that there were two men and myself left of the section. When the Farm was rushed and taken, I found two Lewis gunners and carried until I met Mr McLaren, who told me to get back to the strongpoint. While I was there I was put in charge of a stretcher by Capt. Rome to see that Maj. Gordon was taken to the dressing station. When I returned to Gallipoli, I established myself with the mixture of men on the right of the strongpoint as the place was so crowded and dug in.[25]

McLaren began to consolidate on the northern slope of Hill 35:

We endeavoured to organise a line of men of all battalions, and pushed on along the flat top of the hill being met with heavy rifle and machine gun fire, the great difficulty being

> the control of the line on account of the broken nature of the ground, it being nothing but a mass of deep shell holes. Three verbal messages were sent back by runners, asking for men to be sent forward, but as none appeared and being left alone with my orderly, I pushed over to the left and decided that the best thing to do would be to establish a strong line by the concrete emplacements where a good field of fire could be obtained over the ground in front and to the flanks. I arrived at this decision through seeing the enemy coming over the rise on the left. This line I succeeded in reaching about two hours later and found that the work had commenced, so I took command of the right half and we established it with a strong line, manning it with LGs and 2 machine guns.[26]

One of McLaren's runners was L/Cpl John Burke of 7 Platoon:

> After passing over Hill 35, our men started to fall from the German snipers again. Mr McLaren called me and asked me to find Maj. Gordon and ask him to send up reinforcements as quickly as possible. After a trying time from German snipers and passing through a German barrage of heavies, I delivered the message. I think the reason we had so many casualties was because of the weight the men carried. They could not get up and down quick enough and because of the Bn in front of us not keeping close enough to the barrage when we were at Lens, the barrage was 200 yards in front of us, therefore German snipers were able to set themselves and wait for us to carry on over Hill 35, instead of keeping close to the barrage so as to be upon the enemy before he time to recover.[27]

The problem of weight was insurmountable. Nothing superfluous was carried—the pick or shovel toted by every second man, essential for consolidation. Some voiced complaint about the ineffectiveness of rifle grenades against pillboxes. L/Cpl Henry Eccles later believed:

> One of the weak points in the last attack was the ineffectiveness of all the bombs and rifle grenades carried up and they seemed to be no of use whatsoever against the German pillbox. If we had more snipers and they could get out to the flanks, they would be able to keep the Germans in the pillboxes.[28]

After overcoming Lens, 2Lt Garnsworthy pushed further left, then veered right, centrally along the ridge of Hill 35:

> When I had finished I lost sight of my platoon, but I got together a lot of men and went forward till I came to a strongpoint on the right of Gallipoli [Sulva]. This I took, capturing about 20 prisoners. I then got together another lot of men and went forward. As I went forward I noticed one of our machines come down on my right. Seeing no troops near to help the airman. I made off towards him, but could not get to him owing to a German machine gun firing on us from a 100 yards' range, so I gave it up and started to advance again but could go further owing to being enfiladed from both sides, so stayed at Gallipoli

> which had been taken by the 9th Bn. I then wrote a message and sent it back by one of our men. I then helped the 9th to dig a trench round Gallipoli in case of being counter-attacked, but during the afternoon we were shelled so heavily that the trenches were blown in. we left the machine guns in the dugouts already for action.[29]

'Sulva', ought to have been 'Suvla', but an early misspelling perpetuated.

It was after taking Sulva that Sgt Walter Whitelaw of 16 Platoon became separated from Garnsworthy. He was treating a wounded man in a shell hole, but when he had finished, he found he was alone. Eventually, he returned to Gallipoli, meeting Cpl Thomas Hill and Cpl Colin Bain. The three were ordered to remain with the 1/9th and help consolidate Gallipoli. After the assault on Lens, Hill—commanding 16 Platoon's Lewis section—also became separated:

> After that my section was reduced to one man and myself, and my man got cut off from me. I then carried on with three men out of the 9th King's. the three men and myself attacked a concrete emplacement which was held by two Germans who had a machine gun. I myself shot the two Huns and one of the men fired the MG at a party of Germans which was retiring.[30]

Realising their isolated situation, they returned to Gallipoli.

The attack had become a multitude of small-unit actions—sometimes just two or three men from different battalions. L/Cpl Edward Machin and one of his section pushed on:

> On the morning of the 20th inst., five bombers and myself went into action with 6 Platoon. It was rather too dark at the time to recognise each other at any distance above five yards, so by the time we reached Hill 35 we were separated. Rfn [Henry] Chater and myself were together until we reached Hill 35 on our way, so at that point I got in touch with my section at intervals. Between Hill 35 and Hill 37, Rfn Chater and myself got between a cross fire and a frontal fire, apparently from snipers. We could not locate their positions, but we bombed a large shell hole about 25 yards' distance in front and we had no more sniping from that point. We then came back a little way and worked round to the left. We bombed two suspected positions there, but the sniping continued. Chater and myself got separated as the result of heavy shelling by the enemy. At dusk that night I joined an officer of the 5th L. N. Lancs, 2Lt Provan and together with six other men, dug a strongpoint and remained there until relieved by the South Stafford Regiment.[31]

Another group was led forward by Sgt Thomas Rowe of 'D'. On his own initiative, he collected men from various battalions and attacked a German strongpoint, from which he took ten prisoners and a machine gun. Rowe garrisoned this position, securing it against counterattack—gallantry and leadership that resulted in the DCM.[32]

No. 2 Platoon's 2Lt Ernest Harrop was to the left of Garnsworthy:

> I myself took a small party and pushed on towards Gallipoli. We managed to get to a point in front of and to the right of Gallipoli with very little opposition, but could not get any further owing to MGs and snipers, and also not being in touch with parties on our left and our right. Sometime after, we managed to make our way to one of the concrete places called Gallipoli, where I found a Company-Commander of the 9th King's. here I decided to help him dig a defensive position.[33]

Second-Lieutenant Pilgrim, on Garnsworthy's right, found himself pinned down:

> Reorganised at Lens and found that all officers of my company had become casualties, so collected all the men available and pushed on and met with very heavy machine gun fire and at D19 b. 5.8 ['Pilgrim' in Coordinates Table] found myself with only three riflemen and it was not possible for me to continue forward. I sent back runner to inform Bn HQ my position, but I think he became a casualty and my message was not received. In the meantime, I noticed that our troops had taken Gallipoli, but no reinforcements arrived so I moved round to the side of Hill 35 with the intention of digging in and holding onto the hill. Here I found Capt. Rome and reported to him the situation. I then collected all available men (about 15) [including Henry Chater and Wilfred Hilton] and set them on digging in from Hill 35 towards Gallipoli.[34]

With Pilgrim was L/Cpl Albert Lee of 6 Platoon:

> We were naturally mixed up as the lads were all eager to get forward and I know that the men felt their superiority in morale over the enemy. The first batch we met were absolutely panic-stricken and fairly danced about with fright. We soon reorganised and this was brought about by the good work of Lt Pilgrim, who was in the vicinity. All officers and men worked well. One point to remember was that although we lost the barrage, the men pushed forward by short rushes, which were successful in every case.[35]

Further to the left, L/Cpl John Samuel from 4 Platoon continued his advance:

> One strongpoint was still holding out on our right and some men trying to get closer in to it. Me and the two men left in my section, I gave orders to open fire with their rifles on a loop-hole which I thought they may have been firing out of. Soon after, two Germans dashed out across our front, one with a bandage round the head, they endeavouring to run away to their rear, so I opened fire on them and on the third attempt knocked them out. In the meantime, the strongpoint had been entered. I asked the officer Mr Conibear to come forward, but he was under the impression that it was too early as our barrage was still playing about us to a limited extent. He told me he would go over to some tanks and try to define our position. There was some commotion going on then, around a strongpoint to our left, so I took my two men over. Just as we got there, the German garrison had just surrendered, except one officer who was shot. This strongpoint was in

> the 164 area, but there was very few of the King's Own there, who I believe should have taken it, they had gone more to the left. I being then a junior NCO there, I placed myself and my men under the command of a senior NCO of 9th King's, which was later taken over by an officer of 164 MGC. We assisted in the consolidation of the place and helped to bring heavy rifle and machine gun fire on the enemy in his attempted counter-attacks. I was sent in charge of ration parties and also patrol at night. Until 165 Bde were relieved I was under the orders of our garrison officer, who then gave me a chit and one man who was left to return to my unit.[36]

Conibear was mortally wounded shortly afterwards.

Sgt Hyam found himself, Cpl Corlett, and five men isolated forward of Gallipoli:

> Moving forward, we came upon another hold-up, but this we soon overcame and carried on, until we came upon yet another hold-up, with very heavy sniper fire from the rear of the position. This we overcame and moved forward.
>
> By this time, I found myself with a CSM and some men of the 9th KLR. We were advancing and found that we were an isolated party, that there was nobody on our flanks. Deciding that it was impossible to carry on, as there were only seven all told and we had no support. We fell back on Gallipoli and dug in, making it a strongpoint. Shortly after this, an officer of the 9th came along and took the CSM away. Then the CO of the 9th came along, viewed the position and told me to make the place as strong as possible and hang on. Then, getting in touch with people on our right and left, we settled down to await events.
>
> Soon after this, a 2Lt 9th KLR came along and attached himself to us. Everything went smoothly, with the exception of heavy machine gun and sniper fire, and occasional strafes from the enemy artillery.[37]

At 9.45 a.m., two companies of the 1/5th Loyals were ordered to reinforce the battalion and attack Hill 37, which they succeeded in doing at 11 a.m., but twenty minutes later, they were forced back off the hill. Joining the Loyals in this attack was 2Lt Charles Wallington's 1 Platoon.

One of the day's great tragedies is the fate of 1 Platoon. Described in various sources as all thirty being killed attacking an unnamed strongpoint on the south of Hill 35. Their Platoon-Sergeant was Hugh Elliott, but as twenty-eight of those killed had no company entered into the Casualties Book (only fourteen of the dead are listed as 'A'), it is impossible to identify those from 1 Platoon. However, some of the Platoon survived: L/Cpl Sydney Kelly's Lewis section advanced along the north of Hill 35:

> At Zero I started off with a Lewis gun team and we kept together until we got to Gallipoli. After this place was taken everyone seemed to bunch together, with the result that when we moved forward again, everyone got separated and mixed up. I then went forward with a couple of Lewis gunners from 'B' Coy. until we were told to return to Gallipoli by

> Mr McLaren. I then took up a position on the right of Gallipoli in charge of Mr Hewitt [*sic.*—probably 2Lt Huish]. This position we consolidated there until we were relieved. Of my original team, three were wounded and the rest came back safely.[38]

How they must have felt upon learning that the rest of their platoon was gone can only be imagined.

Sgt Edward Heatley and Cpl Frank Richards, in their isolated position on the right slope of Hill 37, watched the battalion fight their way east:

> From this position we observed our own battalion fighting their way half left from us. On making enquiries from the officer in charge, Capt. Gibson, we found that the 5th were not in touch, either on the right or left and were told to hang on at all costs. Immediately after this, artillery smashed a counter-attack intended for our position. We enquired every day as to the position of the Bn, but the officer in charge could give us no information whatsoever. We remained with the above company until relieved.[39]

At 11.45 a.m., the 1/5th reported that although they held Ditch Trench, there was no one to their left and the Germans appeared to be holding Hill 37 in considerable strength. Brigade received reports that small German posts were still holding out on the east of Hill 35, making all movement difficult. Brig.-Gen. Boyd-Moss ordered Lt-Col. Drew of the 1/9th to gather all available men for two 'mopping-up' waves and thoroughly clear this area, enabling an organised attack against Hill 37. It was not until 2 p.m. that the eastern side of Hill 35 was declared enemy free.[40] It was then that the enemy attempted to counterattack, but were stopped by a barrage from divisional artillery. At 2.30 p.m., Capt. Blackledge—who had taken command after Maj. Gordon's wounding—witnessed two companies of the 1/5th South Lancs moving forward:

> About 11.15 a.m., I received a message from Capt. Rome to say that he was holding Hill 35 with a mixed body of men and that he had made Lens his strongpoint. On hearing this, I went up to find out further information, but was unable at first to find Capt. Rome's post. While looking for it I observed from Hill 35 the advance of two companies of 5/South Lancs, together with some details of 6th and 9th King's towards Hill 37. As this seemed to be progressing satisfactorily, I returned to Bank Farm to report. Later in the afternoon I received more accurate information as to Capt. Rome's whereabouts and I found a strongpoint at a gunpit which was called Lens, [battery position] but the commander, Capt Mallet of the North Lancs, had no information about Capt. Rome [Rome was in Lens].[41]

The 1/5th were ordered to attack Hill 37 from the south as soon as they saw the 1/9th and 1/6th attack from the west.

As the South Lancs advanced, they were joined by various platoons from the battalion, including Harrop's 2 Platoon:

In the afternoon, the South Lancs were seen going through towards Hill 37. I at once got my small party together and joined them. We made our way with little opposition to the forward slope of Hill 37. Here we decided to dig in.[42]

From Gallipoli, Sgt Hyam observed:

Later on in the afternoon I was surprised to see bodies of men moving up towards me in artillery formation. On arriving in line with us, they extended into waves of attack and moved forward towards Hill 37. It was a fine sight to see our men attacking without a protective barrage and they got to their objectives with very little loss, taking numerous prisoners. Our own HQ party under Mr [William] Drew followed in support of the South Lancs. After the South Lancs had established themselves our HQ party fell back and dug in, in line with us.[43]

Hill 37 and Gallipoli Copse were taken by 4 p.m. and the South Lancs began to consolidate.[44] Capt. Rome's work at Lens was also progressing:

I was greatly relieved when Mr McLaren joined me and then two more officers came. I kept pushing forward small parties and also sent up two machine guns to Gallipoli and two Lewis guns. I then gave orders for everybody to dig in and made this position as strong as possible. The Germans were beginning to make things very warm for us, machine gun fire, sniping and shelling. I made my HQ in the middle of the position with two lookout men to watch the situation in front as the situation was very difficult to diagnose. I had a position dug for about 300 yards, shaped like this [sketch map inserted, showing a wide crescent-shaped position, the ends pointing eastwards]—making things as strong as possible.

Owing to the garrison always increasing, as men who had lost direction came in and then amassing as they were reformed and sent forward, it proved a very difficult task to stop crowding, confusion etc. When the enemy attack barrage started we had everything ready, except I should have liked to have been dug in twice as deep. The Germans put down a very heavy barrage and several men got killed and wounded. One case, a direct hit killed a machine gun crew. The men became very nervous and it became very difficult to make them stay where they were, especially on our left as it seemed to get more heavily shelled. After the barrage had been going for about 40 minutes, one of my lookout men said that the SOS had gone up. I got up to have a look round and saw another SOS go up to my front so I at once put up my SOS. Then our barrage started and except for the enemy shelling of our position, there nothing further doing that night.[45]

The 5 p.m. barrage heralded a strong enemy counterattack. Among the defenders was L/Cpl Albert Lee:

We were not long at the Green Line when the Germans attacked. They were in full view in a field of fire of at least 1,000 yards. They came forward in four successive waves and pushed forward to within bombing distance. Up to this time our Lewis guns opened out

> incessantly and the men stood up and used their rifles well. The Germans let us have a few bombs, but our Mills No.5 again showed superiority. I know there was no danger of them meeting at close quarters. They had quite enough. By nightfall, we had reorganised our party and selected a place to entrench, ammunition was brought up and apart from that we had three boxes of German bombs which were a great help. Communication was soon made right and left and we held on until relieved.[46]

Garnsworthy's sentries alerted him to the SOS:

> Between 6 0'clock and 6.30, (p.m.) the SOS was sent up from Hill 37. We then stood-to, but the Germans shelled us so heavily that the men were sent back to the dugouts, standing-to all the time, with two sentries on lookout all the time.[47]

Harrop's men engaged the attackers:

> About 5 p.m., the enemy were seen preparing for a counter-attack, they were coming forward in waves. The SOS signal was put up and every man stood-to. The enemy suffered heavily from our artillery, but many pressed on and advanced towards our hastily dug line. This gave our Lewis guns and men a very good opportunity of showing how deadly these weapons were, which they did with good effect, not one of the enemy reaching our trench. Good work was also done by Mills rifle grenades in scattering parties of the enemy. On both our flanks, the enemy had pushed back our troops and after a consultation with the officers, it was decided to withdraw our garrison to the rear side of the crest to get in touch with the troops on both flanks. This was successfully done and a new line dug about 50 yards from the crest [slightly forward of Lens].[48]

The counterattack got to within 20 yards of British defences on the right and 50 yards on the left—so close that the South Lancs destroyed their maps, codebooks, and all copies of messages sent since Zero.[49] The decision to pull the line back to avoid leaving the flanks in the air was undoubtedly correct. Among those ordered to withdraw to Lens was L/Cpl Alfred Bellshaw, commanding an 'A' Company Lewis section:

> Two Lewis guns started of [*sic.*] 5.40 kept with Mr McLaren until reaching first German strongpoint. Up to reaching this point had one casualty (Rfn [William] Lloyd). After passing this point, got separated from Mr McLaren and placed myself and team under the charge of Sgt [John] Dick. We carried on to next strongpoint. After we were there for some time, Sgt Dick told us to the first strongpoint. I think it was Lens. My team was reduced to two men, the No. 1 of the team was wounded, thereby we lost the gun, but it was afterwards salved. On getting to Lens I found Mr McLaren and Capt. Rome, who told me to keep myself handy and get in shell holes on the left. I done [*sic.*] and also had a number of men from various battalions forming a listening party nearby to see our left flank was not turned, also to watch the enemy did not spring any surprise attacks on us.[50]

Initially, 2Lt Huish established himself on the left of Hill 35:

> When the men who had taken Gallipoli fell back to the position, which was afterwards called Hill 35, I put my men in a shell hole and got the Lewis gun in position, thinking a counter-attack was expected. All information I got led me to believe that our left flank was open, so I set the men to dig a small strongpoint and later managed to attach another Lewis gun to my party [Sydney Kelly's]. The position became untenable in the afternoon, the trench being blown in and I was forced to withdraw to the position on Hill 35, where I was put in charge of a trench by Capt. Rome and remained so until the relief on the night of the 22nd/23rd September.[51]

Lt-Col. McKaig reached Bank Farm at dusk and assumed command. At this time, Capt. Rome held Hill 35 with a mixed force of four officers and 150 men from several battalions, only twelve of whom were from the 1/6th; the rest were spread about Gallipoli, the Capitol, and isolated positions on Hill 37. It was impossible for McKaig to gather the necessary information as to the strength of these isolated bodies, though efforts were made. McKaig, Blackledge, and Capt. Roberts of the 1/9th began to inspect all the posts between Gallipoli and Hill 35 and a decision was made to organise Gallipoli and its assorted outposts into one strongpoint—Hill 35, connected to Sulva, as the other.[52]

The night was quiet, but at 5.30 a.m. on 21 September, enemy guns began to bombard all positions, giving Capt. Rome at Lens an uncomfortable time:

> We dug in still deeper during the night. About half an hour before dawn, the Germans, in answer to our barrage, shelled us this time the heaviest shelling I have ever experienced. We had ten men killed and about seven wounded. During the day we were very bothered by German aeroplanes and everybody remarked on the scarcity of our own planes. The German planes dropped bombs and made things generally very uncomfortable for us.[53]

Rome was not the only officer to complain about the absence of the RFC. Capt. Proctor of 1/4th KORL rather sarcastically commented: 'On this occasion the work of our aircraft was splendid. I can only suggest one improvement and that is their alarm clocks be set for two hours earlier'.[54]

After this early bombardment, there was little hostile fire, though enemy movement was observed at several points—eliciting retribution from divisional artillery. Most defenders continued to consolidate, though some—as Sgt Hyam reported—were employed otherwise:

> On the afternoon of the 21st, we were informed that we were to be relieved at night and were to bury our dead before leaving. This I did by sending out parties of twos in different directions, to search the ground in the vicinity of my post.[55]

The hoped-for relief did not arrive.

Between 5 and 6 p.m., Brigade received numerous reports of enemy massing for another counterattack, and at 6 p.m., the foe began a ferocious creeping barrage along the ridge, reaching Hill 35 at 6.50 p.m. At 7.10 p.m., an SOS rose from the divisional left flank, and another came from the brigade's own left flank. The South African Bde, to 55 Division's right, reported a very large German force advancing along Hill 37. Divisional artillery and the MGC began to sweep the ground in front of British positions as soon as the first SOS was reported, the situation seeming critical—as many as eight SOS rockets in the air at any one time. Around 8 p.m., the counterattack collapsed and British artillery fire gradually dwindled.

The Brigade Narrative noted:

> Shortly afterwards the position was reported to be still held, although the Germans had got right up to our defences in places. Some wounded men of the South Lancs reported that they had been driven back by the Germans after all their ammunition was expended. They joined the supporting troops behind and afterwards, advancing with them, drove back the Germans and restored the line.[56]

L/Cpl Donald McMillan, Rfn John Chater, and Rfn Thomas Haydock from 'B' were in an advanced post, forward of Gallipoli Copse, with 2Lt Johnson of the 1/7th. McMillan wrote:

> During the different counter-attacks we had to lie out about 20 yards in front of the trench. Whilst doing this on the Friday night, [21st] we observed two Germans carrying the Red Cross flag leave these dugouts [the Snag] and advance towards us. Thinking they were giving themselves up, we allowed them to advance, but instead they picked up a sniper we had hit and carried him back with them.[57]

Capt. Rome recorded considerable fire against Lens:

> That night we got heavily shelled again and had another six men and four German wounded killed. The rest of the night was quiet till dawn, when we again got shelled, but this time we only had one man killed and three wounded. During that day we kept very busy getting in wounded and getting bearers to take them down to the dressing station. The stretcher bearers worked very well indeed. We were still bothered with German aeroplanes, but I made all the men lie very low and I think they did not spot us once. That morning we again got very heavily shelled and had a few more casualties.[58]

The 22nd was spent on further consolidation and preparation for relief. It was decided to relieve by areas: Hill 37, Gallipoli Copse, Elms Corner, Gallipoli, and Hill 35 in that order. Guides from each platoon sector reported to Bank Farm at 5 p.m., and were led to Oxford Road to meet guides from 59 Division, by Captains Roberts and Blackledge. As soon as the guides met, Blackledge proceeded to the Transport Lines to prepare accommodation for the battalion.

Sgt Hyam recorded his last day at Gallipoli:

> On the 22nd, at 4 p.m., our artillery had a practice barrage, to which we received no reply. At 6 p.m., there was another practice barrage, to which the enemy replied with a very heavy bombardment, most of which we appeared to get—yet we suffered no casualties. About 10 p.m. we were relieved by the South Staffs Regiment and had a very quiet passage out.[59]

After relief, the battalion occupied huts at Vlamertinghe, and on 23 September, they left for Esk Camp near Watou. Entraining at Peselhoek on 27 September, they reached Bapaume at 2.30 p.m., then marched to huts and tents at Barastre.

The diary notes twenty-nine killed, forty-four missing, and 156 wounded (totalling 229). However, the eventual toll was worse: eighty-one dead and 161 wounded, a total of 242—46 per cent of all who took part, forty-one of whom were 'originals'. Seventy-one of the fatalities were killed in action, only fourteen of whom have a known grave. Out of the 242 casualties, only three are recorded for a date other than 20 September—a detail (considering the after-battle reports) that is patently incorrect. Rfn William Wild was wounded in the thigh on 21 September and evacuated to a London hospital, where he was still an in-patient when he died from pneumonia just after the Armistice. On 22 September, Rfn James Plant was wounded in the face—another 'Blighty wound'—and Rfn William Partington was diagnosed with shellshock and subsequently transferred.

One casualty who does not appear in the table below is twenty-eight year-old Rfn Wilson Wright from 'A', whose stabbing with his own bayonet was designated an accidental injury. Wright explained:

> On 20 September I was one of a garrison in a strongpoint. Whilst moving from one shell-hole to another I placed my rifle, bayonet upwards in the shell-hole. I jumped into the shell-hole and the bayonet caught my foot and cut the boot and the foot. I remained on duty until relieved on 22 September and reported sick on return to camp.[60]

No disciplinary action was taken, his remaining on duty very much indicating this was a complete accident.

One feature from after-battle reports concerned violations of the Red Cross flag. Cpl Herbert Gobie of 'B' wrote that 'Increasing use made by the enemy of white and Red Cross flags. Numbers of white flags seemed to have been left behind by the enemy, several noted around Gallipoli'.[61]

Rfn Ernest Hodgson from 9 Platoon also reported violations:

> I was passing a strongpoint called Gallipoli, when a party of Germans emerged from the strongpoint with Red Cross badges on their arms and one of the rear men was carrying a white flag above his head. They had been using the machine guns of the strongpoint. They were the only men who had been in the strongpoint.[62]

'C' Company's Rfn Daniel Sweeney recounted:

> While I was in the trenches on dates 20th and 21st September there was a strongpoint occupied by Germans who used the Red Cross flag on both dates and they brought out a man, who we supposed was wounded and brought back a stretcher with something on it, which we thought was ammunition. We got very heavy machine gun fire from this point and also continual sniping which accounted for eight of our men being killed and two wounded.[63]

Sgt Hyam and Cpl Corlett signed a joint statement:

> During the day of the 21st September, I noticed a party of Germans coming towards our line, preceded by a white flag with a Red Cross on it. They appeared to be carrying a stretcher. The party went into a dugout about 500 yards to the left front of Gallipoli [Martha House]. I noticed shortly after they left the dugout, sniping became pretty active from that direction, so in all probability, a couple of snipers managed to get into the dugout under the cover of the Red Cross Flag.[64]

KORL also remarked on the intensity of the sniping and MG fire from there.

Cpl Donald Bates provided the final deposition:

> On the 21st September, whilst at the strongpoint Gallipoli Copse, I noticed a party of Germans [bearing a Red Cross flag] advancing towards our left flank about 500-yards away. The whole party entered a dugout, which very soon became active with snipers [Kansas House]. The place had hitherto been quiet. Sometime later a party of Germans left the dugout and appeared to be carrying a stretcher. I judged the enemy had left behind a few men to snipe.[65]

Fatalities from the Battle of the Menin Road Ridge, 20-22 September 1917

Name	Number	Fate
Cpl Bertram Abbott	240469	KIA: 20/9
L/Cpl Allan Creighton Aitken	242466	KIA: 20/9
L/Cpl Sam Annison	242631	KIA: 20/9
Rfn George Washington Ashcroft	331201	KIA: 20/9
Rfn James Barton	242814	KIA: 20/9
Rfn Howard Norbury Boase	241610	KIA: 20/9
Rfn John Bradley	242789	KIA: 20/9
Cpl Ernest Carline	241781	KIA: 20/9
Rfn Thomas Lionel Carter	241428	KIA: 20/9
Rfn Samuel James Cheers	241682	KIA: 20/9
Rfn George Frederick Cheshire	242515	KIA: 20/9
Rfn William Moss Clayton	202414	DOW: 27/9
Rfn George Henry Clegg	242845	KIA: 20/9
Rfn Edgar Collins	50308	KIA: 20/9
2Lt Arthur Edward Conibear		DOW: 14/10
Rfn Joseph Cooke	202709	KIA: 20/9
Rfn Harold Hamer Coupland	242013	KIA: 20/9
L/Cpl John Darcy	200538	KIA: 20/9
Rfn Arthur Llewellyn Davies	204206	KIA: 20/9
Rfn William Davies	241967	KIA: 20/9
Cpl Henry Edgar Dean	241019	KIA: 20/9
L/Cpl Herbert Donaldson	242114	KIA: 20/9
Rfn John Henry Doubleday	331352	KIA: 20/9

L/Cpl William Duggan	52574	KIA: 20/9
Capt. Donald Eastwood		KIA: 20/9
Sgt Hugh Stanhope Elliott	240091	KIA: 20/9
Rfn William Freeman	240893	KIA: 20/9
Rfn James Stanley Frost	332492	KIA: 20/9
Rfn Walter Frost	51136	KIA: 20/9
Rfn Francis Furlong	242850	KIA: 20/9
Rfn Frank Alexander Gammons	202580	KIA: 20/9
Rfn Harold Dale Greaves	242851	KIA: 20/9
Cpl John Nicholls Hadwin	240386	KIA: 20/9
Rfn Morris Herczel	202209	KIA: 20/9
Rfn George Hind	51132	KIA: 20/9
Rfn Norman Hobson	49943	DOW: 9/10
Rfn John Hodgkins	49941	KIA: 20/9
Rfn Willie Hodgson	49942	KIA: 20/9
Rfn Harry Holmes	49945	KIA: 20/9
Rfn Colin Hughes	202947	KIA: 20/9
Rfn Clarence Victor Hunneybell	49948	KIA: 20/9
L/Cpl Thomas Duncan Inkster	241587	KIA: 20/9
Cpl John Francis Jenkins	240288	DOW: 22/9
Rfn Peter Jones	201915	KIA: 20/9
Rfn Valentine Kennedy	331995	KIA: 20/9
2Lt Charles Frederick King		KIA: 20/9
L/Cpl William Arthur Latham	200176	KIA: 20/9
Rfn Thomas Leavy	242742	KIA: 20/9
L/Sgt Richard John Lee	241088	KIA: 20/9
Rfn William Edward Leech	242082	DOW: 21/9
Rfn William Henry Lloyd	241974	DOW: 22/9
Rfn William Wallace Lunt	204264	KIA: 20/9
Rfn John Marsden	242866	KIA: 20/9
Rfn William McDonald	331723	KIA: 20/9
Rfn Michael John McNamara	42853	DOW: 23/9
L/Cpl Walter Henry Newton	241843	KIA: 20/9
Rfn Frank Nixon	268493	KIA: 20/9
Rfn Leo Phillips	26156	KIA: 20/9
2Lt Norman Rutherford Phillips		KIA: 20/9
Rfn Charles Plumb	202226	KIA: 20/9
L/Cpl Alfred George Rigby	240369	KIA: 20/9
Rfn Thomas Roberts	50016	KIA: 20/9
Rfn Herbert Robinson*	240807	KIA: 20/9
L/Cpl Norman Royle	241415	KIA: 20/9
Rfn James Samuel	267058	KIA: 20/9
Rfn Robert Sandmann	260038	DOW: 23/9
Rfn James Scott	243824	DOW: 28/9
L/Cpl Thomas Shallcross	240857	KIA: 20/9
CSM John Alfred Shaw	240179	KIA: 20/9
Rfn Frank Shepherd	203128	KIA: 20/9
2Lt David Herbert Spratt		KIA: 20/9
Rfn Thomas Sullivan	307647	KIA: 20/9
Rfn Arthur Tattersall	242879	KIA: 20/9
Cpl James Townley	241455	DOW: 30/9
Rfn Albert Waddington	241411	KIA: 20/9
Rfn Kenneth Walker	241852	KIA: 20/9
2Lt Charles Harold Wallington		KIA: 20/9
Rfn John Walsh	204454	KIA: 20/9
Cpl Percy Whalley	241716	KIA: 20/9
Rfn Alfred Henry Whittick	307102	KIA: 20/9
Rfn Douglas Spiers Williamson	242889	KIA: 20/9

* = CWGC have 19 September for Robinson's death; however, it is noted in the Casualties Book for 20 September. All DOW are recorded wounded on 20 September.

Wounded during the Battle of the Menin Road Ridge, 20–22 September 1917

Rfn Stephen H. Allen	49894	WIA: 20/9
CSM Charles Bonser Argent	240070	WIA: 20/9
Rfn Arthur Patrick Barry	240400	WIA: 20/9
Rfn John Baxendale	265903	WIA: 20/9
Rfn Fred G. Beardsell	49990	WIA: 20/9
2Lt Arthur Leonard Bemment		WIA: 20/9
Rfn Nathaniel Bent	241774	WIA: 20/9
Rfn Harry Birchall	49982	WIA: 20/9
Rfn John Birchall	49919	WIA: 20/9
Rfn John Birtwistle	28229	WIA: 20/9
Rfn Henry Bishop	27085	WIA: 20/9
Rfn Henry Bond	308204	WIA: 20/9
Rfn Wilfred Bernard Bowden	240140	WIA: 20/9
Rfn Alfred Bradbury	242796	WIA: 20/9
Rfn Alfred Braddock	49925	WIA: 20/9
Rfn Daniel Bragg	241827	WIA: 20/9
Rfn James Henry Bryans	263007	WIA: 20/9
Rfn Alfred Buckley	308092	WIA: 20/9
L/Cpl Cecil Lewis Butler	241692	WIA: 20/9
Rfn Daniel Callaghan	243887	WIA: 20/9
Rfn Cyril Herbert Campbell	51140	WIA: 20/9
Rfn John Greatrex Campbell	269679	WIA: 20/9
Cpl Richard Catherall	241248	WIA: 20/9
Rfn James Arthur Caton	242843	WIA: 20/9
Rfn James Clulo	269612	WIA: 20/9
Rfn William Colclough	269410	WIA: 20/9
2Lt George Herbert Coleman		WIA: 20/9
Rfn John Colley	268486	WIA: 20/9
Rfn John William Cook	242816	WIA: 20/9
Rfn Ernest Edward Corlett	25999	WIA: 20/9
Rfn John Craddock	242842	WIA: 20/9
Rfn John Creer	331908	WIA: 20/9
Rfn Frederick Cullen	332820	WIA: 20/9
L/Cpl Charles Francis Davies	200732	WIA: 20/9
Rfn Ernest Davies	49995	WIA: 20/9
Rfn Francis John Davies	269303	WIA: 20/9
Rfn Cyril Solomon Davis	242715	WIA: 20/9
Cpl John N. Dawson	240251	WIA: 20/9
Sgt John Dick	241096	WIA: 20/9
Rfn J. W. Downs	260016	WIA: 20/9
2Lt William Charles Garfield Drew		WIA: 20/9
L/Cpl John A. Dudson	240714	WIA: 20/9
Rfn Thomas Duffy	30641	WIA: 20/9
L/Cpl H. Edwards	308343	WIA: 20/9
Rfn James Wallace Elston	241451	WIA: 20/9
Rfn C. H. Evans	8853	WIA: 20/9
Sgt Charles Oswald Evans	240463	WIA: 20/9
L/Cpl Hugh Evans	241995	WIA: 20/9
L/Cpl Robert Francis Evans	241970	WIA: 20/9
Rfn Stanley Shepherd Evans	242072	WIA: 20/9
Rfn Fred P. Fellows	49936	WIA: 20/9
Rfn Herbert James Felton	331228	WIA: 20/9
Rfn Francis Albert Ford	242583	WIA: 20/9
Rfn William Henry Ford	49998	WIA: 20/9
Rfn Alfred Foster	332898	WIA: 20/9
Rfn George A. Foster	51521	WIA: 20/9
Rfn Frank Freeman	331655	WIA: 20/9
Rfn Michael Furey	242893	WIA: 20/9
Rfn John H. T. Gardner	50594	WIA: 20/9
Rfn Ellis Garner	242692	WIA: 20/9
Rfn Robert Garnett	241922	WIA: 20/9
Rfn Joseph Gerrard	49939	WIA: 20/9
Rfn Harold Lightfoot Gibbs	241845	WIA: 20/9
Rfn Albert Glover	202040	WIA: 20/9
Maj. Stanley Edgar Gordon		WIA: 20/9
Rfn William Gore	51381	WIA: 20/9
Rfn Harold F. Granger	204131	WIA: 20/9
Rfn Fred Greenwood	242722	WIA: 20/9
Rfn Herbert Greenwood	242723	WIA: 20/9
Rfn Smith Greenwood	242724	WIA: 20/9
Rfn R. Gregson	307082	WIA: 20/9
Rfn Edward James Guy	270087	WIA: 20/9
Rfn Frederick W. Hall	242728	WIA: 20/9
Rfn Ralph Hampson	240880	WIA: 20/9
Rfn Ernest Frank Hancock	235061	WIA: 20/9
Rfn John Henry Harrison	331445	WIA: 20/9

Rfn James Hays	265782	WIA: 20/9
L/Cpl John Robert Hesk	241870	WIA: 20/9
Rfn Ernest Hill	242133	WIA: 20/9
Rfn Wilfred Hilton	242729	WIA: 20/9
Rfn George Hirons	49944	WIA: 20/9
Rfn William Holderness	260024	WIA: 20/9
L/Cpl Walter Hoskyn	241919	WIA: 20/9
Rfn John A. Hughes	240154	WIA: 20/9
Sgt Charles Jackson	240653	WIA: 20/9
Rfn Arthur Jarvis	49951	WIA: 20/9
Rfn Albert Johnson	242008	WIA: 20/9
Rfn Alfred Jones	332813	WIA: 20/9
Rfn Harold F. Kelly	331371	WIA: 20/9
Rfn Septimus Frederick R. Kersey	202111	WIA: 20/9
2Lt W. S. Lawson		WIA: 20/9
Rfn William John Lewis*	240253	WIA: 20/9
Rfn George Lincoln	242860	WIA: 20/9
Cpl William Alexander Mackenzie	240554	WIA: 20/9
Rfn William Marsden	242746	WIA: 20/9
Rfn Absolom Mather	260031	WIA: 20/9
Rfn Robert W. McCormick	8765	WIA: 20/9
Rfn Walter Eugene McEvoy	58487	WIA: 20/9
Rfn A. McKie	242610	WIA: 20/9
Rfn Arthur Meadows	330988	WIA: 20/9
L/Cpl George Henry Miller	240412	WIA: 20/9
Rfn James Owen Morgan	242750	WIA: 20/9
Rfn William Moston	242752	WIA: 20/9
Rfn James Murney	241476	WIA: 20/9
2Lt Fred Rothwell Nield		WIA: 20/9
L/Cpl Michael O'Flaherty	26187	WIA: 20/9
Rfn John O'Hanlon	308975	WIA: 20/9
Rfn William Ormrod	260034	WIA: 20/9
Sgt George Pickworth Owen	240229	WIA: 20/9
Rfn Herbert Palmer**	242869	WIA: 20/9
Rfn John Palmer	332877	WIA: 20/9
L/Cpl John Henry Parker	240638	WIA: 20/9
Rfn Thomas William Parkinson	201462	WIA: 20/9
Rfn William Parry	242675	WIA: 20/9
Rfn Arthur Mitchell Pascoe	242109	WIA: 20/9
Rfn Robert Paul	242788	WIA: 20/9
Rfn George R. Pearson	241607	WIA: 20/9
Rfn Harry Peers	241933	WIA: 20/9
Capt. Robert Cairns Phillips		WIA: 20/9
Rfn Adam H. Potter	51133	WIA: 20/9
Rfn Thomas Povey	331016	WIA: 20/9
Rfn Herbert Prescott	332491	WIA: 20/9
Sgt Albert Robert Rashbrook	240770	WIA: 20/9
Cpl Arthur Regan	242647	WIA: 20/9
Cpl Thomas Arthur Riley	241058	WIA: 20/9
L/Cpl Chamber Edward Ritson	242068	WIA: 20/9
Rfn Arthur Roberts	241483	WIA: 20/9
Rfn Frank Roberts	242270	WAD: 20/9
Rfn Cyril Edgar Robinson	241514	WIA: 20/9
Rfn Robert Robinson	260037	WIA: 20/9
Rfn Thomas Rollerson	242804	WIA: 20/9
Rfn Richard Rudkin	240459	WIA: 20/9
Rfn John Seddon	242686	WIA: 20/9
Rfn Reginald Edwards Sergeant	242607	WIA: 20/9
Rfn Alexander Simon	243639	WIA: 20/9
Rfn Frank Skeats	242876	WIA: 20/9
Rfn Archie McDougal Smethurst	204081	WIA: 20/9
L/Cpl J. V. Smith	241214	WIA: 20/9
Rfn Joseph Victor Stanley	242872	WIA: 20/9
Rfn Thomas William Stockley	49959	WIA: 20/9
Rfn Norman Tate	241888	WAD: 20/9
Rfn Eli Taylor	49957	WIA: 20/9
L/Cpl John Henry Thelwell	241900	WIA: 20/9
Rfn Thomas Thompson	242628	WIA: 20/9
Rfn Thomas H. Tobin	241352	WIA: 20/9
Rfn Walter Turnbull	242877	WIA: 20/9
Rfn David Walders	242819	WIA: 20/9
Rfn Thomas Alfred Waller	34306	WIA: 20/9
Rfn Patrick Walsh	242769	WAD: 20/9
Cpl Francis Augustus Wareham	240612	WIA: 20/9

Rfn William Watkins	332190	WIA: 20/9	Rfn John M. Woodley	242543	WIA: 20/9
Rfn Andrew Horne Watson	240746	WIA: 20/9	L/Cpl Anthony Edgar Wrathall	242053	WIA: 20/9
Sgt George Frederick Webb	240043	WIA: 20/9			
Rfn John Whittle	260041	WIA: 20/9	Rfn William J. Wren	240466	WIA: 20/9
Rfn William Henry Wild	48931	WIA: 21/9	Rfn R. Wright	53254	WIA: 20/9
Rfn Henry Williams	331003	WIA: 20/9	Cpl Thomas Ainscough Wright	242682	WIA: 20/9
Rfn William Williams	325023	WIA: 20/9			

* = Lewis was paralysed from the waist down and died soon after the war.

** = Herbert Palmer was an alias. His full name was Herbert Palmer Seal.

10

28 September 1917—6 December 1917: The Thin Khaki Line

Coordinates for this Chapter

Bird Lane (1)	50°0′18.00″N 3°10′37.20″E	Dove Lane	50°0′42.40″N 3°11′16.70″E
Bird Lane (2)	50°0′25.20″N 3°10′54.50″E	Duncan Post	49°59′14.00″N 3°11′22.50″E
Bird Post	50°0′47.10″N 3°11′7.00″E	Eagle Quarry	50°0′33.70″N 3°11′12.20″E
Birdcage	50°0′43.20″N 3°11′26.00″E	Eagle Trench	50°0′36.90″N 3°11′14.90″E
Blunt Nose	49°59′29.60″N 3°11′57.10″E	Ego Post	49°59′44.10″N 3°11′26.80″E
Cat Post	49°59′3.30″N 3°11′31.60″E	Falcon Sap	50°0′47.40″N 3°11′29.00″E
Catelet Copse	50°0′41.90″N 3°10′20.80″E	Fleeceall Lane	49°59′51.90″N 3°11′12.50″E
Catelet Road	50°1′2.60″N 3°11′21.80″E	Fleeceall Post	49°59′59.40″N 3°11′15.80″E
Crossbill Road	50°0′42.40″N 3°11′3.80″E	Ford Street	49°59′43.30″N 3°11′41.50″E
Cruciform Post	50°0′35.10″N 3°10′35.90″E	Gillemont Farm	49°59′25.60″N 3°12′1.20″E
Daniel Trench	49°59′30.80″N 3°11′47.50″E	Gillemont Trench	49°59′24.10″N 3°12′6.70″E
Dog Trench	49°59′9.80″N 3°11′38.40″E	Glen Lane	49°59′20.50″N 3°11′58.20″E
Doleful Post	49°59′29.10″N 3°11′18.70″E	Grafton Post	50°0′13.40″N 3°10′46.30″E

Grafton Trench	50°0′8.50″N 3°10′51.80″E	11 Post	49°59′21.30″N 3°11′55.00″E
Heythrop Lane	50°0′22.80″N 3°10′23.10″E	13 Copse	50°0′21.00″N 3° 9′46.20″E
Heythrop Post	50°0′23.50″N 3°10′36.10″E	Oldham Street	50°0′32.10″N 3°11′34.90″E
Holts' Bank	50°0′50.10″N 3°10′29.70″E	Ossus Wood	50°0′49.30″N 3°11′11.90″E
Honnecourt Wood	50°2′16.10″N 3°11′17.30″E	Perch Support	50°0′39.10″N 3°11′12.40″E
Island Traverse	49°59′47.90″N 3°11′42.30″E	Perch Trench	50°0′40.30″N 3°11′16.00″E
Ken Lane	49°59′23.80″N 3°10′50.30″E	Priel Cutting	50°0′28.30″N 3°10′9.20″E
Knoll, The	50°0′3.40″N 3°11′51.60″E	Quail Quarry	50°0′38.60″N 3°11′5.90″E
Lark Post	50°0′31.50″N 3°11′9.40″E	RE Trench	49°59′26.50″N 3°11′57.20″E
Lempire HQ	49°59′29.50″N 3°10′19.10″E	Seed Trench	50°0′41.50″N 3°11′18.90″E
Lempire Road HQ	50°0′20.80″N 3°10′19.30″E	Snipe Quarry	50°0′35.40″N 3°11′7.20″E
Limerick Post	50°1′3.90″N 3° 9′52.00″E	Spree Lane	50°0′23.70″N 3°11′45.00″E
Little Priel Farm	50°0′31.10″N 3°10′36.10″E	Stokes Street	49°59′24.00″N 3°12′1.20″E
Macquincourt Trench	50°0′10.80″N 3°12′19.90″E	Stone Trench	50°0′51.00″N 3°11′2.70″E
Malassise Road	50°0′33.40″N 3° 9′59.40″E	Tino Trench	50°0′40.50″N 3°11′38.70″E
New Post	49°58′59.50″N 3°11′34.60″E	Tombois Farm	49°59′56.60″N 3°11′11.20″E
NF Lane	49°59′28.70″N 3°11′54.60″E	Van Lane	49°59′31.20″N 3°12′4.90″E

Despite the recent privations, the division was to relieve 35 Division at Villers Faucon, between Cambrai and Saint Quentin. A French intelligence assessment, estimated that the British offensive in Flanders had put seventy German divisions out of action over the last four months—nearly half their strength on the Western Front.[1] The German Army was, however, far from spent and another British push was planned at Cambrai for November. The 55th Division would have a peripheral role.

On 29 September, Lt-Col. McKaig, 2Lt Daglish (now Adjutant), Maj. Bennet (now 2IC), Capt. Albert Jones, 2Lts Harrop, Killey, and Garnsworthy, and Intelligence-Officer 2Lt Pilgrim visited the trenches held by 17/West Yorks at Lempire. While there, the CO penned a number of recommendations for the New Year Honours, all of which were accepted. Among these was a MiD for Transport-Sergeant George Harries:

> His splendid work as a Sergeant of the battalion for the last two years. In June and July 1917, he never failed to lead his transport through heavy shelling night after night with a minimum of loss. The fact that his battalion has never had to wait for its stores or rations, is largely due to this NCO's efforts.[2]

Another was for CSM John Handley, for his continuous good service and devotion to duty. The MSM was awarded, and before leaving the battalion for commissioning in March 1918, he was also awarded the Belgian *Croix de Guerre*.

The battalion moved to Longavesnes on 1 October, and at 5 p.m. the next day, they set off for the front line at Lempire, relieving the West Yorks at 10.45 p.m. The divisional front was over 14,000 yards of discontinuous line in terrible repair, and with just 9,343 infantrymen, they were stretched.[3] The reality—as noted by Brig.-Gen. Stockwell—worked out at one infantryman per 10 yards of front.[4] The battalion's fighting strength, of twenty-eight officers and 743 men, was well below establishment, forty-two recent replacements hardly denting the losses of 20 September. HQ was in Lempire, with 'D' in reserve around Tombois Farm and the northern part of Fleeceall Lane. 'A', 'B', and 'C' held the front line. The northernmost company in particular was thinly-spread, occupying Grafton Post and a series of scattered, smaller posts along Grafton Trench. To their left was 1/5th KORL, the subsector join at the junction of Bird Lane and Grafton Trench. In the centre, one company held Fleeceall Post and the right-hand company held Ego Post. The 1/5th KLR held the line to their right, the battalion's right bound just past Island Traverse, where Ford Street met the front line.

Their first night passed quietly, though it was extremely cold, dawn revealing a hard frost. Daylight also revealed the dreadful state of their trenches—revetting and draining urgently required. The weather became more unsettled on 3 October, though enemy activity remained low and overnight patrols found nothing to report. A few 77-mm were fired at the road between Lempire and Tombois Farm, though Transport escaped casualties. The 4th was again uneventful.

There were no casualties to enemy action on 5 October, though Grafton Post was lightly shelled in early morning. However, two men were hospitalised with injuries: Rfn Henry Edgar managed to shoot off one of his fingers, for which he was awarded fifty-six days' field punishment, medically downgraded and transferred; the second, twenty-eight-year-old Rfn Thomas Yarrington from Transport, suffered a spiral fracture to his left leg when a mule fell on him. CQMS Albert Hampson witnessed the accident:

> About 9 p.m. on 5 October, Rfn Yarrington was driving a pair of mules and limbered wagon from Batt. HQ to the ration dump near Ego Post. Just as he was approaching the dump,

> his near and riding mule fell owing to the greasy nature of the track. Rfn Yarrington fell with his left leg under the mule and was extricated from this position with some difficulty. He was unable to stand and complained of pains in his left leg between the ankle and knee. I had him carried by stretcher to the Aid Post in Lempire village.[5]

Transport-Officer 2Lt Andrew Lindsay added that heavy rain had made the track particularly slippery. That night saw further shelling of the road leading from Lempire after Transport had completed their run.

There was no discernible enemy activity in the battalion's subsector on the 6th, a situation that continued until relief at 9.45 p.m. On 7 October, they went into reserve at Sainte-Émilie, where Sgt Harry Evans MM departed on the 11th to be an instructor at XIX Corps School.

Remaining at Sainte-Émilie until 12 October, training and large working parties occupied their time. Their next tour in the line was in the notorious Birdcage subsector, to the immediate left of their previous placement. HQ was in Heythrop Lane, which although far from centrally-situated, had suitable dugouts, and 'C' were in support, with two platoons in Cruciform Post, north of Little Priel Farm, the others in Heythrop Post. The other companies manned the front line.

The left of this subsector was defended by Bird Post, just 100 yards from Ossus Wood, whose eastern end was firmly in German lines—its disputed western reaches providing a deadly, booby trap-laden venue for the patrolling activities of both sides. On the right of the line was Eagle Quarry, the largest of three thereabouts—the others titled Quail and Snipe. While quarries gave protection from hostile fire, they presented dangers too, should a sudden attack pen the defenders inside. The Birdcage itself was a salient of semi-destroyed trenches, 150 yards from the nearest German position of Falcon Sap and untenable during daylight. Directly behind the apex of the Birdcage was Seed Trench, which was little better; Perch Trench and Perch Support were home for the front line garrison during the day. Though Eagle Trench and Dove Lane led forward to the Birdcage, neither provided safe passage past the end of Perch Trench.

During the night of 13 October, there was desultory shelling by 77-mm of Little Priel Farm, Bird Lane, and Crossbill Road—the sunken track running north-south immediately behind the front line. Patrols were largely uneventful, though one spotted a small enemy working party between Ossus Wood and the Birdcage.

Concerned about a pre-attack bombardment leading to excessive casualties among front line garrisons, Jeudwine decided to reduce the numbers in these vulnerable positions. Consequently, after dark on 14 October, 'D' withdrew to reserve dugouts along the Malassise Road at Priel Bank—dispositions which also allowed better deployment of troops to plug gaps in the porous front line. The day had been quiet, and though Little Priel Farm and the Birdcage were shelled intermittently, no casualties resulted.

On 15 October, Little Priel Farm was heavily shelled with HE and shrapnel, and at 8.30 a.m., and again after midday, the Birdcage was bombarded by a heavy *Minenwerfer*. This ceased when divisional artillery retaliated, but not before twenty-six-year-old L/Cpl

David Finlay from 'A' was critically wounded in the abdomen. This promising NCO died at Tincourt the next day. A night patrol tried to approach Falcon Sap, but found the garrison there fully alert, so returned.

During the morning 'stand-to' on 16 October, an NCO and two men made a daring daylight reconnaissance of Ossus Wood, discovering a number of slit trenches, though none appeared to have been occupied for a considerable time. Approaching the enemy front line, they observed about forty men standing on their fire-step. When some began to point urgently towards the trio, the patrol beat a hasty retreat. The remainder of the day was fairly quiet, though the rear of Heythrop Post and Eagle Quarry were lightly shelled between 3.45 p.m. and 5 p.m., and at 4 p.m., twelve *Minenwerfer* rounds landed on the rim of Eagle Quarry.

On 17 October, Little Priel Farm received a light shelling—a now-routine activity—and a few medium *Minenwerfer* rounds targeted the Birdcage. At 10 p.m., divisional artillery carried out two four-minute demonstration shoots against German positions in Honnecourt Wood, opposite Villers-Guislain (in the Battalion diary for 16 October, but divisional and brigade documents attribute it to the 17th). The enemy made no reply.

On 18 October, Little Priel Farm, the Birdcage, Eagle Trench, and Eagle Quarry were all subjected to light shellfire, the Birdcage also targeted by mortars. A small night patrol sighted an enemy patrol leaving German lines near Falcon Sap, but lost them when they proceeded south towards Tino Trench. Enemy artillery was more active than usual on 19 October and Bird Post, Little Priel Farm, and Eagle Quarry all received attention, wounding 'A' Company's Rfn Albert Thornton in the right forearm. Night patrols were complicated by a thick mist and one near the left bound glimpsed two separate enemy six-man patrols in No Man's Land around the Catelet Road, 100 yards outside the enemy wire. Twice they attempted to close, but each time swirling mist cloaked the enemy from view.

Enemy artillery remained active on 20 October, Little Priel Farm being shelled, but it was the twenty heavy *Minenwerfer* rounds fired into Eagle Quarry during the morning that wounded two: L/Cpl Reginald Oversby was hit in the hand, arm, and back and Sgt John Coates MM, the left leg—neither returned.

On the morning of 21 October, a daylight patrol reconnoitred the wire in Ossus Wood between 5.15 a.m. and 8.45 a.m., finding nothing new to report. Bird Post was lightly shelled during the day, but the only casualty was accidental: Sgt Walter Hannah was wounded in the arm and back and evacuated home. This NCO would be greatly missed and the culprit, Rfn Charles Seely, was placed under arrest. Hannah's injuries were the result of a single bullet that scored across his back before penetrating his arm.[6] Battalion obviously considered Seely culpable, as he was court-martialled on 6 November, but found 'not guilty'—so there were clearly extenuating circumstances.

Around 3 a.m. on 22 October, thirty gas shells landed near HQ, however, no one was affected. The day is reported quiet in the diary, though the Intelligence Summary paints a somewhat different picture.[7] Though this reports only few rounds of artillery fire directed at the Birdcage, it also details mortar fire against the Birdcage at 10 a.m. and twenty heavy *Minenwerfer* rounds landing inside Eagle Quarry at 11.30 a.m. That night, they were relieved and marched to Épehy, to be conveyed by light railway to Tincourt.

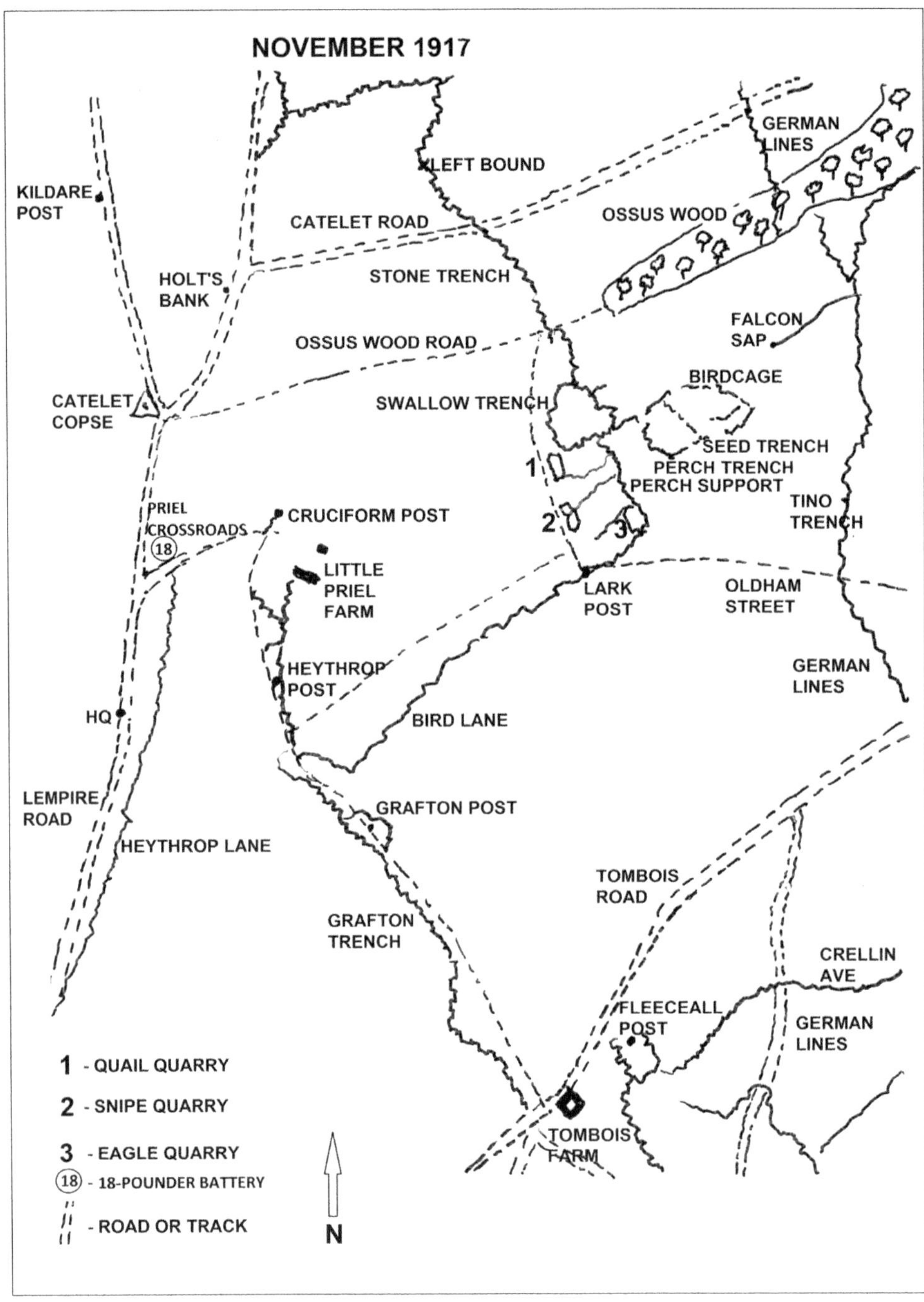
NOVEMBER 1917
LEFT BOUND
GERMAN LINES
KILDARE POST
CATELET ROAD
OSSUS WOOD
HOLT'S BANK
STONE TRENCH
FALCON SAP
OSSUS WOOD ROAD
BIRDCAGE
CATELET COPSE
SWALLOW TRENCH
SEED TRENCH
PERCH TRENCH
PERCH SUPPORT
1
2
3
TINO TRENCH
PRIEL CROSSROADS
18
CRUCIFORM POST
LITTLE PRIEL FARM
LARK POST
OLDHAM STREET
HEYTHROP POST
GERMAN LINES
HQ
BIRD LANE
LEMPIRE ROAD
GRAFTON POST
HEYTHROP LANE
TOMBOIS ROAD
GRAFTON TRENCH
CRELLIN AVE
FLEECEALL POST
GERMAN LINES
TOMBOIS FARM
1 - QUAIL QUARRY
2 - SNIPE QUARRY
3 - EAGLE QUARRY
18 - 18-POUNDER BATTERY
- ROAD OR TRACK
N

The battalion trained there until 1 November. Twenty-one-year-old Rfn Alfred Barnes, attached to 196 MGC, was wounded in the chest on 24 October—an American citizen from Trenton, New Jersey, but resident in Liverpool when he enlisted. Rfn Edward Makinson was classified PB on 30 October, his subsequent attachment to the British Mission in Palestine having unforeseen consequences. Wounded in the Jordan Valley on 10 April 1918, he was captured, spending the rest of the war a prisoner of the Turks.

Late on 1 November, the battalion relieved 164 Bde in the right sector, taking the right of the line at Gillemont Farm from Ford Street to just past New Post. One company was in reserve dugouts in Ken Lane; another in support, with two platoons in Doleful Post; and the others in Duncan Post. 'B' held the left of the line, nearest to Gillemont Farm. One platoon was distributed along Daniel Trench, leading to the left bound; the remainder in the trenches close to the farm—Blunt Nose, NF Lane, RE Trench, and Glen Lane. This subsector was one of the more vulnerable, the eastern ends of Stokes Street, Van Lane, and Glen Lane, all German-held—a series of posts that deterred hostile incursion. The other front-line company was centralised around Cat Post, with one platoon in posts along Dog Trench.

Relief went smoothly, with scant enemy fire that night or during the following day—almost all activity occurring further north. Night patrols were also uneventful, though the Germans in Gillemont Trench bombed their own wire on half a dozen occasions during the night. The 3rd was particularly quiet, and it was not until the early hours of 4 November that change occurred.

At 4 a.m., the enemy began a hurricane bombardment of the battalion's positions and all approaches along the brigade front. For sixteen minutes, 5.9, 4.2, 77-mm and trench mortars blasted the line; simultaneously, three enemy raiding parties entered Glen Lane, either side of No. 11 Post. The SOS had been fired as soon as the bombardment began and two of the raiding parties were beaten off by defensive fire. Cpl Harold Price attacked a group of infiltrators, driving them off with bombs; he and his section hastening their withdrawal with accurate Lewis and rifle fire. Unfortunately, in the minute that the raiders had been in the British line, they succeeded in snatching Riflemen John Bates and Allan Bruce. The only fatality was 'A' Company's twenty-five-year-old Rfn John Houghton, killed by the bombardment. Four Riflemen and recently-arrived 2Lt David Morris were wounded: Percy Blakey, hit in the left hand; Herbert Rallings, in the left shoulder; Frederick Studholme, with a thigh wound; and with a wound to his left arm, James Reynolds. Price was awarded the DCM and promoted 'B' Company's Lewis-Sergeant.

A patrol was hurriedly briefed and despatched in pursuit of the raiders. Although no enemy were located, they returned with a German cap and rifle, grenades, wire-cutters, and a number of opened field dressings, lending credence to the defenders' belief that they had inflicted casualties. The rest of the day was quiet, though twelve overnight patrols were out across the divisional front in case of further incursions. The battalion's line remained undisturbed until 1.30 p.m. on 6 November, when German artillery and trench mortars retaliated to a demonstration shoot against the wire opposite the battalion's line. Dog Trench and Cat Post were both hit, the latter badly damaged. Fortunately, the only casualty was Rfn Thomas Parry attached to 165 TMB, who was wounded at duty. Also with 165 TMB was Cpl Charles Bradshaw, who received a MiD the following day, possibly in connection with the events of the 6th. The battalion was relieved at 9 p.m. and moved to brigade support in Lempire and Sandbag Alley.

Gales and driving rain made 7 November uncomfortable. Artillery batteries near Lempire rendered it a priority target for German artillery, and next day, it was shelled by 5.9 Howitzers throughout the day, 500 rounds fired at Lempire and Ronssoy. This was repeated during the afternoon of 9 November, but the battalion escaped on both days. German fire was much reduced on 10 November, the weather continuing wet and windy.

Around midnight on 11 November, they relieved the 1/9th in the Birdcage, and next day, British guns conducted a program of wire-cutting across the divisional front, one mortar battery blasting a 20-yard wide gap in the wire in front of the Knoll. This provoked an inevitable response, and the Birdcage was targeted by *Minenwerfers* at noon, 2 p.m., and 3 p.m., only ceasing when 165 TMB retaliated against the *Minenwerfers*. Fleeceall Post and Little Priel Farm were also lightly shelled. That night, one patrol ventured along Oldham Street to the enemy wire, finding the sunken track void of enemy posts.

Wire-cutting continued on 13 November and Little Priel Farm, Grafton Trench, Fleeceall Post, and Tombois Farm were all subjected to retaliation and a few light *Granatenwerfers* struck the Birdcage around noon. On 14 November, mist curtailed the wire-cutting, though the MGC carried out a shoot against a German Company HQ in Macquincourt Trench. This was supposed to be in conjunction with artillery, but when their shoot was postponed, no one thought to inform the MGC.[8] German retaliation was slight, with Little Priel Farm lightly shelled and a few *Minenwerfers* on Eagle Quarry.

At 10 a.m. on 15 November, several *Minenwerfer* rounds landed amid 'C' in Eagle Quarry, killing Riflemen Thomas Massey, twenty-six-year-old Frederick Prendergrast, nineteen-year-old Stanley Reid, and twenty-year-old Daniel Sweeney. Riflemen Frank Bradley was wounded in the thigh, Aubrey Downer in the collar-bone, and Charles Padley of 'D'—the only one to return—wounded in the head. Richard Rudkin's facial wound was minor and he remained on duty after it had been dressed. The postponed shoot was carried out that afternoon, but provoked little retaliation. Night patrols observed German wiring parties repairing the damage caused by the divisional guns, one at Oldham Street, the other 500 yards to the right in front of Tino Trench, near its junction with Spree Lane.

Wire-cutting continued on 16 and 17 November, but apart from intermittent fire against the Birdcage and Little Priel Farm, the battalion escaped unmolested. At 6 p.m. on the 17th, they were relieved and travelled to billets in Longavesnes, arriving at 10 p.m.

Of considerable concern to Jeudwine was a German raid against Gillemont Farm at 6.25 a.m. on 18 November. After a heavy bombardment, 200 raiders penetrated 300 yards into the Loyals's defences. After twenty minutes, the raiders were driven out; but damage to the trenches was severe and fifty-five men captured.[9] This led to apprehension that plans for an attack, scheduled for the 20th, may have been compromised.

At 5 p.m. on 19 November, the battalion moved to Sainte-Émilie as divisional reserve for the forthcoming attacks against the Knoll and Gillemont Farm—a diversion for the new British offensive at neighbouring Cambrai. Only 164 Bde could be spared as the others were needed to hold the elongated front. The Liverpool Irish on the left and 2/5th Lancashire Fusiliers on the right would attack the Knoll; 1,200 metres to their south, 1/4th KORL would assault at Gillemont Farm. At the same time, the 1/9th in the Birdcage would raise dummy figures and a tank silhouette above their parapet to draw enemy fire.

Divisional records demonstrate a concern about the potential dangers this operation engendered. Corps had ordered the division's heavy artillery north to support the main attack at Cambrai, leaving just the 18-pounders, mortars, and machine guns as fire support. When 166 Bde were ordered to provide eight Vickers for the operation, the Brigade-Commander warned:

> I would point out that it seems imperative to maintain present distribution of machine-guns on Villers Ridge Subsector, plus a minimum of two guns to fire up Stick and Banteux Ravines, thus leaving only two guns to cover remainder of Brigade front. This I consider totally inadequate.[10]

Maj. Hoare of the 1/9th had similar worries when ordered to provide men for carrying parties:

> To provide a party of 100 other ranks for carrying wire on Z Day it will be necessary for me to withdraw entirely the garrison from Holts' Bank, Cruciform and Heythrop Posts (45 other ranks) and to take two men from every post in the front line.
>
> If in addition, a covering party (say 20 other ranks) is required for the Pioneers and wiring party it will be necessary to withdraw three men from every front line post.
>
> In my opinion this endangers the safety of the Sector and leaves me without any reserve in case of emergency.[11]

As this was merely a diversion, it was considered unnecessary to force it through, or to hold any gains if the cost became too high—the main objective of the attacks having been met in tying down German manpower. Although the German Commander later stated that he had not attached any great importance to the attacks on the Knoll and Gillemont, no enemy assets were redeployed north until much later in the day.[12] This success came at a cost, with 164 Bde suffering 562 casualties, making holding this extended line even more challenging—especially as German retaliatory fire utterly destroyed many stretches of trench.[13] The only battalion casualty was twenty-year-old Rfn Ernest Nadin, attached to 165 TMB. It was January 1918 before his wounds to hand and knee allowed him to rejoin the TMB.

At midnight on 21 November, the battalion was placed at twenty minutes notice to support 166 Bde in case of a German counterattack resulting from the Cambrai operation. At 4 a.m., they were ordered to Épehy, but 'stood-down' at 7.30 a.m., returning to Sainte-Émilie. One who did not travel up with them was Rfn Robert Bradshaw from Formby. Admitted to the Field Ambulance suffering from tetanus, he died two days later.

At 5.45 p.m. on 22 November, the battalion filed up to the line, relieving the 1/9th in the Birdcage at 9 p.m. One company remained in reserve in Priel Cutting; another in support, deploying two platoons in Holts' Bank, one in Cruciform Post and one in Heythrop Post. Of the two front-line companies, one occupied most of the Birdcage and south to Lark Post, the other the left of the Birdcage, Flycatcher Post, nearby Bird Post, with one platoon north of Ossus Wood Road in Stone Trench. HQ's dugout was in Lempire Road.

Although a few rounds targeted Little Priel Farm, the night was quiet and patrols found No Man's Land deserted, though sentries in the enemy front line were very alert and it was not possible to approach closely. Apart from intermittent shelling of Little Priel Farm, the 23rd was calm—though this fire resulted in two Riflemen wounded: David Black was hit in the thigh, evacuated home, and eventually transferred; also wounded in the thigh, though far more seriously, was twenty-seven-year-old Arthur Webster, an injury that proved fatal on 11 December. L/Cpl H. Jones (061) also ended up in hospital, recorded as suffering from an accidental puncture wound to his left thigh.[14] Fifteen patrols were out across the divisional sector—some in daylight—all finding the defenders alert and no indications that the foe was considering the withdrawal Intelligence suggested might occur. Little Priel Farm was again shelled intermittently on 24 November and forty rounds fired at Lempire and Catelet Roads. The only casualty of the day was twenty-year-old Rfn Lawrence Crane, who was killed.

From Brig.-Gen. Stockwell's diary, it is evident that senior officers within the division believed enemy withdrawal was far from likely:

> Reorganisation going on. We have made no progress opposite Cambrai. I think the situation is bad. We have a beastly salient. Talked it over with Divisional Commander. The position is dangerous—if he attacks on our front, or on our left, we have very few men to stop him with & no guns. The Division hold 14,000 yards of front with 4,000 men & about 6 battalions. It strikes me that if I was a Bosch I should go for the Banteux Ravine and cut through.[15]

Jeudwine discussed these fears at length with Corps-Commander Gen. Thomas 'D'Oyly Snow, who concurred.

Apart from intermittent shelling of Little Priel Farm and the Birdcage on 25 November, the day remained quiet. Patrols across the division reported an alert enemy in his front line, but no excursions into No Man's Land by them. Further indications of a possible enemy offensive appeared the next day, when enemy artillery registered the front line and support trenches with high airbursts—fire that appeared to come from new batteries. There was also enemy aerial activity over the front line, of an intensity that denied RFC spotter aircraft opportunity to observe German rear areas. About 8 p.m., it began to snow, but morning rain turned it to slush; by noon, it had gone.

The 27th was generally quiet, with just intermittent harassing fire, and at 4 p.m., the battalion carried out an inter-company relief, 'A' going into Reserve and 'B' into Support. One event which shocked many was the death of L/Sgt William Flynn. The seemingly-healthy twenty-five-year-old dropped dead, from what was discovered at his *post mortem* to be heart disease. In the late afternoon, considerable movement was discerned behind enemy lines, though beyond the range of the only guns available, the 18-pounders. Just eight 6-inch Howitzers provided the heavy artillery for all of VII Corps, and despite repeated requests, the only additional guns allocated to 55 Division was one battery of 18-Pounders.[16, 17]

At 4 a.m. on 28 November, a reconnaissance patrol went to look for enemy movement in Ossus Wood and the front line south of there, but nothing was seen—similar ventures occurring across the divisional front. That day, Jeudwine issued an urgent *Divisional Warning Order*: 'Certain indications during today point to the possibility of enemy making an attack against our front. All troops will be warned to be specially on the alert in the trenches and all posts'.[18] Special officer-led patrols—ordered only to return after dawn—exited across the divisional front, tasked with looking for gaps cut into the enemy wire, and sentries were warned to look for evidence of any gaps cut in their own wire—precautions that were to continue until further notice.

Throughout the day, observers noticed unusual movement behind enemy lines, though hostile artillery fire remained slight. Jeudwine's reaction—when his depleted division was given the additional responsibility of the Villers-Guislain sector that same day—was fairly choleric. His worries about the vulnerability of the Banteux Ravine were great enough for him to ask for a brigade from 12 Division to help defend the Ravine, a request that was initially granted; however, when he visited Maj.-Gen. Scott on 29 November, he was told that it would not now be provided. The CRA, Brig.-Gen. Perreau, had arranged with III Corps for a barrage by their heavy artillery against obvious German assembly positions to take place at 6.30 a.m. on the 30th, but as reported in the *OH*, this was cancelled by III Corps on the night of the 29th—a fateful decision.[19]

However, Jeudwine's papers show that there was more to this than appears. In a later letter to Snow, Jeudwine gave his version:

> I do not agree with Knapp's [Brig.-Gen. Kempster Knapp] account of what passed between himself and me on the night of the 29th. I have a pretty clear recollection of this conversation and this is what I maintain happened. As soon as Perreau, my C.R.A., told me that the assistance of III Corps, Heavy Artillery had been refused. I rang up Burnett-Stuart [Brig.-Gen. Sir John Burnett-Stuart, B.G.G.S. VII Corps] and made the strongest representations with regard to the necessity for our having the fire of heavy artillery on our front. He said that the III Corps would not agree, and when I still pressed he asked if I would speak to Knapp about it. Knapp, who was apparently in the room, came to the telephone and I renewed my protests to him. He did not however meet them in at all a sympathetic spirit. He pointed out that there was no certainty that we were going to be attacked and that if the heavy artillery fired and there was no attack it would be a great waste of ammunition. I admit that I was infuriated at this way of looking at it, and I put the opposite case to him, *viz.*, that if on the other hand there was an attack and no heavy artillery was brought to bear upon it, there would be a great waste of life and that in my

> opinion it was better to waste ammunition than to waste lives. I clearly recollect using practically those very words to him.
>
> I have no recollection of Burnett-Stuart saying to me, as Knapp maintains he did, that if I 'considered the matter imperative he would call up the B.G.S., III Corps and reopen the question'. On the contrary, he (Burnett-Stuart) said that he had done everything he could and that if I was not satisfied would I speak to Knapp. The conversation between Knapp and myself then took place which I have given above.[20]

Enemy troop movement continued into 29 November, but otherwise, the front remained quiet. All special patrols returned through the mist of 30 November, reporting the enemy wire was still intact. At 7.05 a.m., an intense German bombardment opened against the entire front line, all support positions, and all routes forward. Battalion HQ came under a very heavy barrage of gas shells, though the worst of the fire fell on 'C' and 'D' in the front line.

Behind this bombardment, massed waves of infantry assaulted Fleeceall Post, the Birdcage, and Eagle Quarry, and although the SOS was sent, pitifully few guns were available to reply. To the north, in 166 Bde's sector, the situation was most critical, their positions stormed from the front, left, and behind—the mist-shrouded Banteux Ravine having become the highway through British lines that Jeudwine feared.

The initial bombardment smashed the battalion's front line, causing heavy casualties. The Birdcage and Eagle Quarry were quickly overrun—their garrisons, in their inadequate shelters, killed, wounded, or stunned by the ferocity of the fire. Fleeceall Post had slightly longer to react and was able to hold, driving the attackers back to their own lines; Haythrop and Cruciform posts offered stubborn resistance against the enemy advancing towards them up the slight slope, driving off repeated assaults.

In command of Cruciform was twenty-one-year-old Sgt Henry Dodd. When the first of the attackers came through Little Priel Farm towards them, he and his men conducted a fierce defence, pushing the enemy back. The heavy small arms fire alerted HQ to the danger, all telephone wires having been cut. Second-Lieutenant Thomas Bride—with the battalion for just six days—was hurriedly dispatched to Cruciform with his reserve platoon. Although the enemy held Little Priel Farm, this did not go unchallenged and possession see-sawed backwards and forwards throughout the day until, eventually, Sgt Dodd led another counterattack, which cleared and then secured the position against further incursions. Dodd's coolness and determination to hold, despite being under heavy close range small arms fire from three sides, was instrumental in the battalion maintaining their grip there. Had Cruciform fallen, the battalion's left flank would have been open and the foe presented with a route around their rear via Priel Cutting and the Lempire Road. For his courage, Dodd received the MM, though a DCM would not have been out of place.[21] For 2Lt Bride's inspirational leadership in holding Cruciform against repeated attacks, his skilled direction of fire, preventing the enemy overrunning a British gun position in Priel Road, and his personal courage in disregarding the heavy fire, the MC was awarded.[22]

The gun position was a section of D276 Battery RFA, with two 18-pounders dug in at

Priel crossroads. These began firing at 7.10 a.m., but at 7.30 a.m., when the SOS was fired from the Birdcage, an enemy barrage struck their position, wounding the officer in charge. The men cleared out to a flank to avoid the fire and Sgt Thornley, who had taken command, was told by the CO of the TMB to hold position as long as possible—even though the enemy was practically on top of them. Thornley observed a large party of enemy moving along Holt's Bank, and after consultation with Lt-Col McKaig, he had four of his gunners manhandle one of the guns around, engaging the enemy over open sights. They fired twenty rounds of HE before having to take cover from heavy, close-range machine-gun fire, removing the dial sights and breech mechanisms before doing so.

Thornley's communications to the battery were cut, and with no officer available, their OC sent up Sgt Cyril Gourley to take charge, with orders to send information back and keep the guns in action. However, due to the heavy fire from enemy Howitzers, it was not possible to man the guns again until 11 a.m., when the barrage moved south onto the Lempire Road. Lt-Col. McKaig requested that the guns fire against the Birdcage, which they did, one at a time, firing until noon, when McKaig informed them that the enemy were coming in force down Holt's Bank and the Cottesmore Trench Road. One of the guns had been put out of action, but Gourley had the other pulled from its pit, swung around, and engaged the enemy at 400 yards' range. The second round exploded directly in the middle of the enemy party. Gourley and his men were then machine-gunned by three low-flying German aircraft and came under rifle fire from their left flank. Undaunted, they continued firing, getting another twenty rounds off before being forced to take cover again when the aircraft directed 100 rounds of 4.2 onto them. Fifteen minutes later, the gunners recommenced fire, but only got eight rounds off before again being forced once again to take shelter.

At 2 p.m., the RFA sent up Lt Biggart up to take command of the section, but he had only been there half an hour when the enemy was once again observed on, and to the front of, Holt's Bank. The gunners engaged with HE, but after twenty rounds, they were forced to remove the dial sight and take cover after coming under close-range fire from two machine guns to their left. At 4 p.m., large numbers of enemy were seen running over the Villers Ridge from Holt's Bank, and with the 1/6th expecting to be attacked at any moment from the direction of Priel Cutting, the gunners helped the battalion build barricades and carry ammunition and bombs to the forward positions.[23] The gun section was withdrawn after dark, their epic action earning Sgt Gourley the VC and eleven of his men the MM.

The good communications that Lt-Col. McKaig was able to maintain with the gun section and Cruciform Post was accredited to one runner, Rfn Austin Hyde. Despite heavy shellfire and sniping, he repeatedly delivered messages between Cruciform and HQ, and after dark, he guided a number of resupply parties forward with ammunition and food. During the night, he was wounded in the face, but refused to be evacuated until eventually being ordered to by 2Lt Bride. The courage and determination of this soldier, who had joined 'A' Company from the PB Battalion four months earlier, was recognised by the MM.[24] The supply of hot meals to Haythrop and Cruciform Posts was thanks to 'A' Company cook

Rfn Frederick Edwards. Early in the action, he was ordered to make sure that the men had food and was determined that no German was going to put a stop to his culinary activities. A succession of cookhouses were blown in on top of him, but each time, he rescued what he could and set up anew elsewhere. Once the food was prepared—and notwithstanding the danger and difficulty—he personally helped deliver hot meals and tea to both posts, a contributory factor to maintaining morale that cannot be understated and was well-deserving of the MM he was awarded.[25]

Bird Lane was the only communication trench leading from the captured front line, and to prevent the enemy using it to assault Haythrop Post, 2Lt Frank Horton led a party to build and then hold a bombing block 400 yards along it. This small and very isolated garrison caused significant casualties among the enemy in the Birdcage and Eagle Quarry, and consequently came under very heavy artillery fire—though Horton's squad stubbornly held their ground. At one point, the subaltern, who was awarded the MC for his courage and leadership, was buried up to his neck by an exploding shell, but refused to be bowed.[26]

Holt's Bank remained in enemy hands, large numbers having accessed there along the Catelet Valley. When the shelling began, the battalion's reserve company made their way to HQ and one platoon was sent straight up to reinforce Holt's Bank. Unfortunately, it was already too late, the platoon stopped in their tracks by intense enemy fire. For a while, the position appeared precarious—beset from the front, their left flank in the air. Fortunately, the hurried strengthening of this flank, carried out under heavy enfilading machine-gun fire and bombardment, served its purpose.

It was critical that Lt-Col. McKaig discover how far the enemy had penetrated on the battalion's left, and a reconnaissance by 'B' Company's Sgt Francis Gloyne established their exact whereabouts. This information was invaluable, as was the small advance post the NCO established in Catelet Copse. Gloyne held this position, where he was able to establish liaison with the Central Indian Horse until the battalion was ordered to withdraw, being awarded the MM for his work.[27]

Across the divisional front, all available reserves hurried forward. By 9 a.m., the 1/9th were distributed across a number of locations, with the company reinforcing the 1/6th kept in readiness in Priel Cutting and 13 Copse. At 9 p.m., all the 1/9th came under Lt-Col. McKaig's tactical remit.

On the left, 166 Bde struggled valiantly, but it was the gallant counterattack against Vaucellette Farm by the 1/4th Loyals that finally halted the enemy. During the night, hostile artillery fire dwindled and all seemed calm opposite the battalion. To their immediate left was Limerick Post, where a composite force of 1/5th KORL and Liverpool Scottish drove off multiple attacks from the vastly superior numbers surrounding them. At 5 a.m., this small garrison used the cover of darkness to slip back through the enemy, and all, apart from six non-walking wounded, returned safely. The wounded, and two stretcher-bearers who selflessly volunteered to remain with them, were taken prisoner.

In the early hours, two companies of enemy infantry, believing the battalion had abandoned Fleeceall Post, attempted to occupy it. To their consternation, they found that far from being vacant, it was garrisoned by an alert and aggressive force and the battalion took three prisoners from the attackers, who milled around in confusion in No Man's Land after receiving such unexpected resistance.

During the day of 1 December, assisted by the 1/9th and two squadrons of the 38th Central Indian Horse, 166 Bde made an unsuccessful attempt to regain the ground lost to the battalion's immediate left. The night of 1 December was particularly quiet, and at 6 a.m. on the 2nd, the battalion was relieved by the 1/9th and moved to Lempire, where they helped to construct new defences. During the afternoon of 2 December, the lightly-held advance post was forced to temporarily withdraw from Catelet Copse by a strong German attack, but when reinforcements arrived, the 1/9th seized it back. At 9 a.m. on 3 December, the enemy once again took Catelet Copse, but an hour later, it was recaptured—a bloodless victory as the enemy retreated without a fight.

Lt-Col. McKaig received a Bar to his DSO for his leadership. He was tireless in his energy, repeatedly visiting the advanced positions, inspiring all with his courage. Capt. Walter Brownell was also recommended for an 'immediate' MC for his command of Haythrop and Cruciform Posts, but this was not sanctioned as he had been recommended for an MC in the New Year Honours. The recommendations were combined and the MC awarded. Acting 'A' Company CSM Sgt Edward Jones (929) received a Bar to his MM; during the initial bombardment, he had been badly gassed, refused to report sick, and, throughout the heaviest times of the barrage, calmly visited the positions, steadying and reassuring the men.[28] Sadly, some citations are missing from Jeudwine's papers, so the deeds that earned Rfn Henry Rogers (870) his MM are no longer on record.

By 11 p.m. on 5 December, the battalion was relieved and made their way to Villers Faucon in preparation for a move to Péronne, the entire division relieved by midnight of 6 December.

Losses on 30 November were the highest of the war. The diary reported nine officers and 223 men missing, one man killed, and twenty-five wounded, though, with hindsight, the overall total of 253 works out marginally less, with fifty killed and 203 wounded or captured. Although many of the 189 prisoners were wounded prior to capture, apart from a few exceptions, it is not possible to state whom. Five died from their wounds while in German hands, and a further eight died from illness before repatriation. Apart from those with the 'Lifeboat Party', 'C' and 'D' were no more. Other battalions fared worse: on the extreme left of the divisional line, adjacent to the Banteux Ravine, the entire 1/5th South Lancs was lost.

Fatalities, 30 November 1917

Name	Number	Fate
Rfn Isaac Anderson C)	242648	KIA
Rfn Arthur Frederick Banks (A)	240508	KIA
L/Sgt Donald Bates (B)	241660	KIA
Rfn Edward Boon (D)	49920	KIA
Rfn Archibald Breckenridge (C)	241654	KIA
Sgt Joseph Ainge Burden (B)	240331	KIA
Rfn Thomas Burke	308978	KIA

Rfn Taylor Cheetham	51144	KIA
Rfn Arthur Blundell Clee	51380	KIA
L/Cpl William Arthur Copestake	51131	KIA
Rfn John Harold Davies (B)	267594	KIA
L/Cpl Leslie Charles Davies (C)*	241909	DOW: 10/12
Rfn Albert Edward Dixon	49996	KIA
Rfn William Henry Emberson	88055	KIA
Rfn Fred Emmett (C)	242718	KIA
Rfn Noel Harvey Firth	51433	KIA
Rfn Geoffrey Charles Gadsden*	241357	DOW: 4/12
Rfn Frederick Glossop	300006	KIA
Rfn Thomas Arthur Griffiths (A)	241585	KIA
Rfn James Hartley (C)	242735	KIA
Rfn Tom Hartley	26979	KIA
Rfn William Arthur Harton (C)	241353	KIA
Cpl Thomas Hill (D)	241423	KIA
Rfn George Stanley Hughes	242525	KIA
Rfn Joseph Hughes	241208	KIA
Rfn James E. Jenks	27828	KIA
Rfn William Kniveton	49165	KIA
Rfn William Lacey	269950	KIA
Rfn William Francis Lee (B)*	242899	DOW: 9/12
Rfn Albert Locker (D)	242086	KIA
Rfn Terence MacGarrey (C)	242117	DOW: 1/12
Rfn Walter Eugene McAvoy (C)	58487	KIA
Rfn George Edward Norris*	51129	DOW: 10/12
Rfn Edwin George Oakley	51396	KIA
Rfn Thomas Ormerod (C)	242809	KIA
Rfn William James Parry	64908	KIA
Rfn John Parry (D)**	242673	DOW: 3/12
Rfn Joseph Poland*	88758	DOW: 1/12
Rfn James Edward Proffitt	49966	KIA
Rfn John Quinn	242057	KIA
Rfn Walter Gabriel Sinclair	202142	KIA
L/Cpl Henry Skilbeck (C)	242511	KIA
Rfn Thomas Arthur Spurling	235079	KIA
Rfn Fred Starkey (C)	242873	KIA
Rfn John Henry Walker	51401	KIA
2Lt Sidney Herbert Webster		KIA
Rfn Arthur Wilkes	51134	KIA
Rfn Edward Woods	52039	KIA

* = Died from wounds whilst in German hands.

** = Wounded on 1 December 1917.

Died from Illness in German Hands

Rfn Alfred Boardman	88085	28/05/18
Rfn James William G. Brookes (D)	49922	25/12/17
Rfn Thomas Harvey* (C)	305407	27/11/18
Rfn Tom Haywood	88062	27/12/18
Rfn John Hewitt	269422	27/2/18
Rfn William Howarth (D)	242806	3/12/17
Rfn George Frederick Nicholls (D)	242797	10/12/17
Rfn Edward Welsh (D)	242833	24/11/18

* = died just after release.

Wounded or Captured, 30 November 1917

Rfn Frederick Harold Altmann	51376	POW
Rfn Richard Alty	330593	POW
Rfn Russell Scott Anderson (B)	240608	POW
Rfn Robert Ashton (C)*	242831	POW
Rfn John Balshaw	36718	POW
Rfn Stephen Myles Barker (D)	242837	POW
Rfn Robert Barrow (C)	242649	POW
L/Cpl Henry John Beale (B)**	241658	WIA
Rfn Frank Beaumont	49987	POW
L/Cpl Alfred William Belshaw (A)	241712	POW
Rfn Walter Bennett (C)	242798	POW
Rfn Arthur Bevan (C)	241911	POW
Rfn Frederick J. Bibby	51383	POW
Rfn Alfred Boardman	88085	POW
Rfn Thomas Boothby	51422	POW
2Lt Victor R. Bowers		POW
Rfn Alfred Bradshaw	265884	POW
Sgt Frank Watson Bramwell (D)	240397	POW
Rfn James William G. Brookes (D)	49922	POW
Rfn John T. Broomhead	49988	WIA
Rfn Samuel Brown	51424	POW
Rfn Thomas Ralph Brown (C)	241562	POW
Rfn William Henry Bruce	332108	POW
Rfn Alfred Buckley	308092	POW
Rfn Charles E. Cain	260015	POW
L/Cpl Daniel Callaghan	243887	POW
Rfn John Chater (B)	49931	WIA
Rfn Thomas J. Clark (D)	49992	POW
Rfn Harold Joseph Claussen (A)	241222	POW
Rfn William Ernest Cogley (A)	242643	POW
Rfn Robert Metcalfe Cooper (D)	241838	POW
Cpl Thomas William Corlett (B)	240207	POW
Rfn John Thomas Costain (D)	242653	POW
Rfn Fred Coupe (D)	242805	POW
Sgt Harold Crook (C)	240394	POW
Rfn Archibald Crooke (B)	242614	POW
Rfn Fred Cryer	49932	POW
Cpl Arthur Davies (B)	241085	POW
2Lt W. K. Davy		POW
Sgt Tom Clarke Dick (D)	240689	WIA
Rfn Joseph Dilworth (A)	242594	POW
Cpl Alfred Dixon (C)	240635	POW
L/Cpl William Dobby (A)	242627	POW
Rfn Edward S. Dodd	51377	POW
Rfn Samuel Doorbar	49960	POW
Rfn Albert Duckett (B)	242811	POW
Rfn John Dunne (D)	242848	POW
Rfn Charles Lewis Edwards (C)*	241626	POW
Rfn Walter Edwards	17323	POW
Rfn Thomas J. Ellis	240529	WIA
Rfn Albert Morice Evans (D)	260048	POW
L/Cpl William Evans	242560	POW
Rfn Fred P. Fellows	49936	POW
Rfn George Fenton (D)	241948	POW
Rfn John W. Fishwick (A)	30431	POW
Rfn Edward Fletcher	269146	POW
Rfn Reginald Forfar	267145	POW
Rfn George Foulkes (D)	350034	POW
Rfn Charles Gates (D)	242852	POW
Rfn Edward Gent (A)	332289	POW
Rfn Ernest George (A)	242721	POW
Rfn William Giddings	51135	POW
Rfn James Robert Gledson	332729	POW
Cpl Herbert Gobie (C)	240646	POW
Rfn Claud Gorham	88059	POW
Rfn Sidney L. Green	88058	POW
Rfn Albert Thornton Gregson	269885	POW
Rfn Edward James Guy	270087	POW
Rfn Robert Hall (D)	242854	POW
Rfn Arthur Hanmer (C)	242733	POW
Rfn Reginald E. Harris	51386	POW
Rfn William Harrison	49947	POW
Sgt Montague Hart (C)	240315	POW
Rfn David Harvey	50006	POW
Rfn Thomas Harvey (C)	305407	POW
Rfn Thomas E. Haydock (B)	260021	POW
Rfn James Hays	265782	POW
Rfn Tom Haywood	88062	POW
Rfn Herbert Heald	50011	POW
Sgt Edward Heatley (D)	240308	POW

Rfn Henry Charles Helme	51387	POW	Rfn Henry Moss	260030	POW
L/Cpl John Robert Hesk (D)	241870	POW	Rfn William Halewood Murray (C)	241670	POW
Rfn John Hewitt	269422	POW	Rfn Walter Muse	200116	POW
Rfn Wilfred Hilton (B)	242729	POW	Rfn John Musker	30027	POW
Rfn William Holman	200976	POW	Rfn Henry Cecil Rupert Nealy	260033	POW
Rfn George Horn	47468	POW	Rfn James Neary	201521	POW
Rfn William Howarth (D)	242806	POW	Rfn Charles Needs	51414	POW
Rfn Arnold H. Howe	51411	POW	Rfn William Henry Niblett (C)	241363	POW
Rfn John A. Howell	51420	POW	Rfn George Frederick Nicholls (D)	242797	POW
Rfn Philip Howorth (C)	240321	POW	Rfn Herbert Nichols (C)	242868	POW
Rfn Austin O. Hyde (A)	242790	WIA	Rfn Jonathan Nickson (D)	242601	POW
Rfn Thomas Ikin	50014	POW	Rfn John Norminton (C)	241899	POW
Rfn Willie Jennings	51417	POW	Rfn Edwin Norris (B)	241715	POW
Sgt Edward Doyle Jones**	241929	WIA	Rfn Peter O'Rourke (D)	305114	POW
L/Cpl James Johnston (D)	241858	POW	Rfn Arthur J. Padley	50153	POW
Rfn Edward Jones	51378	POW	Rfn Thomas William Parkinson	201462	POW
Rfn Harry Jones	330393	POW	Rfn Joseph Parr	51440	POW
L/Cpl James Albert Jones (C)	241984	WIA	Rfn William John Parry	51398	POW
Rfn James George Kay (C)	242107	POW	Rfn William Charles Passmore (A)	241201	POW
Rfn Arthur G. Keane	51388	POW	Cpl Herbert Peart (C)	241314	POW
Rfn Thomas Kelshaw	306778	POW	Rfn Joseph Robert Phillips (C)	240330	POW
Rfn Cornelius Harry J. Keyte	51389	POW	Rfn William Pickford	50480	POW
Rfn William King	51437	POW	Rfn Robert Pickwell	51397	POW
Cpl Albert Lee (B)	330378	POW	Rfn Thomas Alfred Pulford (B)	241492	WIA
Rfn James Life	260028	POW	Rfn Thomas William Purcell (B)	242760	POW
Rfn Edward M. Lloyd	51438	POW	Rfn James P. Rainford	51443	POW
Rfn Richard Marsh Lyons	240600	WIA	Rfn Thomas Reddington (B)	242762	WIA
Rfn Edward Machin (B)	49953	WIA	L/Cpl William J. Reidy (A)	308889	POW
Sgt Albert Edward MacMaster (D)	240065	POW	Cpl Frank Richards (D)	241427	POW
Rfn Joseph Marrs	51390	POW	Rfn James J. A. Riley	52879	POW
Rfn Charles Frederick Marsh (D)	242341	POW	Cpl Peter Rimmer (A)	242685	POW
Rfn William Thomas Martin	51393	POW	Rfn James Robbins	88067	POW
Rfn William McCall	24072	WIA	Rfn William Rodger (D)	240367	POW
L/Cpl Edward McCarthy	242747	POW	Rfn George W. Rodgers	51382	POW
Rfn James McIlroy (D)	242091	POW	2Lt Edward S. Rogers		POW
L/Cpl James McMahon (C)	241790	POW	Sgt Thomas Rowe (D)	240267	POW
L/Cpl Nathan McManus (C)	241895	POW	Rfn Richard Rudkin (C)	240459	POW
L/Cpl James Melia	48983	POW	Rfn George Runacus (C)	241513	POW
L/Cpl Joseph Molyneux (A)	204539	POW	Cpl George Henry Salt (D)	241426	POW
Rfn Charles Moore	49954	POW	Rfn Alfred Sampson	260074	POW
Rfn Stanley Moore (C)	241820	POW	Rfn John Saunt	88068	POW
Rfn Arthur Morgan	88063	POW	Rfn Hanson Scott	49974	POW

Rfn Charles Seely (B)	331369	POW
Rfn Bartley Shannon	406711	POW
2Lt Herbert J. Sheppard		POW
Rfn James Sleightholme (D)	241698	POW
Cpl William Smallwood (C)	241627	POW
Rfn James Smith (D)	242100	WIA
Rfn James Edward Smith (C)	241811	WIA
2Lt William Reginald Smith (A)		POW
Rfn William Sprang	51445	POW
Rfn Percival Routledge Steffell (C)	241869	WIA
Lt Robert Reginald Stewart (D)		POW
Rfn Frank Stubbs (D)	49970	POW
Rfn Joseph C. Sutcliffe	49972	POW
Rfn William Sutcliffe	49971	POW
Rfn George Tabbernor	49976	POW
Rfn Norman Tate (D)	241888	POW
Rfn Archie Taylor	235030	POW
Rfn William Pierce Taylor (D)	241589	POW
Rfn Albert Terry	260039	POW
Rfn John Thomas (D)	241824	POW

Rfn Thomas William Thomas (C)	241905	POW
Rfn Charles Edward Thompson (A)	241724	WIA
Rfn Walter Thompson (C)	242812	POW
Cpl Ernest Townley (C)	241454	POW
Rfn Sidney Turner	49975	POW
Capt. George Dawson Tyson (C)		POW
Rfn James Upton (A)	241240	POW
Rfn Sydney Upton (D)	242064	POW
Rfn Joseph Vibrans	265384	POW
Rfn Frank Ward	405744	POW
Rfn William Waterhouse (B)	242778	POW
Rfn Charles Reynolds Watkins	51400	WIA
2Lt Cecil Valentine Watts		POW
Rfn Edward Welsh (D)	242833	POW
Rfn William Wheeler	29896	POW
Rfn Edward Williams	242355	POW
Rfn Frederick Williams	267947	POW
Rfn Frank Wilson	51406	POW
L/Cpl Stanley Woodward (C)	242881	WIA
Rfn Herbert Bertram Wren (D)	241877	POW

* = known to have been wounded prior to capture. ** = known to have been gassed.

After the spectacular gains at Cambrai, the reverses of 30 November shocked the British public, regaled with tales of a brilliant victory just ten days earlier. Pressed for answers by concerned politicians, Haig requested an immediate report from Gen. Byng; Haig's subsequent criticisms of the performance of the defenders were based on Byng's report, which led him to believe that the defences were an unbroken line and in good order. As described earlier, this was far from true. Based on this, Haig expressed doubts about the fighting capacity of the defenders:

> Risks had to be taken in reducing forces at some points in order to be strong at others, but the risk taken at Cambrai was not an undue risk for the enemy should not have succeeded in penetrating any part of our defence.[29]

Byng was quick to blame the failure on the poor leadership and fighting ability of soldiers from 55, 12, and 20 Division, particularly junior officers and machine gunners. He further pronounced that no responsibility was attributable to anyone in High Command, and that he and all his subordinate commanders had been happy that there were sufficient troops available to handle any counterattack.

Byng's insistence that none of his subordinate commanders had been unhappy with the number of troops available to them does not hold up in light of Jeudwine's repeated requests for a brigade to cover the Banteux Ravine. The Court of Enquiry in January 1918—careful not to criticise High Command—can only be interpreted as a whitewash. Jeudwine believed the process nothing more than an exercise in self-aggrandisement by Gen. Ivor Maxse, commander of XVIII Corps and member of the Committee of Enquiry. Jeudwine's personal copy of the report was annotated: 'Ivor Maxse again. Personal advertisement'.[30] In summary of his views in a letter to Snow, Jeudwine fumes:

> I have read through the report of the Committee of Enquiry. It is of course Maxse pure and simple, and very poisonous Maxse at that. I find a great many points with which I am in total disagreement: for instance, it is stated near the bottom of Page 5 that there appears to have been a lack of vigilance in the outpost lines. This, as I think you know, I deny altogether. It is further stated here that no SOS signals were sent up. This is of course not the case as you have a copy of a statement from an officer of Artillery in which the reply of the guns to the SOS Signals is referred to. Again, on Page 6, under the heading of 'Warnings from above unheeded', I am as muddled as you are to what is meant by 'Higher Commanders'.
>
> Then at Para. 6 of the note by a member of the Court of Enquiry (same distinguished General again) it is stated that we can 'discover few traces of organised counter-attacks or of methodical resistance'. As you are well aware, the spontaneous counter-attack of the 1/4th Loyal North Lancashires along the Villers-Guislain spur stopped for good the enemy's advance in that direction, and pinned him down with the result of making subsequent counter-attacks by the Guards Division possible. But the whole of this memorandum, the anonymity of which is very lightly veiled, is sheer advertisement and hardly worth taking the trouble to contradict.[31]

The mere fact that Haig felt a Court of Enquiry necessary suggests he was not totally satisfied with Byng's explanation.

The *OH*, published twenty years later, rightly attributed the blame to Byng and his CoS, who should have been aware of the dangers of counterattack through the Banteux Ravine—especially given that Snow had expressed concerns to Third Army about this more than once.[32] Equally, too little artillery had been allocated within the danger area, a problem that could only have been solved at 'Army' level, and yet all requests for additional heavy artillery were turned down. Much of the criticism aimed at the three divisions was based on the assumption that there must have been a lack of vigilance from men in the front line because no SOS signals were supposedly sent; yet officers reported that these signals were fired by the men in the forward trenches—brigade and divisional Signal Logs—which the Enquiry had access to—unambiguously record this. Without their heavy artillery and many of the 18-pounder batteries and mortars put out of action in the initial bombardment, what little fire support was available was too meagre to hinder the advance. The dead ground and weather gave the enemy a strategic advantage, for they could amass safely out of sight of the defenders. Many machine guns were put out of action by the barrage, the surviving gunners either overwhelmed by attackers descending upon them at short range, often from the rear, or fought until their ammunition was exhausted.

Blame clearly rests with Byng, whose focus on the main attack on the 20th was such that, despite warnings from subordinate commanders, he failed to take into account events to its flank—an area he had weakened to provide extra impetus to his main push. The most disappointing aspect of this matter is Byng's attempt to deflect culpability onto those too low in the chain of command to be able to defend themselves against this slur.

This stain to 55 Division's reputation was later rebuffed by the *OH*:

> The 55th Division had no reason to reproach itself. Overwhelmed by numbers and by a vastly superior artillery the troops had shown their quality by standing fast amid their broken defences and resisting as long as resistance was possible.[33]

11

7 December 1917—8 April 1918: Givenchy-lès-la-Bassée

Coordinates for this Chapter

'B' Line	50°32′21.40″N 2°44′56.20″E
Albany	50°31′36.20″N 2°45′1.50″E
Barnton North	50°32′22.30″N 2°45′28.30″E
Barnton Road	50°32′31.60″N 2°45′25.40″E
Barnton Tee	50°32′30.50″N
Brewery	2°45′15.20″E 50°31′24.00″N 2°44′52.40″E
Brewery OP	50°31′23.10″N 2°44′58.80″E
Cailloux Keep North	50°33′2.90″N 2°44′20.00″E
Cailloux Keep South	50°32′57.80″N 2°44′20.70″E
Canadian Orchard	50°32′59.50″N 2°46′3.20″E
canal lock	50°31′19.90″N 2°45′16.10″E
Canal Trench	50°31′24.30″N 2°46′12.60″E
Cover Trench	50°32′55.80″N 2°45′54.20″E
Crater Trench	50°31′49.50″N 2°45′46.60″E
Death or Glory Sap	50°31′19.00″N 2°45′56.60″E
Dover Trench	50°32′53.00″N 2°46′6.60″E
Duck's Bill Extension	50°31′36.00″N 2°46′2.90″E
Festubert Keep	50°32′37.10″N 2°44′9.30″E
Finchley Road (March)	50°31′34.60″N 2°45′51.10″E
Givenchy Keep	50°31′42.50″N 2°45′24.10″E
Gorre Château	50°32′28.10″N 2°41′50.70″E
Gunner Siding	50°31′41.10″N 2°45′22.40″E
Hatfield Road	50°31′41.50″N 2°45′30.90″E
Hilder's Redoubt	50°31′43.40″N 2°45′15.00″E
Le Plantin	50°32′12.60″N 2°44′34.50″E
Le Plantin HQ	50°32′3.50″N 2°44′32.60″E

Loop Road	50°32′10.60″N 2°45′24.00″E	Sap-A	50°31′40.10″N 2°45′51.50″E
Mackensen Trench	50°32′20.80″N 2°45′40.50″E	Sap-B	50°31′41.70″N 2°45′47.70″E
Moat Farm Redoubt	50°31′47.80″N 2°45′11.30″E	Sap-E	50°31′47.20″N 2°45′42.90″E
Orchard Keep	50°31′28.50″N 2°45′30.60″E	Sap-F	50°31′50.80″N 2°45′40.80″E
Orchard Road	50°31′26.90″N 2°45′52.60″E	Sap-I	50°31′55.00″N 2°45′38.50″E
Orchard Road	50°31′26.00″N 2°45′42.90″E	Sap-K	50°31′58.10″N 2°45′34.10″E
Pioneer Trench	50°32′56.20″N 2°44′58.40″E	skeletons	50°31′23.20″N 2°46′9.90″E
Pont Fixe North	50°31′26.50″N 2°44′51.10″E	Spoil Bank	50°31′22.80″N 2°45′25.40″E
Post-10	50°31′38.50″N 2°45′43.40″E	Tortoise	50°31′19.30″N 2°46′8.00″E
Prince's Island	50°32′9.10″N 2°45′26.10″E	Vauxhall Road HQ	50°31′33.90″N 2°44′43.40″E
Quinque Rue	50°33′0.50″N 2°45′43.30″E	Village Line at Festubert	50°32′40.80″N 2°44′18.40″E
Red Dragon Crater	50°31′45.40″N 2°45′47.50″E	Warlingham Crater	50°31′39.60″N 2°45′52.80″E
Regent Street	50°31′51.10″N 2°45′32.00″E	Windy Corner	50°31′43.50″N 2°44′40.10″E
Richmond Trench	50°33′2.40″N 2°45′36.00″E		

The battalion's stay at Péronne was brief, as they moved to Marœuil, north-west of Arras, on 8 December, arriving at 6 p.m. They were joined there by a draft of just thirty men, their fighting strength including this draft just 543. The following day, they moved into huts at 'Y' Camp, the day spent training, generally cleaning up, and replacing kit. On 12 December, the battalion marched to Chelers and onwards to Tangry the following day. The 14th saw a continuation of their travels, this time to Fontaine-lès-Boulans, where they were billeted until 8 February.

Tragically, 6 January saw the death from illness of twenty-one-year-old Sgt Alexander Salmon, who was still an inpatient in Norwich War Hospital after his abdominal wound from September 1916. There was also a change of RSM on 26 January, when James Knight was posted to the Base Depot and CSM Arthur Robinson appointed to replace him. The battalion also lost the services of 'D' Company's Rfn John Hatch—one of the 'originals'—who broke his collarbone in an accident. He and L/Cpl Victor Smith, who dislocated his hip, were sent home.

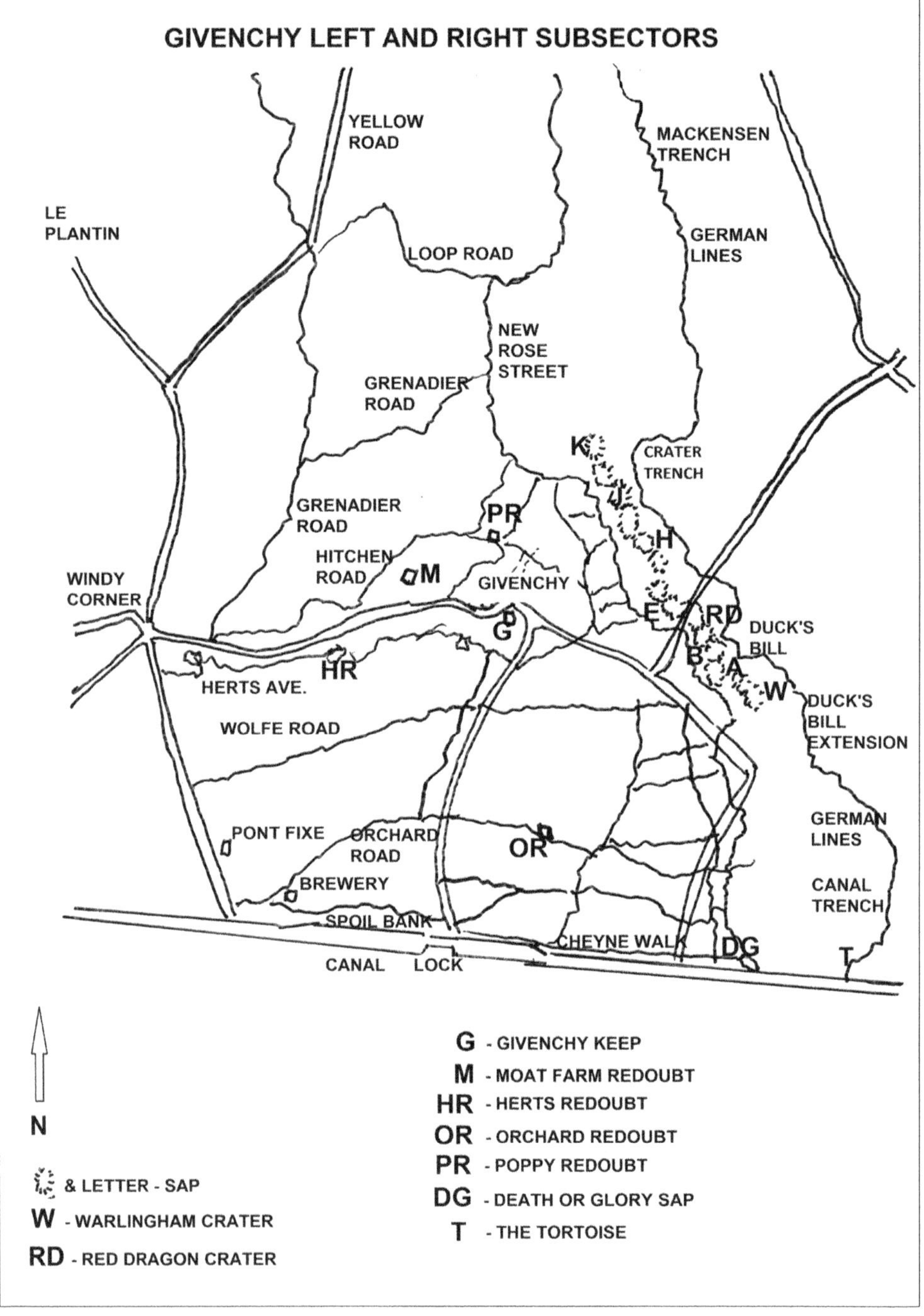
GIVENCHY LEFT AND RIGHT SUBSECTORS
YELLOW ROAD
MACKENSEN TRENCH
LE PLANTIN
GERMAN LINES
LOOP ROAD
NEW ROSE STREET
GRENADIER ROAD
K
CRATER TRENCH
J
GRENADIER ROAD
PR
H
HITCHEN ROAD
M
WINDY CORNER
GIVENCHY
E
RD
DUCK'S BILL
G
B
A
HR
W
HERTS AVE.
DUCK'S BILL EXTENSION
WOLFE ROAD
GERMAN LINES
PONT FIXE
ORCHARD ROAD
OR
CANAL TRENCH
BREWERY
SPOIL BANK
CHEYNE WALK
DG
T
CANAL
LOCK
N
G - GIVENCHY KEEP
M - MOAT FARM REDOUBT
HR - HERTS REDOUBT
OR - ORCHARD REDOUBT
PR - POPPY REDOUBT
DG - DEATH OR GLORY SAP
T - THE TORTOISE
& LETTER - SAP
W - WARLINGHAM CRATER
RD - RED DRAGON CRATER

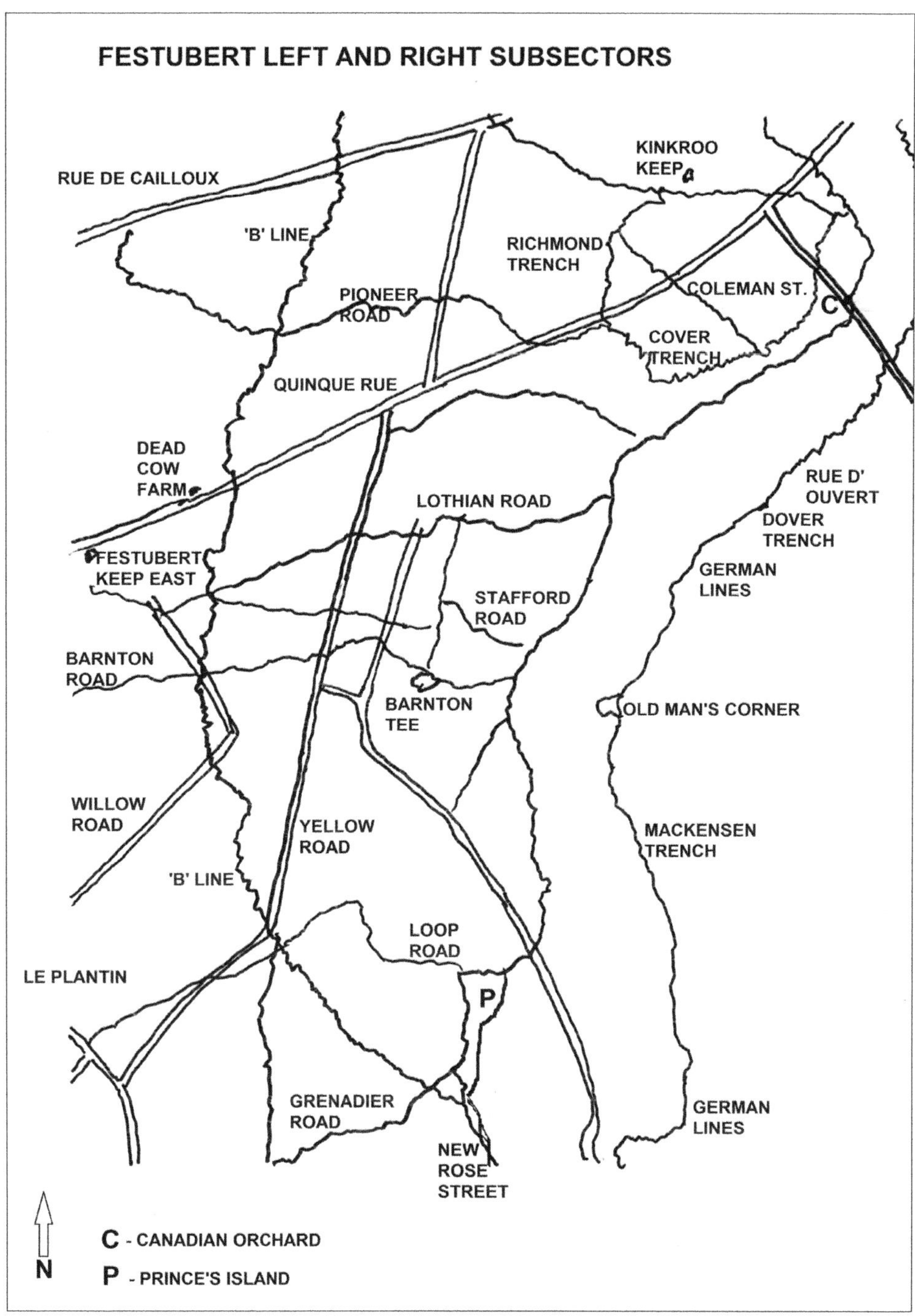
FESTUBERT LEFT AND RIGHT SUBSECTORS
RUE DE CAILLOUX
KINKROO KEEP
'B' LINE
RICHMOND TRENCH
PIONEER ROAD
COLEMAN ST.
C
COVER TRENCH
QUINQUE RUE
DEAD COW FARM
LOTHIAN ROAD
RUE D' OUVERT
DOVER TRENCH
FESTUBERT KEEP EAST
GERMAN LINES
STAFFORD ROAD
BARNTON ROAD
BARNTON TEE
OLD MAN'S CORNER
WILLOW ROAD
YELLOW ROAD
MACKENSEN TRENCH
'B' LINE
LOOP ROAD
LE PLANTIN
P
GRENADIER ROAD
NEW ROSE STREET
GERMAN LINES
N
C - CANADIAN ORCHARD
P - PRINCE'S ISLAND

At the beginning of 1918, the BEF was short of 75,000 infantrymen and also labourers behind the lines. The situation was exacerbated further when Haig was ordered to send five divisions to reinforce the Italian Front. Curbing the supply of reinforcements, as a way of preventing Haig from 'wasting' them on offensives, was a dangerous policy that put the whole outcome of the war in jeopardy.[1] However, organisational changes boosted battalion numbers, when shortages of infantrymen prompted further Government intervention. On 14 January, Division was ordered to reduce the number of battalions to nine. A week later, the Liverpool Irish, 1/9th KLR, and 1/5th Loyals left for 57 Division, where their first- and second-line battalions were amalgamated.[2] The Germans and the French earlier underwent a similar reshuffle, but these changes had been gradual and compensated for by an increase in machine-gun and artillery firepower. With no such cushion in place to compensate British divisions, robbed of 25 per cent of their strength, Haig protested, citing the damaging effects on troop morale that such changes would cause at a time when he believed the enemy was planning a major offensive—but to no avail.[3]

This was the second blow to Haig regarding manpower. Earlier in 1917, at a conference to which Haig had not been invited, the Government had agreed with the French to extend the BEF's line. On 22 December, Haig wrote to the War Cabinet warning that he could not undertake the responsibility of defending the Channel ports if such a proposal went ahead. Thus, at a time of chronic shortages of infantrymen, political interference forced Haig to extend a front with defences in a poor state due to a combination of winter, enemy action, and a lack of available labour to repair them. He was also forced to reorganise his divisions, requiring considerable internal restructuring of staff, whose efforts would have been better employed on strengthening the defences.[4]

Before the Liverpool Irish departed, men surplus to requirements were posted to other battalions of the KLR. In January, the 1/6th welcomed 130 of them. Fortunately, this included some outstanding soldiers; conversely, it is evident the outgoing battalion grasped the opportunity to offload their disciplinary problems and those whose age and fitness made them less suited to an infantry role. When the Rifles returned to the line in February, their strength was a much healthier forty-four officers and 974 men.

On 9 February, the battalion left for Rely and next day for Busnettes, where they were billeted until the 11th. That same day, a reconnaissance party departed for the front line, and on 12 February, the battalion moved to Beuvry. On the 13th, they took over the left subsector at Givenchy (the Battalion diary erroneously states the 'right' subsector). Their left bound was in Barnton North and, though the foremost position on the right bound was Sap-B, the main defensive position there was Post-10, further back on the Hatfield Road. Givenchy had been bitterly contested—the front line dominated by an extensive crater field. Some were German-held, others British-held, though the northerly ones were under disputed ownership, each side holding the lip nearest their own line. Here, the tunnellers fought their deadly subterranean battles on a daily basis.

Their first twenty-four hours in the trenches were quiet, though the enemy shelled Windy Corner with gas shortly before noon. This aptly-named crossroads was a choke-point for ration and working parties, almost impossible to avoid and constantly shelled. Although visibility was poor on 14 February, restricting the view of enemy trenches, one of the battalion's snipers managed to bag a German in Crater Trench. During the afternoon, the enemy sent a number of small balloons floating over the lines. A couple of these, downed by rifle fire, were found to be bearing German newspapers and propaganda leaflets—a welcome source of additional toilet paper.

At 7.15 p.m., an extraordinary act of bravery by Sgt Hugh Sammond undoubtedly saved the lives of another sergeant and an officer. Two rifle grenades were fired by the enemy, one of which landed, fizzing, directly in his trench. Pulling the officer out of the way, the thirty-four-year-old NCO dropped to his knees, groped around in the dark of the bottom of the trench for the grenade, and threw it back out—where it immediately exploded. Sammond was awarded the MM, though, sadly, the father of one from Liverpool did not live long enough to receive the actual medal.[5]

Night patrols found the subsector very quiet, though a single shot and several flares were fired from a German position at the northern tip of Crater Trench, opposite Sap-K (the shallow remnants of the triple-craters of Sap-K are the only visible trace of Givenchy's crater field, now a local fly-tip).

The diary reports 15 February quiet, noting that the rear was heavily shelled, though it was probably the six *Granatenwerfers* that struck Givenchy, where there were a number of defensive keeps, or the eight medium trench mortar rounds that hit Red Dragon Crater that were responsible for their two casualties. Sgt Edward Jones (929) was wounded at duty, but L/Cpl Hugh Evan's spinal wound proved fatal, the thirty-two-year-old dying on 1 April. The 16th was quiet, with only a few *Granatenwerfers* near Hilder's Redoubt, Regent Street, and Hatfield Road at 10 p.m. Although a number of patrols went out overnight, their only item of interest was the sound of talking from three German posts in Crater Trench.

Just 125 yards to the right of Sap-B, the 1/4th Loyals were the victims of a well-planned raid at 3.15 a.m. on 17 February. Under cover of a large smoke bomb—prompting the garrison of Warlingham Crater to don their respirators, believing they were under gas attack—forty raiders rushed them, wounded three of the garrison, and captured the remaining three. Although the Loyals reacted quickly, the raiders escaped with their prisoners.

On 17 February, hostile artillery sent only a few rounds into the battalion's subsector, hitting Gunner Siding, but one slightly wounded Rfn Richard Davis. Three small reconnaissance patrols were out overnight, one near the left bound discovering an enemy wiring party in front of Mackensen Trench, another finding the enemy busy wiring Sap-I. A third patrol examined the triple-crater of Sap-F. Although the battalion held the western lip, the opposite one was German-held and any move into the crater was audacious; between there and the British-held Sap-E were another four small, but disputed craters, and it was from the northernmost of these that the patrol came under machine-gun fire and beat a hasty retreat—fortunately without casualties. The battalion was relieved at 9 a.m. on 19 February and moved to support in the Village Line between Pont Fixe North and Le Plantin, HQ occupying a dugout in Albany. There were three casualties on 19 February, possibly from light shellfire at Windy Corner as they were on their way out of the line. Nineteen-year-old Rfn William Lightfoot was killed and Rfn Leonard Collings wounded in the scalp; L/Cpl Reginald Morris was seriously injured, a shrapnel wound to his upper jaw ending his active service.

In early 1918, Haig was paying much more attention to defence than ever before, suspecting that the enemy may risk all and try to finish the war before the American Expeditionary Force deployed fully. He believed they would endeavour to drive a wedge between the French and British and seize the Channel ports, leaving the Allies with no choice but to sue for peace. Haig was also convinced that, in attempting this, the German Army would be so debilitated that he would be able to deliver a decisive counterattack in Autumn 1918.[6]

Although seriously weakened on the Western Front, the enemy pulled forty-eight divisions from the East—an unthinkable option had Russia still been in the fight. Haig understood that the offensive would breach his front lines, so planned a 'defence in depth', leaving the front line relatively weakly manned, ordering the construction of a series of 'keeps' to form a second and third line.[7] Wire and natural obstacles would funnel attackers into 'zones', where they would be engaged from these keeps. His strategy minimised potential losses during an initial bombardment; moreover, the further the enemy advanced, the less effective his artillery support and the more tenuous his logistical lines would become.

The old front line, its support, and its reserve lines became the 'Forward Zone'. Behind this, the 'Battle Zone' would be constructed on what had been the 'Corps Line', and yet another series of defences further back on the 'Army Line' were redesignated the 'Rear Zone' or 'Green Line'.[8] Due to lack of manpower and time, very little of this work was actually completed. In a conversation with the King during a royal visit to the Front in late March, Haig informed him that his infantry numbered 100,000 less than a year previously; that he was facing a German Army three times the British strength; and that he was expected to defend a front a fifth longer.[9]

The Village Line was key to 55 Division's defences and Jeudwine designated it the 'line of resistance to be denied the enemy at all costs'.[10] It ran through Givenchy and south to Cuinchy—hardly the textbook 'battle zone', being the rear edge of the 'Forward Zone'—but was strategically advantageous, particularly as both ruined villages contained many intact cellars and fortifiable rubble: This was where 55 Division would make their stand. This line consisted of a series of heavily fortified, mutually-supportive strongpoints. Around these were thick belts of wire, slanted to channel attackers into the fields of fire of multiple machine guns enfilading these gaps. In case of tank attack, anti-tank mines were laid in belts behind the front line opposite Givenchy and 18-pounders were sited near the redoubts—Vickers and Lewis guns, with armour-piercing ammunition, positioned nearby. The locally-fabricated mines consisted of a pressure plate on a wooden firing box, connected by instantaneous fuse to a buried trench mortar round.[11] In the high, coarse grass that grew around the strongpoints lurked older, less visible belts of wire.

There is ambiguity as to precisely what is meant by 'Village Line', most sources defining it as the line from Festubert through Le Plantin and Windy Corner to Pont Fixe, yet units themselves sometimes referred to the defensive positions within Givenchy as part of it.[12] In reality, the Village Line near Givenchy was a wide belt where the 'Forward Zone' and

'Battle Zone' merged into one deep stretch—a characteristic of huge relevance in the weeks to come. About 1–2 miles further to the rear, the Green Line was titled the 'Tuning Fork Line' and ran roughly along the line south from Le Touret to the canal just east of its junction with the Canal Beuvry.

Passive defence was only part of Jeudwine's strategy. Each platoon in the line was designated either a 'garrison' or 'counterattack' platoon—any loss of territory to be immediately regained before the foe could consolidate. Still smarting from the events of November, the Divisional-Commander was determined that never again would his division face a similar situation. On receipt of the code word 'Bustle', reserves would rush to pre-prepared defensive positions, which they were expected to have reconnoitred beforehand.

The period of 20–22 February was quiet, though intermittent fire fell across the brigade sector and it was a rare day when Givenchy Keep was not shelled. The garrison was protected in deep-mined dugouts and three deep subways, two of which began at Moat Farm Redoubt, providing both accommodation and safe passage to the various keeps around the village. The only casualty from this fire was Rfn Thomas Flood, who received a slight wound to his right hand on the 21st.

On 23 February, enemy artillery became more active, particularly against Givenchy Keep, which was under fire for most of the day. Jeudwine, concerned that this was the prelude to an attack, ordered extra vigilance in the front line, and to boost the support positions further north, a platoon from 'C' was despatched to Cailloux Keep North. Hostile fire continued to be heavy on the 24th, targeting Givenchy and support positions, such as the Brewery, which was severely damaged by a number of direct hits. Fire slackened on 25 February, and that night, the battalion was relieved, moving to divisional reserve in Gorre. Rfn Albert Alsop—one of the January draft—is recorded wounded in the left thigh by shrapnel on 26 February, but was probably a casualty from the journey out of the line late on 25 February. He returned a month later.

The battalion remained in Gorre until 4 March, mostly training, though on 28 February they were inspected by the Divisional-Commander at Locon. As ever, there were accidents. On 28 February, Rfn James Wall suffered a knee injury, on only his second day with the battalion. Though he soon returned to duty, the injury kept recurring and most of his time with the battalion was spent in hospital, until he was returned to England four months later. Rfn Clifford Ellis suffered accidental burns to his scalp on 2 March and was evacuated home.

On 4 March, the battalion took over the right subsector at Givenchy. HQ occupied a dugout at the junction of Vauxhall Road and Pont Fixe Road; half of 'A' went into dugouts at Windy Corner, the rest at Pont Fixe; and the other companies manned the front line. The left bound was at Sap-A, occupied only at night, posts further back sheltering the garrison during the day. The left company manned from Sap-A to Finchley Road. The right bound of the centre company was at the end of Orchard Road, with the right company occupying positions from there to the canal. Their foremost post, aptly named Death or Glory Sap, projected 60 yards forward of the front line, facing the German-held Tortoise (the coordinates for this sap place it in the canal, as the canal bank was adjusted northwards during post-war reconstruction). The right company's HQ in Spoil Bank afforded a good view over German positions.

Aerial photographs from March 1918 present the sector as a cratered wasteland; however, photographs taken at ground level show otherwise. The canal had lost its water east of the lock, and although undoubtedly boggy, it appears crossable on foot; numerous surviving trees delineated roads behind British and German lines—many still bearing foliage—but of greatest relevance to infantry operations was the waist-high vegetation that covered the pitted surface of No Man's Land, dense enough to allow covert daylight actions. This was certainly a sector where slackness by sentries could be severely punished by the opposition and, equally, gave snipers opportunities to smite the unwary.

Little hostile activity faced the battalion on 4 March, although occasional shelling around Windy Corner was responsible for the gassing of L/Cpl Ernest Farries. The only man lost on 5 March was Rfn Walter Ardern, with the battalion for less than three weeks. His accidental shoulder injury resulted in a medical downgrading and transfer. Overnight patrols were uneventful, apart from considerable speculative machine-gun fire sweeping No Man's Land from a German position in the Duck's Bill Extension. The 'special patrols' all returned safely after dawn, having checked their own and the enemy's wire for breaches—the only item of interest was evidence of fresh excavations at the Tortoise.

On 6 March, Spoil Bank was targeted by six rounds of 15-cm, and Riflemen George Briggs and John Drinkald both suffered shellshock, and though Drinkald rejoined five weeks later, Briggs was medically downgraded and posted to the Base Depot.

The night of 6–7 March saw much heavier fire across the divisional front, especially opposite Le Plantin. This escalated in the early hours, providing cover for a large-scale raid against the 1/5th South Lancs at Barnton Tee at 5.05 a.m., resulting in the capture of sixteen out of the nineteen men in Post 2. Jeudwine was incandescent when he learned that only four of the rifles in the post had been fired; that the officer-led patrol had returned well before dawn; and that contrary to his (Jeudwine's) specific order, the 60-yard gap in the defensive wire in front of Post 2 was a two-day-old breach that had not been repaired. Although the GOC considered dismissing the CO, he decided that in view of the inexperience of the majority in that battalion, it would serve no practical purpose, other than to further demoralise them.

Hostile fire covered the raid and, during 7 March—when the divisional front was pounded for much of daylight—wounded three of the battalion. Neither L/Cpl Cyril Marsden, wounded in the back, nor Sgt James Williams (749), wounded in the right thigh, returned; Rfn William Pierce's face wound was less serious and he was back in May. The night was much quieter, and by 8 March, the situation had reverted to normal. Ten patrols were out across the divisional front during the night of 8–9 March, the battalion's reporting the sounds of work coming from behind Canal Trench, but no other evidence of enemy activity.

On 9 March, a battalion patrol discovered five German and one British skeleton in No Man's Land, and a German rifle, which was brought back ('skeletons' in Coordinates Table). The patrol then moved south, discerning the sounds of an enemy working party at the Tortoise, before returning to their lines. Ground observers in the battalion's line also reported a line of white tape just behind Canal Trench, stretching about 1,000 yards rearward, and this—coupled with increased enemy aerial reconnaissance—led Intelligence to believe that another raid, or even an attack, was intended. Jeudwine issued special orders, warning troops in the front line to be extra vigilant, and night patrols were increased. German fire increased during the afternoon of 10 March and a dozen 10.5-cm struck Orchard Keep at 4.10 p.m., followed twenty minutes later by a number of 10.5-cm on the Keep and Orchard Road. The only battalion casualty was Rfn Robert Evans (587), who received a 'Blighty' wound to the chest.

Enemy mortars targeted Orchard Road at 2.30 p.m. on 11 March, but no casualties ensued. One overnight patrol located a new enemy outpost 200 yards forward of the Tortoise—a sentry there firing white flares into No Man's Land throughout the night. There was another increase in enemy aerial activity on 12 March, but most of the hostile fire was to neighbouring subsectors. Observers managed a clearer look at the tape behind Canal Trench, reporting it had now been raised on 3-foot-high poles, one every 40 yards. That night, patrols described sounds suggestive of a relief under way in Canal Trench.

At various times during the morning and early afternoon of 13 March, Spoil Bank came under fire from 77-mm and 10.5-cm and it was probably these that were responsible for the two wounded Riflemen that day: Ernest Buckley was hit by shrapnel in the right thigh and evacuated home and twenty-two-year-old Frederick Longden affected by gas, spending nearly three months in hospital before being posted to the 1/5th. This was their last night in the line, as they were relieved in the early hours of the 14th.

Now in Support, the battalion moved to just north of the canal, south-west of Gorre, with part of the battalion in the Ferme du Roi. On 13 March, Jeudwine issued 'Operational Order 170'. To 55 Division's left, the line was held by the 1st Portuguese Division and the GOC was seriously concerned about their ability to hold, should the anticipated German offensive strike there. This order—to whichever brigade was in Divisional Reserve—gave notice that, between the hours of 5 a.m. and 9 a.m., they were to be on thirty minutes' readiness to support the Portuguese and one hour's readiness at all other times.[13]

At 7 p.m. on 14 March, the battalion received 'Bustle' and moved to the Tuning Fork Line, two companies going into the Village Line. 'Bustle' was cancelled at 9.30 a.m. and they returned to Gorre. German artillery had been active against the rear overnight and the battalion suffered two casualties. Thirty-year-old Rfn George Ford was only slightly wounded on 14 March, remaining on duty after the shrapnel wound to his neck had been dressed, but in the early hours of 15 March, twenty-seven-year-old Rfn John Rushton was killed. The 15th was also the last day at the front for 'original' Sgt Joseph Smith MM (036). The reason given in the *Casualties Book* for his home posting was 'war worn'. On 16 March, another of the 'originals', Rfn Thomas Fullerton, was admitted to the Field Ambulance, suffering from shellshock, and it was 11 May before he was deemed fit.

The 16th was their last day in Support, and at 10 a.m. the next day, they relieved the 1/5th South Lancs in the right subsector at Festubert. The left company was distributed among posts where the Barnton Road met the front line and the right company dispersed along Loop Road and Prince's Island; the support company occupied the 'B' Line, with the reserve company at Le Plantin. Battalion HQ went into a dugout in Le Plantin.

The battalion had been in position for less than an hour when thirty rounds of 77-mm struck Prince's Island, seriously wounding Rfn Percy Ellercott in the right arm. Hostile fire was mostly at a low level, other subsectors and the rear receiving the lion's share. Patrols found little to report upon, apart from occasional machine-gun fire and flares launched from the German front line. It was not until 19 March that further casualties were incurred, either from random fire or routine targeting of the night-time supply routes. Thirty-seven-year-old Rfn Amos Taylor and twenty-three-year-old Sgt Alexander Wallace were mortally wounded, both dying on 20 March. Rfn Sam Edgeley received a 'Blighty' wound to his shoulder, but the head wound of Rfn Joseph Cooper and elbow wound of Rfn Wilfred Holland—both of whom returned in May—were less serious. Although 20 March was another quiet day, three more were hit: Rfn William Ellison died at Lapugnoy on the 23rd and twenty-year-old Cpl Charles Bradshaw—another of the 'originals' and attached to the TMB—succumbed at Chocques on 21 March. Also attached to the TMB was twenty-seven-year-old Cpl James Dunn, who was killed outright.

At 5 a.m. on 21 March, a heavy bombardment of mustard gas continued for two hours and thirty minutes, resulting in twenty-one casualties from 'B'. Twenty-year-old Rfn William Carless was killed outright and thirty-year-old Rfn William Hargreaves died three weeks later. Of the nineteen wounded, only four returned.

Gas Casualties, 21 March 1918

2Lt Edmund A. Akerman		WIA	Rfn Charles F. Kingston	53456	WIA
Rfn William Bradley	51418	WIA	Rfn Edward Machin	49953	WIA
Rfn William Harold Carless	88864	KIA	Rfn Ernest Morris	308236	WIA
Rfn Henry T. Chater	11952	WIA	Rfn Roland Francis Parkinson	242823	WIA
Rfn John Edward Davies	52561	WIA			
Rfn Richard Davis	88867	WIA	Rfn William Ambrose Quayle	331983	WIA
Rn James Albert Garvey	380481	WIA			
Rfn Charles Graney	26672	WIA	Rfn George F. Rowe	51250	WIA
Rfn William Hargreaves	260026	DOW: 17/4	Rfn Richard Ruth	51110	WIA
Rfn Enoch Harris	266740	WIA	Rfn Sydney Tanner	201922	WIA
Rfn Albert Hesketh	88087	WIA	Rfn John William Wright	11952	WIA
L/Cpl Joseph Hume	64893	WIA			

Patrols on the night of 21–22 March reported large gaps in the enemy wire in front of Mackensen Trench. One patrol found the body of a recently-killed German in No Man's Land. Upon searching the corpse, the only items found were a field dressing and a letter, both of which were brought back. In the early hours of 22 March, a party of enemy were seen trying to mend the gaps in their wire and dispersed by Lewis gun fire. At 8.30 a.m., one of the battalion's snipers observed three men fixing a gap and was able to shoot one, the other two immediately going to ground. That night, a patrol found the enemy repairing this same breach and returned to direct Lewis fire onto them. Hostile artillery remained at a low key, with just the odd round hitting their subsector. The battalion spent 23 March preparing to hand over to the 1/5th, just the usual harassing fire causing minor difficulties. The only casualty prior to their relief at 8 p.m. was Rfn William Anderton, with contusions to his right arm. However, when it was X-rayed, his elbow was found to be fractured and he was sent home.

The battalion was once again billeted in Gorre, the usual training and working parties occupying them. On 24 March, while on a working party, Rfn Ernest Addison was wounded in the right thigh and evacuated home. Intelligence suspected an enemy attack for early on 26 March, and as a precaution, the battalion occupied the Village Line at 10.30 p.m. on the 25th, spending the night there before returning to Gorre in the morning. In the event, all stayed quiet, though Jeudwine remained convinced an offensive was imminent. The only casualty that night was Rfn Thomas McGann, who was gassed, returning to duty a month later.

At 8 p.m. on 27 March, the battalion relieved the 1/7th in the left subsector at Festubert. With the Portuguese to their left, the battalion's dispositions reflected the unease about their neighbours' ability to sustain a German attack. Only one company was deployed to the front line, distributed in posts around Canadian Orchard, Cover Trench, and Richmond Trench. The reserve company was in the Village Line at Festubert, positioned to react to any breakthrough from the north or the east. HQ was in a dugout near the centre of the village. The other two fighting companies were both to the rear of the forward company, placed to block infiltration from the left, the foremost centralised around the junction of the 'B' Line and Pioneer Trench, the other garrisoning Cailloux North and South.

Prior to midnight, more gas targeted the battalion, affecting eight men. Sixteen patrols were out across the divisional front, though those of the battalion were uneventful.

Gas Casualties, 27 March 1918

Rfn John Boyne	59448	Rfn James Ismay	405611
Rfn Martin Downey	308518	Rfn Charles Leeburn	307598
Cpl Jonah Gill	260049	Rfn Frederick William Reynolds	88274
Rfn Charles Godfrey	10427	Rfn John William Ward	88930

At 7.15 a.m. on 28 March, fifteen 10.5-cm rounds struck Canadian Orchard and nearby positions, slightly wounding 2Lt Kenneth Pocklington. More seriously hurt was Rfn H. Fowden, head and arm injuries ending his overseas service. Intelligence warned that information from 'other sources' reported that enemy officers had been observed studying a map and reconnoitring the ground 5,500 yards to the east of the battalion's right bound; another group of map-bearing officers was reported visiting the tower at Illies church, 6,500 yards from British lines—information that could only have strengthened Jeudwine's conviction that the offensive was imminent.

On 30 March, artillery and mortars from both sides engaged in harassing fire. The forward company's positions around Quinque Rue received a number of 77-mm and 10.5-cm shrapnel and gas rounds. L/Cpl Stanley Banks and Riflemen Thomas Briscoe, William Hogan, and William Keneley were all affected by the gas, though only Hogan was evacuated home. Artillery activity increased on the 31st, and all the rear came under short, intense bursts of harassing fire. The whole of the area occupied by the forward company came under sustained fire, resulting in another two gas casualties. Neither Rfn Arthur Furnival nor Rfn James Radford rejoined. Hostile fire slackened on 1 April, though at 9.30 a.m., three *Minenwerfer* rounds struck Canadian Orchard. With serious wounds to his left arm and buttock, 'A' Company's Rfn Edwin Stevenson was evacuated to England; Rfn James Downey's leg wound was treated in France, the Irishman returning in late May. Elsewhere, L/Cpl Harold Taylor, Rfn William Taylor, and Rfn Thomas Cunningham were gassed, all three later returning. The only other casualty was Rfn John White, with accidental injuries—numerous broken ribs, fractured scapula, and contusions to back and chest, suggesting his injuries were probably horse-related.

On 26 March, Divisional HQ made a precautionary move to just outside Les Chaudrons. A raid against a German post earlier that month had seized a map, upon which Divisional HQ in Locon was clearly marked. Further indications of an offensive were picked up on 1 April when an RAF aircraft spotted large troop concentrations heading towards La Bassée from Vendin-le-Vieil.

German guns were less active on 2 April, though another five were evacuated after exposure to mustard gas: L/Cpls William Blewitt, Charles Evans, and Joseph Levey and Riflemen James Corcoran and Daniel McCormick all eventually rejoined. Although night patrols were uneventful, one returned with information that stakes in a length of wire in front of Dover Trench had been marked with whitewash, indicative of a prepared exit point. There was little hostile fire directed towards the battalion for most of 3 April, though between 7 and 8 p.m., Festubert came under heavy gas bombardment, hospitalising Riflemen Samuel Kelly and James Rogerson. That night, another patrol—one of sixteen across the divisional front—revisited Dover Trench. Laying up just outside of the wire, they were able to report that between 11 p.m. and 5 a.m. of the 4th, they had heard the continual sounds of transport and the unloading of heavy material behind German lines—clear evidence of preparations. The gradual awakening of dawn brought no elucidation as mist shrouded enemy lines. Once again on 4 April, enemy artillery engaged in light harassing fire, a high proportion of which was Yellow-X. Riflemen Wallace Kitcher, Thomas Redmond, and John Ford were all treated for the effects, but the latter was the only one not to return. Overnight patrols heard further sounds of transport behind German lines, though visibility remained poor.

There was very little hostile fire on 5 April; nevertheless, 'C' Company's Rfn Charles Robinson received a 'Blighty' wound to his forearm. After dark, the battalion was relieved, HQ, 'B', and 'D' moving to Gorre Château. For 'A', ordered to remain in support for the 1/5th, and 'C', in support at Festubert Keep for the 1/7th, there was little respite. The next three days were quiet, the only loss on 6 April, when Rfn John Norton, attached to 164 TMB, was wounded, dying later that day.

On 6 April, 166 Bde was informed that they would be relieved the following night by 1 Division, 55 Division's sector being adjusted to north of the canal. It was planned that, once relieved, the Brigade would be able to replace the Portuguese on 9 April, and with this in mind, they were brought across the canal on 8 April, a decision that was to have huge significance the following day.

12

9 April 1918—28 July 1918: Kaiserschlacht

Coordinates for this Chapter

1/7th's HQ (Le Plantin)	50°32′3.50″N 2°44′32.60″E	Chelsea Bridge	50°31′56.40″N 2°42′18.30″E
Advanced HQ (9 April)	50°32′34.60″N 2°42′46.20″E	Cheshire Road	50°32′10.80″N 2°44′57.90″E
Barge House (approx.)	50°31′53.30″N 2°42′35.60″E	Coventry Sap	50°31′38.90″N 2°45′43.00″E
Barnton Road	50°32′29.50″N 2°44′35.30″E	Dead Cow Farm	50°32′44.80″N 2°44′49.60″E
Baron Post	50°31′54.30″N 2°43′28.50″E	ditch (Le Plantin road)	50°31′45.40″N 2°44′39.90″E
Bart Post	50°31′57.20″N 2°43′45.70″E	Duke Post	50°32′6.90″N 2°43′28.10″E
Battersea Bridge	50°31′41.70″N 2°43′15.40″E	'E' Keep (approx.)	50°32′45.00″N 2°43′8.00″E
Bayswater Trench	50°31′23.50″N 2°45′33.70″E	Estaminet Corner	50°32′20.80″N 2°43′41.40″E
Berkeley Street	50°31′45.90″N 2°45′37.00″E	Fanshawe Castle	50°31′29.50″N 2°44′35.70″E
Brewery Corner	50°32′58.10″N 2°44′19.20″E	Festubert Central	50°32′38.90″N 2°44′16.30″E
Cambridge Terrace	50°31′35.80″N 2°45′41.10″E	Festubert East	50°32′39.30″N 2°44′36.60″E
Cavan Lane	50°31′49.00″N 2°45′10.00″E	Festubert Switch	50°32′39.40″N 2°43′46.20″E
Charges Street	50°31′48.10″N 2°45′38.60″E	Finchley Road	50°31′33.20″N 2°45′43.20″E

George Road	50°32′15.50″N 2°45′9.40″E	Prince Post	50°32′9.60″N 2°42′56.20″E
German post (13 June)	50°32′4.00″N 2°45′1.50″E	Queen Post	50°32′25.20″N 2°43′19.50″E
Grenadier Road	50°31′49.40″N 2°44′54.40″E	Route 'A' Keep	50°33′1.30″N 2°43′24.40″E
Gunner Siding (July)	50°31′30.80″N 2°45′14.90″E	Southmoor Villas	50°31′46.70″N 2°45′0.70″E
Herts Redoubt	50°31′41.70″N 2°45′3.40″E	Tramway House	50°32′25.60″N 2°44′13.70″E
HQ (23 April)	50°32′11.70″N 2°43′52.80″E	Tuning Fork Keep	50°32′35.20″N 2°43′32.30″E
HQ (7 May)	50°31′33.10″N 2°43′45.50″E	Tuning Fork Switch	50°32′39.30″N 2°43′18.50″E
jctn Half Moon/ Piccadilly	50°31′50.00″N 2°45′34.70″E	Upper Cut	50°31′53.90″N 2°45′26.80″E
King's Road	50°31′46.80″N 2°45′26.40″E	Vauxhall Bridge	50°31′23.40″N 2°44′22.80″E
Le Plantin North	50°32′16.90″N 2°44′30.30″E	Ware Road	50°31′56.50″N 2°45′23.90″E
Lloyd's Avenue	50°32′14.30″N 2°44′34.10″E	Waterloo Bridge	50°31′49.20″N 2°42′46.30″E
Lone Farm	50°31′41.80″N 2°44′1.90″E	Willow Drain	50°31′34.30″N 2°45′49.50″E
Marais South-East Keep	50°32′3.80″N 2°43′39.20″E	Willow Road	50°32′12.60″N 2°44′34.50″E
McMahon Trench	50°32′48.20″N 2°44′13.90″E	Windy Terrace	50°31′44.00″N 2°44′44.00″E
Orchard Post	50°32′46.10″N 2°43′23.40″E	Wolfe Road	50°31′38.50″N 2°45′34.90″E
Piccadilly	50°31′48.50″N 2°45′30.05″E		

At 4.10 a.m. on 9 April, the enemy initiated a very heavy bombardment of all the division's trenches, batteries, and rear areas. Shortly after, Division was informed by the Portuguese that they too were under bombardment. Mixed in with the HE was phosgene, a gas that dispersed more rapidly than mustard, suggestive of a follow-up infantry action. At 4.34 a.m., Jeudwine ordered 166 Bde to their battle positions, and minutes later, 'Bustle' was sent to all units, who proceeded through the thick fog to their designated posts (contemporary documents refer to 'heavy mist', though as visibility was as low as 25 yards and only 40 yards at best, this falls under the modern definition of 'fog').

Immediately as shells began to explode around the billets at Gorre Château, men were roused, told to dress in 'battle order', and make their way to the trenches in nearby Gorre Wood. When 'Bustle' was received, 'B', 'D', and HQ made for their designated positions in single file, one platoon at a time. The first to leave was 2Lt Herbert Fitzgerald's 5 Platoon, who marched along the North Tuning Fork road to 'E' Keep. Fully aware of the road's importance, enemy artillery paid significant attention to it and 5 Platoon suffered half a dozen casualties before arriving at 6.30 a.m. No. 6 Platoon-Commander 2Lt James Pilgrim considered that there were better ways to travel than along a shell-rent road and, avoiding all hostile fire, he navigated his platoon cross-country to Route 'A' Keep, arriving at 7.20 a.m. Nos 7 and 8 Platoon under 2Lt Charles McLean and 2Lt Thomas Bride also used the North Tuning Fork road to access their adjacent positions in the Tuning Fork Switch, though both platoons arrived intact. However, soon after arrival, 8 Platoon came under heavy fire and 2Lt Bride was wounded, Platoon-Sergeant Francis Gloyne taking command—a task he accomplished so successfully that he received a Bar to his MM.[1]

'Bustle' did not go smoothly for all, as 14 Platoon's 2Lt Charles Cole reported:

> On the morning of the 9th inst., about 4.45, I was instructed by Capt. Rome to get the men of my platoon away from Gorre Château, which was being heavily shelled, to a place of safety along the Le Hamel road and proceeded to their quarters, where I gave them instructions where to rendezvous. When all the men had quitted the Château, I made my way towards the Le Hamel road for the purpose of getting them together, but when I reached the road leading round Gorre Château wood, I saw a party of men disappearing round the Y.M.C.A building and thinking they were loose, made my way after them.
>
> They were in fact loose and had been turned off by the shelling. When we had reached the football ground I called a halt and got them together, but despite many attempts, were unable to reach our rendezvous owing to shelling and gas. When it became light and the shelling less severe, we retraced our steps towards the Château and I put the men into trenches and proceeded with a runner (Rfn Walker) to the Château for any further orders which may have been given. Here, I learned that the Bn had gone forward to the 'Bustle' position. I went back, gathered my men and proceeded to my position in the Tuning Fork Line defences, where I found 2Lt Jackson already in position.[2]

Capt. Rome was wounded by artillery on the North Tuning Fork road, so 2Lt John Pilling took over; then, after he too was wounded, 2Lt Alfred Jackson took over 'D' Company (for which he was later recommended for the MC, though it was not sanctioned). Command of Jackson's 13 Platoon passed to L/Sgt James Williams (496).

HQ also suffered on the journey to their advanced HQ, situated in the Corps Signal dugout, behind a ruined farmhouse. While directing the detail into artillery formation, Capt. Albert Jones was killed by a shell; Capt. Blackledge taking over as Adjutant. 'D' took up positions along the Tuning Fork Line, with one platoon in the Tuning Fork Keep.

'A', in support of the 1/5th, and 'C', in support of the 1/7th, immediately 'stood-to' when the barrage began. The twenty-seven men of 1 Platoon, under 2Lt Wilfred Pegge and 2Lt

McDermott's 4 Platoon, occupied Festubert Keep; 2Lt William Skinner's 2 Platoon in McMahon Trench; and No. 3 Platoon, under 2Lt Joseph Dow, manned Festubert Central.

Under intense bombardment from shrapnel, HE, and gas, 2Lt Walter Williams's 10 Platoon 'stood-to' in their positions in the outskirts of Le Plantin, to the right of Willow Road. To his north was 2Lt Henry Miller's 12 Platoon:

> At 4.10 a.m. on the morning of the 9th, the enemy opened a bombardment of gas, shrapnel and HE. My platoon was in reserve at Tramway House. We immediately 'stood-to' awaiting orders. The Company-Commander, not receiving any word, intercepted some men running down the road and afterwards, I immediately received orders to take my platoon up to the Village Line. This I did, leaving my Lewis gun under the charge of the officer in charge of the Convent Observation Post and I received orders to place my platoon in the left flank of Le Plantin North, as this appeared to be the weak spot, being in position about 9.30.[3]

No. 9 and 2Lt Hubert Spary's 11 Platoon took up positions in Le Plantin North.

At 5.49 a.m., Division received a signal from IX Corps intimating that the bombardment may be a raid against the Portuguese, though the last message from their ally, received twenty minutes earlier, stated that there was no infantry action to their front. Jeudwine communicated with his brigadiers, who reported that, apart from the shellfire, all was quiet to their front. At 6.36 a.m., Corps and Division lost signals contact with the Portuguese, Jeudwine therefore ordered 166 Bde to establish contact and determine the situation, warning both 165 and 166 Bde to prepare against an attack from their left.

It is unclear at what time the enemy infantry assault actually began, though the attack on the left preceded that against 164 Bde, adjacent to the canal, which began shortly after 9 a.m. The first indication was the sound of intense small arms fire somewhere to the left, and around 8 a.m., large numbers of Portuguese appeared through the fog, fleeing to the rear in total disarray, many without weapons. Almost the entire Portuguese division had either surrendered immediately or bolted—their reserve brigade taking to their heels as soon as men from the front began to pass through them. Isolated pockets and one strongpoint, manned by men from the 10th Portuguese Regiment, bravely fought on alone until overwhelmed, leaving an enormous gap on 55 Division's left. The enemy poured though this breach, and the left company of 1/5th KORL, ordered up to Le Touret to reinforce the Portuguese, found themselves attacked from their front, left, and rear—the enemy appearing out of the fog just 25 yards from them. Although that company was overwhelmed, the other three put up a stalwart defence, eventually halting the German advance there.

Further south, 165 Bde came under heavy infantry attack shortly after 8 a.m. German guns and mortars had pounded the British front line into oblivion and these posts—suffering many killed or wounded—were overpowered when the enemy appeared out of the fog from behind, having curved south after penetrating the Portuguese line. The front and support lines fell by 8.15 a.m., and at 8.30 a.m., German troops were reported on Quinque Rue, just in front of the 'B' Line defences of the OBL. Soon after, the 'B' Line was attacked and the northern flank turned. An officer from 165 Bde, sent to rally the Portuguese, was forced to give up his efforts after being threatened with bayonetting.[4] At the 1/7th's HQ, word was received at 9.10 a.m. that Prince's Island had been captured, and at 9.30 a.m., the enemy reached George Road.

Sgt Ernest Hodgson of 9 Platoon recalled:

> My platoon officer, with one Sgt and a Cpl went out on patrol. The Sgt came back wounded and reported that the enemy were between the OBL and the front line. About 8 a.m. the mist lifted and it was then that we first caught sight of the enemy advancing towards us in extended order. My platoon officer then gave orders to fire.[5]

Second-Lieutenant Spary described his morning:

> At 4.10 a.m. on the morning of the 9th the bombardment opened by the enemy consisted of gas, HE and shrapnel. Realising that this preceded an attack, we stood-to in the breastworks at Le Plantin North. The only casualty was my platoon-sergeant.
>
> At about 7 a.m. the barrage lifted and nothing could be seen of the enemy, owing to a very heavy thick mist. From information gained from a patrol from the platoon, the enemy were in the OBL and a party of 125 were advancing towards our position.
>
> A little later, this party was seen advancing through the mist in extended order and I gave the order to fire. The enemy appeared to be taken greatly by surprise and the casualties were very heavy.
>
> The mist had by this time lifted and I took two L/Cpls out in front and brought in 44 prisoners and three officers. We made seven journeys out and each time brought in wounded, and also an MG and about 5,000 rounds of ammunition.[6]

Spary's 7 a.m. patrol was just himself and L/Cpl William Huggonson. The pair waited at the OBL until the enemy was almost on them before returning. Huggonson went out again later, and accounted for several of the enemy, who were sniping at them from shell holes, receiving the MM for this and his earlier patrol.[7] Although Spary failed to specify times, his later sorties probably occurred late morning—visibility only beginning to clear around 10 a.m., returning to normal around noon. Later that day, Spary was wounded in the back by shrapnel, but refused to leave his platoon for treatment until 13 April, earning an MC for his courage and determination.[8]

One of the two NCOs that Spary took forward later that day was L/Cpl Arthur McMillan. When their Platoon-Sergeant was killed, he had stepped into the breach, making an invaluable contribution to the effective action of the platoon. At one point, he had gone out single-handed during daylight to bring in a number of prisoners, and when ammunition began to run low, he dashed back through the barrage to collect more. His MM was hard-earned.[9]

No. 10 Platoon engaged the enemy from their position to the right of Willow Road, as 2Lt Williams reported:

The shelling continued without any developments until 7 a.m., when it appeared to lift. At 10 a.m., touch was obtained with the enemy, who were seen proceeding in the vicinity of Willow Road towards our position. Fire was immediately opened by Lewis guns and rifles. Patrols were sent out on my left and right. Observation was bad owing to a heavy mist which did not lift until midday. Heavy casualties were seen to be inflicted on the enemy.[10]

Sgt Henry Beale described 3 Platoon's action:

A heavy mist made observation very difficult and our own wire being invisible, a very keen lookout was kept. The mist lifted slightly and a small party of enemy infantry were seen advancing in the direction of McMahon Trench. Lewis gun and rapid rifle fire was immediately opened on them, inflicting casualties and dispersing the remainder of the party.

Shortly after, the operations extended to our own frontage and a small party of Germans were seen advancing with machine guns. The enemy opened fire, sweeping the parapet with his machine guns and casualties were inflicted upon the garrison.

The garrison opened rapid fire and the enemy was effectively quietened. The mist lifting, we were able to observe for a distance of ¼ mile, when two machine guns and a number of men (apparently dead) were seen lying outside our wire. A party of men went out, and on approaching the Germans, discovered them to be alive. A sharp fight ensued, in which we killed all but three, who were taken prisoner. Two machine guns were also brought in.[11]

Second-Lieutenant Skinner encountered the enemy around the same time:

After being bombarded by gas and explosive shells for 4 or 5 hours, the enemy were eventually seen advancing and after a continuous burst of Lewis gun and rapid fire, the remnants of the enemy were observed digging in immediately in front of our strong belt of wire, which was about 100 yards from the trench.[12]

Of the two companies in 'Bustle' positions around the Tuning Fork, only Pilgrim's 6 Platoon was in imminent peril, as Route 'A' Keep was forward of the other positions, their left flank wide open. In a bitter struggle, lasting less than two hours, his platoon lost half their men:

Up to 10 a.m., the Keep was heavily shelled with 5.9s and 4.2s. Owing to the heavy mist I could not see our wire, so I posted two sentries out near the wire. At 11 a.m., these men reported that the enemy was coming down the road singing and about 50 strong. When they got within 20 yards of the Keep, 1 M.G., 1 L.G. and 8 rifles opened fire and inflicted heavy casualties amongst them.

After very heavy bombing from my flanks, I was eventually driven out at 11.45, leaving one man behind (seriously wounded). Total casualties, 2 killed, 10 wounded. With the remaining 12 men I reported to Bn HQ and was detailed to report to [D Coy] 5th King's at Festubert and was then ordered to reinforce Festubert Central.[13]

The successful evacuation of so many wounded was quite a feat, Rfn Walter Poore showing tremendous courage during this phase. Already the recipient of the MM from his time with the Liverpool Irish, he carried one casualty from the keep to the safety of a shell hole, dressed his wounds, and returned for another. Under ceaseless machine-gun fire, he crawled to within 20 yards of the keep, retrieving another man. Pilgrim recommended him for the DCM, though it was downgraded to a Bar to his MM.[14]

With his meagre force, Route 'A' Keep was untenable for Pilgrim and no blame was attributed for withdrawing. In fact, he was recommended for the MC for his fine example during the heavy bombardment of Festubert Central and his energy and disregard to danger—repeatedly organising the rebuilding of the defences when they were obliterated by shellfire. Sadly, it was not approved.[15]

The only fire support for Pilgrim came from 5 Platoon in 'E' Keep, though as Sgt Silvester Morris commented: 'The enemy were fired on by the platoon at about 700 yards range during their attack on "A" Keep, but offered a very indistinct target'.[16]

At 11.25 a.m., 165 Bde informed Division that the whole of the OBL appeared to be in enemy hands, though the Village Line was holding. At 11.50 a.m., Lt Adam ordered 1 Platoon forward to reinforce the 1/5th in Cailloux Keep. Second-Lieutenant Pegge wrote:

> I reported to Mr Bond at Cailloux Keep and my Lewis gun section and one rifle section took up their position in Cailloux South. My other rifle section was put in Cailloux North. The enemy were then occupying shell holes about 60 yards from the wire in Cailloux South and about 100 yards to the left of Cailloux North. Heavy rifle and MG fire was brought to bear upon him and grenades were used to move the enemy from shell holes which were occupied.[17]

Second-Lieutenant D. McDermott was also ordered forward:

> I received orders to take my platoon to reinforce Festubert East. We proceeded to the trench in artillery formation, suffering two casualties on the way up. On my platoon reaching its position [2 p.m.] I reported to Capt. Russell of the 1/5th KLR. He placed me under the command of 2Lt Hamer, the OC of Festubert East.
>
> On our arrival in the trench we were just in time to catch an enemy MG team in our wire, firing through one of our MG emplacements into the trench. We killed all this team by our rifle fire, capturing the MG. The enemy bombarded us throughout the day with 15″ and 5.9 shells. When the mist cleared we caught large numbers of the enemy in the open on our left flank, many of which we killed with rifle and MG fire.[18]

'A' Company's other platoons remained where they were for the time being, as did all of 'C'.

In the late afternoon, the other three 'B' Company platoons were sent to further reinforce the 1/5th (6 Platoon was already with them). Sgt Morris reported:

> [No. 5 Platoon] remained at E Keep until about 5 p.m., losing 1 killed and 1 wounded during its occupation of the Keep. At about 5 p.m. (9th April) the platoon left the Keep

and moved up the North Tuning Fork Road to Festubert to reinforce the 5th KLR. On its arrival there, we were taken to a position about 400 yards to the north and shown a line of shell holes, which we were told was our position, thus forming a defensive flank facing north.[19]

At 6 p.m., 7 Platoon repositioned via Festubert Corner to form a defensive flank to the left. Sgt Gloyne reported a similar task for 8 Platoon on the right:

> Later in the day, about 5.30 p.m., we received orders to reinforce the 5th King's by Cailloux Keep. Our work was to form a defensive flank for Cailloux, McMahon and Festubert Keeps. We did this by connecting shell holes, thus forming a rough trench.[20]

'D' reinforced the 1/7th in the early evening, as indicated by 2Lt Cole:

> I remained in this position—the left of the north Tuning Fork Line—until the evening, when Capt. Blackledge came along and instructed me to gather the whole of the remaining men of D Company together and report to him at Bn HQ. I reported to him as instructed, stating that I had 50 NCOs and men with me, and I then received further instructions to report to the CO 1/7th KLR in the Village Line as quickly as possible. I made the journey by the North Tuning Fork road-Village Line without casualty and reported as requested. Here, the party was placed under the command of OC C Company 1/7th KLR and allotted a position lining the Village Line from Windy Corner to Le Plantin S., having connection with the Lancashire Fusiliers on the right and C Company 1/7th KLR on the left.[21]

Upon arrival, Sgt Williams's 13 Platoon was sited in a ditch on the Le Plantin road, just north of Windy Corner. Second-Lieutenant Sprigings's 16 Platoon remained in support, in open ground just behind the 1/7th's HQ in Le Plantin. The rest of 'D' were placed northwards along the Le Plantin road.

By now, the dangerous situation on the division's right was under control. During the morning, large numbers of enemy penetrated to Windy Corner and beyond, but a stubborn defence by 1/4th KORL, who refused to give up isolated posts—even when surrounded—and a series of counterattacks by them and the Fusiliers, regained all but one post in the crater field. Because of the danger posed here, the Rifles had been held where they were in case they were needed to plug gaps on the right. Consequently, no efforts had been made to retake Route 'A' Keep, though its German garrison was kept pinned down by rifle and machine-gun fire. It was intended to counterattack the Keep at dawn on 10 April, but the necessity of utilising two companies for this venture brought about its postponement.

Further north, hostile artillery fire against 165 Bde had been murderous and the vast majority of casualties were from this, though enemy sniping was also problematic. German infantry made a number of attempts to break the line during the evening. At 7.30 p.m., 1 Platoon repulsed an attempt to rush Cailloux South, driving off the attackers with well-directed bombs. No. 2 Platoon was also attacked:

> Nothing further happened, apart from our continuous sniping till dusk, when the alarm was given and after a short burst of rapid fire nothing could be seen, but a patrol being sent out, a badly wounded German was brought into the trench, where he expired. Nothing of importance was found on the body, beyond the usual identification and dry rations for the following day.[22]

All four 'A' Company platoons deployed numerous patrols overnight, men not occupied thus busy improving their makeshift defences ravaged by the bombardment. The 1/5th's report, written by Lt Hamer, records that 4 Platoon provided men for a small advance post in a ditch. This came under machine-gun fire from a gun situated somewhere to their rear—where exactly was never established—killing two and wounding one.[23]

In their somewhat exposed position on the left flank of Le Plantin North, 12 Platoon observed a party of enemy moving down the Barnton Road and engaged them with effective enfilading fire.

To the rear of the 1/5th, in the Tuning Fork Switch, was Liverpool Scottish, who had been brought up earlier that day and attached to 165 Bde. Although there was a gap between them and the 1/5th, it was well covered by machine guns and isolated posts in the gap. To the left of Liverpool Sottish, 166 Bde continued to hold, with 1/5th KORL and two companies of 1/5th South Lancs. The extreme left of the divisional line, up to the Canal de la Lawe, was held by the divisional-pioneers, three RE field companies, and 251 Tunnelling Company—all in an infantry role. To their rear, a battalion-sized composite force of Portuguese had been held at gunpoint by the HQ detail of 1/5th KORL, when they retreated through their position, warned that they would be shot if they tried to leave. Brig.-Gen. Kentish reported:

> The urgency of digging in on the line of the Loisne river appeared to me to be obvious and the Portuguese collected by the King's Own, being the only troops available, but at the same time showing a very ardent desire to withdraw to the rear, I sent Capt. Kerr my Staff-Captain and Capt. Abercrombie, my Brigade-Major, to organise them and warn them that any soldier attempting to retire would be instantly shot. This they did, and placing British officers and NCOs with them they were able to get them to carry out my instructions.[24]

In addition, every available man was collected from Transport Lines to boost defences, the line across the other side of the Lawe held by 51 (Highland) Division brought forward to plug the gap.

Fortunately, shellfire slackened during the night, but the relentless pounding had taken its toll, and as dawn rose on the 10th, 2Lt Sprigings learnt he was the only officer for 15 and 16 Platoon, as both 2Lt William Hutton and 2Lt John Pilling (doubling up as Company-Commander) had been wounded. Pilling had received a serious arm wound early in the afternoon of the 9th, but refused to be evacuated. However, during the night, he collapsed and was carried to the Aid Post, his arm later amputated. For his courage and determination, the young subaltern received the MC.[25] Sprigings was ordered to remain at the Bath House with his men, ready to immediately reinforce any weak point in the line.

At 4 a.m. on 10 April, the entire line 'stood-to' in case of a continuation of the assault, but no attacks were forthcoming. Patrols from each post remained out until it was light, and shortly after dawn, Sgt Hodgson took a couple of men forward, returning soon after with a German machine gun and a signal lamp—probably abandoned during the 8 a.m. attack of the previous day.

Initially on 10 April, enemy attempts to continue the offensive concentrated around Loisne, endeavouring to turn the division's left flank, where, at 7.40a.m., large numbers attacked under the cover of a heavy bombardment. Despite suffering heavy casualties, the garrison of Loisne had beaten off the attack by 9.30 a.m. Until the previous evening, Loisne Central had been held by twenty men of the RFA and a Lewis. Providentially, a company of Liverpool Scottish was sent to bolster the defence and it was they and a company of the 1/5th South Lancs who blunted this attack.

Around 10 a.m., artillery began to pound the battalion again, and between 11 a.m. and 2.30 p.m., the enemy made a number of half-hearted efforts to attack the Cailloux keeps and Festubert—easily beaten off by the 1/5th, with the help of 7 and 8 platoons. During this attack, 2Lt Charles McLean amazed his men by calmly walking from shell hole to shell hole, encouraging them on and directing their fire (he later led a party of men in a successful counterattack against one of the Cailloux keeps, earning the MC for these actions).

No. 4 Platoon in Festubert East were also attacked, as 2Lt McDermott reported:

> On the 10th we were bombarded continuously all day. An enemy party attempted to approach our position during the afternoon, but was driven off by our LG and rifle fire, leaving many dead behind him.[26]

Occupying an advance post on the right was L/Cpl Harry Thomas. He and his small party from 4 Platoon repulsed numerous attacks, though twice the enemy managed to enter their position. Thomas drove them back out again into the open with volleys of bombs, where they were dealt with by Vickers and Lewis fire. Later, he took a patrol out and personally brought back a German machine gun under enemy fire, receiving the MM for his courage.[27]

Hostile artillery continued throughout the day, and at 4 p.m., two 5.9 rounds hit 1 Platoon in Cailloux South, knocking out the entire Lewis Section and half the Rifle Section. Rfn Thomas Elston, the No. 1 on the Lewis, was buried and the gun-NCO killed; after he was dug out, Elston took over, and despite being buried again, he insisted on remaining with the gun once he had been freed. His Lewis was still in action when the platoon was relieved on 13 April and he was awarded the DCM for his fine example.[28] On three occasions that day, the breastworks commanded by L/Cpl William Ledgerwood were flattened by shellfire. Each time, he showed considerable coolness and disregard to enemy fire as he organised their rebuilding, and when the NCOs in charge of two nearby posts became casualties, he took over their positions too. Ledgerwood successfully held all three positions against enemy attacks on the 11th and was recommended for the DCM, though this was later reduced to the MM.[29]

Sgt Beale's 3 Platoon, in Festubert Central, also took a beating from shellfire:

> Visibility was very good and we were subjected to a terrific artillery fire and more casualties were inflicted upon the garrison. Reinforcements arrived at dusk and they, with the remainder of the garrison, proceeded to rebuild our battered breastworks. Patrols were sent out at night, but encountered no enemy parties.[30]

Fearsome though this bombardment was, it paled into insignificance compared to that at 6 a.m. the following morning—its scale described by Beale as 'unprecedented'.

During the day, the gap between Festubert and the Tuning Fork was effectively plugged by the construction of two posts: Orchard Post and an unnamed post between Tuning Fork Keep and Festubert Keep. The 'unnamed post' (in coordinates table as Festubert Switch) prevented enemy intrusions between Route 'A' Keep and Festubert. As if German fire was not bad enough, twice that afternoon four RAF aircraft bombed and then machine-gunned Brigade positions (No. 2 Squadron had been given the incorrect position for British lines).[31]

At 6.47 p.m., the whole Village Line came under very heavy Howitzer fire, and at 7 p.m., the enemy attacked Loisne, gaining a temporary foothold before being driven out—twenty-one Germans and two machine guns being captured. Just after 8 p.m., 165 Bde HQ lost contact with both Cailloux keeps and Festubert East and became concerned that these positions, whose defences had been practically obliterated by the day's shellfire, had been taken. Fortunately, this was not the case and contact was regained by runner thirty-five minutes later. The defences of Cailloux North, however, were considerably weakened: two Vickers, a pair of Lewis guns and their crews, having been annihilated. Further south, Sgt Williams took out a ten-man patrol from 13 Platoon along Cheshire Road, as far as the OBL, finding the enemy holding in strength just to the east. That night, the Tuning Fork was reinforced by a company of 13/KLR and six additional Vickers.

Forward Observers reported enemy infantry massing south of Le Touret, and divisional artillery was brought to bear on the area. On the Division's extreme left around Mesplaux, the situation became grave during the late morning, the overstretched defenders gradually being pushed back, though the line eventually held.

The 165th Bde's positions came under heavy artillery fire soon after dawn on 11 April, resulting in numerous casualties. No. 4 Platoon in Festubert East lost three Vickers and a Lewis to shellfire. Commander of 5 Platoon, 2Lt Herbert Fitzgerald, was seriously wounded by a low-bursting shrapnel shell, dying soon afterwards. Although 'SDGW' denotes him as 'KIA' and CWGC record him for 9 April, Platoon-Sergeant Silvester Morris and 2Lt McLean both attest he was 'wounded' during the morning of 11 April.[32] Another loss was 3 Platoon's 2Lt Joseph Dow: badly gassed during the journey forward on 9 April, he had clung on as long as possible, but allowed himself to be evacuated that evening. Sgt Beale took over and was later awarded a DCM for his leadership. Every time shells blew away

3 Platoon's breastworks, Beale calmly organised their rebuilding in a slightly different location, husbanding his men as best he could.[33]

Although McDermott attributes the following action to the 12th, he was in error and the events are from 11 April (he may be forgiven as he was writing in mid-August):

> At dawn on the morning of the 12th, [*sic*] we dispersed an enemy working party by rifle fire. During the afternoon of the 12th, [*sic*] the shell fire reached such a pitch as to make the uninhabitable, as we only had two fire bays left. The OC [Lt Hamer] decided to leave this position and occupy Festubert East Support. We were just leaving the trench when we were attacked by the enemy from the rear and right flank. We put out a party of 1 MG and about six riflemen to cover our withdrawal and the enemy were successfully driven off.[34]

Once again, 1 Platoon came in for punishment:

> At 7.10 a.m., the enemy opened heavy artillery fire on Cailloux South, which continued until 11 a.m. The shelling was renewed at 12.30 p.m. and was kept up till close on 4.30 p.m.
>
> Cailloux North was then attacked from the left flank and the defenders withdrew into the shell holes. A party of 25–30 enemy, assisted by their bombers, forced their way into Cailloux South, coming in from the bushes on the right flank. Our artillery opened on Cailloux and the remainder of the garrison in the South Keep occupied the shell holes in front of the Village Line during the shelling.[35]

The last to leave Cailloux North were 2Lt Pegge and L/Cpl John Tilley—the only two of the garrison not to be killed or wounded. They hurled bombs at the attacking enemy, until overwhelming odds forced their withdrawal; both participated in the later counterattack, with Tilley receiving the MM.[36]

To augment their Howitzers, the Germans brought up a number of 77-mm, which very effectively engaged British positions over open sights. No. 8 Platoon, in its shell holes to the flank of Cailloux, gave as much fire support as possible, but were unable to stop the attack. In McMahon Trench, 2 Platoon also engaged a party of approximately fifty, who were advancing southwards to the right of Cailloux Keep.[37] When Cailloux South fell, Lt John Little and CSM Edward Chatten manned the small OP at Brewery Corner, just 50 yards away. The pair kept up continuous, accurate rifle fire against the infiltrators, inflicting severe casualties and effectively preventing them consolidating—remaining there until the foe brought artillery to bear against the ruined house that was the OP. Another rewarded for his courage was Sgt Henry Dodd, who, after the wounding of CSM John Tennant, became acting CSM. Due to the shortage of officers, he too commanded a party during the later counterattack, earning a Bar to his MM.

The officer in charge of the 'unnamed post', 2Lt Lester Shaw of the Liverpool Scottish, showed considerable initiative when the two Cailloux posts fell, taking his men forward to keep the enemy in Route 'A' Keep pinned down.

As soon as they were informed of this loss, Divisional Howitzers bombarded both Cailloux posts and Lt Adam organised a counterattack, with a composite force from 1, 7, and 8 Platoons. Unfortunately, some Howitzer rounds fell short, forcing men in the shell holes to pull back slightly until the guns ceased fire at 7 p.m. and the counterattack began. Lt Little commanded the right flank of the attack and CSM Chatten, standing in the open as he hurled bombs at the enemy, inspired all. The simultaneous arrival of two platoons from 13/KLR to the west of Festubert—ordered up there by Lt-Col. McKaig—helped encourage enemy withdrawal. No Germans were captured, though they left four dead behind when they retreated. The remainder of the night was spent strengthening the defences in the keeps. Adam and Little were awarded the MC and Chatten the MM.[38]

In the early hours of 12 April, 'A' and 'B' were relieved by 13/KLR and went to Tuning Fork North. HQ was also relieved, returning to Gorre Château, with Lt-Col. McKaig assuming command of the Gorre defences—though this was short-lived. Although the château itself was heavily shelled between 7 p.m. and 8 p.m., no casualties resulted as the men had been kept clear of this obvious target.

Losses had been considerable, and although most platoon reports did not detail their losses, 2Lt Pegge was the exception:

> My losses were as follows:
> Killed: L/Cpl [Andrew] Speedie, Rfn [Charles] Bowen, Rfn [Herbert] Butler, Rfn [Thomas] Geraghty, Rfn [Thomas] Clague.
> Died of Wounds: Rfn [Charles] Moorhouse, Rfn [James] Clulo, Rfn [John] Ritchie
> Wounded: Sgt [Henry] Daniels, L/Cpl [Thomas] Barrow, Rfn [Clement] Jones
> Shell shock: Rfn [Frank] Roberts [recorded WIA with contusions to the head]
> Missing: Rfn [Harry] Banks.[39]

Though most casualties were listed for 9 April, based on platoon reports, many actually occurred on other dates.

One man of interest from above is nineteen-year-old Charles Bowen. As Pegge reported him as 'killed', this was clearly confirmed, unlike Banks, whose death was then unknown. It is inconceivable that the five 'known dead' were not given a battlefield burial, their subsequent lack of a known grave hardly surprising given the intensity of later fighting. What does beggar belief is Bowen's supposed burial in Serre Road No. 2 on the Somme—the idea that his body was discovered at Festubert in 1920, then taken to the Somme for reburial is frankly ludicrous. A study of the Graves Registration form for Plot 1, Row 'E', at Serre No. 2 shows that initially the body was attributed to '1943 Bowen Pte'. The typed '1943' was later crossed out and '88851' written in.

Sadly, despite forwarding comprehensive evidence to CWGC, it was decided insufficient to categorically prove that it is not Charles Bowen at Serre. Unfortunately, the tag detailing the information used to identify the body was buried with him, though I suspect a semi-legible marking on a piece of kit provided the name 'Bowen' and the number '1943'. This number is significant as '19435' Pte Robert Bowen of 2/Yorkshire Regt was killed near

Serre on 1 July 1916 and has no known grave—it is not unreasonable to assume that he is the actual occupant of Grave 11.

Throughout their time under fire, 'B' Company's Lewis-NCO, Cpl Frederick Joughin DCM, repeatedly left cover to visit the guns in his company, checking their condition, and whenever guns suffered complicated stoppages—however heavy the fire—he left cover to rectify the problem, keeping all the guns in action. For his invaluable services, he was recommended for an MM, though it was not approved.[40]

At 9.30 p.m. on 12 April, HQ moved to Le Plantin North to relieve the 1/7th's HQ, and though they were shelled on the way forward, they avoided casualties: 'A' and 'B' returned to the Tuning Fork Switch. On the night of 13-14 April, 'C' was ordered to join 'A' Company of the 1/7th in the Tuning Fork Line; 'D' moved to the Village Line to relieve 'C' Company of the 1/7th (contemporary records exhibit considerable contradictions, regarding company locations for the 1/6th between 13 and 15 April. The positions described here are taken from individual platoon reports).

German guns continued to seek out targets across the divisional front and further casualties ensued. No. 14 Platoon in the Cheshire Defences (midway between Le Plantin North and South) were bombarded by 5.9 and 8-inch shells, one blowing 2Lt Cole to the ground and wounding him in the face. Picking himself up, the young subaltern insisted on remaining and continued to encourage his men on, only accepting treatment when the platoon was relieved on the night of 15-16 April. Although recommended for the MC, it was not approved.[41] The ferocity of enemy shellfire may be gauged by words, such as 'unprecedented', which, coming from men who had experienced the wrath of German artillery on the Somme, Ypres, and Épehy, is some testament.

Every available body was fed into the line when the scale of the assault became understood, whatever their experience. Recently-commissioned John Lowe and James Fenn arrived from England late on the night of 13 April and were immediately put to use in the OP at Danesbury House, to the right of Lloyd's Avenue. Next morning, the pair were sent to join 'D', Lowe getting 15 Platoon.

Under such heavy fire, it took a special brand of courage to brave open ground—valour exemplified by runners, stretcher-bearers, and supply parties on a regular basis. By the end of 9 April, the only remaining runner from 'B' was Rfn George Rogers. Notwithstanding the fate suffered by his comrades, for the whole time 'B' manned the line, he continued to defy shell and machine-gun fire to ply his trade, despite his utter exhaustion. His courage and fortitude were rewarded with the MM.[42]

Two stretcher-bearers similarly recognised were Riflemen John Mayors and John Cullen. Mayors, already the holder of the MM, showed extraordinary courage on 9 April. The ferocious bombardment resulted in many casualties in his section of trench—held by a joint force of the battalion and the 1/5th—and he treated many wounded from there. Once these were dealt with, he left cover to search for additional casualties, bringing several back, who would undoubtedly have died had Mayors not found and treated them. For eight hours he endured these risks, until a bursting shell severely wounded him in the thigh.[43] His selfless actions resulted in a Bar to his MM. At thirty-six, John Cullen was the oldest in 2 Platoon and designated a stretcher-bearer. Acting entirely on his own initiative, he established a small dressing station to the rear of McMahon Trench, where he attended men from many units. When time allowed, he brewed dixies of tea, and despite heavy fire, he carried the precious brew to the exposed advanced posts. Despite exhaustion, Cullen maintained this service without rest over four days.[44]

Although not in the firing line, 'C' Company cook L/Cpl George Marsden was still in great risk at Le Plantin. On 9 April, his cookhouse received a direct hit and, although he was unwounded, the cookhouse was destroyed. Rescuing what he could from the debris, he set about building another. Almost immediately, this was destroyed, the only salvageable items being three dixies. Despite these limitations, he succeeded in supplying hot food at all times during the day and night, bringing up and cooking the rations under exceptionally heavy fire for six days. As his citation avowed; 'His untiring efforts undoubtedly helped very considerable in keeping the men fit to stand the heavy shellfire to which they were subjected'.[45]

Transport-Sergeant William Burbage was recognised with the MSM:

> His services were valuable in organising parties for carrying bombs and S.A.A. through heavy shelling, and in supervising the distribution of them on arrival to the front line troops. He was responsible for the successful carriage of rations and tea to the most advanced posts.[46]

Also acknowledged was A/RSM Arthur Robinson. As a 'warranted' rank, this meant the MC:

> This Warrant Officer showed continuously the highest qualities of courage and devotion to duty under fire. When the enemy's advance threatened the left of the position he collected the Battalion Headquarters details, formed a defensive flank with them, and succeeded in stopping the enemy's advance.
>
> His knowledge of the position of bomb, S.A.A. and water dumps was of the greatest help, and he worked at distributing these for three days and nights under extremely heavy shellfire.
>
> On one occasion he remained at a bomb store in a house and issued bombs to our counter-attacking parties for half an hour after the house had been fired by an incendiary shell. This action was of invaluable assistance in maintaining the supply.[47]

Capt. Blackledge, though recommended for the DSO, was awarded a Bar to his MC for his work as Adjutant, which included a number of reconnaissance missions made at great personal risk.[48] It is probable that the MMs for Rfn Harry Evans (808), Sgt Alexander McKnight, and Cpl Thomas Morris (887) were also awarded for this battle, though their citations have not survived.

After relief on the night of 15–16 April, the battalion marched to Beuvry, where they boarded lorries for Auchel, remaining in billets there, training and refitting until the 23rd.

In total, the battalion suffered 212 casualties, fifty-seven of whom were fatalities. Both those reported missing turned up a month later, though the *Casualties Book* does not elaborate as to where they had been. No disciplinary action was taken, so they must have been 'claimed' by another unit. Four men were captured, but no records survive to indicate if they were wounded prior to this. Of the 149 wounded, ten were from gas, three with shellshock, and 136 with penetrating wounds. Nineteen of the casualties were 'originals'. One man not in the table below is Rfn Thomas Reynolds—also an 'original'—who shot himself in the foot on 11 April. His FGCM sentenced him to the standard fifty days' field punishment. Most 'originals' still ranked 'Rifleman' were in Transport or Stores, so it is possible his weapon handling may have been somewhat 'rusty'. Another not in the table is Sgt Thomas Page. He was admitted to hospital on 18 April, suffering from shellshock—undoubtedly due to the pounding between 9 and 15 April—his condition severe enough for medical discharge.

Casualties, 9-14 April 1918

Rfn Alfred Felix Aberg	88842	DOW: 10/4
Rfn James Abram	242702	WIA: 9/4
Rfn William Ankers	46730	WIA: 9/4
Cpl Colin James Macbeth Bain	240633	WIA: 9/4
Rfn Harry Banks	242817	KIA: 9/4
Rfn Sidney Bann	241690	WIA: 9/4
L/Cpl Thomas William Barrow	241828	WIA: 9/4
Rfn James Louis Barton	64779	KIA: 9/4
Rfn Thomas Frederick Beatty	12739	Gas: 10/4
Sgt Edward Benson	330512	WIA: 9/4
L/Cpl Reginald Bibby	265799	SS: 11/4
Rfn William George Binnall	260051	KIA: 9/4
Rfn Harold Birkett	88844	WIA: 9/4
Rfn Hugh A. Blunt	85314	WIA: 9/4
Rfn Ernest Booth	88845	WIA: 9/4
Rfn Charles Ernest Bowen	88851	KIA: 9/4
Rfn Joseph Bowne	241520	WIA: 9/4
2Lt Thomas Bride		WIA: 9/4
Rfn Cecil James Brookes	88850	WIA: 9/4
Rfn James Henry Brown	242836	Gas: 9/4
Rfn Frederick Burdett	84823	WIA: 9/4
Rfn Jeffrey Burke	306586	WIA: 9/4
L/Cpl Arthur George Burne	268380	KIA: 9/4
Rfn John Henry Burrows	242650	WIA: 9/4
Rfn Herbert Butler	88836	KIA: 9/4
Rfn Thomas Carey	51410	WIA: 9/4
L/Cpl Arthur Ernest Carr	243895	KIA: 9/4
Rfn Vincent Joseph Christian	49502	WIA: 9/4
Rfn Thomas Edwin Clague	51430	KIA: 9/4
Rfn Henry Clayton	88858	WIA: 9/4
Rfn Albert Clifton	85363	KIA: 9/4
Rfn Edgar Clowes	241148	WIA: 9/4
Rfn James Clulo	269612	DOW: 11/4
2Lt Charles Frank Cole		WIA: 14/4
Rfn Harry Collinson	72524	WIA: 9/4
L/Cpl James Connolly	51805	Gas: 9/4
Rfn George Benjamin Copley	268342	WIA: 9/4
Sgt Henry Cornall	305976	WIA: 9/4
Rfn Henry Coulthard	203275	WIA: 9/4
Rfn John Davies Cowan	240089	WIA: 11/4
Rfn Charles Douglas Cowles	85415	WIA: 9/4
Rfn John Craddock	242842	WIA: 9/4
Rfn James Daley	240310	WIA: 9/4
Sgt Henry Daniels	241673	WIA: 9/4
Rfn Stanley Davenport	88869	KIA: 9/4
Rfn Charles Davies	13438	WIA: 9/4
Rfn David W. Davies	51385	WIA: 9/4
L/Cpl John Davies	240847	Gas: 9/4
Rfn John I. Davies	54471	WIA: 9/4

L/Cpl William Edward Deacon	267210	WIA: 9/4
Rfn James Dearden	380540	KIA: 9/4
Rfn Leo Delaney	23172	WIA: 9/4
Rfn William Dewhurst	305710	KIA: 9/4
Rfn Arthur T. Dodd	88870	WIA: 9/4
Rfn Hilton Donnelly	88871	DOW: 15/4
Rfn Harry A. Doran	380095	WIA: 9/4
2Lt Joseph Alexander Dow		Gas: 9/4
Rfn Charles Dower*	41622	MIA: 9/4
L/Cpl Arthur Draper	50998	WIA: 9/4
Sgt Samuel Dresser	7617	Gas: 9/4
Rfn William Charles Duckett	240256	WIA: 9/4
Rfn John Easterby	49718	DOW: 14/4
Rfn Alexander Edwards	307880	WIA: 9/4
Rfn F. Ellis	265881	WIA: 9/4
Rfn Charles Saville Elsy	49935	WIA: 9/4
Rfn Fred Elvey	87244	WIA: 9/4
Rfn James Entwistle	90388	KIA: 9/4
Rfn William Evans	88879	WIA: 9/4
Rfn Arthur Everall	380077	WIA: 9/4
Rfn Charles Fagan**	307337	WIA: 9/4
Rfn John Fairclough	240438	WIA: 9/4
Rfn James Farrell	86649	WIA: 9/4
Rfn Michael Feeney	307113	KIA: 10/4
Rfn Albert J. Fellows	50000	WIA: 9/4
2Lt Herbert Fitzgerald		KIA: 11/4
Rfn Richard J. Fitzsimons	86687	WIA: 9/4
Rfn Alfred Fletcher	202548	WIA: 9/4
Rfn James Fletcher	242720	KIA: 9/4
Rfn Thomas Flood	48963	KIA: 9/4
Rfn John Foster	243798	KIA: 9/4
Rfn Albert Freer	88280	WIA: 9/4
Rfn Frank Gale****	88886	KIA: 9/4
Rfn Joseph Gale	34958	WIA: 9/4
L/Cpl Frank Gascoigne	240389	WIA: 9/4
Rfn George Gascoigne	242089	WIA: 9/4
Rfn Thomas Geehan	407016	WIA: 9/4
Rfn Thomas Geraghty	50583	KIA: 9/4
Rfn John Gillibrand	48811	WIA: 9/4
L/Cpl Victor Glover	88887	WIA: 9/4

Sgt James Thomas Gooderham	381446	KIA: 9/4
Rfn John Gorick	90971	WIA: 9/4
Rfn W. O. Gough	59539	WIA: 9/4
Rfn Alfred M. Hagerty	43480	WIA: 9/4
Rfn Archibald Malcolm Haig	51830	DOW: 11/4
Rfn Cuthbert Hall	242694	WIA: 9/4
Rfn Harry Halpin	94272	WIA: 9/4
Rfn Hugh Ragsdale Hammersley	309020	WIA: 9/4
Sgt John Simon Hancock	241604	KIA: 9/4
Rfn Alfred Hanson	49745	WIA: 9/4
L/Cpl James Harding	13845	WIA: 9/4
Rfn William Harris	242663	WIA: 11/4
Rfn Stanley Harrison	86463	KIA: 14/4
Rfn Samuel Haw	87008	WIA: 9/4
Rfn James Hayes	36675	KIA: 9/4
Rfn Bernard Healey	50337	WIA: 9/4
Rfn Joseph Robert Heaney	242036	KIA: 9/4
Rfn William Thomas Herridge	204606	WIA: 9/4
L/Cpl Peter P. Holt	52145	WIA: 9/4
Rfn Thomas N. Hopkins	87204	WIA: 9/4
Rfn John Hornby	94270	WIA: 9/4
Rfn Cyril C. Horrobine	51014	WIA: 9/4
Rfn Louis Humphreys	51436	WIA: 9/4
Rfn James Hunter	94268	DOW: 12/4
Rfn Henry Hurry	235099	WIA: 9/4
2Lt William Stanley Hutton		WIA: 11/4
Rfn John Jackson	94289	WIA: 9/4
Rfn Robert James	94288	KIA: 9/4
Capt. Albert Edward Jones		KIA: 9/4
L/Cpl Clement Joseph Jones	270116	WIA: 9/4
Rfn George Jones	94274	KIA: 9/4
Rfn Henry Jones	242897	WIA: 9/4
Rfn George Kellett	87243	WIA: 9/4
Rfn Harold Kelly	94281	WIA: 9/4
Rfn Charles Barker Kendall	240174	WIA: 9/4
Cpl Leslie Kenrick	200363	WIA: 9/4
Rfn Joseph William Kightley	85369	WIA: 10/4
L/Cpl Charles Henry Lucock	240379	WIA: 9/4

A/Cpl Henry Neal Malone	240378	WIA: 9/4
Rfn John Henry Marsden***	242793	POW: 9/4
L/Cpl David Charles Marsh	240788	Gas: 10/4
Rfn Frederick Henry Marsh	25494	DOW: 17/4
Rfn Ernest Mason	240281	WIA: 9/4
L/Cpl George Edward Maycock	51147	WIA: 9/4
Rfn John Mayors	308388	WIA: 9/4
Rfn Alexander McDowell	332021	KIA: 9/4
Rfn Ernest Metcalf	85447	WIA: 9/4
Rfn Charles Ernest Moorhouse	330824	DOW: 9/4
Rfn William John Morgan	64955	WIA: 9/4
Rfn William Morris	240150	WIA: 9/4
Rfn Tom Morton	56408	WIA: 9/4
Rfn Patrick Mullins	85470	KIA: 9/4
Rfn Arthur Swale Myers	32623	KIA: 9/4
Rfn James Nolan	305222	WIA: 9/4
Rfn James Nuttall	91460	WIA: 9/4
Sgt William O'Hare	94284	WIA: 9/4
Rfn Herbert Palmer	242869	KIA: 9/4
Rfn Fred Parkinson	88088	KIA: 9/4
Rfn John Peebles*	331917	MIA: 9/4
Rfn Egbert L. Philson	51442	WIA: 9/4
Rfn William John Pickett	381124	KIA: 9/4
2Lt John Francis Pilling		WIA: 9/4
Rfn Harry Pointon	85402	WIA: 9/4
Cpl Denis Joseph Powell	380712	WIA: 9/4
Rfn Albert Rankin	41446	KIA: 9/4
Cpl James Readdie	241755	WIA: 9/4
Rfn James Reid	41859	WIA: 9/4
Rfn Joseph Reil	203333	WIA: 9/4
Rfn David Ivor Richards	353010	Gas: 9/4
L/Sgt Thomas Arthur Riley	241058	WIA: 9/4
Rfn John Edward Ritchie	242765	KIA: 9/4
Rfn Bernard Roberts	32714	DOW: 12/4
Rfn Frank Roberts	242270	WIA: 9/4
Rfn Frank Henry Roberts	241695	WIA: 9/4
Rfn Thomas Charles Roberts	240860	WIA: 9/4
Rfn Robert Robertson	57567	WIA: 9/4
Capt. Thomas Edward Rome		WIA: 9/4
Rfn John Rose	13999	WIA: 9/4
Sgt Ernest Rowbottom	240365	WIA: 9/4
Rfn William John Rowlands	51121	WIA: 9/4
Rfn Stanley Ruscoe	56094	KIA: 9/4
Rfn Charles F. Rutz	88907	WIA: 9/4
Cpl Thomas Sadler	260047	KIA: 9/4
Sgt Hugh Sammond	22829	KIA: 9/4
Rfn Fred Sanderson	12167	Gas: 9/4
Rfn Polito Santos	50631	WIA: 9/4
Rfn Joseph Shone	201905	POW: 9/4
Rfn Francis B. Skuce	51107	WIA: 9/4
Rfn James Richard Slade	49969	WIA: 9/4
Rfn George Slobon	39077	WIA: 9/4
Rfn Frank James Slocombe	58049	KIA: 11/4
Lt Charles Ernest Smith		KIA: 13/4
Rfn Harry Smith	85032	WIA: 9/4
2Lt Hubert George Spary		WIA: 9/4
L/Cpl Andrew Speedie	38869	KIA: 9/4
Rfn Henry Spencer	85452	WIA: 9/4
Rfn Ernest Spink	50215	WIA: 9/4
Rfn Charles William Steen	241504	POW: 9/4
L/Cpl Joseph Cuthbert Sutton	241628	KIA: 11/4
Cpl Myles James Swinnerton	305596	WIA: 9/4
CSM John Charles Tennant	23843	WIA: 9/4
Rfn Clement Thomas	34398	KIA: 9/4
Rfn Evan Fraser Thoms	57576	KIA: 9/4
L/Cpl Frank Thoms	57577	SS: 13/4
Rfn William Tyrer	52831	KIA: 9/4
Rfn Albert Walker	308510	Gas: 9/4
Rfn Hugh Walker	50219	WIA: 9/4
Rfn William Michael John Ward	240845	POW: 9/4
Cpl Walter Webb	85920	WIA: 9/4
Sgt James Weightman	201507	WIA: 9/4
Rfn Joseph Wild	31433	WIA: 9/4
Rfn Henry William	49127	WIA: 9/4
Rfn Albert Williams	240309	DOW: 13/4
Rfn Ivor John Williams	41244	WIA: 9/4
Rfn Joseph Williams	200896	WIA: 9/4
Rfn Robert George Williams	241796	WIA: 9/4
Rfn Thomas J. Williams	84558	WIA: 9/4

L/Cpl Thomas John Williams	200696	WIA: 9/4	L/Cpl James Lancelot Woodward	51402	KIA: 9/4
Rfn Arthur J. Wilson	85180	WIA: 9/4	Rfn William Worswick	242774	WIA: 9/4
L/Cpl Stanley Wilson	240431	WAD: 9/4			
Rfn Henry Wood	51056	SS: 13/4			

* = turned up nearly a month later. ** = attached to Divisional HQ.

*** = attached to the TMB. **** = fatally gassed.

With over 3,000 casualties, 55 Division was considerably weakened, though the battalion received 206 reinforcements by the end of the month, two of whom were familiar faces: CSM Charles Argent and CSM John Moss had both been posted to 12/KLR on 1 April, but returned on the 22nd.

On 23 April, the battalion marched to Verquin and onwards to Verquigneul the following day. Training continued in the vicinity of the village, preparing for their return to the line on the 27th. That evening, they relieved Liverpool Scottish on the right at Festubert: 'A' took the left front, with 'D' in support to them; 'C' to the right front, with 'B' in support. HQ occupied a concrete dugout, 400 yards south of Estaminet Corner.

Their first night in the line was quiet: the only casualty on 27 April being Rfn George Lindsey, accidentally wounded in the right knee by a premature rifle grenade detonation. Between 6 p.m. and midnight on the 28th, considerable 'searching fire' by 4.2, 5.9, and 77-mm probed the left of the line as far back as Estaminet Corner. Festubert and Le Plantin were also targeted for much of the day by an 8-inch Howitzer, a round hitting every four minutes. A number of casualties ensued, the most severe being nineteen-year-old Rfn Jack Harrison, who died the next day, and nineteen-year-old Rfn William Jefferson, hit in the chest and right leg, dying on 4 May. Rfn Percy Blakey was wounded in the left hand; Cpl Henry Lane—another of the 'originals'—in the right arm; Rfn James Muir in the knee; and Rfn George Watson in the jaw. With the battalion for just ten days, Rfn John Hochkins was treated for lacerations to his forehead. Although he returned to duty a few days later, he was later admitted to hospital, suffering from epilepsy and was medically discharged. Patrols found little to report, apart from numerous German flares fired from Barnton Trench.

For much of 29 April, the enemy fired mustard gas into the battalion's subsector, though HE and shrapnel fire was reduced. L/Cpl Christopher Cope was wounded in the right foot by shrapnel, the other casualties were all from gas, and on 30 April, the continued use of gas resulted in a further losses.

Casualties, 29-30 April 1918

L/Cpl Christopher C. Cope	49917	WIA: 29/4	Rfn John R. Green	86677	WIA: 30/4
Rfn William Edwin Durant	306906	WIA: 29/4	Rfn James H. Hey	87062	WIA: 29/4
Rfn John B. Ewing	87270	WIA: 29/4	Rfn Robert Hodges	85970	WIA: 29/4
Rfn Edward Gossage	51256	WIA: 29/4	Rfn William G. Howard	85975	WIA: 30/4

Rfn George Isherwood	94273	WIA: 30/4	L/Sgt Arthur McMillan	242672	WIA: 30/4
Rfn Owen Jones	64878	WIA: 30/4	Cpl Walter O'Connor	242050	WIA: 30/4
2Lt John William Turner Lashmar		WIA: 30/4	Rfn Eugene Patrick Power	204358	WIA: 30/4
			Rfn George Wright	305721	WIA: 30/4

Hostile fire slackened on 1 May, and after dark, the battalion were relieved and moved to support. HQ went into a dugout 250 yards to the north-east of Battersea Bridge; 'A' were in Le Préol South (modern day Le Préolan); two platoons from 'B' held Marais South-East Keep, the others, nearby trenches; 'C' were in Le Préol North, north-east of Waterloo Bridge; and 'D' were based at the Tuning Fork Switch, south of Estaminet Corner. The break was brief, and after dark on 2 May, they returned to the left subsector at Givenchy. Unfortunately, while 55 Division had been out of the line, another German attack had seized the entire crater field and southwards, almost to the canal. Death or Glory Sap, though still British-held, was even more out on a limb.

'D', 'B', and 'C' held the front line. 'D' Company's positions, centred around Grenadier Road, now faced north due to the German gains of 9 April. 'B' Company's platoons orientated both north and east, were centred around Upper Cut. 'C' held the old front line, near Charges Street. Although 'A' were in support, their leading platoon in Ware Road was in the front line, sandwiched between 'D' and 'B'. HQ occupied a dugout on the Cuinchy road, 300 yards south of Windy Corner. Although the diary reports no casualties, records show that one of the 'originals', Rfn John Richards, was wounded by gas.

The diary refers to 3 May as a 'quiet day', with 'slight artillery activity', but between 3.15 p.m. and 4 p.m., it was anything but. In retaliation for divisional 'heavies' targeting the Crater Field, German 77-mm, 4,.2 and 5.9 fired upon 'A' Company in Herts Redoubt, Givenchy Keep, and King's Road. 'D' Company's platoons in Cavan Lane and Moat Farm were also hit, and *Minenwerfers* targeted Givenchy Keep and 'A' in Piccadilly. At various times during the day, an 8-inch Howitzer also fired into the subsector. Thirty-nine-year-old Rfn John Wilson was killed outright and Rfn John Jackson died from his head wound on 1 June (both from 'D'); also killed were twenty-five-year-old CQMS John Baines and Rfn Richard Davenport. CQMS Robert Hull was wounded in the face, shoulder, and foot—a 'Blighty' wound that ended his time with the battalion. Also wounded were 2Lt Hubert Kershaw, Rfn Samuel Southern—whose arm wound resulted in medical discharge—and 'original' Rfn James Burke, with contusions to his side and right arm. The loss of two CQMSs and an older man suggests the stores, adjacent to HQ, were hit. Night patrols found little to report, though enemy working parties, seen in Sap-K and Sap-I, were dispersed with Lewis and rifle fire.

There was only desultory shelling on 4 May; however, this changed the next day. Throughout the afternoon, an 11-inch Howitzer targeted Windy Corner and Moat Farm Redoubt—which was practically demolished, burying fourteen men, ten of whom were never recovered. The Redoubt, only 25 yards square, consisted of a concrete bomb and small arms ammunition store in the centre, surrounded by breastwork traverses. Some overhead cover was provided on the surface by a few half-elephant shelters, but the main refuge was a couple of deep dugouts. These provided good protection against a 5.9, but a direct hit by an 11-inch Howitzer round—probably fused to penetrate before exploding—was un-survivable and dugout and men were obliterated. The four who were dug out, three of whom were wounded, were probably in the adjacent trench, which was also badly damaged. The only man to rejoin was Rfn Richard Lea. Suffering shock and contusions, it was seven weeks before he returned, though fate was not to be denied in the long run.

Casualties from Moat Farm, 5 May 1918

Rfn Albert Ball	331810	WIA	Rfn Archibald Goodwin	99508	KIA
L/Cpl John Edwards Burke	240683	WIA	L/Cpl William Gore	51381	KIA
Rfn Harold Caldwell	85958	KIA	Rfn Clarence Hopkinson	86494	KIA
Rfn Edwin Chapman	86801	KIA	Rfn Richard Lea	405862	WIA
Rfn Edmund Evans	90378	KIA	Rfn Frank Leach Lynch	94293	KIA
Rfn Charles Edward Gamble	99507	KIA	Cpl James Parkinson	35960	KIA
Rfn Jack Gilliver	99509	KIA	Rfn Lewis Rimmer	241056	WIA

Throughout the night of 5–6 May, 77-mm and 4.2 targeted Windy Corner and Givenchy church. *Minenwerfers* sought out the garrisons of Moat Farm, Givenchy Keep, and Herts Redoubt between 8 a.m. and 9 a.m. on 6 May, and Moat Farm again at 3.30 p.m., another four being wounded: 2Lt McDermott's wound—suffered in Moat Farm—kept him from duty until late August; the foot wound of L/Cpl Richard Evans and thigh wound of Rfn Rowland George were 'Blighty' ones; though Sgt William McCudden, with contusions to his back, returned a month later. Also hospitalised, with severe hand injuries after a bomb accident, was Rfn John Rose. Although the battalion placed a listening patrol and one small reconnaissance patrol out overnight, their only report was hearing the sound of German sentries chatting to each other in Sap-K.

That night, the battalion were relieved and moved into support on the northern bank of the canal. 'A' manned Pont Fixe; 'B' and 'C' in Canal Bank (either side of Westminster Bridge); and 'D' in Windy Corner. HQ went to a dugout a few hundred yards down from the bridge. The battalion were not there long, marching to Beuvry on 8 May, where they travelled by bus to Vaudricourt. Their stay in support had been long enough to suffer another four casualties from 'D'. Twenty-six-year-old L/Cpl George Thomas was killed outright; Cpl George Alexander was wounded in the face, arm, and chest and eighteen-year-old Rfn John Morton was wounded in the head—both died on 9 May; and Rfn Fred Myers was wounded in the head, back, and legs and evacuated home.

The morning of 9 May was taken up with training, and during the afternoon, they marched to Labourse. At 10.30 p.m., the battalion was told to prepare for 'Bustle' and 'stood-to' from midnight to 8 a.m., on thirty minutes' notice to move; at noon, this was increased to two hours' notice and the battalion was able to resume training on the 11th.

It was not until the night of the 14th that they returned to the line, this time to the left subsector at Festubert. The only casualty up until midnight was Mancunian Rfn Abraham Lazarovitch, who received a minor wound to the hip. In this subsector, most platoons were placed to defend an attack from the left flank. 'D' were the right front company, though three of their platoons were actually arraigned along the defensive line south of Estaminet Corner, with only one to the rear of Festubert, facing northwards, to the east of 'B' Company. The actual east-facing front line was held by five Lewis sections. 'D' were around Cailloux, three of their platoons aligned northwards, the other holding four posts in the front line. 'C' Company's platoons were grouped around Estaminet Corner itself, with Battalion HQ in the South Tuning Fork Road.

Enemy artillery fire increased on 15 May, the effects mostly felt in other sectors, nonetheless, the battalion suffered four casualties: twenty-two-year-old 2Lt Walter Williams and eighteen-year-old Rfn Leonard Malkin were both killed, and Rfn John Fisher was wounded in the right hand and Rfn Joseph McDevitte in the thigh, hand, and ankle. Intelligence believed, based on reports from escaped prisoners, the resurgence of German fire was to disguise the withdrawal of guns—increasing the rate of fire of the remaining batteries to mask this. Just in case it was prescient of a renewed offensive, eighteen patrols entered No Man's Land overnight.

Although artillery fire remained heavy during the night, it was focused further south and the battalion escaped without loss. The 16th was quiet, though Estaminet Corner was shelled at various times during the morning and afternoon. That night, the battalion was relieved and moved into support, with 'A' and 'D' in Le Préol North, 'B' in the Tuning Fork Line, and 'C' in the Lone Farm locality. HQ occupied a dugout near Battersea Bridge.

At 2.30 a.m. on 17 May, the sounds of considerable movement of transport was heard from behind enemy lines, activity that continued until 4 a.m. Apart from a few Blue-X shells on Cailloux during the night, there had been little enemy fire, but at 4.15 a.m., this all changed, when the enemy barraged the whole divisional front. This lasted for twenty minutes, but no infantry attack followed. The only battalion loss casualty was Rfn William Bourne, who was killed. The remainder of that day saw only light harassing fire in the forward areas, though German artillery continued to bombard battery positions.

On 18 May, the battalion returned to the right subsector at Festubert. 'B' took the left front, with 'D' in support. The right front was manned by 'C', with 'A' in support and HQ in Duke Post in Addison Road. Four Riflemen were wounded on 18 May, two of whom were attached to 419 Field Company RE at the time. Thirty-year-old Martin Downey was seriously injured in the right arm and evacuated home; Lewis Martin's eye wound was minor, but he was posted to the 1/5th after leaving hospital; and Alfred Royden's chin wound was insignificant and he was back with his platoon six days' later. The fourth, Robert Thomas, spent four days at the Field Ambulance after being gassed.

Although 19 May was mainly quiet, an 8-inch Howitzer shelled Le Plantin, wounding four: Rfn John Cowan's arm wound was slight and he remained on duty once it was dressed; Rfn John Bridge's wound on his left thigh was also minor and he returned six days' later; and L/Cpl Thomas Lapworth and Rfn Martin McGae both suffered serious arm wounds. That night, a battalion patrol spotted a wiring party in front of the OBL, returned, and directed Lewis fire onto the enemy, who withdrew in disarray. Although German artillery and mortars engaged in considerable activity during the night, this was mainly directed elsewhere.

On 20 May, the battalion was relieved by 1/5th KORL—though this was more a tactical adjustment than a relief—166 Bde taking over Festubert and 165 Bde moving south to relieve 164 Bde at Givenchy. The battalion occupied the left-subsector: 'C' held the left front (facing north); 'D' the centre; 'A' the right; and 'B' the keeps in and around Givenchy. A few Blue-X shells hit Herts Redoubt during the night, Rfn Thomas Redmond spending four days with the Field Ambulance being treated for the effects of gas and abrasions to his right shin. Also wounded was Rfn Alexander Edwards, whose hand wound kept him from duty for a month. Givenchy was also on the receiving end of a few Blue-X rounds during the morning of 21 May, but most of the fire was HE and shrapnel. The battalion's rear received intermittent bursts of harassing fire, but it was the front line that came under the heaviest fire, from 4.2 and 5.9 shells between 6 p.m. and 7.30 p.m.

Rfn Edgar Ward was admitted to hospital with second-degree burns to hand and wrist. His pal, Rfn William Butler, was with him in the Signallers' Dugout, shared with the 1/5th:

> Rfn Ward and myself were making tea on a 'Tommy's cooker. When lifting the dixie off, the cooker overturned and immediately the whole table went up in a blaze. We put some sandbags on but they got burnt and the place filled with smoke. Ward got his hand and arm badly burnt. The fire got too much for the two of us so we rushed off to HQ and reported. The table had a German oilsheet on it as a tablecloth.[49]

Ward added that the cooker ignited 'spirit from Primus lamp belonging to 1/5th KLR signallers, which was on table nearby. In hurrying through flames to escape from dugout, burns occurred, on left wrist and hand'.

The rear was very heavily shelled during the night of 21–22 May, Gorre falling victim to an almost unbelievable 10,000 Yellow-X rounds. Enemy artillery was active against Givenchy and Windy Corner intermittently throughout 22 May, Howitzers seeking targets in the British line; the rear areas were beset throughout the day and night. During the evening, the battalion was relieved and moved to support. 'A' and three platoons of 'D' went to dugouts at Pont Fixe; 'B' took up positions along the canal bank, with 'C' and 'D' Company's remaining platoon at Windy Corner. HQ was once again at Westminster Bridge.

The battalion suffered a number of casualties on 22 May, and though the only fatality was Rfn Robert Spilsbury, only two of the eleven wounded returned. At least two of these casualties occurred at Southmoor Villas prior to relief, where L/Cpl Kehoe earned his MM:

> This NCO was in charge of the signal station at Southmoor Villas, Givenchy, when a heavy shell blew in the cellar in which the signal station was situated, burying the occupants and instruments. Although wounded in the arm, he dug out one of the signallers who had been wounded and buried, after first extracting himself from the debris. The enemy still

> continued to shell the place, but alone he dug out and repaired his wires and instruments and was successful in re-establishing communications with Brigade HQ in about fifteen minutes from the time it was interrupted. In spite of his wound, he remained alone at his post until relieved.[50]

Fortunately, the 23rd was casualty-free.

Casualties, 22 May 1918

Rfn Joseph Barron	51408	WIA	L/Cpl Joseph Meade Kehoe	240655	WAD
2Lt Joseph Alexander Dow		WIA	Rfn George McCallum	51392	WIA
Rfn Kershaw Fletcher	49938	WIA	Cpl William Nelson	51976	WIA
Rfn Cuthbert Greaves	47019	WIA	Rfn George Pearson	330659	WIA
Rfn William Hacking	92003	WIA	Rfn Robert Spilsbury	332761	KIA
Rfn Albert Edward Jones	240168	WIA	Rfn Frank Townson	85952	WIA

The battalion returned to the line on 24 May, relieving the 1/5th in the right subsector at Givenchy. All four companies manned the front line, in order from left to right: 'C', 'D', 'A', and 'B'. HQ was in Fanshawe Castle. Between 11 p.m. and 12.15 a.m. on 24 May, both subsectors were heavily shelled, and throughout the 24th, light shelling continued, the only casualty being Rfn William Moore, with a 'Blighty' wound to the chest. The only other sufferer was Rfn Allen Holt, though the twenty-six-year-old was a victim of his section-commander, Cpl Thomas Kennedy. While on a working party in Bayswater Trench at 11.30 p.m., Kennedy—swinging a pickaxe in the dark—managed to catch Holt on the hand with it. The injury was not serious and Holt returned next day.

German fire slackened on 25 May, though there were still two Riflemen wounded, neither of whom returned. Frederick Foden was hit in the left ankle and Harry Halpin in the neck. Hostile artillery had been fairly active during 26 May, but after dark, the fire included a number of Blue-X and Yellow-X rounds, one of which badly affected Rfn Clifford Bromley, who was evacuated home. The 1/4th KORL arrived to relieve the battalion late that night, though the relief was not completed until 3.15 a.m. on the 27th. The battalion went straight to 'Bustle' positions, until ordered to billets at Drouvin at 5.30 a.m. For some, however, their stay in harm's way was prolonged. Half of 'A' went to Vauxhall Bridge and half of 'D' to Westminster Bridge, both furnishing bridgehead garrisons.

The battalion remained at Drouvin, rotating the bridgehead platoons, and it was while on this duty that Rfn Samuel Hewitt was wounded in the left knee on 29 May; on 31 May, Rfn Ernest Benson was also wounded in the left knee. The only other casualty was Rfn Thomas Green, accidentally wounded in the buttock after a bomb-training mishap on 27 May. On 30 May, twenty-year-old Rfn Joseph Watson was admitted to hospital with a high temperature, dying from acute encephalitis on 4 June. While at Drouvin, CQMS Herbert Davies received a MiD, though unfortunately his citation has not survived.

On 1 June, the battalion travelled by bus to Annequin, then marched to the right subsector at Festubert to relieve Liverpool Scottish. 'B' occupied the left front, with 'D' supporting them; on the right front was 'C', with 'A' in support. HQ went to Battersea Bridge. There was considerable hostile shellfire after dark and the battalion suffered twelve casualties in the hours leading up to midnight. Four were killed outright and twenty-eight-year-old CSM Morris Humphreys was mortally wounded.

Casualties, 1 June 1918

Name	Number	Status
Rfn Hartley Dean Bancroft	88848	KIA
Rfn John T. G. Edwards	88873	WIA
Rfn William Glover	69911	WIA
Rfn Edwin Grimshaw	88888	KIA
CSM Morris Humphreys	240295	DOW: 4/6
Rfn Walter Jackson	242858	WIA
Rfn George Alfred Mark Lanceley	99585	KIA
Sgt Herbert L. Macnicoll	241392	WIA
Rfn Henry W. Mason	99596	WIA
Rfn Herbert McConnell	381042	WIA
Rfn Richard Welton	86681	KIA
L/Cpl Joseph W. Wood	50994	WIA

German fire subsided on 2 June, with just harassing fire during daylight, though in the early hours, Festubert was targeted by Blue-X rounds and Rfn Thomas Eastham spent a week at the Field Ambulance as a result, and Riflemen Wilson Eccleston and David Hughes were wounded at duty. A similar pattern emerged on 3 June, with numerous Blue-X shells mixed in with HE and shrapnel during the early hours, the volume of fire diminishing during daylight. The only gas casualties were Riflemen John Anglesey and William French, the latter acute enough to be evacuated home. The other five casualties were all victims of general shellfire, L/Cpl Stanley Wilson the only fatality. The most seriously injured was Sgt Francis Gloyne, whose skull was fractured, a great loss to the battalion; he was joined on the hospital ship by Rfn John Dodd, who was wounded in the forearm. Rfn William Beach and L/Cpl Arthur Good both remained on duty once their wounds were dressed. Although the battalion's night patrols were uneventful, patrols from other sectors reported that the enemy was becoming much more aggressive in No Man's Land.

During the night of 3–4 June, the rear areas in the south of 55 Division's sector came under very heavy fire from Blue-X shells, though on the battalion's positions, it was mainly HE and shrapnel. HQ moved to Westminster Bridge on 4 June, though the bridge itself had been destroyed by shellfire the previous night. Rfn John Eyres was wounded on 4 June, returning in September after recovery from his buttock wound. Wounded in the thigh by one of five bombs dropped at Haillicourt that night was Rfn Clement Fletcher, attached to Divisional Transport.[51]

Hostile fire was scant on 4 June, though after dark, it escalated considerably, Beuvry alone hit by 4,000 rounds of Yellow-X. The battalion's rear was targeted by 10.5 and 15-cm, gas mixed in with HE and shrapnel. During the early hours of 5 June, Riflemen John Hornby and Joseph Schofield were gassed; Le Plantin also came under fire from

Minenwerfers. One patrol, on the left of the subsector, encountered an enemy patrol in No Man's Land and shots were exchanged, with shouts heard from the enemy as they retreated. Hostile artillery was quiet overnight on 5–6 June, and no further casualties ensued. The battalion's patrol found the body of a long-dead German in No Man's Land, in front of Le Plantin South. From his ID disc, it was established that he was from the 'Class of 1919'—a very young casualty of war. Apart from this, the patrol was routine, unlike the 1/9th to their right, who got into a bombing match with an aggressive German patrol close to their lines.

Artillery activity remained low during daylight on 6 June and the subsector received little fire. Although the battalion's night excursions were uneventful, the enemy attempted to ambush patrols in both Givenchy subsectors, and during the afternoon of 7 June, they made a successful silent raid against a post in Berkeley Street, capturing some of the garrison. The 7th heralded a slight increase in enemy artillery, but it remained well below the intensity of earlier that month. At 4.15 p.m. on 8 June, the enemy attempted another silent raid, this time against Orchard Road Post, which was beaten off without loss. Later that night, the battalion were relieved and moved to Givenchy support.

'A' manned Pont Fixe, 'B' went to Windy Corner, 'C' to the canal bank, and 'D' sent three platoons to Pont Fixe and one to Windy Corner; HQ occupied a dugout at Fanshawe Castle. The five wounded from 8 June are probably from the move out of the line prior to midnight. Rfn Arthur Hill was wounded in the buttock and evacuated home; Rfn Douglas Hill fell victim to a gas shell, and though he returned to duty in September, his stay in hospital was considerably lengthened after contracting dysentery there. A/Cpl William Sleigh's arm wound was not serious, though Rfn H. Holden, wounded in the right knee, and William Hurst, wounded in the right arm and scalp, were evacuated home.

Between 2.50 and 6 a.m. on 9 June, there was a very heavy bombardment, approximately 1,000 Blue and Yellow-X shells falling in concentrated bursts on Pont Fixe, Fanshawe Castle, and Windy Corner. Amid the gas, shrapnel and HE also caused casualties, Rfn Robert McGuire being lost to the battalion with an eye wound. Rfn Thomas Wilkinson's thigh wound was only minor and he remained on duty after it was dressed, though, unfortunately, it became infected and he was admitted to hospital on the 16th, rejoining in July. The concentration of the gas had not been realised and it was only hours later that men began showing symptoms. Two eighteen-year-olds, Riflemen Fred Newbon and Alfred Royden, died later in hospital, as did nineteen-year-old Rfn John Mather.

It is not possible to reconcile the casualty numbers in the diary against records in the *Casualties Book*, and neither fits comfortably with reported dates of gas shelling in Intelligence Summaries. Taking the dates in latter as accurate, it is probable that all those recorded in the *Casualties Book* as wounded by gas between 9 and 13 June are victims from the shelling during the early hours of the 9th—only documented on the day their symptoms became manifest (the dates below are those in the *Casualties Book*). Admitted to the Field Ambulance on 11 June, though probably victims from the 9th, were eighteen-year-old Riflemen Herbert Griffiths and John Hubbard and nineteen-year-old Edwin Johnson—all three died.

Only a few HE and shrapnel rounds struck battalion positions on 10 June, though Rfn George Hayes was wounded in wrist, shoulder, and back and Sgt Ernest Rowbottom in the right leg—a 'Blighty' wound that ended his service with the battalion. Far more seriously wounded was Rfn Charles Thompson, who died later that day.

'B' in particular were considerably weakened, and when the battalion relieved the 1/5th at 11.30 p.m. on 11 June, they remained at Windy Corner. 'D' Company of the 1/5th continued to man the Givenchy keeps until the Rifles were relieved on 14 June. Although the diary of the 1/6th states that 'C' manned the left front, 'D' the centre and 'A' the right front, the 1/5th's diary chronicles that both their 'A' Company (on the left front) and 'D' Company remained in the line—which, considering the number of gas casualties suffered by the Rifles, is probably correct—'C' Company of the 1/6th staying in Le Plantin under the 1/5th.

Some non-gas casualties were suffered on 11 June, L/Cpl Joseph Levey being the most critical, his wounds to chest, right arm, and leg proving fatal the following day. Attached to Divisional HQ, Rfn John Campbell was wounded at duty and Rfn Bernard Goldman accidentally injured his fingers—an injury complicated by infection—and it was September before he returned. The Intelligence Summary for 12–13 June refers to enemy artillery activity as 'abnormally quiet', a situation that continued during the day of 13 June, lending credence to most, if not all, of the battalion's gas casualties originating on 9 June.[52] Only scattered fire fell across Givenchy on 12 June, wounding two Riflemen. Walter Knaggs was hit in the shoulder and evacuated home, but the head wound of twenty-year-old Frederick Sage proved fatal on 17 July.

Gas Casualties, 9-13 June 1918

Rfn William Henry Aitchison	22303	WIA: 11/6
Rfn James Henry Alderson	53013	WIA: 13/6
Rfn Joseph Allen	86626	WIA: 11/6
Rfn Charles D. Armstrong	85442	WIA: 13/6
Rfn G. Arnold	308513	WIA: 11/6
Rfn James Ashton	56062	WIA: 11/6
Rfn George Astley	51128	WIA: 11/6
L/Cpl Ernest Ault	305040	WIA: 11/6
A/Cpl Frank B. Barlow*	85959	WIA: 9/6
Rfn Thomas Barrett*	35163	WIA: 9/6
Sgt Henry John Beale	241658	WIA: 11/6
Rfn Thomas Bradshaw Beesley	242590	WIA: 11/6
Rfn William John Bennison	51426	WIA: 11/6
Rfn William George Bentley	85191	WIA: 13/6
Rfn Albert Victor Bradwell*	307797	WIA: 11/6
L/Cpl Thomas William Brewer*	240493	WIA: 10/6
Rfn William Thomas Bullock	86596	WIA: 11/6
Cpl David Canning	305801	WIA: 11/6
Rfn Leonard Cartwright*	11351	WIA: 10/6
Rfn John Charnley	88862	WIA: 13/6
Rfn Joseph Charnley	84111	WIA: 9/6
Rfn Frank Clarke	85404	WIA: 11/6
Rfn Ernest Seddon Clarkson	308820	WIA: 13/6
Rfn Joseph Cooper	51143	WIA: 11/6
Cpl Jonathan Crellin	380445	WIA: 11/6
Rfn John Henry Crompton	85225	WIA: 11/6
Rfn William Crowe	325217	WIA: 11/6
Rfn Benjamin Cunliffe	260010	WIA: 11/6
Rfn Thomas Cunningham*	88861	WIA: 10/6
Rfn Charles Dower*	41622	WIA: 11/6

Rfn Patrick Doyle*	51432	WIA: 9/6
Rfn Thomas Edwards*	26179	WIA: 10/6
Rfn Thomas Elston	332968	WIA: 11/6
Rfn Harry Fielding	101290	WIA: 11/6
Rfn Abraham Fletcher	88268	WIA: 11/6
Rfn Wilfred Flindle	86557	WIA: 11/6
Rfn Joseph Flynn*	267057	WIA: 11/6
Rfn Samuel M. Fox*	50510	WIA: 11/6
Rfn Alfred Fyles	32561	WIA: 11/6
L/Cpl William James Gale	17340	WIA: 11/6
Rfn Thomas Edward Gallamore	99518	WIA: 11/6
Rfn Frederick Gardiner	101293	WIA: 11/6
Rfn Joseph Gettings	99513	WIA: 9/6
Rfn John Gillibrand*	48811	WIA: 10/6
Rfn Joseph Gilmore	101294	WIA: 11/6
Rfn Arthur T. Glover*	87106	WIA: 11/6
Rfn James Gornall*	101296	WIA: 11/6
Rfn Norman Benjamin Gray*	99519	WIA: 10/6
Rfn Walter Green	85472	WIA: 11/6
Rfn William Green	101297	WIA: 13/6
Rfn Walter Greenwood*	57648	WIA: 11/6
Rfn Herbert Stanley Griffiths	86844	DOW: 22/6
Rfn Ivan Grindell	99515	WIA: 9/6
Rfn Norman Hall*	94265	WIA: 10/6
Rfn James Hallum*	203320	WIA: 9/6
L/Cpl James Harding	13845	WIA: 10/6
Rfn William John Harding*	87158	WIA: 9/6
Rfn Robert Harrison*	86755	WIA: 10/6
Rfn Frederick Hawley	57154	WIA: 13/6
Rfn Joseph Hayden	88890	WIA: 13/6
Rfn George Heslop*	99534	WIA: 11/6
Rfn Patrick B. Hickey*	24125	WIA: 13/6
Rfn Edward Higginbotham	101305	WIA: 11/6
Rfn Alfred Hill	101301	WIA: 13/6
Rfn George Arthur Hinchliffe	99538	WIA: 13/6
Rfn Edward Henry Hole	101308	WIA: 11/6
Rfn Albert Holt	99525	WIA: 13/6
Rfn Thomas E. H. Howard*	86464	WIA: 13/6
Rfn John Joseph Hubbard	99522	DOW: 20/6
Rfn David M. Hughes*	101310	WIA: 10/6
Rfn Frank Hughes*	87154	WIA: 11/6
Rfn William Charles Henry Hulme	99539	WIA: 10/6
L/Cpl Joseph Hume	64893	WIA: 11/6
Rfn William H. Hunt*	85435	WIA: 9/6
Rfn Fred Hutchinson*	86491	WIA: 9/6
Rfn Albert Jackson	86542	WIA: 11/6
L/Cpl Harold T. Jarman*	94290	WIA: 9/6
Rfn James Jessop	99559	WIA: 13/6
Rfn Edwin Johnson	94277	DOW: 25/6
Rfn Arthur Edward Jones*	88071	WIA: 11/6
Rfn Charles Owen Jones*	94287	WIA: 9/6
Rfn Edward Jones	94276	WIA: 11/6
Rfn Rees Jones	86759	WIA: 11/6
Rfn William Jones*	94275	WIA: 11/6
Rfn Robert Alexander Joseph*	241764	WIA: 10/6
Rfn Peter Keay*	99575	WIA: 11/6
Rfn Bernard Kelly	85921	WIA: 11/6
Rfn William Kent	99569	WIA: 11/6
Rfn Albert Victor King	308597	WIA: 11/6
Rfn Stephen Lamb	99581	WIA: 11/6
Rfn Reginald Lambert*	242041	WIA: 11/6
L/Cpl George Benjamin Langhorne	241803	WIA: 11/6
Cpl William Ledgerwood	240439	WIA: 11/6
Rfn Sidney Frank Lloyd	94294	WIA: 9/6
Rfn Edward Machin	49953	WIA: 13/6
Rfn Albert Mason*	99603	WIA: 10/6
Rfn John Thomas Mather	86565	DOW: 16/6
Rfn William McCormick	307058	WIA: 11/6
Rfn Francis McDaid	85173	WIA: 11/6
Rfn Thomas McGann	52206	WIA: 11/6
Rfn John Thomas Midworth*	88271	WIA: 11/6
Rfn Norman W. Milnes	99595	WIA: 11/6
Rfn John William Mitchell	72435	WIA: 13/6
Sgt Silvester Samuel Morris	380962	WIA: 9/6
Rfn Oscar Mustin	88064	WIA: 11/6
Rfn James Naylor	201829	WIA: 11/6
Rfn Fred Newbon	87002	DOW: 12/6
Rfn Frank Nicholls	86578	WIA: 11/6

Rfn John O'Hare	85962	WIA: 13/6	Rfn Fred Sanderson*	12167	WIA: 11/6
Rfn Joseph W. Palfreyman*	95496	WIA: 13/6	Rfn Polito Santos*	50631	WIA: 11/6
Cpl James Arnold Plint	240429	WIA: 10/6	Rfn Asa Sayles*	325068	WIA: 9/6
L/Cpl Walter Poore	307095	WIA: 10/6	Rfn Peter Seville	305665	WIA: 11/6
Rfn Thomas Powell	94283	WIA: 11/6	L/Cpl Charles Skewes	241299	WIA: 11/6
Rfn William Ambrose Quayle	331983	WIA: 11/6	Rfn Arthur Skinner	85409	WIA: 10/6
Rfn Fred Railton	242051	WIA: 11/6	Cpl Ezra James Smalley	44505	WIA: 11/6
Rfn Harry Rainey	94000	WIA: 11/6	Rfn William Edward Smith*	88918	WIA: 9/6
Rfn David Ivor Richards	353010	WIA: 10/6	Rfn James Snelgrove*	59255	WIA: 11/6
Rfn John Henry Richards	240242	WIA: 11/6	Rfn Frank Thoms	57577	WIA: 13/6
Rfn Robert Rigby	84784	WIA: 13/6	Rfn Arthur Walker	242331	WIA: 11/6
Rfn Charles Roberts*	380881	WIA: 11/6	Rfn John William Ward	88930	WIA: 11/6
Rfn John Murray Roberts	242763	WIA: 10/6	Cpl Cecil Harry West	240222	WIA: 10/6
L/Cpl John R. Roberts	85500	WIA: 13/6	Sgt James Henry Wilde	23456	WIA: 11/6
L/Cpl Frank Roe*	307987	WIA: 10/6	Rfn Henry William*	49127	WIA: 10/6
Rfn George Rogers	88910	WIA: 13/6	Rfn John Reginald Williams	241851	WIA: 11/6
Rfn Henry Rogers	87870	WIA: 13/6	Rfn Samuel Williams*	240572	WIA: 10/6
Rfn Henry Edward Rogers	307655	WIA: 11/6	Rfn Richard A. Woodeson	88937	WIA: 13/6
Rfn Alfred Royden	86590	DOW: 18/6	Rfn Walter Charles Wright	267927	WIA: 13/6
Rfn Leonard R. F. Sampson	90977	WIA: 13/6			

* = Men who never returned to the battalion. Brewer, Plint, Samuel Williams, Ledgerwood, and John Richards were 'originals'.

Although only six fatalities resulted from gas, the overall toll of 147, forty-six of whom never returned, was a casualty rate almost as high as in a set-piece battle.

The battalion faced an aggressive enemy and another daylight raid was attempted on 13 June. This time their selected target was the post at the junction of Half Moon Trench and Piccadilly. The small raiding party of an officer and three men, all wearing British helmets and partial British uniforms, was engaged with rifle fire and bombs, wounding three of the raiders, though they managed to regain their own lines—an attempt that emphasised the importance of sentries staying alert.

German incursion efforts resumed at midnight on 13 June when a group attempted to raid Coventry Sap from the west. This was just to the right of the battalion and the raid was repulsed. Barely ten minutes later, the battalion launched their own foray against a German post north of Grenadier Road. Although this was beyond the battalion's left bound, the 1/5th South Lancs—in the process of relieving Liverpool Scottish there—had been warned. The thirty-eight-strong raiding force was led by 2Lt John Lowe, assisted by Cpls George Butler, William Huggonson, and Harry Thomas.

Shortly before the planned Zero of 2.10 a.m., division artillery began a wire-cutting barrage, then, boosted by machine guns, switched to a box-barrage, isolating the objective. When the raiders rushed their target, 2Lt Lowe and Cpl Butler—the first into the post—were somewhat disconcerted to find it vacant. Nonetheless, they went off in search.

Not far away, they discovered a pocket of enemy sheltering in a shell hole and a sharp firefight ensued. The German NCO in charge of the group shot and wounded 2Lt Lowe, Butler returning fire until the adversary fell. Another two of the enemy were also killed before the surviving pair surrendered to Butler. Cpl Thomas's Group secured the nearby communication trench, where they established a block 50 yards beyond the post, holding this against a strong German counterattack. When the withdrawal signal was given, Thomas was the last to exit enemy lines.

The prisoners' interrogation established that they were actually a six-man patrol from 1 Company, 98 IR, tasked with establishing if British posts forward of Le Plantin South were occupied. The enemy had only just left their line when the barrage began, one of their patrol running back—only to flee straight into a shell. The remainder took cover in the shell hole where Lowe and Butler encountered them. Thomas was awarded a Bar to his MM and Butler the MM; Lowe, who despite his wound remained on duty until relieved, gained the MC. The raid was thought a considerable success, as much useful intelligence was gained from the prisoners.

German artillery did not retaliate, possibly as they had an operation of their own planned for the early hours of 14 June. At 2 a.m., they made another sortie against Coventry Sap—this time from the north—faring no better and suffering additional casualties. At dawn, the 1/7th held their fire when German stretcher-bearers entered No Man's Land to retrieve their wounded. Routine harassing fire during 14 June resulted in another two casualties. Rfn Ernest Buckley was killed and another wounded. The two wounded ORs (one from the raid, the other from shellfire) were Rfn Harry Tighe, wounded in the right thigh, and Rfn Richard Bradshaw, wounded in the abdomen.

The battalion was relieved on 14 June and moved to 'Bustle' positions in the Beuvry-Cambrin Reserve Line, and at 5 a.m. the next morning, they became divisional reserve at 'W' Camp, east of Vaudricourt, where they were joined by the rump of 'B' and 'C'. The only casualty from the early hours was L/Cpl Samuel Stain, who received a minor shrapnel wound to his left knee. Although they remained out of the line until 20 June, working parties suffered casualties. On 17 June, Rfn Frank Green was treated for the effects of gas, rejoining the following day; on 19 June, Rfn Alfred Horne was admitted to hospital after exposure to lachrymatory gas—though it was nearly three months before he was fit. A number were gazetted for awards at this time: L/Cpl Henri Paul for the MM and C/Sgt Ernest Thomas and CSM John Moss for the MSM, though their citations do not survive.

Although some of the gas casualties returned and 160 new arrivals joined before their return to the front, the battalion was still undermanned, their '*Return*' for the week ending 29 June, noting a mere 572 officers and men.[53]

On 20 June, the battalion boarded the light railway at Hairpin Corner for Empire Siding at Le Quesnoy. From there, they marched to the left subsector at Festubert to relieve Liverpool Scottish, HQ going to Duke Post. Company dispositions resembled a right-angled triangle, the vertical side facing east. 'D', clustered at the apex, garrisoned Cailloux—the enemy to their fore and on both sides—though the distribution of their platoons suggests that the north was considered the direction of greatest danger. To their south, and occupying the base of this triangle, was 'A' in Festubert—their platoons placed to face an eastern threat. The third of the forward companies, 'B', were central to the hypotenuse. 'C' manned the reserve line, north of Estaminet Corner. Although hostile artillery fire was light, the battalion suffered one casualty before midnight: Rfn Ronald Dewar—who had only arrived that morning—spent the shortest time with the battalion of anyone—his scalp wound occasioning two months in hospital and transfer to the RE. One patrol from 'A' discovered a five-strong enemy working party in the OBL near Dead Cow Farm, but were spotted as they approached, the foe quickly retreating.

Routine harassing fire on 21 June was responsible for the death of twenty-six-year-old L/Cpl Frederick Davies. Patrols ventured forward again after dark, but no sign of the enemy was to be found. Despite little hostile fire on 22 June, another two casualties were suffered: twenty-year-old Manxman Rfn William Harper was killed and Rfn Leslie Jeeves very seriously wounded in the left thigh by multiple shrapnel balls. On 23 June, before the battalion was relieved and moved into the Festubert support line, Cpl William Caldwell received a 'Blighty' wound to the left knee.

HQ was once again at Waterloo Bridge; 'A' and 'B' in the centre locality of the Tuning Fork Line; and 'C' divided between Lone Farm, King Post, and Marais South-East, with two Lewis sections in Bart Post and Baron Post. 'D' were also split, with two platoons in Prince Post, the others in Queen Post and the Tuning Fork Line. The move to the rear was far from a passage to safety, and during the morning of 24 June, Barge House came under fire, eliciting ten casualties among a working party there.

Working Party Casualties, 24 June 1918

Sgt Robert Cliffe	200663	WIA	Rfn Robert Miller	330682	WIA
Rfn John Faulkner	101291	DOW: 25/6	L/Cpl Andrew Murphy	242260	WIA
Rfn Charles Henry Fazackerley	101289	WIA	Rfn Patrick Stanton	29417	WIA
			Rfn Robert D. Thomas	83043	WIA
Rfn Richard Harrison	85234	WIA	L/Sgt John Tilley MM	240129	DOW: 25/6
Rfn John Douglas Holden	331218	WIA			

More working parties were demanded on 25 June, and later that day, another two casualties were sustained by men so employed, both 'Blighty' cases. Riflemen William Smith (735) was wounded in the shoulder and right arm and George Thompson hit in the right arm. The battalion was relieved on 26 June and bivouacked in the woods at Bellenville, south of the canal. After spending the day resting, they left at 9.45 p.m. on 27 June to relieve the Fusiliers in the right subsector at Givenchy. All four companies manned the front line, half their strength forward, the rest in support—positioned from left to right: 'C', 'D', 'B', and 'A', with HQ in Windy Terrace.

There was scant fire during the night, and patrols encountered no enemy. During light shelling of Pont Fixe and Spoil Bank in the morning of 28 June, Rfn Joseph Goodman was wounded in the left hand and evacuated home (Goodman served under the alias 'Cringle'). He was the sole casualty due to enemy action, though Rfn Henry Spencer, posted in a week earlier, managed to shoot himself in the foot—clearly considered carelessness, his FGCM awarding only twenty-one days' field punishment. The rest of the day was reasonably quiet and there was little German fire overnight. This situation continued on 29 June, the only casualty being Rfn Joseph Joughin of 'D', wounded by routine harassing fire while in Cambridge Terrace.

Early in the morning of 30 June, a sentry in Death or Glory Sap spotted an enemy soldier to the front of his position and opened fire. The man cried out, fell, and was not seen to move again. Hostile artillery and mortar fire was at its usual levels and three Riflemen suffered 'Blighty' wounds: Nelson Balding was hit in the chest; Frederick Barton in both legs; and John Hudson, the left knee. As midnight approached, 2Lt Charles Cole briefed his three men for 'D' Company's reconnaissance patrol, scheduled for the early hours of 1 July.

Cole, Cpl Thomas Kennedy, L/Cpl Jonathan Powell, and Rfn Patrick Moore exited via the block in Finchley Road. Unbeknownst to them, they had been spied by an enemy sentry and 130 yards into their journey, at the junction of Finchley Road and Willow Drain, were met by a salvo of bombs and machine-gun fire from German posts to either side. Powell—to the rear—witnessed his comrades fall, but miraculously unharmed, managed to make his way back to the block. 'D' Company CSM, thirty-three-year-old John Chadwick, alerted by the outbreak of fire, collected a rescue party. Meeting Powell on his way back, the CSM got the details and led his men towards the casualties, only to be driven off by heavy fire. Once the rescue party was safely back, Chadwick returned alone, crawling to within 6 feet of Kennedy's body before coming under a hail of machine-gun fire and bombs from the enemy, who called upon him to surrender. His mission clearly impossible, the CSM returned. Lt-Col. McKaig recommended him for the MM—a recommendation endorsed by Brig.-Gen. Boyd-Moss and Jeudwine—but it was turned down by Corps, 'with regret', because, 'as a warrant officer, is not eligible for the MM'.[54] Kennedy was the only fatality; Cole and Moore spent the rest of the war in captivity (the battalion erroneously documented these casualties for 30 June).

German artillery was more active than usual during the morning of 1 July, but quietened down in the afternoon, though the Battalion diary refers to it as a 'quiet day'. The Intelligence Summary reported the 100 mortar rounds fired at Orchard Keep as 'normal'.[55] Thankfully, no casualties resulted; however, Rfn Harry Hughes, who had joined the battalion from England on 18 April, was admitted to hospital on 1 July, suffering from debility. In September, a London hospital diagnosed shellshock and he was medically discharged and given a pension.[56] After dark, hostile fire was just the routine harassment, and unlike the previous night, patrols were uneventful.

On 2 July, intermittent shelling was experienced throughout the sector and hostile mortar fire increased considerably, and though this was mainly from light mortars, forty heavy *Minenwerfer* rounds also struck battalion lines. 'A' Company's position at Death or Glory Sap was particularly badly hit, the first round burying the entire Lewis team. While the rounds were still falling, Cpl William Roberts went to their assistance, dug out the four buried men, then continued digging until he unearthed the gun. Taking it into the nearest shelter, he stripped, cleaned, and reassembled it, bringing it back into action—deeds rewarded with the MM.[57] The three casualties that day were Cpl Wilfred Hayseldine, hit in the right thigh; Rfn Samuel Kelly wounded in the shoulder; and Rfn Charles Mackay, the left forearm. The remainder of 3 July saw mostly harassing fire, though 200 rounds of 5.9 hit Windy Corner over the day. Late that night, the battalion were relieved and left for their 'Bustle' positions, prior to becoming divisional reserve. Though enemy guns targeted the rear as they filed back, they escaped without loss.

For most of 4 July, they occupied positions along the Beuvry–Cambrin Line, though at 5 p.m., they began a journey to 'W' Camp, remaining there until the 9th. Training and working parties dominated, many of the latter involving supply runs to the front line. Only four replacements arrived during this period. On 9 July, the battalion boarded busses at Drouvin, bound for Beuvry. Once there, they marched into support at Festubert: 'A' and 'B' in Le Préol North; 'C' to Lone Farm and King Post; and 'D' to Queen Post and Prince Post. HQ's dugout was midway between Chelsea and Battersea bridges.

On 12 July, the battalion relieved the 1/5th in the left subsector at Festubert. Riflemen Edward Buckley and Samuel Haw were both recorded 'wounded at duty' on the 12th, but the only man requiring hospital treatment was Cpl Edward Colley, whose thigh wound meant two months in hospital. 'A' were in reserve in the Tuning Fork Switch; 'B' in Cailloux; 'C' at Festubert; and 'D' in the north-west locality, along Festubert Switch. The night and following day were quiet, hostile fire well below normal, remaining so until the morning of 15 July saw a slight increase. The diary reports one man wounded on 14 July and another on the 15th, though the *Casualties Book* records both L/Cpl Harold Thompson and Rfn Stephen Ashcroft for the 15th, their leg wounds requiring evacuation home. Relieved late on the 15th, the battalion moved to 'Bustle' positions.

On the night of 16 July, they relieved the 1/4th Loyals in the left subsector at Givenchy. 'C' manned the keeps, 'B', 'A', and 'D' the left, centre, and right of the front line; and HQ was in Windy Terrace again. The only casualty due to enemy action was Rfn Egbert Philson—wounded in face and hand—though he returned three weeks later. Joining him at the Field Ambulance was Rfn Robert Bevan, who had lacerated his foot on the sharp edge of a biscuit tin while washing his feet. The 17th was mainly quiet until after dark, when the usual harassing fire began. Windy Corner was hit by 77-mm and Moat Farm, Wolfe Road, and Herts Keep were all targeted by 4.2 and 5.9. The only casualty on 18 July was Rfn Albert Rushworth, whose minor knee wound was probably from that evening, when enemy artillery considerable upped its rate of fire—over 500 rounds of 4.2 striking the forward area.

During the afternoon of 19 July, shellfire once again intensified, Pont Fixe and Wolfe Road receiving most. The battalion was relieved that night and moved into the Givenchy support. The only casualty of that day was Rfn James Corcoran, who was gassed after dark. HQ was once again in Barge House; 'A' and three platoons from 'C' in Pont Fixe; 'B' protecting Westminster and Vauxhall bridges; and 'D' and the remaining 'C' Company platoon at Windy Corner Terrace.

The first casualties occurred on the 20th. Rfn Thomas Williams (851) was evacuated home and Bernard Walsh's arm wound kept him from duty for a fortnight. Also lost was Capt. James McLaren, sent home by a medical board after his health deteriorated. Rfn Thomas Ebbs was wounded in the left leg on 21 July, but returned to duty in October. On 22 July, the battalion was ordered into divisional reserve at Drouvin, but 'stood-to' in their 'Bustle' positions until 5 a.m. on 23 July. The only casualty before they left for Drouvin was Rfn Norris Jones, evacuated home with serious contusions to both legs.

The battalion remained at Drouvin until 29 July, training and providing the manpower for numerous working parties. Three casualties occurred on these: Rfn John Drinkald was admitted to hospital with shellshock on 28 July, and he was transferred to an anti-aircraft unit after leaving the IBD; Rfn Robert Williams (843) was hit in the head and left leg and evacuated home; and Rfn John Ryan suffered a minor scalp wound.

13

29 July 1918—11 November 1918: The Hard Road to Victory

Coordinates for this Chapter

advanced post 1	50°32′7.10″N 2°45′44.90″E	Div. left on 8 November	50°35′27.80″N 3°19′13.10″E
advanced post 2	50°31′59.90″N 2°45′46.50″E	Eitel Alley South	50°33′1.30″N 2°46′21.00″E
advanced post 3	50°32′5.80″N 2°46′7.00″E	Escaut crossing point	50°35′44.00″N 3°24′39.00″E
Bois de L'Hospice	50°33′9.30″N 3°0′1.00″E	Ferme du Baron	50°35′14.40″N 3°17′53.60″E
Brewery, the	50°33′6.70″N 2°44′50.40″E	Flat Farm	50°32′39.70″N 2°47′14.80″E
Brickfields	50°32′31.60″N 2°46′39.40″E	Fort de Seclin	50°33′20.96″N 3°3′12.33″E
brickworks	50°32′50.40″N 2°47′19.30″E	Fort de Vendeville	50°33′58.00″N 3°4′57.60″E
Bridge View	50°31′52.30″N 2°42′37.80″E	German telephone exch.	50°33′21.80″N 2°47′23.20″E
Canteleux	50°31′48.40″N 2°46′43.40″E	Hantay Château	50°31′58.40″N 2°51′36.90″E
Canteleux Alley	50°31′41.40″N 2°46′44.70″E	Indian Village	50°33′18.10″N 2°45′1.00″E
crossroads (30 Oct.)	50°36′0.70″N 3°21′38.40″E	La Bassée Alley South	50°32′10.00″N 2°47′22.00″E
Cupola Alley	50°31′58.90″N 2°46′31.20″E	La Croix de Pierre	50°35′7.90″N 3°20′33.00″E
Deadman's Trench	50°32′1.40″N 2°45′31.10″E	left bound 25 September	50°33′37.10″N 2°47′13.30″E

Les Ewuis Farm	50°32′27.40″N 3°0′33.00″E	Setchell's post	50°32′9.40″N 2°47′3.50″E
lunatic asylum	50°35′45.30″N 3°23′23.30″E	Shetland Trench	50°33′9.20″N 2°45′29.30″E
New Rose Street	50°31′58.50″N 2°45′23.20″E	Spartan Trench	50°33′8.60″N 2°47′15.70″E
Nora Trench	50°33′26.80″N 2°47′4.60″E	Stone Bridge	50°31′47.60″N 2°42′42.30″E
Pic-au-Vent	50°35′11.94″N 3°21′2.97″E	Stork Trench	50°32′55.10″N 2°46′26.60″E
Pioneer Dump	50°33′26.00″N 2°47′11.70″E	tannery	50°34′38.60″N 3°20′25.70″E
Plain Alley	50°31′24.70″N 2°46′42.80″E	Tube Station Post	50°33′29.50″N 2°45′24.70″E
Sap-H	50°31′53.50″N 2°45′38.60″E	Turn Table	50°32′2.20″N 2°46′54.00″E
Serpent Trench	50°33′17.90″N 2°46′29.90″E	Violaines Trench	50°32′14.30″N 2°46′19.30″E

On 29 July, the battalion relieved the 1/5th South Lancs in the right subsector at Festubert, two companies at the front, the rest in support. 'D' took the positions on the left, from Barnton Road down to the northern half of Le Plantin North. Supporting them in the Tuning Fork Switch was 'B'. On their right, one platoon of 'A' held the remaining part of Le Plantin North, another in Cheshire Road, the rest in the Tuning Fork Switch with 'C'; HQ were at Battersea Bridge. The only casualty prior to midnight was Rfn Harold Bell, who was gassed, rejoining in September. The battalion's only night patrol encountered an enemy patrol of four or five men, who left the scene rapidly when the Riflemen approached.

Little hostile fire struck the front line on 30 July, though the rear areas were still hazardous, Cpl George Maycock suffering a 'Blighty 'wound to the leg. The last day of July continued in much the same manner, and although their patrols were uneventful, prisoners captured by others from the division offered useful intelligence; reporting low manning levels in their outpost line—just behind the OBL—and considerable casualties from British artillery among the garrisons in their main line of resistance. One prisoner, a lightly-wounded aspirant officer from 31 RIR, stated that his regiment were about to withdraw from the outpost line opposite the Givenchy right-subsector. Jeudwine wasted no time, and during daylight on 31 July, the OBL from the north of Death or Glory Sap to just south of the crater field was reoccupied and consolidated. By the end of August, the division would be fighting a very different type of warfare.

The final casualty before relief on 3 August was Rfn Joseph Hughes (537), wounded in the left knee by shrapnel and evacuated home. After 1/5th South Lancs took over, the battalion moved into Givenchy support, HQ in Barge House; 'A' at Westminster Bridge, 'B' in Windy Corner Terrace (with one platoon from 'D' Company); and 'C' and 'D' at Pont Fixe.

Although 4 August began quietly, at 7.30 p.m., the whole sector came under heavy artillery fire, Pont Fixe being badly hit. Second-Lieutenant James Fenn was wounded in this initial outbreak of fire, and in the early hours of 5 August, L/Cpl William Halsall suffered a serious hand wound and Rfn Charles Poole was wounded through both thighs, dying later that day.

On 6 August, the battalion relieved the 1/5th in Givenchy's left subsector: 'A', 'B', and 'C' holding the front; 'D' occupying the keeps; and HQ in Windy Terrace. The Givenchy battalions had been tasking daylight patrols for over a week without issue, though an attempt to seize Warlingham Crater was abandoned due to accurate sniping from Red Dragon Crater. Shortly before their relief by the battalion, a sergeant from the 1/5th went out alone in the afternoon, and after a brief exchange of fire, he snatched a German corporal from New Rose Street, bringing the prisoner back intact.

During daylight on 7 August, 2Lt John Lashmar and seven men patrolled as far as the junction between Fife Road and the OBL, finding no trace of the enemy. Night patrols were equally uneventful. Throughout the morning of 8 August, Pont Fixe and Windy Corner were shelled, hostile fire across the Givenchy sector being slightly above normal, resulting in six casualties, though once the hand wound of L/Sgt James Williams (496) was dressed, he remained on duty. The most seriously injured was twenty-three-year-old Rfn Charles Nessling. With the battalion for just a fortnight, he died at the Aid Post. Neither Rfn William Simpson, wounded in the right arm, nor Rfn John Taylor, wounded in the ankle, returned. Riflemen Joseph Dwyer, hit in the knee, and George Mason, wounded in the fingers, were back before the end of the month.

The 9th was quiet, and that night, the battalion were relieved, moving to their 'Bustle' positions. At 5 a.m. on 10 August, they marched to Vaudricourt. Training and working parties occupied their time until their return to the line on 15 August, though there were no casualties. William Bullock, one of those gassed in June, was declared a deserter from his convalescence camp on 12 August. Far from being a deserter, he had been admitted to 56 General Hospital with gastro-enteritis and it was the camp's administration procedure that was lacking, not the unfortunate Rifleman. Thankfully, the mess was sorted out, but not until 7 October, a week after he had rejoined the battalion. The only victim from the working parties was Rfn Arthur Fazackerley, with an accidental injury. He and another were carrying a roll of barbed wire on a length of angle iron. As the leading man put his end down, the angled iron swung up and caught Fazackerley on the left eyelid, cutting it badly.

On 15 August, the battalion relieved 1/5th KORL in the left subsector at Festubert: 'B' were on the left front at Cailloux, with 'C' to their right in Festubert; in support, 'A' occupied the Tuning Fork Switch and 'D' Festubert Switch. HQ were once again in Duke Post. The night began quietly enough, but at 3 a.m. on 16 August, the enemy began a heavy bombardment of 4.2 and 77-mm across the entire sector. Amid the HE and shrapnel were a considerable number of Blue, Green, and Yellow-X shells, and L/Sgt Albert Smith (250) was evacuated home suffering from the effects (he was gazetted for the MM on 11 December). Also wounded was Rfn Bertie Russell, a minor shrapnel wound to the left buttock necessitating a fortnight off duty. Rfn Rowland Wood, attached to the TMB, received a 'Blighty' wound to the face.

All diaries deemed 17 August a quiet day, and it was probably just one unlucky round responsible for the eight casualties: Riflemen Fred Hudson, Richard Potter, George Simcox, and John Tipping were all killed; the four wounded—Riflemen George Bottomley, Frederick Lane, Raymond Newberry, and Thomas Warren—recovered from their injuries and rejoined the battalion.

On the evening of 18 August, the battalion moved into support; HQ going to Bridge View; 'A' and 'B' to Le Préol North; 'C' to Lone Farm and King Post; and 'D' to the Tuning Fork Switch. Their respite was quiet and casualty-free, but also brief, as they returned to the line on the night of 20 August.

Relieving 1/4th KORL in the right subsector of Givenchy, 'A', 'B', 'C', and 'D' were arraigned left to right, with HQ in Fanshawe Castle. Four casualties were suffered before midnight: Rfn Frederick Hawley was killed; Thomas Lynch received a 'Blighty' wound to his scalp; Richard Roberts's back wound only kept him from duty for ten days; and Jack Jones was classed as 'wounded at duty'. These four were victims of routine shellfire, and though Fanshawe Castle was targeted by Blue-X at 3.10 a.m. on 21 August, no casualties resulted. Hostile fire continued at routine levels throughout this tour and patrols were similarly uneventful, apart from an enemy wiring party seen opposite the middle of the subsector on the night of 22–23 August.

The enemy was suspected of being up to something however, as signallers in the Brigade Listening Station reported that enemy 'power-buzzer' messages the previous night had been five times the usual activity level—Division tasking twenty-seven overnight listening posts as a precaution. Riflemen Fred Aspinall and Robert Mawdsley both suffered 'Blighty' wounds on 23 August; another loss was twenty-three-year-old subaltern 2Lt Walter Cottier, who died in hospital from illness.

The battalion was relieved by a joint force from 1/4th Loyals and 1/4th KORL on the night of 23 August, the latter (in conjunction with the Fusiliers) having an attack arranged for 7.20 a.m. on the 24th. This audacious daylight operation, conceived by Brig.-Gen' Stockwell, planned to seize the Crater Field without preliminary bombardment. Succeeding spectacularly, by the end of the day all objectives were taken at a cost of twenty lives, half of whom were victims of a British Howitzer firing short. The division had secured a significant tactical advantage, dominating the entire crater field—a valuable stepping stone for advance.

Upon relief, the battalion became divisional reserve at West Camp. Two more 'originals' were lost before moving to Givenchy support at 3 p.m. on 27 August: Cpl Sydney Hancock was wounded in the left knee during a working party on 26 August and Rfn Cecil Raley MM accidentally injured on 27 August—lacerations to face and hand keeping him from duty until early December. Rfn David Evans suffered an accidental leg injury on 28 August, resulting in his evacuation home.

'A' manned Herts Redoubt and Windy Terrace; 'B', Spoil Bank and Pont Fixe; 'C', Pont Fixe and the Brewery; and 'D' at Windy Corner. HQ was once again in Barge House. During the night, bursts of fire fell on Pont Fixe, Windy Corner, and Barge House, but no casualties resulted. The 28th was quiet, though after dark, hostile fire against the roads and tracks around Givenchy increased. Although the fire slackened during 29 August, intermittent harassing fire wounded Rfn Frank Brayshaw, though the injury to his right leg was minor.

After dark, a number of officers and SNCOs reconnoitred the left subsector, where thanks to the seizure of the craters, new positions awaited. Sadly, their reconnaissance coincided with a burst of 5.9 fire against the craters, killing former Rifleman, twenty-six-year-old Lt Thomas Phillips, a serious loss to the battalion.

After dark on 30 August, enemy artillery was very active against the craters and its approaches, but the battalion's relief of the 1/7th went smoothly. On the left, 'B' manned the OBL and New Rose Street; in the centre, 'C' occupied Deadman's Trench down to Sap-H; the right, from Sap-H to Sap-F, was held by 'A'; 'D' providing support in Moat Farm and Givenchy Keep; and HQ were in Windy Terrace.

During the morning of 31 August, the craters were heavily shelled by 4.2 and 5.9, wounding Rfn Harry Fielding in the nose and 'C' Company's Sgt Ernest Hodgson in the thigh—a 'Blighty' wound that ended his overseas service. Later that night, Rfn William Batten was gassed, being transferred after leaving hospital.

German defences either side of the canal were offset and Intelligence believed the enemy may straighten their line by either withdrawing his forces north of the canal or, less likely, advance in the south. Consequently, patrols were pushed out eastwards to establish advance posts. The battalion, tasked with setting up two, encountered no opposition. On the left, one was 400 yards forward of Deadman's Trench; the right-hand one was 400 yards forward of Sap-K (advanced posts 1 and 2 in the Coordinates Table). One patrol penetrated 300 yards behind enemy lines without encountering a single German. To their right, the 1/5th occupied the Tortoise, but were later obliged to withdraw because of enfilading machine-gun fire from south of the canal.

Intermittent shelling of the craters resulted in no casualties on 1 September, and that night, another post was established 200 yards further forward of where the patrol had penetrated the previous night (advanced post 3). Between 11 a.m. and 3 p.m. on 2 September, New Rose Street and the craters were shelled by 4.2 and 5.9, killing twenty-eight-year-old Sgt James Wilde and wounding Rfn Jack Hawcock in the left hand. Tragically, they were not the only casualties, as a bomb accident killed twenty-three-year-old L/Cpl Joseph Hume, an only son who was also engaged to be married. Badly wounded in the same accident were Riflemen David Davies (768) and William Green (314). That night, the battalion was relieved, moving straight back into the line in the left subsector at Festubert.

'D' manned the left front in Cailloux and Festubert Switch, supported by 'B', who were also in the Switch; the right front was held by 'A', placed around the Festubert locality, supported by 'C' in the Tuning Fork Switch. HQ was in Duke Post.

Early in the morning of 3 September, 46 Division to the left began a limited advance and 165 Bde was ordered to keep in touch and seize the OBL and Indian Village. The battalion pushed a two-company force forward. Scouting patrols blazed the trail for the attacking platoons; Cpl George Butler commanded one. They were only 80 yards from German positions (the Brewery) when very heavy machine-gun and rifle fire opened up, wounding two of his men. With the help of another man, Butler managed to carry thirty-year-old L/Cpl William Redmond—his right leg smashed by a bullet—across 100 yards of open ground through a hail of fire. Redmond's injury was severe, his leg amputated at the thigh, and Butler received a Bar to his MM.[1]

Platoon scout Rfn Benjamin Kempster located a previously-unknown German post, and after working out the best way to approach it unseen, he returned with the information. This position was easily overrun and the platoon pushed on to their ultimate objective, Indian Village. L/Cpl Donald Laurie, in charge of the rifle section, was tasked with taking Indian Village. Unfortunately, machine-gun fire from there completely pinned down their Lewis section. Laurie pushed on alone and engaged the enemy at close range with rifle fire, allowing the Lewis section to make their move. Laurie then took his section around the German position, cutting off their retreat and forcing the surrender of five survivors. He and Kempster both received the MM.[2]

Another scout to be awarded the MM was Rfn Stanley Jepson:

> During an advance his platoon reached a point two hundred yards inside the enemy outpost line, from which they were able to gain valuable information as to the enemy's positions. Rfn Jepson volunteered to carry this information back and did so in spite of very heavy fire from machine-guns and snipers. This journey of several hundred yards under close fire from the enemy he repeated three times, bringing back each time information of great assistance to his company-commander.[3]

'A' Company were on the right of the advance, and for thirty-one year-old Cpl John Hulme's section, things went badly in the late morning. Ordered to establish contact with the company to his left, they approached Shetland Trench, where they believed that company had reached. Here they were almost surrounded by a much stronger enemy patrol, who opened fire at close range. Hulme fell mortally wounded and all the others, apart from thirty-one-year-old Rfn Harold Broom, were also wounded. In spite of the heavy fire, Broom carried back Rfn Albert Cooper—who had received a serious buttock wound—receiving the MM for his courage. All, apart from Hulme, made it to safety.[4]

By 11.50 a.m., all objectives were secured and liaison with 46 Division was established at Tube Station Post. Apart from Redmond, the battalion suffered another nine wounded—though not all from Hulme's patrol, which was probably only four or five strong. Of the others, Rfn Richard Woodeson was wounded in the thigh, leaving hospital the following month; Rfn John Stewart's leg wound kept him from duty for a fortnight, as did the foot wound of L/Cpl Albert Loynes; Rfn Wilfred Ashby was wounded in the elbow; L/Cpl Albert Huxley and Riflemen John Jackson (289) and Thomas Lowe hit in the shoulder; and the last of the casualties, Rfn Harold Ogden, suffered a head wound that kept him from duty until four days after the Armistice. Hulme died in German hands the following day and was buried near the German aid post at Gondecourt. Another loss that day was Rfn Edward Southern, admitted to hospital with influenza, he died on 26 November.

Although there was little hostile fire during the afternoon of 3 September, at 8.30 p.m., 165 Bde's positions and the craters were heavily shelled—fire that probably accounted for some of those above. Festubert and the OBL also came under heavy gas bombardment during the early hours of 4 September. Astonishingly, considering that the battalion suffered sixty-two gas casualties, the diary records 'casualties nil'—an unbelievable omission. Of these, no fewer than twenty-six died and, out of thirty-six survivors, only sixteen returned.

The division continued pressuring the enemy on 4 September, the battalion pushing platoons towards Rue de Marais. The scouts of 2Lt Wilfred Pegge's 1 Platoon located an enemy position in their line of advance and returned to brief Pegge, who then made his own reconnaissance. Armed with this knowledge, Pegge sent L/Cpl James Nichols's section around the flank, while the rest pinned the enemy down. Nichols and his men managed to work their way behind the post without the defenders being aware; once they realised that they were surrounded, they surrendered without a fight. This attack was carried out without a single loss to the platoon. The prisoners were keen to talk, and when Pegge questioned them about the dispositions of the rest of their company, they obligingly pointed these out on his map. Pegge took his platoon forward to verify the information, which turned out to be accurate. In total, they penetrated 800 yards past the enemy outpost line—1,500 yards forward of the battalion's outposts. Pegge was awarded the MC and Nichols the MM for their successful mission.[5]

In places, the battalion faced heavy fighting, especially around Serpent Trench and Eitel Alley South, which were held in strength. During this engagement, L/Cpl Albert Johnson (008) was killed and three wounded: Cpl Albert Johnson (052), with a very minor knee wound; Rfn Fred White, shot through both legs; and Rfn George Woodward, shot through the right shoulder. The diary reports that posts were built in Canadian Orchard and New Rope Trench, and although the latter does not feature on divisional maps, Intelligence Summaries record the battalion building posts in Stork Trench and on the outskirts of Rue de Marais; they also established liaison with the left division, 660 yards forward of Tube Station Post.

Gas Casualties, 4 September 1918

Rfn George Barraclough*	105584	WIA	Rfn William M. Craven	32819	WIA
Rfn Charles J. Beardmore*	58767	WIA	Rfn Albert Crowther	105605	DOW: 11/9
Rfn Charles Boggild	305743	DOW: 12/9	Rfn John Charles Curfew	105608	WIA
Rfn Frederick Bowler	241102	WIA	Rfn John T. Curley*	235589	WIA
Rfn William Henry Brookes	105586	DOW: 12/9	Rfn Thomas Curwen	105606	DOW: 8/9
Rfn Joseph Clarke*	31705	WIA	Rfn John Darcy	88868	WIA
Rfn Thomas Clayton*	888663	WIA	Rfn James Downey	50323	DOW: 8/9
Rfn John Collinge	105591	DOW: 9/9	Sgt Samuel Dresser*	7617	WIA
Rfn John Connor	41915	DOW: 8/9	Rfn D. B. Elrod*	99489	WIA
Rfn Alfred Corbett	88860	DOW: 6/9	Rfn John Farrell*	13143	WIA
Rfn James Coulton	35970	DOW: 8/9	Rfn Harry Faulkner	50278	DOW: 6/9
Rfn Thomas Crabtree	105604	DOW: 6/9	Cpl Ernest Fisher	23001	DOW: 9/9

Rfn Thomas Patrick Fullalove	87240	DOW: 6/9
Rfn Thomas Edward Gallamore*	99518	WIA
Rfn Sydney Goodill	99514	WIA
Rfn Arthur E. Gough	99511	WIA
Rfn William Green	101297	DOW: 8/9
Cpl Robert Grice	260018	DOW: 6/9
Rfn John Harrison	242665	DOW: 9/9
Rfn Ernest Haude	82688	WIA
Rfn Samuel Haw	87008	DOW: 6/9
Rfn Norman Hinchcliffe	99533	DOW: 8/9
Rfn George Arthur Hinchliffe	99538	WIA
Rfn Albert Holt	99525	DOW: 11/9
Rfn Albert Jackson*	86542	WIA
Rfn John R. Jaeger*	214237	WIA
Rfn James Jolly*	95166	WIA
Rfn Arthur Jones*	308376	WIA
Sgt William Jones	57980	DOW: 15/9
Rfn Francis John Kellow	381862	DOW: 8/9
Rfn John Lawson*	91053	WIA
Rfn Sidney Frank Lloyd	94294	WIA
L/Sgt Charles Percy Loades	328011	DOW: 7/9
Rfn Charles David Lomas	87120	DOW: 7/9
Rfn Edward Machin	49953	WIA
Rfn John Mackarell*	14684	WIA
Rfn William Matthews	105536	WIA
Rfn Charles Munt*	308849	WIA
Rfn Michael Murray*	94282	WIA
Rfn Oscar Mustin*	88064	WIA
L/Cpl Robert Prescott	307525	WIA
Rfn William Ambrose Quayle	331983	WIA
Rfn Albert S. M. Smith*	82808	WIA
L/Cpl George W. Sowerby*	57840	WIA
L/Cpl Samuel Stain	87867	DOW: 8/9
Rfn Michael Summers*	267159	WIA
Rfn James Thompson	47368	DOW: 8/9
Rfn Bernard James Walsh	305343	WIA
Rfn Charles Ward	86622	DOW: 7/9
Rfn Stanley T. Wright	23657	WIA
Rfn William H. Wright	50176	WIA

* = wounded who did not return.

During daytime on 5 September, the battalion were relieved and moved into support, with HQ at Battersea Bridge. 'A' were distributed along Festubert East, South Tramway Trench, and the Tuning Fork Switch; 'B', at Lone Farm and the Reserve Line; 'C', in the Reserve Line and Tuning Fork Switch; and 'D', in the two Cailloux Keeps, McMahon Post, and Festubert Central. Harassing artillery fire wounded three: L/Cpl William Gale, suffering from multiple shrapnel wounds, was evacuated home, as was Rfn John Judson, with a serious thigh wound, and Rfn Cornelius Ledger's forearm wound kept him from duty until late October. The battalion's time in support was quiet, and on 8 September, 165 Bde became Corps Reserve at 'W' Camp, remaining there until the 14th.

Some working parties were caught by gas as they toiled in the dark. On 10 September, Rfn Joseph Kelly became the first victim, returning in late October. On the 12th, it was Rfn James Laver, who only rejoined after the Armistice. Four Riflemen were gassed on 13 September; Archibald Cooper and Benjamin Kempster both rejoining, though Herbert Longmire was evacuated home and Edward Fitzsimmons medically downgraded and posted to a Kitchen Company in Boulogne.

On 14 September, they marched to the front via Le Préol, relieving the Fusiliers in the outposts on the very right of the divisional line. The war had moved on, the front line now on the fringes of Canteleux, only a mile west of the church in La Bassée. 'C' took the left front in Violaines Trench, with 'D' to their right in Cupola Alley. 'B' were in Canteleux

Alley, with 'A' on the right front in Plain Alley, their right bound at the canal. The only casualty prior to midnight was Rfn Harry Carr, badly wounded in the hand and face by a rifle grenade.

Hostile artillery was very active during the night of 14–15 September, shrapnel, HE, and Yellow-X fired in abundance, though most landed behind the battalion. Givenchy and the craters were shelled again during the morning of 15 September, the intensity increasing during the night. Though the fire to the rear was mainly from 4.2 and 5.9, the battalion's outposts were subjected to 200 rounds of 77-mm in the early hours of 16 September, wounding Rfn Gilbert Chisholme in the wrist. The only other casualty that day was Rfn Hew Stevenson, who was a very long way from the front. One of the 'originals', twenty-four-year-old Stevenson must have been overjoyed to be granted home leave on 16 September, but at Calais that night, he was buried when German aircraft bombed the area. Although he was dug out physically unharmed, the experience triggered a nervous breakdown and he was medically discharged and pensioned for shellshock. Tragedy also struck for one in the front line, though it would be several days before Oldham man Rfn Fred Sykes would learn that Ruth, his nine-year-old daughter, had died from TB. The thirty-eight-year-old father of five from 'C' was granted compassionate leave.

Late on the 16th, 'A' was withdrawn to Cheyne Walk and Bayswater and 'B' to Piccadilly and Givenchy to make room for the 1/5th, who were to assault Canteleux Trench in front of La Bassée, at 5.20 a.m. on 17 September. The attack went well, taking their objectives with light casualties and seizing thirty-three prisoners. German artillery had been fairly active during the night, Blue-X and Yellow-X rounds amid the numerous 4.2 and 5.9 shrapnel and HE. When the divisional guns began their preliminary bombardment for the attack, German artillery responded in kind—most of its fire directed at the Rifles. It is probable that all the battalion's casualties for 17 September, listed below, came from this retaliation and not from later fighting patrols (the exception being L/Cpl George Fairclough, attached to 165 TMB, who as a gas casualty, was probably a victim of earlier fire).

Casualties, 17 September 1918

Rfn Albert Alsop	88843	WIA	Rfn Richard Lea	405862	KIA
Rfn William Aspden	38323	WIA	Rfn Rowland Lister	99588	WIA
Rfn Matthew Downey	306838	WIA	Rfn John Riley	27827	WIA
L/Cpl George Albert Fairclough	241798	Gas	Sgt John Thomas Ryan	19657	KIA
			Rfn George Wilson	88276	KIA
Rfn Herman Haworth	94264	KIA	Rfn John C. Woods	50686	WAD

Later that afternoon, the 1/6th pushed out fighting patrols from 'C' and 'D' in the direction of Brickfields and Violaines. Commanding one of 'D' Company's patrols was 2Lt John Setchell. He led his twelve men down La Bassée Alley, where they later established a post. About 450 yards along, he reached the junction of La Bassée Alley and La Bassée Alley

South, electing to clear to the right before continuing. Creeping along, they encountered a sentry, who was silently captured, and, shortly after, another, who was similarly disposed of. The trench contained two pillboxes—both occupied. The five-man garrison of the first surrendered, as did the second, containing another nine; all sixteen prisoners were brought back safely to British lines and provided some very useful information. Setchell was awarded the MC for this successful action.[6]

A post under the command of L/Cpl James Wareing was established in one of these pillboxes, but upon searching it, he found it was wired for demolition. Intelligence had warned about booby traps, but notwithstanding this and his limited knowledge of explosives, Wareing found and cut all the wires leading to the charge and removed the detonators—an act for which he received the MM.[7] Although his actions may seem foolhardy, in view of the amount of enemy retaliatory fire, he felt it imperative to get his section into cover as quickly as possible and not wait—for what could have been hours—for the RE to defuse it.

Another patrol, commanded by 2Lt Samuel Lee, advanced along Cupola Alley, 300 yards to Setchell's right. His point man informed the subaltern about a sentry ahead, in a position known as Turn Table. Lee crawled forward alone to reconnoitre the position and was within 30 yards when the sentry spotted him and pulled out a grenade. Lee snapped off a quick shot, hitting the sentry in the right arm, the grenade falling to the ground—fortunately for the foe, it was before he had pulled the cord. Lee rushed the post, captured the sentry, and then chased after the other six from the garrison, who had fled when he opened fire. Although he managed to shoot one, the rest escaped. Lee was also awarded the MC.[8]

Enemy artillery constantly targeted 165 Bde throughout the night of 17 September and for much of the following day. Although mostly 4.2 and 5.9, some 77-mm and scattered Yellow-X shells struck the battalion's line, but only two casualties resulted, both on the 18th: Rfn John Cain was gassed and Rfn Nicholas Finlay wounded in the arm, neither seriously.

On 18 September, 'C' and 'D' were relieved and joined the others in support. 'A' were in Cheyne Walk and Bayswater, 'B' in the southern craters (Red Dragon–Warlingham), 'C' in Gunner Siding, and 'D' in Pont Fixe. HQ occupied Barge House. There was only scattered shelling overnight and on the 19th, most falling to the north of them. Their only casualty that day was Rfn William Cross, evacuated home after being gassed.

Two casualties occurred on 20 September, though only one was due to enemy action. Rfn James Morgan suffered lacerations from being blown into barbed wire by a shell, and although initially recorded as wounded at duty, he was later admitted to the Field Ambulance, only returning in December. The other, Rfn Abraham Lazarovitch, sliced his hand with an axe while cutting wood and did not return until after the Armistice. Later that day, the battalion moved into Corps Reserve at Drouvin Camp, where they remained until 23 September. Although numerous working parties were demanded, only Rfn William Morgan was wounded, his gassing severe enough to warrant evacuation home.

On 23 September, the battalion boarded the light railway at Hairpin Junction, detraining at Le Préol bridge. From there, they marched to relieve Liverpool Scottish in the outpost line at Festubert. The 24th was quiet, their only casualty was Rfn Frederick Barret, who fell, injuring his back and right leg. The battalion was ordered to make a two-company attack on the morning of 25 September, in conjunction with 19 Division to their left.

At 8.30 a.m., 'A' and 'B' left their jumping-off positions. Less than two hours later, they were in possession of the La Bassée road, from the left divisional bound to the German telephone exchange. Most of the enemy were still sheltering in their dugouts when the attackers reached them and surrendered without resistance. The right company pushed up Spartan Trench, capturing the brickworks north of Violaines. By the early afternoon, Flat Farm was also secured and both companies were busy consolidating—seventy-one prisoners in the bag. A weak counterattack at 10.30 a.m. was easily beaten back.

Few casualties occurred in the advance, but German artillery ferociously bombarded their gains and casualties were numerous. At 6.30 p.m., the enemy counter-attacked under cover of a heavy barrage and the left company was forced to withdraw 250 yards. It was an orderly, fighting withdrawal, commanded by Capt. Adam, who despite being wounded, displayed great leadership in reorganising the defences at Nora Trench and halting the counter-attack—actions rewarded by the MC.

At 3.30 a.m. on the 26th, the battalion attacked again, retaking all the territory lost the previous day and another twenty-eight prisoners. During the assault on Pioneer Dump, CSM Chadwick charged ahead—armed with just a revolver—and cleared an enemy bombing block, his persistent courage finally recognised with a DCM. Tragically, he died from illness in January 1920.

Once again, casualties during the actual infantry action were low, but later artillery fire took a heavy toll. Losses totalled sixty-three, thirteen of whom were fatalities, and it is probable that all those taken prisoner were wounded prior to capture, though Rfn John Kettle's death in German hands was from illness. The bravery of a number was recognised, though their citations have not survived: Sgt Samuel Davey and Riflemen Thomas Foggo, Albert Freer, George Hardwick, Percy Murtagh, Bertie Russell, and Louis Rubens were all awarded the MM. That evening, the battalion moved into reserve after relief by the 1/5th, who continued the advance next day.

Casualties, 25-26 September 1918

Name	Number	Status
Capt. Emmanuel Christo Adam*		WIA: 25/9
L/Cpl William Henry Aitchison	22303	WIA: 25/9
L/Cpl Abraham Aulie	14209	WIA: 25/9
L/Cpl Harry Baldwin	59354	WIA: 25/9
Rfn Harold Bell	90816	POW
Rfn Charles Bethell	90382	KIA: 26/9
Rfn Harry Bill	267864	WIA: 25/9
Rfn Thomas Arthur Black	105585	WIA: 25/9
Rfn Edward Bond	12857	WIA: 26/9
L/Cpl Llewellyn Bradley	85968	WIA: 25/9
L/Cpl Harold Broom	51619	DOW: 5/10
Rfn James J. Burke	308961	WIA: 25/9
Rfn William Carney	242711	WIA: 25/9
Rfn James Clarke	105603	WIA: 26/9
Rfn Frederick Stanley Clayton	241989	WIA: 25/9

Sgt Robert Cliffe	200663	WIA: 25/9	Rfn John Herbert M. Kettle	99578	D: 11/10
L/Cpl George Benjamin Copley	268342	WIA: 25/9	Rfn Charles Henry Knott	82870	WIA: 26/9
			Rfn Arthur Maltby	99591	KIA: 25/9
Cpl Jonathan Crellin	380445	WIA: 25/9	Sgt Edward McInroy	305173	KIA: 26/9
Sgt Arthur Cuerden	405236	WIA: 25/9	2Lt Charles John McLean		WIA: 25/9
L/Cpl Walter Edward Davies	88837	WIA: 25/9	L/Cpl Henry Murphy	11380	WAD: 26/9
Rfn Hartley Downs	308087	WIA: 26/9	Rfn Frank Nicholls	86578	WIA: 25/9
Rfn Francis Henry Dowsett	242522	WIA: 25/9	Rfn William Carr Nicholson	99604	WIA: 25/9
Rfn William Eyles	86812	WIA: 25/9	Rfn Vincent E. Pike	86562	WIA: 25/9
Rfn Arthur Fazackerley	332894	WIA: 25/9	Rfn James Ramsden	49968	KIA: 25/9
Cpl John Fell	308275	WIA: 25/9	Rfn Harry Pointon**	85402	WIA/POW
2Lt F. W. H. Garnham		WIA: 25/9	Cpl James Readie	241755	WIA: 25/9
Rfn Charles Robert Gatland	105499	KIA: 26/9	Rfn Thomas Francis Reynolds*	240172	DOW: 26/9
Rfn Albert Gibson	308380	WIA: 25/9			
Rfn Cuthbert Greaves	87019	WIA: 26/9	Rfn David Ivor Richards	353010	KIA: 26/9
Rfn William Bryan Griffith	101292	KIA: 26/9	Rfn Frederick William Roberts	88066	WIA: 26/9
Rfn Hervey Hartley	99542	WIA: 25/9			
Sgt Gerald Ernest Hemingway	31822	DOW: 26/9	Rfn Peter Seville	305665	WIA: 25/9
			Cpl Ezra James Smalley	44505	KIA: 26/9
Cpl William James Herbert*	240458	WIA: 25/9	Rfn Gifford Smith	88914	WIA: 25/9
Cpl Richard Neville Hesketh	88834	KIA: 26/9	Rfn William Swainbank	72456	WIA: 25/9
Rfn Alfred Horne	86488	WIA: 25/9	Rfn John William Ward	88930	WIA: 25/9
Rfn Mark Reginald Hughes	99521	WIA: 25/9	Sgt James Weightman	201507	WIA: 26/9
L/Cpl Thomas Dugdale Jackson	85185	POW	Cpl William Wilson	330088	WIA: 25/9
			Rfn William Worthington	88935	POW
Rfn Joseph J. Johnson	87123	KIA: 26/9	Rfn Frederick Wroe	12389	WIA: 25/9
Rfn William Keneley	330675	WIA: 25/9			

All who died from wounds are recorded wounded on the 25th.

* = an 'Original'. ** = Pointon is recorded in the *Casualties Book* as being wounded and missing on 29 September—he was almost certainly a casualty of the 25th.

'A' went to the Tuning Fork Keep and Reserve Line; 'B' around Cailloux; 'C', in the vicinity of Le Plantin; and 'D' about Barnton Road. HQ occupied a dugout in Duke Post. The 27th was quiet, though Rfn Thomas Robinson suffered a shrapnel wound to the shoulder. The battalion was relieved on 29 September, but not before five were gassed during an early morning bombardment of the rear with Blue, Yellow, and Green-X shells: Cpl James Jackson and Riflemen Alexander Carr, William Carr, Arthur Dixon, and George Scrivener were all affected. After relief, the battalion went into billets in the Rue de Lille in Béthune, where they remained until 3 October.

While they were out of the line, the CO made recommendations for the New Year's Honours. Among these, QM Maj. Edward Goulding received the OBE for his unfailing determination to put the welfare of the men above his own and for personally supervising the delivery of vital supplies under heavy shellfire. RQMS McWean received the MSM for similar reasons. Mentioned in Dispatches were Cpl John Braithwaite, Rfn Walter Roberts, and Capt. Adam.

Division planned to capitalise on any general German withdrawal—to be triggered by a telegram containing the code name 'Scurry', followed by the Divisional Objective and the time the advance was to begin. Each unit would then move to predetermined starting positions. To facilitate this, brigades were reorganised, battalions divided into 'Advanced Guard' and 'Main Party'. Additionally, each brigade-commander had at his disposal elements of 'C' Sqn, King Edward's Horse; one section of RE; an 'Investigation Party' from the Tunnelling Company; an 18-pounder battery; a section of 4.5-inch Howitzers; a mobile section of medium trench mortars; a company from the MG Battalion; and a proportion of the Field Ambulance.

Behind the lines, working parties feverishly laboured, improving roads for the large amount of wheeled traffic needed to support an advance, and surfacing other tracks for pack animals to follow.[9] No full 'Scurry' was sent, as the method of German withdrawal didn't allow Corps to issue a definite order for advance at a specific time, but the codename was used to order an advance and the arrangements worked perfectly. The intention was to maintain pressure on the retreating enemy, but not to force the engagement of the entire division, as the number of divisions available within Fifth Army were inadequate for a full-scale offensive.

Late on 2 October, a captured German officer revealed that the expected enemy withdrawal to the Haute Deûle Line had begun at 4 a.m., so at 5 a.m. on 3 October, the battalion received 'Scurry'. 'A' deployed around Pont Fixe, 'B' at Le Plantin, 'C' around Lancaster Post, 'D' to Estaminet Corner, and HQ in Lone Farm. Next day, the battalion moved to the La Bassée-Aubers Line, with 'A' and 'C' south of the La Bassée-Canteleux Road, the others to the north of it, with HQ in Bath Road.

During 3–4 October, the division advanced 5 miles, encountering little resistance, casualties correspondingly light. Most enemy positions had either been blown, booby-trapped, or wired for demolition. West of Salomé, the roads were heavily cratered and the RE and Pioneers filled in thirty-two craters in 14 miles, allowing supplies and artillery to keep pace with the advance. The battalion also received their final draft prior to the Armistice, when fifty-six men joined on 4 October. On the 5th, the battalion relieved 1/4th KORL in the outpost line on the right of the divisional advance, rather inconveniently split by the canal. To the north of the canal, 'C' occupied the eastern end of Petit Hantay, 'B' providing support in the western end of the village and HQ in Hantay Château. Across the canal, 'A' was in the outskirts of Billy-Berclau, with 'D' in support.

There was negligible hostile fire during the day on 6 October, but as night fell, very heavy machine-gun fire was directed against all supply routes. HQ in Hantay Château came under intermittent shelling for most of 7 October and Rfn James Naylor was wounded in the ankles, though he returned later that month. The only other casualty was Rfn George Harrison, who accidentally shot himself in his left hand while cleaning his rifle—a lapse that saw his evacuation home after just three days with the battalion and a lenient fourteen days' field punishment for his carelessness.

On 8 October, the battalion were relieved and went into support billets in Salomé. Sadly, prior to their relief, they suffered three casualties: 2Lt Henry Miller and Rfn Albert Wilson were both wounded—the latter with a 'Blighty' wound to the left leg—and nineteen-year-old Rfn Richard Jones was killed. It was not until 15 October that the battalion returned to the line.

The front remained fairly constant until 10 October, stiff enemy resistance and German flooding of the low ground to the west of Don delaying advance. Hostile fire had increased considerably and a large number of fires and explosions were seen behind enemy lines—suggestive of further organised withdrawal. Jeudwine began to plan a forced crossing of the Haute Deûle Canal to coincide with a push by 74 Division to their left, who would force the canal at Haubourdin. On 13 October, information from prisoners indicated a possible withdrawal to the east of Lille that night, but overnight patrols probing enemy defences found them holding their usual posts. A large-scale raid by the 1/5th to the south-west of Don railway station at 9.30 p.m. captured twenty prisoners, who confirmed that withdrawal was expected any day. Late on 14 October, the Corps to the right succeeded in crossing at Pont-à-Vendin and Meurchin. The 74th Division also succeeded in pushing their line forward, when the enemy to their front withdrew; on the divisional front, however, the enemy held firm. During the afternoon of 15 October, determined action by the advanced guard of the 1/5th KLR and 1/4th Loyals, they succeeded in driving the enemy across the canal.

In view of these advances, late on 15 October, the battalion was brought forward from Salomé to La Place, resting there for two hours before preparing to leapfrog through the 1/5th, who had crossed the canal that night. It was 4 a.m. on 16 October when the battalion crossed to take over the lead, a single plank spanning the waterway. 'A' and 'D' under Capt. Richard Rathbone headed for Annœullin and 'B' and 'C' under Capt. Blackledge, to Allennes-les-Marais; HQ remained at Don station. The advance against Allennes was delayed by heavy machine-gun fire, though at 9 a.m., the enemy in Annœullin set fire to the village and retired upon Rathbone's approach. Clearing the village, Rathbone swung round and pushed towards Allennes, where their imminent approach, and pressure from Blackledge's force, precipitated German withdrawal. 'B' then shifted east, occupying Herrin before noon. By the evening, 'B' held position in Herrin, with 'A' to the north of the village; 'C', 'D', and an advanced Battalion HQ, in Allennes. Although there were no casualties due to enemy action, another two men were accidentally injured: Rfn William Hulme was accidentally stabbed in the foot by another man's bayonet and Rfn Frederick Wilkinson shot himself in the right hand—though the injury was minor and he returned five weeks later.

At 6 a.m. on 17 October, the battalion continued their push, meeting no resistance in Gondecourt, before advancing across the Houplin-Gondecourt Road, their objective a rough line from the Bois de L'Hospice down to Les Ewuis Farm. They gained this at noon, and at 2 p.m., they pushed patrols into Seclin—the first place where they found civilians still in their homes. The remainder of the battalion then advanced and occupied the Fort de Seclin. It was only when they pushed on against Grand Ennetières that they encountered stubborn resistance, which was overcome by 4.30 p.m. By the evening, 'A' occupied the Fort de Vendeville, HQ and 'B' were in Seclin, and 'C' and 'D' in Grand Ennetières, which was shelled that evening, though the only casualties were civilian.[10]

Seven were wounded during the fighting, though the most seriously injured was twenty-nine-year-old Rfn George Hewitt, whose abdominal wound proved fatal on the 22nd. Rfn Walter Phillipson was the only one to rejoin the battalion, his arm wound allowing his return to duty on 6 November. Cpl Leonard Collings MM, L/Cpl John Carrington, and Riflemen Joseph Allen, Henry Fidoe, James Hamer, and John Mitchell were all evacuated home.

At 8 a.m. on 18 October, the 1/7th leapfrogged through, continuing towards the high ground east of Fretin; an hour later, the 1/5th also marched through, taking position east of Grand Ennetières. At 10 a.m., HQ, 'A' and 'B' moved to Grand Ennetières, where the whole battalion was billeted. Fretin and Grand Ennetières were both heavily shelled by 4.2 Howitzers at 2 p.m., though the battalion escaped without loss.

Overnight, the divisional crossed the La Marcq river and the battalion was billeted in Fretin, their journey eastwards continuing at 7 a.m. on 20 October, firstly through Péronne-en-Mélantois, then over the river at Bouvines, onto Cysoing, reaching Quennaumont at 10.30 a.m. The rest here was brief, as at 1.30 p.m., they marched through Bourghelles, Wannehain, then Maraîche, where they were billeted. The *Casualties Book* documents two fatalities for 20 October, both killed in action: Riflemen Walter Hyde and Albert Oxspring (Oxspring is recorded for the 19th by CWGC).

On 21 October, the battalion was relieved and went into Corps Reserve in the western edge of Bourghelles. Although there were no casualties from enemy action, nineteen-year-old Rfn George North was admitted to hospital suffering from Spanish influenza, dying on the 29th. The battalion remained in billets until 26 October, training in the new 'open' warfare.

From 23 October, it became clear that the enemy was determined to hold the bridgehead west of Tournai. Jeudwine ordered that it was now Corps policy not to attack this bridgehead, so rather than continuing the general advance, a main line of resistance was to be constructed west of Froidmont in case of counterattack, with divisional artillery, machine guns, and mortars continuing to harass the foe.[11] The rapid progress proved challenging for logistics, though sufficient water, food, and ammunition continued to reach the front line and the guns were able to keep pace. Considerable ingenuity, however, was needed to maintain communications:

> The rate of the advance of III Corps has outstripped the maximum speed of construction of overhead telegraph routes, and it's necessary to concentrate the work of all Signal Service personnel on the construction of one main forward route.... In order, as far as possible, to meet the requirements of headquarters and units not now on the telephone, a Public Call Telephone has been installed just inside the doorway of the Corps Headquarters château.[12]

On 26 October, the battalion relieved the Fusiliers in reserve at Froidmont. Enemy artillery was fairly quiet during daylight, but after dark, activity increased considerably. With no obvious fixed positions, much of this fire was speculative—mainly directed at villages. Many of the rounds were gas, causing appalling casualties among civilians, who lacked protection. On 27 October, the only casualty from the battalion was Rfn Charles Hudson, though his gassing was minor.

On 28 October, the battalion relieved 1/4th KORL in the outposts. 'B' on the left front, 800 yards north of Pic-au-Vent, had their platoons widely spaced. They were supported by 'D' in La Croix de Pierre. 'A', on the right front, held defensive positions in and around Ere, with 'C' in support at the crossroads 1,200 yards east of Froidmont. HQ set up in the tannery near the crossroads. The diary refers to two wounded that day, though no entries in the *Casualties Book* support this. The battalion sent two daylight patrols out on the 29th, both of whom discovered that the enemy still held their line, though neither suffered loss. Sadly, a 'B' Company patrol was far less fortunate in the early hours of 30 October, coming under heavy machine-gun fire, which hit six Riflemen.

The diary refers to this fire coming from a crossroads in square U.27c (there are no crossroads in that square and it is 4,000 yards behind the lines of the neighbouring division). The probable position was the crossroads in square O.27c, where an enemy machine gun had been reported by KORL the previous night, 600 yards north-east of 'B' Company's left platoon. Twenty-six-year-old William Williams (023) was killed, and nineteen-year-old Ivan Grindell was mortally wounded, dying later that day. John Hornby and William Spence both suffered 'Blighty' wounds; Frederick Ellison, wounded in the right shoulder, rejoined in late November; and J. Lamb was able to continue on duty once his wound was dressed.

Later that day, the battalion was relieved and pulled back to Esplechin as reserve (the diary states Froidmont, though the Divisional dispositions map, shows the battalion billeted in the northern part of Esplechin). Back in Oswestry, Rfn Wilfred Barton—posted there after recovering from his 1917 wounding—died from influenza at the hospital on 30 October. The last day of October was quiet and casualty free, though intermittent shelling on 1 November resulted in the evacuation of Rfn Alfred Shaw with a thigh wound. Another move took place on 3 November, when the battalion manned the main line of resistance, from just north of Froidmont to the divisional bound south-east of Haudion. HQ moved into the Ferme du Baron, midway between Lamain and Esplechin.

Enemy artillery fire increased on the 4th, though the only casualty was RQMS Thomas McWean on 5 November, with a 'Blighty' wound to the left leg, suffered when Froidmont was lightly shelled during the evening. 'A' Company's CQMS, Albert Hampson took over as RQMS. It was not until 7 November that the battalion returned to the outpost line, with 'D' on the left front, supported by 'B', and 'C' on the right front, supported by 'A'. HQ was once again in the tannery.

The enemy began his expected withdrawal across the Escaut at 4.30 a.m. on 8 November; however, it was only after the battalion realised enemy positions seemed abnormally quiet that a series of small patrols were despatched by both forward companies. When these reported the enemy gone, strong fighting patrols were sent out and given the western bank of the Escaut as their objective. 'D' experienced some slight opposition, but despite this, they and 'C' had passed beyond Faubourg-Saint-Martin and the lunatic asylum by 7 a.m., establishing positions close to the river bank at 8 a.m. Heavy enemy machine-gun fire swept all approaches to the river, halting further progress. Hot on the heels of the advance was Lt-Col. McKaig and a small escort from HQ, reaching Tournai at 7.45 a.m. to be greeted by the delighted burgomaster. The rest of the battalion, following behind, were east of Ere at 8.30 a.m. Their advance had been somewhat quicker than 74 Division to their left, so once Tournai was entered, they swept round to the left to secure the town. As soon as 74 Division arrived, the Rifles handed over their positions and prepared to continue their advance.

The locals obligingly pointed out the positions of German machine guns on the eastern bank, and while the men rested, officers and SNCOs reconnoitred the approaches and suitable crossing places. During the afternoon, the companies moved to the selected crossing point, south of Tournai. Enemy machine guns continued to target the approaches and 100 4.2 Howitzer rounds fired into Tournai caused eight casualties: nineteen-year-old Rfn John Harrison was killed outright and twenty-two-year-old Rfn Robert Quayle critically wounded in the thigh and lower jaw, injuries that proved mortal next day; they were the last two fatalities before the Armistice. Only Rfn Leonard Butter, wounded in the buttock, rejoined. L/Cpl Richard McCullagh, one of the 'originals' and a signaller with 'A', had got through the entire war without so much as a scratch. To be wounded just three days before the Armistice was most unlucky. Although the injury to his left foot was minor, he contracted influenza four days before Christmas and was evacuated home—thankfully, he survived. The other casualties, Riflemen Thomas Bailey, John Bradley, Thomas Eastham, and Thomas Halligan, all boarded hospital ships for England.

Preparations for the three-company crossing continued, the assault scheduled for 11 p.m., under Capt. Blackledge, whose advanced headquarters were near the crossing-point. 'C', who were not involved, brought three collapsible boats and a light bridge forward. Once a bridgehead was established, the RE would construct a pontoon bridge, allowing heavier traffic across. By 11 p.m., German machine-gun fire had ceased and the far bank was silent. The boats were launched and men began to be ferried over. To their great relief, they found the enemy had withdrawn. By dawn, 'A', 'B', and 'D' were safely on the eastern bank and the RE had completed their bridge. Platoons, pushed out in a screen 2,000 yards ahead, encountered no opposition.

At 9.30 a.m., the 1/7th passed through the battalion, who moved to billets at the château at Vaulx. Only sporadic hostile artillery fire was experienced during the 9th, but this resulted in their last casualty from enemy action. L/Sgt Albert Simm was wounded in the wrist and hand and evacuated home. By 2 p.m., both brigades from 55 Division had reached their second objective, east of Barry, and were in touch with the enemy, who were retreating.

The divisional advance was now spearheaded by two units: Stockwell's Force and Legard's Force. The former, commanded by Brig.-Gen. Stockwell, consisted of 164 Bde HQ, 'C' Sqn King Edward's Horse, 'A' Company of VII Corps' Cyclist Battalion, and 'A' Battery from 275 Bde RFA. Legard's Force, attached from 9th Cavalry Bde, was of a similar composition, the cyclists providing the infantry element for both battle groups. Stockwell crossed the river at 3 p.m., followed shortly afterwards by Legard. Stockwell reached the western outskirts of Leuze at 8.30 p.m., encountering considerable machine-gun and mortar fire, so held position for the night.

The enemy continue his withdrawal during the night, and early on 10 November, Legard reported that Leuze was clear of the enemy, though the delighted locals informed them that there were still small numbers 4 miles along the road in Ligne. The 165th Bde continued their advance at 8 a.m. on 10 November, the 1/7th leading and the battalion following in their wake. At 9.25 a.m., the 1/7th entered Leuze and by 10 a.m., Legard's Force had quashed the opposition in Ligne and was advancing on Villers-Saint-Amand. At 12.25 p.m., Legard reached Ath, where further progress was checked by heavy machine-gun fire sweeping the canal bridges.

The battalion halted in Leuze for dinner, and at 2 p.m., they were ordered to billet for the night in Ath. At 4.30 p.m., while still *en route*, their orders were amended and they were directed to about-turn and occupy billets in Grandmetz. Once again, their orders were changed when they were intercepted and told to billet in Ligne. However, as they marched through Chapelle-à-Wattines, they were met by the billeting party, bearing the news that no accommodation was available in Ligne. Lt-Col. McKaig took an executive decision and billeted his now-exhausted men in Chapelle-à-Wattines.

Since crossing the Escaut, the division had advanced 13 miles along the main Tournai-Brussels Road, despite the enemy rendering the road impassable to all but men on foot and pack transport. In that distance, the Pioneers and RE filled in twenty-two large craters and defused 500 mines.[13]

Jeudwine ordered that no attempts be made to force the crossings of the River Dendre and the canal in Ath and that night, he and the brigade-commanders planned an assault crossing, using their entire infantry force; this was facilitated by the full might of divisional artillery. However, this was made redundant thanks to a daring action by a Lewis team from the Fusiliers. At 5.30 a.m. on 11 November, the Germans were still manning the iron bridge, which was wired for demolition. By clever use of cover, the Lewis team worked their way into a house overlooking the bridge and drove off the enemy with accurate fire, preventing them from detonating the charge. The Fusiliers rushed the bridge, securing a bridgehead and allowing Legard to move through to continue the advance.

At 8.30 a.m., the battalion was ordered to move on Ath and began their march. Battalion commanders were discussing details for the attack at a conference in Villers-Saint-Amand when, at 9.05 a.m., a verbal message about a ceasefire was passed to Divisional HQ at Barry, necessitating a hurried phone call to the conference and various staff officers frantically trying to contact the forward troops, ordering them to hold position. Legard's cavalry were 7 miles east of Ath before they halted.[14]

The battalion paused near Ligne, awaiting Lt-Col. McKaig's return from the conference and were resting on the sides of the road when a cavalry unit passed, imparting rumours that the enemy had withdrawn. At 10.25 a.m., an orderly galloped towards them from the front, repeatedly yelling something, but it was not until he got nearer that the men towards the front of the battalion could make out the words, 'Cease Fire, Cease Fire'. His message was met with considerable enthusiasm, but until it was corroborated, the battalion took no action. Confirmation came five minutes later, when Lt-Col. McKaig rode up, bearing the news that a 'cease fire' would begin at 11 a.m.—news greeted with 'tremendous cheering'.[15]

The battalion was ordered to Meslin-L'Évêque and set off at 10.45 a.m., passing the Divisional-Commander, who took their salute. The roads were lined with cheering civilians, and at 11 a.m., they halted and the buglers blew the 'Cease-Fire' before the march continued. At 1.45 p.m., Meslin-L'Évêque was reached and men billeted around the village.

14

Epilogue

The response to the news of a cease-fire, as chronicled in the diary, must be treated with a modicum of scepticism. A similar reaction—as 'officially' noted in many diaries—is not always borne out by the individual recollections of those from the same battalions. Undoubtedly pleased that the war had apparently ended, most were too exhausted and too conscious of the losses and hardships endured along the way to be overly elated. Of the 1,125 who boarded SS *City of Edinburgh* in February 1915, just ninety-nine heard the bugles sound. The reception back in England was far less muted. Norman Ellison, a clerk in the Depot at Heaton Park, recalled:

> Manchester went completely wild that day. The camp was thrown open and nearly everyone streamed down to the centre of the city. No trams were running and all the pubs were closed. Piccadilly and the main thoroughfares were tightly jammed with cheering crowds: it was pandemonium. One incident has remained in memory throughout the years: two sailors jigging on the roof of a taxi cab when it collapsed and they disappeared inside.[1]

A number of awards were gazetted in the Birthday Honours for 1919, most of which have already been narrated. One so far omitted was a DCM for Cpl Walter Parker, attached to the TMB:

> His gallantry and distinguished service during the last six months. He has invariably shown great coolness and initiative under fire, and on several occasions, when in isolated positions, has proved himself a very useful commander of men. His work at all times has been admirable, and in particular during recent minor operations he has rendered very valuable service.[2]

The battalion remained at Meslin until 15 December. It must be understood that the Armistice was merely a cease-fire, consequently, training continued; though, as it became clearer that the Armistice would hold, it became secondary to other activities. Discipline and military efficiency had to be maintained, but it was a difficult balancing act for commanders to ensure that too much did not have precisely the opposite effect to that intended.

Understandably, men wanted to return to home as soon as possible, but under the circumstances, it was not yet possible to demobilise in large numbers. The delay caused considerable ill-feeling among some and, invariably, there were those who voted with their feet: two of the 1918 arrivals deserted—both were caught and punished; a third was given twenty-eight days' field punishment for altering the date of attestment in his Pay Book—a pointless subterfuge, as the date was recorded in many other documents.

Sports, training, and general military life still carried their risks, even if the fighting was over. On 3 December, Rfn James Kelly had a very lucky escape when he negligently discharged his rifle while attempting to unload it. The wounds to thumb and index finger were minor and he returned to duty two days later. On 22 November, Rfn John Darcy was accidentally burned in the face, spending three weeks in hospital. Injured in the same incident was Rfn Bernard Goldman, whose burns to hand and face were more serious and he was evacuated home. On 13 December, Cpl James Wareing accidentally broke his collar bone, though his stay in hospital was prolonged when he contacted Spanish influenza there—though he survived. Others were less fortunate: thirty-year-old L/Cpl George Ford died from influenza at Terlincthun on 28 November. Some perished at home from illness or conditions caused by their military service: twenty-two-year-old Rfn Reginald Waring had been medically discharged in May 1917 after a heart defect was diagnosed; although a pre-existing condition, it was aggravated by his service and proved fatal on 19 December. On 5 January 1920, thirty-nine-year-old Rfn Herbert Cowan, one of the 'originals', died in Liverpool. During his service, he had seemed remarkably robust—just six days with the Field Ambulance in June 1917, suffering from a high temperature—however, his commemoration by CWGC means that his service was seen as a contributory factor to his premature demise.

Sport and education became crucial in the following months: Jeudwine wanted his men, who had toiled so hard, to return to civilian life with better skills than when they had enlisted. Courses in mathematics and English were run, men being able to take recognised examinations in these; trade and professional courses were also organised, instructors found from the vast pool of skills available within the military. Refresher courses were also available for those already qualified in various trades, but whose civilian skills had become somewhat rusty during their time with the colours.

On 7 December, the battalion marched to the Ath–Tournai Road, the division lining the road to welcome His Majesty the King. Accompanied by the Prince of Wales, Prince Albert, and Maj.-Gen Jeudwine, the monarch walked the length of the division to enthusiastic cheering from all ranks. Upon their departure, the battalion marched to Ath, where they broke for lunch and the battalion was dismissed—no doubt to the great benefit of local estaminets. On 15 December, they marched to Enghien and onwards through Lembecq the next day, eventually reaching Uccle, where they were billeted. The final divisional-parade was on 3 January, the third anniversary of its formation, when they were inspected by King Albert of Belgium at the Bois de la Cambre, just outside Brussels.

Some battalions joined the occupation force in Germany, though the 1/6th remained in Uccle until the end of April 1919. By then, almost all had been demobbed and it was just a cadre that returned to the civic reception in Liverpool, where they were joined by former members of the battalion. Lt-Col. McKaig remained CO until 1928—twelve years from when he first took command. The short, but distinguished life of the Rifles effectively ended in 1936, when it became a Territorial anti-aircraft unit. After a number of designation changes, it finally disbanded in March 1955.

Although many re-engaged post-war, the majority went back to rebuilding the lives so precipitously interrupted in 1914. For most, their priority was the present and the future, drawing a veil over the horrors of the past—with varying degrees of success. In the immediate post-war years, many bereaved families visited the old battlefields to seek out the soil where their loved ones had perished. Many old soldiers visited too: Norman Ellison returned to the Salient in 1922 and an anonymous account of his trip, entitled 'Along the Road to Pop: A soldier revisits a land of ghosts: some memories of a tragic pilgrimage', was published in the *Echo* in 1924.[3] Despite the sombre title, his article was upbeat, concentrating on happier memories rather than the suffering.

The 1920 publication of a history of the 2/6th prompted some veterans of the 1/6th to express the opinion that the story of their hardships should also be recorded, and in 1927, Col. McKaig and Norman Ellison published a joint letter in the *Echo*, asking for diaries and accounts of their service from anyone who had served with the battalion.[4] From the material received, interviews, his own diary, and the 'Edmonds' copy of the war diary, Ellison began to compose a battalion history. Eventually, he had penned some 40,000 words and submitted these to Col. Harrison, Col. McKaig, Lt-Col. Wainwright, and Maj. Blackledge—all of whom approved his work. Unfortunately, the costs of printing effectively doomed the project and it was decided that a shorter account in *The Greenjacket* would suffice; sadly, this publication suffered a premature demise in July 1928, the battalion's story ending abruptly at September 1916. In 1970, Ellison wrote in the foreword of his *Miscellany* of his intention to deposit the typed version of his *1914-1919 Diary*, the completed part of the *Battalion History* and his collection of newspaper cuttings and 'oddments relevant to the battalion' with the Liverpool Record Office, as 'I cannot equate with equanimity, their destruction on my death'.[5] In April 1958, Ellison had added a foreword to his *1914-19 Diary*:

> I have underwritten deliberately, as I realise how utterly impossible it is to convey the horrors of modern warfare to the reader who has no experience of them. Compiling this book has given me a great deal of personal satisfaction. If it has any value at all, it will not be now but say fifty years hence, when, should it survive, it will enable posterity to read how war took a very ordinary young man from an office-desk and turned his well-ordered life upside-down.[6]

I sincerely hope that this volume goes some way towards fulfilling his aspiration.

Although many met for a pint with old pals, the first reunion was not until 24 February 1933, organised after a series of meetings between Lt-Col. Wainwright, Norman Ellison, and Russell Anderson MM. The success of this first gathering promulgated the organisation of the Liverpool Rifles Association in 1934. Although the natural choice for the first President would have been Lt-Col. Wainwright, he had passed away three months after the 1933 reunion, so the most-senior of the former COs, Col. Davison, was chosen, with Maj. Adam elected Chairman, Russell Anderson the Secretary, and Norman Ellison the Treasurer. At these dinners, the Chairman engaged the company's attention with the ship's bell from SS *City of Edinburgh*, which was presented to the Association when this Liverpool-registered ship was scrapped. Apart from a pause brought about by rationing during the Second World War, the Association met on the nearest Friday to 24 February. In 1970, 100-old comrades attended, though the only founding member still alive was Ellison, Anderson having died in 1958; gradually, they became fewer and the Association died with them.

The Association was not the only 'old comrades' organisation as, in 1930, Ellison and a group of like-minded pals formed the 'Old Insufferables', meeting every Armistice night until Ellison's death in December 1976. This small band—usually around a dozen—were not solely limited to the Rifles, as other veterans from their circle of friends joined them. The meetings were light-hearted; for example, in 1934:

> 'Skip' Roberts had converted the bare whitewashed cellar of his house [Sydenham Avenue, Aigburth] into a very realistic billet. Straw upon the floor, puttees, shirts, pants etc., drying on a line across the room, a brazier, boots, tin-hats, coats and rats too, closely-shuttered windows labelled 'NOT TO BE OPENED. UNDER ENEMY OBSERVATION' and other appropriate touches—the rat nibbling a broken loaf for example—combined to make a great turn-out. Friend Tristram again photographed the group—a particularly happy effort. We were glad to see member Norman Wigzell down again from Birmingham [Wigzell saw home service with the battalion].
>
> Rations over, the remainder of the evening was spent upstairs with the song book and the gramophone. The draw brought George Preston's name out of the hat [Cheshire Regiment]. At half after midnight, two car-loads passed through the new Mersey Tunnel to Wallasey—and so ended one of the most successful of our gatherings.[7]

One other reunion must not be omitted: at the Stork Hotel on 20 March 1936, 6 Platoon got the slap-up meal promised by Platoon-Commander Lt Frederick Bardsley-Powell. Twenty of the platoon were there to dine.

Many went onto distinguished careers post-war, so many that it would be impossible to do justice to them here. However, it would be unfair not to narrate some of Norman Ellison's achievements, as his foresight and dedication in preserving so much material is beyond value. After the war, he worked in an uncle's paper manufacturing business, but in later years, he was able to combine his love of writing and nature. To many readers of a 'certain age', he will be more familiar as 'Nomad', the prolific writer and broadcaster, with over 300 broadcasts—mainly on BBC Radio's *Children's Hour*, which he participated in from 1946 through to 1960.

APPENDIX I

How Long Did the Battalion Spend in the Front Line?

Days Activity	1915	1916	1917	1918	TOTAL	% of TIME
Travelling	14	13	14	5	46	5%
Rest/Intensive Training	77	55	126	55	313	23%
Reserve/Support	111	172	124	135	542	40%
Front Line	107	126	101	120	454	32%

APPENDIX II

Analysis of Statistics

	1/6th KLR	1/5th KORL	1/4th KORL
% of men killed	17.6%	24%	24.6%
% battle casualties (dead and wounded)	60.1%	63%	67%
When did men become a casualty?			
Within first three months in the trenches.	55%	61%	51.3%
Between four and six months in the trenches.	18%	19%	16.4%
Between seven and twelve months in the trenches.	13%	14%	15.4%
Over twelve months in the trenches.	14%	6%	16.9%

For comparison purposes, these tables include data from both KORL battalions in 55 Division, based upon statistically significant samples from surviving service and pension records—approximately 1,700 in total. The data from the 1/6th is from the three volumes of the *Casualties Book* and, as such, is complete and not a statistical sample.

The higher fatality rate of the KORL reflects the battalion-sized attacks both carried out soon after their initial deployment, distinct from the 1/6th, whose first attack was company-sized. However, the analysis of how long men spent in the trenches before becoming a casualty demonstrates that, for all three battalions, vital experience gained in the first three months made all the difference. If men survived their initial apprenticeship, their chances of becoming a casualty diminished considerably.

One source of casualty that was not taken into account when compiling these statistics was accidental wounds—whether self-inflicted, the result of premature detonation, or carelessness by a comrade. The weapon handling of some left much to be desired, and out of the 4,047 who served overseas with the battalion, no fewer than forty-six were shot, stabbed, or blown up by themselves or careless comrades.

% Hospitalisation-other than gas/GSW	1/6th KLR	1/5th KORL	1/4th KORL
Scabies	2.4%	4.4%	7.7%
Shellshock	3.4%	3.2%	4%
Trench foot	0.4%	2.7%	2.5%
Trench Fever	6.4%	6.4%	8%
Trench nephritis	0.4%	0.8%	1.1%
ICT	6.4%	6.1%	4.8%
Seasonal influenza	6%		
Spanish influenza	1.8%		
Myalgia/Rheumatism/Sciatica/Arthritis	2.7%		
DAH/VDH/Cardiac Murmur	1%		

The causes of hospitalisation are broadly similar, though it is fair to say that the Rifles appear less prone to some afflictions. Compared to KORL, they seem almost immune to trench foot, however, there are good reasons for this disparity. Both KORL battalions spent the winter of 1915 in notoriously wet trenches, unlike the Rifles, who were in the much drier conditions at Vaux and then as Army Troops behind the line. The overwhelming majority of trench foot cases for all three battalions were prior to joining 55 Division.

Compared to many, the original battalion was remarkably well behaved, reflecting their initial recruitment of men from professional and white-collar occupations. Once this changed, disciplinary charges rose accordingly, though a number of hardened troublemakers—inherited when the two battalions of the Liverpool Irish were amalgamated—saw a considerable rise in both minor and serious disciplinary charges. Over the course of the war, one officer and thirty-nine men were court-martialled. One man was found not guilty, the others received a variety of punishments. Only two were sentenced to be shot, one for his third desertion, the other for sleeping on sentry—neither sentence was carried out. Ten were charged for self-inflicted shootings, three of which were indisputably deliberate; seven for sleeping on sentry duty; eleven for desertion; one for leaving his post; and eleven for a variety of other offences. The majority of deserters were not first offenders, and though most were released from custody early, one remained in prison until 1921, after starting a mutiny in his military prison.

APPENDIX III

Battalion Roll

Key

If an officer is shown with a number, then this was his number in the battalion prior to commissioning. Men with the rank 'DVR' are drivers of the ASC who deployed to France with the battalion in February 1915.

* - deployed to France with the battalion in February 1915.

** - deployed to France with the battalion in February 1915 and still with them on 11 November 1918.

R - RAMC

H - Home Service only with battalion

Abbey*	H.	Rfn	2407	Adams	Vivian M.	Rfn	241625
Abbott*	Bertram	Cpl	240469	Adamson	Frederick E.	Rfn	3980
Abbott*	George N.	Rbfn	240353	Adamson	John	Rfn	330676
Aberg	Alfred F.	Rfn	88842	Addison	Charles H.	Rfn	88840
Abernethy	Frank	Rfn	241669	Addison	Ernest	Rfn	47620
Abraham	Reginald	Rfn	242605	Ainslie*	Kenneth	Rfn	1873
Abram	James	Rfn	242702	Ainsworth	Albert	Rfn	242700
Achorn	John T.	Rfn	306859	Ainsworth	Henry	Rfn	241979
Ackroyd	Alfred	Rfn	51141	Airey	John	Rfn	242044
Ackroyd**	Ernest	Rfn	241038	Aitcheson	Frederick W.	L/Cpl	242033
Acornley	Arthur	Rfn	306176	Aitchison	Thomas H. G.	Rfn	241180
Adam	Emman. C. M.	Capt.		Aitchison	William H.	L/Cpl	22303
Adams	Arthur	Rfn	49980	Aitken	Allan C.	L/Cpl	242466
Adams*	Charles F.	L/Cpl	240896	Aitken	William R.	Rfn	88841
Adams*	Clarence	Rfn	1295	Aked	Leslie	Rfn	241611
Adams	Harold	A/Cpl	240740	Akerman	Edmund A.	2Lt	
Adams	Herbert	Rfn	241966	Alcock	Charles	Rfn	4044
Adams	Joseph C.	Rfn	241367	Alcock	Charles M.	Rfn	242140
Adams	Robert J.	Rfn	85509	Alcock	Harry	Rfn	4097

Alderson	Frederick H.	Rfn	3478	Argent**	Charles B.	CSM	240070
Alderson	James H.	Rfn	53013	Argue	Robert H.	Rfn	4154
Alderton	Thomas E	Rfn	85359	Argue*	Thomas C.	Cpl	240596
Alexander*	Albert E.	Rfn	1872	Armitage	John A.	Rfn	49981
Alexander*	Charles	Rfn	1177	Armstrong	Charles D.	Rfn	85442
Alexander	George	Cpl	330846	Armstrong*	James	Rfn	240159
Alexander**	Leonard V.	Rfn	240625	Armstrong*	John	Rfn	240480
Alexander	William	Rfn	105535	Arnold	G.	Rfn	308513
Allan	James	Rfn	3812	Arthur	Henry H.	Rfn	241872
Allan	Stanley H.	Rfn	4092	Ashbrook	John B.	Rfn	241762
Allen	Albert L.	Rfn	88839	Ashby	Oswald R.	Rfn	242276
Allen*	Arthur J.	Rfn	2963	Ashby	Wilfred F.	Rfn	95552
Allen	Frederick	Rfn	241647	Ashcroft	George W.	Rfn	331201
Allen*	Harold A.	Rfn	1484	Ashcroft	Joseph W.	Rfn	330266
Allen*	James	Rfn	240269	Ashcroft	Stephen	Rfn	267310
Allen	Joseph	Rfn	86626	Ashley	George K.	Rfn	241412
Allen	Samuel	Rfn	51780	Ashton	James	Rfn	56062
Allen	Stephen H.	Rfn	49894	Ashton	Julian	Rfn	241935
Allen*	Sydney R.	Rfn	2003	Ashton	Robert	Rfn	242831
Allman	John	Rfn	305919	Ashton	Thomas	Rfn	260002
Alsop	Albert	Rfn	88843	Ashurst	Thomas R.	Rfn	242125
Altmann	Frederick H.	Rfn	51376	Ashworth	James	Rfn	242703
Alty	Richard	Rfn	330593	Ashworth*	Ronald	Rfn	2059
Ambrose	Robert W. H.	Rfn	3609	Aspden	William	Rfn	38323
Anderson*	Charles	Rfn	1245	Aspell	Stanley G.	Rfn	3063
Anderson	Isaac	Rfn	242648	Aspinall	Edward G.	Rfn	4531
Anderson**	John F.	Rfn	240268	Aspinall	Fred	Rfn	381584
Anderson	Leonard	L/Cpl	240047	Aspinall	William	Rfn	242475
Anderson*	Russell S.	Rfn	240608	Astley	George	Rfn	51128
Anderson*	Thomas J.	Cpl	240401	Aston*	William	Sgt	63
Anderson	Vernon	Rfn	108324	Atherton*	John B.	Rfn	240127
Anderton	William	Rfn	306245	Atkin	Rowland	Rfn	49918
Andrews**	Arthur E.	WO2	240705	Atkinson	Gilbert	Rfn	51407
Anforth	John	Rfn	242701	Atkinson	Michael U.	Rfn	241526
Anglesey	John	Rfn	241235	Atkinson	Thomas W.	Rfn	52254
Angus	John W.	Rfn	47198	Aulie	Abraham	L/Cpl	14209
Ankers	William	Rfn	46730	Ault	Ernest	L/Cpl	305040
Annesley*	Richard T.	Sgt	1191	Austin*	Joseph B.	Rfn	2077
Annett	William	Rfn	330949	Avery*	H.	Rfn	2711
Annison	Harold E.	Rfn	3589	Aynsley*	William H.	Rfn	240778
Annison	Sam	L/Cpl	242631	Ayre (Hare)	Charles W.	Rfn	4096
Annison*	Thomas G.	Rfn	2408	Bacon	Francis H.	2Lt	
Appleton	Edward	Sgt	22602	Baddeley**	Rowland F.	L/Cpl	240162
Ardern	Walter	Rfn	92010	Bailey	J. H.	Rfn	37156

Bailey	James W.	Rfn	242834	Bardsley-Powell*	Frederick S. E.	Lt	
Bailey	Joseph	Rfn	243756	Bardwell*	Herbert M.	L/Cpl	1532
Bailey	Thomas H.	Rfn	94488	Barford	Valentine E.	Rfn	240785
Bain*	Colin J. M.	Cpl	240633	Bark*	Norman	Rfn	1893
Baines*	Francis S.	L/Cpl	1869	Barker	Frederick J.	Rfn	241456
Baines	John C.	CQMS	22005	Barker	Harold G	Rfn	85327
Baines*	John S.	Rfn	1870	Barker*	James W.	Rfn	240815
Baker	Arthur	L/Cpl	241882	Barker	Stephen M.	Rfn	242837
Baker*	James	Rfn	1868	Barlow	Frank B.	A/Cpl	85959
Baker	Matthew	Rfn	241645	Barnard	George	Rfn	241464
Baker	Thomas	Rfn	242832	Barnes	Abraham	Rfn	109093
Baker*	Thomas	Rfn	1424	Barnes	Alfred B.	Rfn	241901
Baker*	Walter S.	Rfn	2392	Barnes	Frederick	Rfn	242833
Balding	Nelson	Rfn	263014	Barnes*	George	Rfn	2286
Baldwin	Harry	A/Cpl	59354	Barnes*	William A.	L/Cpl	240158
Bale	John	Rfn	109058	Barnett	James	Rfn	241030
Balfour*	Alexander	Rfn	240933	Barnett[H]	James	RSM	unk
Ball	Albert	Rfn	331810	Barnett	William F.	Cpl	241591
Ball*	Richard H.	Rfn	2455	Barnshaw*	Harry G.	Rfn	1692
Ball*	Reginald H.	L/Cpl	2226	Baron	Simeon	Rfn	88267
Ball	Thomas S.	L/Cpl	241086	Barraclough	George	Rfn	105584
Ball	Wilfred	Rfn	241639	Barrand*	Eric I. J.	Rfn	240450
Ball	William	Rfn	241703	Barrett	Frederick	Rfn	86539
Ballinger	Frederick C.	Rfn	242887	Barrett	Robert	Capt.	
Ballock	William J.	Rfn	3219	Barrett	Thomas	Rfn	35163
Balmer	George	Rfn	204776	Barron	Joseph	Rfn	51408
Balmforth	Alfred	Capt.		Barrow	Robert	Rfn	242649
Balshaw	John	Rfn	36718	Barrow	Thomas W.	L/Cpl	241828
Bamber	Henry	L/Cpl	405253	Barry*	Arthur P.	Rfn	240400
Bamfield	Archibald	Rfn	49928	Barton	Frank	Rfn	49923
Bancroft	Hartley D.	Rfn	88848	Barton	Frederick	Rfn	88743
Banister	John A. W.	Sgt	380704	Barton	Gilbert	Rfn	53012
Banks*	Arthur F.	Rfn	240508	Barton	James	Rfn	242814
Banks	Harry	Rfn	242817	Barton	James L.	Rfn	64779
Banks	Hartley	Rfn	242801	Barton	Wilfrid	Rfn	260009
Banks	Leonard	Rfn	51142	Baster*	Herbert H.	2Lt	240350
Banks	Stanley	L/Cpl	260004	Batcheldor*	George	Rfn	1684
Bann	Sidney	Rfn	241690	Bate	Walter	Rfn	51688
Banner	Frederick	Rfn	3743	Bates	Donald	L/Sgt	241660
Banning*	Joseph	L/Cpl	240958	Bates	John L.	Rfn	51139
Bannon*	Thomas P.	Rfn	1986	Batson*	Charles	L/Sgt	186
Barber*	Ernest A.	Rfn	2037	Battarbee*	George H.	A/Cpl	240177
Barber	George	Rfn	87048	Batten	William	Rfn	87869
Barber*	Wilfred	Cpl	1326	Battersby	Fred	Rfn	242840

Batty*	James H.	Rfn	240574
Baugh	Fred	Rfn	241840
Baugh	William E.	Rfn	330693
Baxendale	John	Rfn	265903
Baxendale	Peter	Rfn	108929
Bayliss*	George W.	L/Sgt	1189
Beach	William	Rfn	350002
Beale	Henry J.	Sgt	241658
Bean*	Arthur G.	Rfn	241160
Bean	John G.	L/Cpl	241503
Beard	Horace O.	Rfn	49929
Beardmore	Charles J.	Rfn	58767
Beardsell	Fred G.	Rfn	49990
Beattie	John E.	Rfn	5370
Beatty	Thomas F.	Rfn	12739
Beaumont	Frank	Rfn	49987
Beausire*	Percy James	Cpl	2198
Bebbington	Herbert	Rfn	300466
Becconsall	John	L/Cpl	305774
Beck	Thomas W.	2Lt	
Beck	Walter	Rfn	107871
Beech	William E.	Rfn	37559
Beechey*	Claude G.	CSM	36
Beecroft	Francis E.	Rfn	242704
Beesley	Thomas B.	Rfn	242590
Beeston*	Ernest	L/Sgt	2295
Bell	Harold	Rfn	90816
Bell*	John	Cpl	2438
Bell*	John H.	Rfn	240877
Bell*	Robert	L/Cpl	240444
Bell	Thomas T.	Rfn	331878
Bellerby	Herbert	L/Cpl	49834
Bellion*	William	Rfn	1456
Belshaw	Alfred W.	L/Cpl	241712
Bemment	Arthur L.	2Lt	
Bennet**	Ernest W. K.	Maj.	
Bennett	Arthur	Rfn	85192
Bennett	Frederick	Rfn	266562
Bennett	Job H.	Rfn	1992
Bennett	Thomas J.	Rfn	268633
Bennett	Walter	Rfn	242798
Bennetts	Sidney F.	2Lt	
Bennison	William J.	Rfn	51426
Benson	Edward	Sgt	330512
Benson	Ernest	Rfn	88852
Benson	Joseph	Rfn	80721
Benson*	Robert H.	Rfn	240472
Bent*	A.	Rfn	1929
Bent	Nathaniel	Rfn	241774
Bentley	Edwin	Rfn	305867
Bentley*	Frederick	Rfn	2721
Bentley	William G.	Rfn	85191
Bentley	William R.	Rfn	242684
Berry	Loes W.	Rfn	49092
Bethell	Charles	Rfn	90382
Bettesworth*	Harold	Rfn	1178
Bevan	Arthur	Rfn	241911
Bevan	Robert J.	L/Cpl	266855
Beveridge*	Thomas S.	Rfn	240058
Bibby	Frederick J.	Rfn	51383
Bibby*	George F.	Rfn	240215
Bibby	Reginald	L/Cpl	265799
Bibby	Thomas	Rfn	241917
Bickley	Samuel	Rfn	242839
Bicknell	Thomas	Rfn	242706
Bill	Harry	Rfn	267864
Bingham*	Arthur C.	Rfn	240336
Bingham*	Percy Alex	Rfn	240542
Binnall	William G.	Rfn	260051
Binns	Herbert C.	Rfn	84872
Birch*	Frederick	Rfn	2183
Birchall	Harry	Rfn	49982
Birchall	John	Rfn	49919
Bird	Albert A.	Rfn	241098
Bird*	Percy G.	Rfn	1727
Birkett	George	Capt.	
Birkett*	George B.	Cpl	240605
Birkett	Harold	Rfn	88844
Birt	Frank	Rfn	49989
Birtwistle	John	Rfn	28229
Bishop	Henry	Rfn	27085
Bisset	Kenneth	2Lt	
Black	David	Rfn	22930
Black*	David S.	Rfn	240556
Black	John H	Rfn	59412
Black	Thomas A.	Rfn	105585
Blackburn*	Eric	Rfn	2099
Blackburn*	Gray	Rfn	2083

Blackburn*	Leonard	Rfn	1511	Bottomley	George	Rfn	88846
Blackledge**	Geoffrey G.	A/Maj.		Bottrill*	Stephen N.	Cpl	240524
Blake	John	Rfn	13315	Boult*	Reginald H. S.	2Lt	
Blakemore	John Albert	Rfn	242890	Boumphrey[H]	Norman R.	Rfn	240869
Blakey	Percy	Rfn	49985	Bounds	Albert E.	Rfn	241728
Blanchard	Vernon S.	Rfn	48346	Bounds	Arthur	Rfn	242838
Bland*	William W.	Rfn	1427	Bourne	William H.	Rfn	95497
Bleakley	Thomas	Rfn	109096	Bowden*	Wilfred B.	Rfn	240140
Blewitt	William H.	L/Cpl	260249	Bowen	Charles E.	Rfn	88851
Blinkhorn	George	Rfn	241590	Bowen	William	Rfn	88856
Blood*	Arthur G.	L/Cpl	240451	Bowers	George	Rfn	305425
Blood	J.	Rfn	49986	Bowers	Percy	Rfn	325047
Blount*	Harold	Rfn	240447	Bowers	Victor R.	2Lt	
Blundell	John R.	Rfn	241864	Bowes	John	Rfn	241477
Blundell	William J.	Rfn	241815	Bowler	Frederick	Rfn	241102
Blunt	Hugh A.	Rfn	85314	Bowman*	Edward F.	Cpl	1500
Blyde*	John	Rfn	240682	Bowman**	Tom J.	Sgt	240014
Blythe*	Ernest	Sgt	1265	Bown*	Albert	Cpl	240924
Blythe*	Frederick J.	Rfn	2548	Bowne	Joseph	Rfn	241520
Blythe	John	Rfn	4636	Box	Thomas	Rfn	29759
Boag	Arthur J.	Rfn	242273	Boyd*	Arthur D.	A/Cpl	240266
Boardman	Alfred	Rfn	88085	Boyd	Joseph P.	Rfn	4253
Boase	Howard N.	Rfn	241610	Boydell	Edward	Rfn	240862
Boff	William	Rfn	268972	Boyle	Austin	Rfn	330174
Boggiano	Albert E.	Rfn	241745	Boyne	John	Rfn	59448
Boggild	Charles	Rfn	305743	Boys*	Charles D. B.	Rfn	1887
Bolton	William	L/Cpl	2390	Bradbury	Alfred	Rfn	242796
Bond	Edward	Rfn	12857	Braddock	Alfred	Rfn	49925
Bond	Henry	Rfn	308204	Bradley	Frank	Rfn	242709
Bond*	Lionel G. F.	2Lt	2015	Bradley*	George H.	Rfn	240721
Bond	Robert	Rfn	242683	Bradley	John	Rfn	242789
Bonner	Samuel	Rfn	242069	Bradley	John	Rfn	109073
Bonser	Harold	Rfn	88052	Bradley	John W.	L/Cpl	260008
Booker	Hedley	Rfn	242886	Bradley	Llewellyn	L/Cpl	85968
Boon	Edward	Rfn	49920	Bradley*	Max E.	Rfn	240398
Boote	George W.	Rfn	49983	Bradley	Walter	Rfn	331204
Booth	Ernest	Rfn	88845	Bradley	William	Rfn	51418
Booth	George L.	Rfn	49927	Bradshaw	Alfred	Rfn	265884
Booth	Whiteley	Rfn	49930	Bradshaw*	Charles H.	Cpl	240532
Booth	William	Rfn	51427	Bradshaw**	Henry H.	C/Sgt	240062
Boothby	Thomas	Rfn	51422	Bradshaw	Richard	Rfn	300019
Bore	Charles	L/Cpl	241912	Bradshaw	Robert	Rfn	242616
Bott*	George G. R.	Rfn	2391	Bradwell	Albert V.	Rfn	307797
Botting	Charles W.	Rfn	4343	Bragg	Daniel	Rfn	241827

Braithwaite	William	Rfn	3577
Braithwaite*	James M.	Rfn	2144
Braithwaite**	John E.	Cpl	240141
Braithwaite	Walter	Rfn	88084
Bramley*	Thomas T.	Rfn	240306
Bramwell*	Frank W.	Sgt	240397
Brand	Christopher	A/Cpl	51150
Brasher	Horace J. L.	Rfn	105588
Brayshaw	Frank	Rfn	306285
Breckenridge	Archibald	Rfn	241654
Breese	Frank U.	Rfn	240846
Breingan*	David W.	Rfn	240432
Brennan	Christopher	Rfn	242523
Brennan	Thomas	Rfn	260007
Bretherick*	Harold	A/Cpl	240865
Bretherton	Richard	Rfn	242705
Brewer	Alfred	Rfn	53043
Brewer*	Thomas W.	L/Cpl	240493
Bricknell	Frederick H.	Rfn	242782
Bride	Thomas	2Lt	
Bridge	John	Rfn	87015
Brierley	Samuel	Rfn	108690
Brierton	Francis X.	Rfn	3557
Briggs	Albert E.	Rfn	235567
Briggs	Charles A.	Rfn	49991
Briggs*	Egbert	Sgt	1863
Briggs	George W.	Rfn	49926
Briggs*	H.	Rfn	2027
Briggs	James	Rfn	242707
Briggs	Thomas	Rfn	242708
Briscoe	Thomas	Rfn	14554
Britton	Harold W.	2Lt	
Broad	Alfred H.	2Lt	
Broadbent*	George E.	Rfn	2161
Broady	Atho J.	Rfn	3622
Brock	George A.	Rfn	49984
Brocklehurst*	Edward H.	Capt.	
Brogden	John	Rfn	88847
Bromley	Clifford	Rfn	32862
Brooker*	Eric P.	L/Cpl	240254
Brookes	Cecil James	Rfn	88850
Brookes	James W. G.	Rfn	49922
Brookes	William H.	Rfn	105586
Brooks	Frederick	Rfn	242835
Broom	Harold	L/Cpl	51619
Broom*	John	Rfn	2459
Broomhead	John T.	Rfn	49988
Broster*	William C.	Sgt	2061
Brough	Samuel	L/Cpl	331298
Brough*	Frank L.	Rfn	240153
Brown	Albert H.	Rfn	3513
Brown	Alfred M.	Rfn	204263
Brown	Ernest K.	Rfn	88853
Brown	Henry	Rfn	241694
Brown	Henry J.	L/Cpl	91227
Brown	James H.	Rfn	242836
Brown	James R.	Rfn	235284
Brown	John	Rfn	3970
Brown	John	Rfn	269735
Brown*	Keith H.	Rfn	1482
Brown	Norman	Rfn	99428
Brown	Percy H.	Rfn	85401
Brown	Richard	Rfn	39197
Brown	Samuel	Rfn	51424
Brown*	Stanley J.	L/Sgt	240518
Brown	Teddie	Rfn	49924
Brown	Thomas H.	Rfn	16224
Brown	Thomas R.	Rfn	241562
Brown	Walter	Rfn	241444
Brown	William R. L.	Rfn	4128
Browne	Charles	Rfn	260003
Browne*	Richard M.	Lt	2034
Brownell**	Walter R.	A/Capt.	1861
Brownfield*	George H.	Rfn	240396
Brownrigg	Alfred T.	Rfn	240784
Bruce	Allan L.	Rfn	241842
Bruce	William H.	Rfn	332018
Bruckshaw	William	Rfn	34494
Brundell	James W. G.	Rfn	241032
Brunner*	Eric W. D.	Rfn	2416
Bryans*	James H.	Rfn	263007
Bryans*	Joseph C.	Sgt	240246
Bryning	Arthur C.	Rfn	240298
Bryson*	Thomas W.	L/Cpl	240699
Buckley	Alfred	Rfn	308092
Buckley	Arthur	Rfn	49921
Buckley*	Edmund C. G.	Capt.	
Buckley	Edward	Rfn	88849

Buckley	Eric K.	2Lt	
Buckley	Ernest	Rfn	51798
Buckley	Ernest	Rfn	85468
Buckley	William	Rfn	109029
Bullock	Frederick J.	Rfn	241931
Bullock	William T.	Rfn	86596
Burbage**	William P.	Sgt	240701
Burden*	Joseph A.	Sgt	240331
Burdett	Frederick	Rfn	84823
Burge	Arthur	Rfn	240969
Burgess	Arthur	Rfn	88053
Burke	James J.	Rfn	308961
Burke	Jeffrey	Rfn	306586
Burke*	John E.	L/Cpl	240683
Burke	Thomas	Rfn	308978
Burlin*	Henry	Rfn	240395
Burne	Arthur G.	L/Cpl	268380
Burnham	W. A.	Rfn	60760
Burns	John	Rfn	200659
Burns	John T.	Rfn	242696
Burrows	Alfred B.	Rfn	260005
Burrows	John H.	Rfn	242650
Burrows	John W.	Rfn	86490
Burrows	Neville R.	A/C/Sgt	242134
Burtinshaw	John A.	L/Cpl	2535
Burton	Geoffrey B.	Lt	
Bush	George	Rfn	49493
Bush	Samuel	Rfn	305155
Bushell*	Arthur	Sgt	1675
Bushell	Charles	Rfn	331716
Butler	Albert	Rfn	88855
Butler	Cecil L.	L/Cpl	241692
Butler	George	Sgt	51729
Butler	Herbert	Rfn	88836
Butler*	Robert W. F.	Rfn	2132
Butler	William	Rfn	242606
Butler*	William E.	RSM	10720
Butter	Leonard	Rfn	88854
Buttery	Charles H.	2Lt	
Bygroves	Charles E.	Rfn	241553
Cadman*	Albert G.	Sgt	240289
Caffal*	Samuel	Rfn	1146
Cain	Charles E.	Rfn	260015
Cain	John	Rfn	94208
Cain	Peter	Rfn	3867
Caine	Rufus	Rfn	51409
Caird*	Charles D. B.	L/Cpl	1859
Cairns	Leonard G	Rfn	85443
Cairns*	Thomas S.	Rfn	2159
Cairns	William	Rfn	95502
Caldwell	Harold	Rfn	85958
Caldwell	William J.	Cpl	92200
Callaghan	Daniel	L/Cpl	243887
Callon	George E.	Rfn	242332
Callow	Edward	Rfn	241566
Calvey[H]	Thomas	Cpl	240087
Cama*	Vincent	Rfn	2692
Camm	Joseph	Rfn	241441
Campbell	Cyril H.	Rfn	51140
Campbell	Duncan	Rfn	240858
Campbell	John	Rfn	305157
Campbell	John G.	Rfn	269679
Canning	David	L/Sgt	305801
Cape	John	Rfn	242803
Capper*	Walter L.	Rfn	380978
Capstick	Frederick	Rfn	242791
Cardew	Arthur B.	Lt	
Carey	Thomas	Rfn	51410
Carless	William H.	Rfn	88864
Carline	Ernest	Cpl	241781
Carlisle*	William	L/Cpl	564
Carney	William	Rfn	242711
Carpenter	Frederick A. J.	Rfn	380304
Carpenter*	John E.	Rfn	1990
Carr	Albert G.	Rfn	241678
Carr	Alexander	Rfn	266567
Carr	Arthur E.	L/Cpl	243895
Carr	Harry	Rfn	105602
Carr	John	Rfn	242651
Carr	John H.	L/Cpl	18705
Carr	Stanley R.	Rfn	108395
Carr	Thomas P.	L/Cpl	240125
Carr	William	Rfn	20830
Carrington	John W.	L/Cpl	306203
Carruthers	Arthur	Rfn	105593
Carte	William W.	Rfn	242841
Carter	Alfred G	Rfn	41101
Carter**	Edgar	Rfn	240165

Surname	Forename	Rank	Number
Carter	George	Rfn	241644
Carter	J. L.	Rfn	241769
Carter	James H.	Rfn	48658
Carter	Samuel J.	Rfn	241643
Carter	Thomas L.	Rfn	241428
Cartwright	Edward	Rfn	51428
Cartwright	J. H.	2Lt	
Cartwright	Leonard	Rfn	11351
Carver	Jack	Rfn	94182
Caryl**	John H.	Rfn	240055
Cashin	William E.	Rfn	4645
Casson	John	Pte	5205
Castle	Charles	Rfn	4424
Catherall	Richard	Cpl	241248
Caton	James A.	Rfn	242843
Catterall	Harold	Rfn	88857
Caunce	James E.	Rfn	4309
Cavanagh*	Frederick G.	Sgt	39
Cearns	Joseph	Rfn	241708
Cederberg*	Emil H.	Rfn	240975
Chadwick	John	CSM	300203
Chadwick	William	Rfn	242820
Chambers	Martin	Rfn	86414
Chambers	Thomas G.	Rfn	242124
Chandler	Percival	Rfn	241468
Chaplin	Henry L.	Rfn	51429
Chapman	Edward	Rfn	242635
Chapman	Edwin	Rfn	86801
Chapman	Harvey	Rfn	105589
Chapman	John E.	Rfn	308397
Chapman	Thomas E	Rfn	85364
Chappell*	Colin	Rfn	2238
Charles	George	Rfn	241001
Charnley	John	L/Cpl	88862
Charnley	Joseph	Rfn	87111
Charnock	John	L/Cpl	260013
Chater	Henry T.	Rfn	49993
Chater	John	Rfn	49931
Chatten	Edward W. G.	CSM	26524
Chavasse	Geoffrey D.	Lt	
Cheater	Edgar	Rfn	64787
Cheers	Samuel J.	Rfn	241682
Cheetham	Taylor	Rfn	51144
Cheshire	George F.	Rfn	242515
Chester	Joseph	Rfn	305716
Chesworth	Thomas	Rfn	241637
Childs	F.	2Lt	
Chipchase	Joseph R.	Rfn	269976
Chisholme	Gilbert	Rfn	241044
Christian	Vincent J.	Rfn	49502
Churchill	William	Rfn	105601
Clague	Thomas E.	Rfn	51430
Clague	William E.	Rfn	30805
Clare	Daniel	Rfn	331069
Clark	Andrew	Rfn	241761
Clark	E. B.	Rfn	3749
Clark	Leonard	Rfn	241920
Clark*	Robert S.	Rfn	240311
Clark	Thomas J.	Rfn	49992
Clark	Wilkinson M.	Rfn	49700
Clark*[R]	William A.	Pte	1546
Clark	William H.	Rfn	88054
Clarke*	Alfred H.	Cpl	2820
Clarke	Alfred J.	L/Cpl	240483
Clarke	Frank	Rfn	85404
Clarke*	Henry P.	Rfn	1220
Clarke	Hugh A.	L/Cpl	241934
Clarke	James	Rfn	105603
Clarke	Joseph	Rfn	31705
Clarke	Peter	Rfn	241816
Clarke*	Thomas A.	Rfn	240552
Clarkson	Ernest S.	Rfn	308820
Clarkson*	Joseph A	Rfn	2203
Claussen	Harold J.	Rfn	241222
Clayton	Frederick S. E.	Rfn	241989
Clayton	Henry	Rfn	88858
Clayton	Horace	Rfn	308017
Clayton	James	Rfn	241665
Clayton	Thomas	Rfn	88863
Clayton	William M.	Rfn	202414
Cleator	William K.	Rfn	4433
Cleaver	Ernest C.	Rfn	241116
Clee	Arthur B.	Rfn	51380
Clegg	George H.	Rfn	242845
Clegg	John	Rfn	242067
Clegg	William	Rfn	242713
Clements	Jules C.	2Lt	
Clephan*	Richard J.	Rfn	1628

Clewis	John J	Rfn	51403
Cliffe	Alfred H.	Rfn	3049
Cliffe	Robert	Sgt	200663
Clifton	Albert	Rfn	85363
Clinch**	Ernest	Rfn	240507
Close	William	Rfn	88859
Clothier	Basil	Cpl	1395
Clough*	Gordon	Rfn	1894
Clough	John	Rfn	242712
Clowes	Edgar	Rfn	241148
Clulo	James	Rfn	269612
Coates	Henry G.	Rfn	4847
Coates	John B.	Sgt	241788
Cochrane	James	L/Cpl	241809
Cockburn	Herbert J.	Rfn	241719
Cockburn*	Laurence B.	L/Cpl	1469
Cockburn*	Stanley G.	Cpl	1470
Cogley	William E.	Rfn	242643
Colclough	William	Rfn	269410
Cole	Charles F.	2Lt	
Coleman	George H.	2Lt	
Coleman	John F.	L/Cpl	50723
Collard	A. J.	Rfn	4441
Colley	Douglas J.	2Lt	
Colley	Edward C.	L/Sgt	16959
Colley	Geoffrey A. D.	2Lt	
Colley	John	Rfn	3955
Colley	John	Rfn	268486
Colley*	Thomas T.	Rfn	240446
Collier	Harold	Rfn	260012
Colligan	Henry	L/Cpl	267952
Colligan*	Robert	Rfn	240349
Collinge	John	Rfn	105591
Collings	Leonard	Cpl	21859
Collins	Edgar	Rfn	50308
Collins*	Ernest A.	Rfn	240703
Collins	Joseph F. F.	Rfn	267834
Collins	Percy	Rfn	3934
Collinson	Frank	Rfn	241857
Collinson	Harry	Rfn	72524
Collinson	Leonard M.	Rfn	4560
Collister	Thomas J.	Rfn	202413
Colquhoun**	Arthur S.	Rfn	240512
Colquhoun	Thomas	Rfn	47132
Conibear	Arthur E.	2Lt	
Conlon	Richard	Rfn	241890
Connell	Arthur	Rfn	87013
Connolly	Anthony	Rfn	243881
Connolly	James	L/Cpl	51805
Connor	John	Rfn	41915
Conroy[H]	Peter	Rfn	1475
Conway	John J.	Rfn	242121
Conway	Michael	Rfn	242652
Cook*	Frederick	Rfn	1858
Cook*	Gerald N.	Rfn	2090
Cook	John W.	Rfn	242816
Cooke*	Harry	Sgt	240187
Cooke	Joseph	Rfn	202709
Cookson	Percy S.	Maj.	
Coop	Joseph	Rfn	85951
Cooper	Albert	Rfn	105607
Cooper	Archibald	Rfn	86919
Cooper	Colin H. B.	2Lt	
Cooper*	Frank P.	Rfn	1997
Cooper*	John	Rfn	240481
Cooper	Joseph	Rfn	51143
Cooper	Joseph M.	Rfn	88865
Cooper	Robert	Rfn	4585
Cooper	Robert M.	Rfn	241838
Cope	Christopher C.	L/Cpl	49917
Cope*	Frank	Rfn	240465
Copestake	William A.	L/Cpl	51131
Copland	James	Cpl	21712
Copley	George B.	L/Cpl	268342
Corbett	Alfred	Rfn	88860
Corby	John J.	Rfn	51431
Corcoran	James	Rfn	53624
Cordon**	Robert	Rfn	240593
Corlett	Ernest E.	Rfn	25999
Corlett*	Thomas W.	Cpl	240207
Cornall	Henry	Sgt	305976
Cornes*	William	Rfn	2399
Cornet	George B.	Rfn	242844
Cornish*	Norman J.	L/Cpl	1961
Corran*	Robert D.	Rfn	240630
Corrigall*	John	L/Cpl	240566
Corrin	Harold	Rfn	4555
Coslett*	Fred H.	Cpl	240051

Costain	John T.	Rfn	242653	Crocker*	Leonard N.	Rfn	2089
Costello*	Arthur F.	Rfn	1629	Cromack	Norman	Rfn	105600
Costin	William	Rfn	241652	Crombie	Alfred	L/Cpl	260014
Cottam	James D.	Rfn	86489	Cromer*	Albert E.	Rfn	240116
Cottier	Ernest F.	Cpl	21477	Crompton	John H.	Rfn	85225
Cottier	Walter K.	2Lt		Crook*	Harold	Sgt	240394
Coulthard	Henry	Rfn	203275	Crook*	William	Dvr	726
Coulton	James	Rfn	35970	Crooke	Archibald	Rfn	242614
Coupe	Fred	Rfn	242805	Cropper	James	Rfn	242714
Coupland	Harold H.	Rfn	242013	Crosby	Herbert E.	Rfn	2705
Courtie	David	Rfn	241616	Cross*	Benjamin	CQMS	218
Courtney*	Bernard S. S.	Rfn	1677	Cross*	Charles	Rfn	2388
Cousins[H]	George H.	A/WO2	240779	Cross	James O.	Rfn	4635
Cowan**	Harold G.	L/Sgt	240166	Cross	Norman C.	Rfn	241729
Cowan**	Herbert	Rfn	240499	Cross	William	Rfn	105590
Cowan*	John D.	Rfn	240089	Crossley	Ernest	Rfn	51423
Cowan*	Richard I.	Cpl	240477	Crouchley*	John	Rfn	2483
Coward	Ernest	L/Cpl	86609	Crowe	William	Rfn	325217
Cowderoy	George F.	Rfn	201181	Crowther	Albert	Rfn	105605
Cowell	Joseph	Rfn	241889	Crowther	Henry	Rfn	242807
Cowell	Robert M.	Rfn	4567	Crowther*	Thomas A.	A/Cpl	359050
Cowell	Thomas	Rfn	242710	Croxton	Donald S.	Rfn	240805
Cowins*	Henry	Rfn	240254	Cryer	Fred	Rfn	49932
Cowles	Charles D.	Rfn	85415	Cubbin	Herbert	Rfn	3837
Cowman	Frederick G.	2Lt	241010	Cuerden	Arthur	Sgt	405236
Cox[H]	Alfred L.	Rfn	240681	Cullen	Frederick	Rfn	332820
Cox*	Arnold H.	Rfn	2386	Cullen	John	L/Cpl	332186
Cox	John W.	Rfn	49994	Culverwell	Albert B.	Rfn	3452
Cox*	Reginald F.	Rfn	2815	Culwick*	E.	Rfn	240121
Crabb*	Alexander	Rfn	1557	Cummings	John W.	Rfn	87872
Crabtree	Thomas	Rfn	105604	Cunliffe	Benjamin	Rfn	260010
Craddock	John	Rfn	242842	Cunningham	Thomas	Rfn	88861
Crafter*	Hilton C.	Rfn	2521	Curfew	John C.	Rfn	105608
Craig	Thomas R.	Rfn	241024	Curley	John T.	Rfn	235589
Crane	Lawrence	Rfn	87871	Curran	Robert	Rfn	241003
Crane	Thomas	Rfn	241575	Currie*	Theodore	Rfn	240577
Craven	William M.	Rfn	32819	Cursi*	Paul D.	Rfn	371
Crawford	John	Rfn	59227	Curtis**	John W.	Rfn	240409
Crawley	Frederick	Rfn	260011	Curwen*	Robert	L/Cpl	2063
Crean*	James	Rfn	2278	Curwen	Thomas	Rfn	105606
Crebbin*	John	Rfn	240419	Curwen*	William H.	L/Cpl	241026
Creer	John	Rfn	331908	Cuthbertson	William A.	Rfn	241040
Crellin	Jonathan	Cpl	380445	Daggers*	Harold	Rfn	240259
Critchley	William	Rfn	300217	Daglish	Robert S.	2Lt	

Dailey*	William E.	Rfn	240848	Davies	John	Rfn	79453
Dales	David F.	Rfn	48582	Davies	John E.	Rfn	52561
Daley*	James	Rfn	240310	Davies	John G.	Rfn	3366
Dalgarno*	James H.	Sgt	243891	Davies	John H.	Rfn	267594
Dalrymple	Thomas	Rfn	3581	Davies	John I.	Rfn	54471
Dalton	John	Rfn	18984	Davies*	John T.	Rfn	1747
Daniels	Frederick C.	Rfn	241199	Davies	John W.	Rfn	241930
Daniels	Henry	Sgt	241673	Davies	Leslie C.	L/Cpl	241909
Danily*	John	Cpl	240555	Davies	Mark	Rfn	20922
Darcy	John	L/Cpl	200538	Davies*	Reginald E.	Rfn	2057
Darcy	John	Rfn	88868	Davies*	Thomas H.	Sgt	240083
Darlington	Herbert L.	Rfn	1183	Davies	Walter E.	L/Cpl	88837
Darwen	Thomas	Rfn	260017	Davies	Walter S.	L/Sgt	241834
Davenport	Richard	Rfn	94278	Davies	William	Rfn	241967
Davenport	Stanley	Rfn	88869	Davies*	William	Rfn	3487
Davey*	Albert E.	Rfn	240520	Davies	William H.	Rfn	242618
Davey	Samuel F.	Sgt	242561	Davies	William H.	Rfn	241992
Davidson	George	Rfn	3887	Davies*	W. W.	Rfn	2104
Davidson	Thomas	Rfn	305888	Davis	Cyril S.	Rfn	242715
Davidson	William H. H.	Capt.		Davis*	Herbert L.	Rfn	243883
Davies	Arthur	Cpl	241085	Davis*	Nathan	Rfn	240537
Davies	Arthur E.	Rfn	242322	Davis*	Philip	Rfn	240132
Davies	Arthur L.	Rfn	204206	Davis	Richard	Rfn	88867
Davies	Brynmore	Rfn	242023	Davison*	Henry	Lt-Col.	
Davies	Charles	Rfn	13438	Davy	W. K.	2Lt	
Davies	Charles F.	L/Cpl	200732	Dawson**	George L.	Sgt	240264
Davies*	Charles M.	Cpl	240687	Dawson	John	Rfn	241435
Davies	David O.	Rfn	82768	Dawson*	John N.	Cpl	240251
Davies	David W.	Rfn	51385	Dawson	Joseph A.	Rfn	241320
Davies	Ernest	Rfn	49995	Dawson*	Thomas	Rfn	1182
Davies	Francis J.	Rfn	269303	Deacon	William E.	L/Cpl	267210
Davies*	Frank A.	Rfn	2092	Dean	John A.	Rfn	242827
Davies	Frank L.	Cpl	241418	Dean*	Eric Victor	Rfn	240984
Davies	Frederick	L/Cpl	266471	Dean*	Ernest N.	Rfn	1487
Davies	George	Rfn	88072	Dean*	Henry E.	Cpl	241019
Davies*	Guy L.	Rfn	2086	Dean	Thomas	Rfn	109071
Davies	Gwilym R.	Rfn	241898	Deane*	Harold	Rfn	1656
Davies	Harold	Rfn	241421	Deane	Oliver E.	Rfn	242654
Davies	Harry	Rfn	90742	Deane*	Wellesley V.	Rfn	1880
Davies*	Herbert L.	Rfn	240531	Dearden	James	Rfn	380540
Davies*	Herbert T.	CQMS	240008	Delaney	John	Rfn	36526
Davies	Jack	Rfn	202386	Delaney	Leo	Rfn	23172
Davies	John	L/Cpl	240847	Dennett*	Francis G.	Rfn	2114
Davies	John	Rfn	2914	Denyer	Percy E.	Rfn	242824

Desages*	Wilfred R.	Rfn	240345
DeValve	Harold	Rfn	241737
DeValve*	Leslie G.	L/Cpl	240231
Dewar	Donald	Rfn	88131
Dewhurst	Henry	Rfn	43032
Dewhurst	William	Rfn	305710
Dick	John	Sgt	241096
Dick*	Tom C.	Sgt	240689
Dickinson*	John R.	Cpl	947
Dicks	Arthur	Rfn	52018
Diggle*	John H.	Rfn	2510
Dilworth	Joseph	Rfn	242594
Dilworth	William	Rfn	4438
Disley**	Thomas C.	Rfn	240240
Dixon	Albert E.	Rfn	49996
Dixon*	Alfred	Cpl	240635
Dixon	Arthur	Rfn	41177
Dixon*	Charles L.	Rfn	240551
Dixon*	Herbert S.	Sgt	240686
Dixon*	John H.	Rfn	1854
Dixon	Robert H.	Rfn	242847
Dixon**	Walter S.	Rfn	240160
Dobby	William	L/Cpl	242627
Dobell**	Alfred T.	2Lt	
Dobell*	Robert L.	Capt.	
Dobie	Charles	Rfn	50997
Dobson*	J. G.	Rfn	2858
Dodd	Arthur T.	Rfn	88870
Dodd	Edward S.	Rfn	51377
Dodd	Henry E.	Sgt	241084
Dodd*	James	Rfn	1246
Dodd	John	Rfn	25511
Dodsworth*	David J.	L/Cpl	241450
Dodsworth*	Eric D.	Rfn	1722
Doherty	Edward	Rfn	91633
Doidge**	Alfred E.	Cpl	240392
Donaldson	Herbert	L/Cpl	242114
Donaldson*	Jonathan D.	Rfn	1434
Donnahey	James	Rfn	330201
Donnan*	Joseph G.	Sgt	357
Donnelly	Charles	Rfn	242655
Donnelly	Hilton	Rfn	88871
Doody*	Alfred H.	Rfn	240109
Dooley	Herbert J.	Rfn	241738

Doorbar	Samuel	Rfn	49960
Doran	Alfred	Rfn	242491
Doran	Harry	Rfn	3804
Doran	Harry A.	Rfn	380095
Dossor*	Norman W.	Cpl	240702
Double	Ernest E.	Rfn	50999
Doubleday	John Henry	Rfn	331352
Dovaston	Charles	Rfn	15778
Dow	Joseph A.	2Lt	
Dower	Charles	Rfn	41622
Dowling*	Gerald W.	Rfn	1907
Downer	Aubrey F. C.	Rfn	51384
Downes	Frederick W.	L/Cpl	91194
Downey	James	Rfn	50323
Downey	Martin	Rfn	308518
Downey	Matthew	Rfn	306838
Downey	Michael	Rfn	307076
Downie*	George G.	Rfn	1255
Downs	Hartley	Rfn	308087
Downs	J. W.	Rfn	260016
Downs	James T.	Rfn	49933
Dowsett	Francis H.	Rfn	242522
Doyle	J.	Rfn	5410
Doyle	John	Rfn	241813
Doyle*	John P.	Rfn	1852
Doyle*	John S.	Rfn	240861
Doyle	Patrick	Rfn	51432
Doyle	Samuel	Rfn	241867
Doyle*	William P.	Rfn	1384
Draper	Arthur	L/Cpl	50998
Draper	Robert E.	Rfn	241453
Draycott*	Joseph M.	Rfn	2234
Dresser	Samuel	Sgt	7617
Drew	William C. G.	2Lt	
Drinkald	John J.	Rfn	88866
Drummond*	William A.	L/Cpl	1483
Drysdale	Eric	Rfn	305197
Duckett	Albert	Rfn	242811
Duckett	Arthur	Rfn	3539
Duckett*	George	Rfn	2170
Duckett*	William C. G.	Rfn	240256
Dudson	John A.	L/Cpl	240714
Duffin	Frederick G.	Rfn	241941
Duffy	John	Rfn	242657

Duffy*	Robert	Rfn	240285
Duffy	Samuel C. R.	Cpl	240232
Duffy	Thomas	Rfn	30641
Duffy	William	Rfn	242891
Dugdale	Lionel A.	2Lt	
Duggan	William	L/Cpl	52574
Duke	William	Rfn	241338
Dunn	James	Cpl	241078
Dunn	John	Rfn	242716
Dunn	Newsham	Rfn	307877
Dunn	Rufus	Rfn	242846
Dunne	John	Rfn	242848
Dunning*	Thomas	Rfn	2133
Dunwell*	Leslie G.	Rfn	240586
Durant	William E.	Rfn	306906
Durham	James	Rfn	242096
Dutton	Edward	L/Cpl	242106
Dutton*	Ernest	L/Sgt	240261
Dutton*	George C.	Sgt	240085
Dutton*	John	L/Cpl	240853
Dwine	William	Rfn	260059
Dwyer	Joseph	Rfn	105609
Dyall**	Charles	Cpl	240108
Dyall*	Frank	Cpl	240258
Dyson	David Henry	Rfn	50506
Eagles	George	Rfn	267549
Eaglesfield*	William J.	Sgt	240117
Earl*	James M.	Rfn	240564
Earle	Robert	Rfn	242892
Easterby	John	Rfn	49718
Eastham	Thomas W.	Rfn	88086
Eastwood*	Donald	Capt.	1769
Eastwood*	Richard C.	Rfn	2145
Ebbs	Thomas	Rfn	305731
Eccles	A. G.	Capt.	
Eccles*	Henry C.	Rfn	240102
Eccleston*	Reginald D.	Rfn	2102
Eccleston	Thomas H.	Rfn	88872
Eccleston	Wilson	Rfn	241718
Eckford	Bernard	Rfn	3892
Eden	William	Rfn	242799
Edgar	Henry S.	Rfn	59343
Edgar	John	Rfn	88880
Edge[H]	Thomas H.	Rfn	240213
Edgeley	Sam	Rfn	88874
Edkins*	Clement W. R.	Capt.	240322
Edmonds	Herbert V. F.	Rfn	29110
Edmondson*	John D.	Rfn	1764
Edwards*	Albert C.	Sgt	240082
Edwards	Alexander	Rfn	307880
Edwards*	Arthur M.	Rfn	2775
Edwards*	Arthur W.	Sgt	1052
Edwards	Charles L.	Rfn	241626
Edwards	David W.	Rfn	241940
Edwards	Edward S.	L/Cpl	241114
Edwards**	Frederick T.	Rfn	240320
Edwards	George	Rfn	330233
Edwards	Graeme H.	Rfn	202261
Edwards	H.	L/Cpl	308343
Edwards	Henry	Rfn	241776
Edwards**	Herbert L.	Rfn	240317
Edwards	John T. G.	Rfn	88873
Edwards	Percy	Rfn	241812
Edwards	Richard J.	Rfn	241801
Edwards*	Sidney C.	Rfn	1559
Edwards	Thomas	Rfn	26179
Edwards	Thomas	Rfn	23655
Edwards	Walter	Rfn	17323
Edwards	Walter	Rfn	94678
Edwards	William	Rfn	241804
Edwards	William G.	Rfn	201950
Egan	William	Rfn	267194
Egerton	Sydney A.	Rfn	51002
Eglin	Nathan	Rfn	90232
Eivers*	James J.	Cpl	240341
Eldridge*	Ernest J. M.	Rfn	2300
Elias	Reginald R.	Rfn	88838
Ellercott	Percy J.	Rfn	51003
Elliott	Ernest	Rfn	12395
Elliott*	Hugh S.	Sgt	240091
Elliott	James	Rfn	240765
Ellis	Charles F.	Rfn	41858
Ellis	Clifford	Rfn	49997
Ellis	F.	Rfn	265881
Ellis	Roland F.	L/Cpl	235590
Ellis*	Thomas J.	Rfn	240529
Ellis	Vernon H.	L/Cpl	88881
Ellison	Charles H.	Rfn	241671

Ellison*	Christopher G.	Rfn	1381	Evans	Hugh	Rfn	242849
Ellison	Frederick W.	Rfn	22065	Evans	James H.	Rfn	88876
Ellison	Hubert E.	Rfn	85953	Evans	James P.	Rfn	241783
Ellison*	Norman F.	L/Cpl	240479	Evans	John H.	Sgt	241422
Ellison	William	Rfn	88877	Evans	Joseph	Rfn	241323
Elrod	D. B.	Rfn	99489	Evans	Lewis C.	Rfn	242083
Elston	James W.	Rfn	241451	Evans*	Peter	Rfn	1995
Elston	Thomas	Cpl	332968	Evans	Richard	Rfn	242143
Elsworth[H]	Francis J.	Sgt	240189	Evans	Richard E.	L/Cpl	242540
Elsworth	John	L/Cpl	94553	Evans	Robert	Rfn	52587
Elsy	Charles S.	Rfn	49935	Evans	Robert F.	L/Cpl	241970
Elvey	Fred	Rfn	87244	Evans*	Stanley P.	Rfn	1341
Emberson	William H.	Rfn	88055	Evans	Stanley S.	Rfn	242072
Emberton	Victor	A/Cpl	241938	Evans*	Thomas	L/Cpl	240470
Emblen	David F.	Rfn	4223	Evans	William	Rfn	242660
Embley	Edward	Rfn	242717	Evans	William	L/Cpl	242560
Emery	Thomas	Rfn	202281	Evans	William	Rfn	88879
Emmett	Fred	Rfn	242718	Evans*	William D.	Rfn	2782
Emmett	Robert	Rfn	241793	Evans	William H.	Rfn	88878
Emmott	Jonathan	Rfn	94279	Evans[R]	William L.	Lt	
Entwistle	James	Rfn	90388	Evanson	John	Rfn	88875
Entwistle	James	Rfn	108256	Everall	Arthur	Rfn	380077
Epstein*	Isidor	A/Cpl	240595	Everett	Alfred J.	Rfn	235297
Escolme	Harold	Rfn	242593	Ewing	John B.	Rfn	87270
Espley	William H.	Rfn	49934	Exley	George	Rfn	202552
Essery*	John H.	Cpl	240533	Eyles	William	Rfn	86812
Evans	Albert M.	Rfn	260048	Eyres	John E.	Rfn	14134
Evans	C. H.	Rfn	8853	Fagan	Charles	Rfn	307337
Evans	Cecil	Rfn	19641	Fairbairn*	Arthur W.	Rfn	1329
Evans	Charles	L/Cpl	242658	Fairbairn*	William R.	Rfn	1330
Evans	Charles E.	Rfn	3777	Fairchild	William	Rfn	405093
Evans*	Charles O.	Sgt	240463	Fairclough	George A.	L/Cpl	241798
Evans*	David G.	Rfn	1849	Fairclough*	John	Rfn	240438
Evans	David H.	Rfn	241794	Fairclough*	William	L/Cpl	240589
Evans	Edmund	Rfn	90378	Fairclough	William R.	Rfn	5398
Evans*	Edward R.	Rfn	240464	Fairhurst	Jack D.	L/Cpl	241177
Evans	Eric Ben	Rfn	241545	Fairhurst	John	2Lt	
Evans*	Francis G.	L/Cpl	240291	Fairhurst	L.	L/Cpl	51405
Evans*	Frank A.	Rfn	240325	Farley	Edward	Rfn	307133
Evans*	Frank E.	L/Cpl	240390	Farley	Robert	Rfn	89128
Evans	George P.	Rfn	242659	Farnham	Henry C.	L/Cpl	240917
Evans	Harry	Rfn	86598	Farr	Tom	Rfn	86474
Evans	Harry E. V.	L/Cpl	241808	Farrell	James	Rfn	86649
Evans	Hugh	L/Cpl	241995	Farrell	John	Rfn	13143

Farrell	Kevin	Rfn	21821	Finlay	Nicholas T.	Rfn	29213
Farrell	Louis F	Rfn	85463	Finnegan	Robert	Rfn	242098
Farrell*	Paul	Rfn	240843	Firth*	Edward	Cpl	240165
Farrell*	William G.	Rfn	2139	Firth	Noel H.	Rfn	51433
Farries	Ernest R.	Cpl	88835	Fisher	Ernest	Cpl	23001
Faulkner	Charles E. A.	Rfn	241921	Fisher	John	Rfn	86495
Faulkner	Harry	Rfn	50278	Fisher*	Robert H.	Rfn	2121
Faulkner	John	Rfn	101291	Fisher	Thomas	Rfn	241908
Fawcett*	Stanley	Rfn	240414	Fishwick	John W.	Rfn	30431
Fawcitt**	John H.	Rfn	240526	Fitton*	Arthur J.	Rfn	1940
Fay	Stephen	Rfn	86719	Fitton	Ernest	Rfn	94748
Fazackerley	Arthur	Rfn	332894	Fitzgerald	Charles W.	Rfn	4099
Fazackerley	Charles H.	Rfn	101289	Fitzgerald	Herbert	2Lt	
Fazackerley*	Harold D.	Rfn	2218	Fitzmaurice*	Andrew M.	Cpl	240303
Fazakerley*	John G.	Sgt	240101	Fitzsimmons	Edward	Rfn	308881
Fearnett	John	Rfn	16174	Fitzsimmons	Thomas	Rfn	19152
Fearnley	Arthur	Rfn	50002	Fitzsimons	Richard J.	Rfn	86687
Fearon	Thomas	Rfn	241087	Flanagan	Bernard	Rfn	201985
Feathers	Sam	Rfn	50001	Flannery	Thomas	Rfn	37744
Feeney	Thomas	Rfn	242719	Fletcher	Abraham	L/Cpl	88268
Feeney (Fenney)	Michael	Rfn	307113	Fletcher	Alfred	Rfn	202548
Fell	John	Cpl	308275	Fletcher	Clement	Rfn	307889
Fell	William	Rfn	241748	Fletcher	Edward	Rfn	269146
Fell*	William R.	Rfn	2134	Fletcher*	George	L/Cpl	240798
Fellows	Albert J.	Rfn	50000	Fletcher	George A.	Rfn	88882
Fellows	Fred P.	Rfn	49936	Fletcher	James	Rfn	242720
Fellows	William	Rfn	87868	Fletcher	Kershaw	Rfn	49938
Felton	Herbert J.	Rfn	331228	Fletcher*	Reginald P.	Rfn	1192
Fenn	James B.	2Lt		Flindle	Wilfred	Rfn	86557
Fenton	George	Rfn	241948	Flitcroft	James	Rfn	109048
Ferguson*	Charles	Rfn	240937	Flood	Thomas	Rfn	48963
Ferguson*	Charles H.	Cpl	240571	Flynn	James R.	Rfn	109044
Ferguson	George	Rfn	84890	Flynn	Joseph	Rfn	267057
Ferguson*	M.	Rfn	2311	Flynn	William	L/Sgt	50995
Ferguson**	Peter	L/Cpl	240979	Foden	Frederick G.	Rfn	88883
Ferriday	John	Rfn	5550	Foden*	H. H.	Rfn	2201
Ferris	James P.	Rfn	109021	Foggo	Thomas R.	Rfn	16814
Fidoe	Henry	Rfn	51004	Fontannaz*	Albert E.	Rfn	2282
Fielding	Harry	Rfn	101290	Forbes	Gordon	Rfn	305493
Finch	Leslie H.	Rfn	86569	Ford	Francis A.	Rfn	242583
Findlow	John W.	Rfn	3769	Ford	Frederick N.	Rfn	242074
Findlow*	Thomas G.	Rfn	2381	Ford	George C.	L/Cpl	242661
Fineburg	Myer	Rfn	241297	Ford	John F.	Rfn	53460
Finlay	David W.	L/Cpl	242577	Ford*	William F.	Rfn	240809

Ford	William H.	Rfn	49998
Foreman	Tom	L/Cpl	88057
Forfar	Reginald	Rfn	267145
Forryan	Arnold F.	Rfn	88056
Fosbrook	Fred	Rfn	49937
Fosbrooke*	Ernest L.	Rfn	240297
Foss*	George G.	Rfn	1405
Foster	Alfred	Rfn	332898
Foster*	Douglas B.	Cpl	1689
Foster	Eric C.	L/Cpl	242136
Foster	Fred	Rfn	241699
Foster	Frederick W.	Rfn	86509
Foster	George A.	Rfn	51521
Foster	James O.	Rfn	241623
Foster	John	Rfn	243798
Foster	William	Rfn	241680
Foulkes*	Fred	Rfn	1587
Foulkes	George	Rfn	350034
Foulkes	Isaac	Cpl	242646
Fowden	H.	Rfn	86972
Fowler*	Albert	Rfn	2316
Fowler	William	Rfn	242039
Fowler	William W.	Rfn	332370
Fox	Francis H.	Rfn	242894
Fox	H.	Rfn	108692
Fox*	Harry	Rfn	1443
Fox	John B.	Rfn	240334
Fox	Samuel M.	Rfn	50510
Foxcroft	Ernest	Rfn	241605
Foxe*	Vincent J.	Rfn	240233
Fraser*	Frank	Rfn	240618
Freeman	Frank	Rfn	331655
Freeman	William	Rfn	240893
Freer	Albert	Rfn	88280
Freestone	Arthur H.	2Lt	
Freestone	Frederick	Rfn	235022
French	William A.	Rfn	307385
Fricker	John E.	Rfn	3781
Frost	James S.	Rfn	332492
Frost	Walter	Rfn	51136
Froude*	George	Cpl	1348
Frumin	Isaac	Rfn	94615
Fry*	Joseph	Rfn	240547
Fulham	Thomas	Rfn	109088

Fullalove	Thomas P.	Rfn	87240
Fullerton	Frank C.	Cpl	31138
Fullerton**	Thomas C.	Rfn	240224
Furey	Michael	Rfn	242893
Furlong	Francis	Rfn	242850
Furniss*	Thomas M	Rfn	2127
Furnival	Alfred	Rfn	49999
Fyfield	Frank	Rfn	23626
Fyles	Alfred	Rfn	32561
Gaddas	Thomas R.	Rfn	242004
Gadsden	Geoffrey C.	Rfn	241357
Gale	Frank	Rfn	88886
Gale	Joseph	Rfn	34958
Gale	William J.	L/Cpl	17340
Gallagher	Murdock	Rfn	58633
Gallamore	Thomas E.	Rfn	99518
Gallie	James I.	Rfn	241963
Galloway*	W. J.	Rfn	1847
Gamble	Charles E.	Rfn	99507
Gammons	Frank A.	Rfn	202580
Gardiner	Frederick	Rfn	101293
Gardner	George A.	L/Cpl	56907
Gardner	Harry L.	2Lt	
Gardner	John H. T.	Rfn	50594
Garland	Frank W.	Rfn	3586
Garlick	Jacob A.	Cpl	15430
Garner	Ellis	Rfn	242692
Garnett	Harry	Rfn	242105
Garnett	Robert	Rfn	241922
Garnett*	William F.	Sgt	61
Garnham	F. W. H.	2Lt	
Garnsworthy	Randall	2Lt	
Garrahan	Gilbert	Rfn	331082
Garside	F. Charles	Lt	
Garvey	James A.	Rfn	380481
Gascoigne*	Frank	L/Cpl	240389
Gascoigne	George	Rfn	242089
Gater	Harry	Rfn	99517
Gates	Charles	Rfn	242852
Gatland	Charles R.	Rfn	105499
Gauntlett	Edgar J.	Rfn	4072
Gawthrop	George G.	Rfn	242895
Geehan	Thomas	Rfn	407016
Geekie*(AOC)	William	S/Sgt	1312

Geldard	Edward	Rfn	3883	Godfrey	Reginald J.	Rfn	241213
Gent	Edward	Rfn	332289	Godfrey	Sidney	Rfn	241184
George	Ernest	Rfn	242721	Goffey	George	Rfn	241636
George	Rowland	Rfn	99512	Goffey	William	Lt	
Geraghty	Thomas	Rfn	50583	Goldman	Bernard	Rfn	87057
Gerrard	Joseph	Rfn	49939	Good	Arthur	A/Cpl	48714
Gettings	Joseph	Rfn	99513	Good*	F. Charles	Rfn	1188
Gibbs*	Harold	Rfn	1417	Good*	George	L/Sgt	240021
Gibbs	Harold L.	Rfn	241845	Gooderham	James T.	Sgt	381446
Gibson	Albert	Rfn	308380	Goodill	Sydney	Rfn	99514
Gibson	Alexander	Rfn	3937	Goodman	Joseph F.	Rfn	13344
Gibson*	George H.	Rfn	240521	Goodman*	William B. L.	Rfn	1905
Gibson*	William S.	Rfn	1943	Goodwin	Archibald	Rfn	99508
Giddings	William	Rfn	51135	Goodwin	Gerald F.	Rfn	240931
Gilbert*	John G.	Rfn	1324	Goodwin	William J.	Rfn	268706
Gilbert*	Richard	Rfn	1663	Goodyear*	James H.	Rfn	1700
Gilchrist*	A. J.	Dvr	727	Gordon*	Stanley E.	Maj.	
Giles	John	Rfn	87834	Gore	Charles T.	CQMS	94280
Gill	John C.	Rfn	240743	Gore*	Frank H.	Rfn	727
Gill	Jonah	Cpl	260049	Gore*	George A.	Rfn	1198
Gillibrand	John	Rfn	48811	Gore	William	L/Cpl	51381
Gillies	Angus S.	Rfn	242642	Gorham	Claud	Rfn	88059
Gilliver	Jack	Rfn	99509	Gorick	John	Rfn	90971
Gilmore	Joseph	Rfn	101294	Goring	William T.	Rfn	99510
Gittins	Samuel E.	Rfn	241923	Gornall	James	Rfn	101296
Gladwinfield*	Charles	Rfn	2129	Gossage	Edward	Rfn	51256
Gladwinfield	Joseph	Rfn	241693	Gough	Arthur E.	Rfn	99511
Glassbrook	William L.	Rfn	105587	Gough	W. O.	Rfn	59539
Glazebrook*	Edward C.	Rfn	1765	Goulding*	Edgar A.	Sgt	143
Gledson	James R.	Rfn	332729	Goulding**	Edward S.	Maj.	QM
Glendenning*	Robert J.	Sgt	1116	Grace	Michael	Rfn	242638
Glossop	Frederick	Rfn	300006	Graham	Arthur	Rfn	51434
Glossop	Harry	Rfn	101295	Graham*	Malise R.	Rfn	2318
Glover	Albert	Rfn	202040	Graham*	Philip W.	Cpl	242486
Glover	Arthur T.	Rfn	87106	Graham	Thomas	Rfn	58694
Glover*	John Vivian	Rfn	240694	Graham	Walter	Rfn	72658
Glover	Thomas	Rfn	242784	Graham	William	Rfn	242725
Glover	Victor	L/Cpl	88887	Grainger	William	Rfn	3446
Glover	William	Rfn	69911	Graney	Charles	Rfn	26672
Gloyne*	Francis E.	Sgt	240149	Granger	Harold F.	Rfn	204131
Goadby	Lawrence H.	Rfn	240713	Grant*	Alexander H.	Cpl	1174
Gobie*	Herbert	Cpl	240646	Gratton*	John W.	Rfn	2321
Goddard	Robert F.	Rfn	51138	Gray	Norman B.	Rfn	99519
Godfey	Charles	Rfn	10427	Gray	Richard	Rfn	51145

Gray*	William B. L.	Rfn	240126
Gray*	William H.	Rfn	240611
Grayson	Arthur	Rfn	90233
Greaves	Cuthbert	Rfn	87019
Greaves	Harold D.	Rfn	242851
Green	Alfred	Rfn	240247
Green	Charles H.	Rfn	50003
Green	Frank	Rfn	86493
Green	George	Rfn	260019
Green	Harold	Rfn	332731
Green	John H. T.	Rfn	241437
Green	John R.	Rfn	86677
Green*	Percy C.	Rfn	2319
Green*	Robert E.	Rfn	1171
Green	Sidney L.	Rfn	88058
Green	Thomas	Rfn	88892
Green	Thomas H.	Rfn	88060
Green	Thomas W.	Rfn	99516
Green	Walter	Rfn	85472
Green	William	Rfn	101297
Green	William A.	Rfn	12314
Greenall	James	Rfn	86832
Greenhalgh	Maurice L.	2Lt	
Greening	William H.	Rfn	242035
Greenland*	Richard	Rfn	2110
Greenwood	Fred	Rfn	242722
Greenwood	Herbert	Rfn	242723
Greenwood	John M.	L/Cpl	101299
Greenwood	Smith	Rfn	242724
Greenwood	Walter	Rfn	57648
Gregg	Harold	Rfn	88889
Gregg	Reginald A.	2Lt	
Gregory	Robert	Rfn	242687
Gregson	Albert T.	Rfn	269885
Gregson	Frank	Lt	
Gregson	Hugh	Rfn	242624
Gregson	R.	Rfn	307082
Gregson	Thomas	Rfn	308022
Greig	Robert G.	Rfn	88884
Greville*	Dudley	Rfn	1313
Grice	Arthur Cyril	Rfn	203443
Grice	Robert	Cpl	260018
Grice	Robert	Rfn	101298
Grieve	Harold	L/Cpl	21717
Griffies*	Frank V. K.	Rfn	2929
Griffin	Charles E.	L/Cpl	85886
Griffin	Edgar T.	Rfn	88885
Griffin*	Edward S.	2Lt	240700
Griffith	William B. L.	Rfn	101292
Griffiths*	Arthur	Sgt	927
Griffiths*	Edmund B.	Sgt	1331
Griffiths*	Edward	L/Cpl	240388
Griffiths*	Evan	L/Cpl	240909
Griffiths	Herbert S.	Rfn	86844
Griffiths*	James H.	Rfn	1982
Griffiths*	Richard	L/Cpl	240163
Griffiths	Robert	Rfn	241069
Griffiths	Samuel	Rfn	85466
Griffiths	Thomas A.	Rfn	241585
Griffiths	Thomas H.	Rfn	101300
Griffiths	William	Rfn	4494
Griffiths*	William	Rfn	240050
Griffiths	William E.	Rfn	241841
Grimshaw	Edwin	Rfn	88888
Grindell	Ivan	Rfn	99515
Grinton*	John R. M.	Rfn	240647
Grogan	James	Rfn	241860
Grosvenor	Thomas E.	Rfn	50004
Grove	James P.	2Lt	
Guest	George	Rfn	241918
Guilbert	Sydney	Rfn	3666
Guy	Edward J.	Rfn	270087
Guy	Samuel	Rfn	241632
Hackett	Joseph	L/Cpl	94431
Hacking	William	Rfn	92003
Hadfield	John P.	Rfn	26122
Hadwin*	John N.	Cpl	240386
Hagerty	Alfred M.	Rfn	43480
Haggis	John	Rfn	50334
Hague	Harry W.	Rfn	101303
Haig	Archibald M.	Rfn	51830
Haigh	Fred W.	Rfn	50012
Haines[H]	Harold S.	Rfn	unk
Hale	John	Rfn	242662
Hales	Ralph W.	CQMS	23944
Halford	Rupert	Sgt	22391
Halford	William	Rfn	305437
Hall	Cuthbert	Rfn	242694

Hall*	Eaton	Rfn	2292	Harding	James	L/Cpl	13845
Hall	Frederick W.	Rfn	242728	Harding**	Lawrence	Rfn	240519
Hall	Norman	Rfn	94265	Harding	William J.	Rfn	87158
Hall	Robert	Rfn	242854	Hardman	Stanley	Rfn	3518
Hall	Robert H.	Rfn	3506	Hardwick	George	Rfn	99520
Hall**	Thomas	Rfn	240170	Hardy	Bert	Rfn	85326
Hall	Wilfred W.	Rfn	4059	Hardy	Edwin	Rfn	99523
Hall	William R.	Rfn	201333	Hardy	John	Rfn	105592
Hallam*	John	Rfn	240636	Hardy	Victor G.	2Lt	
Hallam**	William A.	Sgt	240335	Hardy	William	Rfn	200187
Halligan	Thomas	Rfn	31456	Hargraves*	Frank	L/Cpl	1704
Hallum	James	Rfn	203320	Hargreaves	Reginald	Rfn	240186
Halpin	Harry	Rfn	94272	Hargreaves	Robert	Rfn	242736
Halsall*	Archibald R.	Rfn	2508	Hargreaves	William	Rfn	260026
Halsall	William	L/Cpl	265724	Harp	Samuel	Rfn	49940
Hamar	Douglas	Rfn	241740	Harper	Percy J.	A/Cpl	241786
Hamer	James	Rfn	86975	Harper*	Thomas	Rfn	2148
Hammersley	Hugh R.	Rfn	309020	Harper	William R.	Rfn	59312
Hammond	Leonard	Rfn	101302	Harraden*	Herbert R.	Sgt	1843
Hamnett*	Thomas H.	Rfn	2327	Harries**	George C.	Sgt	240068
Hampson*	Albert W.	RQMS	240045	Harris	Enoch	Rfn	266740
Hampson*	Ralph	Rfn	240880	Harris	Ernest	Rfn	300289
Hampton	Robert	Rfn	94269	Harris*	Frederick D.	Rfn	240816
Hampton	Sydney C.	Rfn	4053	Harris*	Philip	Rfn	1890
Hancock	Ernest F.	Rfn	235061	Harris	Reginald E.	Rfn	51386
Hancock	John S.	Sgt	241604	Harris	Thomas	Rfn	305036
Hancock*	Sydney	Cpl	240078	Harris	William	Rfn	242663
Hancock	Tom	Rfn	99550	Harrison	Albert	Rfn	242612
Hand	Harry	Rfn	50007	Harrison	Arthur	Rfn	306782
Handley*	John	Rfn	240720	Harrison	Arthur P.	Cpl	15504
Handley*	John S.	WO2	240111	Harrison	Edgar K.	Rfn	242052
Handley	William	Rfn	242825	Harrison	Ernest	Rfn	4168
Hankey[H]	James R.	Sgt	380966	Harrison*	Eustace J.	Lt-Col.	
Hankin	Thomas	Rfn	241780	Harrison	Fred	L/Cpl	242664
Hankinson	Samuel	Rfn	242856	Harrison	George	Rfn	109051
Hanmer	Arthur	Rfn	242733	Harrison*	George	Lt	1368
Hannah	Arthur	Rfn	242734	Harrison	Harold	Rfn	4447
Hannah*	Walter B.	Sgt	240443	Harrison	Henry	L/Cpl	85446
Hanson	Alfred	Rfn	49745	Harrison*	Herbert M.	Rfn	1555
Hanson	Charles	Rfn	51907	Harrison	Jack	Rfn	309023
Hanson	Harry	Rfn	242726	Harrison	John	Rfn	242665
Hanson	Herbert R.	Rfn	50009	Harrison	John	Rfn	101304
Harding*	Eric S. M.	Rfn	1844	Harrison	John H. T.	Rfn	331445
Harding**	Frank N.	Rfn	240194	Harrison	Richard	Rfn	85234

Harrison	Richard H.	Rfn	203617
Harrison	Robert	Rfn	86755
Harrison	Stanley	Rfn	86463
Harrison	William	Rfn	49947
Harrison*	William H.	Rfn	2403
Harrison*	William L.	Cpl	1285
Harrop**	Ernest B.	Lt	240557
Hart	John	Rfn	4069
Hart*	Montague	Sgt	240315
Hartley*	Cyril	Rfn	1403
Hartley*	Harry	Rfn	240431
Hartley	Hervey	Rfn	99542
Hartley	James	Rfn	242735
Hartley	John	Rfn	242830
Hartley*	Robert H.	Sgt	240583
Hartley	Tom	Rfn	49946
Hartley	Tom	Rfn	26979
Harton	William A.	Rfn	241353
Harvey	David	Rfn	50006
Harvey	Frederick G.	Rfn	406206
Harvey	James	Rfn	3884
Harvey*	John R. R.	Rfn	2052
Harvey	Thomas	Rfn	305407
Harwood*	Percy H.	Rfn	240606
Harwood	Thomas	Rfn	241926
Harwood	Unwin	Sgt	94271
Haskey	Charles	Cpl	307907
Haswell*	Charles	Rfn	240883
Hatch*	Charles J.	Rfn	240637
Hatch*	John F.	Rfn	240652
Hatte*	William F. S.	L/Cpl	2149
Haude	Ernest	Rfn	82688
Haw	Samuel	Rfn	87008
Hawcock	Jack	Rfn	99530
Hawitt*	Arthur M.	Rfn	2787
Hawitt*	Thomas H.	Rfn	2323
Hawkins**	William H. P.	Rfn	240522
Hawksley*	Harold	Rfn	240569
Hawksworth*	Matthew	2Lt	2593
Hawley	Frederick	Rfn	57154
Haworth	Franklin W.	Rfn	241479
Haworth	Harry	Rfn	15989
Haworth	Richard S.	Rfn	3083
Haworth	Herman	Rfn	94264
Haworth*	Reginald	Rfn	2174
Hay**	George A.	Rfn	240293
Hayden	Joseph	Rfn	88890
Haydock	Thomas E.	Rfn	260021
Haydon[H]	Henry J.	Sgt	240029
Hayes	A.	2Lt	
Hayes	George H.	Rfn	99528
Hayes	James	Rfn	36675
Hayes*	Thomas	Bugler	1199
Hayes	William	Rfn	308551
Haygarth	William	Rfn	243641
Hayhurst*	John	Cpl	240060
Hayhurst*	John	Rfn	1733
Haynes*	Allen S.	Rfn	1731
Haynes	Eric S.	Rfn	4545
Hays	James	Rfn	265782
Hayseldine	Wilfred	Cpl	94297
Hayston	Harry	Rfn	260020
Hayton	William M.	A/Cpl	46321
Hayward*	John P.	Rfn	1288
Hayward*	Richard M.	L/Cpl	1507
Haywood*	George B.	Rfn	1430
Haywood	Tom	Rfn	88062
Hazeltine	William	Rfn	242857
Hazlewood	Wilfred E.	A/L/Cpl	88061
Heald	Herbert	Rfn	50011
Healey	Bernard	Rfn	50337
Heaney	Joseph R.	Rfn	242036
Heap*	Frederick M.	Rfn	1457
Heatley*	Edward	Sgt	240308
Heaton	Edward B.	Rfn	241742
Heaton*	William E.	L/Sgt	1335
Hegarty	John	L/Cpl	242695
Helm	William	Rfn	242822
Helme	Henry C.	Rfn	51387
Hemingway	Gerald E.	Sgt	21822
Hemmings	Algernon C.	Rfn	99544
Henderson	Arthur N.	L/Cpl	2895
Henderson*	John L.	Rfn	241068
Henderson*	William F.	Rfn	2893
Hennessey*	John B.	Rfn	1837
Hennessey*	Joseph A.	Rfn	240384
Henning	William	Rfn	241398
Henri	Paul	L/Cpl	241676

Henry*	Norman	Cpl	1911	Hill	Walter P.	2Lt	
Henry**	William W.	CQMS	240385	Hill*(ASC)	William H.	Farrier	5178
Henson	Edward J.	Rfn	242666	Hill	William J.	Rfn	242021
Henson	Herbert	Rfn	99546	Hillyard	Harry	Rfn	99543
Hepworth	William C.	Rfn	4455	Hilton	Isaac L.	Rfn	242828
Herbert	John J.	Rfn	307911	Hilton	Wilfred	Rfn	242729
Herbert*	William J.	Cpl	240458	Hinchcliffe	Norman	Rfn	99533
Herczel	Morris	Rfn	202209	Hinchliffe	George A.	Rfn	99538
Herridge	William T.	Rfn	204606	Hinchliffe	Harry	L/Cpl	99532
Herschell	Ernest	Capt.		Hind	George	Rfn	51132
Hesk	John R. R.	L/Cpl	241870	Hinmars	Charles D.	Rfn	3626
Hesketh	Albert	Rfn	88087	Hinton	J.	Rfn	3445
Hesketh	Peter	Rfn	241438	Hipwell*	William E.	Rfn	56
Hesketh	Richard N.	Cpl	88834	Hird	Edward	Rfn	266389
Hesketh	Stanley R.	Rfn	330269	Hirons	George	Rfn	49944
Heslop	George	Rfn	99534	Hirst	Harold	Rfn	241620
Hester	James	Rfn	87156	Hisley*	Charles J.	Rfn	240383
Hewitson*	Thomas	L/Sgt	240156	Hitch	William H.	Rfn	49742
Hewitt	Ernest	Rfn	50013	Hitchen	Ernest	A/Cpl	241684
Hewitt	George B.	Rfn	91634	Hitchman*	Thomas B.	Rfn	1428
Hewitt**	James	Rfn	240875	Hitchmough	Henry	Rfn	241617
Hewitt	John	Rfn	269422	Hitchon	Albert E.	Rfn	90209
Hewitt	Samuel	Rfn	99547	Hoare	Ernest	Rfn	241193
Hewitt	Samuel W.	Rfn	86018	Hobson	Norman	Rfn	49943
Hewitt	William H.	Rfn	241756	Hochheimer	Walter	Rfn	101306
Hey	James H.	Rfn	87062	Hochkins	John	Rfn	86480
Heyworth	Norman	L/Cpl	86785	Hockless	William	Rfn	99549
Hickey	Patrick B.	Rfn	24125	Hodges	Harold R.	Rfn	242126
Hickling	Tom	Rfn	88073	Hodges	Robert	Rfn	85970
Higgin*	Walter W.	Lt		Hodgkins	John	Rfn	49941
Higginbotham	Edward	Rfn	101305	Hodgson	Albert C.	Rfn	241668
Higgins*	John P.	Rfn	2076	Hodgson	Arthur	A/Cpl	50008
Higgins*	William S.	Rfn	2067	Hodgson	Ernest J.	Sgt	201460
Hill	Alfred	Rfn	101301	Hodgson	Mark	Rfn	4491
Hill	Arthur	Rfn	241805	Hodgson	Willie	Rfn	49942
Hill	Arthur	Rfn	99540	Hodson*	Edward W.	2Lt	240614
Hill	Charles	Rfn	99527	Hodson	James	Rfn	24639
Hill	Charles D.	Rfn	4215	Hodson	John	Rfn	260022
Hill	Douglas	Rfn	86857	Hodson	John	Rfn	331802
Hill	Ernest	Rfn	242133	Hoey	Thomas	Rfn	101307
Hill	Herbert W.	Rfn	308027	Hogan	William	Rfn	305147
Hill	Norman G.	Rfn	241609	Holcroft	Peter	Rfn	24190
Hill	Thomas	Cpl	241423	Holden	A.	Rfn	3930
Hill*	Thomas R.	L/Sgt	2421	Holden	H.	Rfn	99536

Holden	John	Rfn	260023	Horton	Frank	2Lt	
Holden	John D.	Rfn	331218	Hoskyn	Walter	A/Cpl	241919
Holden	William	Rfn	242813	Hotchkiss	Harry	Rfn	241875
Holden	William E.	L/Cpl	241818	Hotchkiss*	William	Rfn	88703
Holderness	William	Rfn	260024	Hough	Albert	Rfn	260025
Holding	Charles A.	Rfn	241961	Houghton*	Benjamin R.	Rfn	240995
Holding	Robert	Rfn	242896	Houghton*	Frederick	Rfn	2200
Hole	Edward H.	Rfn	101308	Houghton	John R.	Rfn	241231
Holgate*	Gordon	L/Cpl	240514	Houghton*	Sydney B.	Rfn	1832
Holland	Ernest	Rfn	50010	Houston**	James	Rfn	240901
Holland	Wilfred	Rfn	51435	Howard	Charles H.	Rfn	3397
Hollinghurst*	Herbert	L/Cpl	240580	Howard	Charles W.	Rfn	328004
Hollis	John	Rfn	242738	Howard*	Daniel	Rfn	1836
Hollows	Arthur	Rfn	109011	Howard	George	Rfn	99548
Holman	William	Rfn	200976	Howard	James	Rfn	109064
Holmes**	Frank	C/Sgt	240489	Howard	Stanley	Rfn	242853
Holmes	Harry	Rfn	49945	Howard	Thomas E. H.	Rfn	86464
Holmes	Reginald J.	Rfn	4476	Howard	William G.	Rfn	85975
Holt	Albert	Rfn	99525	Howarth	Frank	Rfn	99541
Holt	Allen	L/Cpl	268435	Howarth	Frederick	Rfn	109091
Holt	Edward	Rfn	242730	Howarth	Thomas	Rfn	85966
Holt	Herbert	Rfn	88269	Howarth	William	Rfn	242806
Holt	Peter P.	L/Cpl	52145	Howarth	William	Rfn	50519
Holt*	Alfred	Rfn	2030	Howarth	George	Rfn	242737
Honderwood*	Robert S.	Rfn	240745	Howe	Arnold H.	Rfn	51411
Hooper*	Ernest J.	Rfn	2098	Howe	Robert J.	Rfn	51146
Hoose	Reuben	Rfn	241362	Howe*	Allen H.	Rfn	1279
Hope	Harold	Rfn	94266	Howell	John A.	Rfn	51420
Hopkins	Thomas N.	Rfn	87204	Howlett	Allan	Rfn	51016
Hopkinson	Clarence	Rfn	86494	Howorth*	Philip	Rfn	240321
Hopley*	Robert J. J.	Rfn	2332	Howson	William H.	Rfn	242731
Horan*	John	Sgt	240650	Hoyle	Herbert	Rfn	99531
Horn	George	Rfn	47468	Hubbard*	Henry	Rfn	2821
Hornby	Albert W.	A/Cpl	241071	Hubbard	John J.	Rfn	99522
Hornby	John	Rfn	94270	Huddlestone	William A.	Rfn	99535
Hornby*	Roland G.	Rfn	1725	Hudson	Arthur	Rfn	3644
Horne	Alfred	Rfn	86488	Hudson	Charles	Rfn	101309
Horner*	Arthur O.	Rfn	240559	Hudson	Fred	Rfn	94267
Horner	Samuel	Rfn	242855	Hudson	John E.	Rfn	99524
Horrobine	Cyril C.	Rfn	51014	Hudson	John E.	Rfn	241433
Horrocks	Thomas	Rfn	45845	Huggonson	William	L/Sgt	51969
Horsfall*	Douglas B.	Rfn	240208	Hughes	Alfred	Rfn	240953
Horsfall*	John B.	Sgt	1429	Hughes	Charles W.	Rfn	241029
Horton	Arthur	L/Cpl	51069	Hughes	Colin	Rfn	202947

Hughes	David M.	Rfn	101310
Hughes*	Edward H.	Rfn	1176
Hughes	Ernest V.	Capt.	
Hughes	Frank	Rfn	87154
Hughes	Frederick T.	Rfn	4277
Hughes*	Geoffrey	Lt	
Hughes*	George	Rfn	1569
Hughes	George	Rfn	3984
Hughes	George	Lt	
Hughes	George S.	Rfn	242525
Hughes	Harry T.	Rfn	86559
Hughes*	James W.	A/Cpl	240490
Hughes*	John A.	Rfn	240154
Hughes	John R.	Rfn	241663
Hughes	Joseph	Rfn	3771
Hughes	Joseph	Rfn	241208
Hughes	Joseph	Rfn	99537
Hughes	Mark R.	Rfn	99521
Hughes	Peter	Rfn	99545
Hughes	Robert	Rfn	58669
Hughes[H]	Robert A.	Sgt	240020
Hughes[H]	Robert E.	Rfn	1833
Hughes	Thomas	Rfn	242637
Hughes*	Thomas A.	L/Cpl	240907
Hughes	Thomas H.	Rfn	241837
Hughes	Walter Peter	Rfn	241498
Hughes	William H.	Rfn	242727
Huish	Wilfred C.	2Lt	
Hull*	Robert J.	CQMS	240033
Hulme	John S.	Cpl	14296
Hulme	Jonathan	Rfn	242667
Hulme	Joseph H.	Rfn	1766
Hulme	R. T.	Rfn	5495
Hulme	William C. H.	Rfn	99539
Hume	Joseph	L/Cpl	64893
Hume*	William W. K.	Cpl	240034
Humphreys	Louis	Rfn	51436
Humphreys*	Morris	CSM	240295
Humphreys*	Trevor	Rfn	1480
Humphries	Ephraim J.	Rfn	50005
Hunneybell	Clarence V.	Rfn	49948
Hunt	William H.	Rfn	85435
Hunter	James	Rfn	94268
Hunter*	John H.	Rfn	1831
Hunter*	William C.	Rfn	1505
Hurley	Thomas W.	Rfn	242732
Hurry	Henry	Rfn	235099
Hurst	William	Rfn	86764
Huston**	Frederick	Rfn	240695
Hutchinson	Fred	Rfn	86491
Hutchinson*	Stanley R. A.	Rfn	1336
Hutton	William S.	2Lt	
Huxley	Albert	L/Cpl	59927
Hyam*	Herbert	Sgt	240081
Hyde	Austin O.	Rfn	242790
Hyde*	Henry E.	Rfn	2813
Hyde	Walter	Rfn	49737
Hyland	William J.	Rfn	109022
Hyman	Harry	Rfn	4572
Hyslop*	Arthur L.	L/Cpl	1740
Ikin	Harold	Rfn	241777
Ikin	Thomas	Rfn	50014
Illingworth	Fred	Rfn	99553
Illingworth*	Frederick D. R.	L/Sgt	1397
Imlach*	Henry T.	Sgt	102
Inkster	Thomas D.	L/Cpl	241587
Ion	Joseph E.	Rfn	241236
Ireland	William	Rfn	331544
Irwin	Alfred E.	Rfn	99551
Irwin	Innes E.	L/Cpl	3468
Isaacs	Joseph	Rfn	241928
Isherwood	George	Rfn	94273
Isherwood	George P.	Rfn	99552
Isherwood	James	Rfn	29058
Ismay	James	Rfn	405611
Issett	Samuel	Rfn	88074
Jackson	Albert	Rfn	86542
Jackson	Alfred C.	2Lt	
Jackson	Charles	Rfn	4526
Jackson*	Charles	Sgt	240653
Jackson	Harold H.	2Lt	
Jackson	James J.	Cpl	12100
Jackson	John	Rfn	94289
Jackson*	John Brian	Rfn	240567
Jackson*	Joseph	Rfn	240977
Jackson*	Robert A.	Rfn	240442
Jackson	Thomas D.	L/Cpl	85185
Jackson	Walter	Rfn	242858

Jackson	William	Rfn	241925	Johnson	Edwin	Rfn	94277
Jackson	William	Rfn	260027	Johnson	Ernest J.	Rfn	99557
Jackson*	William	Rfn	1208	Johnson*	George	CSM	240016
Jackson	Zachariah	Cpl	56082	Johnson*	Harris Y.	Rfn	1476
Jaeger	John R.	Rfn	241237	Johnson	Henry	Rfn	268046
James	Allan G.	2Lt		Johnson*	Henry W.	CSM	18
James*	Edwin	Rfn	240945	Johnson	Hugh C.	Rfn	241733
James	Frank W.	Rfn	241855	Johnson	Joseph	Cpl	19875
James	Frederick G.	Rfn	94622	Johnson	Joseph J.	Rfn	87123
James	George W.	Rfn	242668	Johnson*	Percival T.	A/Cpl	240167
James	Mark Ewart	L/Cpl	86527	Johnson*	Percy W.	L/Cpl	241481
James	Robert	Rfn	94288	Johnson	R.	Rfn	50015
James*	Robert R. C.	Sgt	240619	Johnson*	Reginald H.	Rfn	2729
Jameson	James A.	Rfn	332564	Johnson	Robert	Rfn	108695
Jamieson*	John	L/Cpl	950	Johnson	Thomas	L/Cpl	26519
Jarman	Harold T.	L/Cpl	94290	Johnson	Walter	Rfn	99558
Jarvis	Arthur	Rfn	49951	Johnson	William	L/Cpl	99566
Jarvis	Arthur	Rfn	94435	Johnston*	Hugh S.	Rfn	241324
Jarvis	Harry	Rfn	99556	Johnston	James	L/Cpl	241858
Jarvis	William S.	Rfn	332330	Jolly	James	Rfn	95166
Jeeves	Leslie W. R.	Rfn	99561	Jones	A. H.	Rfn	3861
Jefferson	William E.	Rfn	93948	Jones*	Albert	Rfn	2162
Jeffes*	Edward W. B.	Cpl	137	Jones*	Albert E.	Rfn	240168
Jenkins	George	Rfn	4685	Jones	Albert E.	Capt.	
Jenkins*	James A.	Rfn	1830	Jones	Alfred	Rfn	332813
Jenkins*	John F.	Cpl	240288	Jones	Alfred E.	Rfn	59367
Jenkins	William A.	Rfn	242420	Jones*	Alfred H. H.	Sgt	78
Jenks	James E.	Rfn	27828	Jones	Arthur	Rfn	4245
Jennings*	Edward	Sgt	240296	Jones	Arthur	Rfn	308376
Jennings	George	Rfn	86379	Jones	Arthur E.	Rfn	88071
Jennings	Harry	Rfn	59538	Jones	Charles O.	Rfn	94287
Jennings	Thomas	Rfn	49949	Jones	Charles S.	Rfn	99567
Jennings	William	Rfn	49950	Jones	Clement J.	L/Cpl	270116
Jennings	Willie	Rfn	51417	Jones	Deiniol G.	Rfn	241902
Jepson	Stanley	Rfn	99560	Jones*	Edgar	A/Cpl	241420
Jerrett	Harold	2Lt		Jones*	Edgar M.	Rfn	2010
Jessop	James	Rfn	99559	Jones	Edward	Rfn	242740
Jevons	Ellis	Rfn	4351	Jones	Edward	Rfn	51378
Jinks	Arthur W.	Rfn	51020	Jones	Edward	Rfn	94276
Johnson	Albert	L/Cpl	242008	Jones*	Edward A.	Rfn	240408
Johnson	Albert	Cpl	260052	Jones	Edward D.	WO2	241929
Johnson	Arthur S.	Rfn	242014	Jones	Ernest	Rfn	4603
Johnson	Arthur S.	Rfn	241962	Jones*	Ernest B.	Rfn	241557
Johnson	Donald C. M.	2Lt		Jones*	Ernest H.	Rfn	240604

Jones*	Ernest L.	Rfn	240598
Jones*	Frank A.	Rfn	1942
Jones*	Frank E.	Rfn	240841
Jones	Frederick	Rfn	87245
Jones	Frederick C.	Rfn	242129
Jones	Geoffrey	Rfn	241700
Jones	George	Rfn	94274
Jones*	George B.	L/Cpl	240227
Jones	George H.	Rfn	3991
Jones*	George H.	L/Cpl	824
Jones	George W.	L/Sgt	15722
Jones*	Griffith	Rfn	2192
Jones	Griffith P.	Rfn	241593
Jones**	H.	L/Cpl	240061
Jones	Harry	Rfn	330393
Jones	Henry	Rfn	242897
Jones	Henry W.	Rfn	242465
Jones*	Herbert B.	Sgt	240009
Jones	Hugh E.	Rfn	241759
Jones	Hughie	Rfn	241563
Jones*	Iorwerth Ap G.	Rfn	240824
Jones	Ivor	Rfn	2062
Jones*	J.	Rfn	3540
Jones*	J.	Dvr	730
Jones*	J. R.	Dvr	724
Jones	Jack	Rfn	99555
Jones	James A.	L/Cpl	241984
Jones	John A.	Rfn	241750
Jones	John A.	Rfn	3982
Jones*	John R.	Rfn	2853
Jones	Joseph	Rfn	241629
Jones*	Joseph H.	L/Sgt	240180
Jones*	Lewis V. H.	A/Cpl	240243
Jones	Norris	Rfn	49754
Jones	Owen	Rfn	64878
Jones	Peter	Rfn	201915
Jones*	Pierce	Rfn	2056
Jones	Rees	Rfn	86759
Jones	Richard J.	Rfn	242092
Jones	Richard P.	Rfn	99563
Jones	Robert	Cpl	263011
Jones*	Robert A.	Rfn	240407
Jones*	Robert H.	Rfn	2533
Jones*	Robert L.	Rfn	1230
Jones	S.	Rfn	5585
Jones*	Stanley	Rfn	837
Jones*	Stanley	Cpl	2165
Jones*	Stanley T.	Rfn	2051
Jones*	Stanley W. E.	Rfn	2079
Jones	Thomas	Rfn	242506
Jones	Thomas A.	2Lt	
Jones*	Thomas E.	Rfn	240744
Jones*	Thomas L.	Rfn	1988
Jones*	Trevor A.	Rfn	1351
Jones*	Trevor P. G.	Rfn	240212
Jones[H]	Vernon H.	Rfn	1926
Jones	W.	Rfn	4231
Jones	Wilfred	Rfn	241720
Jones	William A.	Rfn	241881
Jones**	William A.	L/Cpl	240301
Jones	William	Rfn	94275
Jones	William	Rfn	57248
Jones	William	Sgt	57980
Jones*	William H.	Cpl	240494
Jones	William H.	Rfn	56707
Jones	William H.	Rfn	241619
Jones	William J.	Cpl	15105
Jones	William J.	Lt	
Jones	William J.	Rfn	15522
Jones*	William R.	Rfn	240128
Jones*	William R.	Rfn	2210
Joseph	Robert A.	Rfn	241764
Joughin*	Frederick C.	Sgt	241471
Joughin	John H.	L/Cpl	241042
Joughin	Joseph	Rfn	241879
Joughin	William G.	L/Cpl	42618
Jowett*	Robert	Rfn	2745
Joynson*	Harry L.	L/Cpl	2044
Judge	John	Rfn	99564
Judson	John	Rfn	99565
Jump*	Robert	Rfn	1289
Kane	George	Rfn	332858
Kane	James F.	Rfn	241846
Kavanagh	Archibald	A/Cpl	242898
Kay	Harry C.	Rfn	242329
Kay	James G.	Rfn	242107
Kay*	Thomas	Rfn	2135
Kaye*	Thomas	Rfn	2038

Keane	Arthur G.	Rfn	51388
Kearne	Percy	Rfn	407043
Keates	George H.	L/Cpl	241070
Keay	Peter	Rfn	99575
Keegan*	Harold R.	Rfn	240510
Keegan	Herbert J.	Rfn	242043
Keeton	Richard	Rfn	4013
Kehoe	Joseph M.	L/Cpl	240655
Kelf	Ernest J.	Rfn	51022
Kellett	George	Rfn	87243
Kelley*	Cedric	Rfn	2436
Kellow	Francis J.	Rfn	381862
Kelly	Bernard	Rfn	85291
Kelly	Harold	Rfn	94281
Kelly	Harold F.	Rfn	331371
Kelly	James	Rfn	305597
Kelly	John	Rfn	99571
Kelly	Joseph	Rfn	21068
Kelly	Robert	Rfn	242629
Kelly	Samuel	Rfn	38454
Kelly	Sydney	L/Sgt	241942
Kelshaw	Thomas	Rfn	306778
Kemp*	Charles K. N.	L/Cpl	240452
Kemp	John	Rfn	94592
Kemp*	John L.	L/Sgt	240182
Kempe*	Reginald H. S.	L/Sgt	2070
Kempster	Benjamin	Rfn	331473
Kendal	John	Rfn	242741
Kendall*	Charles B.	Rfn	240174
Keneley	William	Rfn	330675
Kennedy	Thomas M.	Cpl	267839
Kennedy	Valentine	Rfn	331995
Kennedy		Rfn	109076
Kenny	Leo	Rfn	242859
Kenny	Thomas	L/Cpl	308977
Kenny	William	Rfn	99577
Kenrick	Leslie	Cpl	200363
Kenshole	Edward H.	2Lt	
Kent*	James H.	Rfn	2337
Kent*	Richard H.	L/Cpl	240404
Kent	William	Rfn	99569
Kenyon*	William Y.	Rfn	240825
Kermode*	Alfred H.	Cpl	240282
Kermode*	James F.	Rfn	1610
Kerr*	Douglas	Rfn	240382
Kerr	John H.	Rfn	241139
Kerr	Walter	Rfn	305377
Kerruish*	John W.	Rfn	241687
Kersey	Septimus F. R.	Rfn	202111
Kersey	Walter G.	Rfn	4187
Kershaw	Arnold	Rfn	94291
Kershaw	Hubert	2Lt	
Kettle	John H. M.	Rfn	99578
Kewish*	E.	Rfn	2151
Key*	George L.	Rfn	2287
Key*	Herbert W.	A/Cpl	240475
Keyte	Cornelius H. J.	Rfn	51389
Kidd*	John C.	Sgt	240381
Kiernan	George W.	Rfn	37382
Kightley	Joseph W.	Rfn	85369
Killey	James B.	Lt	
Kilner*	Norman L.	Rfn	1542
King	Albert V.	Rfn	308597
King	Arthur	Rfn	99568
King	Charles F.	2Lt	
King*	Imrie A.	Rfn	240491
King[H]	James A.	Rfn	unk
King*	John H.	Rfn	3130
King*	John J.	Rfn	240136
King*	Robert H.	Rfn	3129
King	William	Rfn	51437
Kingston	Charles F.	Rfn	53456
Kinsey[H]	Francis O.	Rfn	240820
Kinvig	William	Rfn	5423
Kirby	Arthur	Rfn	4213
Kirby	William J.	Rfn	330559
Kirkbridge*	Jackson W.	Rfn	240358
Kirkland	Henry	Rfn	4051
Kirkland	Thomas	Rfn	50947
Kirkwood	Alex	Cpl	241960
Kirwan	Gerald	Sgt	306891
Kisby	William R.	Rfn	99572
Kissack*	Edward J.	Rfn	2302
Kitchener	George	L/Cpl	57960
Kitcher	Wallace A.	Rfn	15301
Kitson*	Francis H.	Rfn	1745
Knaggs	Walter	Rfn	99576
Kneale	George	Rfn	35683

Kneale	John Fred	2Lt	241111
Kneale	Sydney J.	L/Cpl	241110
Kneebone	Thomas	L/Cpl	99570
Kneen	Thomas M.	Rfn	242566
Knight	Edward	Rfn	50099
Knight*	James A.	RSM	240011
Knight	James W.	Rfn	51419
Knight	John T.	Rfn	99574
Kniveton	William	Rfn	49165
Knott	Charles H.	Rfn	82870
Knowlson**	Ellis	Rfn	240923
Kovachich	Edward G.	Rfn	405614
Kramer	James	Rfn	99572
Kydd*	Frederick J.	Rfn	1296
Lace*	Philip W.	Rfn	1678
Lacey	William	Rfn	269950
Laing	H.	Rfn	200885
Lamb	J.	Rfn	307622
Lamb	Stephen	Rfn	99581
Lamb*	W. E.	Rfn	240173
Lambert	Reginald	Rfn	242041
Lancaster*	Joseph	Rfn	1933
Lanceley	George A. M.	Rfn	99585
Lane	Frederick H. J.	Rfn	57937
Lane*	Henry J.	Cpl	240578
Langham*	William F.	Rfn	1564
Langhorne	Cyril V.	A/Cpl	240764
Langhorne	George B.	Cpl	241803
Lapworth	Thomas H.	L/Cpl	61265
Lashmar	John W.T.	2Lt	
Latham**	Thomas B.	Rfn	240902
Latham	William A.	L/Cpl	200176
Laurie	Donald	L/Cpl	15735
Laver	James H. S.	Rfn	99586
Lavery	Harry	Rfn	241916
Lavin*	C.	Rfn	2255
Law	David A.	Rfn	96764
Law	John	Rfn	86665
Lawes	Arthur H.	Rfn	241939
Lawrence	Charles	Rfn	3894
Lawson	John	Rfn	91053
Lawson	W. S.	2Lt	
Lawson*	William	Rfn	1237
Lawton	Byron	Rfn	241356
Lawton*	George	Rfn	1201
Lax	George A.	Rfn	85012
Lazarovitch	Abraham	Rfn	332697
Le Rougetel*	Arthur	L/Cpl	1268
Lea*	Alfred	Rfn	2962
Lea	Richard	Rfn	405862
Leach	Arthur	Rfn	23085
Leamey**	James	Rfn	241230
Leatherbarrow*	E. J.	WO2	240004
Leaver*	Harry R.	L/Cpl	2472
Leavy	Thomas	Rfn	242742
Ledger	Cornelius	Rfn	99582
Ledgerwood*	William	Cpl	240439
Ledsham	William H.	Rfn	3488
Lee	Albert	Cpl	330378
Lee*	Albert V.	Rfn	2163
Lee*	Harold	L/Cpl	2766
Lee	Harry T.	Rfn	242743
Lee	John J.	L/Cpl	242118
Lee	Norman	Rfn	99587
Lee*	Percy	Rfn	1974
Lee	Richard J.	L/Sgt	241088
Lee	Samuel	2Lt	
Lee	Victor	2Lt	
Lee	William F.	Rfn	242899
Leeburn	Charles	Rfn	307598
Leech	William E.	Rfn	242082
Leeks	Fred	L/Sgt	51137
Lees*	Frederick D.	Sgt	240380
Leeson	Arthur	Rfn	109023
Leigh	James	Rfn	85432
Leigh	Richard F.	Rfn	242131
Leigh**	Robert	Rfn	241007
Leigh	Thomas S.	Rfn	241651
Leighton*	Arthur	Rfn	1338
Lennan	Alfred	Rfn	105498
Lennie*	George H.	Rfn	2563
Lester	James	Rfn	94296
Lester	Reginald W.	Rfn	241432
Lester	Thomas	Rfn	3531
Letheren[H]	Cyril V.	Rfn	1548
Levens	Thomas	Rfn	52299
Lever	Thomas P.	Rfn	242007
Levey	Joseph	L/Cpl	308776

Lewis	Aaron O.	Rfn	94292
Lewis[H]	Cecil M.	Rfn	1985
Lewis*	David R.	Sgt	1106
Lewis	Edward C.	Rfn	241622
Lewis*	Herbert O.	Sgt	240133
Lewis*	Hugh B.	L/Cpl	240405
Lewis*	Humphrey	Cpl	240601
Lewis	Maurice R.	2Lt	
Lewis	Robert	Rfn	241800
Lewis*	Thomas	Cpl	87
Lewis*	Wilfred	Sgt	240023
Lewis*	William J.	Rfn	240253
Leyland	Harold	Rfn	330759
Life	James	Rfn	260028
Liggett*	Harold W.	Rfn	2199
Lightbourn	Herbert	Rfn	107969
Lightfoot	William	Rfn	88270
Lilley*	William D.	Cpl	1303
Lincoln	George	Rfn	242860
Lindburg	Thomas H.	Rfn	241410
Lindsay	Andrew A.	Lt	
Lindsay*	Gerald W.	Rfn	1736
Lindsay	W.	Lt	
Lindsey	George E.	Rfn	94295
Linekar*	Francis R.	Rfn	1914
Lister	Rowland	Rfn	99588
Lister*	Herbert	Rfn	240476
Litchfield*	John R.	L/Cpl	240534
Little	John H. M.	Lt	
Little	Thomas G.	Rfn	243640
Liversidge[H]	Harry K.	Rfn	1824
Lloyd*	Clifford U.	Rfn	2213
Lloyd	Edward M.	Rfn	51438
Lloyd	Frederick D.	Rfn	241831
Lloyd	Percy	Rfn	50255
Lloyd	Richard	Rfn	241792
Lloyd	Sidney F.	Rfn	94294
Lloyd	William H.	Rfn	241974
Lloyd*	Samuel T.	Rfn	1614
Lloyd*	Sydney	Rfn	2208
Loades	Charlie P.	L/Sgt	328011
Locker	Albert	Rfn	242086
Lodge	Alfred	Rfn	241958
Lofthouse	C. Thornton	2Lt	
Lomas	Charles D.	Rfn	87120
Lomas	Fred	Rfn	87000
Lomax	Lewis	Rfn	94752
London	Albert	Rfn	99579
Lonergan	William	Rfn	241603
Long	Frank W.	Rfn	242670
Long*	John J	Rfn	2339
Long**	Joseph W.	Rfn	240032
Longden	Frederick E.	Rfn	268404
Longmire	Herbert J.	Rfn	99580
Longmore	J. T.	Rfn	49952
Longstaff	Arthur M.	Rfn	4307
Longworth	Robert W.	Rfn	3393
Longworth	W.	Rfn	242272
Loughran*	Frank	Rfn	240346
Lovett	Harold J.	Rfn	4275
Lovgreen	Theodore J.	Sgt	240031
Lowe	John F.	2Lt	
Lowe*	John W.T.	Rfn	240484
Lowe	Thomas	Rfn	308033
Lowe*	William W.	Rfn	1826
Lowes**	George F.	Rfn	240441
Loynd	Arthur	Rfn	242744
Loynes	Albert	Cpl	99584
Lube*	James E.	Cpl	240416
Lucas	Alexander	Rfn	241705
Lucas	John H. M.	Rfn	5501
Lucock*	Charles H.	L/Cpl	240379
Luke*	William S.	Cpl	240175
Lunt	James E.	Rfn	242681
Lunt**	Arthur L.	Rfn	240329
Lunt*	Arthur T.	Rfn	1696
Lunt	William W.	Rfn	204264
Lupton*	Reginald B.	Rfn	2723
Lymn*	Clifford	Rfn	2926
Lynch	Frank L.	Rfn	94293
Lynch	George	Rfn	305782
Lynch*	James W.	Rfn	240707
Lynch	Joseph	Rfn	4646
Lynch	Thomas	Rfn	99583
Lyons*	Richard M.	Rfn	240600
Lyth*	Edward	Rfn	2950
MacGarrey	Terence	Rfn	242117
Machin	Edward	Rfn	49953

Mackarell	John	Rfn	14684
Mackay	Charles	Rfn	405072
Mackenzie	Charles H.	L/Cpl	91220
Mackenzie*	John L.	Rfn	2304
Mackenzie*	William A.	Cpl	240554
MacMaster*	Albert E.	Sgt	240065
Macnicoll	Herbert L.	Sgt	241392
Madden	Charles	Rfn	242862
Madden	William G.	Rfn	243894
Madoc-Jones*	Gwilyn	Rfn	61885
Magee	Thomas	Rfn	242016
Maggi*	Norman P.	Sgt	240092
Makinson	Edward	Rfn	260032
Malkin	Leonard	Rfn	99601
Malone*	Henry N.	A/Cpl	240378
Maltby	Arthur	Rfn	99591
Mangan	William A.	Rfn	241409
Mann*	Charles G.	Rfn	240157
Mann	John	Rfn	241389
Mansell*	Harry L.	L/Cpl	240536
Mansergh*	Harry R.	Rfn	1262
Marginson	James	Sgt	260001
Marland*	George	Rfn	240286
Marriott	Joseph A.	Rfn	99602
Marrison*	John	Sgt	32
Marrs	Joseph	Rfn	51390
Marsden	Cyril	L/Cpl	18871
Marsden*	George	L/Cpl	240052
Marsden*	Harold E.	Rfn	240790
Marsden	John	Rfn	242866
Marsden	John H.	Rfn	242793
Marsden	Thomas J.	Cpl	2865
Marsden	William	Rfn	242746
Marsden	William	Rfn	3868
Marsh	Charles F.	Rfn	242341
Marsh	David C.	L/Cpl	240788
Marsh	Frederick H. J.	Rfn	25494
Marsh	George W.	Rfn	99590
Marsh	Thomas	Rfn	109069
Marshall	Albert E.	Rfn	64994
Marshall*	James L.	Sgt	221
Marston	Charles A.	Rfn	241964
Marten	Charles	Rfn	3178
Martin	George F.	Rfn	241459
Martin	Henry	Rfn	91525
Martin	James	Rfn	242863
Martin*	John	Dvr	729
Martin*[R]	John G.	Maj.	
Martin	Lewis A.	Rfn	88893
Martin**	Stanley D.	Rfn	240425
Martin	William T.	Rfn	51393
Marwood*	Cecil E.	Cpl	1657
Masding	Stanley H. P.	2Lt	
Mason	Albert	Rfn	99603
Mason	Albert E.	Rfn	240916
Mason	Charles	Rfn	306111
Mason*	Ernest	Rfn	240281
Mason	Ernest A.	Rfn	241414
Mason	George H.	Rfn	99593
Mason	Henry W.	Rfn	99596
Mason*	William J.	A/Cpl	240768
Massey	George	Rfn	241601
Massey	Thomas E.	Rfn	51425
Massey*	Henry T.	Rfn	2343
Massey**	Joseph	Rfn	240603
Mather	Absalom	Rfn	260031
Mather	John T.	Rfn	86565
Mathers	John	Rfn	242671
Matthews	Harry	Rfn	381015
Matthews	Thomas J.	Rfn	242625
Matthews	William	Rfn	105536
Matthews	William H.	Sgt	241856
Maude	Reginald	Rfn	241683
Maudsley	Albert E.	Rfn	242505
Maudsley*	John	Rfn	2131
Mawdsley	Robert	Rfn	41450
Maxfield	Matthew H.	Rfn	2555
Maxwell	Herbert	Rfn	50617
Maxwell	James	Cpl	240747
Maybury	Richard L.	Rfn	241635
Maycock	George E.	Cpl	51147
Mayell	Harry	Rfn	51413
Mayes	Herbert T.	Rfn	241448
Mayor	Robert	Rfn	90900
Mayors	John	Rfn	308388
McAleavy	Owen J	Rfn	307644
McAllester	Herbert	Rfn	3082
McAuley	John	Rfn	10560

McBeath*	Brian E.	Rfn	1673	McGrath	Peter H.	L/Cpl	99597
McCabe	Harold	Rfn	330569	McGregor	George	Rfn	201055
McCall	James H.	L/Cpl	53069	McGregor	John	Rfn	305528
McCall	William	Rfn	24072	McGuire	Robert	Rfn	269357
McCallum	George	Rfn	51392	McIlroy	James	Rfn	242091
McCann	Joseph	Rfn	241417	McInroy	Edward	Sgt	305173
McCarthy	Edward	L/Cpl	242747	McKaig**	John B.	Lt-Col.	
McConnell	Herbert	Rfn	381042	McKaig*	Wallace R.	2Lt	1729
McConnell**	Stanley	Rfn	240377	McKellar	James	Rfn	241662
McCorkindale	Edward G.	Rfn	241424	McKeon	Charles	Rfn	47004
McCormick	Daniel	Rfn	88757	McKie	A.	Rfn	242610
McCormick	Robert W.	Rfn	8765	McKinlay	Thomas	Rfn	242867
McCormick	William	Rfn	307058	McKnight	Alexander	Sgt	330132
McCudden	William C.	Sgt	330690	McLaren	James A.	Capt.	
McCullagh*	Richard	L/Cpl	240226	McLaughlin*	Henry V.	L/Cpl	240131
McDaid	Francis	Rfn	85173	McLean	Arthur	Rfn	3498
McDermott	D.	2Lt		McLean	Charles J.	2Lt	
McDermott	Thomas J.	Rfn	202740	McLean*	Thomas	L/Cpl	2040
McDevitte	Joseph T.	Rfn	99594	McLoughlin	John	Rfn	241768
McDonald	Henry	Rfn	99600	McMahon	James	L/Cpl	241790
McDonald	William	Rfn	331723	McManus	Nathan	L/Cpl	241895
McDonnell*	Francis	Rfn	2709	McMeakin*	Thomas J.	Rfn	2288
McDonnell	William	Rfn	3086	McMillan	Arthur	Sgt	242672
McDonough	Thomas	Rfn	305385	McMillan	Donald	L/Sgt	241592
McDowell	Alexander	Rfn	332021	McMillan	George	2Lt	
McElhinney	Leonard C.	Rfn	242058	McMullin	Alfred	Rfn	405298
McElhinney*	George C.	Rfn	203972	McNair*	Robert	L/Cpl	2305
McEvoy	Walter E.	Rfn	58487	McNamara	Michael J.	Rfn	42853
McEwen**	John Henry	Rfn	240462	McQuarrie	William N.	Rfn	34854
McGae	Martin	Rfn	37546	McVay	John	Rfn	242861
McGann	Peter	Rfn	380440	McVittie	William	Rfn	39487
McGann	Thomas	Rfn	52206	McWean*	Thomas	RQMS	240005
McGeachin*	Charles S.	Cpl	240142	McWilliam*	James	L/Sgt	1645
McGee	James B.	Rfn	99592	Meadowcroft	William	Rfn	51148
McGeorge*	Martin	Rfn	240192	Meadows	Arthur	Rfn	330988
McGeorge*	Thomas S.	L/Cpl	240621	Meadows	James	Rfn	109070
McGill*	Edward	Sgt	1076	Meers*	Albert F.	Rfn	2972
McGill*	John P.	Sgt	240077	Melia	James	L/Cpl	48983
McGivering**	Donald	Rfn	240527	Mellen	Harold	Rfn	56670
McGivern	Joseph	Rfn	242826	Mennell	Thomas	Rfn	86570
McGough	James	Rfn	242748	Meredith	James	Rfn	5620
McGowan	Eugene	Rfn	27287	Mernock	James	Rfn	242697
McGrath*	Henry	Rfn	1215	Merrigan	Joseph	L/Cpl	2976
McGrath*	John J.	Rfn	2137	Merriman*	Cecil H.	2Lt	2016

Merron*	John B.	Rfn	1486	Molyneux*	Robert	Rfn	2117
Metcalf	Ernest	Rfn	85447	Monk	Henry	Rfn	242818
Metcalfe	Dudley W.	Rfn	242888	Monks	Harold W.	Sgt	305851
Metcalfe	Henry P.	Rfn	51391	Montgomery*	William S.	Capt.	
Middleton	Archibald J.	Rfn	3234	Moody	William H.	Rfn	241844
Middleton*	Albert E.	Rfn	1980	Moor	Arthur B.	Rfn	241458
Middleton	Frederick	Rfn	94446	Moore	Charles	Rfn	49954
Middleton*	Geoffrey V.	Sgt	2028	Moore	Ernest	Rfn	242062
Midgeley	H.	Rfn	242749	Moore	Ernest	L/Cpl	51031
Midworth	John T.	Rfn	88271	Moore	Patrick	Rfn	38704
Millar*	Walter	Cpl	240216	Moore	Robert	Rfn	47798
Millard	George B.	Rfn	241613	Moore	Stanley	Rfn	241820
Millard*	Robert A.	Cpl	240410	Moore	William A.	Rfn	331585
Miller*	Alfred E.	Rfn	240889	Moorhouse	Charles E.	Rfn	330824
Miller	George G.	Rfn	88272	Moran	Thomas	Rfn	3818
Miller*	George H.	L/Cpl	240412	Morgan	Arthur	Rfn	4347
Miller	Henry F. S.	2Lt		Morgan	Arthur	Rfn	88063
Miller*	Leonard B.	Rfn	1259	Morgan	George	Rfn	85381
Miller	Robert	Rfn	330682	Morgan	James O.	Rfn	242750
Miller*	Wilfred H.	Rfn	1261	Morgan	John	CQMS	23121
Miller	William D.	Cpl	240989	Morgan*	Samuel D.	Sgt	668
Millington	James	Rfn	381416	Morgan	Thomas J.	Rfn	3757
Millington	John	Rfn	242045	Morgan	William J.	Rfn	49008
Mills	John	Rfn	3723	Morgan	William J.	Rfn	64955
Milnes	Norman W.	Rfn	99595	Morley	Henry	Rfn	331425
Milnes*	Percy J.	Rfn	925	Morley	James	Rfn	85290
Milroy	William J.	Rfn	242821	Morriarty	William	Rfn	200761
Milton	Maurice H.	Rfn	50022	Morris	Arthur	Rfn	85049
Milton*	John H.	Sgt	971	Morris	David L.	2Lt	
Minshall*	Alfred L.	L/Sgt	240376	Morris	Edward E.	Rfn	4426
Mitchell*	Alfred H.	Sgt	1236	Morris*	Edward T.	Sgt	240046
Mitchell	Ernest	Rfn	49955	Morris	Ernest	Rfn	308236
Mitchell	John W.	Rfn	72435	Morris*	George E.	Rfn	240292
Mitchell	Leslie	L/Cpl	86021	Morris	Myer	Rfn	241825
Mitchell*	William	A/Cpl	1934	Morris	Peter	Rfn	242865
Mitton	William	Rfn	93974	Morris	Reginald B.	L/Cpl	52850
Moah*	James	Rfn	1820	Morris	Rupert	Rfn	84882
Moffat*	Robert	Cpl	240040	Morris	Silvester S.	Sgt	380962
Moir	John D.	Rfn	241945	Morris	Thomas	Rfn	242504
Mole	Richard R.	Rfn	241373	Morris	Thomas J.	Cpl	241887
Molyneux*	Benjamin	Rfn	2303	Morris	Thomas S.	Rfn	241143
Molyneux	D.	Rfn	242751	Morris	Wilfred	Rfn	51439
Molyneux	Joseph	L/Cpl	204539	Morris**	William	Rfn	240150
Molyneux	Joseph S.	L/Cpl	241914	Morris	William G.	Rfn	260029

Morrish*	Richard G.	L/Cpl	1642	Myers	Arthur S.	Rfn	32623
Morson	John W.	Rfn	242690	Myers	Fred	Rfn	87001
Morton*	Alfred E.	Sgt	245	Myerscough**	Luke	Rfn	240659
Morton**	Charles E.	Cpl	240420	Mylrea*	John L.	Rfn	240836
Morton	John H.	Rfn	99598	Nadin*	Albert C.	Rfn	240235
Morton	Tom	Rfn	56408	Nadin*	George H.	Rfn	240797
Morton	William	Rfn	4417	Nadin	Ernest	Rfn	242754
Moscrop*	Joseph A.	CSM	243896	Nash	Henry	Rfn	305744
Moses	Malcolm H.	Rfn	241993	Naylor	James	Rfn	51394
Moses	Walter H.	Rfn	241648	Naylor	James	Rfn	201829
Moss	Ernest	L/Cpl	330118	Neale*	Charles H.	Rfn	240926
Moss	Henry	Rfn	260030	Neale*	Robert	Rfn	2517
Moss*	John A.	CSM	240090	Nealy	Henry C. R.	Rfn	260033
Moss*	Maurice E.	2Lt	1463	Neary	James	Rfn	201521
Moss	William	Rfn	241404	Needs	Charles	Rfn	51414
Moston	William	Rfn	242752	Neely*	Ernest	Rfn	240283
Mostyn	Edward O.	Cpl	242002	Neil	George P.	Rfn	269343
Mottershead	George R.	Rfn	242576	Nelson	Thomas H.	L/Cpl	240957
Moulton*	Arthur B.	Sgt	136	Nelson	William	Cpl	51976
Mountford*	John W.	Rfn	2781	Nessling	Charles L.	Rfn	381986
Mountney	William B.	Rfn	99589	Newberry	Raymond J.	Rfn	51395
Muir*	Frank W.	Rfn	2229	Newbon	Fred	Rfn	87002
Muir	James K.	Rfn	241361	Newham	Henry	Rfn	4688
Muirhead	John	Rfn	266482	Newton	Walter H.	L/Cpl	241843
Mullins	Patrick	Rfn	85470	Niblett	William H.	Rfn	241363
Mundy	William E.	Rfn	86476	Niblock	Arthur W.	Rfn	26635
Munt	Charles	Rfn	308849	Nicholl*	James V.	Rfn	240661
Murdoch*	Hugh	Rfn	2344	Nicholls	Frank	Rfn	86578
Murney	James	Rfn	241476	Nicholls	George F.	Rfn	242797
Murney*	Thomas P.	Rfn	240375	Nichols*	Charles T.	Rfn	1497
Murphy	Andrew	Cpl	242260	Nichols*	Frederick R.	L/Cpl	240218
Murphy*	Francis	Sgt	240582	Nichols	Herbert	Rfn	242868
Murphy	Henry	L/Cpl	11380	Nichols	James R.	Cpl	242032
Murray*	Bertram	L/Cpl	1683	Nicholson	John	Rfn	99605
Murray	Michael	Rfn	94282	Nicholson	John	Rfn	331722
Murray	William	Rfn	3831	Nicholson	William C.	Rfn	99604
Murray	William H.	Rfn	241670	Nickels*	Colmar R.	Cpl	1734
Murrow*	Ralph G.	Cpl	240316	Nickson	Arthur G.	Rfn	241741
Murtagh	Percy	Rfn	307510	Nickson	Jonathan	Rfn	242601
Muse	Walter	Rfn	200116	Nield	Fred R.	2Lt	
Musk	Frederick G.	Rfn	242753	Nieman	Richard	Rfn	242508
Musker	John	Rfn	30027	Nightingale*	Robert J.	Rfn	2142
Mustin	Oscar	Rfn	88064	Nixon	Charles	Rfn	49961
Mycock	James	L/Cpl	45505	Nixon	Frank	Rfn	268493

Noke	Harold	Rfn	88891
Nolan	David	L/Cpl	241347
Nolan	James	Rfn	305222
Norman*	George	Rfn	241025
Norman	Isiah	Rfn	34140
Norman*	William H.	Sgt	240741
Norminton	John	Rfn	241899
Norris	Edwin	Rfn	241715
Norris	George E.	Rfn	51129
Norris	Thomas	Cpl	241107
North	George	Rfn	99606
Norton	John	Rfn	49170
Nowell	Walter	Rfn	242755
Nuttall	Fred	Rfn	242756
Nuttall	James	Rfn	91460
Nuttall	James H.	Rfn	50672
Oakes	James	Cpl	305494
Oakley	Edwin G.	Rfn	51396
O'Brien	Peter J.	2Lt	
O'Connor	Walter	Cpl	242050
Oddy*	Charles	Rfn	2261
O'Donnell*	F. G.	Sgt	1465
O'Donnell*	Walter	L/Sgt	240516
O'Donovan	John	Rfn	308980
O'Dwyer	Lawrence	Rfn	241731
O'Flaherty	Michael	L/Cpl	26187
Ogden	Harold	L/Cpl	308803
Ogden	Horace W.	Rfn	22204
Ogden	William E.	2Lt	
O'Hanlon	John	Rfn	308975
O'Hare	John	Rfn	85962
O'Hare	William	Sgt	94284
O'Keefe*	Stephen	Cpl	1719
Oldfield	David	Rfn	242800
Oldham	Ernest	Rfn	4205
Oldham	Lawrence G.	Rfn	4312
O'Leary	Alfred G.	Rfn	242075
Oliver	Arthur	Rfn	242792
Oliver	Edmund	Rfn	242010
Oliver*	Edward L.	Lt	
O'Neill	Thomas W.	Rfn	242757
Onions	Joseph W.	Rfn	3773
Orange	Sidney A.	Rfn	308053
O'Reilly	J.	Rfn	201915
Orfanes	Nicholas	Rfn	305100
Ormerod	Thomas	Rfn	242809
Ormrod	William	Rfn	260034
O'Rourke	Peter	Rfn	305114
Osborne	Francis J.	Sgt	50026
O'Shaughnessy	John	Rfn	243880
O'Sullivan*	Jeremiah J.	Rfn	1752
Oswald	Harold R.	2Lt	
Ovenden	Charles	Rfn	3208
Oversby	Reginald	L/Cpl	49962
Owen	Evan T.	Rfn	268336
Owen[H]	Francis J.	Rfn	1579
Owen*	George P.	Sgt	240229
Owen	Glyn	Rfn	330754
Owen*	John G.	Rfn	240502
Owen	John R.	Cpl	241927
Owen*	Thomas B.	Cpl	240094
Owen*	William H.	Rfn	2347
Owen	William L.	Rfn	241972
Owens	David J.	Rfn	241666
Owens	Ernest W.	A/Cpl	241416
Owens	John G.	Rfn	266612
Owens	Robert	Rfn	241064
Owens	Samuel N.	L/Cpl	3000
Owens	William E.	Cpl	240950
Oxenbould*	Basil H.	2Lt	2033
Oxenham	John E.	Rfn	105408
Oxspring	Albert	Rfn	99599
Padley	Arthur J.	Rfn	50153
Padley	Charles	Rfn	241753
Pagan	David	Rfn	41839
Page	Thomas	Sgt	10907
Page*	Thomas H.	Rfn	240402
Pain*	Ernest H.	Rfn	243884
Paisley	Blaylock	Rfn	242758
Pakenham-Walsh*	Conrad M.	Rfn	1724
Palfreyman	George	Rfn	3851
Palfreyman	Joseph W.	Rfn	95496
Palmer	Herbert	Rfn	242869
Palmer	John	Rfn	332877
Parker*	Albert G.	Rfn	1553
Parker	John	Rfn	49965
Parker*	John H.	A/Cpl	240638
Parker	Milford G.	Rfn	4100

Parker**	Walter E.	Cpl	240664	Patton	Henry	Rfn	242132
Parker	Wilfred	Rfn	330297	Paul	Robert	Rfn	242788
Parker	William	L/Cpl	241377	Paynter	George	Rfn	4028
Parkhouse	Marvyn	Cpl	16864	Paynter	William H.	Rfn	241113
Parkins	Joseph H.	Rfn	240990	Peach	George F.	Rfn	241847
Parkins	Robert W.	L/Cpl	242567	Peachey	Edward L.	Rfn	95499
Parkinson	Francis H.	Rfn	241340	Peacock*	Cyril	Rfn	240241
Parkinson	Fred	Rfn	88088	Peacock	Edward G.	Rfn	51185
Parkinson	Harold	Rfn	109062	Peake*	Edward M.	Rfn	240344
Parkinson	James	Cpl	35960	Pearce*	Robert G.	Rfn	240561
Parkinson	Roland F.	Rfn	242823	Pearce*	Thomas H.	Rfn	240257
Parkinson	Thomas W.	Rfn	201462	Pearson	Andrew V.	Rfn	3923
Parkinson	William B.	Rfn	3895	Pearson	Arthur	Rfn	49779
Parks*	James B.	Cpl	240197	Pearson	George	Rfn	330659
Parr	Joseph	Rfn	51440	Pearson	George R.	Rfn	241607
Parrington	Edgar	Rfn	241128	Pearson	George W.	Rfn	51035
Parrington*	Eric R.	Rfn	2520	Peart	Herbert	Cpl	241314
Parrington	William H.	Rfn	242066	Peat	Enoch H. E.	Rfn	51036
Parry	Albert L.	Rfn	241405	Peck	Harold	Rfn	202985
Parry*	Bernard	L/Cpl	240095	Peck*	Stanley	Rfn	2068
Parry	Charles	Rfn	201696	Peebles	John	Rfn	331917
Parry*	Ernest	L/Cpl	2348	Peers	Andrew	Rfn	242070
Parry	Fred	Rfn	51034	Peers	Harry	Rfn	241933
Parry*	Harry B.	2Lt	240842	Peet	George	Rfn	241951
Parry*	John	Rfn	1402	Pegge	Wilfred J.	2Lt	
Parry	John	Rfn	242673	Pennington	George C.	Rfn	85450
Parry*	John H.	Rfn	240882	Pennington*	John H.	Sgt	240115
Parry	Robert	Rfn	330063	Pennington*	Percy S.	L/Cpl	240114
Parry	Thomas G.	Rfn	242674	Penrice	Walter	2Lt	
Parry**	Thomas J.	Cpl	240511	Percy	William H.	L/Sgt	241073
Parry**	Thomas S.	Rfn	240500	Periton*	Reginald C.	Rfn	1479
Parry	Thomas W.	Cpl	305209	Perry[R]	Alan Cecil	Capt.	
Parry	William	Rfn	242675	Peterson*	Thomas R.	Sgt	240373
Parry	William J.	Rfn	64908	Philipps*	Thomas H.	Rfn	240615
Parry	William J.	Rfn	51398	Phillingham*	John	Rfn	2633
Parslow*	Charles	Rfn	241098	Phillips	A.	Rfn	90194
Parsons	Joseph W.	Rfn	241711	Phillips	Frank D.	Rfn	242063
Partington	William	Rfn	260035	Phillips	George T.	Rfn	241817
Pascoe	Arthur M.	Rfn	242109	Phillips	Harold	Rfn	241381
Pascoe	Wallis T.	Rfn	49958	Phillips*	Herbert D.	Rfn	2617
Passmore	William C.	Rfn	241201	Phillips*	Joseph R.	Rfn	240330
Paterson	H.	Rfn	241994	Phillips	Leo	Rfn	26156
Paton*	James	Lt	1367	Phillips*	Norman R.	2Lt	2306
Paton*	William L.	L/Sgt	1276	Phillips	Ottowell	Rfn	51441

Phillips	Robert C.	Capt.	
Phillips*	Thomas	Lt	2350
Phillipson	Walter	Rfn	109020
Philson	Egbert L.	Rfn	51442
Phipps*	Robert	L/Cpl	240144
Phythian	John R.	Rfn	242676
Pickering	George	Rfn	50156
Pickering	Robert J.	Rfn	242473
Pickett	William J.	Rfn	381124
Pickford	William	Rfn	50480
Pickles*	George W.	Rfn	240210
Pickwell	Robert	Rfn	51397
Pierce*	George A.	Cpl	240333
Pierce*	Jonathan M.	Rfn	1193
Pierce	William	Rfn	52948
Pike	Vincent E.	Rfn	86562
Pilgrim	James	2Lt	
Pilling	Arthur B.	Rfn	3593
Pilling	Edward A.	2Lt	
Pilling*	John E.	Cpl	240230
Pilling	John F.	2Lt	
Pilling	William	Rfn	85058
Pim*	Mortimer	Rfn	1658
Pimlett	Richard A.	Rfn	241565
Pinches*	John E.	Rfn	2678
Pinnington*	Sydney	Cpl	545
Pinnock*	James H.	Rfn	240372
Pitt	Frank	2Lt	
Place	Robert W.	Rfn	242759
Plant	James	Rfn	49964
Plant	Joseph S.	Rfn	4182
Plant*	William J.	Rfn	240221
Platt	Samuel	Rfn	242578
Platt*	Richard	Rfn	1742
Plews	Joseph H.	Rfn	241882
Plint**	James A.	Cpl	240429
Plumb	Charles	Rfn	202226
Plumer	John	Cpl	4457
Plummer	George V.	Rfn	3845
Pocklington	Kenneth D. B.	2Lt	
Poindestre**	Charles E.	Rfn	240448
Pointer*	John S.	Rfn	1901
Pointon	Harry	Rfn	85402
Poland	Joseph	Rfn	88758
Pollack	Arthur	Rfn	268901
Poole	Charles	Rfn	49963
Poole	Edwin	Rfn	242626
Poole	Henry	Rfn	4095
Poole	Joseph H.	Rfn	241397
Poole	Tom	Rfn	4064
Poore	Walter	Cpl	307095
Porteous*	William	Cpl	1643
Porter	Charles	Rfn	109031
Porter	Harold M.	Rfn	4255
Porter	John H.	Rfn	242030
Porter	Percy	Rfn	381272
Porter*	Thomas B.	Rfn	2221
Postlethwaite*	Percy	L/Cpl	1967
Potter	Adam H.	L/Cpl	51133
Potter*	John C.	Rfn	240665
Potter	Richard W.	Rfn	300550
Pover	George	Rfn	241907
Povey	Thomas	Rfn	331016
Powell	Denis J.	Cpl	380712
Powell	E.	Rfn	241735
Powell	Jonathan D.	Rfn	23167
Powell*[R]	Reginald J.	Pte	1548
Powell	Thomas	L/Cpl	94283
Powell	William	Rfn	109078
Power	Eugene P.	Rfn	204358
Prendergrast	Frederick	Rfn	241343
Prescott	Herbert	Rfn	332491
Prescott	Herbert	Rfn	86841
Prescott	Robert	L/Cpl	307525
Preston	John R.	Rfn	3447
Preston*[R]	Robert S.	Pte	1531
Price	Gilbert	Rfn	241460
Price	Harold E.	Sgt	242130
Price	Patrick	Rfn	52703
Price	Robert J.	Rfn	51404
Price	Thomas	Rfn	241751
Prichard**	Robert	Rfn	240161
Priestley	H.	2Lt	
Prince*	Frederick J.	Rfn	240867
Pritchard	Albert	Rfn	241326
Pritchard	Enrique G.	Rfn	54488
Pritchard	Ernest G.	L/Sgt	240859
Pritchard	Gwelym J.	Rfn	242001

Pritchard	Reginald E.	Rfn	3903
Proffitt	James E.	Rfn	49966
Proudfoot	Henry	Rfn	3766
Proudlove*	Walter M.	Rfn	1737
Prout	Thomas P. V.	Rfn	241371
Pryce*	Charles	Rfn	240759
Puddicombe	John F.	L/Cpl	241612
Pugh	Edward D.	Rfn	86548
Pugh*	Herbert E.	Rfn	1299
Pulford	Thomas A.	Rfn	241492
Punt*	Robert W. F.	Rfn	2409
Purcell	John	Rfn	11054
Purcell	Joseph	Rfn	241452
Purcell	Thomas W.	Rfn	242760
Purdon*	Cecil H.	A/Cpl	240550
Purdon*	Harold R.	Cpl	240548
Purdon*	Robert G.	Sgt	1203
Purnell	W. G.	2Lt	
Purvis*	Reginald C.	Rfn	1811
Pye	John	Rfn	242870
Pye**	William A.	Rfn	240138
Pyke	Henry	Rfn	240876
Qualtrough	Edward	Rfn	241516
Quarrie*	Robert H.	Rfn	240666
Quayle*	Charles	L/Cpl	240205
Quayle	John H.	Rfn	242761
Quayle	Robert A.	Rfn	36884
Quayle	William A.	Rfn	331983
Quilliam*	Richard P.	Rfn	2284
Quinlan*	James L.	Sgt	240371
Quinn	James R.	Rfn	86618
Quinn	John	Rfn	242057
Quirk	Walter W.	L/Cpl	241339
Radford	James	Rfn	50629
Railton	Fred	Rfn	242051
Railton	Robert E.	Rfn	4048
Rainey	Harry	Rfn	94000
Rainford	James P.	Rfn	51443
Raley**	Cecil	Rfn	240959
Rallings	Herbert	Rfn	51130
Ralph	Joseph	L/Cpl	242113
Ralphs	Herbert	Rfn	242608
Ramsden	James	Rfn	49968
Ramsden*	Walter F. S.	Cpl	1908
Randles*	Samuel	Rfn	240348
Randles*	William J.	Rfn	240145
Rankin	Albert	Rfn	41446
Rankin	James	Rfn	3596
Rankmore*	Albert E.	WO2	240038
Rashbrook*	Albert R.	Sgt	240770
Rathbone	Richard R.	Capt.	
Rattray*	Arthur	Rfn	1375
Rattray*	Edward B.	Rfn	1305
Rawcliffe	Arthur C.	Rfn	241631
Rawlings	Frederick C.	Rfn	94001
Rawlins	Thomas A.	Capt.	
Rawlins*	Eric L.	Rfn	1809
Rawlinson*	Harry	Cpl	240238
Raws*	William	Rfn	2235
Rawsterne	John	Rfn	88273
Raymond*	William D.	Rfn	2080
Readdie	James	Cpl	241755
Readle*	George	Rfn	1898
Reamsbottom*	Norman S.	Rfn	2258
Reddington	Thomas	Rfn	242762
Redfearn*	William G.	Rfn	240406
Redhead	William	Rfn	241932
Redmond*	John D.	Rfn	240706
Redmond	Thomas	Rfn	11520
Redmond	William	L/Cpl	332363
Rees	Charles W.	Rfn	242514
Rees	Leslie J.	Rfn	1807
Rees	Thomas	L/Cpl	13466
Rees	William G.	Rfn	260010
Reese	Richard T.	2Lt	
Reeves*	Henry E. A.	Sgt	240319
Reeves	Walter H. R.	Rfn	94512
Regan	Arthur	Cpl	242647
Regan[H]	Frank	Rfn	240106
Reid	James	Rfn	41859
Reid	Stanley	Rfn	88722
Reidy	William J.	L/Cpl	308889
Reil	Joseph	Rfn	203333
Reinecke*	Charles	Rfn	240146
Relton**	James	Rfn	240411
Renton	George	Rfn	51444
Revill*	Mark	Rfn	2291
Reynolds	Frederick W.	Rfn	88274

Reynolds[H]	Henry R.	Rfn	1806	Roberts	Ellis	Rfn	86298
Reynolds	James	Rfn	242333	Roberts*	Ernest	Rfn	240558
Reynolds*	Thomas F.	Rfn	240172	Roberts	Frank	Rfn	242270
Reynolds	William	Rfn	204353	Roberts	Frank H.	Rfn	241695
Rhodes	Percy	Rfn	242698	Roberts	Frederick W.	Rfn	3959
Richards	David I.	Rfn	353010	Roberts	Frederick W.	Rfn	88066
Richards	Frank	Cpl	241427	Roberts*	Harold D.	Cpl	766
Richards*	John H.	Rfn	240242	Roberts*	Henry N.	Sgt	1325
Richards	William N.	Rfn	268506	Roberts*	Herbert W.	Sgt	240066
Richmond*	Henry R.	Rfn	2567	Roberts*	Ivor G.	Rfn	2704
Rickard*	William	Cpl	240668	Roberts	James	Rfn	405649
Riddell	John M.	Rfn	240898	Roberts	John	Sgt	241679
Riddell	Walter H. R.	Rfn	200198	Roberts*	John C.	Sgt	240201
Riddick*	Thomas	Rfn	2105	Roberts	John G.	Rfn	241799
Rideal	Samuel	2Lt		Roberts	John M.	Rfn	242763
Rider	Arthur	Rfn	3529	Roberts	John R.	L/Cpl	85500
Ridge*	Fergus H.	L/Cpl	932	Roberts	Norman P.	Rfn	240873
Rigby*	Alfred G.	L/Cpl	240369	Roberts*	Percy J. E.	Rfn	2415
Rigby	Charles	Rfn	308316	Roberts	Richard	Rfn	85650
Rigby*	George A.	Rfn	2360	Roberts	Robert D.	Rfn	242003
Rigby	Michael	Rfn	201179	Roberts**	Robert L.	Rfn	240742
Rigby	Robert	Rfn	84784	Roberts	Thomas	Rfn	50016
Rigby*	Thomas F.	Sgt	240313	Roberts*	Thomas A.	Rfn	2111
Riley	James J. A.	Rfn	52879	Roberts*	Thomas C.	Rfn	240860
Riley	John	Rfn	27827	Roberts*	Thomas E.	Rfn	240813
Riley	Thomas	Rfn	331518	Roberts*	Thomas W.	Rfn	2013
Riley	Thomas A.	Sgt	241058	Roberts*	Walter E.	Rfn	240137
Rimmer	John R.	Rfn	47182	Roberts	Walter R.	Rfn	241584
Rimmer	Lewis	Rfn	241056	Roberts	William	Sgt	267682
Rimmer	Peter	Cpl	242685	Roberts*	William	Rfn	2150
Rimmer	William	Rfn	307810	Roberts	William H.	Rfn	72717
Rimmer	William G.	Rfn	3956	Roberts*	William M.	Rfn	2458
Riordan*	James K.	Rfn	240454	Roberts	William P.	Cpl	23883
Rishton	Charles	Rfn	242241	Roberts*	William W.	Rfn	2277
Ritchie	John E.	Rfn	242765	Robertson*	Alexander H.	Rfn	2251
Ritson	Chamber E.	L/Cpl	242068	Robertson*	George	Rfn	359100
Robbins	James	Rfn	88067	Robertson	James	Rfn	330199
Roberts*	Alexander S.	Rfn	2783	Robertson	Robert	Rfn	57567
Roberts	Arthur	Rfn	241483	Robertson*	William	Cpl	1471
Roberts	Arthur	Rfn	85457	Robertson*	William D.	Rfn	240530
Roberts	Bernard	Rfn	32714	Robinson*	Alfred	Rfn	2172
Roberts	Charles	Rfn	380881	Robinson**	Arthur	WO1	240017
Roberts*	Cyril J.	Rfn	1327	Robinson	Charles	Rfn	241977
Roberts**	Edmund A.	Rfn	240368	Robinson	Cyril E.	Rfn	241514

Robinson	Frank A.	Rfn	72457
Robinson	Greig N.	Rfn	241739
Robinson	Harold P.	2Lt	
Robinson*	Harry W.	Rfn	1659
Robinson	Herbert	Rfn	240807
Robinson*	J.	Rfn	1937
Robinson	John	Rfn	240710
Robinson	John R.	Rfn	3625
Robinson*	Norman	Rfn	1334
Robinson**	Reginald	Sgt	240211
Robinson	Robert	Rfn	260037
Robinson	Robert	Rfn	307182
Robinson	Robert J.	L/Cpl	240641
Robinson	Thomas E.	Rfn	85289
Robinson	W.	Rfn	3814
Robinson*	Wilfred	Rfn	240314
Robinson*	Wilfred E.	2Lt	1760
Robinson*	William	Rfn	2081
Robley	John Elliot	Rfn	3438
Robson*	Harold	Rfn	240800
Roche	Joseph	L/Cpl	26136
Roche*	Walter G.	Rfn	1184
Rock	George	Rfn	49562
Rodger	William	Rfn	240367
Rodgers	Alfred H.	Rfn	240667
Rodgers	George W.	Rfn	51382
Roe	Frank	L/Cpl	307987
Rogers	Arthur	Rfn	241968
Rogers	Edward S.	2Lt	
Rogers	Geoffrey P.	Capt.	
Rogers	George	Rfn	88910
Rogers	Henry	Rfn	87870
Rogers	Henry E.	L/Cpl	307655
Rogers	William B.	Rfn	3363
Rogerson	James	Rfn	49176
Rogerson	Leonard	Rfn	90245
Rollerson	Thomas	Rfn	242804
Rome*	Thomas E.	Capt.	
Ronald*	Nigel B.	Lt	
Ronaldson*	James	L/Cpl	240323
Rooley	Arthur J.	Rfn	49967
Rooney	Lawrence	Rfn	270009
Roper*	Elijah	CSM	240049
Rose	Fred	Rfn	109013
Rose	John	Rfn	13999
Ross**	Andrew R.	Rfn	240366
Ross	George J.	Rfn	3852
Ross*	Joseph F.	Rfn	1609
Ross*	Norman D.	Rfn	2075
Rothwell	Charles	Rfn	85444
Rothwell	G.	Lt	
Rothwell*	William J.	Cpl	240908
Rourke	Herbert	Rfn	4414
Rowan*	Maxwell H	Rfn	1834
Rowbottom*	Alfred	Lt	1799
Rowbottom	Ernest	Sgt	240365
Rowe*	George A.	Rfn	240015
Rowe	George F.	Rfn	51250
Rowe	John	Rfn	93997
Rowe*	Thomas	Sgt	240267
Rowland	Harold C.	Rfn	241983
Rowland	Henry	Rfn	108652
Rowland	John R.	Rfn	308282
Rowland*	Stanley	Rfn	1798
Rowland*	William H.	Rfn	240328
Rowlands*	George	Cpl	240324
Rowlands	William J.	Rfn	51121
Rowley*	Gerald	Rfn	240426
Roycroft	Henry	Rfn	260036
Royden	Alfred	Rfn	86590
Royle*	Alfred	Rfn	2398
Royle*	Henry H. E.	L/Sgt	1347
Royle	Norman	L/Cpl	241415
Royston	Joseph W.	Lt	
Ruane	Thomas J.	Rfn	241031
Rubens	Louis	Rfn	57996
Rudd*	Frank	Rfn	240617
Ruddle*	Francis T.	Rfn	2541
Ruddock	John R.	Rfn	3989
Rudkin	Richard	Rfn	240459
Runacus	George	Rfn	241513
Rundle*	James R.	Sgt	240079
Ruscoe	Stanley	Rfn	56094
Rushton	John	Rfn	33380
Rushworth	Albert	Rfn	59065
Russell	Bertie	Rfn	88065
Russell*	Edward A.	Rfn	240270
Russell	George	Rfn	88510

Russell	Hubert T. D.	Rfn	242764
Russell	John	Rfn	3792
Russell**	John N.	CQMS	240364
Russell*	Raymond	Cpl	240430
Ruth	Richard	Rfn	51110
Rutherford	James P.	Rfn	3741
Rutter	Edward	Rfn	109077
Rutz	Charles F.	Rfn	88907
Ryan	Edward	Rfn	241519
Ryan	Edward	Rfn	4460
Ryan	John T.	Sgt	19657
Ryder	Arthur	Rfn	51421
Sadler	Thomas	Cpl	260047
Sagar	John W.	Rfn	48991
Sage	Frederick G.	Rfn	50966
Salmon*	Alexander F.	Sgt	240188
Salt	George H.	Cpl	241426
Salthouse	William	Rfn	305794
Sammond	Hugh	Sgt	22829
Sampson	Alfred	Rfn	260074
Sampson	Edward W.	Rfn	4173
Sampson	Leonard R. F.	Rfn	90977
Samuel	James	Rfn	267058
Sanderson	Fred	Rfn	12167
Sandmann	Robert	Rfn	260038
Sanne	Alfred	Rfn	242477
Santos	Polito	Rfn	50631
Saunt	John	Rfn	88068
Savage*	Edmund D.	Sgt	2270
Savage	Frederick	Rfn	4258
Savage	Robert	Rfn	241850
Sayer	Ernest	Sgt	241536
Sayles	Asa	Rfn	325068
Scallion	John	L/Cpl	265490
Scantlebury*	Archibald	Rfn	2691
Scarff	Frank V.	Rfn	241865
Scarlin[H]	Arthur H.	Rfn	1224
Schofield	Joseph	Rfn	86834
Scholefield*	Herbert W.	Rfn	240919
Schonewald*	Henry	Rfn	1888
Schwadahl	Erik E.	Rfn	3713
Scoins*	Arthur G.	A/Cpl	240505
Scorgie*	Charles G.	Rfn	2082
Scott	Gilbert L. S.	Rfn	241722
Scott	Hanson	Rfn	49974
Scott	James	Rfn	243824
Scott*	Percy W.	Rfn	2480
Scott	William	Rfn	241866
Scott-Barrett*	Hugh	Capt.	
Scrivener	George H.	Rfn	33114
Scroggie	David	Rfn	242691
Searle	William T.	Rfn	241723
Seddon	John	Rfn	242686
Seely	Charles	Rfn	331369
Sefton*	Herbert	Rfn	240528
Seiler	Christian	Rfn	4423
Sephton	George	Rfn	330151
Sergeant	Reginald E.	Rfn	242607
Setchell	John	2Lt	
Seville	Peter	Rfn	305665
Shallcross*	Thomas	L/Cpl	240857
Shane	John	Rfn	307240
Shannon	Bartley	Rfn	406711
Shannon	George	Rfn	240280
Sharp	John	Rfn	242871
Sharp	John C.	Rfn	15495
Sharples	Frank E.	L/Cpl	242005
Shaw	Alfred	Rfn	21059
Shaw*	Arthur N.	Rfn	2365
Shaw	Ernest	Rfn	50111
Shaw	Harold	Rfn	87996
Shaw*	John A.	CSM	240179
Shaw*	Phillip	L/Sgt	1759
Shaw	Thomas	Rfn	48990
Shayler	William	Rfn	405188
Shear	Abram H.	Rfn	49340
Shepherd	Frank	Rfn	203128
Shepherd*	Richard V.	Rfn	240628
Shepherd	Walter	Rfn	241833
Shepherd	William	Cpl	88894
Sheppard	Herbert J.	2Lt	
Sheridan*	Alexander P.	Rfn	2120
Shields*	William	Rfn	1876
Shipham*	Arthur C. L.	Rfn	2623
Shipsides	Edward	Rfn	242900
Shone	Joseph	Rfn	201905
Shore	George T.	L/Cpl	3288
Short	Matthew	Rfn	50163

Short	Reginald	Rfn	51379
Shuffleton	James	Rfn	19935
Sidebotham**	William M.	Sgt	240840
Sides	Archibald	Rfn	241714
Silcock	Harry O.	Rfn	242108
Simcox	George	Rfn	94514
Simister	Reginald	Rfn	4049
Simm	Albert E.	L/Sgt	305476
Simon	Alexander	Rfn	243639
Simpson	Charles	Rfn	49973
Simpson	Henry	Rfn	20772
Simpson*	James H.	Sgt	240123
Simpson	Stanley	Rfn	85434
Simpson	Thomas H.	Rfn	308252
Simpson	William	Rfn	49789
Simpson	William A.	CSM	200627
Sinclair	Walter G.	Rfn	202142
Skafte*	Charles W.	Sgt	975
Skeats	Frank	Rfn	242876
Skeldon	Norman.	Rfn	3522
Skewes	Charles	Cpl	241299
Skewes	Harold	Rfn	241594
Skilbeck	Henry	L/Cpl	242511
Skinner	Albert S.	Rfn	3605
Skinner	Arthur	Rfn	85409
Skinner	William O.	2Lt	
Skuce	Francis B.	Rfn	51107
Skyner*	John S.	Rfn	1454
Slack*	Harry	Rfn	2260
Slade*	George P.	Rfn	240671
Slade	James R.	Rfn	49969
Sleigh	William J.	A/Cpl	51149
Sleightholme	James	Rfn	241698
Slobon	George	Rfn	39077
Slocombe	Frank J.	Rfn	58049
Smalley	Ezra J.	Cpl	44505
Smallshaw	Henry	Rfn	109047
Smallwood	William	Cpl	241627
Smart	John	Sgt	94286
Smart	Philip H.	Rfn	241167
Smedley	Arthur	Rfn	242766
Smethurst	Archie M.	Rfn	204081
Smith*	A.	Rfn	240122
Smith	Albert	Rfn	240789
Smith	Albert	Sgt	308250
Smith*	Albert E.	Rfn	3122
Smith	Albert S. M.	Rfn	82808
Smith*	Allan W.	2Lt	1359
Smith	Arthur	Rfn	241667
Smith	Bernard F.	Rfn	51044
Smith	C.	Rfn	4360
Smith	Charles	Rfn	242783
Smith*	Charles D.	Rfn	1524
Smith	Charles F.	Lt	
Smith*	Charles F.	Lt	1360
Smith	Douglas	Rfn	4593
Smith	Edward C.	2Lt	
Smith	Frederick P.	Rfn	241564
Smith	Gifford	Rfn	88914
Smith*	Graham E.	Rfn	1996
Smith	Harry	Rfn	85032
Smith	Henry	Sgt	16213
Smith	Horace	Cpl	240252
Smith*	Ireson	Rfn	1795
Smith	J. V.	L/Cpl	241214
Smith*	J. W.	Rfn	2108
Smith	James	Rfn	242100
Smith	James	Rfn	242875
Smith	James E.	Rfn	241811
Smith*	John E.	Sgt	240074
Smith*	Joseph W.	Sgt	240036
Smith**	Percy	Rfn	240449
Smith*	Rowland	Rfn	2177
Smith*	Samuel T. H.	Rfn	240594
Smith	Thomas	Rfn	242902
Smith*	Thomas B.	L/Sgt	240063
Smith	Thomas H.	L/Cpl	305301
Smith	Victor G. C.	L/Cpl	235057
Smith	William	Sgt	241778
Smith	William	Rfn	241878
Smith	William	Rfn	52735
Smith	William E.	Rfn	88918
Smith**	William E.	Rfn	240587
Smith*	William R.	2Lt	1763
Smitheringale	William	Rfn	109032
Smyth	George J.	2Lt	
Smythe*	Harold W.	Rfn	240515
Snelgrove	James	Rfn	59255

Southern	Edward	Rfn	38590
Southern	F.	Rfn	5448
Southern	Samuel	Rfn	51399
Southworth	Robert	Rfn	88913
Sowerby	George W.	L/Cpl	57840
Spargo*	Hubert J.	L/Sgt	1141
Spary	Hubert G.	2Lt	
Spear*	John H	Rfn	240626
Speed	Archibald G.	Rfn	4137
Speedie	Andrew	L/Cpl	38869
Spence	Alexander M.	Rfn	240588
Spence	John	Rfn	3258
Spence	William	Rfn	37216
Spencely[H]	H. D.	Lt-Col	
Spencer	Henry	Rfn	85452
Spencer	Henry	Rfn	305602
Spencer	Herbert B.	2Lt	
Spencer*	James	Rfn	2184
Spencer	Sam	Rfn	87373
Spencer	Thomas E.	Rfn	241849
Spencer	Thomas H.	Rfn	4407
Spencer	William	L/Cpl	242689
Spilsbury	Robert	Rfn	332761
Spink	Ernest	Rfn	50215
Sprang	William	Rfn	51445
Spratt	David H.	2Lt	
Sprigings	Reginald H.	2Lt	
Springer	Lazarus	Rfn	105501
Spurling	Thomas A.	Rfn	235079
St George	Harold E.	2Lt	
Stacey	Harry	Rfn	241787
Stafford*	Herbert C.	L/Cpl	240363
Stafford	Lawrence	Rfn	242677
Stafford	Leonard	Rfn	109010
Stain	Samuel	L/Cpl	87867
Standring	John W.	Rfn	109090
Stanley	Joseph V.	Rfn	242872
Stansfield*	Vincent	L/Cpl	240275
Stanton	Patrick	Rfn	29417
Starkey	Fred	Rfn	242873
Stead**	Ernest	Rfn	240099
Stead**	George	Sgt	240071
Stead*	Robert W.	Rfn	1466
Steadman*	George W.	Rfn	1668
Steadman	Thomas	Rfn	3742
Stedman**	Henry J.	Sgt	240771
Steen	Charles W.	Rfn	241504
Steffell	Percival R.	Rfn	241869
Steinberg	I. R.	Rfn	84984
Stenhouse*	Alan H.	Lt	
Stent	Sydney	Rfn	241996
Stephens	George H.	Rfn	3944
Stephens	Henry	Rfn	307814
Stephenson*	William G.	Sgt	240073
Stern*	John R.	CSM	59
Sterry	Arthur V.	Rfn	241810
Stevens*	Herbert L.	Rfn	240486
Stevenson	Edwin	Rfn	241674
Stevenson*	Hew	Rfn	240672
Steward	C. T.	Lt	
Stewart*	George P.	Rfn	1723
Stewart	John	Rfn	331798
Stewart	John	Rfn	405191
Stewart	John S.	CQMS	202483
Stewart	R. G.	Rfn	201032
Stewart	Robert R.	Lt	
Stilliard	Rupert J.	2Lt	
Stirk*	Harold	Rfn	1531
Stockdale	George H.	Rfn	201874
Stockdale*	William	Rfn	2072
Stockley*	Charles T.	Rfn	1415
Stockley	Thomas W.	Rfn	49959
Stockton	Frederick	Rfn	241650
Stoddart	Joseph	Rfn	307155
Stopforth	Richard	Rfn	242009
Stott	John	Rfn	242808
Stott	W.	Rfn	242810
Strange	Alfred	Rfn	242678
Strange	Charles	Rfn	4329
Strefford	Thomas	Rfn	241315
Stroh	Alfred	Rfn	331779
Strutt	John	L/Cpl	3507
Stubbs	Frank	Rfn	49970
Studholme	Frederick W.	Rfn	406018
Sullivan	Thomas	Rfn	307647
Summer*	Sydney T.	Rfn	2364
Summers	Michael	Rfn	267159
Summerskill*	Henry	Rfn	1515

Sumner	William H.	Rfn	242128
Sundwall	Herbert H.	Rfn	241689
Sutcliffe	Joseph C.	Rfn	49972
Sutcliffe*	Stephen	L/Cpl	240810
Sutcliffe	William	Rfn	49971
Sutton	Joseph C.	L/Cpl	241628
Swainbank	William		72456
Swaine	John S.	Rfn	242592
Swallow*	Thomas	Rfn	1464
Swan*	Percy S.	Rfn	2141
Sweeney	Daniel D.	Rfn	242901
Swift[H]	James	Rfn	4867
Swift*	John	Rfn	1885
Swinnerton	Arthur W.	Rfn	3758
Swinnerton	Myles J.	Cpl	305596
Swinney	Henry A.	Rfn	57846
Swire	James B.	Rfn	242787
Sye	John K.	Rfn	242679
Sykes	Albert J. M.	Rfn	240473
Sykes	Fred	Rfn	242874
Tabbernor	George	Rfn	49976
Taberner	James	Rfn	308063
Taggart*	William H.	Sgt	242904
Talbot	John	Rfn	105427
Tankard*	Charles	Rfn	240971
Tanner*	Clement	A/WO1	240300
Tanner	George	Rfn	381915
Tanner	Sydney	Rfn	201922
Tarbet*	Claude E.	Rfn	2367
Tate	Norman	Rfn	241888
Tattersall	Arthur	Rfn	242879
Taylor*	Albert	Rfn	1650
Taylor	Amos	Rfn	48993
Taylor	Archie	Rfn	235030
Taylor	Arthur R.	Rfn	53619
Taylor**	Cuthbert G.	Rfn	240440
Taylor	Edward	Rfn	241791
Taylor	Edward	L/Cpl	203324
Taylor*	Edward S.	Rfn	1478
Taylor	Eli	Rfn	49957
Taylor	Frederick	Rfn	241749
Taylor	Frederick	Rfn	265976
Taylor	George W.	Rfn	380059
Taylor*	Gilbert L.	A/Cpl	240337
Taylor[H]	Gordon	Rfn	3102
Taylor	Harold	Sgt	19077
Taylor*	Harold	Rfn	240757
Taylor	Harry	Rfn	330521
Taylor*	Henry J.	Rfn	3094
Taylor*	Hubert J.	Rfn	240501
Taylor	John	Rfn	49845
Taylor	Joseph	Rfn	52867
Taylor	Richard	Rfn	242767
Taylor	Richard	Rfn	86496
Taylor	Ronald F.	Rfn	242279
Taylor*	Samuel	Cpl	240044
Taylor*	Stanley W.	L/Cpl	1743
Taylor	William	L/Cpl	52863
Taylor	William P.	Rfn	241589
Taylor	William R.	Rfn	63847
Teague*	Thomas E.	Cpl	1638
Teall	George H.	Maj.	
Teece	John	Rfn	241906
Telford*	Charles D.	Rfn	1790
Tellett	Albert	Rfn	241638
Temple[H]	John H.	Capt.	
Ten-Broeke*	Bertram St-L.	Rfn	2050
Tennant	John C.	CSM	23843
Terry	Albert	Rfn	260039
Terry*	Harry M.	Rfn	240620
Thacker	William H.	Rfn	85216
Theakstone*	Marmaduke	Rfn	240340
Thelwell	John H.	L/Cpl	241900
Thistlewood*	William M.	L/Cpl	1789
Thomas	Clement	Rfn	34398
Thomas*	Ernest H.	A/C/Sgt	240130
Thomas	George N.	L/Cpl	242097
Thomas	Harold F. G.	2Lt	
Thomas*	Harry P.	Sgt	240485
Thomas	James H.	Rfn	3942
Thomas	John	Rfn	241824
Thomas	John A.	Rfn	308329
Thomas	Oswald	Rfn	305464
Thomas	Philip	Rfn	406619
Thomas	Robert D.	Rfn	83043
Thomas	Robert J.	Rfn	42880
Thomas	Samuel	Rfn	241896
Thomas	Thomas W.	Rfn	241905

Thomas*	William E.	Rfn	1382	Tomkinson	Richard	Rfn	203571
Thomas*	William H.	Rfn	2239	Tomlinson	Charles O.	L/Cpl	267634
Thomas*	William J.	Rfn	2049	Tonkinson	Thomas H.	Rfn	204717
Thompson	Charles	Rfn	20044	Topping*	Charles	Cpl	1071
Thompson	Charles E.	Rfn	241724	Topping*	Frederick	Rfn	240362
Thompson	George W.	Rfn	51931	Towers	Frank	Rfn	260040
Thompson*	Hans E.	L/Cpl	244792	Towers	William	Rfn	4345
Thompson	Harold	L/Cpl	306570	Townley	Ernest	Cpl	241454
Thompson	James	Rfn	47368	Townley	James	Cpl	241455
Thompson*	John	Rfn	1922	Townsend*	John G.	Rfn	1572
Thompson*	John H.	C/Sgt	240110	Townshend*	Alfred D.	Rfn	1661
Thompson	Thomas	Rfn	242628	Townson	Frank	Rfn	85952
Thompson	Walter	Rfn	242812	Travill*	Robert	Rfn	240536
Thompson	William	Rfn	4380	Treacy*	Eric H.	Rfn	2681
Thompson*	William	Rfn	240988	Treen	Arthur	Rfn	87759
Thompson*	William R.	Rfn	811	Tremayne*	Harry	L/Cpl	240413
Thoms	Evan F.	Rfn	57576	Trench*	John R.	Capt.	
Thoms	Frank	L/Cpl	57577	Troughear*	Ernest W.	Cpl	240327
Thomson	James M.	Rfn	241595	Troughton	Harry	Rfn	241319
Thomson	John	2Lt		Trumbell	Donaldson	Rfn	85465
Thomson	Josiah F.	Rfn	241772	Tudor*	Cecil	Rfn	240195
Thorburn*	Ronald D. V.	Sgt	240436	Tuke	Frank	Rfn	27938
Thorne	George	Rfn	86807	Tunna	John	Rfn	4032
Thornhill	Henry J.	Rfn	242878	Tunstall*	Thomas R.	Rfn	240839
Thornton	Albert E.	Rfn	241721	Turford*	James	Sgt	240305
Thornton	John L.	Rfn	3395	Turnbull	Walter	Rfn	242877
Thorp	Frank E.	Rfn	2546	Turner	Charles	Rfn	51050
Thursby	Rowland	Rfn	84783	Turner	Clifford J.	Rfn	240888
Thwaite	John	Rfn	49977	Turner*	Joseph R.	Rfn	1566
Thwaite	Thomas P.	Rfn	242880	Turner	Sidney	Rfn	49975
Tibbells*	Charles	L/Cpl	569	Turner	Thomas B.	Rfn	241726
Tighe	Harry	Rfn	88290	Turner*	William A.	Maj.	
Tilley*	John	L/Sgt	240129	Turnock	Rushton	Rfn	4556
Timuthy*	H.	L/Cpl	240903	Tushingham**	Robert	Rfn	240237
Tindall	John W.	Rfn	88069	Tushingham*	Thomas	Rfn	1713
Tinker	George	Cpl	241655	Twentyman	Philip	Rfn	240914
Tipping	John	Rfn	267424	Twiss*	William H.	Rfn	2064
Tobias*	Simon	Rfn	240456	Twist	Samuel	Rfn	242815
Tobin	Thomas H.	Rfn	241352	Tyrer**	Charles M.	Sgt	240610
Todd*	Murray	2Lt		Tyrer	Richard	Cpl	22559
Todd*	William	Rfn	2366	Tyrer	William	Rfn	52831
Todhunter*	Walter H.	Cpl	240541	Tyson	Bernard J.	Rfn	4432
Todman	Arthur	Rfn	242768	Tyson	David A.	Rfn	241876
Tolson	Fred H.	Rfn	49978	Tyson*	Edward H.	Capt.	

Tyson	George D.	Capt.		Walley*	Ronald S.	Rfn	1741
Tyson	Ralph	Rfn	242122	Wallington	Charles H.	2Lt	
Tytler*	Ernest	L/Cpl	240513	Wallis*	Harry	Rfn	1158
Underwood	Arthur C.	L/Cpl	2041	Walls	Arthur C.	Rfn	88227
Unwin*	Frank	Rfn	240064	Walls	Samuel	Rfn	4630
Unwin	Robert J.	Rfn	242903	Walmsley	Ernest B.	Rfn	84771
Upton	James	Rfn	241240	Walsh	Bernard J.	Rfn	305343
Upton	Sydney	Rfn	242064	Walsh	John	Rfn	204454
Valentine	Howard	Rfn	3611	Walsh	Patrick	Rfn	242769
Vance	Reginald B.	Rfn	94027	Walton*	William T.	Rfn	1963
Verdin*	Joseph	L/Sgt	240067	Warbrick	John H.	Rfn	242321
Vernon	Cyril H.	2Lt		Warburton*	Alsager	Capt.	1732
Vibrans	Joseph	Rfn	265384	Warburton	John	Rfn	242773
Vick	Henry J.	Rfn	241696	Warburton**	John T.	Sgt	240756
Viets	John	Rfn	242781	Warburton	Thomas	Rfn	88940
Viggars**	Thomas	Rfn	240118	Ward	Charles	Rfn	86622
Waddington	Albert	Rfn	241411	Ward	Edgar L.	Rfn	267945
Waddington*	Herbert M.	L/Sgt	240533	Ward	Frank	Rfn	405744
Waddington	John J.	Rfn	241985	Ward	John	Rfn	242782
Wade	James A.	Rfn	59352	Ward	John W.	Rfn	88930
Wainwright	Edward P.	Rfn	4012	Ward*	Leslie H.	Cpl	240622
Wainwright*	Richard	Maj.		Ward	Robert	Lt	
Wainwright	Thomas	Rfn	3979	Ward	William M. J.	Rfn	240845
Wakeham	Arthur R.	Rfn	241154	Ward*	William R.	WO2	11
Walders	David	Rfn	242819	Wareham*	Francis A.	Cpl	240612
Walkden	Charles	L/Cpl	19869	Wareing	James	Cpl	27824
Walker	Albert	Rfn	308510	Waring	John F.	Lt	
Walker	Arthur	Rfn	242331	Waring	Reginald P.	Rfn	240460
Walker	Charles	Rfn	105537	Warner**	William H.	Rfn	240359
Walker*	Ernest N.	Rfn	240704	Warnock	William	Rfn	95498
Walker	Frederick B.	2Lt		Warren	Thomas E.	Rfn	200865
Walker*	Herbert C.	Rfn	2312	Waterhouse*	Archie B.	Rfn	1494
Walker	Hugh	Rfn	50219	Waterhouse	William	Rfn	242778
Walker	John H.	Rfn	51401	Watkins	Charles R.	Rfn	51400
Walker	Kenneth	Rfn	241852	Watkins	William	Rfn	332190
Walker*	Raymond W.	Rfn	2214	Watkinson*	William R.	Rfn	4466
Walker	Robert	Rfn	52760	Watkinson*	William R.	Rfn	356090
Walker	Walter	Rfn	22876	Watson*	Albert	Sgt	240143
Wall	James	Rfn	260250	Watson*	Andrew H.	Rfn	240746
Wallace	Alexander	Sgt	200122	Watson	Edgar J.	Lt	
Wallace	George R.	Rfn	332629	Watson	George A.	Rfn	88070
Wallace	Harold John E.	Rfn	242471	Watson*	John Noel	Rfn	1778
Wallace	Norman	Rfn	3745	Watson	Joseph	Rfn	85068
Waller	Thomas A.	Rfn	34306	Watson	Octavius	Rfn	241653

Watt*	William	Sgt	3126
Watts	Cecil V.	2Lt	
Watts	H. S. V.	2Lt	
Watts	John R.	Rfn	235335
Weall	Fred B.	Rfn	260042
Weaver	John	Rfn	241311
Webb	Walter	Cpl	85920
Webb*	George F.	Sgt	240043
Webster	Arthur S.	Rfn	241862
Webster	Henry	Sgt	24465
Webster*	Herbert J.	L/Sgt	240343
Webster	Percy	Rfn	269406
Webster	Robert	L/Cpl	15365
Webster*	Sidney H.	2Lt	240355
Webster*	William	Rfn	240468
Wedgwood*	Bertram H.	Capt.	
Wedlake*	Fred H.	Rfn	1753
Weightman	James	Sgt	201507
Weir**	James E.	Rfn	240616
Weissenberg	Harold E.	Rfn	241688
Weld*	John J. H.	L/Sgt	240421
Weld-Blundell*	Louis J.	Rfn	1913
Wells	Archibald	Rfn	241839
Wells	Thomas D.	Rfn	3860
Welsh	Edward	Rfn	242883
Welton	Richard	Rfn	86681
Wentworth	Robert E.	Rfn	243877
Wess**	Herbert	Rfn	240585
West*	Cecil H.	Sgt	240222
West*	Donald W.	Rfn	1785
West	George H.	Rfn	87727
West*	Harry G.	Rfn	1783
Westall	Langford	Rfn	95688
Westby*	George H. A.	Capt.	
Westlake	Edward	Rfn	52013
Westray	Francis A.	Rfn	3935
Whalley	Percy	Cpl	241716
Whalley	Thomas B.	Rfn	241509
Whamond	George H.	Rfn	242884
Wheeler	William	Rfn	29896
Whinyates*	Harold B.	Rfn	240354
Whitby*	William N.	Rfn	2789
White	Fred	Rfn	242776
White	Fred	Rfn	36757
White*	James	L/Sgt	240181
White	John	Rfn	308083
White	Samuel	Rfn	242882
White	Thomas	Rfn	109034
White*	Thomas N.	L/Cpl	2248
Whiteford*	Sydney	L/Cpl	240076
Whitehall	Herbert	Rfn	330837
Whitehead	Harry	Rfn	268444
Whitehead	William	Rfn	242680
Whitehouse*	George E.	Rfn	2575
Whitehurst	John G.	Cpl	240723
Whitehurst*	Edward O.	Rfn	1594
Whitelaw**	Walter G.	Sgt	240093
Whiteside*	Herbert	Rfn	1925
Whiteway	Edward L.	L/Cpl	15440
Whitfield*	Richard	Rfn	240602
Whitford*	John	Rfn	1197
Whittaker	Arthur	Rfn	109095
Whittaker	Charles	Rfn	242770
Whittaker*	James	Rfn	241018
Whittaker	Thomas	Rfn	35025
Whittaker	William	Rfn	50293
Whitter	Thomas	Rfn	242779
Whittick	Alfred H.	Rfn	307102
Whittle	John	Rfn	260041
Whittle*	John R.	Cpl	1447
Whitty*	Richard	Rfn	240445
Whitworth	Allan	L/Cpl	50831
Whybrew	William	Rfn	325081
Whyman*[R]	W.	Cpl	1434
Wiggins*	Thomas A.	L/Sgt	240326
Wigzell	Norman	Rfn	unk
Wilbraham	Harry	Rfn	330869
Wilcock	Charles	Rfn	242786
Wild	H.	Rfn	242688
Wild	Joseph	Rfn	31433
Wild	William H.	Rfn	48931
Wilde	James H.	Sgt	23456
Wilde	William J.	Rfn	242795
Wilding	George	Rfn	305808
Wilkes	Arthur	Rfn	51134
Wilkin	Joseph T.	Rfn	243636
Wilkins*	Frederick E.	Rfn	240357
Wilkinson*	Arthur G.	Rfn	241023

Wilkinson	Charles A.	Rfn	243637	Williams	Thomas	Rfn	240178
Wilkinson	Douglas S.	Rfn	4537	Williams	Thomas	Rfn	18851
Wilkinson	Frederick	Rfn	241615	Williams	Thomas J.	Rfn	84558
Wilkinson	Herbert	Rfn	88139	Williams	Thomas J.	L/Cpl	200696
Wilkinson	Thomas	Rfn	242777	Williams	Walter	2Lt	
Willcox*	Harold	CSM	240022	Williams	William	Rfn	325023
William	Henry	Rfn	49127	Williams*	William A.	Rfn	241054
Williams*	Albert	Rfn	240309	Williams	William D.	Rfn	242047
Williams*	Alexander	Rfn	240609	Williams	William G.	Rfn	4024
Williams*	Arthur	Rfn	1775	Williams*	William G.	Cpl	2045
Williams	Arthur	Rfn	108677	Williams*	William G.	Rfn	240041
Williams	Arthur L.	Rfn	2659	Williams	William H.	Rfn	83041
Williams	Arthur S.	Rfn	4503	Williams*	William J.	Rfn	2164
Williams*	Charles G.	Sgt	240039	Williams*	William L.	Rfn	2871
Williams*	D. G. Bryn	Rfn	240562	Williams*	William R.	Rfn	2279
Williams	David C.	Rfn	240549	Williamson	Douglas S.	Rfn	242889
Williams*	David T.	A/Cpl	240748	Wills*	Henry N.	Rfn	240422
Williams	Edward	Rfn	242355	Wilmot	James R.	Rfn	242478
Williams	Edward	Rfn	51359	Wilson	A. M.	Rfn	241466
Williams	Edwin	Rfn	241685	Wilson	Abraham	Rfn	242772
Williams	Frank	Rfn	4667	Wilson	Albert	Rfn	88944
Williams*	Frank	Rfn	2188	Wilson*	Alfred	Rfn	2363
Williams*	Frank A.	WO2	24	Wilson*	Arthur	Rfn	2771
Williams	Frederick	Rfn	267947	Wilson	Arthur J.	Rfn	85180
Williams*	Harold H.	Rfn	1891	Wilson*	Arthur S.	L/Sgt	240356
Williams*	Harold M.	Rfn	1586	Wilson*	Charles L.	Rfn	2197
Williams	Henry	Rfn	331003	Wilson*	David	Sgt	240478
Williams**	Herbert	Sgt	240072	Wilson*	David H.	Rfn	240338
Williams	Hugh K.	L/Cpl	241075	Wilson	Eric	Rfn	3820
Williams	Ivor J.	Rfn	41244	Wilson	Francis G.	Rfn	241915
Williams	James	L/Sgt	16496	Wilson	Frank	Rfn	51406
Williams	James	Sgt	381749	Wilson*	Frank M.	Cpl	240591
Williams	James	Rfn	12664	Wilson	George	Cpl	61632
Williams	John	Rfn	241661	Wilson	George	Rfn	88276
Williams	John L.	Rfn	2841	Wilson*	Henry	Rfn	1575
Williams	John R.	Rfn	241851	Wilson	Herbert W.	Rfn	3188
Williams	Joseph	Rfn	200896	Wilson	John	Rfn	3460
Williams*	Joseph T.	Rfn	240098	Wilson*	John E.	Rfn	240590
Williams	Llewellyn	Rfn	241789	Wilson*	Stanley	L/Cpl	240435
Williams	Owen J.	Rfn	242885	Wilson*	Thomas W.	Lt	
Williams	Robert	Rfn	56843	Wilson	William	L/Cpl	331462
Williams	Robert C.	Rfn	241736	Wilson	William	Cpl	330088
Williams	Robert G.	Rfn	241796	Wilson	William	Rfn	108694
Williams*	Samuel	Rfn	240572	Wilson*	William	Sgt	240279

Windsor	Leonard	Rfn	241614
Winn*	Harold J.	Cpl	240417
Winstanley*	Stanley W.	Rfn	240509
Winstanley*	Vivian	Rfn	240497
Winter*	William H.	Sgt	240037
Wise	Walter W.	Rfn	4443
Withers	Hugh R.	2Lt	
Withey	Joseph H.	Rfn	53496
Witton	Frederick W.	Rfn	86469
Wood	Albert E.	Rfn	88942
Wood	Henry	Rfn	51056
Wood*	J.	Rfn	2025
Wood**	James H.	L/Sgt	240107
Wood	John H.	Rfn	41557
Wood	Joseph W.	Cpl	50994
Wood	Rowland	Rfn	49956
Wood	William	Rfn	88275
Woodeson	Richard A.	Rfn	88937
Woodley	John M.	Rfn	242543
Woodmansey	Frederick G.	Rfn	241596
Woods	Edward	Rfn	52039
Woods**	Edward	Rfn	240119
Woods	Hugh G.	L/Cpl	15467
Woods	John C.	Rfn	50686
Woods*	John J.	Rfn	2222
Woods*	Richard A.	Rfn	2065
Woods*	William H.	Rfn	263006
Woodward	Daniel B.	Rfn	42718
Woodward	George	Rfn	332845
Woodward	James L.	L/Cpl	51402
Woodward	Stanley	L/Cpl	242881
Woodyer*	William	Rfn	1536
Wooler*	Harry	CQMS	240035
Wooley	J. E.	Rfn	1928
Woosey	Harold	L/Cpl	241953
Worrall	Frederick E. R.	Rfn	405208
Worsnip	Tom	Rfn	109089
Worstall	Samuel	RQMS	22585
Worswick	William	Rfn	242774
Worthington*	James R.	Sgt	240019
Worthington	Samuel	Rfn	242775
Worthington	William	Rfn	88935
Wragge	George A.	Rfn	49979
Wrathall	Anthony E.	L/Cpl	242053
Wren	Herbert B.	Rfn	241877
Wren	William J.	Rfn	240466
Wrest	Frank	Rfn	267602
Wright	Albert E.	Rfn	241034
Wright	Albert V.	Rfn	5435
Wright	Francis N.	Rfn	241969
Wright*	Frederick H.	Rfn	1702
Wright	George	Rfn	305721
Wright	Georges	2Lt	
Wright	James	Rfn	242771
Wright	John	Rfn	35682
Wright	John W.	Rfn	11952
Wright	R.	Rfn	53254
Wright	Stanley T.	Rfn	23657
Wright	Thomas A.	Cpl	242682
Wright	Walter C.	Rfn	267927
Wright	William H.	Rfn	50176
Wright	William W.	Rfn	240925
Wright	Wilson	Rfn	269598
Wrightson	Laurence	Rfn	3375
Wroe	Frederick	Rfn	12389
Wyldes	Thomas	Rfn	49377
Yarrington*	Thomas E.	Rfn	240579
Yates	George B.	Rfn	3967
Yates*	Hermann S.	Sgt	652
Yates	John W.	Rfn	267694
Yates	Samuel	Rfn	308277
Yearsley	William	Rfn	3584
Yendall	Wilfred	Rfn	332078
Yorke*	Donald	L/Cpl	1649
Young*	Herbert	Cpl	240539
Young	Joseph	Rfn	43490
Young*	Sydney W.	Rfn	1686
Young	William	2Lt	
Yoxall	Joseph	Rfn	242785
Zacharias*	Francis H.	Sgt	921

Endnotes

Chapter 1

1. Westlake R., *The Territorial Battalions* (London: Guild Publishing, 1986), pp. 29-31.
2. *Liverpool Echo*, 21 August 1914.
3. *Regulations for the Territorial Force and for County Associations* (London: HMSO, 1908), para. 274.
4. Excerpt from *The Territorial*, (1927) *The Liverpool Rifles—a Miscellany, Ellison Papers.*
5. *Letter from RSM James Barnett to Lt-Col. McKaig*, 28 November 1927, *Ellison papers.*
6. *Ibid.*
7. *Liverpool Echo*, 3 August 1914.
8. *Ibid.*, 4 August 1914.
9. *Letter from RSM James Barnett to Lt-Col. McKaig*, 28 November 1927, *Ellison papers.*
10. *Liverpool Echo*, 13 August 1914.
11. *Ibid.*, 12 August 1914.
12. *1914-1919 Diary, Ellison Papers*, p. 3.
13. *Sussex Express, Surrey Standard and Kent Mail*, 3 September 1914.
14. Sydney William Young, WO 363.
15. George Walter Pickles, WO 364.
16. George Robertson, WO 363.
17. *Liverpool Echo*, 15 September 1914.
18. *1914-1919 Diary, Ellison Papers*, insert after p. 6.
19. *Liverpool Echo*, 6 October 1914.
20. *Sussex Express, Surrey Standard and Kent Mail*, 10 September 1914.
21. *Ibid.*
22. *Surrey Mirror*, 18 September 1914.
23. *1914-1919 Diary, Ellison Papers*, p. 5.
24. *Sussex Express, Surrey Standard and Kent Mail*, 24 September 1914.
25. *Ibid.*
26. *Transcription of newspaper report of the Inquest.* Francis John Owen, WO 363.
27. *Liverpool Daily Post and Mercury*, 10 October 1914.
28. *1914-1919 Diary, Ellison Papers*, p. 8.
29. *Sussex Express, Surrey Standard and Kent Mail*, 16 October 1914.
30. *1914-1919 Diary, Ellison Papers*, p. 11.
31. Simpkins P., *Kitchener's Army* (Barnsley: Pen & Sword Military, 2007), p. 42.
32. *1914-1919 Diary, Ellison Papers*, p. 7.

33. *Ibid.*, pps. 7-8.
34. *Liverpool Echo*, 22 December 1914
35. *1914-1919 Diary, Ellison Papers*, pp. 9-10.
36. *Liverpool Daily Post and Mercury*, 13 January 1915.
37. *Ibid.*, 22 December 1914.
38. *Ibid.*, 5 November 1914.
39. War Diary of Headquarters 5 Division. General Staff, WO 95 1512-1_3
40. War Diary of 1/6th King's Liverpool Regiment, WO 95 1572-3.

Chapter 2

1. War Diary of 1/6th King's Liverpool Regiment, WO 95 1572-3.
2. *1914-1919 Diary, Ellison Papers*, p. 14.
3. *The Liverpool Rifles—a Miscellany, Ellison Papers.*
4. Alexander Stuart Roberts, WO 364.
5. Lewis Vernon Jones, WO 363.
6. Excerpt from *The Greenjacket, (1926), pp. 8-9, the Liverpool Rifles—a Miscellany, Ellison Papers.*
7. War Diary of Headquarters 5 Division. General Staff, WO 95 1511-2_1.
8. *Excerpt from The Greenjacket, (1926) p. 9, the Liverpool Rifles—a Miscellany, Ellison Papers.*
9. *Ibid.*
10. War Diary of 15 Infantry Brigade, WO 95 1566-2.
11. War Diary of Headquarters 28 Division. General Staff, WO 95 2267-4_2.
12. *1914-1919 Diary, Ellison Papers*, p. 18.
13. War Diary of 1/Dorsetshire Regiment, WO 95 1572-2_1.
14. War Diary of Headquarters 28 Division. General Staff, WO 95 2267-4_2.
15. *1914-1919 Diary, Ellison Papers*, p. 30.
16. *Liverpool Echo*, 12 April 1915.
17. Wyrall, E., *The History of the King's Regiment (Liverpool) 1914-1919 Volumes 1-3* (Uckfield: Naval and Military Press. 2002 reprint), p. 118.
18. *Excerpt from The Greenjacket, (1926) p. 12, the Liverpool Rifles—a Miscellany, Ellison Papers.*
19. *The Liverpool Rifles—a Miscellany, Ellison Papers.*
20. *1914-1919 Diary, Ellison Papers*, p. 25.
21. Fred Hector Westlake, WO 363.
22. *1914-1919 Diary, Ellison Papers*, p. 31.
23. War Diary of Headquarters 28 Division. General Staff, WO 95 2267-4_1.
24. *Liverpool Echo*, 8 April 1915.
25. *Ibid.*, 27 March 1915.
26. *The Liverpool Rifles—a Miscellany, Ellison Papers.*
27. *Liverpool Echo*, 8 April 1915.
28. *Ibid.*, 12 May 1915.
29. *Excerpt from The Greenjacket, p. 16,* (1927) *The Liverpool Rifles—a Miscellany, Ellison Papers.*
30. *Ibid.*
31. *Ibid.*
32. *The Liverpool Rifles—a Miscellany, Ellison Papers.*
33. Excerpt from *The Greenjacket, (1926) p. 18, The Liverpool Rifles—a Miscellany, Ellison Papers.*

34. War Diary of Headquarters 5 Division. General Staff, WO 95 1512-1_1.
35. *1914-1919 Diary, Ellison Papers*, pps. 35-36.
36. *Liverpool Echo*, 6 May 1915.
37. *The Liverpool Rifles—a Miscellany, Ellison Papers.*
38. *Liverpool Echo*, 6 May 1915.
39. *1914-1919 Diary, Ellison Papers*, pp. 36-37.
40. *The Liverpool Rifles—a Miscellany, Ellison Papers.*
41. *Liverpool Daily Post and Mercury*. 18 May 1915.
42. Charles Wilfred Skafte, WO 363.
43. War Diary of 1/Norfolk Regiment, WO 95 1573.
44. *1914-1919 Diary, Ellison Papers*, p. 37.
45. *Ibid.*, p. 39
46. *The Lancaster Observer and Morecambe Chronicle*, 7 May 1915.
47. *Ibid.*, 14 May 1915.
48. War Diary of 15 Infantry Brigade, WO 95 1566-2.
49. 'A' & 'Q' Diary 5 Division, WO 95 1517-3.
50. War Diary of Headquarters 5 Division. General Staff, WO 95 1512-1_3
51. *1914-1919 Diary, Ellison Papers*, p. 41.
52. *Letter from Frank Evans, 1914-1919 Diary, Ellison Papers*, insert after p. 44.
53. War Diary of 15 Infantry Brigade, WO 95 1566-2.
54. Excerpt from *The Greenjacket, (1926) p. 19, The Liverpool Rifles—a Miscellany, Ellison Papers.*
55. *Liverpool Echo*, 13 May 1915.
56. *Letter from Capt. Trench to Lt-Col McKaig*, 11 June 1916, *Ellison Papers*
57. War Diary of 15 Infantry Brigade, WO 95 1566-3.
58. War Diary of 1/Dorsetshire Regiment, WO 95 1572-2_1.
59. *The Liverpool Rifles—a Miscellany, Ellison Papers.*
60. Excerpt from *The Greenjacket, (1926) p. 20, The Liverpool Rifles—a Miscellany, Ellison Papers.*
61. Charles Douglas Smith, WO 364.
62. *'A' Company Report 5 May 1915*, War Diary of 1/6th King's Liverpool Regiment, WO 95 1572-3
63. Excerpt from *The Greenjacket, (1926) p. 21, The Liverpool Rifles—a Miscellany, Ellison Papers.*
64. *'C' Company Report 5 May 1915*, War Diary of 1/6th King's Liverpool Regiment, WO 95 1572-3.
65. *Letter from William Wilson to Norman Ellison*, 2 March 1974, *Ellison Papers.*
66. *The Liverpool Rifles—a Miscellany, Ellison Papers.*
67. Excerpt from *The Greenjacket, (1926) p. 24, The Liverpool Rifles—a Miscellany, Ellison Papers.*
68. *'C' Company Report 5 May 1915*, War Diary of 1/6th King's Liverpool Regiment, WO 95 1572-3.
69. *Liverpool Echo* 12 May 1915.
70. Excerpt from *The Greenjacket, (1926) p. 24, The Liverpool Rifles—a Miscellany, Ellison Papers.*
71. *The Liverpool Rifles—a Miscellany, Ellison Papers.* (page unnumbered)
72. Excerpt from *The Greenjacket, (1926) p. 22, The Liverpool Rifles—a Miscellany, Ellison Papers.*
73. War Diary of Headquarters 5 Division. General Staff, WO 95 1512-2.
74. *Liverpool Echo* 17 May 1915.
75. Edmonds J. E., *Official History of the Great War, Military Operations France and Belgium,*

1915. Volume 1 (Uckfield: Naval & Military Press, 2009), p. 305.

76. War Diary of Headquarters 5 Division. General Staff, WO 95 1512-2.
77. War Diary of Headquarters 5 Division. General Staff, WO 95 1512-2
78. *Liverpool Echo*, 21 May 1915.
79. Edmonds, *op. cit.*, p. 306.
80. War Diary of 15 Infantry Brigade, WO 95 1566-3.
81. Stanley Tynemouth Jones, WO 363.
82. Sydney Pinnington, WO 363.
83. War Diary of Headquarters 5 Division. General Staff, WO 95 1512-2.
84. Excerpt from *The Greenjacket, (1927) p. 13, The Liverpool Rifles—a Miscellany, Ellison Papers.*
85. 'A' & 'Q' Diary 5 Division, WO 95 1517-3.
86. War Diary of 15 Infantry Brigade, WO 95 1566-3.
87. *1914-1919 Diary, Ellison Papers*, pp. 49-50.
88. *The Liverpool Rifles—a Miscellany, Ellison Papers.*
89. *Daily Orders*, 5 Division, WO 95 1517-5_1.
90. War Diary of 15 Infantry Brigade, WO 95 1566-3.
91. *Signal* dated 9 June 1915, War Diary of 15 Infantry Brigade, WO 95 1566-3.
92. War Diary of 15 Infantry Brigade, WO 95 1566-3.
93. *1914-1919 Diary, Ellison Papers*, pp. 50-51.
94. *Lt Blackledge's Report to the Adjt.* 23 June 1915, War Diary of 1/6th King's Liverpool Regiment, WO 95 1572-3.
95. *War Diary of 15 Infantry Brigade*, WO 95 1566-3.
96. *The Liverpool Rifles—a Miscellany, Ellison Papers.*
97. Excerpt from *The Greenjacket, p. 14,* (1928) *The Liverpool Rifles—a Miscellany, Ellison Papers.*
98. George Duckett, WO 364.
99. Atenstaedt R. L., *Trench fever: the British medical response in the Great War* (Journal of the Royal Society of Medicine. Published online November 2006. Institute of Medical & Social Care Research, University of Wales, Bangor, 2006).
100. *1914-1919 Diary, Ellison Papers*, p. 53.
101. War Diary of Headquarters 5 Division. General Staff, WO 95 1512-3_1.

Chapter 3

1. *1914-1919 Diary, Ellison Papers*, p. 59.
2. David Conway Williams, WO 363.
3. *1914-1919 Diary, Ellison Papers*, pp. 57-58.
4. War Diary of Headquarters 5 Division. General Staff, WO 95 1512-3_1.
5. Excerpt from *The Greenjacket, (1927) p. 18, The Liverpool Rifles—a Miscellany, Ellison Papers.*
6. *Ibid.* pp. 17-18.
7. *1914-1919 Diary, Ellison Papers*, pps. 63-64.
8. Richard Spencer Haworth, WO 363.
9. *Excerpt from The Greenjacket, (1927) p. 18, The Liverpool Rifles—a Miscellany, Ellison Papers.*
10. *1914-1919 Diary, Ellison Papers*, pp. 62-63.
11. *1914-1919 Diary, Ellison Papers*, pp. 61-62.
12. George Barnes, WO 363.
13. *1914-1919 Diary, Ellison Papers*, pps. 68-70.

14. Gibbs, P., *Now it can be Told* (New York: Garden City Publishing Co., 1920), Part 2, XII.
15. Excerpt from *The Greenjacket, (1927) p. 22, The Liverpool Rifles—a Miscellany, Ellison Papers.*
16. *1914-1919 Diary, Ellison Papers*, pp. 67-68.

Chapter 4

1. Excerpt from *The Greenjacket,* (1927) p. 21, *The Liverpool Rifles—a Miscellany, Ellison Papers.*
2. *1914-1919 Diary, Ellison Papers*, p71.
3. *Ibid*, pp. 72-73.
4. *Ibid*, pp. 73-74.
5. Excerpt from *The Greenjacket,* (1927) p. 22, *The Liverpool Rifles—a Miscellany, Ellison Papers.*
6. *Excerpt from The Greenjacket,* (1928) p. 10, *The Liverpool Rifles—a Miscellany, Ellison Papers.*
7. *War Diary of Headquarters 55 Division. General Staff,* WO 95 2899-1.
8. Excerpt from *The Greenjacket,* (1927) p. 23, *The Liverpool Rifles—a Miscellany, Ellison Papers.*
9. War Diary of Headquarters 55 Division. General Staff, WO 95 2899-1.

Chapter 5

1. Excerpt from *The Greenjacket,* (1928) p. 10, *The Liverpool Rifles—a Miscellany, Ellison Papers.*
2. *1914-1919 Diary, Ellison Papers*, p. 79.
3. *Ibid*, pp. 79-80.
4. Excerpt from *The Greenjacket,* (1928) p. 11, *The Liverpool Rifles—a Miscellany, Ellison Papers.*
5. War Diary of Headquarters 55 Division. General Staff, WO 95 2899-1.
6. *Intelligence Summary noon 7 March 1916—noon 8 March 1916*. War Diary of Headquarters 55 Division. General Staff, WO 95 2899-2-1.
7. War Diary of 165 Infantry Brigade, WO 95 2925-1.
8. *Recommendations for Awards, Jeudwine Papers*. 356FIF/6/1/12.
9. *Intelligence Summary noon 11 March 1916—noon 12 March 1916*. War Diary of Headquarters 55 Division. General Staff, WO 95 2899-2-1.
10. Coop J. O., *The Story of the 55th (West Lancashire) Division* (Liverpool: Liverpool Daily Post, 1919), p.184.
11. *1914-1919 Diary, Ellison Papers*, pp. 81-82.
12. War Diary of Headquarters 55 Division. General Staff, WO 95 2899-2-1.
13. *Intelligence Summary noon 26 April 1916—noon 27 April 1916*. War Diary of Headquarters 55 Division. General Staff, WO 95 2899-2-2.
14. William Lawrie Paton WO 363.
15. *Intelligence Summary noon 22 May 1916—noon 23 May 1916*. War Diary of Headquarters 55 Division. General Staff, WO 95 2899-3.
16. *Intelligence Summary noon 6 June 1916—noon 7 June 1916*. War Diary of Headquarters 55 Division. General Staff, WO 95 2899-4_1.
17. *Intelligence Summary noon 1 June 1916—noon 2 June 1916*. War Diary of Headquarters 55 Division. General Staff, WO 95 2899-4_1.

18. *Account of Raids 28 June 1916*. War Diary of Headquarters 55 Division. General Staff, WO 95 2899-4_1.
19. *Ibid*.
20. *Liverpool Echo* 26 August 1916.
21. *Account of Raids 28 June 1916*. War Diary of Headquarters 55 Division. General Staff, WO 95 2899-4_1.
22. *Ibid*.
23. *Smoke Barrage for Z Day*, War Diary of 165 Infantry Brigade, WO 95 2925-1.
24. *Intelligence Summary noon 30 June 1916—noon 1 July 1916*. War Diary of Headquarters 55 Division. General Staff, WO 95 2899-4_2.
25. War Diary of Headquarters 55 Division. 'A' & 'Q' Branch, WO 95 2909-5.
26. War Diary of Headquarters 55 Division. 'A' & 'Q' Branch, WO 95 2909-3_1.
27. Henry Theodore Imlach, WO 363.
28. Excerpt from *The Greenjacket*, (1928) p. 15, *The Liverpool Rifles—a Miscellany, Ellison Papers*.

Chapter 6

1. Excerpt from *The Greenjacket*, (1928) p. 16, *The Liverpool Rifles—a Miscellany, Ellison Papers*.
2. *Ibid*.
3. Brian Elstob McBeath, WO 363.
4. *Operation Order No. 49*, War Diary of 165 Infantry Brigade, WO 95 2925-2_1.
5. *Report of Action by Lt-Col Shute*, War Diary of 165 Infantry Brigade, WO 95 2925-2_1.
6. *Recommendations for Honours and Awards, Jeudwine Papers*,356 FIF/6/6/17/1-11.
7. *Report of Action by Lt-Col Shute*, War Diary of 165 Infantry Brigade, WO 95 2925-2_1.
8. Excerpt from *The Greenjacket*, (1928) p. 17, *The Liverpool Rifles—a Miscellany, Ellison Papers*.
9. *Report of Action by Lt-Col Shute*, War Diary of 165 Infantry Brigade, WO 95 2925-2_1.
10. War Diary of Headquarters 55 Division General Staff, WO 95 2900-2_1.
11. Excerpt from *The Greenjacket*, (1928) p. 17, *The Liverpool Rifles—a Miscellany, Ellison Papers*.
12. *Recommendations for Honours and Awards, Jeudwine Papers*, 356 FIF/6/6/17/1-11.
13. War Diary of Headquarters 55 Division. General Staff, WO 95 2900-2_1.
14. *Message from Brig.-Gen. Duncan*, War Diary of 165 Infantry Brigade, WO 95 2925-2_1.
15. *Report of Action by Lt-Col Shute*, War Diary of 165 Infantry Brigade, WO 95 2925-2_1.
16. War Diary of 1/7th King's Liverpool Regiment, WO 95 2927.
17. War Diary of Headquarters 55 Division. General Staff, WO 95 2900-2_1.
18. *Signal flimsy*, War Diary of 165 Infantry Brigade, WO 95 2925-2_1.
19. *Message timed 3.20 a.m. 12 August*, War Diary of 165 Infantry Brigade, WO 95 2925-2_1.
20. *Situation Report 13 August*, War Diary of 165 Infantry Brigade, WO 95 2925-2_2.
21. *Operation Order No. 52*, War Diary of 165 Infantry Brigade, WO 95 2925-2_1.
22. *Situation Report 13 August*, War Diary of 165 Infantry Brigade, WO 95 2925-2_2.
23. War Diary of Headquarters 55 Division. 'A' & 'Q' Branch, WO 95 2908-5.
24. War Diary of 1/5th King's Liverpool Regiment, WO 95 2926-1.
25. War Diary of Headquarters 55 Division. General Staff, WO 95 2901-1_1.
26. *Operation Order No. 39*, War Diary of 165 Infantry Brigade, WO 95 2925-3.
27. *Daily Report B 6/7 September*, War Diary of 165 Infantry Brigade, WO 95 2925-3.
28. William Harold Thomas, WO 363.
29. War Diary of 1/5th King's Liverpool Regiment, WO 95 2926-1.

30. *Summary of Operations 5-11 September,* War Diary of 165 Infantry Brigade, WO 95 2925-3.
31. *Report by 5th Kings on Last Night's Operation,* War Diary of 165 Infantry Brigade, WO 95 2925-3.
32. *Operations: 9 September, 6th (Rifle) Battalion the King's Liverpool Regiment,* War Diary of 165 Infantry Brigade, WO 95 2925-3.
33. War Diary of 2/Kings Royal Rifle Corps, WO 95 1272/1-6.
34. *Summary of Operations 5-11 September,* War Diary of 165 Infantry Brigade, WO 95 2925-3.
35. War Diary of Headquarters 55 Division. General Staff, WO 95 2900-2_3.
36. *Letter* from Elijah Roper to Miss Paton, 9 October 1916.
37. War Diary of Headquarters 55 Division. General Staff, WO 95 2901-1_1.
38. Frank Williams, WO 363.
39. Excerpt from *The Greenjacket,* (1928) p. 19, *The Liverpool Rifles—a Miscellany, Ellison Papers.*

Chapter 7

1. *1914-1919 Diary, Ellison Papers*, p. 91.
2. *Diary of Clifton Inglis Stockwell,* October 1916.
3. *Divisional Intelligence Summary 10 a.m. 29 October to 10 a.m. 30 October,* War Diary of Headquarters 55 Division. General Staff, WO 95 2901-1_1.
4. War Diary of 165 Infantry Brigade, WO 95 2925-4.
5. *Honours and Awards, Jeudwine Papers*, 356 FIF/6/3/11.
6. *Ibid.*
7. War Diary of Headquarters 55 Division. 'A' & 'Q' Branch, WO 95 2909-2.
8. Henshaw T., *The Sky Their Battlefield II* (High Barnet: Fetubi Books, 2014), p63.
9. *Volume 1, Casualties Book* pp. 77, 80.
10. *Ibid.* p83.
11. *1914-1919 Diary, Ellison Papers*, pps. 95-96.
12. War Diary of Headquarters 55 Division. General Staff, WO 95 2902-1_1.
13. War Diary of Headquarters 55 Division. General Staff, WO 95 2902-2_1.
14. *Honours and Awards, Jeudwine Papers*, 356 FIF/6/3/11.
15. War Diary of Headquarters 55 Division. General Staff, WO 95 2902-2_2.
16. *Honours and Awards, Jeudwine Papers,* 356 FIF/6/6/17.
17. *Ibid.*
18. War Diary of Headquarters 55 Division. General Staff, WO 95 2902-4_2.
19. *Honours and Awards, Jeudwine Papers*, 356 FIF/6/6/17.
20. *Ibid.*
21. *Ibid.*
22. John Clough, WO 363.
23. *Ibid.*
24. Isaac Foulkes, WO 363.
25. *Ibid.*
26. *Ibid.*
27. *Diary of Clifton Inglis Stockwell,* May 1917.
28. Alexander Simon, WO 363.
29. Hodgkinson A., *The King's Own 1/5th Battalion, TF in the European War 1914-1918* (Lancaster: The King's Own Royal Regimental Museum, 2009), p. 57.
30. *Honours and Awards, Jeudwine Papers,* 356 FIF/6/3/11.

31. *Ibid.*
32. *Honours and Awards, Jeudwine Papers,* 356 FIF/6/6/17.

Chapter 8

1. *Narratives of 'D' Company 1/6th Battalion, the King's (Liverpool) Regiment.* 356/FIF/2/2/10 *Jeudwine Papers.*
2. *Narratives of 'B' Company 1/6th Battalion, the King's (Liverpool) Regiment.* 356/FIF/2/2/8 *Jeudwine Papers.*
3. *Ibid.*
4. *Narratives of 'D' Company, op. cit., Jeudwine Papers.*
5. *Ibid.*
6. *Ibid.*
7. *Ibid.*
8. War Diary of Headquarters 55 Division. General Staff, WO 95 2903-2_1.
9. *Narratives of 'A' Company 1/6th Battalion, the King's (Liverpool) Regiment.* 356/FIF/2/2/7 *Jeudwine Papers.*
10. *Ibid.*
11. *Narratives of 'D' Company, op. cit., Jeudwine Papers.*
12. *Ibid.*
13. *Ibid.*
14. *Ibid.*
15. *Ibid.*
16. *Narratives of 'A' Company, op. cit., Jeudwine Papers.*
17. *Ibid.*
18. *Narratives of 'D' Company, op. cit., Jeudwine Papers.*
19. *Ibid.*
20. *Ibid.*
21. *Ibid.*
22. *Ibid.*
23. *Narratives of 'B' Company, op. cit., Jeudwine Papers.*
24. *Ibid.*
25. *Ibid.*
26. *Ibid.*
27. *Ibid.*
28. *Ibid.*
29. *Narratives of 'C' Company 1/6th Battalion, the King's (Liverpool) Regiment.* 356/FIF/2/2/9 *Jeudwine Papers.*
30. *Ibid.*
31. *Ibid.*
32. *Narratives of 'D' Company, op. cit., Jeudwine Papers.*
33. *Ibid.*
34. *Narratives of 'B' Company, op. cit., Jeudwine Papers.*
35. *Ibid.*
36. *Narratives of 'C' Company, op. cit., Jeudwine Papers.*
37. *Ibid.*
38. *Ibid.*
39. *Ibid.*
40. *Narratives of 'D' Company, op. cit., Jeudwine Papers.*
41. *Ibid.*

42. *Narratives of 'B' Company, op. cit., Jeudwine Papers.*
43. *Narratives of 'C' Company, op. cit., Jeudwine Papers.*
44. War Diary of Headquarters 55 Division. General Staff, WO 95 2903-2_1.
45. *Narratives of 'B' Company, op. cit., Jeudwine Papers.*
46. *Ibid.*
47. *Narratives of 'D' Company, op. cit., Jeudwine Papers.*
48. *Narratives of 'B' Company, op. cit., Jeudwine Papers.*
49. *Narratives of 'C' Company, op. cit., Jeudwine Papers.*
50. *Narratives of 'D' Company, op. cit., Jeudwine Papers.*
51. *Narratives of 'B' Company, op. cit., Jeudwine Papers.*
52. *Narratives of 'D' Company, op. cit., Jeudwine Papers.*
53. *Ibid.*
54. *Ibid.*
55. *Narratives of 'C' Company, op. cit., Jeudwine Papers.*
56. *Narratives of 'B' Company, op. cit., Jeudwine Papers.*
57. *Narratives of 'D' Company, op. cit., Jeudwine Papers.*
58. *Ibid.*

Chapter 9

1. War Diary of Headquarters 55 Division. General Staff, WO 95 2903-4_1/2.
2. *Narratives of officers, 1/6th Battalion, the King's (Liverpool) Regiment.* 356 FIF/2/2/52 Jeudwine Papers.
3. Edmonds J. E., *Official History of the Great War, Military Operations France and Belgium, 1917. Volume 2* (Uckfield: Naval & Military Press, 2009), p. 251.
4. *Narratives of Officers, op. cit., Jeudwine Papers.*
5. *Narratives of 'B' Company, 1/6th Battalion, the King's (Liverpool) Regiment.* 356 FIF/2/2/54 *Jeudwine Papers.*
6. *Narratives of 'A' Company, 1/6th Battalion, the King's (Liverpool) Regiment.* 356 FIF/2/2/53 *Jeudwine Papers.*
7. *Narratives of Officers, op. cit., Jeudwine Papers.*
8. *Narratives of 'B' Company, op. cit., Jeudwine Papers.*
9. *Ibid.*
10. *Narratives of Officers, op. cit., Jeudwine Papers.*
11. *Narratives of 'D' Company, 1/6th Battalion, the King's (Liverpool) Regiment.* 356 FIF/2/2/56 *Jeudwine Papers.*
12. *Narratives of 'A' Company, op. cit., Jeudwine Papers.*
13. *Narratives of 'B' Company, op. cit., Jeudwine Papers.*
14. *Narratives of 'D' Company, op. cit., Jeudwine Papers.*
15. *Narratives of 'C' Company, 1/6th Battalion, the King's (Liverpool) Regiment.* 356 FIF/2/2/55 *Jeudwine Papers.*
16. *Narratives of Officers, op. cit., Jeudwine Papers.*
17. *Narratives of 'C' Company, op. cit., Jeudwine Papers.*
18. *Narratives of 'D' Company, op. cit., Jeudwine Papers.*
19. *Narratives of Officers, op. cit., Jeudwine Papers*
20. *Ibid.*
21. *Ibid.*
22. *Narratives of 'D' Company, op. cit., Jeudwine Papers.*
23. *Narratives of 'C' Company, op. cit., Jeudwine Papers.*
24. *Narratives of Officers, op. cit., Jeudwine Papers.*

25. *Narratives of 'A' Company, op. cit., Jeudwine Papers.*
26. *Narratives of Officers, op. cit., Jeudwine Papers.*
27. *Narratives of 'B' Company, op. cit., Jeudwine Papers.*
28. *Ibid.*
29. *Narratives of Officers, op. cit., Jeudwine Papers.*
30. *Narratives of 'D' Company, op. cit., Jeudwine Papers.*
31. *Narratives of 'B' Company, op. cit., Jeudwine Papers.*
32. *London Gazette* 6 February 1918.
33. *Narratives of Officers, op. cit., Jeudwine Papers.*
34. *Ibid.*
35. *Narratives of 'A' Company, op. cit., Jeudwine Papers.*
36. *Ibid.*
37. *Narratives of 'C' Company, op. cit., Jeudwine Papers.*
38. *Narratives of 'A' Company, op. cit., Jeudwine Papers.*
39. *Narratives of 'D' Company, op. cit., Jeudwine Papers.*
40. *War Diary of 165 Infantry Brigade,* WO 95 2925-4.
41. *Narratives of Officers, op. cit., Jeudwine Papers.*
42. *Ibid.*
43. *Narratives of 'C' Company, op. cit., Jeudwine Papers.*
44. *War Diary of 1/5th South Lancashire,* WO 95 2929.
45. *Narratives of Officers, op. cit., Jeudwine Papers.*
46. *Narratives of 'B' Company, op. cit., Jeudwine Papers.*
47. *Narratives of Officers, op. cit., Jeudwine Papers.*
48. *Ibid.*
49. *Narrative of Operations, War Diary of 1/5th South Lancashire Regiment,* WO 95 2929-2.
50. *Narratives of 'A' Company, op. cit., Jeudwine Papers.*
51. *Narratives of Officers, op. cit., Jeudwine Papers.*
52. *Ibid.*
53. *Ibid.*
54. *Narratives of 'C' Company, op. cit., Jeudwine Papers.*
55. *Ibid.*
56. *War Diary of 165 Infantry Brigade,* WO 95 2925-4.
57. *Narratives of 'B' Company, op. cit., Jeudwine Papers.*
58. *Narratives of Officers, op. cit., Jeudwine Papers.*
59. *Narratives of 'C' Company, op. cit., Jeudwine Papers.*
60. *Wilson Wright.* WO 363.
61. *Narratives of 'B' Company, op. cit., Jeudwine Papers.*
62. *Ibid.*
63. *Narratives of 'C' Company, op. cit., Jeudwine Papers.*
64. *Ibid.*
65. *Ibid.*

Chapter 10

1. *The Allied Offensive in Flanders,* War Diary of Headquarters 55 Division. General Staff, WO 95 2904-1.
2. *Recommendations for Honours and Awards.* 356 FIF/6/4/25 *Jeudwine Papers.*
3. *Diary of Clifton Inglis Stockwell,* 24 November 1917.
4. *Ibid.*, 18 November 1917.
5. Thomas Edward Yarrington. WO 363.

6. Walter Bishop Hannah. WO 363.
7. War Diary of Headquarters 55 Division. General Staff, WO 95 2904-1.
8. War Diary of Headquarters 55 Division. General Staff, WO 95 2904-2_2.
9. War Diary of Headquarters 55 Division. General Staff, WO 95 2904-2_1.
10. War Diary of Headquarters 55 Division. General Staff, WO 95 2904-2_2.
11. *Ibid.*
12. Miles, W., *Official History of the Great War, Military Operations France and Belgium, 1917 Volume 3* (Uckfield: Naval & Military Press, 2009), p. 96.
13. War Diary of Headquarters 55 Division. 'A' & 'Q' Branch, *WO 95 2910-1.*
14. *Casualties Book, Volume 1*, p.146.
15. *Diary of Clifton Inglis Stockwell,* 24 November 1917.
16. Miles, *op. cit.,* p. 299.
17. *Ibid.,* pp. 166-7.
18. *Ibid.*, p. 373.
19. *Ibid.*, p. 172.
20. *Letter to General Snow,* 356 FIF/8/2, *Jeudwine Papers.*
21. *Recommendations for Honours and Awards.* 356 FIF/6/17/1-11 *Jeudwine Papers.*
22. *Ibid.*
23. *Precis of Narrative of Operations, D276 Battery RFA,* War Diary of Headquarters 55 Division. General Staff, WO 95 2904-3.
24. *Recommendations for Honours and Awards,* 356 FIF/6/17/1-11, *Jeudwine Papers.*
25. *Ibid.*
26. *Ibid.*
27. *Ibid.*
28. *Ibid.*
29. Miles, *op. cit.*, p. 295.
30. *Annotations to Report of Court of Enquiry,* 356/FIF/8/2/2, *Jeudwine Papers.*
31. *Letter from General Jeudwine to General Snow,* 356/FIF/8/3, *Jeudwine Papers.*
32. Miles, *op. cit.*, pp. 298-9.
35. *Ibid*, pp. 184-5.

Chapter 11

1. Edmonds, J. E., *Official History of the Great War, Military Operations France and Belgium, 1917. Volume 2* (Uckfield: Naval & Military Press, 2009) p. 470.
2. Coop, *The Story of the 55th (West Lancashire) Division* (Liverpool: Liverpool Daily Post, 1919), pp. 85-86.
3. Edmonds, *op. cit.*, pp. 470-471.
4. *Ibid*, pp. 472-473.
5. *Honours and Awards, Jeudwine Papers*, 356 FIF/6/6/17.
6. Reid, W., *Architect of Victory—Douglas Haig* (Edinburgh: Birlinn, 2006), p. 409.
7. *Ibid.*, p. 424.
8. Edmonds, *op. cit.*, p. 477.
9. Reid, *op. cit.*, p. 428.
10. Edmonds, *op. cit.*, p. 161.
11. War diary of Headquarters 55 Division. General Staff, WO 95 2905_4.
12. Coop, *op. cit.*, p. 91.
13. War diary of Headquarters 55 Division. General Staff, WO 95 2905_4.

Chapter 12

1. *Honours and Awards, Jeudwine Papers*, 356 FIF/6/6/17.
2. Narratives of the 1/6th Liverpool Rifles, War Diary of 165 Infantry Brigade, WO 95 2925-5_1.
3. *Ibid.*
4. War Diary of 165 Infantry Brigade, WO 95 2925-5_1.
5. Narratives of the 1/6th Liverpool Rifles, *op. cit.*
6. *Ibid.*
7. *Honours and Awards, Jeudwine Papers*, 356 FIF/6/6/17.
8. *Ibid.*
9. *Ibid.*
10. Narratives of the 1/6th Liverpool Rifles, *op. cit.*
11. *Ibid.*
12. *Ibid.*
13. *Ibid.*
14. *Honours and Awards, Jeudwine Papers*, 356 FIF/6/6/17.
15. *Ibid.*
16. Narratives of the 1/6th Liverpool Rifles, *op. cit.*
17. *Ibid.*
18. *Ibid.*
19. *Ibid.*
20. *Ibid.*
21. *Ibid.*
22. *Ibid.*
23. Narratives of the 1/5th King's Liverpool Regiment, War Diary of 165 Infantry Brigade, WO 95 2925-5_1.
24. War Diary of Headquarters 55 Division. General Staff, WO 95 2905_3.
25. *Honours and Awards, Jeudwine Papers*, 356 FIF/6/6/17.
26. Narratives of the 1/6th Liverpool Rifles, *op. cit.*
27. *Honours and Awards, Jeudwine Papers*, 356 FIF/6/6/17.
28. *Ibid.*
29. *Ibid.*
30. Narratives of the 1/6th Liverpool Rifles, *op. cit.*
31. War diary of Headquarters 55 Division. General Staff, WO 95 2905_5.
32. Narratives of the 1/6th Liverpool Rifles, *op. cit.*
33. *Honours and Awards, Jeudwine Papers*, 356 FIF/6/6/17.
34. Narratives of the 1/6th Liverpool Rifles, *op. cit.*
35. *Ibid.*
36. *Honours and Awards, Jeudwine Papers*, 356 FIF/6/6/17.
37. Narratives of the 1/6th Liverpool Rifles, *op. cit.*
38. *Honours and Awards, Jeudwine Papers*, 356 FIF/6/6/17.
39. Narratives of the 1/6th Liverpool Rifles, *op. cit.*
40. *Honours and Awards, Jeudwine Papers*, 356 FIF/6/6/17.
41. *Ibid.*
42. *Ibid.*
43. *Ibid.*
44. *Ibid.*
45. *Ibid.*
46. *Honours and Awards, Jeudwine Papers*, 356 FIF/6/5/17.
47. *Ibid.*

48. *Honours and Awards, Jeudwine Papers*, 356 FIF/6/6/17.
49. Edgar Lacey Ward, WO 363.
50. *Honours and Awards, Jeudwine Papers*, 356 FIF/6/6/17
51. War Diary of Headquarters 55 Division. General Staff, WO 95 2906-2-1.
52. *Ibid.*
53. War Diary of Headquarters 55 Division. 'A' & 'Q' Branch, WO 95 2910-3_1.
54. *Honours and Awards, Jeudwine Papers*, 356 FIF/6/6/17.
55. War Diary of Headquarters 55 Division. General Staff, WO 95 2906-2-1.
56. Harry Trevor Hughes, WO 364.
57. *Honours and Awards, Jeudwine Papers*, 356 FIF/6/6/17.

Chapter 13

1. *Honours and Awards, Jeudwine Papers*, 356 FIF/6/6/17.
2. *Ibid.*
3. *Ibid.*
4. *Ibid.*
5. *Ibid.*
6. *Ibid.*
7. *Ibid.*
8. *Ibid.*
9. 55 Division Narrative of Operations. 24 August-11 November 1918. 356/FIF/3/3/1. *Jeudwine Papers.*
10. War Diary of Headquarters 55 Division. General Staff, WO 95 2907-1-1.
11. 55 Division Narrative of Operations. 24 August–11 November 1918. *Op. cit.*
12. War Diary of Headquarters 55 Division. General Staff, WO 95 2907-1-3.
13. 55 Division Narrative of Operations. 24 August–11 November 1918. *Op. cit.*
14. *Ibid.*
15. *War Diary of 1/6th King's Liverpool Regiment,* WO 95 2926-2_2.

Epilogue

1. *1914-1919 Diary, Ellison Papers,* p. 98.
2. *London Gazette* of 3 September 1919.
3. *Newspaper clipping, 1914-1919 Diary, Ellison Papers.*
4. *The Liverpool Rifles—a Miscellany, Ellison Papers.*
5. *Ibid.*
6. *1914-1919 Diary, Ellison Papers.*
7. *Minutes of the Old Insufferables*, Ellison Papers.

Bibliography

Published Sources

55th (West Lancashire) Division Trench Orders (Lancaster: King's Own Museum, 2013)

Ainslie, G. M., *Hand Grenades, A handbook on Rifle and Hand Grenades* (London: Chapman & Hall, 1917)

Coop, J. O., *The Story of the 55th (West Lancashire) Division* (Liverpool: Liverpool Daily Post, 1919)

Edmonds, J. E., *Official History of the Great War, Military Operations France and Belgium, 1915. Volume 1* (Uckfield: Naval & Military Press, 2009); *Official History of the Great War, Military Operations France and Belgium, 1915. Volume 2* (Uckfield: Naval & Military Press, 2009); *Official History of the Great War, Military Operations France and Belgium, 1917. Volume 2* (Uckfield: Naval & Military Press, 2009); *Official History of the Great War, Military Operations France and Belgium, 1918 Volume 2* (Uckfield: Naval & Military Press, 2009)

Gibbs, P., *Now it can be Told* (New York: Garden City Publishing Co., 1920)

Henshaw, T., *The Sky Their Battlefield II* (High Barnet: Fetubi Books, 2014)

Hodgkinson, A., *The King's Own 1/5th Battalion, TF in the European War 1914-1918* (Lancaster: The King's Own Royal Regimental Museum, 2009)

Miles, W., *Official History of the Great War, Military Operations France and Belgium, 1916 Volume 2* (Uckfield: Naval & Military Press, 2009); *Official History of the Great War, Military Operations France and Belgium, 1917 Volume 3* (Uckfield: Naval & Military Press, 2009)

Notes for Infantry Officers on Trench Warfare (Uckfield: Naval & Military Press, 2008)

Reid, W., *Architect of Victory-Douglas Haig* (Edinburgh: Berlinn Ltd, 2006)

Regulations for the Territorial Force and for County Associations (London: HMSO, 1908)

Simpkins, P., *Kitchener's Army* (Barnsley: Pen & Sword Military, 2007)

War Office, *General Staff. Infantry Training (4-Company Organisation)* (London: HMSO, 1914)

Westlake, R., *The Territorial Battalions* (London: Guild Publishing, 1986)

Wyrall, E., *The History of the King's Regiment (Liverpool) 1914-1919 Volumes 1-3* (Uckfield: Naval and Military Press. 2002 reprint)

Newspapers, Web Pages, and Periodicals

Atenstaedt, R. L., *Trench fever: the British medical response in the Great War* (Journal of the Royal Society of Medicine. Published online November 2006. Institute of Medical & Social

Care Research, University of Wales, Bangor, 2006); *The medical response to trench nephritis in World War 1* (Kidney International, published online 5 July 2006. Institute of Medical & Social Care Research, University of Wales, Bangor, 2006)
Lancaster Observer and Morecambe Chronicle, 1915
Liverpool Echo, 1914–1919
Liverpool Daily Post and Mercury, 1914–1919
Surrey Mirror, 1914
Sussex Express, Surrey Standard, and Kent Mail, 1914.
Baker, C., *The Long, Long Trail*, www.1914-1918.net/
The Greenjacket, 1926-1928
The Territorial, (date unknown)

Unpublished Sources

Burial Returns. Commonwealth War Graves Commission
Medal Index Cards WO 372 (National Archives)
Officers' Service Records, WO 374 (National Archives)
Officers' Service Records, (WO 339). The National Archives
Pension Records, WO 364 National Archives)
Service Records, WO 363 (National Archives)
Private Diary of Clifton Inglis Stockwell. (Stockwell Family)
The Jeudwine Papers, 356/FIF (Liverpool Record Office)
The Ellison Papers, (Liverpool Record Office)
War Diary of 83 Infantry Brigade, WO 95 2273 (National Archives)
War Diary of 85 Infantry Brigade, WO 95 2278 (National Archives)
War Diary of 165 Infantry Brigade, WO 95 2925 (National Archives)
War Diary of 166 Infantry Brigade, WO 95 2928 (National Archives)
War Diary of 15 Infantry Brigade, WO 95 1566 (National Archives)
War Diary of 1/5th King's Liverpool Regiment, WO 95 2926-1 (National Archives)
War Diary of 1/6th King's Liverpool Regiment, WO 95 1572-3 (National Archives)
War Diary of 1/6th King's Liverpool Regiment, WO 95 2926-2 (National Archives)
War Diary of 1/7th King's Liverpool Regiment, WO 95 2927-1 (National Archives)
War Diary of 1/8th King's Liverpool Regiment, WO 95 2983-5 (National Archives)
War Diary of 1/5th South Lancashire Regiment, WO 95 2929-2 (National Archives)
War Diary of 1/Bedfordshire Regiment, WO 95 1570 (National Archives)
War Diary of 1/Cheshire Regiment, WO 95 1571 (National Archives)
War Diary of 1/Dorsetshire Regiment, WO 95 1572-2 (National Archives)
War Diary of 2/Kings Royal Rifle Corps, WO 95 1272/1-6 (National Archives)
War Diary of 1/Norfolk Regiment, WO 95 1573 (National Archives)
War Diary of 1/5th South Lancashire, WO 95 2929 (National Archives)
War Diary of 1/4 King's Own (Royal Lancaster) Regiment, KO 1017/64 (King's Own Museum, Lancaster)
War Diary of the 1/5th King's Own (Royal Lancaster) Regiment, WO 95 2274-3 (National Archives)
War Diary of the 1/5th King's Own (Royal Lancaster) Regiment, WO 95 2930 1-4 (National Archives)
War Diary of 1/York and Lancaster Regiment, WO 95 2275 (National Archives)
War Diary of Headquarters 5 Division. General Staff, WO 95 1512 (National Archives).
War Diary of Headquarters 5 Division. General Staff, WO 95 1513 (National Archives)
'A' & 'Q' Diary 5 Division, WO 95 1517-3 (National Archives)

Daily Orders, 5 Division, WO 95 1517-5_1 (National Archives)
War Diary of Headquarters 28 Division. General Staff, WO 95 2267 (National Archives)
War Diary of Commander Royal Engineers, 28 Division. General Staff, WO 95 2270-2 (National Archives)
War Diary of Headquarters 55 Division. General Staff, WO 95 2899–2904 (National Archives)
War Diary of Headquarters 55 Division. 'A' & 'Q' Branch, WO 95 2908–2910 (National Archives)

Index